D0211913

EX LIBRIS

SOUTH ORANGE
PUBLIC LIBRARY

Encyclopedia of Archaeology

History and Discoveries

Encyclopedia of Archaeology

History and Discoveries

Volume I, A–D

Edited by Tim Murray

A B C ☙ C L I O
Santa Barbara, California • Denver, Colorado • Oxford, England

REF
930.1
ENC
V.1 A-D

Copyright © 2001 by Tim Murray

All rights reserved. No part of this publication may be reproduced, stored in a
retrieval system, or transmitted, in any form or by any means, electronic, mechanical,
photocopying, recording, or otherwise, except for the inclusion of brief quotations in
a review, without prior permission in writing from the publishers.

Library of Congress Catalog Card Number

Encyclopedia of archaeology : History and discoveries / edited by Tim Murray.
    p. cm.
Includes bibliographical references.
    ISBN 1-57607-198-7 (hardcover : alk. paper) — ISBN 1-57607-577-X (e-book)
    1. Archaeology—History—Encyclopedias. 2. Archaeologists—Biography—Encyclopedias.
3. Antiquities—Encyclopedias. 4. Historic sites—Encyclopedias. 5. Excavations (Archaeology)—
Encyclopedias. I. Murray, Tim, 1955–
    CC100.E54 2001
    930.1—dc21   20011002617

05 04 03 02 01 00 99 10 9 8 7 6 5 4 3 2 1

ABC-CLIO, Inc.
130 Cremona Drive, P.O. Box 1911
Santa Barbara, California 93116–1911

This book is printed on acid-free paper ∞.
Manufactured in the United States of America

Advisory Board

K.-C. Chang
Harvard University

Douglas R. Givens
Peabody Museum, Harvard University

Leo Klejn
European University, St. Petersburg

Colin Renfrew
University of Cambridge

Alain Schnapp
Université de Paris 1 Pantheon-Sorbonne

Bruce G. Trigger
McGill University

To my family

Contents

Preface and Acknowledgments

This project was begun in 1992, with the first two volumes (*The Great Archaeologists*) being published in 1999. The three volumes that comprise *History and Discoveries* conclude the *Encyclopedia of Archaeology*. When this project was first conceived I drew up a very long list of countries, people, sites, techniques, methods, theories, issues, styles and traditions of archaeology that I thought provided a comprehensive picture of the evolution of archaeology. As in most projects of this magnitude, the *Encyclopedia of Archaeology* of necessity changed during the protracted and often difficult journey to publication. The result retains my initial goals: to provide the most in-depth, authoritative, and through reference work on the history of archaeology.

What I see in all five volumes, but in particular the three that comprise *Histories and Discoveries* is simply a watershed in the history of archaeology. Never before has it been possible for us to contemplate the unity and diversity of archaeology on this scale. It is now more often being observed (indeed Bruce Trigger does so in these volumes) that the history of archaeology is beginning to play a significant role in debates about archaeological theory and the philosophy of archaeology. The entries in these volumes provide a wonderful source of inspiration and information for those fundamental debates, the outcomes of which will directly affect the ways in which human beings search for an understanding of themselves.

The five volumes represent over a million words of text and the direct and indirect contributions of hundreds of people around the world. It is appropriate to begin these acknowledgments by recognizing the work of the contributors whose names are to be found in the following pages. This encyclopedia is their work. The entries to this encyclopedia were written between 1993 and 2001 and are a reflection of the state of knowledge about the histories of sites, regions, countries, and personalities at the time when they were written. Many of the entries in *History and Discoveries* were translated into English from French, German, Russian, and Spanish. Although the names of the translators are listed at the end of each relevant entry, it is also important to acknowledge that their work has broadened and deepened this history of archaeology.

A large number of the contributors to these volumes were identified by the very many colleagues who used their networks to track people down. I was often touched by the willingness of colleagues from around the world to help, indeed some who at very short notice came up with superb contributions because those who had originally been contracted failed to deliver. I owe particular debts of gratitude to Peter Bellwood, Ian Hodder, Gordon Willey, Peter Robertshaw, Scott Raymond, Wil Roebroeks, Steve Shennan, Richard Bradley, Mark Leone, T. G. H. James, Barry Cunliffe, Rosemary Joyce, Henry Cleere, Barry Kemp, Derek Roe, W. Y. Adams, Helen Clarke, Thurstan Shaw, Robert Bednarik, Georg Kossack, H. G. Niemeyer, Gina Barnes, Peter White, J. Jefferson Reid, David Webster, Warwick Bray, Anna Roosevelt, Miriam Stark, Heinrich Härke, and T. Patrick Culbert.

The administrative and secretarial staff of the Archaeology Program at La Trobe University, Stella Bromilow and Ros Allen, have been a tower of strength during the project.

I have said before that it was Kristi Ward (then of ABC-CLIO) who made it possible for me to publish the kind of book that these five volumes have turned out to be. Her successor at ABC-CLIO, Kevin Downing, has carried the brunt of all the pressure that this kind of project generates. He has been an excellent editor—patient and impatient, understanding, never losing sight of the destination and being prepared to use (most) means to get us there. It was an entirely unexpected bonus to see him converted to the wonder of Australian Rules football. Of course it would have been perfect if he had chosen to support Essendon rather than Geelong, but the cup is half full anyway.

Three other people have been instrumental in getting the project to completion. Wei Ming, the technical officer in the Archaeology Program at La Trobe University, is responsible for the maps. Their quality is testimony to his great skill, but they do not of themselves reveal Wei Ming's patience and ability to perform miracles. I am very fortunate indeed to have in him such a talented and dedicated colleague.

Susan McRory was responsible for the production side at ABC-CLIO. Her organizational abilities, and her commitment to getting the details as right as we could make them, are awe-inspiring. There is absolutely no doubt that we would not have these books without her.

The same can be said of Susan Bridekirk. Susan has performed the role of research assistant and editor with tremendous skill and dedication. During the past four years of the project she has worked in libraries in England, France, and Australia researching the history of archaeology, and she has made a fundamental contribution to the writing and editing of many of the texts in these volumes. I am deeply grateful to the Vice-Chancellor of La Trobe University (Professor Michael Osborne) and the Dean of its Faculty of Humanities and Social Sciences (Professor Roger Wales) for making it possible for Susan Bridekirk to join the project.

My family have borne the distractions of the past ten years with more grace and good humor than I deserve, and I hope that by dedicating *History and Discoveries* to them I can give something back.

Tim Murray
Melbourne, Australia
2001

Introduction

Many of the points I have wanted to make about the importance and value of the history of archaeology have already been made in the introduction to *The Great Archaeologists* (the first two volumes of the *Encyclopedia of Archaeology*). In those first volumes I was concerned mainly with exploring the role of biography in writing the history of archaeology, and in coming to grips with the great diversity in approach taken by the contributors to those volumes. The essays in *The Great Archaeologists* have attracted considerable attention (most of it very good), but one comment made by an eminent historian of archaeology struck a particular chord. Contemplating the richness of new information about something that he felt we knew reasonably well, he was moved to remark that in recent decades the history of archaeology had really come of age.

I think that he meant this in two ways. First, that archaeologists were now sufficiently confident about the value of their discipline and its perspectives to seek a deeper understanding of its history—an understanding that had the clear potential to challenge disciplinary orthodoxies. Second, that the sheer scale of archaeology practiced at a global scale gave rise to many interesting questions about the unity of the discipline. In the early 1980s Bruce Trigger and Ian Glover pursued some of these questions in two editions of the journal *World Archaeology* that were devoted to the exploration of "regional traditions" in archaeology. What Trigger and Glover (and the contributors to their project) were keen to establish was whether the diversity of experience among archaeologists and the societies they served had led to real differences in approach and purpose among nations or groups of nations such as "Anglo-Saxon" or "Francophone," "First World," "Second World" or "Third World," "Colonialist" or "Postcolonialist."

While the first two volumes of this encyclopedia amply demonstrated the diversity of personal histories among influential archaeologists and antiquarians over the past four centuries, they pointed to significant commonalities as well. This notion that there are questions, issues, and fundamental activities, such as classification, that lie at the heart of a discipline like archaeology supports the view that it is possible for archaeologists to communicate with each other (however imperfectly) and to share knowledge. This theme of unity in diversity (and the ambiguities that arise from it) is even more strongly supported in the final three volumes of the encyclopedia that together comprise *History and Discoveries*.

In these volumes we have histories of archaeology as it has been practiced in most parts of the world, biographies of significant archaeologists in addition to those included in the first two volumes of the project, and histories of significant sites, debates, techniques, methods and issues that are central to the global practice of the discipline. Notwithstanding the perception of commonalities, the impression of diversity is also very strong indeed, and the notion of there being different regional traditions in archaeology is strongly exemplified. The same is true for the practice of particular kinds of archaeology, be it of simple or complex societies, or of particular technologies or site types. For example, the pattern of research into the prehistoric and historical archaeology of settler societies such as Canada, the United Sstates of America, Australia, and New Zealand is different from that in other postcolonial societies.

Yet at the same time one is struck by the things archaeologists share—a concern with locating, recovering, and making sense of evidence of past human lives and an understanding that making the human past intelligible is a significant cultural function, no matter what society archaeological research is being conducted in. Certainly the histories that comprise these volumes make it very clear that since the nineteenth century archaeology has played a significant role in the cultural lives of nations, and that in doing so it has been frequently put to use to serve nationalist agendas—whether these are in China, Russia, Australia or the countries of Europe, the Americas, or Africa.

Thus while archaeologists might share a commitment to revealing the importance of the human past they have frequently done so in different ways and to meet different cultural and political ends. Many of the histories presented here explore the interplay between the work of archaeologists as "objective" scientists and the social and cultural contexts within which they work. In doing so they reveal theoretical and methodological connections between archaeologists that have also played a fundamental role in the creation of archaeology. The tensions between local and global archaeologies revealed by the entries in these volumes seem to me to be a true reflection of the experience of many contemporary archaeologists, and they pose a strong challenge to the discipline in future decades.

Encyclopedia of Archaeology

History and Discoveries

Abercromby, Lord John (1841–1924)

A Scottish antiquary, the secretary of the SOCIETY OF ANTIQUARIES OF SCOTLAND, and its president from 1913 to 1918, Abercromby is most famous for his typological analyses published in *Bronze Age Pottery of Great Britain and Ireland* (1912).

In 1904 Abercromby used the term *beaker* to describe the decorated, handleless pottery drinking vessels used all over Europe between 4000 and 2000 B.C. He argued that the appearance of beakers in northern and western Europe could only be understood in relation to changes in similar assemblages from southeast and central Europe. While Abercromby's beaker typology remained unchanged until quite recently, his explanation of their uniform spread has been disproved. Abercromby argued for a putative "Beaker folk" who migrated all over Europe with their pottery. It is now thought that it was the pottery style that migrated alone—that the beakers were an interregional and even international style of artifact that were traded over long distances and were widely recognized male status objects used in drinking rituals. Abercromby argued that cultural uniformity meant social and ethnic uniformity—an argument that was later used by some archaeologists to support Nazi ideology in Germany. Nonetheless Abercromby's "new" approach to archaeological evidence (one that still finds support among some archaeologists) was more international than most approaches to the same evidence in England during this time.

Abercromby's influence was virtually confined to Scotland. His bequest to the University of Edinburgh in 1916 endowed the chair of archaeology that still carries his name. VERE GORDON CHILDE was the first appointment to the Abercromby Chair in 1927, and STUART PIGGOTT succeeded him.

Tim Murray

See also Britain, Prehistoric Archaeology

Absolute Dating Techniques
See Dating

Abu Simbel

Situated in Lower Nubia (Egypt), the site of Abu Simbel comprises two temples cut from living rock during the reign of the pharaoh Ramses II, thirteenth century B.C. The temples feature major works of sculpture, in particular seated figures of Ramses II and standing figures of Ramses and his queen, Nefertari.

The integrity of the temples was threatened by rising waters of the Nile River because of the construction of the a new Aswan High Dam and the creation of Lake Nasser in the 1960s. In a model of international cooperation, the United Nations Educational, Scientific, and Cultural Organization (UNESCO) made possible a large-scale survey and excavation of sites that were to be inundated by Lake Nasser and, perhaps more spectacularly, the dismantling and reassembly of the temples at a new site created above the water line. The rescue project lasted from 1960 to 1980.

Tim Murray

See also Egypt: Predynastic; Nubia

Abydos, Egypt (Spectrum Colour Library)

Abydos

A major site in Upper Egypt, Abydos, which lies west of the Nile near al-Balyana, was a royal burial site of the first two dynasties and later a major place for the worship of the god Osiris. Excavation of Abydos was begun at the end of the nineteenth century by Emile-Clément Amélineau, but the site is most directly associated with SIR WILLIAM MATTHEW FLINDERS PETRIE. Grave sites from the archaic period and stelae and ritual architecture of the nineteenth dynasty have been discovered, and excavations continued at Abydos throughout the twentieth century.

Tim Murray

See also Egypt: Predynastic; French Archaeology in Egypt and the Middle East

Acosta, Jorge R. (1904?–1975)

Acosta was born in China, the son of distinguished Mexican diplomat Alfonso Villalobos. He lived and studied for many years in England, where he attended St. Johns College, Cambridge (1924–1925) and befriended classmate and future Mayanist JOHN ERIC THOMPSON. Acosta's career as an archaeologist lasted nearly fifty years, from 1928 to 1975.

The long list of sites and regions where Acosta did fieldwork is impressive: Zacaleu, GUATEMALA; Mountain Cow, BELIZE (with Thompson); MONTE ALBÁN, Monte Negro, and other centers in Oaxaca; CHICHÉN ÍTZA; Uxmal; PALENQUE; Tres Zapotes (Veracruz); Cholul; Ixcateogpan (Guerrero); Tenayuca; and TEOTIHUACÁN. His most important investigations focused on three ancient cities, Monte Albán, Tula, and Teotihuacán, where he spent years doing research. In the course of other projects he discovered the famous mural sequence of drinking figures inside the Great Pyramid of Cholula and at Uxmal (Yucatán). He directed an architectural restoration program that greatly influenced the theory and practice of cultural patrimony conservation in MEXICO. He discovered the ceremonial cave under the Pyramid of the Sun at Teotihuacán that probably played a key role in the founding and the general structural plan of that ancient city. His restoration of the Palace of Quetzalpopalotl at Teotihuacán has been considered excessive by some specialists, but it constituted a major success in making a 1,500-year-old building understandable for thousands of visitors.

Acosta's investigations in Oaxaca with Alfonso Caso and IGNACIO BERNAL during three decades were fundamental for the development of Mexican archaeology and produced several classic reports, including *The Ceramics of Monte Albán* (1967) and, on Tula, *Revista Mexicana de Estudios Antropologicos*. While Acosta directed his most consequential field seasons at Tula, he was also the field director of Caso's program at Monte Albán.

On the basis of his work at Tula, Acosta's name can be added to the very short list of archaeologists who have rediscovered major ancient civilizations. Acosta proved that ruins at Tula, in the modern Mexican state of Hidalgo, were in fact those of the legendary city of Tollan, capital of the Toltec Empire during the tenth and eleventh centuries A.D. The major part of Acosta's work at Tula was devoted to the excavation and restoration of many of the buildings on the main plaza. These were some of the best investigations of pre-Hispanic architecture ever conducted in Mexico. Acosta's program at Tula functioned as field training for young archaeologists and anthropologists. He died in Mexico City on March 5, 1975.

Roberto Cobean and
Alba Guadalupe Mastache Flores

See also Toltecs

References
For references, see *Encyclopedia of Archaeology: The Great Archaeologists, Vol. 1*, ed. Tim Murray (Santa Barbara, CA: ABC-CLIO, 1999), pp. 425–440.

Adams, Robert McCormick (1926–)

Born in Chicago and educated in a progressive environment, Robert McCormick Adams developed an interest in archaeology that can be traced to childhood experiences in the American Southwest. He served in the U.S. Navy during World War II and subsequently enrolled at the University of Chicago to study social sciences. In 1950, Adams, with Linda and ROBERT BRAIDWOOD, participated in an excavation at JARMO in Iraq. During fieldwork there Adams met the social anthropologist Fredrik Barth, and Barth convinced Adams to continue with graduate school. Important intellectual influences on Adams at the University of Chicago came from the social anthropologist Fred Eggan, with his stress on the comparative method, and from Robert Braidwood, who advocated a multidisciplinary approach to prehistoric archaeology. Adams was also influenced by the work of V. GORDON CHILDE and his concern with technology, demography, internal social organization, and social evolution. Another critical influence was the New World archaeologist GORDON WILLEY, who had done pioneering reconnaissance surveys in the VIRÚ VALLEY of PERU, using settlement patterns and demography.

In the field of Near Eastern history, Adams worked with the Danish Sumerologist Thorkild Jacobsen, who had worked on archaeological projects sponsored by the University of Chicago's ORIENTAL INSTITUTE. Jacobsen was not only an expert in third millennium B.C. history and the Sumerian language, he was also an avid reader and writer in the philosophy of history. Adams's interest and training in ecology came in part from his studies and collegial relationships with Sherwood Washburn and Clark Howell in the Department of Anthropology at Chicago and from Washburn's running argument with the social anthropologist Robert Redfield.

Adams received his M.A. at Chicago in 1952, writing on Jarmo pottery and stone vessel industries, and while he was working toward his doctorate, he was appointed to a combined position divided between the Oriental Institute and the Department of Anthropology. Adams received his Ph.D. in 1956 and held this same combined position for the duration of his academic career at Chicago.

Adams undertook fieldwork in MEXICO and then returned to fieldwork in Iraq in the 1950s and 1960s, where he continued to work until the 1970s when politics made it impossible to continue working there. This massive amount of fieldwork and surveying have resulted in substantial and significant publications. One of the first of Adams's articles, with Jacobsen, was published in *Science* in 1958, and it reached a large public, including archaeologists, anthropologists, and historians as well as students of Near Eastern history and culture. That article was an indication of the direction his career was to take. Formally, it reported on a study of the feasibility of new irrigation schemes, deep drainage, and other agricultural projects that could be mobilized as a result of the new oil revenues flowing into Iraq, but the authors provided a historical background to the project and explained why land that was once productive had gone to ruin.

Adams's essays in *City Invincible: A Symposium of Urbanization and Cultural Development in the Ancient Near East* (1960) and his book *The Evolution of Urban Society: Early Mesopotamia and Prehispanic Mexico* (1966) feature concerns with comparative social theory, ethnographic analogy, and a long-term historical lens. These elements were to characterize all his subsequent writing.

The Evolution of Urban Society, which became an instant classic in anthropology, provided a detailed comparison between the two best-known cases of the evolution of ancient states and so fulfilled Eggan's requirement for "controlled comparison" as the hallmark of anthropological analysis. In its day, the book represented the best that anthropological archaeology had to offer. It identified similarities in development among different ancient states while not unduly reducing the differences and diversity among states. It showed that archaeologists were the anthropologists who could actually study the evolution of states while social anthropologists who had done most of the talking and writing about social evolution had no way to test any of their views. The book made famous Childe's list of the traits of ancient states, which had been published in an obscure essay, even though it seriously qualified Childe's discussion.

Adams decisively influenced the course of social evolutionary theory with his argument against Karl Wittfogel's assertion that the requirements of large-scale irrigation caused the rise and determined the character of ancient

states. By ranging through major New World examples as well as adducing the appropriate Mesopotamian data, Adams demonstrated that large-scale irrigation was the consequence, not the cause, of dynastic states.

More than thirty years after the publication of the book, Adams's ideas are still pertinent and challenging. The transformations in social organization that accompanied the new political and economic relations in early states, a subject taken up by Adams in his chapter on kin and class, have been much debated. His exploration of the ideological forms of political leadership as contested ground, and hence as engines of change, was advanced by archaeologists in the late 1980s and early 1990s as a principle object of research.

Land behind Baghdad: A History of Settlement of the Diyala Plains (1965) was the result of an international development project in the Diyala River basin from new directions in settlement pattern studies. Among them Adams added, crucially, the employment of aerial photos, detailed ethnographic and historical documentation, and a commitment to a long-term historical perspective (which he developed quite independently from the work of French historian Fernand Braudel). Adams's archaeologial purview—proceeding from the prehistoric Ubaid period to A.D. 1900 (ca. 7,000 years)—and his abundant and appropriate use of specialized geomorphological, ethnographic, and historic data make his case for a holistic comprehension of the past.

Whereas *Land behind Baghdad* focused on post-Mesopotamian settlement patterns, *The Uruk Countryside: The Natural Setting of Urban Societies* (1972) transformed extant knowledge of early urbanization in MESOPOTAMIA. This book was jointly authored with German archaeologist Hans J. Nissen and comprises two interrelated leitmotivs. The first is the development of southern Mesopotamia into the first urban society in world history. The second is the puzzling fact that today, this same region is virtually empty of towns and intensive agriculture. The book's conclusion is a meditation on the destablizing force of central government.

The same two themes remain central in the

book *Heartland of Cities: Surveys of Ancient Settlement and Land Use on the Central Floodplain of the Euphrates* (1981) in which Adams established an almanac of modern and ancient climatic conditions and agricultural productivity in Mesopotamia as a natural and technological setting for further investigation. The interaction between human beings and their environment resulted in an early urbanism in which city-states attempted to achieve stability over an often politically autonomous and resilient countryside. As the larger and more centralized states of late antiquity were able to maximize the production of cereals and other crops, they minimized the flexibility of a pastoralist-urban life and increased the potentialities of salinization, which turned land into swamps and brought about a massive demographic decline. A classic scenario of increasing short-term gains at the expense of long-term survival is played out to a sorrowful end.

Adams's work has shown that in all the superficially mundane activities of locating sites, seriating objects, and connecting them to stratified material and reconstructing settlement patterns—the very stuff of archaeology—the subject of social change could be apprehended. Today, archaeologists devise survey projects of great sophistication and detail and through their work have transformed our knowledge of regions throughout the world. Although Willey in Peru and William Sanders and colleagues in Mexico were also pioneers of systematic settlement surveys, Adams's work has arguably had the greatest impact on this form of research. Adams not only explored the relation between environmental and human social systems better than others but also analyzed and dignified the activities of the archaeological worker in two ways that became critical in the late twentieth century, both to archaeologists and to their colleagues.

First embedded in the intellectual milieu of anthropologists and historians and often regarded more as technicians than as thinkers, archaeologists corporately earned respect through the persuasive intellectuality of Adams's work. His research is judged to be an original contribution to social knowledge and, in particular, to social evolutionary theory. Adams's research em-anates from arduous fieldwork and the synthesis of disparate fields of expertise whose breadth no one else has been able to match or, it seems, even imagine. Second, Adams's work has never given the impression of being dispassionate scholarship that is disassociated from the world in which his research was done and that has nothing to say to the people of Iraq or to the makers of modern western policy.

In 1984, at the height of his distinguished career at the University of Chicago—where he had been a professor in the Oriental Institute (and its sometime director), professor of anthropology, dean of the division of social sciences, and provost of the university—Robert Adams became secretary of the SMITHSONIAN INSTITUTION in Washington, D.C., and served in that position until his retirement in 1994. While at the Smithsonian, Adams was also on the staff of the Departments of Near Eastern Studies and Anthropology at Johns Hopkins University. After his retirement from the Smithsonian he became adjunct professor in the Department of Anthropology at the University of California, San Diego.

Norman Yoffee

References

For references, see *Encyclopedia of Archaeology: The Great Archaeologists, Vol. 2,* ed. Tim Murray (Santa Barbara, CA: ABC-CLIO, 1999), pp. 808–810.

Africa, East, Later

Research on the later archaeology of East Africa has ranged from the need to understand the late Pleistocene and Holocene artifact traditions and linguistic groups in the region (Bower, Nelson, Waibel, and Wandibba 1977; Isaac, Merrick, and Nelson 1972; L. S. B. Leakey 1931, 1935; M. D. Leakey 1945; M. D. Leakey and L. S. B. Leakey 1950; Phillipson 1977a, 1977b, 1985; Soper 1971a, 1971b; Sutton 1966, 1972), the reconstruction of the environmental changes for the period based on analysis of pollen cores from highland lakes and limnological analysis of lakes in the area (Butzer, Isaac, Richardson, and Washbourne Kamau 1972; Isaac, Merrick, and Nelson 1972; Livingstone 1980; Hamilton 1982; Richardson and Richardson 1972), the techniques of artifact making (Kiriama 1986;

Schmidt 1978), and the collection of oral traditions in order to verify the existence of various archaeological entities (Schmidt 1978). These investigations have produced enough information to outline climatic and vegetation shifts in the region, especially during the late-Pleistocene and early-Holocene periods, and have also helped in defining the major cultural entities of the region. Thus, the major theoretical orientation of most of these studies has been culture historical as well as ecological in reconstruction.

The first systematic study of the later prehistory of East Africa was started in the 1920s by LOUIS S. LEAKEY, who at the time was concentrating his work in the area of Lake Nakuru and Lake Naivasha in Kenya. The principal aim of his work, as was the case elsewhere at that time, was to try to reconstruct the region's cultural history using archaeological evidence. Leakey was most concerned with looking at the origins of food production in the region. The presence of polished ax heads, stone bowls, pottery, and human burial sites in the area led Leakey to refer to this industry as Neolithic, and he named it Njoroan after the present-day Njoro township, where it was first identified. Leakey thought this culture had intruded into the area from the Sudan (L. S. B. Leakey 1931). Calling this industry Neolithic was in line with the practice elsewhere, notably in the Near East and Europe, of assigning any industries with pottery and polished artifacts to the Neolithic period. According to Leakey, the pottery, stone bowls, and polished artifacts had been used for the preparation of domesticated cereals, which meant that their presence in the region indicated the practice of some sort of agriculture (L. S. B. Leakey 1931).

Apart from reconstructing the culture sequence, Leakey was also concerned with trying to ascertain the racial or linguistic group of the makers of the cultures. Thus, on the basis of the oral history of the Kikuyu tribe, Leakey attributed these early Neolithic sites to the mythical Gumban people, who were supposed to have preceded the Kikuyu. The Gumban cultures were divisible into two, Gumban A and Gumban B. The former was characterized by pottery that was internally scored and had extensive exter-

nal decoration, a motif Leakey described as basketlike. This culture was represented at the Makalia burial site and Stable's Drift on the Nderit River. Gumban B, on the other hand, was characterized by the presence of well-made stone bowls, pestle rubbers, and obsidian artifacts as well as pottery that had a roulette decoration. The type site for this culture was the Nakuru burial site and present-day Lion Hill near Lake Nakuru.

MARY LEAKEY was the next person to concentrate on researching the Neolithic, and like her husband, she centered her work in the Naivasha and Nakuru lake basins. She excavated the Hyrax Hill cemeteries as well as an Iron Age settlement on the site, and later she excavated a Neolithic crematorium at Njoro, now commonly referred to as the Njoro River Cave. The Hyrax Hill site was a combined settlement and burial site in which males were buried with no grave goods while females were buried with grave goods such as beads, pottery, and stone vessels. In her report, Mary Leakey (1943) suggested that a site should be designated as Neolithic if it had polished artifacts, pestle rubbers, stone bowls, or systematic burials. She further argued that the presence of cultivation and/or animal husbandry in the form of domestic plants or animals was not necessary in order for a site to be considered Neolithic. This definition was later to prove crucial in the identification of new Neolithic cultures at Hyrax Hill and Njoro River Cave.

The Njoro River Cave site yielded about eighty cremated human burials and large amounts of grave goods, among which were stone bowls, grindstones, pestle rubbers, flaked stones, stone beads, stone pendants, pottery, remains of a gourd basket, and an elaborately decorated and carbonized wooden vessel. Leakey assumed that the Njoro River Cave culture had a genetic relationship with the Mesolithic culture named Elmenteitan, and she thus described the culture as evolved Elmenteitan.

Subsequent research did not yield more sites with finds similar to those of the Njoroan culture, so the term was dropped. The research, however, did reveal two more cultures—the Tumbian and the Kenya Wilton C, which were considered to be Neolithic. The Tumbian was named after Tumba in modern Congo (formerly Zaire), where it was reported, and it is characterized by polished stone ax heads. Similar artifacts found in the Ugandan and Kenyan Lake Victoria basin were attributed to this culture. The Kenyan Wilton C was also identified in the Lake Victoria basin but on shell mounds. The Tumbian was subsequently renamed Sangoan and is now attributed to the middle Stone Age.

Research in Uganda by T. P. O'Brien and E. J. Wayland revealed three Neolithic cultures named Kageran, Wilton Neolithic A, and Wilton Neolithic B. The Kageran culture, named after River Kagera on the banks of which it was found, was characterized by cores, choppers, scrapers, and flakes. The characteristic features of Wilton Neolithic A, found at the Nsongezi rock shelter, were pottery, backed blades, crescents, and thumbnail scrapers. The pottery was decorated by codrouletting, herringbone, and crosshatching designs. The Wilton B was identified near Mt. Elgon on the Uganda/Kenya border, and it was characterized by currents, burins, and thumbnail scrapers. In Uganda, the thumbnail scrapers were indicators of the Neolithic period since most sites in the country did not have polished stone artifacts, stone bowls, or pottery.

During the 1960s and 1970s, research on the Neolithic period continued in the Naivasha and Nakuru basins and in other parts of the Kenyan and Tanzanian highland regions. Barbara Anthony and Mark Cohen excavated a farm site where they recovered flaked stones, pottery, stone vessels, and faunal remains, which included domestic stock. A University of California team led by GLYN ISAAC attempted to relocate the site of Long's Drift in Kenya, previously excavated by Leakey, but instead discovered a site they named Prolonged Drift. This site yielded numerous flaked stone vessel fragments, pottery, and faunal remains, some of which were of domestic stock. Further south in Tanzania (then Tanganyika), Hans Reck had excavated burial mounds in the Ngorongoro Crater from 1915 to 1916 and discovered beads similar to those found at the Njoro River cave site. Sassoon excavated the Engaruka ruins and cairns in Tanzania, though these cairns were discovered to be purely Iron Age.

A number of rock-shelter sites in the Lake Victoria region, especially around the Winam Gulf, were excavated by C. Gabel between 1966 and 1967, and these yielded flaked stones and pottery as well as wild and domestic animal remains. At Lothagam in northern Kenya, Larry Robbins excavated a site that yielded pottery, flaked stones, and abundant faunal remains, most of which were aquatic. Robbins also recovered a number of bone harpoons. John Bower excavated the site of Seronera on the Serengeti plains in central Tanzania, and Golden and Odner excavated the Narosura site in southwestern Kenya. Both the Seronera and Narosura sites yielded stone vessels, pottery, flaked stones, and wild and domestic fauna. Harry Merrick and Michael Gramly also excavated the Lukenya hills east of Nairobi, where they recovered domestic stock and wild animal remains, pottery, flaked stones, and stone vessels. Onyango Abuje began working in the Naivasha and Nakuru basins.

Most, if not all, of the research just described was concerned with tracing the origins of food production (Neolithic) in East Africa. The aim was not to synthesize the finds on a regional basis, but to see whether one could locate the exact location where the process may have started or intruded into the region. Thus, between the 1920s and 1950s, *Neolithic* was an acceptable term for the cultures that were unearthed. After the 1950s, however, most researchers started arguing that no part of sub-Saharan Africa had gone through a Neolithic stage, and such names as stone-bowl cultures, terminal-late Stone Age, and late–Stone Age food-producing cultures were suggested instead. In the early 1970s, however, the tide turned back, and most archaeologists reverted to the use of the term *Neolithic* but with specific definitions. For instance, it was argued that because of the preponderance of domestic fauna among the stone-bowl cultures of the central Rift Valley, the cultures of the area should be named "pastoral Neolithic," a period defined as being characterized by a later Stone Age technology and a pastoral economic base relying heavily on domestic cattle and sheep and goats (Bower and Nelson 1978).

Most of the research documented above was done mostly on a site and not on a regional scale. However, in 1964 John Sutton attempted a regional synthesis of Neolithic pottery by reclassifying the pottery hitherto known into three categories: A, B, and C. Class A was Elmenteitan pottery, which was confined to the sites of Gambles cave II, the Njoro River Cave, the Naivasha Railway rock shelter, and Long's Drift. Class B comprised the Gumban A and Hyrax Hill pottery while all the roulette-decorated pottery, some of which belonged to Gumban B and Lanet ware, was grouped as class C. Class A was considered to be the oldest, and Sutton believed it had been made and/or used by hunter-gatherer communities. Class C on the other hand was the youngest and was believed to have been associated with iron-using communities.

A better regional synthesis of Neolithic pottery was produced by Simuyu Wandibba (1977), who used the key attributes of decorative techniques motifs and vessel shapes. As a result of this synthesis, five Neolithic wares were identified: Nderit, Narosura, Maringishu, Akira, and Elmenteitan or Remnant ware. Wandibba attempted to order the wares into a provisional chronological sequence on the basis of the stratigraphic sequence and radiometric dates and suggested that Nderit ware was the oldest, followed by Narosura, Maringishu, Elmenteitan, and eventually Akira.

The relationship among the various Neolithic entities has been a contentious issue among researchers mainly because there was no unified approach in defining such entities. Nonetheless, since the early 1980s, there has been agreement about naming the lithic industries, with somewhat less unanimity regarding the naming and chronological ordering of the ceramic entities. Stanley Ambrose (1984b, 1985) has examined the relationship between the various East African Neolithic sites in terms of their chronology, pottery, lithic artifacts, economy, and geographic distribution. According to Ambrose, there were three broad Neolithic groups, which could have been contemporaneous: the Savanna Pastoral Neolithic, the Elmenteitan, and the Eburran. The Eburran had previously been named "Kenya Capsian" by Louis and Mary

Leakey (1931), but according to Ambrose (1980), it was a long-lived tradition indigenous to the central Rift Valley of Kenya.

Ambrose (1984a, 1984b) defined five phases of the Eburran, with the first four occurring around 1200 B.P., and the last, which is associated with ceramics and domestic animals, occurring about 3000 B.P. Although most Eburran sites are found in ecotones between forest and savanna, Ambrose (1984a, 1984b) argues that the Hyrax Hill Neolithic village and the Crescent Island causeway at Lake Naivasha, both found in open grasslands, are Eburran 5 sites. Both sites contain ceramic styles and lithic artifact technology found in savanna pastoral Neolithic sites. Ambrose contends that there are continuities from the early-Holocene Eburran technology and the Eburran 5 sites, and he argues that the Eburran 5 represents an adaptation of indigenous foragers to a stock-rearing way of life introduced into the region by immigrant herders.

The Elmenteitan, which had earlier been recognized by L. Leakey (1931) as part of the Middle Stone Age, was documented by later researchers as a distinctive lithic entity with an exclusively covarying ceramic style (Ambrose 1980, 1984a; Collett and Robertshaw 1983b; Nelson 1980). Using comparative metric studies of the stylistic aspects of the lithic assemblages, Ambrose characterized the Elmenteitan lithic industry as possessing large microlithic blade blanks and finished tools with a standardized size in geometric microliths. The ceramics associated with the Elmenteitan were called Remnant ware (after the type site) by Wandibba (1977) and Elmenteitan by D. Collett and P. Robertshaw (1983b). Unlike the other surviving Neolithic ceramics, the vessels often have lugs, are usually undecorated, and are mainly bowl forms in varying sizes.

The Savanna Pastoral Neolithic (SPN) on the other hand includes some sites referred to by L. S. B. Leakey as Kenya Wilton and some containing what Leakey called "Gumban A" pottery as well as other ceramic styles. The grouping is nonuniform in lithic terms so that most scholars now use a geographic/economic term instead of an industrial name derived from a type site.

The SPN sites nevertheless are distinguishable from Elmenteitan occurrences by virtue of their smaller and differently derived microlithic blanks, smaller scraper forms, and somewhat larger geometric microliths.

Pottery from SPN sites includes beakerlike containers and bowls of varying sizes with both open and narrow mouths. Decoration is also common and varied. The classification and dating of SPN ceramic styles, some of which temporally succeed one another, have been controversial. Bower and Nelson (1978) and also Wandibba (1980) proposed a set of terms for "wares" defined by wall thickness, finishing, and decorative motifs. Collett and Robertshaw (1983b), on the other hand, undertook a four-variate cluster analysis of ceramics from sites at which vessel form could be reconstituted and revised the Neolithic classification system. Their analysis yielded four main clusters, one of which included pottery from all three sites with Elmenteitan lithics as well as from Deloraine farm, a very early (1100 B.P.) Iron Age site thought to represent the transition of a local stone-using population to iron technology. One of the remaining three clusters contains Nderit ware ceramics as well as other forms, and the same sample also included material from east of Lake Turkana. Collett and Robertshaw chose to call this the Olmalenge tradition. Another cluster, called the Oltome by Collett and Robertshaw, contains ceramics most commonly referred to as Kansyore ware. The last cluster, called the Oldishi tradition, includes materials from sites on Crescent Island and its causeway.

The introduction of new terminology by Collett and Robertshaw is indicative of the confusion and controversy that still surround the study and classification of the Neolithic period in East Africa. The main center of these studies revolves around the issue of indigenous versus foreign origins of the culture. One group, composed mostly of indigenous archaeologists such as Onyango Abuje and Wandibba (1980), argues for a local origin. These archaeologists believe that the indigenous population of East Africa domesticated at least some of the livestock and a majority of the crops (millets, sorghums, yams, etc.) that are currently grown in Africa.

The other group, composed almost exclusively of foreign archaeologists, argues that the Neolithic cultures of East Africa intruded into the region. The intruders, who may have come from the northeast, were Caucasoid and brought with them the art of animal husbandry and perhaps crop production as well (Ambrose 1984b, 1986b; Cole 1963; L. S. B. Leakey 1931, 1935; M. D. Leakey 1945; Sutton 1973). Whichever argument is correct, various analyses have shown that geographic proximity had a strong influence on the closeness of clustering within the major divisions, which may reflect varied intensities of communication within local versus regional populations.

Analyses of SPN sites by Ambrose and De Niro have been interpreted to indicate that the SPN makers were more heavily reliant on animal products and, hence, more heavily committed to pastoralism than were the makers of Elmenteitan artifacts. Robertshaw and Collett (1983a) on the other hand, stress that a good number of the sites could have supported rainfall-dependent farming and that some artifacts may be agricultural implements.

Since 1971, when the first unequivocal faunas of domestic animals were identified by Odner (1971) and Gramly (1972), most terminal–Stone Age researchers have focused on the identification and study of such fauna. Those who have been on the forefront of this kind of study are Diane Gifford-Gonzalez (1984, 1985), F. Marshall (1986), Bernard Mbae (1986), Karega Munene, and, to a lesser extent, Robertshaw. The aim of this work has been to provide a picture of the use of domestic and wild animals by early food producing peoples and their contemporaries. Cattle, sheep, goats, and donkeys have been identified at Neolithic sites with camels entering relatively late in the cultural sequence in the drier regions of northern Kenya (Barthelme 1977).

The 1960s saw not only the emergence of independent East African states but also the establishment of fully fledged universities and university colleges in the region. Within these institutions, there was an urgent need to restructure the curriculum in order to reflect the new status of the territories and the aspirations of the nationals. One area of immediate concern was the restructuring of history departments and curricula in order to give more emphasis to local history, the existence of which had hitherto been denied by the colonialists. The major focus of this restructuring was along the lines of evidence that could be used to reconstruct African history. Evidence comprised oral traditions, linguistics, and archaeology among other disciplines.

In archaeology, the period that mattered most was the Iron Age because it was thought that it was the only period that could provide evidence that was directly linked to present-day societies. During the period following independence, there was thus a proliferation of writings by indigenous historians whose main focus was on marrying the oral traditions, archaeology, and local histories (e.g., Muriuki 1974). Within archaeology itself, the pioneering work on the Iron Age was undertaken by the British Institute in Eastern Africa, which was established in 1960 for the sole purpose of conducting research into the later prehistory of East Africa. In 1966, the institute established the Bantu Studies Research Project (BSRP), and its aim was to elucidate, using archaeology, the expansion of Bantu speakers into the region, as had been proposed by linguists.

Using ceramics and the evidence of iron smelting from most early–Iron Age sites, the BSRP gave credence to linguistic arguments that it was the Bantu-speaking people who were responsible for the introduction of iron working techniques into East Africa (Phillipson 1976a, 1976b, 1977a, 1977b). However, the ceramic groups that were thus used had subjective affinities such as key attributes like decoration and shape. These affinities led to the delineation of typological ceramic sequences, which were later grouped together by time and space to postulate linear sequences of population movement. For example, it was argued that all early–Iron Age ceramics had the same decoration, techniques, motifs, and pottery shapes and that this fact was an indication that these ceramic entities had been manufactured by Bantu speakers (Phillipson 1977a, 1977b, 1985; Soper 1971a, 1971b). These studies were based on a naïve concept of culture that argued that style or culture was determined by society (linguistic group). This argument overlooks the fact that despite having the same socialization process, individuals within a given society or culture have their own tendencies that may affect the way they make their material culture.

The tendency to rely on ceramics as the main basis of studying the early Iron Age started to change in the late 1970s when the American researcher Peter Schmidt turned his attention to the study of the technological process of iron smelting. His main task was to reconstruct the techniques used in smelting, and the construction of the furnace and fuel used within both ethnographic and archaeological contexts, in order to understand whether these techniques could have been imported from elsewhere. The same approach was used by H. Kiriama (1986). Results from both studies indicated that during the early Iron Age, preheating a furnace enabled the production of carbon steel and that, in fact, this process had not been done anywhere else (Kiriama 1987; Schmidt 1978). These studies tried to negate the concept that ceramics can be equated with cultural entities and that, therefore, Bantu speakers were responsible for the introduction of iron work into the region. Instead, it was argued that ceramics and their styles are entities that, first and foremost, have utilitarian functions, and that when they are used to negotiate social relationships, it is done not at the societal but at the individual level. Groups of individuals at the village or craft level may use the style of their ceramics to show their relations with one another and not necessarily to indicate their ethnic affiliations.

It has also been shown that the various Bantu-speaking groups had different attitudes and norms toward iron smelting and toward smelter and iron implements so that it becomes impossible to group these societies into a broad cultural group (Kiriama 1992). The overall argument in these studies is that the technological and social realms within which the ceramics and iron smelting and tools were made and used should be studied and critically analyzed before any theories as to their origins are advanced.

The so-called later Iron Age has not been exhaustively studied. Sites in this category are varied and scattered and are mostly found in both the open savanna and the forested ecotones. In some instances, these sites are assumed to be manifestations of the direct ancestors of the groups of people who are living in these areas, and they have thus been linked to oral traditions. The use of oral traditions as a source of information for archaeology started becoming fashionable in the 1960s, especially after urgings from Jan Vansina about the necessity of undertaking interdisciplinary approaches that used archaeology, oral traditions, historical linguistics, and ethnographic data as sources in studying African history (Vansina 1965, 1967). As a result, M. Posnansky used oral traditions to corroborate his excavation findings at the Ankole capital site of Bwenyorere (Posnansky 1967). Oral traditions have also been used in locating archaeological sites (Schmidt 1983a, 1983b; Wandibba 1977) and in explaining the history and functions of sites (Scully 1969, 1979; Sutton and Robert 1968).

Coastal archaeological sites were believed to be different and separate from sites in the interior, despite the fact that in most cases coastal and interior sites were contemporaneous. This belief was due to the fact that the archaeologists who originally researched the coastal sites were mostly foreigners and tended to regard the coastal settlements as foreign, having been founded by commercial merchants from the Persian Gulf (e.g., Chittick 1984). Later research that was conducted mostly by indigenous archaeologists has shown that the coastal settlements were intrinsically local in origin and relied on the local populations and resources for their foundation and sustenance (e.g., Abungu 1989; Mutoro 1987). Foreign merchants only enhanced the stature of these settlements and enabled them to be linked to the metropolitan commercial centers.

The existence of a large number of linguistic groups within East Africa, and local archaeologists' concerns about the establishment of a cultural sequence, prompted an attempt to correlate various archaeological entities with particular language families (Ambrose 1982, 1984a, 1984b; Phillipson 1977). Ambrose (1982, 1984b) and

Robertshaw (1989) have linked the Elmenteitan and SPN archaeological entities to linguistic groups that are thought to have entered Kenya at some point in the later-Holocene period. Sutton (1966, 1986), Odner (1971), and Ambrose (1982, 1984a) have argued that the SPN represents the original incursion of the earliest food producers, the southern Cushitic speakers, into eastern Africa. The Elmenteitan has been commonly linked with southern Nilotic speakers on the basis of ethnohistory, ceramic continuities (Robertshaw 1989), and reconstructions of the timing of migrations and intergroup contacts (Ambrose 1982; Ehret 1974, 1976).

Ambrose (1982) contends that the Eburran 5 sites were created by indigenous peoples, possibly Khoisan speakers, who led a foraging lifestyle but were forced to adapt to food producing ways of life because of competition from immigrant farmers and herders. L. Shepartz (1988), however, argues that while indigenous peoples may be represented on the Neolithic record, their remains show no distinctive Khoisanoid features.

Soper (1971a, 1971b, 1982) and Phillipson (1977, 1985) contend that the early–Iron Age artifacts were the work of the Bantu speakers. Their argument is based on the fact that iron working, mud-built settlements, and some ceramics made their first appearance in the archaeological record at the same time the Bantu speakers did. They argue that this fact is enough to justify the correlation of the Bantu speakers with the early Iron Age.

Most archaeologists working in East Africa have seldom explicitly discussed their base assumptions for giving priority to one raw material, such as ceramics, over another for inferring shared cultural attributes. Nor has there been detailed discussion of the reasoning behind correlating linguistic and/or ethnic affiliations to archaeological traditions or phases. Ethnographic evidence suggests that correlation of ceramic or lithic technology with linguistic family or of either of these with demes or ethnic groups may overly simplify complex and mutable social interactions (Hodder 1982; Kiriama 1997). It may be more productive to recast the questions of terminal–Stone Age/Iron Age population interactions in East Africa in terms that are determined less by implicit assumptions concerning language, culture, and genetics.

Indigenous Archaeologists

Only Kenyan and Tanzanian universities have active archaeology programs in East Africa, although similar programs are offered by history departments. Most indigenous archaeologists in these countries have concentrated on either the terminal–Stone Age or Iron Age periods (Abungu 1989; Kiriama 1984, 1986, 1992; Masao 1979; Mutoro 1987; Onyango Abuje 1976; Wandibba 1977, 1984). Indigenous archaeologists have concentrated on the later periods because most of the lecturers at the universities were more interested in these periods and they tended to encourage their students to undertake projects in their areas of specialization. It should be noted that, first, despite the prominence of East Africa as a cradle of mankind, none of the people conducting research in the early periods taught at local universities, let alone encouraged local students to undertake study projects in this area. Second, the early period has been seen as not being controversial and as not having enough to do with the history of the local populace and the definition of nation states. Thus, local archaeologists have been encouraged to concentrate on the later periods in an effort to negate colonial and racist propaganda that only began with the intrusion of the white man.

Onyango Abuje (1976) and Onyango Abuje and Wandibba (1979) were the first local archaeologists to argue for the local origins of food production. They also maintained that the term *Neolithic,* discarded as not being fit for African food producing societies, should be retained as food producing societies in eastern Africa had the same characteristics as those in Europe. Onyango Abuje (1976) in particular argued for a total indigenous evolution of the East African Neolithic culture, contending that the populations that independently invested in and developed food producing skills were not Caucasoid immigrants but African in origin. He further argued that these people domesticated some livestock and the majority of the crops that are currently grown in Africa. Wandibba (1977, 1980) undertook a reanalysis of the pottery in the Rift Valley of Kenya and showed that the pottery was particular to the given areas where it was found; thus, there was no likelihood of its importation by immigrants. Karega Munene, on the other hand, used an evolutionary-ecological model to argue for a home-grown Neolithic culture. According to him, the domestication of plants and animals was the result of an adaptive response to stress caused by specific historic situations. In other words, the East African population domesticated plants and animals independently as a response to specific local situations and needs.

Even with regard to the Iron Age, local indigenous archaeologists have been involved in disproving the migrationist theories of earlier archaeologists. S. Lwanga-Lunyiigo (1976), for example, argues that Bantu speakers appeared on the East African scene very early and that the postulated expansion from West Africa never took place. He maintains that it is difficult to spot the exact origin of Bantu speakers, that iron smelting was an independent East African innovation, and that the interlacustrine area was the center from which metallurgy, ceramics, and agricultural techniques spread to central and southern Africa. Kiriama (1986, 1987, 1993), on the other hand, has used a technological and contextual approach to argue for the local invention of ironworking techniques. Analyzing iron slag from an early–Iron Age site in Kenya, Kiriama (1987) has shown that there was preheating of furnaces during the prehistoric period, which enabled the ironworkers to attain high furnace temperatures and thus produce high carbon steel. He has also used a contextual approach (Kiriama 1993) to show that various Bantu speakers used their ceramic and iron implements differently. This work negates the argument for common Bantu origin, and Kiriama proposes that the social realm within which ceramics and iron objects were created and used should be studied if we are to understand the origins and spread of ironworking. The social context within which an item of material culture functions can enable one to understand the similarities and differences that exist among various societies.

It is the same story on the coast where the indigenous archaeologists (Abungu 1989; Mutoro 1987) have tried to show that coastal settlements were not foreign but local in origin. Felix Chami (1992) has shown that on the southern Tanzanian coast there was continuous occupation of sites starting from the first millennium A.D. to around the twelfth to fifteenth centuries. Furthermore, he shows the presence of grinders used for bead manufacture as well as marine shell and glass in sites that are about 55 kilometers away from the sea. In addition, there are similarities between littoral and hinterland ceramics, which Chami argues is indicative of both cultural and economic affiliation between the littoral and its immediate hinterland. This evidence contradicts the hitherto held opinion that the coast was culturally different from its hinterland (Horton 1984).

What is remarkable about the coastal studies by indigenous archaeologists is their attempt, not to rely on the standing structures hitherto used by most foreign archaeologists, but to use the nonvisible settlements, those thought to have been occupied by local inhabitants, including migrants and traders, as well. Notable among indigenous archaeologists is Paul Msemwa (1988, 1990) who has looked at refuse disposal within coastal settlements and used the results as a base in explaining the archaeological record of the area. It is also noteworthy that local pottery, which had previously been ignored when constructing coastal chronology—the earlier chronology was based on imported Arabic/Persian (Islamic) and Chinese pottery—is now being used as an important variable in chronological construction. The danger, however, of using pottery typology to date sites is not taking into account the problem of human scavenging activities. Old potsherds have frequently been found incorporated into later sites through human activities of recycling and reuse. Likewise, later human activities in older settlements occasionally mix up the archaeological record. For instance, at Kilwa, in southeastern Tanzania, carbon–14 dating contradicted the principle of superposition, with charcoal samples taken from

lower levels being much younger than samples taken from the upper levels (Chittick 1966a, 1966b, 1967). It is noteworthy that Msemwa questions this disturbed nature revealed by carbon–14 dates and is looking at site formation processes as a way of developing an alternative chronology of coastal sites.

Almost all the studies that have been done in East Africa are bereft of theoretical discussion. The exceptions are Msemwa (1989), and Kiriama (1993). Msemwa used the general systems theory in modeling the use of the Rufiji River in Tanzania by the Warufiji people. In his study, Msemwa divided the river into ecosystems with each ecosystem being defined by a configuration of landscape and soil types, subsistence activities, distance from the sea, and means of communication. Using this model, Msemwa found that despite the fact that Mafia Island had all the advantages of the other coastal settlements, Mafia did not grow into an important center. Msemwa argues that this was a result of a lack of adequate resources, such as freshwater, and of the presence of malarial mosquitoes. He theorizes that emphasis should be placed on the relationship between resource availability and the patterning of settlement locations, particularly the nature of those resources.

Kiriama (1992) went further and used the food systems research paradigm to study not only coastal settlements but also their relationship with the hinterland. Since food systems research is concerned with changes in food systems over the long term, its application assists in understanding how settlement sizes were affected by the intensification or abatement of food resources or how food production in a particular region contributed to the migration and subsequent settlement of the area. Kiriama argues that the availability or lack of resources in the hinterland affected the setting up, sustenance, and eventual decline of some of the settlements on the coast. In other words, instead of looking at extraneous factors for the origins and subsequent decline of East African coastal settlements, researchers should look at developments in the hinterland.

Other foreign researchers have used the new archaeology paradigm in the region, not to try to understand the past of the communities concerned, but to prove their theories (Herbich 1988; Hodder 1982, 1986).

Herman Ogoti Kiriama

See also Africa, East, Prehistory; Africa, Horn of; Africa, South, Prehistory; Swahili Coast of Africa

References

Abungu, G. H. O. 1989. *Communities on the River Tana, Kenya: An Archaeological Study of Relations between the Delta and River Basin, A.D. 700–1890.* Ph.D. dissertation, University of Cambridge.

Ambrose, S. H. 1980. "Elmenteitan and Other Late Pastoral Neolithic Adaptations in the Central Highlands of East Africa." In *Proceedings of the Eighth Pan-African Congress of Prehistory and Quaternary Studies—Nairobi 1977,* 279–282. Ed. R. E. Leakey and B. A. Ogot. Nairobi: Inernational Louis Leakey Memorial Institute for African Prehistory.

———. 1982. "Archaeological and Linguistic Reconstructions of History in East Africa." In *The Archaeological and Linguistic Reconstruction of African History,* 104–157. Ed. C. Ehret and M. Posnansky. Berkeley: University of California Press.

———. 1984a. "Holocene Environments and Human Adaptations in the Central Rift Valley, Kenya." Ph.D. dissertation, University of California, Berkeley.

———. 1984b. "Introduction of Pastoral Adaptations to the Highlands of East Africa." In *From Hunters to Farmers,* 212–239. Ed. J. D. Clark and S. Brandt. Berkeley: University of California Press.

———. 1985. "Excavations at Maasai Gorge Shelter, Naivasha, Kenya." *Azania* 20: 2967.

Barthelme, J. 1977. "Holocene Sites North-east of Lake Turkana: A Preliminary Report." *Azania* 12: 33–41.

Bower, J. R. F., and C. M. Nelson. 1978. "Early Pottery and Pastoral Cultures of the Central Rift Valley, Kenya." *Man* 13: 554–566.

Bower, J. R. F., C. M. Nelson, A. F. Waibel, and S. Wandibba. 1977. "The University of Massachusetts Late Stone Age / Pastoral Neolithic Comparative Study in Central Kenya." *Azania* 12: 119–146.

Butzer, K. W., G. Ll. Isaac, J. L. Richardson, and C. K. Washbourne Kamau. 1972. "Radiocarbon Dating of East African Lake Levels." *Science* 175: 1069–1076.

Chami, F. 1992. "Current Archaeological Research in the Bagamoyo District, Tanzania." In *Urban Origins in Eastern Africa, Proceedings of the 1991 Workshop in Zanzibar,* 16–34. Ed. P. J. J. Sinclair and A. Juma.

Chittick, H. N. 1966a. "Unguja Ukuu: The Earliest Imported Pottery and an Abbasid Dinar." *Azania* 1: 161–163.

———. 1966b. "Kilwa: A Preliminary Report." *Azania* 2: 1–36.

———. 1967. "Discoveries in the Lamu Archipelago." *Azania* 2: 37–67.

———. 1974. "Excavations at Aksum, 1973–74: A Preliminary Report." *Azania* 9: 159–205.

———. 1984. *Manda: Excavations at an Island Port on the Kenya Coast.* Memoir no. 9. Nairobi: British Institute in Eastern Africa.

Cole, S. 1963. *The Prehistory of East Africa.* Harmondsworth, UK: Penguin.

Collett, S., and P. Robertshaw. 1983a. "Pottery Traditions of Early Pastoral Communities in Kenya." *Azania* 18: 107–125.

———. 1983b. "Problems in the Interpretation of Radio Carbon Dates: The Pastoral Neolithic of East Africa." *African Archaeological Review* 1: 57–74.

Ehret, C. 1974. *Ethiopians and East Africans: The Question of Contacts.* Nairobi: East African Publishing House.

———. 1976. "Linguistic Evidence and Its Correlation with Archaeology." *World Archaeology* 8: 518.

Gifford-Gonzalez, D. 1984. "Implications of a Pastoral Neolithic Faunal Sample from Central Kenya." In *From Hunters to Farmers,* 240–251. Ed. J. D. Clark and S. Brandt. Berkeley: University of California Press.

———. 1985. "The Faunal Remains from Maasai George Rock Shelter and Marula Rock Shelter." *Azania* 20: 69–89.

Gramly, M. R. 1972. "Report on the Teeth from Narosura." *Azania* 7: 87–91.

Hamilton, A. C. 1982. *Environmental History of East Africa.* London: Academic Press.

Herbich, I. 1988. "Differentiating between the Social Contexts of Manufacture and Use in an African Society and the Question of Stylistic Signalling of Ethnic Boundaries." Paper presented at the fifty-third annual meeting of the Society for American Archaeology, Phoenix, AZ.

Hodder, I. 1982. *Symbols in Action.* Cambridge: Cambridge University Press.

————. 1986. *Reading the Past*. Cambridge: Cambridge University Press.

Horton, M. 1984. "The Early Settlement of the Northern Swahili Coast." Ph.D. dissertation, University of Cambridge.

Isaac, G. Ll., H. V. Merrick, and C. M. Nelson. 1972. "Stratigraphic and Archaeological Studies in the Lake Nakuru Basin, Kenya." *Palaeoecology of Africa* 6: 225–232.

Karega-Munene. 1993. "Neolithic/Iron Age Subsidence Economies in the Lake Victoria Basin of East Africa." Ph.D. dissertation, University of Cambridge.

Kiriama, H. O. 1984. "Fabric Analysis of Nderit Ware." B.A. thesis, University of Nairobi.

————. 1986. "Prehistoric Iron Smelting Technology in East Africa." M.Phil. thesis, University of Cambridge.

————. 1987. "Archaeometallurgy of Iron Smelting Slags from a Mwitu Tradition Site in Kenya." *South African Archaeological Bulletin* 42: 125–130.

————. 1992. "Farming Systems Research and Its Implications for Urban Origins in East Africa." In *Urban Origins in East Africa, Proceedings of the 1991 Workshop in Zanzibar*. Ed. P. J. J. Sinclair and A. Juma. Paper no. 8.

————. 1993. "The Iron Using Communities in Kenya." In *The Archaeology of Africa*. Ed. T. Shaw et al. One World Archaeology Series vol. 20. London: Routledge.

Leakey, L. S. B. 1931. *The Stone Age Cultures of Kenya*. Cambridge: Cambridge University Press.

————. 1935. *The Stone Age Races of Kenya Colony*. Oxford: Oxford University Press.

Leakey, M. D. 1943. "Notes on the Ground and Polished Stone Axes of East Africa." *Journal of the East African and Uganda Natural History Society* 17: 182–195.

————. 1945. "Report on the Excavations at Hyrax Hill, Nakuru, Kenya Colony, 1937–38." *Transactions of the Royal Society of South Africa* 30: 271–409.

Leakey, M. D., and L. S. B. Leakey. 1950. *Excavations at the Njoro River Cave*. Oxford: Oxford University Press.

Livingstone, D. A. 1980. "Environmental Changes in the Nile Headwaters." In *The Sahara and the Nile*, 335–355. Ed. M. A. J. Williams and H. Faure. Rotterdam: A. A. Balkema.

Lwanga-Lunyiigo, S. 1976. "The Bantu Problem Reconsidered." *Current Anthropology* 17: 282–286.

Marshall, F. B. 1986. "Aspects of the Advent of Pastoral Economies in East Africa." Ph.D. dissertation, Department of Anthropology, University of California, Berkeley.

Masao, F. 1979. *The Later Stone Age and the Rock Paintings of Central Tanzania*. Wiesbaden: Stones.

Mbae, B. 1986. "Aspects of Maasai Ethnoarchaeology: Implications for Archaeological Interpretation." M.A. thesis, University of Nairobi.

Msemwa, P. J. 1988. "A Review of Shell Fish Collecting Studies along the Coast of Tanzania." In *Urban Origins in Eastern Africa, Project Proposal and Workshop Summaries*. Ed. P. J. J. Sinclair and S. Wandibba. Stockholm: Swedish Central Board of Antiquities.

————. 1989. "Modelling: An Attempt at Locational Analysis of Settlements on Rufiji Drainage Basin, Tanzania." In *Urban Origins in Eastern Africa, Project Proposal and Workshop Summaries*, 129–140. Ed. P. J. Sinclair and S. Wandibba. Stockholm: Swedish Central Board of Antiquities.

————. 1990. "The Determinants of Secondary Refuse Disposal Patterns: An Ethnoarchaeological Study." In *Urban Origins in Eastern Africa, Proceedings of the Harare and Great Zimbabwe Congress*, 116–120. Ed. P. J. Sinclair and G. Pwiti.

Muriuki, G. 1974. *A History of the Kikuyu*. Nairobi: East African Publishing House.

Mutoro, H. W. 1987. "An Archaeological Study of the Miji Kenda Kaya Settlements on the Hinterland Kenya Coast." Ph.D. dissertation, Department of Anthropology, University of California, Los Angeles.

Nelson, C. M. 1980. "The Elmenteitan Lithic Industry." In *Proceedings of the Eighth Pan-African Congress of Prehistory and Quaternary Studies—Nairobi 1977*, 275–278. Ed. R. E. Leakey and B. A. Ogot. Nairobi: International Louis Leakey Memorial Institute for African Prehistory.

Odner, K. 1971. "An Archaeological Survey of Iramba, Tanzania." *Azania* 6: 151–198.

Onyango-Abuje, J. D. 1976. "Reflections of Culture Change and Distribution during the Neolithic Period in East Africa." *Hadith* 6: 14–30.

Onyango-Abuje, J. D., and S. Wandibba. 1979. "The Palaeoenvironment and Its Influence on Man's Activities in East Africa during the Latter Part of Upper Pleistocene and Holocene." *Hadith* 7: 24–40.

Phillipson, D. W. 1976a. "The Early Iron Age in Eastern and South Africa: A Critical Reappraisal." *Azania* 11: 1–23.

———. 1976b. *The Prehistory of Eastern Zambia.* Nairobi: British Institute in Eastern Africa.

———. 1977a. *The Later Prehistory of Eastern and South Africa.* London: Heinemann.

———. 1977b. "The Excavation of Gobedra Rock Shelter, Axum: An Early Occurrence of Cultivated Finger Millet in Northern Ethiopia." *Azania* 12: 53–82.

———. 1985. *African Archaeology.* Cambridge: Cambridge University Press.

Posnansky, M. 1967. "The Iron Age in East Africa." In *Background to Evolution in Africa.* Ed. W. W. Bishop and J. D. Clark. Chicago: University of Chicago Press.

Richardson, J. L., and A. E. Richardson. 1972. "The History of the African Rift Lake and Its Climatic Implications." *Ecological Monographs* 42: 499–534.

Robertshaw, P. T. 1989. *A History of African Archaeology.* London: Currey.

Schmidt, P. R. 1978. *Historical Archaeology: A Structural Approach in an African Culture.* Westport, CT: Greenwood Press.

———. 1983a. "An Alternative to a Strictly Materialist Perspective: A Review of Historical Archaeology, Ethnoarchaeology, and Symbolic Approaches in African Archaeology." *American Antiquity* 48: 62–79.

———. 1983b. "Cultural Meaning and History in African Myth." *International Journal of Oral History* 4: 167–183.

Scully, R. T. K. 1969. "Fort Sites of East Bukusu, Kenya." *Azania* 4: 105–114.

———. 1979. "Nineteenth Century Settlement Sites and Related Oral Traditions from the Bungoma Areas, Western Kenya." *Azania* 14: 81–96.

Shepartz, R. L. 1988. "Who Were the Later Pleistocene Eastern Africans?" *African Archaeological Review* 6: 57–72.

Soper, R. C. 1971a. "Early Iron Age Pottery Types from East Africa: Comparative Analysis." *Azania* 6: 39–52.

———. 1971b. "A General Review of the Early Iron Age in the Southern Half of Africa." *Azania* 6: 5–37.

———. 1982. "Bantu Expansion into East Africa: Archaeological Evidence." In *The Archaeological and Linguistic Reconstruction of African Prehistory,* 223–238. Ed. C. Ehret and M. Posnansky. Berkeley: University of California Press.

Sutton, J. E. G. 1966. "The Archaeology and Early Peoples of the Highlands of Kenya and Northern Tanzania." *Azania* 1: 37–57.

———. 1973. *The Archaeology of the Western Highlands of Kenya.* Memoir no. 3. Nairobi: British Institute in Eastern Africa.

———. 1986. "The Irrigation and Soil-Conservation in African Agricultural History." *Journal of African History* 25: 25–41.

———. 1989. *Excavations at Aksum: An Account of Research at the Ancient Ethiopian Capital Directed in 1972–4 by S. C. Munro-Hay.* London: British Institute in East Africa.

———. 1990. *A Thousand Years of East Africa.* Nairobi: British Institute in Eastern Africa.

Sutton, J. E. G., and A. D. Roberts. 1968. "Uvinza and Its Salt Industry." *Azania* 21: 27–52.

Vansina, J. 1965. *Oral Tradition: A Study in Historical Methodology.* Chicago: Aldine.

———. 1967. "The Use of Oral Tradition in African Culture History." In *Reconstructing African Culture History.* Ed. C. Gabel and N. R. Bennett. Boston: Boston University Press.

Wandibba, S. 1978–1979. "An Attribute Analysis of the Ceramics of the Early Pastoralist Period from the Southern Rift Valley, Kenya." M.S. thesis. University of Nairobi.

———. 1980. "The Application of an Attribute Analysis to the Study of the Later Stone Age/Neolithic Pottery Ceramics in Kenya (Summary)." In *Proceedings of the Eighth Pan-African Congress of Prehistory and Quaternary Studies—Nairobi, September 1977,* 283–285. Ed R. E. Leakey and B. A. Ogot. Nairobi: The International Louis Leakey Memorial Institute for African Prehistory.

———. 1984. "Petrological Investigation of Pottery in Kenya." Report prepared for the Ford Foundation.

Africa, East, Prehistory

Africa is renowned for its diverse and bountiful fossil record of human and nonhuman ancestors that spans some 50 million years, including Eocene primates from the Fayum deposits of Egypt and a sundry group of hominids (members of the family Hominidae, which is the taxonomic family to which humans and their immediate ancestors belong) that made their evolutionary appearance some 5 million years ago in the Middle Awash of Ethiopia. Tracing humans' ancestral beginnings to this region is but

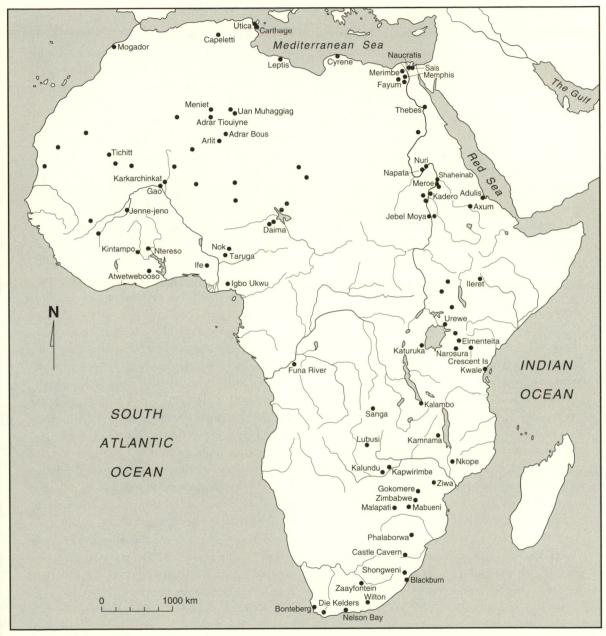

Utica
Carthage
Capeletti
Mogador
Leptis
Mediterranean Sea
Cyrene
Naucratis
Sais
Merimbe
Memphis
Fayum
Thebes

Meniet
Uan Muhaggiag
Adrar Tiouiyne
Adrar Bous
Arlit
Tichitt
Karkarchinkat
Gao
Jenne-jeno
Nuri
Napata
Shaheinab
Meroe
Kadero
Adulis
Axum
Jebel Moya
Daima
Kintampo
Ntereso
Nok
Taruga
Ife
Atwetwebooso
Igbo Ukwu

Ileret

Urewe

Katuruka
Elmenteita
Narosura
Crescent Is
Kwale

N

Funa River

Kalambo

SOUTH

Sanga

Kamnama

ATLANTIC

Lubusi
Nkope

OCEAN
Kalundu
Kapwirimbe
Gokomere
Ziwa
Zimbabwe
Malapati
Mabueni

INDIAN

OCEAN

Phalaborwa

Castle Cavern

Shongweni
Blackburn
Zaayfontein
Wilton
Die Kelders
Bonteberg
Nelson Bay

Red Sea

The Gulf

0   1000 km

Archaeological Sites in Africa

one reason why prehistoric East Africa, of all African regions, deserves special recognition. East Africa is also the birthplace of a rich technological history that has produced: (1) evidence of a technological threshold with the oldest known stone tools at 2.6 million years ago from the Gona deposits at Hadar (Harris 1983; Semaw et al. 1997); (2) possibly the earliest evidence for controlled use of fire in Kenya at 1.4 million years ago (Harris 1982; Gowlett 1992); and (3) equally importantly, the region is besieged with vital archaeological sites that are of paramount importance in defining Early Stone Age (Early Paleolithic) and Middle Stone Age (Middle Paleolithic) industries throughout Africa (Clark 1969; Leakey 1971; Harris 1978; Leakey and Roe 1994; Isaac 1997). Most of what is known today about East African prehistory resulted from the research of a handful of widely acclaimed archaeologists over the last fifty years.

The History of East African Prehistoric Discoveries

In 1893, geologist J. W. Gregory first recognized the contributive importance of East Africa to better understanding the evolutionary history of ancient technologies when he found evidence of "paleoliths" in and around an ancient lake in Maasai country (Cole 1965). In the twentieth century, German entomologist Kattwinkel noted the presence of fossils in 1911 at a rift escarpment known to the Maasai as Olduway, which shortly led German paleontologist Hans Reck to continue work at Olduway (later called OLDUVAI GORGE). Reck noticed that important paleontological localities occur where the Side Gorge meets the Main Gorge. But with World War I beginning, his work came to an abrupt halt. When the war came to an end, extensive archeological research resumed across all of Africa, especially in East Africa. Yet the main scientific quest was not to discover more forgotten material cultures; rather, current scientific interests strove to elucidate past climatic events in order to better understand the chronological framework of the fossil and archaeological records that were already known. This is exactly what prompted E. J. Wayland to survey Uganda while he served as

the Director of Geological Survey of Uganda. In 1934, he reported an ancient split-pebble industry based on rolled material taken from the Kafu River in western Uganda, which was later extended to include other Ugandan sites, such as Kagera Valley and Nsongezi, by South African archeologist C. van Riet Lowe. It was the nature of the sedimentary record that led Wayland to describe environmental intervals he called "pluvials," literally meaning *rains*, that he thought would link Europe's four-glacier concept to Africa. Today, the Kafuan industry is not recognized as a legitimate stone-tool technology because the stone tools (split-pebbles) are the result of natural fractures, most likely caused by the river environment from which they were found, and the pluvial concept is long forgotten. Wayland was also responsible for describing the Sangoan and Magosian Middle Paleolithic industries from type-sites also located near the Kafu River; the Sangoan is still recognized as a legitimate industry, but Magosian tools fall within the range of variation of an Acheulean-Levallois techno-complex.

Prior to the time that the Kafuan industry made its debut, another famous paleoanthropologist and prehistorian, L. S. B. LEAKEY, was working fervently at stone tool sites in Kenya, dinosaur sites in Tanzania (then Tanganyika), and hominid-bearing deposits in South Africa. After getting his field techniques down in Tanzania and describing simple stone tool manufacture and more recent stone tool technologies of Kenya, in 1931 he organized an expedition to Olduvai Gorge with the help of Hans Reck. He quickly recognized the significance of the stone tools found in the layer cake stratigraphy deposits that ranges in date from 1.9 million years ago at the base, to 1.8 million years ago at Bed I, to recent at Bed IV. Before long, Leakey was back at Olduvai, and from 1935 to 1958 he and members of his team had many celebrated accomplishments in terms of collecting fossil mammals and plenty of stone tools, but had discovered no stone tool maker. That wouldn't come until 1959 when his wife, MARY LEAKEY, discovered Zinjanthropus (*Australopithecus boisei*), a.k.a. the nutcracker man and, as no surprise, Louis's stone tool maker. Over the decades, the meticulous excavations at Olduvai by Mary and Louis Leakey would engender incredible hominid discoveries and significant advances facilitating phylogenetic inferences of which particular hominids generated flaked stone technologies. In general, the Leakey's connubial commitment to research was well received, but it was Mary Leakey's work in particular that would ultimately change the course of human evolutionary studies recording the evidence of an ancient past and of how to interpret human prehistory in East Africa. The simple flake and core industry found at Olduvai Gorge became known as the Oldowan Industrial Complex (see below). In earlier deposits, the Leakeys also came across larger tools and cores that were worked on both sides, hence the name biface. Handaxes, picks, and cleavers are all bifaces and resemble the Acheulean industry from Europe. The size of the tool/core and the amount of bifacial flaking would determine the category of flaked stone technology. Acheulean is found at Olduvai Gorge, but intermediate industries are also recognized.

From 1953 to 1966, J. D. CLARK, Director of the National Museum of Zambia, excavated an open-air stratified Pleistocene site in Zambia near Tanzania called Kalambo Falls. This site produced Acheulean, Sangoan, and Epipaleolithic industries that are believed to range in age from the Middle Pleistocene to recent. In 1961, Clark became faculty at the University of California at Berkeley. This marked a paramount period in prehistory studies in East Africa. It was during Clark's tenure at Berkeley that many talented students would undertake archeological training in East Africa—they were to influentially dominate the field for the next thirty years. A protégé of Louis Leakey, South African archaeologist GLYN ISAAC, received his Ph.D. from Cambridge in 1961. He is best known for his work in East Africa, especially at OLORGESAILIE, which is an Early to Late Pleistocene locality in southern Kenya dated to 1.2 to .05 million years ago, and the Koobi Fora field school that he managed alongside Richard Leakey. Various layers at Olorgesailie dated to 780 thousand years ago are inundated with Acheulean handaxes and some skeletons of *Theropithecus oswaldi leakeyi,* which suggests that hominids may

have hunted these now-extinct especially large species of baboons. According to archaeologist Rick Potts of the National Museum of Natural History, Washington, D.C., who has been the principal investigator at Olorgesailie since the unexpected death of Glyn Isaac in the mid-1980s, the site documents an important character suite of Pleistocene large mammals including the last known occurrences of *Elephas recki* and *Hipparion.*

Continuing in the Berkeley tradition during the 1970s, J. W. K. Harris, a doctoral student of J. D. Clark and Glyn Isaac, investigated the Karari escarpment located on the eastern border of Lake Turkana and discovered an archaeological site composed of single platform core/scrapers. Because it was different from the Early Oldowan Industry and Developed Oldowan A & B recovered from Beds I, II, and III, Harris named this innovative technological complex the Karari Industry (Harris 1978). Karari sites are typically concentrated within channel gravels and floodplain silts in the lower portion of the Okote member of the Koobi Fora Formation, which is dated to 1.6 million years ago. Harris is also responsible for the discovery of the oldest known stone tools, which were collected in situ in the Kada Hadar Member of the Gona sequence of Hadar, Ethiopia, dated to 2.6 million years ago. The simple flake pebble tool industry at Gona is typically Oldowan. In the late 1980s, Harris also turned his attention to the Western Rift Valley, where he discovered another Late Pliocene–Early Pleistocene open-air site known as Senga–5 in Congo (formerly Zaire) (Harris et al. 1987). Senga–5 has produced numerous small quartz flakes and simple pebble cores. These are difficult to date through sedimentary analytical techniques; biostratigraphy of associated fauna suggests correlation with the Omo sequence of the Eastern Rift Valley, dated to 2.3 to 1.9 million years ago. Harris also concerned himself with tracing the origins of fire technology in the fossil record, with the earliest evidence of fire use by hominids coming from East Africa at 1.4 million years ago at FxJj 50 and Chesowanja, Kenya (Harris 1982). J. W. K. Harris, now at Rutgers University, has many former and current students working in East Africa continuing his legacy.

Early Paleolithic and Middle Paleolithic Industrial Complexes

Until very recently, African simple flake and small pebble tool technologies were vaguely separated into the Early Stone Age (ESA), while the larger bifacially worked cores and flakes were referred to as the Middle Stone Age (MSA); comparable technologies throughout Europe are known as Early Paleolithic (EP) and Middle Paleolithic (MP), respectively. To lessen confusion, ESA and MSA categories are sometimes interposed with the—just as vague—European system of classification. The only practical classification system is one that critically assesses true industrial complexes (e.g., Oldowan, Karari, Developed Oldowan, and Acheulean) or degree of technological innovation, such as J. D. Clark's Mode 1–5 preparative frameworks.

Early Paleolithic (ca. 2.5 million–250,000 years ago; e.g., Oldowan, Developed Oldowan, Karari, Acheulean, Mode 1, and Mode 2)

The earliest flaked stone technology consisting of split cobbles and simple flakes made mostly of trachyte, rhyolite, basalt, and quartz come from the Gona sequence of Ethiopia dated at 2.6 million years ago and the Hadar sequence, both within the Kada Hadar Member of the Hadar Formation, dated at 2.3 million years ago. Although Gona has the oldest known stone tools, the Kada Hadar stone flakes were recovered on surface and in situ where the A.L. 666 maxilla (upper jaw) attributed to early *Homo* was discovered (Kimbel et al. 1996). In addition, stone tools dated at 2.3 million years ago have also been recovered from the Omo deposits in southern Ethiopia and at Lokalalei, West Turkana, from the Nachukui Formation.

Oldowan Industrial Complex—Early Oldowan is a lithic industry based upon artifact assemblages from Bed 1 and Bed 2 at Olduvai Gorge (Leakey 1971). Overall the Oldowan complex consists of modified (deliberate flaked) pieces of stone or battered cobbles that are classified into several types: hammerstones, choppers, scrapers, discoids, polyhedrons, spheroids, subspheroids, burins, and protobifaces. Overall assemblages are classified by artifact type and relative frequency. For instance, typical Oldowan assemblages are localized and consist of 28 to 79 percent choppers made from varied resources (e.g., quartzite and chert) and in proximity to raw sources. Less than 28 percent of choppers for all tools/cores in assemblages may be indicative of a more progressive lithic complex. Two examples that are thought to lead to the Acheulean Industry are:

(1) Developed Oldowan A—Lithic industry based upon artifact assemblages from upper Bed I, lower Bed II at Olduvai Gorge. Artifact assemblages have low frequency of choppers, and a greater abundance of spheroids, subspheroids, and small scrapers. In addition, protobifaces (a small core not extensively worked on both sides) appear in the record.

(2) Developed Oldowan B—Lithic industry based upon artifact assemblages from lower Bed II through middle Bed III at Olduvai Gorge (Leakey and Roe 1994) and from Melka Kontouré of Central Ethiopia ca. 1.7 to 0.1 million years ago. Artifact assemblages have a greater frequency of core forms (discoids and choppers), and the first appearance of a small bifaces (albeit few in number). Many have argued that this industry can be subsumed in the Acheulean industry; however, Mary Leakey maintained that the Developed Oldowan B is consistent with Oldowan tool traditions.

Acheulean Industry—Lithic industry originally based upon large bifaces found at St. Acheul (France), but in Africa this industry is based upon artifact assemblages from upper Bed II at Olduvai Gorge and at Konso (Ethiopia), Olorgesailie, and Melka Kontouré—to name a few of the more important sites. Artifact assemblages are composed of large bifaces, like handaxes, picks, and cleavers, and all show a high degree of standardization, something that was missing form earlier flake stone techno-complexes. Isaac (1977) suggests that African Acheulean is characterized by the use of very large flakes (less than 10 centimeters in length). Earlier Acheulean at Olduvai utilized smaller cores when preparing bifaces.

Middle Paleolithic (ca. 200–35 thousand years ago; Levalloisian-type cores, Mode 3 preparation)

Levallois-type cores are prepared by an elaborate technique named after a Parisian suburb where flakes of this kind were first recognized. Levalloisian cores take a lot of core preparation to get the perfect striking platform in order to generate a flake with a predetermined shape. Typically, Levalloisian flakes are very thin. In addition, there is an increase in retouched flake tools in the Middle Paleolithic. This industrial period also bears witness to improved hunting techniques as reflected by faunal remains. Sites include Gademotta (Ethiopia), Diré-Dawa (Port-Epic, Ethiopia), Katanda (Congo), and Kapthurin (Kenya).

Summary

East Africa is the birthplace of our earliest ancestors and the oldest known stone technology, but, more importantly, this region provides the earliest evidence of a creative pulse that catapulted our ancestors on a evolutionary trajectory never before witnessed in the history of life. It is not surprising that with the formal acquaintance of different hominid groups sharing ecological niches within the rapidly changing environments of East Africa, groups were forced to compete amongst one another and other animals for available resources. It would only be a question of time until the advent of a flaked stone technology would spawn a crucial advantage for the maker and users of the stone tools to out-compete one other and other primates for food (and water) by expanding dietary breadths and significantly contributing to their survival during times of environmental stress. The significance of flaked stone technologies, however, lies not within the corpus of edification that results when one bashes two pebbles together, but the necessary mental faculties and imaginative capabilities of first conceptualizing stones that possess the mechanical properties that facilitate knapping. When this happened, the overall hominid bauplan was changing course. Encephalization in the Family took off, and nothing short of a major hominid radiation occurred throughout Africa. With the bashing of two rocks a few million years ago, it seems our evolutionary path was reflexively set in stone.

Ken Mowbray

See also Africa, South, Prehistory

References

Clark, J. D. 1969. *The Prehistory of Africa.* New York: Praeger.

Cole, S. 1963. *The Prehistory of East Africa.* New York: New American Library of World Literature.

Gowlett, J. A. J. 1993. *Ascent to Civilization: The Archeology of Early Humans.* New York: McGraw-Hill.

Harris, J. W. K. 1978. *The Karari Industry: Its Place in East Africa Prehistory.* Ph.D. dissertation, University of California. Ann Arbor, MI: University Microfilms.

———. 1982. "Quest for Fire: The Chesowanja Evidence." *Anthro Quest* 24: 9–10.

———. 1983. "Cultural Beginnings: Plio-Pleistocene Archaeological Occurrences from the Afar, Ethiopia. *African Archaeological Review* 1: 3–31.

Harris, J. W. K., et al. 1987. "The Setting, Context, and Character of the Senga–5A Site, Zaire." *Journal of Human Evolution* 16: 701–728.

Isaac, G. L. 1977. *Olorgesailie: Archaeological Studies of Middle Pleistocene Lake Basin in Kenya.* Chicago: Chicago University Press.

———. 1997. *Koobi Fora Research Project, Volume 5, Plio-Pleistocene Archaeology.* Oxford: Clarendon Press.

Kimbel, W. H., et al. 1996. "Late Pliocene Homo and Oldowan Tools from the Hadar Formation (Kada Hadar Member), Ethiopia." *Journal of Human Evolution* 31: 549–562.

Leakey, M. D. 1971. *Olduvai Gorge, Vol. 3, Excavations in Beds 1 and 2.* Cambridge: Cambridge University Press.

Leakey, M. D., and D. A. Roe. 1994. *Olduvai Gorge: Excavations in Beds III, IV, and the Masek Beds, 1968–1971.* Cambridge: Cambridge University Press.

Semaw, S., et al. 1997. "2.5-Million-Year-Old Stone Tools from Ethiopia." *Nature* 385: 333–336.

Africa, Egypt

See Egypt: Dynastic; Egypt: Predynastic

Africa, Francophone

Historical self-criticism has seldom been strong among French prehistorians. A rare instance is F. Audouze and ANDRÉ LEROI-GOURHAN's article (1981) entitled "France: A Continental Insularity," and if we accept the premise of that title, then the archaeology of francophone Africa can best be characterized as the marginalized within the insular. Vast portions of ex-French colonies have yet to be trod upon by a prehistorian, but marginalization has an even deeper foundation in the institutionalized scorn for theory, a French national style that is exaggerated when exported to francophone Africa. As P. de Maret despairs, "From a theoretical point of view, apart from the rather pointless discussion over nomenclature, the archaeologists hardly seemed to concern themselves with larger explanatory models" (Maret 1990, 134).

Yet, as de Maret's pronouncement upon his colleagues in central Africa suggests, self-criticism is franker in Africa than perhaps in any other part of the loose commonwealth of French-speaking nations called La Francophonie. This is one of the several paradoxes (and hidden strengths) of francophone African archaeology. Criticism goes well beyond claims of inadequate methods and meager results. Africans have leveled charges that an effort to train a cadre of indigenous prehistorians, educated in France, was a cynical effort to maintain metropolitan influence, an effort begun only when independence was recognized as an inevitability. Local prehistorians accuse the large French-funded projects of the late 1970s and 1980s of overwhelming African national research priorities, yet some of those same massive-budget projects have been models of interdisciplinary research. France has also funded several national site inventories, a national priority in many countries. Paradoxes are legion in the history of archaeological research in francophone Africa.

It is quite true that theory is dismissed as an "Anglo-Saxon aberration," yet francophone Africa has been a proving ground for several of the most global theoretical positions as the focus of debates going back to the nineteenth century. An epic struggle between *Kulturkreise* and culture evolution raged in the forests of central Africa. Proponents of a very narrow reading of culture particularism debated a diffusionist form of culture evolutionism championed by the ABBÉ HENRI BREUIL for several decades fol-

lowing World War I, and today, a variety of national styles (German empiricism, Anglo-American processual and postprocessual archaeology, and Soviet-style Marxist-Leninist archaeology) vie with recent trends in "French pragmatics" for the intellectual loyalty of a new generation of African prehistorians.

Most research has been conducted by amateurs using methods antiquated even by metropolitan standards. Yet cream does rise, and the history of each region can boast a handful of crossover practitioners from fields as diverse as medicine, administration, and public works who became infected with a passion for prehistory. Such amateurs set for themselves the highest standards of data collection and analysis. It is quite true that the Bordesian quantitative analysis reforms have been incompletely assimilated and that the days of obsession with "belles pieces" (aesthetically pleasing specimens) are not far past, yet innovations in ethnoarchaeology and in the social and technical analysis of stone tool manufacturing known as *chaines operatoires* have been imported into France from francophone Africa.

It is also true that the large majority of the techniques of excavation and surface survey are still far from what they could be. Yet the French have created opportunities for the prompt publishing of research monographs by their nationals and by citizens of their ex-colonies that are the envy of the rest of the archaeological world. It is also quite true that post–cold war changes in the political balance among nations have led to a reassertion of France's claim to exclusive monetary and cultural influence over the lands of La Francophonie, yet there are few other places in the world where so many national styles comingle—as do Malian, French, English, Norwegian, German, American, Swiss, and Dutch in the middle Niger of Mali; Cameroonian, French, Belgian, American, and English in the so-called proto-Bantu homeland of Cameroon; or Madagascan, French, Swedish, and American on the island of MADAGASCAR.

Francophone Africa is a vast area with a rich and astonishingly diverse (and largely unappreciated) past. There are two natural breaks in the history of investigations. It is important to understand that France has perhaps never fully recovered from its loss of talent in World War I and that that war broke colonial efforts into two segments. A third phase of investigations is the postindependence emergence of African national research aspirations.

Pre-1914: Africa Intrudes upon the Prehistorian's Consciousness

The Maghrebian states of Algeria, Morocco, and Tunisia are the exception to the rule of marginalization even during the pre-1914 period. Large corps of colonial amateurs scoured the countryside around the major cities of Constantine, Tebessa, Oran, and Tunis. They established societies of *prehistoire* (Stone Age) and *archeologie* (classical archaeology), and each had its own publications, the first of which, the *Journal de la Societe Archeologique de Constantine,* was founded in 1894. Exceptionally, French professionals were attracted to North Africa, and one of them, P. Pallary, published the first monographic regional synthesis in 1909. For decades, the attraction for amateur, professional, and the whole of the metropolitan establishment was the so-called Capsian-Aurignacian debate.

Resemblances between the blade component of the Maghrebian Capsian and the European Aurignacian periods were remarked upon as early as 1890. It was, however, the professional prehistorian Jacques de Morgan who started the debate by claiming that the similarities were the result of independent development under similar environmental conditions. This position was consistent with the cultural evolutionist, paleoethnological school of GABRIEL DE MORTILLET, but de Morgan was immediately criticized by some professional archaeologists such as Louis Capitan. De Morgan was particularly criticized by local amateur archaeologists who argued not only that a land bridge had once spanned the Mediterranean but also that North Africa was the source of the technological advances made during the Upper Paleolithic period. Breuil himself provisionally accepted the position of de Morgan's opponents in 1912. Most influential among these amateurs was Albert Debruge, who described what he believed to be Neanderthaloid skeletal remains as "ancient Aurignacian." These remains

were found during his 1912, 1914, and 1923 excavations at the important site of Mechta El Arbi.

It was not until the 1940s that the Capsian was finally accepted as being much more recent than the Aurignacian. Significantly absent from the debate was the question of the advisability of classifying local assemblages in terms of the dominant tool typology of France. The bane of francophone African archaeology until very recently was this modified evolutionary presumption, that the stages of the French Paleolithic period anticipated identical or analogous stages elsewhere and that such stages could be recognized by a relatively few type tools *(fossiles directeurs).*

A racist view of the world lay behind the making of highly subjective surface collections of "belles pieces" in the forested lowland basin of central Africa. Bored stones and fine-ground stone axes had been carried back to French-occupied territory by early explorers (e.g., H. M. Stanley and G. Schweinfurth), and this tradition was continued by the administrators and engineers of the early days of French and Belgian colonialism. These collections of artifacts became primary evidence for the theories of cultural evolutionists such as E. Dupont, the head of the Belgian Royal Institute of Natural Sciences. These evolutionists argued that all people throughout the world went through the same stages in the manufacturing of implements and tools, based on the similarity of African stone tools and those found in Europe. They also argued that different people passed from manufacturing stage to manufacturing stage at a faster or a slower rate determined by their race, their environment, or both. Well into the twentieth century, ethnographies of stone tools using "contemporary ancestors, such the forest Pygmies," were used to illustrate the lifestyles of Paleolithic peoples.

Stone and metal tools were displayed in the Central African Geological Exhibition at King Leopold II's imperialistic showpiece, the 1897 Brussels International Exhibition. Two years later, one of the geologists responsible, X. Stainier, published *L'Âge de la Pierre au Congo,* in which he sought to demonstrate the backwardness of the African peoples. For Stainier, African prehistory simply replicated (albeit more recently and at a slower pace) the distant past of Europe. Similar conclusions were drawn by V. Jacques in his 1901 and 1904 studies of all the randomly collected "belles pieces" from Congo now in the Tervuren Museum in Belgium (the inheritor of the site and collections of the 1897 International Exhibition). The Tervuren collection included 655 tools collected by a police captain at Tumba, in what was the Belgian Congo, and these tools would shortly become the focus of a decisive theoretical debate that helped push the whole of African archaeology (anglophone and francophone) away from grand syntheses and toward ever-more particularistic obsessions with nomenclature.

The tombs of Madagascar attracted some attention when colonial rule was imposed, as the conqueror, Gallieni, recommended that the newly founded Académie Malgache choose as its first research priority the monuments and cities of the coast. In 1898, the head of the Académie Malgache, A. Jully, synthesized reports made by amateurs rummaging through the tombs—which continued to be looted for the western art market until World War II. In 1908, P. Callet published the oral traditional history of Madagascar, and it assigned periodic Arab contact as being responsible for all change and progress on the island. There has been little archaeology proper on Madagascar, and researchers showed little interest in the internal dynamics of state formation or human impact on the native megafauna until the postindependence period.

Finally, and ironically, the West African nations that composed the Afrique Occidentale Française (AOF) contain some of the world's richest troves of lithic and metal archaeological remains, yet archaeological research in these countries remained amateur in nature and at very low density—even less so, perhaps, than in the Afrique Equatoriale Française (AEF) between Niger and Congo. Not surprisingly, the lower Senegal River (especially Saint-Louis at the mouth of the river) and the three communes near the temperate Cap Vert location of Dakar) was the first and more intensively explored (results were first published in 1851).

More "belles pieces," generally collected by soldiers, explorers, and administrators in the desert north, found a home in the newly founded (1878) Musée d'Ethnographie du Trocadero (now the Musée de l'Homme) in Paris. There they were studied and results were published by others—such as the founder of the Trocadero museum, Ernest Hamy, and the holder of the first chair of anthropology, Raymond Verneau—who had no firsthand experience in West Africa and certainly no appreciation for the context of the pieces. The museum sponsored collection and excavation campaigns in the Sahara (1870–1890 by F. Fernand) and the lakes region of the middle Niger (in the early 1900s by Lieutenant L. Desplagnes), and it published the unusually precise 1893–1899 excavation reports by L. Mouth (1899) of work at the Guinean Kakimbon rock shelter. However, analysis rarely went beyond speculation about the race of the toolmakers or inserting the finds into cultural-typological stages based upon the European sequence, with changes in the assemblage attributed to the intrusions of new people.

The excavations of Lieutenant Desplagnes at the tumuli of Killi and El Oualadgi are the exceptions of the period. Although this work was certainly not up to modern standards, it was exceptionally well recorded. The trenching of the large mounds was supervised, and Desplagnes kept and published the extensive notes he had taken during the excavations. Many of the finds were eventually properly cataloged in the Trocadero museum. Desplagnes alone among his contemporaries provided enough contextual information to allow subsequent republication and reinterpretation of these important sites.

Unfortunately, Desplagnes subscribed to the hyperdiffusionist thesis that all change, all "progress," in sub-Saharan Africa was derived from the north, especially as the result of race mixing between the Hamites of Semitic, Sumerian, and Berber origins. The highly influential Maurice Delafosse believed in the civilizing influence of the Egyptians and Phoenicians and that Ghana, the first of the great western Sudan empires, was founded by Judeo-Syrians. Nevertheless, Delafosse was basically sympathetic to Africans, and he fought against the current fashion of considering the continent to be without history by demonstrating the importance of West African cities and their great empires. His efforts led the Académie des Inscriptions et Belles Lettres to cosponsor Desplagnes at El Oualdgi and to send Bonnel de Mezieres to the presumed capital of Ghana. Still, the interpretive paradigm (of outside stimulation leading to the emergence of historical states and cities) was fixed and remained unchallenged during the following post–World War I period; indeed, it underlay much of postindependence research. This paradigm described the area's history as unprogressive local populations forming advanced political forms and urban centers only after contact with traders or colonists from the "centers of radiation" across the Sahara.

High Colonialism: Local Particularism from World War I to 1960

The paradigm of Arab cultural stimulation provided a backdoor for the legitimacy and, incidentally, the professionalization of West African prehistory that began in the 1930s. Although on the extreme periphery of the areas covered by Gabriel Camps's prehistory and history of North Africa (1980), the towns and states of the southern desert and the Sahel were, nevertheless, worthy of attention as legitimate parts of the Islamic Arab-Berber world.

It is important to note that the purpose of archaeological work at those sites was to confirm a particular location as a place named in the Arabic chronicles, to recover (cross-datable) North African imports, and to expose monumental stone-built structures (especially mosques). Major "medieval" sites investigated during this period include, in Mauritania, Azugi (by Theodore Monod and Raymond Mauny), Tegdaoust in Mauritania (by Mauny), and the presumed capital of Ghana, Koumbi Saleh (by Lazartigues, Thomassey, and Mauny; Mauny and Szumowski); in Mali, Gao (by le Pontois, Kikoine, and Michel; Bartoli; Mauny), Teghaza (by Langlais and Bessac; de Beauchene; Bourgrat), Tadmekka (by Lhote; Mauny), Timbuktu (by Mauny); in Guinea, the presumed capital of Mali, Niani (by Cooley and Binger; Vidal; Gaillard; Montrat; Mauny); and in Niger, Takedda (by Lieutenant Roy; Lombard; Lhote; Mauny).

Raymond Mauny pulled together these disparate archaeological efforts, along with Arab and European documentary sources and oral traditions, in his masterly *Tableau Géographique de l'Ouest Africain au Moyen Age* [A Geography of West Africa during the Middle Ages, 1961], which remains the prime secondary source on the latest prehistory and early history of West Africa.

Mauny's career is illustrative of the professional winds tugging at all of francophone Africa. Trained as a lawyer-administrator, he arrived in Senegal in 1938, the founding year of the premier African research center, the Institut Français d'Afrique Noire (IFAN). By 1947, an avocational historical bent had matured, and he headed the prehistory and proto-history ("metal age and medieval") department at IFAN. Mauny took a polymath's interest in all periods (lithics and rock art included), visited most known sites, hounded amateur excavators for their unpublished field notes, compiled answers to questionnaires sent to administrators, and displayed his exceptionally interdisciplinary vision in over 220 articles and several synthetic monographs.

If not brilliant, Mauny's excavations were at least up to the standards of most other professionals in francophone Africa (and no worse than even some today). Mauny recruited George Szumowski for IFAN at Bamako (Mali), and he dug innumerable (and poorly published) *petits sondages* (test pits dug nonstratigraphically) in the many habitation sites of the middle Niger (Mema, Mopti), near Segou, and in many rock-shelter deposits near Bamako. Similar work was done, for example, by P. Jouenne and J. Joire on the megalithic and earthen monuments of Senegal and by Mauny and a host of administrators on the tells and tumuli in the lakes region of the middle Niger. Were these efforts better than amateur scratchings? Stratigraphic excavation was the exception, no ceramic sequences or formal pottery typologies were developed, and the recording of the Sahara's prolific rock art was generally inadequate (except by Monod). And in lithic studies, with the exception of Laforgue and Hubert, there was no critique of the continuing reliance upon haphazard surface collections and *fossiles directeurs* derived from the European sequences.

Modern mosque in Jenné, Mali, in the Sudanic style (© *Nik Wheeler / CORBIS*)

Needless to say, across Africa colonialism came and went, but there was no training of a national corps of African archaeologists. And with the very rare exception of Mauny (who fought hard for the preservation of Sudanese-style building in Mali), the colonial authorities failed to stop blatant acts of cultural sabotage. The hiring of villagers to pillage middle Niger tells for their terracotta statuettes began during this period, and in 1931–1932, a journalist, H. Clerisse, butchered Tondidarou, West Africa's largest megalithic site. But West Africa was not alone in this decimation of sites.

A decade later and across the continent, two students spent two months conducting the massacre of some 600 Madagascan tombs. The loss of these tombs was all the more grave because of the lack on the island of even a single self-taught amateur archaeologist. The situation was similar in Afrique Equatoriale Française and in many parts of central Africa (Gabon, French Congo, Rwanda, Burundi), where the occasional geologists or priests continued to assemble the odd surface collections. The most significant work was that of J.-P. Lebeuf along the plain around Lake Chad. He was one of the pioneers in the use of oral tradition and ethnography to provide explanations, in terms of local legends, for the ethnic relations and migrations to some 1,200 "Sao" habitation mounds. Congo fared somewhat better, largely because the few amateurs there turned professional found themselves embroiled in the great Tumba controversy, a theoretical debate with international implications.

The pre–World War I "belles pieces" collection from Tumba became the core of O. Menghin's classic *Kulturkreis,* the Tumbian culture. As a leader of the Vienna culture-circle school, Menghin stressed geographical classification (forested lowlands, in this case) and diffusion or migration of homogeneous, extremely conservative cultural entities out of a very few cultural homelands. His Tumbian ("pig-raiser culture") was homogeneous from the French Congo to Angola. It was an arrow and spearhead, biface and blade culture and had barely evolved from the great hand-axe industry period. Soon, throughout forested Africa the term *tumbian* was applied to axe, large flake, and pick

assemblages (now known as Sangoan, Lupemban, and early Tshitolian).

It did not take long, however, for archaeologists building local sequences to begin to question the coherence of the Tumbian. In 1934–1935, a medical assistant, F. Cabu, organized a systematic collection within four kilometers of canal projects, and his acute observations demonstrated the mixed nature of the Tumba-type collection. Other geologists, G. Mortelmans and L. Cahen, or priests (such as Père Anciaux de Faveaux) became interested in prehistory, and their controlled excavations and local sequences bore out Cabu's conclusions. If their concerns were particularistic and nomenclatural, their methods were a great improvement. Unlike professional archaeologists of the period, they were not slavishly chained to European sequences. At the first Pan-African Congress of Prehistory in 1947, Cabu, his southern African colleagues, and Breuil argued that the Tumbian was a stratigraphically mixed product of racist thinking. They recommended that the term be eliminated. Despite LOUIS LEAKEY's objection, the Pan-African Congress voted for this recommendation in an all-too infrequent show of francophone-anglophone cooperation.

The slow march of professionalism continued in central Africa. Local sequences and definition of facies of the middle–Stone Age Sangoan and Lupemban and several later–Stone Age industries continued to be refined by Mortelmans, L. Cahen, and Bequaert. In 1950, de Heinzelin conducted the first fully controlled excavations in that part of the continent at Ishango, and he introduced a Bordesian quantitative approach to his lithics. Beginning in 1953, the Institute for Scientific Research in Central Africa supported many years of archaeological and physical anthropological research in Rwanda and Burundi by Hiernaux.

The amiability of relations between these researchers and their anglophone counterparts in southern Africa was particularly striking during this time, and was aided enormously by the sense of community fostered by the early Pan-African congresses. The only other part of colonial Africa where individual researchers were similarly able to escape isolation was in North Africa. Between active local research societies (especially in Oran, Constantine, and Tebessa) and the great interest in Maghrebian prehistory taken by leading figures in France (e.g., MARCELLIN BOULE, editor of *L'Anthropologie*), the Bordesian analytical revolution penetrated faster in North Africa. The abundance of local sequences, most unusually for Africa, was complemented by several generations of regional syntheses (Vaufrey in 1955, Balout in 1955, Camps in 1974, Hugot in 1979). The downside was a marked deference to the European stages and typological terms.

The remnant Aurignacian question was put to rest by R. Vaufrey, who demolished the landbridge thesis and showed that the Capsian geometrics and microburins were of Mesolithic (Tardenoisian) age. From the 1930s, under Lionel Balout of the Musée Bardo in Algiers, students such as G. Souville, G. Camps and H. Camps, J. Tixier, and H. Huget received training that stressed the inadequacy of the diagnostic or index artifact. The typological work of R. de Bayle de Hermens (Capsian), H. Camps-Fabrer (bone), and J. Tixier (epipaleolithic) was particularly exacting. Unfortunately, the pace of research in North Africa slowed appreciably as a result of the violence of national independence and the economic and political conditions of the modern Maghrebian states.

Postindependence: Emergence of National Research Goals after 1960

Although the pace of research diminished after independence, there was also a break with traditional North African research in the form of greater internationalization and greater institutional support. Most work continues along the typological direction set by J. Tixier (experimental knapping) and L. Balout (refined local sequences and classification), but some of their younger colleagues (G. Aumassip, A. Gautier, A. Muzzolini, and C. Roubet) have tried to go beyond lithics to a reconstruction of past ways of life. Perhaps these efforts would be more advanced were more North Africans at the forefront of research, but such is not the case despite the opening of serious instruction at the University of Algiers in 1952. Instead, the weight of research is directed toward environ-

mental adaptation or processes, such as the origin of food production, and has shifted east to Libya and more especially to the Egyptian western desert and the prehistoric Nile Valley.

The biggest difference between international efforts in the MAHGREB—such as projects run by the Canadian D. Lubell and the German B. Gabriel—and efforts that have a more traditionally typological thrust is a greater appreciation of interassemblage, intersite, and interregional diversity. The Bordesian quantitative standards have been accepted with a Bordes-like resistance to functional studies. In rock art, too, there is an overwhelming tendency by otherwise outstanding observers such as Italian archaeologist Alfred Muzzolini to look for regions of coherent, homogeneous style or design choice—which are thought to be characteristic of bounded, coherent peoples. Change in art style is presumed to be evidence of migration or of population swamping. Still, the institutional support of Mahgrebian research continues, and the Centre Algérien de Recherches Anthropologiques, Préhistoriques et Ethnographiques, and the Laboratoire d'Anthropologie et Préhistoire et d'Ethnologie of the University of Provence sponsor new research. One clearly sees the integration of older typology and emerging processual concerns in the *Encyclopédie Berbere,* compiled on a continuing basis by G. Camps, and in the journal *Sahara* begun by Muzzolini in 1988.

If the overall effect of independence has been a diminution of research in Congo (formerly Zaire), there has been much new high-quality work in the surrounding central African nations, and the influences of internationalization and greater institutional support are as evident here as they are in North Africa. Although there was not a single archaeologically trained Congolese national at independence, the situation has slowly improved with a steady trickle of students returning from the Free University of Brussels and with the establishment, in 1975, of the Institute of the National Museums of Zaire (IMNZ). The IMNZ is charged with regulating excavations and antiquities generally and has the enormous ongoing task of stemming the free flow of art and antiquities out of the country.

The first director, L. Cahen, organized several projects, but Stone Age research was dealt a psychological blow in 1978 when Cahen's stratigraphical work at Gombe Point showed that materials can be carried great vertical distances by the ubiquitous Kalahari Sands, which threw into doubt many earlier associations. In the northeastern part of the country, F. van Noten's meticulous work in Matupi Cave revealed microliths dating to 40,000 B.P.

In central Africa, however, the research focus has shifted to late-archaic *Homo sapiens* adaptations in the Semliki Valley (Congo), to the Iron Age, and to the beginnings of the so-called Bantu expansion. As early as 1953, Hiernaux suggested that the appearance of iron and dimple-based pottery could be associated with linguist J. Greenberg's Bantu complex of languages. International research on the linking or disassociation of food production, iron, and particular ceramic types with peoples speaking Bantu languages took off in the late 1950s and 1960s. However, the Bantu hypothesis and the increasing prestige of work on the Iron Age did stimulate work in countries that had almost been completely ignored archaeologically, i.e., in the Central African Republic, Rwanda, and Burundi (linguistic archaeology) and especially in Gabon where the well-funded International Centre for Bantu Civilisations was founded in 1985.

Work in Congo on the presumed ancestors of ethnographic peoples and, particularly, the spectacular excavations at Sanga in the Upemba Depression must be mentioned. This large cemetery was discovered by Maesen of the Tervuren Museum, and preliminary excavations by Hiernaux and Nenquin were undertaken in the 1950s. But it was through an intensive campaign begun in 1974 by Pierre de Maret that we have come to appreciate the 1,000-year sequence of burials and the evidence therein of local growth of social stratification, chieftaincy, and external relations that would anticipate the historical expansion of the Luba empire.

By the 1970s, the search for Iron Age origins and for the "proto-Bantu" homeland had turned to Cameroon. In the southeastern part of that country, there has been an international frenzy of overlapping and generally collaborative research by Cameroonian (R. Asombang and J.-M. Essomba), Belgian (de Maret at Shum Laka and Obobogo), American (Schmidt), French (Warnier, Marliac), Canadian (David), and English (Michael Rowlands) archaeologists. The research continues and is a prime example of the intellectual excitement engendered when historians, linguists, and archaeologists, all from different national research traditions, apply themselves to testing various models and hypotheses for a complex prehistoric process. Since 1983, the German River Reconnaissance Project led by M. Eggert has doggedly surveyed the Congolese river system to extend the search for the first ceramic-producing inhabitants of the equatorial rain forest.

Elsewhere, in the former Afrique Equatoriale Française, work by Lebeuf on the "Sao" of the Lake Chad floodplain continued after national independence. His migration perspective was supplemented by environmentally oriented work on related mounds by G. Connah at Daima in Nigeria and, more recently, by A. Holl's mortuary sociology at Houlouf in northern Cameroon. Noteworthy also are the late–Stone Age and Iron Age surveys of F. Treinen-Claustre in northeastern Chad and the extensive use of aerial photography by A. Marliac to map Iron Age settlement patterns in northern Cameroon.

Despite these advances in central African prehistory, the postindependence years there cannot compare to the expansion of archaeological research in Madagascar and West Africa. Madagascar and the Comoros Islands had almost no systematic archaeology before 1966 when Pierre Verin began work at seaport sites to investigate the date of first migrations. The Centre d'Art et d'Archéologie at the University of Madagascar organized research into past human geography, which included an aerial photographic survey of more than 16,000 fortified sites by A. Mille. In 1975, Henry Wright produced the first ceramic sequence for the islands, bringing his considerable experience in MESOPOTAMIA to bear on the problem of Malagasy state formation. One of his students, Suzanne Kus, has devoted an ethnoarchaeological career to the exploration of the deep-time cosmological ordering of space. These projects demonstrate the fallacy of the argument that processual studies must wait in francophone Africa until the basic culture-history sequences have been established. Certainly, studies of process cannot go far without a basic chronological and spatial framework, but the two can be married very profitably.

Perhaps nowhere else does one see this marriage of culture history and theoretical orientation better than in West Africa. Archaeology in francophone West Africa got off to a shaky beginning in the early 1960s, partly because some newly independent countries such as Guinea and Mali were quite hostile to outside researchers and research and partly because very few resources were available for pure research. Now, however, the twin pillars of internationalization and greater institutional support of archaeology are of the highest caliber in West Africa.

It is true that much of the postindependence research continues to be little further advanced theoretically than that of the preceding period. The prevailing types and classification logic of lithic and rock-art studies continue to be of strict European derivation. Function of assemblages is ignored in the search to define geographically widespread, temporally stable traditions. Most regional surveys continue to ignore variability within regional traditions or broad facies. In some surveys, sites not of the target tradition are not even recorded.

In the early historic (proto-historic) period, continuity with an older research paradigm is seen most clearly in "medieval" trade town research. Vast resources have been devoted to extensive areal exposure of the stone architecture at second millennium A.D. sites such as the Mauritanian Tegdaoust, Azugi, and Koumbi Saleh; the Guinean Niani; Mali's Gao; and Niger's Azelik and Marandet. The purpose of this research was to confirm these sites as the trade centers mentioned by various Arab geographers or travelers (e.g., Tegdaoust as al-Bakri's eleventh-century Awdaghost). This orientation makes it difficult to use the data from these sites to talk about processes of culture contact because indigenous quarters are ignored and, with the exception of Tim Insoll's recent work at

Gao, we lack even the most basic ceramic and other artifact sequences.

The final continuity with the colonial period can been seen in the orientation of many of the regional site inventories and salvage surveys to which much national research effort and much foreign funding have been dedicated. Sites are classified by site morphology or by arbitrarily assigned diagnostic surface finds, and survey essentially becomes an exercise in placing points on a map. Often the salvage pressures and the lack of funds preclude any other approach, as in the case of B. Gado's exemplary Niger River survey upstream of Niani and, since 1975, his salvage of the important terracottas associated with necropolises in the Kareugourou region. However, surveys that have had a more processual orientation illustrate how much more could have been accomplished by extensive and adequately funded inventories in, for example, the lower reaches of the Senegal River valley or the lakes region of Mali's middle Niger.

A classic example of how survey, although birthed in a salvage situation, can illuminate larger processual issues is the interdisciplinary research conducted in the Agades Basin of Niger by Suzanne Bernus, Eduard Bernus, and Pierre Gouletquer. The detail of site recording, the combination of multidisciplinary paleoenvironmental work, and the supplementary ethnoarchaeological work on camel pastoralism and specialist (copper) production make this project stand out. The Agades Basin project, however, is just one of several recent projects that have gone beyond mere site and artifact cataloging toward an ever more detailed understanding of late-Pleistocene and Holocene adaptations in the Sahara and the Sahel. These archaeological data complement the spectacular Saharan paleoclimatic information developed since 1980, particularly from lake level, diatom, and palynological sources.

At times, fine archaeological and physical anthropological work is appended to projects that are principally geomorphological and climatological in thrust. The best example is the interdisciplinary interpretation of human colonization of the Sahara and adaptation to its changing environments developed by a team led by the geologist Nicole Petit-Maire. Weaving together all aspects of climate, environment, and human and animal adaptations along the Mauritanian coast and, in particular, in the Malian Sahara from ca. 10,000 to 3500 B.P., it provides hitherto unavailable details about regional microclimates and micro-adaptations. It also contains the curious and yet-to-be explained fact that human colonization of the formerly superarid Malian Sahara began only after 7000 B.P., almost two millennia after the onset of pluvial conditions.

Several other smaller projects focus on specific human adaptations: the Berkeley excavations at Adrar Bous (Air, Niger), led by J. DESMOND CLARK, provide information about Saharan cattle pastoralism; Andy Smith's Karkarichinkat (Tilemsi Valley, Mali) study of adaptations to cyclical climatic change includes the development of domestic bulrush millet from a system of seasonal wild grain harvesting; the highly emotional debates about the articulation of the Tichitt (Mauritanian Hodh) cliff and lakeside sites between P. Munson (sequential evolution of grain and cattle food production from a generalized lacustrine system) and A. Holl (components in a relatively stable seasonal round); and the Senegalese coast microenvironmental study by Linares de Sapir.

One of the most interesting developments in adaptation studies is the recent reassessment of the ideas advanced in the 1970s by Gabriel Camps and John Sutton that the pluvial Sahara and Sahel were home to a fundamentally homogeneous lacustrine way of life based upon fishing, hunting aquatic mammals, and gathering lakeside grasses. As early as 1963, Allan Gallay documented the great diversity of Neolithic occurrences in the Malian Azawad but shied away from interpreting these as the remains of contemporaneous, specialized communities. By the mid-1980s, it was apparent that generalized aquatic exploitation sites were the exception and not the rule in the Sahara, but it was unclear whether the specialized sites represented a time-progression of adaptation to increasing desiccation, seasonal components in a seasonal round, or another adaptation altogether. The third alternative has been suggested by work by J.-P. Maitre in the Hoggar Mountains of Niger and,

most convincingly, by the Malian-American team of T. Togola and K. MacDonald in the Mema and Douzena region of Mali. They believe they have evidence of contemporaneous, articulated specialist communities in the late–Stone Age—the presumed ancestors of the articulated, clustered communities of the early–Iron Age in the floodplains of the Senegal and Niger.

Large-scale processual studies have looked at demography and the social and pyrotechnical aspects of metal production. Working within the framework of a physical anthropological study of coherence and duration of ethnic groups, a Dutch team lead by R. Bedaux recovered skeletons and laboriously excavated cave deposits in the Bandiagara cliffs of Mali and at the middle Niger sites of Galia and Doupwil. Preservation in the Tellem caves was quite exceptional and allowed the recovery of organic material, such as wood and textiles, that contributes to an unusual view of the rich material culture of the first millennium A.D. In Senegambia, the demographers V. Martin and Ch. Becker integrated the results of their exhaustive survey of post Late Stone Age sites and funerary monuments into their ethnohistoric and ethnographic study of modern ethnic group distributions and movements.

Perhaps the best examples of the salubrious effects of the internationalization of francophone West African archaeology are to be seen in studies of metal production and settlement studies (particularly the origins of urbanism). A principal focus of the Agades Basin project was the evolution of copper and bronze production in this important raw material source region. Studies of iron have been particularly stimulated by communication across regions and across national research traditions. Some iron studies focus on the problem of when and where it first appeared and if it was of indigenous origin (e.g., G. Quechon and J.-P. Roset in the Niger Termit massif; D. Grebenart at the Tigidit cliffs of Niger), while other researchers in Togo (de Barros and Goucher), the Mema of the middle Niger (Haaland), and along the middle Senegal (D. Robert and M. Sognane; B. Chavane, H. Bocoum, and D. Killick) have investigated the organization and environmental consequences of industrial-scale production. Ethnographers and ethnoarchaeologists have linked studies of ancient iron production to those of the social role of blacksmiths (E. Bernus and N. Echard). Particularly noteworthy is the work on the ancient linkage of social and production concerns by the Senegalese archaeologist H. Bocoum, who is in the vanguard of a new French theoretical paradigm, the *chaines operatoires*.

Research on West African ceramics has also profoundly influenced the direction of French research. On the side of microexamination, there is the experimental physics conducted on Malian lakes region ceramics by the Group Nucleaire d'Orsay (Fontes, Person, Saliege). Concerning interpretation of ethnicity and symbolism of identity, the pioneering work on (Malian) Sarakole pottery by the Swiss A. Gallay (and of various middle Niger groups by E. Huysecom and A. Mayor) has stimulated an interest in ethnoarchaeology in France. T. Togola has begun a study of the technical and social organization of gold production in the famous Bambouk fields of western Mali, and processual studies of settlement evolution and early urbanism have had the most profound impact on the understanding of the early history of West African societies.

Beginning at JENNÉ-JENO (middle Niger) in the late 1970s and continuing up to 1994 with a program of multisite coring (including the present town of Jenné), S. McIntosh and R. McIntosh used controlled stratigraphical excavation, complemented by regional survey, to show that considerable revisions were needed in the historians' conclusion that towns, heterogeneous populations, and long-distance trade were a late (early-second millennium) gift from traders coming across the Sahara. The Jenné-jeno research was just the first glimpse of extensive east-west trade networks, urbanism (often taking a distinctive clustered form), and occupational specialization that developed during the first millennium. The fact that these were indigenous developments was confirmed by subsequent surveys and excavations along the middle Niger by the McIntoshes (at Dia in 1986–1987 and Timbuktu in 1983–1984), by T. Togola at the clustered Akumbu and Boundouboukou sites in the Mema (late 1980s), by the (1982–1987) Malian Institut

des Sciences Humaines inventory project (Sanogo, Dembele, Raimbault) in the lakes region immediately upstream of the Niger Bend, and (since 1989) by the Dutch Projet Togue (van der Waals) in the upper inland delta floodplain.

Since 1990, the McIntoshes and their Senegalese collaborator, H. Bocoum, have repeated this successful settlement pattern examination in the middle Senegal Valley in a 460-square-kilometer region flanked by the excavated sites of Cubalel and Sioure and, upstream, at the hinterland of the large site of Sincu Bara. Small early–Iron Age settlements evolved into specialized iron production centers and habitation clusters here as well. However, true urbanism and social complexity appear to have developed genuinely late. Members of the middle Senegal Valley team, I. Thiaw and D. Wolfman, initiated the first application of archaeomagnetic dating to francophone Africa with a dating curve covering the first to the fourteenth centuries A.D.

Conclusion: The Politics of Internationalization

The relationship between France and its ex-colonies continues to be debated, and if anything, the debate became more heated after the end of the cold war. Some people question whether that relationship has retarded democracy in Africa ("Dangerous Liaisons" 1994) and, in a similar vein, whether the close cleaving of francophone African archaeologists to metropolitan paradigms and methods has retarded an appreciation of the richness and originality of the continent's past. Two hotly debated issues are critical to the future of internationalization of francophone African archaeology: the exclusivity of La Francophonie and the traditional French distrust of theory.

The concept of La Francophonie goes beyond the ideal of a geopolitical commonwealth of French-speaking nations. Particularly when applied to Africa, it refers to the sentimental assertion that France's ties to its ex-colonies are charmed, and quite unlike those of other ex-colonial powers, because of a unique spiritual understanding. Idealized in France, the concept is often vilified in Africa as a justification of enforced economic and cultural dependency. Irrespective of the value of the opposing positions in the debate, persistent complaints of paternalism by African archaeologists forced the French minister of cooperation to convene a dedicated conference of francophone African and French archaeologists in May 1978 to try to repair relations.

As a result of that conference, France agreed to fund concrete programs to better train African students, to establish cooperative research budgets, to create subventions for scientific and popular publication, and to promulgate rules about the full publication of research results and about the final disposition of artifacts. Many of these promises have been kept, and there has been laudable support for African publications (for example, Editions Karthala), the Malian program of site inventory (Inventaire des Sites Archéologiques de la Zone Lacustre), and the highly successful salvage operations in the Agades Basin (Programme Archéologique d'Urgence, Niger). Less successful, however, has been the response to the principal demand of the African participants in the 1978 conference, namely, to respect local research priorities.

Among those local priorities are more research on the recent past (counter to the general French passion for the Stone Age), ethnoarchaeology, preservation of historic monuments, help in establishing a basic series of radiocarbon dates, and, especially, abandonment of the neo-evolutionary stadial (Neolithique, medieval) and artifact sequences that ultimately say more about European concepts of prehistory than about African realities. Perhaps the major focus of African disappointment on the issue of respect for local research priorities are the "cooperants," French researchers seconded to African research institutes for the purpose of teaching and pursuing joint research. Many cooperants have done fine work and are generous. What Africans notice, however, is how few truly collaborative projects involve cooperants and how little effort has been taken—as in French national policy—to sensitize cooperants to African sensibilities about paternalism (the unspoken but implicit sense that "I know better what they need to do"). France has not always

sent out its best, and too often, a cooperant retains de facto control over research budgets. In recent years, the program has been eliminated or severely curtailed in, for example, Senegal, Mauritania, and Mali.

The flip side of paternalism is, of course, exclusivity. Exclusivity in archaeology is, at least, the logical extension of the complaint of Audouze and Leroi-Gourhan that French archaeology is a "continental insularity." French Africanist archaeologists are no less dismissive than their metropolitan counterparts of what they consider to be the myopic empiricism of German archaeologists and the excessive theorizing on the part of their English and American counterparts. Jean Devisse (1981, 8 n. 29) reflects on this prevailing sentiment: "Le besoin de 'modèles'—ou de problematique—très acceptable pour un esprit de culture anglo-saxonne devient vite dangereux dans les régions de culture 'française' où la tentation est constante d'absolutiser l'hypothèse de travail pour en faire une certitude démontre" ("the need for models, or a problematic, very acceptable for the Anglo-Saxon cultural spirit, becomes quickly dangerous in the regions of French culture where the constant temptation is to absolutely hypothesize how the work is carried out to make it demonstrably certain"). Devisse's prescription for researchers in La Francophonie is to go into the field unshackled by hypotheses or research designs, collect facts that will speak for themselves, and make logical deductions from the very nature of things—precisely the argument made by the Viennese Wm. Schmidt when responding to criticism that his Kulturkreise were purely imaginary entities.

Such statements show a profound misunderstanding of theory and hypothesis building, not as an edifice to be proved, but as causal propositions to be falsified. Such fear of theory shows a profound misunderstanding of the decentralized nature of the academy and of research funding in the United States and Britain. There, the research structure is very different from the authoritarian, core, and top-heavy nature of research in France (where the word baronial is often used). To those who know the beginnings of "the new archaeology," it will come as no surprise that the researchers who claim to be theory free in fact traffic in hidden paradigms and hypotheses: Arab civilization as the deus ex machina for the complexation of society south of the Sahara or in Madagascar, ceramic or lithic "families" corresponding to bounded peoples or ethnic groups, or the presumption that all lithic sequences of the Old World replicate stages already revealed and interpreted in France.

Francophone Africans express resentment when this contempt for theory becomes a tool for exclusivity, for the argument that access to different national research styles should be limited. Because the minister of cooperation controls publishing subvention funds, some African archaeologists feel penalized when they have difficulty publishing their experiments in "Anglo-Saxon" hypotheses or models. There is widespread resentment by those returning with an American Ph.D. for the way they are treated initially by their home research institutes, where the local "barons" are French trained.

All of this feeling comes together under a growing impression of recolonization. Arguments for mystical linkage and intellectual exclusivity certainly do not encourage international cooperation or collaboration, and such positions contradict one of the principal arguments of this article, namely, that francophone African archaeology has advanced most quickly in places such as the Malian middle Niger and Madagascar where respect for local research priorities combines with the creative tension of multiple national research styles. There is the very real danger that an exclusive concept of La Francophonie will frustrate the ability of archaeologists to demonstrate the world-class nature of prehistoric processes in francophone Africa.

Roderick Jacques McIntosh

See also Africa, Sahara; Africa, Sudanic Kingdoms; Bordes, François; French Archaeology in Egypt and the Middle East; Graebner, Fritz; Jenné and Jenné-jeno; Maghreb; Rock Art

References

Antipolis, S. 1978. *Les recherches archéologiques dans les états d'Afrique au sud du Sahara et à Madagascar.* Paris: CNRS.

Audouse, F., and A. Leroi-Gourhan. 1981.

"France: A Continental Insularity." *World Archaeology* 13: 170–189.

Balout, L. 1955. *Préhistoire de l'Afrique du Nord, essai de chronologie.* Paris: Arts et Metiers Graphiques.

Camps, G. 1974. *Les civilisations préhistoriques de l'Afrique du Nord du Sahara.* Paris: Doin.

Clark, J. D. 1970. *The Prehistory of Africa.* London: Thames and Hudson.

Clist, B. 1989. "Archaeology in Gabon, 1886–1988." *African Archaeological Review* 7: 59–95.

Close, A. 1988. "Current Research and Recent Radiocarbon Dates from Northern Africa, III." *Journal of African History* 29: 145–176.

Cornevin, M. 1993. *Archéologie Africaine.* Paris: Maaisonneuve et Larose.

"Dangerous Liaisons." 1994. *Economist* 332, no. 7873 (23 July): 21–23.

Devisse, J. 1981. "La recherche archéologique et sa contribution à l'histoire de l'Afrique." *L'Archéologie en Afrique,* Special number of *Recherche, Pedagogie et Culture* 55: 3–8.

Dewar, R. E., and H. T. Wright. 1993. "The Culture History of Madagascar." *Journal of World Prehistory* 7, no. 4: 417–466.

Lanfranchi, R., and B. Clist. 1991. *Aux origines de l'Afrique centrale.* Libreville: Centre International des Civilisations Bantu.

McIntosh, S. K. 1994. "Changing Perceptions of West Africa's Past: Archaeological Research since 1988." *Journal of Archaeological Research* 2, no. 2: 165–198.

McIntosh, S. K., and R. J. McIntosh. 1988. "From Stone to Metal: New Perspectives on the Later Prehistory of West Africa." *Journal of World Prehistory* 2, no. 1: 89–133.

Maret, P. de. 1985. "Recent Archaeological Research and Dates from Central Africa." *Journal of African History* 26: 129–148.

———. 1990. "Phases and Facies in the Archaeology of Central Africa." In *A History of African Archaeology,* 109–134. Ed. Peter Robertshaw. London: James Currey.

Mauny, R. 1961. *Tableau géographique de l'Ouest Africain au Moyen Age, d'après les sources écrites, la tradition, et l'archéologie.* Memoire of the Institut Fondamental d'Afrique Noire, no. 61. Dakar: Institut Français d'Afrique Noire.

Muzzolini, A. 1986. *L'Art rupestre préhistorique des Massifs Centraux Sahariens.* No. 16. Oxford: British Archaeological Reports.

Phillipson, D. W. 1985. *African Archaeology.* Cambridge: Cambridge University Press.

Robertshaw, Peter, ed. 1990. *A History of African Archaeology*. London: James Currey.

Roubet, C., H.-J. Hugot, and G. Souville. 1991. *Préhistoire Africaine: Mélanges offerts au doyen Lionel Balout*. Paris: Editions A.D.P.F.

van Noten, F., ed. 1982. *The Archaeology of Central Africa*. Graz: Akademische Druck- und Verlagsanstalt.

Vaufrey, R. 1969. "Préhistoire de l'Afrique: Au Nord et à l'Est de la grande forêt." Tunis: Institut des Hautes Études de Tunis.

Africa, Horn of

The Horn of Africa includes the modern states of Eritrea, Ethiopia, Djibouti, and Somalia. The region consists of temperate highlands surrounded by arid and semiarid lowlands and cut by a rift generating the Danakil Depression. The Horn is inhabited by Cushitic-, Semitic-, Omotic-, and marginally Nilo-Saharan-speaking peoples. The region has the longest cultural record in the world, from the earliest steps in human evolution to the present.

The Horn of Africa is one of the richest regions in Africa with respect to archaeological remains. They cover practically the whole time span from the beginning of the early Stone Age to the nineteenth century, and they reflect the very complex cultural history of the region. Despite this richness, archaeology in the Horn is still in its infancy and in many aspects backward when compared with other African regions. The Horn region is still largely unexplored archaeologically, and what work has been done has focused on only a few specific topics (early prehistory, rock art, megaliths, early historical monuments, medieval monuments), which has resulted in a very fragmentary view of the past of the region (Anfray 1990; Brandt 1986; Clark 1954).

Archaeological research in the Horn has a quite long history, with the earliest records of ancient monuments in northern Ethiopia and Eritrea going back to the early sixteenth century (Anfray 1963; Brandt and Fattovich 1990; Fattovich 1992; Mussi 1974–1975; Michels 1979). In a strictly historical perspective, three main phases (explorative, descriptive, interpretative) can be distinguished in the development of archaeological research in the region.

The explorative phase (ca. 1520–1900) was characterized by the activity of travelers and explorers who focused their attention on the ancient monuments visible in northern Ethiopia and Eritrea, mainly at Aksum, which was the capital of an early Christian kingdom dating to the first millennium A.D. The most eminent ones were F. Alvarez in the sixteenth century; C. J. Poncet in the seventeenth; J. Bruce in the eighteenth; and H. Salt, E. Ruppel, Th. Lefebvre, A. Raffray and G. Simon, and Th. Bent in the nineteenth. These explorers contributed to the popularization, at least in academic circles in Europe, of the existence of an ancient civilization in the region, and they set the foundations for historical archaeology in the Horn.

The descriptive phase (ca. 1900–1950) was characterized by the first semisystematic excavations and reconnaissances conducted by professional archaeologists in different regions of the Horn. G. Revoil was the first traveler to record the occurrence of ancient sites in northern Somalia in the late nineteenth century, and only Salt and Bent suggested some hypotheses about the origins of Ethiopian civilization (Brandt and Fattovich 1990; Fattovich 1992).

In Ethiopia and Eritrea, the most representative of these archaeologists were R. Bourg de Bozas (1906) and HENRI BREUIL and Pierre Teilhard de Chardin, (Breuil 1934; Breuil, Teilhard de Chardin, and Wernet 1951), who collected the first Stone Age evidence in southern and eastern Ethiopia and rock-art evidence in eastern Ethiopia; H. Neuville (1928) and F. Azais (Azais and Chambard 1931), who investigated the megalithic monuments (dolmens, tumuli, stelae) in eastern, central, and southern Ethiopia; R. Paribeni (1907), E. Littmann, S. Krencker, and Th. von Lupke (1913), G. Dainelli and O. Marinelli (1912), and S. M. Puglisi (1940), who conducted surveys and excavations in Eritrea and Tigray (northern Ethiopia) and provided relevant knowledge of the ancient Aksumite civilization; A. A. Monti della Corte (1940), G. Bianchi Barriviera (1962, 1963), A. Mordini (1961, Mordini and Matthews 1959), and D. Buxton (1946, 1947, 1971), who systematically explored the medieval rock-hewn churches in northern Ethiopia.

There were also interesting contributions to archaeology in Eritrea by a few Italian residents on the plateau (A. Piva, G. Davico, and V. Franchini), and information about lithic industries collected by Italian officers and residents in Ethiopia after the occupation of the country was published by A. C. Blanc (1955, Blanc and Tavani 1938). This research largely expanded the knowledge of ancient Ethiopia, but it was descriptive and typologically oriented, and there was no real effort to build cultural sequences. Only C. Conti Rossini (1928) attempted to set the different kinds of archaeological evidence into a coherent historical context.

In this phase, British scholars (J. W. Crowfoot, L. P. Kirwan, and A. J. Arkell) also started to explore the northwestern Ethiopian-Sudanese lowlands (Arkell 1954; Crowfoot 1911). These investigations revealed the occurrence of late prehistoric, Hellenistic, and early Islamic sites in the lowlands and on the Red Sea coast. In Somalia, relevant research was conducted by Italian (G. Stefanini and N. Puccioni, L. Cipriani, E. Cerulli, and P. Graziosi), French (P. Teilhard de Chardin), and British (C. Barrington, A. T. Curle, and J. D. Clark) scholars. In particular, during the 1930s, Cerulli and Curle recorded the occurrence of ancient indigenous and early Islamic monuments in northern Somalia, Graziosi (1940) carried out systematic excavations in southern Somalia, and Clark (1954) provided the first comprehensive outline of the Stone Age sequence in the Horn.

The interpretative phase (from ca. 1950) started with the creation of the Ethiopian Institute of Archaeology, based in Addis Ababa under the supervision of French scholars, in 1952. This phase is characterized by large-scale excavations at the major sites as part of well-defined research projects aimed at enlightening the different periods of regional prehistory and ancient history. A relevant aspect of this phase is a more direct involvement of local scholars with the research and conservation of the archaeological heritage. The most important aspect of this phase has been the attempt by different scholars to suggest a reconstruction of the region's past from a cultural-historic and/or a processual perspective (see Anfray 1968, 1990;

Begashaw 1994; Brandt 1984, 1986; Clark 1988; Fattovich 1988, 1990a; Michels 1994).

In Ethiopia and Eritrea, a crucial role was played by the resident French Archaeological Mission, cooperating with the Ethiopian Institute of Archaeology, under the successive direction of J. Leroy, J. Leclant, J. Doresse, H. de Contenson, and F. Anfray, with R. Schneider as epigrapher. These scholars mainly contributed to an outline of the early historical cultural sequence in northern Ethiopia and Eritrea on the basis of fieldwork at sites such as Aksum, Haulti, Melazo, Yeha in northern Ethiopia and Matara in Eritrea (see Anfray 1968, 1990). In the field of historical archaeology, other important contributions derived from the excavations at Aksum in northern Ethiopia and its immediate surrounding area made by N. H. Chittick (1974; Munro-Hay 1989) and L. Ricci (Ricci and Fattovich 1988) as well as from a survey of the Aksum-Yeha region made by J. Michels (1994). In the early 1970s, C. Lepage (1975) resumed the systematic study of the rock-hewn churches in northern Ethiopia. Attention was also paid to the megaliths of eastern, central, and southern Ethiopia by R. Joussaume (1980) and F. Anfray (1982) and to the rock art by P. Graziosi (1964) and P. Cervicek (1971). G. Bailloud, J. Dombrowski (1970), C. Roubet (1970), J. Gallagher (1972), H. Faure (Faure, Gasse, Roubet, and Taieb 1976), and D. W. Phillipson (1977) contributed to the knowledge of the late prehistory of the country.

By the mid-1960s, greater interest in the Stone Age developed due to fieldwork of J. Chavaillon (1968, 1988) at Melka Konture in central Ethiopia, the International Omo Project in the Omo Valley (Coppens, Howell, Isaac, and Leakey 1976), F. Wendorf in the Rift Valley (Wendorf and Schild 1974), and J. D. Clark in the Afar (Brandt 1980; Clark and Williams 1978). In the early 1970s, the first chair of Ethiopian archaeology anywhere in the world was established in Naples, Italy, at the Istituto Universitario Orientale, and in the mid-1970s, human paleontology become the main field of research after the discovery of the earliest hominid remains in the Afar (eastern Ethiopia) by D. Johanson and M. Taieb. In the 1980s, archaeological research was practically suspended in Ethiopia, with only some paleoanthropological fieldwork being conducted in the Omo Valley (Fleagle et al. 1994). Since 1992, archaeological and paleoanthropological fieldwork has been resumed by R. Fattovich and K. A. Bard (1993) and D. W. Phillipson (1994) at Aksum; R. Joussaume and J. Chavaillon in central and southern Ethiopia; S. A. Brandt in southwestern Ethiopia; and J. D. CLARK, D. Johanson, and T. White in the Rift Valley.

In the late 1960s and 1980s, systematic surveys and excavations were conducted in the middle Atbara Valley and the Gash Delta on the Sudanese side of the northern Ethiopian-Sudanese lowlands by J. Shiner (1971) and A. E. Marks, A. M. Ali, and R. Fattovich (Fattovich 1991, 1993a; Fattovich, Marks, and Ali 1984). These investigations, focusing mainly on the late prehistory and early history of the region, made evident the crucial role of the lowlands in the diffusion of food production toward the plateau and in the process of state formation in northern Ethiopia and Eritrea. This research suggested that the land of Punt, frequented by the Egyptians in the third and second millennia B.C., was located in the northwestern Ethiopian-Sudanese lowlands and on the northern Ethiopian plateau (Fattovich 1993b).

In the 1970s and 1980s, proper archaeological investigations were also carried out in the territory of Djibouti by the French scholars Ph. Roger, C. Thibauld, and M. Weidmann (1975) and J. Chavaillon (1987) on the Stone Age; R. Grau, P. Bouvier, and R. Joussaume (1988) on rock art and late prehistory; and J. Leclant and H. Labrousse (Labrousse 1978) on early historical coastal sites. In Somalia, archaeological investigations were resumed in the 1960s and 1970s by British, Russian, Somali, Swedish, American, and Italian scholars. Particularly relevant were the investigations of S. A. Brandt (Brandt 1988; Brandt and Brooke 1984) and M. Mussi (1987; Coltorti and Mussi 1987), who provided fresh evidence concerning the prehistory of northern and southern Somalia; N. H Chittick (1969, 1976), who conducted an exhaustive survey of Roman and Islamic coastal sites; and S. Jonsson (1983), who surveyed late

prehistoric and Islamic sites in northern and central Somalia.

Archaeological research in the Horn of Africa has been affected by environmental, political, cultural, and ideological factors. The main environmental factors are the vastness of the plateau, the difficult access to it, and an almost total lack of good roads until very recently. These factors compelled travelers and scholars to limit their investigations to the more accessible areas and along the main roads. More distant regions, such as the Omo Valley, were not systematically explored before the 1960s.

Political factors also played a crucial role in the history of the investigations. During the explorative phase, particularly in the nineteenth century, investigations were directly connected to European, mainly British and French, attempts to expand political and economic influence in the region because of its strategic position along the Red Sea. In this phase, archaeological work was part of a broader program aimed at getting more information about the region, from geography and environment to culture and history. Such investigations were restricted to the northern plateau as a consequence of the need to establish contacts with the Ethiopian Christian state. The same trend characterized the descriptive phase, when the French were particularly active and Italian work began as a direct consequence of colonial policy. After World War II, the whole of Ethiopia, including Eritrea, was opened for archaeological research, and an international effort to reconstruct the past of the country started; research in Somalia was interrupted up to the 1960s. The war in Eritrea in the 1960s and the political instability following a coup in 1974 progressively closed Ethiopia to archaeological investigations, and there was an almost complete suspension of any activity up until the early 1990s. Archaeological investigations were again interrupted in Somalia in the late 1980s because of civil war.

From a cultural point of view, archaeology in Ethiopia was long regarded as a marginal sector of Ethiopian studies, which until recently focused mainly on the study of the Semitic Christian culture. The interest of scholars was thus focused on the ancient historical remains in the northern regions, where the cradle of Christian culture was located, and on the medieval rock-hewn churches. Moreover, until recently, the research was heavily affected by a dominant "paradigm"—mainly southern Arabian—origin of Ethiopian civilization, and archaeological evidence was basically used to support that theory. Prehistoric investigations arose from the background of African archaeology, which traditionally emphasized the study of Stone Age and rock art, so they were devoted mainly to the study of the early prehistory and marginally to rock art in an effort to set the Ethiopian evidence in the general framework of the African cultural sequence. Only very recently have there been some attempts to investigate late prehistory in order to clarify the processes that led to the development of Ethiopian cultures.

Ideological factors are important in the history of the investigations in Ethiopia and Eritrea. During the time when Ethiopia was a monarchy, historical archaeology was largely supported because it glorified the ancient origins and long history of the Solomonid dynasty. Stone Age archaeology was less well accepted in this period, as its findings could weaken the biblical view of history defended by the Orthodox Church. During the Menghistu regime (1974–1991), early prehistory and human paleontology were stressed and identified with Ethiopian archaeology as they gave the nation prestige as the cradle of mankind. Today, new interest in late prehistoric and historical archaeology is rising in Ethiopia and Eritrea as the result of a debate about a cultural policy aimed at creating a national identity in those countries, for archaeology is considered to be the main way to reconstruct the cultural history of individual ethnic nationalities and their mutual interactions. A cultural policy is also forcing archaeologists in Ethiopia to engage in debates about the meaning of the archaeological evidence, such as the inference of ethnic continuity in specific areas. Such inferences require very careful interpretations.

The combined result of all four factors is a very unbalanced picture in terms of explored areas and investigated periods. At present, only a few regions have been carefully explored in central Eritrea; northern, eastern, central, and southern Ethiopia; and northern and southern Somalia. Most discoveries have been unsystematic, and in many cases the simple occurrence of a site was only recorded. So far, very few systematic surveys have been carried out, few sites have been properly excavated, and very few detailed stratigraphic sequences are available.

The early and middle Stone Age in the Rift Valley and on the Somali plateau, and the pre-Aksumite and Aksumite periods (ca. 1000 B.C.–A.D. 1000) on the northern Ethiopian plateau, have been the main areas of investigation. Late prehistory (ca. 10,000–2000 B.C.) and later periods (ca. A.D. 1000–1600) on the plateau have been almost completely neglected by scholars except for studies of rock art, megaliths, and rock-hewn churches. Islamic archaeology has been practically ignored.

Nevertheless, archaeological investigations in the Horn of Africa have enabled scholars to outline the main trends of the cultural history in the region. At present, the oldest known remains of hominids, which date to about 4 million years ago, have been discovered in the Afar. The earliest evidence of lithic tools, going back to 2.3 millions years ago, has been collected in the Omo Valley, and traces of one of the earliest spatially organized settlements, dating back to Oldowan times (ca. 1.8 million years ago), have been found at Melka Konture in the middle Awash Valley. These results have confirmed that the Horn of Africa was most likely the cradle of mankind, or at least a region where very important human physical and cultural evolutionary steps occurred.

Later Stone Age microlithic industries, dating back to the early to middle Holocene epoch (ca. 10,000–4000 B.C.), have been recorded, both on the Ethiopian plateau and in Somalia. These industries suggest that hunting and gathering people with different lithic traditions occupied the region at that time (Brandt 1986; Clark 1954; Faure, Gasse, Roubet, and Taieb 1976).

Food-producing peoples appeared in the region during the middle Holocene epoch (ca. 4000–1000 B.C.), and domestic cattle and possibly wheat and barley were introduced into the highlands from the western lowlands between ca. 3500 and 1500 (Clark 1988; Fattovich 1988). It is possible that there were some independent attempts to domesticate local plants, as groups living in eastern Ethiopia may have been pre-adapted to food production since the late Pleistocene epoch, about 11,000 years ago (Clark and Prince 1978), and ensete (false banana) might have been domesticated locally in southern Ethiopia at an early date (Brandt 1984).

At least two major centers of peopling arose as a consequence of the new adaptive strategy of food producing. These were located along the northwestern Ethiopian-Sudanese lowlands and on the eastern Ethiopian plateau. The Ethiopian-Sudanese lowlands were occupied by pastoral and agropastoral peoples with an indigenous cultural tradition partly connected with the traditions of the middle Nile Valley (Fattovich 1990a). The eastern Ethiopian plateau was occupied by a pastoral people with Afro-Arabian traditions, as documented by Ethiopian-Arabian rock drawings. By the late third millennium B.C., this population had spread progressively toward southern Ethiopia, northern Somalia, and Eritrea (Cervicek 1971). Rock drawings in the Ethiopian-Arabian style also suggest that peoples with similar cultural traditions were living in eastern Ethiopia and central Arabia from the mid-third to the second millennia B.C. (Cervicek 1979).

An Afro-Arabian interaction sphere most likely began in the seventh millennium B.C. as a consequence of the obsidian trade from Africa to Arabia. In the mid-third to the mid-second millennia, it apparently included the whole region stretching from the northwestern Ethiopian-Sudanese lowlands to the eastern Rift Valley, Djibouti, Aden, and northern Yemen. At this time, the groups living along the Ethiopian-Sudanese lowlands acted as intermediaries between the northern Ethiopian plateau and southern Arabia and the Nile Valley, connecting the Horn of Africa to Egypt. In the mid-second millennium B.C., the interaction sphere was intensified by the development of an Afro-Arabian cultural complex along the opposite shores of the Red Sea, from the southern Saudi coast to the Eritrean coast and Aden. At present, the archaeological evidence suggests that the south-ernmost limit of Egyptian trade, Punt, was located in the western lowlands and on the northern Ethiopian plateau (Fattovich 1993b). In the early first millennium B.C., with the rise of the southern Arabia states, Eritrea and northern Ethiopia (Tigray) were included in the Sabaean area of influence, and an Ethiopian-Sabaean culture appeared in the region (Anfray 1990; Fattovich 1990b).

From the archaeological evidence, four stages can be distinguished in the development of complex societies in northern Ethiopia (Fattovich 1988, 1994). Chiefdoms appeared in the northwestern Ethiopian-Sudanese lowlands and perhaps on the Eritrean plateau in the late-third to second millennia B.C. as a consequence of the inclusion of these regions in the interchange circuit between Egypt and the Horn of Africa. An Ethiopian-Sabaean state arose on the plateau in the mid-first millennium B.C. when the region was included in the area of southern Arabian political and economic expansion. After the decline of the Ethiopian-Sabaean state in the third to second centuries B.C., petty kingdoms most likely emerged on the plateau, but any archaeological evidence of them is still very scarce. Yet it is known that a form of urban society probably survived in central Eritrea. Finally, a new kingdom, with its capital at Aksum, arose on the plateau at the end of the first millennium B.C. and dominated the region up to the eighth and ninth centuries A.D. Christianity became the formal religion of the kingdom in the fourth and fifth centuries A.D.

So far, no real effort has been made to investigate the dynamics of state expansion in the Middle Ages using archaeological evidence, and scholarly interest in that period has focused mainly on the study of the rock-hewn churches (Anfray 1990). These monuments suggest a cultural continuity between the Aksumite and post-Aksumite periods, up to the thirteenth century A.D., and the distribution of the monuments enables scholars to follow the progressive expansion of Christianity southward in the first half of the second millennium A.D. Development of the Ethiopian state during the fourteenth to seventeenth centuries is still totally unexplored archaeologically.

Monumental stelae in the Royal Necropolis of Mai Heja at Aksum, Ethiopia (© Roger Wood / CORBIS)

Archaeological investigations of early Islamic evidence are practically nonexistent. The scarce available evidence suggests that there were Islamic communities along the Red Sea coast, in the western Ethiopian-Sudanese lowlands, and on the southeastern plateau between the eighth and twelfth centuries A.D. The dynamics of peopling on the southern and western plateau before the mid-second millennium B.C. are still practically unknown in terms of any archaeological evidence.

Up to now, only the megalithic stelae in central and southern Ethiopia have been investigated in a systematic way (Anfray 1982; Azais and Chambard 1931), and that research shows that the stelae in central Ethiopia might go back to the early second millennium A.D. The age of the monuments in southern Ethiopia is still uncertain.

The origins of the Nilo-Saharan peoples living along the Ethiopian-Sudanese borderland are still obscure, not only from the archaeological point of view. Archaeological investigations carried out along the northwestern Ethiopian-Sudanese lowlands might suggest that at least a few of these people, such as the Kunama in western Eritrea, belong to a very ancient indigenous stock that has occupied the area since the fifth millennium B.C. The origins of the Somali people are still completely unknown archaeologically.

Rudolfo Fattovich

See also Africa, East, Later; Africa, East,
Prehistory; Swahili Coast of Africa

References

Anfray, F. 1963. "Histoire de l'archéologie éthiopienne." *Tarik* 1: 17–21.

———. 1968. "Aspects de l'archéologie éthiopienne." *Journal of African History* 9: 345–366.

———. 1982. "Les steles du sud. Shoa et Sidamo." *Annales d'Ethiopie* 12: 43–221.

———. 1990. *Les anciens Ethiopiens.* Paris: A. Colin.

Arkell, A. J. 1954. "Four Occupation Sites at Agordat." *Kush* 2: 33–62.

Azais, F., and R. Chambard. 1931. *Cinq annes de recherches archéologiques en Ethiopie.* Paris: P. Geuthner.

Begashaw, K. 1994. "The Evolution of Complex Societies in North Western Ethiopia along the Ethio-Sudanese Border." In *Proceedings of the Eleventh International Conference of Ethiopian Studies—Addis Ababa 1991,* 1:47–62. Ed. B. Zewde, R. Pankhurst, and T. Beyene. Addis Ababa University, Addis Ababa: Institute of Ethiopian Studies.

Bianchi Barriviera, G. 1962. "Le chiese in roccia di Lalibela ed altri luoghi del Lasta." *Rassegna di Studi Etiopici* 18.

———. 1963. "Le chiese in roccia di Lalibela ed altri luoghi del Lasta." *Rassegna di Studi Etiopici* 19: 5–118.

Blanc, A. C. 1955. "L'industrie sur obsidienne des îles Dahlac (Mer Rouge)." In *Actes du IIe Congres Panafricain de Préhistorie Algier 1952,* pp. 355–357. Paris.

Blanc, A. C., and G. Tavani. 1938. "Contributo alla conoscenzadela preistoria della Somalia e dell'' Ogaden (A.O.I.)." *Atti della Societa Toscana di Scienze Naturali* 47: 1–10.

Bourg de Bozas, R. 1906. *Mission scientifique de Bourg de Bozas: Communications adressées en cours de route à la Société de Géographie.* Paris: F.R. de Rudeval.

Brandt, S. A. 1980. "Archaeological Investigations at Lake Besaka, Ethiopia." In *Proceedings of the Eighth Pan-African Congress of Prehistory and Quaternary Studies—Nairobi 1977,* 239–243. Ed. R. E. Leakey and B. A. Ogot. Nairobi.

———. 1984. "New Perspectives on the Origins of Food Production in Ethiopia." In *From Hunters to Farmers,* pp. 173–190. Ed. J. D. Clark and S. A. Brandt. Berkeley: University of California Press.

———. 1986. "The Upper Pleistocene and Early Holocene Prehistory of the Horn of Africa." *African Archaeological Review* 4: 41–82.

———. 1988. "Early Holocene Mortuary Practices and Hunter-Gatherer Adaptations in Southern Somalia." *World Archaeology* 20, no. 1: 40–56.

Brandt, S. A., and G. A. Brooke. 1984. "Archaeological and Palaeoenvironmental Research in Northern Somalia." *Current Anthropology* 25, no. 1: 119–121.

Brandt, S. A., and R. Fattovich. 1990. "Late Quaternary Archaeological Research in the Horn of Africa." In *A History of African Archaeology,* pp. 95–108. Ed. P. Robertshaw. London: J. Currey.

Breuil, H. 1934. "Peinture rupestres préhistoriques du Harrar." *L'Anthropologie* 46: 473–483.

Breuil, H., P. Teilhard de Chardin, and P. Wernet. 1951. "Le Paleolithique du Harrar." *L'Anthropologie* 55: 219–230.

Buxton, D. 1946. "Ethiopian Rock-hewn Churches." *Antiquity* 20: 60–69.

———. 1947. "The Christian Antiquities of Northern Ethiopia." *Archaeologia* 92: 1–42.

———. 1971. "The Rock-hewn Churches of Tigre Province (Ethiopia)." *Archaeologia* 102: 33–100.

Cervicek, P. 1971. "Rock Paintings of Laga Oda (Ethiopia)." *Paideuma* 17: 126–136.

———. 1979. "Some African Affinities of Arabian Rock Art." *Rassegna di Studi Etiopici* 27: 5–12.

Chavaillon, J. 1968. "Melka Kontoure, gisement paléolithique d'Ethiopie." In *La Prehistoire, problemes et tendances,* pp. 117–124. Paris.

———. 1987. "Le site de dépecage pleistocene a Elephas recki de Barogali (Republique de Djibouti): Nouveaux résultats et datation." *Comptes Rendues de l'Academie des Sciences, Paris* 305: 1259–1266.

———. 1988. "Le Gisement paléolithique de Melka Kontoure." In *Evolution et Culture: Proceedings of the Eighth International Conference of Ethiopian Studies—Addis Ababa 1984,* pp. 47–54. Ed. T. Beyene. Addis Ababa University, Addis Ababa: Institute of Ethiopian Studies.

Chittick, N. H. 1969. "An Archaeological Reconnaissance of the Southern Somali Coast." *Azania* 4: 115–130.

———. 1974. "Excavations at Aksum: A Preliminary Report." *Azania* 9: 159–205.

———. 1976. "An Archaeological Reconnaissance in the Horn: The British-Somali Expedition 1975." *Azania* 11: 117–134.

Clark, J. D. 1954. *Prehistoric Cultures of the Horn of Africa.* Cambridge: University Press.

———. 1988. "A Review of the Archaeological Evidence for the Origins of Food Production in

Ethiopia." In *Proceedings of the Eighth International Conference of Ethiopian Studies—Addis Ababa 1984,* pp. 55–70. Ed. T. Beyene. Addis Ababa University, Addis Ababa: Institute of Ethiopian Studies.

Clark, J. D., and G. R. Prince. 1978. "Use-Wear on Later Stone Age Microliths from Iaga Oda, Haraghe, Ethiopia, and Possible Functional Interpretations." *Azania* 13: 101–110.

Clark, J. D., and W. A. Williams. 1978. "Recent Archaeological Research in Southeastern Ethiopia (1974–1975)." *Annales d'Ethiopie* 11: 19–42.

Coltorti, M., and M. Mussi. 1987. "Late Stone Age Hunter-Gatherers of the Juba Valley." *Nyame Akuma* 28: 32–33.

Conti Rossini, C. 1928. *Storia d'Etiopia.* Bergamo: Istituto italiano d'arti grafiche.

Coppens, Y., F. Clark Howell, G. Ll. Isaac, and R. E. F. Leakey. 1976. *Earliest Man and Environments in the Lake Rudolf Basin.* Chicago: University of Chicago Press.

Crowfoot, J. W. 1911. "Some Red Sea Ports in the Anglo-Egyptian Sudan." *Geographical Journal* 37: 523–550.

Dainelli, G., and O. Marinelli. 1912. *Risultati di un viaggio scientifico nella Colonia Eritrea.* Florence: Firenza Tip, Galletti e Cocci.

Dombrowski, J. 1970. "Preliminary Report on Excavations in Lalibela and Natchabiet Caves." *Annales d'Ethiopie* 10: 21–29.

Fattovich, R. 1988. "Remarks on the Late Prehistory and Early History of Northern Ethiopia." In *Proceedings of the Eighth International Conference of Ethiopian Studies—Addis Ababa 1984,* pp. 85–104. Ed. T. Beyene. Addis Ababa University, Addis Ababa: Institute of Ethiopian Studies.

———. 1990a. "The Peopling of the Northern Ethiopian-Sudanese Borderland between 7000 and 1000 BP: A Preliminary Model." *Nubica* 1, no. 2: 3–45.

———. 1990b. "Remarks on the Pre-Aksumite Period in Northern Ethiopia." *Journal of Ethiopian Studies* 23: 1–33.

———. 1991. "Ricerche archeologiche italiane nel delta del Gash (Kassala), 1980–1989: Un bilancio preliminare." *Rassegna di Studi Etiopici* 33: 89–130.

———. 1992. *Lineamenti di storia dell'archeologia dell'Etiopia e della Somalia.* Napoli: Instituto universitario orientale.

———. 1993a. "Excavations at Mahal Teglinos (Kassala) 1984–1988: A Preliminary Report." *Kush* 16: 225–287.

———. 1993b. "Punt: The Archaeological Perspective." In *Atti del VI Congresso Internazionale di Egittologia,* pp. 399–403. Torino, Italy: International Association of Egyptologists.

———. 1994. "The Contribution of the Recent Field Work at Kassala (Sudan) to Ethiopian Archaeology." In *Etudes ethiopiennes,* 1:43–51. Ed. D. Lepage. Paris, France: Editions Recherche sur les civilisations.

Fattovich, R., and K. Bard. 1993. "Scavi archeologici nella zona di Aksum: C. Ona Enda Aboi Zague (Bieta Giyorgis)." *Rassegna di Studi Etiopici* 35: 41–72.

Fattovich, R., A. E. Marks, and A. M. Ali. 1984. "The Archaeology of the Eastern Sahel, Sudan: Preliminary Results." *African Archaeological Review* 2: 173–188.

Faure, H., F. Gasse, C. Roubet, and M. Taieb. 1976. "Les formations lacustres holocenes (argilles et diatomees) et l'industrie epipaleolithique de la region de Logghia (basin du Lac Abbe)." In *Proceedings of the Seventh Pan-African Congress of Prehistory and Quaternary Studies—Addis Ababa 1971,* pp. 391–403. Ed. B. Abebe et al. Addis Ababa University, Addis Ababa: Institute of Ethiopian Studies.

Fleagle, J. G., et al. 1994. "New Palaeontological Discoveries from Fejej, Southern Omo, Ethiopia." In *Proceedings of the Eleventh International Conference of Ethiopian Studies—Addis Ababa 1991,* 1:15–22. Ed. B. Zewde, R. Pankhurst, and T. Beyene. Addis Ababa University, Addis Ababa: Institute of Ethiopian Studies.

Gallagher, J. 1972. "A Preliminary Report on Archaeological Research near the Lake Zuai." *Annales d'Ethiopie* 12: 13–18.

Graziosi, P. 1940. *L'Eta della Pietra in Somalia.* Florence: G. C. Sansoni.

———. 1964. "New Discoveries of Rock Paintings in Ethiopia, I-II." *Antiquity* 38: 91–98, 187–190.

Jonsson, S. 1983. *Archaeological Research Co-Operation between Somalia and Sweden.* Stockholm.

Joussaume, R. 1980. *Le megalithisme en Ethiopie.* Addis Ababa University, Addis Ababa: Institute of Ethiopian Studies.

———. 1988. *Mission Archéologique en République de Djibuti.* Paris.

Labrousse, H. 1978. "Enquêtes et découvertes d'Obok a Doumeira." *Annales d'Ethiopie* 11: 75–77.

Lepage, C. 1975. "Le premier art chrétien d'Ethiopie." *Dossiers de l'Archéologie* 8: 34–57.

Littmann, E., S. Krencker, and Th. von Lupke. 1913. *Deutsche-Aksum Expedition, I–IV.* Berlin: G. Reimer.

Michels, J. W. 1979. "Aksumite Archaeology: An Introductory Essay." In *Axum,* pp. 1–34. Ed. Y. M. Kobishchanov. University Park: Pennslyvania State University Press.

———. 1994. "Regional Political Organization in the Aksum-Yeha Area during the Pre-Aksumite and Aksumite Eras." In *Etudes éthiopiennes,* 1:61–80. Ed. C. Lepage. Paris, France: Editions Recherche sur les civilisations.

Monti della Corte, A. A. 1940. *Lalibela.* Rome: Società italiana arti grafiche.

Mordini, A. 1961. "L'architecture chrétienne dans l'éthiopie du Moyen Age." *Cahiers d'Etudes Africaines* 2: 166–171.

Mordini, A., and D. Matthews. 1959. "The Monastery of Debra Damo." *Archaeologia* 7: 46–48.

Munro-Hay, S. 1989. *Excavations at Aksum.* London: British Institute in East Africa.

Mussi, M. 1974–1975. "Etat des connaissances sur le Quaternaire de la Somalie." *Quaternaria* 18: 161–183.

———. 1987. "Buur Medow 1: A LSA Site in the Middle Juba Valley." *Nyame Akuma* 28: 33–37.

Neuville, H. 1928. "Contribution à l'étude des megalithes abyssins." *L'anthropologie* 38: 255–288.

Paribeni, R. 1907. "Ricerche sul luogo del Monumenti antichi." 17: 497–523.

Phillipson, D. W. 1977. "The Excavations of Gobedra Rock-Shelter, Axum." *Azania* 12: 53–82.

———. 1994. "The Significance Aksumite Stelae." *Cambridge Archaeological Journal:* 189–210.

Puglisi, S. M. 1940. "Primi risultati delle indagini compiute dalla Missione Archeologica di Aksum." *Africa Italiana* 8: 95–153.

———. 1946. "Industria litica di Akssum nel Tigrai Occidentale." *Rivista di Scienze Preistoriche* 1: 284–290.

Ricci, L., and R. Fattovich. 1988. "L'antica Adulis. Scavi archeologici nella zona di Aksum: B. Bieta Giyorgis." *Rassegna di Studi Etiopici* 31:123–197.

Roger, Ph., C. Thibauld, and M. Weidmann. 1975. "Sur la stratigraphie du Pleistocene dans le centre et le sud du T.F.A.I." In *Afar Depression of Ethiopia,* pp. 221–227. Ed. A. Pilger and A. Rosier. Stuttgart: Schweizerbart.

Roubet, C. 1970. "Prospection et découvertes de documents préhistoriques en Dankalie (Ethiopie septentrionale)." *Annales d'Ethiopie* 8: 13–20.

Shiner, J., ed. 1971. *The Prehistory and Geology of Northern Sudan.* Dallas.

Wendorf, F., and R. Schild. 1974. *A Middle Stone Age Sequence from the Central Rift Valley, Ethiopia.* Warsaw: Ossolineum.

Africa, Maghreb

See Maghreb

Africa, Nubia

See Nubia

Africa, Sahara

Apart from some hints of legendary origins provided by Arab historians, two sets of factors precipitated the birth of a Saharan archaeology. First, Napoleon's campaign in Egypt, the craze for "Egyptian antiquities," and JEAN-FRANCOIS CHAMPOLLION's decipherment of Egyptian hieroglyphics in 1822 that marked the beginning of a prestigious discipline, Egyptology. Second, Algeria was occupied by the French in 1830, just as E. Geoffroy Saint-Hilaire, G. Cuvier, and J. BOUCHER DE PERTHES were laying the foundations of two new disciplines within France, animal paleontology and prehistory. The existence of a proper Saharan rock art was also discovered: the engravings of the Monts des Ksour (Saharan Atlas), first mentioned in 1847 by army officers Jacquot and Koch, and also those of the Mathendous, in Libya, where the German explorer Heinrich Barth identified an engraving known as the "Garamantic Apollo" in 1850. Other nineteenth-century explorers (H. Duveyrier in Algeria, G. Nachtigal in the Tibesti, KARL RICHARD LEPSIUS in Nubia, E. von Bary in the Air Mountains) mentioned rock pictures. In 1898 Foureau, with Lamy and a strong escort, headed a remarkable scientific expedition that traveled from Algiers to the Congo. He registered the prehistoric sites he encountered and collected artifacts. The publication of his travels and discoveries marked the end of the era of the

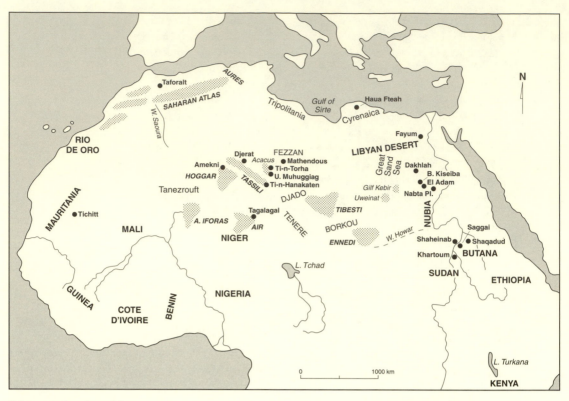

Saharan Archaeological Sites

explorers, whether adventurers or scientists. The discipline of Saharan prehistoric archaeology had been founded.

The First Half of the Twentieth Century: Diffusion, Classification, and Chronology

At the beginning of the twentieth century the French penetrated more deeply into the Hoggar. However, archaeological research in French-speaking Africa concentrated almost wholly on the Maghreb until 1920 to 1930. There, rich historical civilizations and prehistoric cultures were found that looked similar to European ones. They were studied in the same way, with the same words, and with the same goal of organizing the finds into sets of synchronous elements that constituted "stages," analogous with geological and paleontological stages. Then the stages were ordered into chronological sequences. Later on Saharan archaeology was built upon the same fundamental concepts. The first things looked for were the links with Maghreb cultures and the influence, thought to be evident, of pharaonic civilization.

The rock art of the Saharan Atlas was the topic of the first synthesis by G. B. Flamand, *Les Pierres Ecrites* ("Engraved Stones") published after his death in 1921. The classification it proposed is crude: an earlier group in naturalistic style, called "prehistoric," but already recognized as "Neolithic," and a later group in schematic style, called "libyco-berber," with pictures of horses, camels, and inscriptions in the Libyan alphabet. These two groups, which were later named "Precameline" and "Cameline," constituted the fundamental frame of reference for all Saharan classifications.

In 1925 another important work appeared— L. Frobenius and H. OBERMAIER's *Hadschra Maktouba,* which focused on the engravings of the Saharan Atlas. Frobenius was searching Africa for proof of the "Hamitic hypothesis," although neither he nor anybody else ever found it. This theory, developed by C. G. Seligman and others, was in vogue at the time and held that "civilization" had been diffused south of the Sahara (read in the Africa of the Negroes) by either the oriental or northern Hamites, who were pas-

Giant buffalo (ca. 4000–2000 B.C.), Oued Djerat (Tassili, Algeria), about 125 cm. in length (Alfred Muzzolini)

toral peoples and state founders (Egyptians, Ethiopians, Bejas, and Semites), in other words by the white race. Seligman went so far as to specify that the incoming Hamites were pastoral "Europeans." The virtual parallel with the colonization, or "civilizing," of Africa by Europeans went without saying!

Another widely shared but unsubstaniated thesis was diffusionist in nature. People were trying to find out whether the art of the Spanish Levant derived from Saharan art or vice versa. Indeed, many scholars, among them ABBÉ BREUIL, in contrast with Flamand, argued a Paleolithic age for the art of the Saharan Atlas. Breuil was seeing things on a grand scale, linking three arts: the European Paleolithic art of the Magdalenian caves and that of the allegedly Paleolithic Levant with Saharan art, which was often linked with the Capsian period. The latter was linked by Breuil and others to the European Aurignacian, and with South African art that many thought to be very old. All three were said to have exchanged stylistic conventions and themes. Links were also made with predynastic Egypt.

This diffusionist way of thinking always had deep influences on Saharan research. In the long run the accumulation of documentary evidence, obviously different over the diverse regions, and later carbon–14 dates led to the abandonment of Breuil's grandiose but false theories of relationships between Spain, Sahara, and South Africa. But the idea that cultural features could be pan-Saharan—that at least the whole Sahara could be treated as a single culture area—per-

Jackal-headed man (ca. 4000–2000 B.C.), Mathendous (southwest Libya), about 100 cm. in height (Alfred Muzzolini)

sisted, albeit on a reduced scale. Even today some researchers are quick to assert derivation or origin, without proof of the reality of transmission, as soon as they perceive an analogy (whether real or simply coincidental) between two sets of flints, two ceramic decorations, or two rock-art themes in two geographically distinct parts of the Sahara.

As for the general archaeology in the Sahara south of the Saharan Atlas, surface collections continued to accumulate due to the lack of excavation. In addition to Acheulean tools, the Aterian stone-tool industry, specific to the whole of northern Africa characterized by Levallois flakes, had also been found in the Sahara. But the blades, bladelets, and microlithic industries constituting the Iberomaurusian (or Oranian) and the Capsian of the Maghreb, industries then poorly defined chronologically as Aurignacian or Mesolithic, were lacking in central and southern Sahara. A well-characterized Ne-

olithic, with geometric microliths and pottery, was found abundantly throughout the Sahara and was transgressive above older layers. However, in 1933 Raymond Vaufrey demonstrated the faulty linkage between the Capsian and the Aurignacian. On the contrary, the Capsian of the Maghreb, always stratigraphically above the Pleistocene layers, was found to continue in the form of microlithic survivals within the flint assemblages of Neolithic layers. This led Vaufrey to create the concept of the Neolithic Capsian tradition (NCT), within which he included the whole Neolithic of the Maghreb, the Sahara, and some extensions into tropical Africa.

From the 1930s on knowledge of Saharan rock art also grew. In 1932 the young T. Monod published his work on the engravings of the Ahnet Massif (Hoggar) and proposed a general pan-Saharan classification of the engravings, based on the diffusionist concepts of the period. Like Obermaier, Monod defined stages by means of styles and techniques (and not by fauna, as is often wrongly written), and he added to each stage, a *fossile-directeur* (marker fossil). His aim was to imitate the traditional and efficient methods used by geologists and paleontologists to characterize a stage. However, the analogy was deceptive. The fossile-directeur constituted only a sort of a posteriori label, not a discriminating criterion. After some rearrangements the sequence became the classic one, which Henri Lhote adopted and popularized and which is still widely used, in spite of diverse reservations and corrections made later on. The sequence includes: the Bubaline school (only engravings, in naturalistic style and with ancient buffaloes), the Bovidian school (mainly paintings, in naturalistic style and with domestic cattle), the Caballine school (in schematic style and with horses), and the Cameline school (in crude geometric style and with camels). These schools were also considered periods.

Vaufrey's important publication of this period, *L'art rupestre nord-africain* (Cave Art of Northern Africa, 1939), put an end to the controversy over the age of Saharan art. Vaufrey argued that the rock-art sites were not Paleolithic because (as already mentioned by Flamand) ceramics had been found in almost all of the rock-art sites of the Saharan Atlas. He also defended his views on "Egyptian affinities" with rock art, attributed to his NCT where Egypt was regarded as the inspiration and the colonizer.

Libya, an Italian colony since 1912, began to be studied for its prehistory and rock-art sites. A. Desio and P. Graziosi published various sites, mainly rock-art sites, and Graziosi took up that focus again in 1942 in a classical synthesis entitled *L'arte rupestre della Libia* (cave art of Libya). Another classic work of this time was Frobenius's *Ekade Ektab* (1937) on the Mathendous engravings.

The Tassili paintings had been known since 1910, but their importance was not recognized until the 1930s. In 1932 the Tamadjert paintings were discovered, and in 1933 the extraordinary Oued Djerat group. This resulted in several reconnaissance missions to the Djerat, in which the young naturalist, Henri Lhote participated. But World War II halted all projects in central Sahara.

The First Half of the Twentieth Century: The Eastern Sahara Opens

Other Saharan regions had been neglected, and it was not until the 1930s that some reports on the art of Tibesti, Borkou, and Ennedi began to appear. Engravings from Nubian rocks, with their pharaonic boats, were also reported. But between the Nile and the Tibesti stretched 1,000 kilometers of Libyan Desert, the Great Sand Sea—an eternal no-man's-land.

Yet it was not quite absolute desert. The Gorane caravans spoke of a permanent spring in a mountain situated halfway between the Nile and Kufra. In 1923 an Egyptian, Hassan-Bey, crossed from Sollum, on the Mediterranean, to Darfour with a caravan of camels. On his way he recognized the Uweinat granite massif, where there is, in fact, water, and he remarked on its rock art. This was crucial for the development of Saharan research because with this central watering point, the eastern desert was no longer impenetrable. By 1924 Prince Kemal-el-Din reached Uweinat by tractor and described the paintings of the important site of Karkur Talh. During the following decade the rock art of Uweinat as well as that of the neighboring

massif, the Gilf Kebir, were studied by many English missions. The Gilf Kebir was supposed to contain the legendary oasis Zerzura, but its location remains a mystery. Barbary sheep still live in the Gilf Kebir.

From 1938 to 1939 the first synthesis on Nubian engravings by Hans A. Winkler was published. His interpretative schemes, based on "autochthonous" and "Eastern Invaders," considered bold at the time, have become progressively unacceptable. Immediately after World War II two books on central Sudan appeared, and both had great impact: *Early Khartoum* (1949) and *Shaheinab* (1953), both by A. J. Arkell. They were the first reports of true excavations in Sahara—modern, scientific, and multidisciplinary efforts that went beyond mere surface collection. Work on the two Sudanese sites of Khartoum and Shaheinab finally put to rest the Hamitic hypothesis. Indeed, they proved the undoubted antiquity of a Nilotic culture (but not an Egyptian one) and of a "civilization" in black Africa. The discovery of the Sudanese sites had great significance, equivalent to GERTRUDE CATON-THOMPSON's proof, twenty years earlier, that the ruins of GREAT ZIMBABWE were not Phoenician or Sabean but the product of an authentic indigenous African culture.

Arkell's work greatly excited Africanists. Some indulged in lyricism, within the context of the fashionable diffusionist tradition, and changed the details of Hamitic theory to that of a mysterious "Sudanese crucible" where an "African Neolithic" was forged, sending its "civilizing" influence toward the west and across the immense Sahara.

Since 1950: The Central and Western Sahara and the Origin of the Saharan Neolithic

During the immediate postwar period and in the 1950s and 1960s, all the states that occupy the Sahara gained their political independence in one way or another. In 1956 the Centre Algérien de Recherches Anthropologiques Préhistoriques et Ethnographiques (CRAPE) was founded in Algiers. Travelers' reports and the occasional surface collection of tools (e.g., those of the Missions Berliet Tassili-Tchad in 1959 and 1960) gave way to stratigraphical excavations on known habitation sites such as HAUA FTEAH (Cyrenaica), Amekni (Hoggar), Acacus, Tassili, and Grotte Capeletti (Aures).

The major problem that inspired all of these excavations was the elucidation of the origins of the Saharan Neolithic. The Capsian period, as Vaufrey envisaged it within his vast Neolithic Capsian tradition (a concept dismissed by L. Balout), was revised. C-14 dates showed that the Saharan Neolithic was much older than had been expected, with ceramics appearing as recently as the middle of the eighth millennium B.C. at El Adam (in the Egyptian Western Desert) and at Tagalagal. Domestic animals were known from the fifth millennium B.C. and perhaps earlier in the Egyptian Western Desert. The concept of a *sui generis* Saharan early Neolithic, called "*Neolithique Saharo-Soudanais*" by G. Camps and "Aqualithic" by J. E. G. Sutton, took shape. It was a Neolithic of the fairly wet phase at the beginning of the Holocene, and its ceramics included the wavy-line motif and rocking impressions. In this Neolithic (the word simply means "with pottery" for Francophones), domestic animals are considered later than pottery, contrary to evolution noted in the Middle East. Saharan proto-historic periods remain obscure. Ancient Libyan inscriptions, plentiful in the Sahara and more plentiful still in the Maghreb, remain undeciphered.

Other work, without neglecting the cultural aspects of the sites studied, has been aimed principally at formulating climatic and ecological reconstructions. In this domain German geographers have been particularly active, notably in Libya (W. Meckelein, B. Gabriel, H.-J. Pachur, H. Hagedorn, and so on), in Mauritania and northern Mali (N. Petit-Maire), and on the fluctuations of the Holocene Paleo-Chad (H. Faure and J. Maley).

As for rock art, at last the Tassilian paintings have come to the forefront. After his earlier discovery of the Oued Djerat, the explorer Brenans traveled through the Tassilian plateau and filled his notebooks with drawings of this art. These notebooks eventually ended up in the possession of Breuil and Lhote and were presented at the Geological Conference of Algiers in 1952, in the form of two separate and different communications by Lhote and Abbe Breuil.

Henri Lhote undertook important rock-art expeditions between 1956 and 1959. With a team of painters, he made detailed color copies of this art, which were exhibited in Paris in 1959. Since then Lhote has been recognized as the best connoisseur of the rock art of the Tassili, the Hoggar, and the Saharan Atlas and also, more recently, of that from the Air Mountains. Before his death in 1991 he published a considerable amount of material on the subject. Two books (Lhote 1973, 1976) notably popularized the "frescoes of the Tassili" and contributed enormously to the popularization of Saharan cultural tourism. Another discoverer and important author is Gal P. Huard, whose publications have made known sites in Nubia and the Tibesti. The rock art of the Acacus, which differ very little from those of Tassilian, were recorded in the same way by F. Mori, who published them in 1965 in a handsome album.

Until recently studies on Saharan rock art have remained largely in a descriptive phase, through inventories, classifications of schools, and the positioning of these schools in first a relative and then an absolute chronology. Controversies persist about the emic reality of these schools, which are essentially defined according to the criterion of style and chronology. Supporters of a "short" chronology entirely within the Neolithic (the position of the present writer, who claims that the totality of Saharan rock art cannot go back beyond about 4000 B.C.) remain opposed to those who support a "long" chronology. For instance, F. Mori continues to argue for an Upper Pleistocene age for early Saharan rock art. The present writer has also challenged the traditional Monod-Lhote sequence, claiming the so-called Bubaline period to be of Bovidian age.

Problems of interpretation have not been resolved. In 1966 a learned Fulah, Hampate Ba, and an ethnologist, G. Dieterlen, argued that some Tassilian frescoes were the result of the myths of present-day Fulani people, without establishing the reality of this transmission through time. Since then many researchers have expressed enthusiastic views about this exciting in-

Scene with camels (ca. 0 B.C.), In-Itinen (Tassili, Algeria), painting in ochre color. Total length of the scene about 150 centimeters (Alfred Muzzolini)

terpretation. Gal Huard tried to group together all rock art into vast pan-Saharan cultures, such as a pre-Neolithic "Culture des Chasseurs" (culture of hunters) and then a Neolithic "Culture des Chasseurs-Pasteurs" (hunters and pastoralists). But these grandiose structures are open to criticism.

Only recently, in a remarkable and copiously documented study by J.-L. Le Quellec (1993), has an effort been made to interpret some thematic classes, using entities borrowed from the history of religions and supposed to be common to all cultures: the categories of the sacred and its symbols.

The Eastern Sahara since 1950

In the late 1960s, several modern excavations just north of Khartoum, at Chador, Saggai, and El Kadada, tried to define more precisely the Mesolithic and the Neolithic described by Arkell. The Neolithic of Shaheinab was found to begin very early, somewhere around 4000 B.C.

Systematic excavations and large-scale surveys were also undertaken, mainly in the Western Desert of Egypt, just north of the border with the Sudan, by the Combined Prehistoric Expedition (Wendorf, Schild, and Close 1984). Several sites, spread from 150 to 500 kilometers from the Nile—notably, Bir Tarfawi and Bir Sahara for the Paleolithic and Nabta Playa and Bir Kiseiba for the Neolithic—have yielded surprising results. Some are of very old occupation, from the Acheulean and then the Mousterian and Aterian, with fauna both from savannah and steppe. A very long hiatus followed, as everywhere else, corresponding to the post-Aterian Hyperarid phase, and a Holocene reoccupation has been noted from around 7800 B.C.

From as early as 7500 to 7000 B.C., there are a few bone fragments of small-sized cattle, ecologically unexpected in a desert biotope and incompatible with other wild fauna recorded at the same site. For these reasons A. Gautier argued that the cattle were domestic, existing a good millennium before the first domestic cattle in the Middle East and three millennia before those from the Neolithic of Merimde in Egypt—a proposition that has aroused controversy. Toward 6000 B.C. ceramics appeared, along with the traces of village structure at

Nabta Playa. However, dozens of living sites of a similar age were discovered between the Nile and the Libyan border, in the Dakhlah oasis, and in the Sudanese Wadi Howar and its surroundings by an important German expedition led by R. Kuper. This picture of a steppe that was relatively inhabited and traveled through during the wet phase of the early and middle Holocene, at least from 6000 to 5000 B.C., will probably prove to be identical to that of the entire Libyan Desert and the plains north of the Tibesti.

Throughout this period of the early Holocene, up to about 4000 B.C., Egypt apparently was a relatively poor province archaeologically because the Neolithic in the Fayum and at Merimde occurred near 4000 B.C., that is, not earlier than at Khartoum. The most important change to the conceptual field of Saharan prehistorians over the last decades is the vision of an Africa with precociously fragmented populations.

The majority of Saharan archaeological studies are concentrated on the periods of the early and middle Holocene. Recent proto-historic periods are, as already pointed out, relatively less studied. It follows that, contrary to what can be noted in sub-Saharan Africa, this prehistoric research, essentially focused on the Neolithic period, is regarded by indigenous people as an intellectual exercise. Although admittedly useful to the understanding of humankind and human evolution, it has no links with their own ethnic or current national identity. Perhaps this is why there are still very few indigenous researchers—far too few to solve such vast problems. Meanwhile, mass tourism has increased, endangering rock art and rock paintings. And because most countries of northern Africa are burdened by war, rebellion, or bandits, they are unable to offer researchers the security needed to conduct their studies.

Alfred Muzzolini

See also Africa, Francophone; Africa, Sudanic Kingdoms; Maghreb; Rock Art

References
Arkell, A. J. 1949. *Early Khartoum.* London: Oxford University Press.
————1953. *Shaheinab.* London: Oxford University Press.
Flamand, G. B. M. 1921. *Les Pierres Ecrites (Hadjret Mektuba).* Paris: Masson.
Frobenius, L. 1937. *Ekade Ektab. Die Felsbilder Fezzans.* Leipzig: Harrassowits.
Frobenius, L., and H. Obermaier. 1925. *Hadschra Maktouba.* Munich: Wolff.
Graziosi, P. 1942. *L'arte rupestre della Libia.* Naples: Edizioni Mostra d'Oltremare.
Le Quellec, J.-L. 1993. *Symbolisme et art rupestre au Sahara.* Paris: L'Harmattan.
Lhote, H. 1973. *A la decouverte des fresques du Tassili.* [1st ed., 1958.] Paris: Arthaud.
————. 1976. *Vers d'autres Tassilis.* Paris: Arthaud.
Monod, T. 1932. *L'Adrar Ahnet.* Travaux et Memoires de l'Institut d'Anthropologie 19. Paris.
Mori, F. 1965. *Tadrart Acacus.* Turin: Einaudi.
Muzzolini, A. 1986. *L'art rupestre préhistorique des massifs centraux sahariens.* British Archaeological Reports, Cambridge Monographs in African Archaeology 16. Oxford: B.A.R. International Series 318.
Vaufrey, R. 1939. *L 'art rupestre nord-africain.* Archives de l'Institut de Paleontologie Humaine, 20. Paris: Masson.
Wenforf, F., R. Schild, and A. E.Close. 1984. *Cattle-Keepers of the Eastern Sahara: The Neolithic of Bir Kiseiba.* Dallas, TX: Southern Methodist University, Department of Anthropology.
Winkler, H. A. 1938 and 1939. *Rock-Drawings of Southern Upper Egypt,* vols. 1 and 2. London: Egypt Exploration Society.

Africa, South, Historical

Close to the shores of False Bay in the Cape Town suburb of Muizenberg stands what is believed by many people to be the oldest extant nonindigenous dwelling in South Africa. Dated through the Deeds Office, Cape Town, to 1673, the Posthuys (Post House), formed part of a VOC (Verenigde Oostindische Compagnie, Dutch East India Company) outpost. Fittingly, perhaps, it was also the earliest colonial site to be excavated (in the 1970s) by an archaeologist, in this case, Hennie Vos. When offered a post at the Stellenbosch Museum forty kilometers east of Cape Town shortly afterward, Vos naturally concentrated his further efforts in and around that town, doing any archaeological work that came to hand. This included a great deal of rescue archaeology, and Vos has played a major role

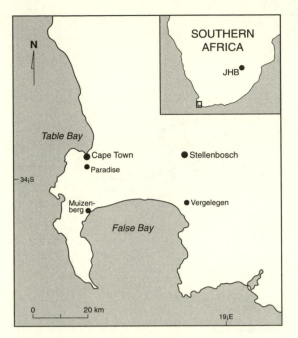

South African Historical Archaeological Sites

in creating an awareness among the general public of the value of archaeological surveys before old buildings are destroyed and/or restructured.

In the early 1980s, an archaeologist from the University of Cape Town, Sharma Saitowitz, extended Vos's work at the Posthuys before going on to research the nineteenth-century Woodstock glass factory. The latter was the first venture into what would become known as industrial archaeology in South Africa.

Along with archaeologist Gabeba Abrahams-Willis's appointment to a post at the South African Cultural History Museum during the early 1980s came her enthusiastic investigation of the potential for historical archaeology in Cape Town and her important venture into cultural resource management. Her dogged insistence that material culture relics from the colonial past be preserved for posterity astonished developers, who hitherto had been ignorant or uncaring of their value. A number of historical features have been salvaged through her efforts.

Meanwhile, from 1980 until 1983, the Department of Archaeology at the University of Cape Town was engaged in small-scale but systematic excavations at the VOC outpost of Paradijs (Paradise) in the Newlands Forest. Reports of these activities suggested a sequence of

deposits at Paradijs and therefore the possibility of uncovering a succession of building phases.

It is clear that interest in the archaeology of Cape colonialism had been awakened. The gradual easing into historical archaeology received a boost in 1984 when the renowned U.S. historical archaeologist JAMES DEETZ was invited to lecture at the University of Cape Town. Deetz's inspiring lecture series on his own pioneering work in the United States coincided with Martin Hall's decision to transfer his main interest from early–Iron Age farming communities in southern Africa to the colonial past and the impact of European expansion on the indigenous populations. Soon after his appointment as a lecturer at the University of Cape Town (where he became a full professor in 1991), Hall set about establishing historical archaeology as a subdiscipline. In the late 1980s, he gathered together interested postgraduate students to form a Historical Archaeology Research Group (HARG) and to begin the first large-scale excavations at the colonial site of Paradijs. This undertaking eventually resulted in nine seasons of fieldwork between 1985 and 1989.

Although the number of artifacts recovered was not excessive—owing, at least in part, to the situation of the site on a slope and the fact that the site was not bounded—the samples were large enough to enable comparisons with collections from other sites, and the tobacco pipe-stem count proved sufficient to be of use in working out a chronology for the various building phases. The changes in the buildings have proved to be invaluable for students interested in the development of what is generally called "Cape Dutch architecture." The pattern of development defined after excavations at Paradijs, and interpreted as indicating a change in the mode of dwelling at the Cape during the eighteenth century, was confirmed in 1987 when a second rural dwelling complex was excavated near the town of Stellenbosch.

One of the main aims of historical archaeologists at the University of Cape Town has been to gain an understanding of the position of the underclass in Cape colonial society. Ranking was important in Europe during the seventeenth and eighteenth centuries, and a VOC list

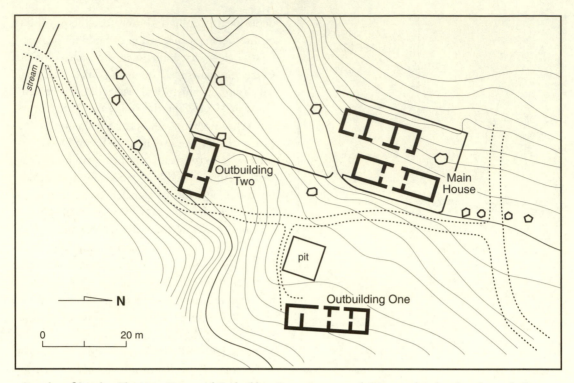

Site plan of Paradise. The Main House and Outbuilding One were excavated. (Historical Archaeology Research Group, University of Cape Town)

by rank was drawn up in 1718 and updated in 1755. Beginning with the governor-general of Netherlands India, it continued all the way down to the third watch. The upper echelons of Cape colonial society comprised the highest company officials, their friends and relations, a few of the wealthier local residents, and visitors who enjoyed relatively high social status in Europe. The "underclass," as Hall uses the term, included everyone below a certain rank within the company, such as ordinary soldiers and sailors, and also people not on the company's payroll who provided the community with menial services: artisans, fishermen, laundresses, seamstresses, and so on. Also included were the lowest of the low: slaves, Khoikhoi servants, habitual drunks, and vagrants. These were people who, for the most part, lived, labored, and hung about in the tawdry back streets and small alleyways not shown on the carefully gridded maps of the town the VOC presented to the civilized world (Hall 1991). Excavations over several seasons at 91 Bree Street have revealed how the neat and regular facade of this large, upper-

class town house cloaked unsavory activities in the backyard where overcrowded outbuildings provided lodgings for those unable to afford anything better.

The excavations mentioned above, as well as several others in both the city and its outlying areas, laid the foundation for analytical and interpretative work, some of which remains to be done and much of that which has been completed exists only in the form of unpublished theses and reports. An example is the work of Jane Klose, who has identified, classified, and cataloged excavated ceramics. This work is of global significance as it facilitates the comparison of Cape finds with those in other settings around the colonial world.

Before the advent of historical archaeology in South Africa, interest in Cape material culture centered on what came to be known as Cape Dutch architecture. Beginning in 1900, with the publication of drawings of old Cape houses by Alice Fayne Trotter, this interest has resulted in numerous popular books, compiled for the most part by architects. The value of these

Part of the backyard of 91 Bree Street, Cape Town (Photo Yvonne Brink)

Typical mid-eighteenth-century gabled Cape farmhouse (Photo Yvonne Brink)

works should not be underestimated. Besides providing a printed record of the most important extant eighteenth-century Cape dwellings, they serve as basic reading matter for historical archaeologists. The books have their limitations, however, as their focus is very much on only one feature of the Cape house—the gable. Almost every author worked out his or her own typology of the Cape gable with the primary aim of tracing its origins to Europe. Among those who found the prototypes of Cape gables in the Netherlands was the renowned architect Sir Herbert Baker, and under his influence, Cape architecture generally came to be considered as being fundamentally Dutch. Baker's obsession with this one feature of the Cape house caused him to play down very real differences he had noted when comparing Dutch floor plans with those of Cape houses—somewhat glibly attributing them to differences in climate and building materials (Baker 1900). Yet marked differences between the more-opulent Cape dwellings and those in the Netherlands are apparent even from a fairly superficial examination.

However, when we compare simple farm buildings, such as those still found in villages along the Cape west coast, with very old farm complexes along the coastal lowlands of many parts of Europe, the differences are far less noticeable. This fact has been pointed out by the architectural historian James Walton, who was not interested in the grand homes of the gentry but instead studied the architecture of the underclass. Walton traveled extensively examining and recording humble structures such as labor-

ers' cottages and outbuildings in many small towns and hidden valleys, and it was he who first suggested that a simpler form of architecture underlies the Cape country manor house. He believed that the traditional so-called letters-of-the-alphabet forms (i.e., inverted T-, L-, and H-shaped dwellings) developed from single-, two-, or three-roomed longhouses by the adding on of rooms behind the transverse main axis and at right angles to it (Walton 1965). Excavations at Paradijs and elsewhere confirmed Walton's arguments to a large extent, which strengthened Hall's belief that changes in Cape architecture strongly pointed toward local development of a whole new mode of dwelling through the eighteenth century.

This thinking resulted in HARG's moving on from discovering, recognizing, and describing artifactual patterning to engaging in more-sophisticated and theoretically orientated ways of interpreting data and finding meaning in the past. Coining the term *building power,* Hall proceeded, inter alia, to examine the symbolic aspects of official buildings, most notably the Castle in Cape Town, which he saw as a symbol of Dutch colonial aspirations and power (Hall, Halkett, Huigen van Beek, and Klose 1990).

For Yvonne Brink, the patterning in material culture use (especially architecture) raised questions that needed answers if one were to make sense of the emergence at a particular time of a form of vernacular architecture that is unique to the Cape of Good Hope. Brink believes both architectural form and close readings of all manner of documents reveal tense relationships between company and colonists,

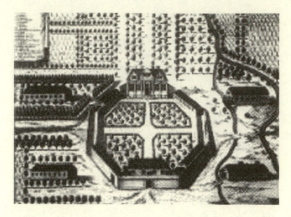

Early-eighteenth-century drawing of the Vergelegen estate (Cape Archives)

especially the free burgher farmers. The latter were company employees who contracted out of company service from 1657 onward to farm on their own account. The crucial role played by land, the symbolism involved in the layout of farm complexes, and the linking of these with questions of personal identity and status are central themes in this work, which is argued out against a background of compatible forms of hermeneutic theory (Brink 1997).

Antonia Malan's research began as an application of Deetz's approach to probate inventories with the aim of discovering how Cape colonial people utilized internal space and how this use of space informs us about social values and lifeways. Her work is comprehensive in that it covers both the Dutch and the British periods of occupation and deals with dwellings of the poor as well as those of the wealthy. Using both documentary material and archaeological excavation, she attempts to reconstruct the story of a whole eighteenth-century city block to demonstrate how rich and poor mixed and moved in and out over a long period in this part of the town (Malan 1998). Of late, Malan has been using narrative based on archaeological knowledge, but blending fact and fiction innovatively, in an attempt to reproduce something of the spirit of Cape slave life and to capture something of the identity of slaves as people.

This kind of innovation is necessary for the historical archaeology of Cape slavery, because thus far, the marks of slavery in the archaeological record have proved to be elusive. It is not at all clear to archaeologists why this should be so, but part of the problem is that Cape slaves were housed very differently from their counterparts who lived on the large slave plantations of the Americas. Even though the term *slave quarters* appears in probate inventories and other documents, small-scale archaeological investigations on suburban properties (for example, by Hall at Taborah and Brink at Saint Cyprian's School) where slave quarters are believed to have existed have yielded no artifactual evidence that even remotely points in the direction of a slave signature or suggests any form of slave resistance. Similarly, virtually nothing about Cape slavery has come to light from any large-scale excavations—not even from the site of Vergelegen near Somerset West.

At that opulent early-eighteenth-century country estate of Governor Willem Adrian Van der Stel, a building clearly marked on contemporary documents as a slave lodge was excavated by Markell during the 1990s. In such a specific context it was hoped that evidence of slave lifeways and owner-slave relationships would be found, but such was not the case. A great deal was learned about the architecture and its changes through time, but there was again no artifactual evidence that could be said to characterize slavery or slave resistance. The ceramic assemblage, for instance, typically comprised Chinese and Japanese porcelains supplemented with coarse earthenwares and some stoneware from Germany and China (Markell 1993). One surprising find in the slave lodge, however, was the skeleton of a woman buried under a floor. Isotopic analysis of teeth and bones (Sealy, Morris, Armstrong, Markell, and Schrire 1993) registered a childhood diet different than that of northwestern Europeans of the time and probably reflects a tropical origin. The most that can be said is that this finding would be consistent with a slave identity.

Slaves were divested of their identities and listed in official documents as movable property along with goods and animals. Most often they were not allowed to keep their own names but were given new ones by their owners. Since they were seen as objects rather than as people, it was not deemed necessary for them to have possessions of their own other than a minimum amount of clothing. At present, it appears that they slept in, or outside the doors of, their owners' bedrooms or in kitchens, passages, or outbuildings—wherever they could find a corner to lie down. They had no personal space in which to hide personal treasures. They appear to have used the family's discarded (or perhaps sometimes stolen) eating utensils and spent what free time they had in backyards or on the street. What might well have been treasured objects are occasionally found—quartz crystals, pieces of coral, ostrich eggshell and glass beads, cowries and other shells from tropical waters—but it is not possible to attribute these specifically to slaves.

Even so, considering the large numbers of slaves from Africa and Asia resident in the Cape, where they soon outnumbered their owners, archaeologists are forced to face the fact that they may be doing something wrong. Hall and Markell (1993) have suggested that either the outlines of slave identity have not been preserved, and will therefore never be found, or we need a more-sophisticated methodology to trace such outlines.

Nevertheless, research on slavery in South Africa continues. Using isotopic analysis and ethnography, Cox has been able to establish that skeletal remains discovered near the old VOC battery of Fort Knokke are those of slaves. The study of archival documents enabled her to identify the Portuguese ship on which these slaves were being transported to Brazil when it was wrecked in Table Bay in 1818 (Cox and Sealy 1997), and further research on this material might reveal more about these unfortunate people. Hopefully, too, the excavations under the directorship of Gabeba Abrahams-Willis on the old VOC Slave Lodge (now the home of the South African Cultural History Museum) will yield information that has hitherto remained hidden. A final point of interest regarding slavery at the Cape is that historians and archaeologists are cooperating in the establishment of a slave route for tourists under the auspices of the United Nations Educational, Scientific, and Cultural Organization.

Related to interest in the archaeology of the underclass at the Cape is what is generally and somewhat loosely termed *contact archaeology,* meaning the study of contact situations between colonists and local people whose ancestors inhabited the Cape for thousands of years prior to its occupation by Europeans. The oppression suffered by these people and the devastating effect of colonialism on their cultures constitute the main themes of this work.

Thanks to many years of archaeological research by prehistorians, much is known about the lifeways of the two groups of indigenous people encountered by Europeans in the western Cape, even before the establishment of a halfway station by the VOC in 1652. John Parkington from the University of Cape Town and Hilary and Janette Deacon from the University of Stellenbosch focused on the stone-tool-using hunter gatherers known as the San (called Bushmen by white colonists). The interests of Andrew Smith, also from the University of Cape Town, lie with the nomadic pastoralists, the Khoikhoi, who were organized into clans and moved around the western Cape utilizing its rich resources to the benefit of their large herds of cattle and sheep. Understanding interactions between Khoisan (the indigenous poeoples) and colonists means relying heavily on the work of these prehistorians.

The first major work on a historical contact site was carried out by Carmel Schrire when she excavated a (then) remote outpost occupied by VOC soldiers at Churchaven on Langebaan Lagoon (Schrire, Cruz-Uribe, and Klose 1993). Excavators uncovered the foundations of a lodge, a roughly constructed fort on the shoreline, and a third very small building, the use of which remains unknown. These seventeenth-century structures are among the earliest erected by colonists at the Cape. This work is also important because it provides evidence for the tensions inherent in contact situations. Furthermore, Schrire's argument—that by this time clear distinctions between hunter-gatherer and pastoralist groups had already been obliterated—set off a debate that remains unresolved but, in the manner of debates, is encouraging further research. Finally, by way of a gentle reprimand, Hall and Markell (1993) have pointed out the importance of the attention Schrire paid to the uppermost levels of occupation and what they can reveal about indigenous-colonial interaction. Too often, levels containing artifacts of colonial origin have been labeled "disturbed" and disregarded in analyses.

The work of HARG was planned and coordinated with the aim of gaining as much knowledge as possible in the shortest possible time. Urgency was necessary because of the vast amount of large-scale reconstruction and development taking place in the city and its surroundings. Although there was some awareness of the importance of preserving colonial heritage, the contribution historical archaeology could make was not realized in the mid-1980s, and little, if any, excavation was undertaken. Restoration of buildings was placed almost solely in the hands of architects. If any research was done at all, it centered around information lodged in the Deeds Office. Finds were not systematically collected, analyzed, and interpreted, and the context went unrecorded. The result was the virtual destruction of too many important historical sites.

Fortunately, this situation has improved greatly as is demonstrated by a flourishing Contracts Office that is loosely affiliated with and operating out of the University of Cape Town's Department of Archaeology. A similar arrangement exists at the University of the Witwatersrand in Johannesburg. Most developers and their architects now work more closely with contract archaeologists and appreciate the importance of archaeological surveys being conducted before development begins. What is more, stricter legislation now governs the disturbance of all archaeological material, and the appointment of professional archaeologists to senior posts on the National Monuments Council, the body that oversees heritage matters, ensures that the laws are more strictly enforced.

Exciting recent work by the Contracts Office includes the uncovering of part of an early-eighteenth-century VOC fortification, the Chavonnes Battery, on the Cape Town waterfront. In nearby Cobern Street, a number of skeletons have been unearthed from unmarked burial grounds. Analysis of the numerous grave goods, combined with isotopic analysis, will inform us of burial practices in the early days of the colony. More recently, other skeletons have come to light on the waterfront from a site not marked as a cemetery on the available maps.

Until the nineteenth century, intercontinental travel was, of course, only possible by sea, and because of the notoriously dangerous seas off the coast of southern Africa, many ships were lost. These wrecks have provided rich pickings for treasure hunters, but here, too, the situation has improved considerably since the late 1980s when a professional maritime archaeologist, Bruno Werz, began operating out of Cape Town. Like developers, maritime salvage operators have begun to appreciate the value of preservation and what historical archaeology is about. Confrontation has largely been eliminated and replaced with cooperation.

One of the most important projects undertaken by Werz was the underwater excavation of the VOC ship *Oosterland,* which sank in Table Bay in 1697. Remains of the rich cargo (including oriental ceramics, spices, dyes, and tropical woods) as well as objects used on the ship (items of clothing, cutlery, baskets, cannons, guns) were brought to the surface with the assistance of divers who were not trained archaeologists. While their skills were being utilized, they were educated in the principles of historical archaeology and the value of systematic underwater excavation. This type of training has done much to foster good relations between maritime salvage operators and divers on the one hand and professional archaeologists on the other. Another outcome of Werz's work is that several students have shown an interest in specializing in maritime archaeology.

The Dutch occupation of the Cape came to an end with the bankruptcy of the VOC in 1795. At the request of the Batavian government, the British took over the Cape and held it in custody until 1803, when it once more reverted to Dutch rule. This reversion was to be no more than a brief interlude, however, as the colony fell permanently to the British in 1806.

Although HARG's research program began with the Dutch period, there has always been a strong interest in the British occupation as well. This focus is, again, in no small measure owing to Deetz who, after his visit, set about researching British settler sites near Grahamstown in Eastern Cape Province. A structural study of the architecture and layout of the small town of Salem enabled his team to show how the culture of the homeland had been transformed locally through the combination of elements from the British Georgian order with older, eighteenth-century Cape elements (Winer and Deetz 1990). Part of Deetz's aim was to compare collections, mainly ceramic ones, with collections from British settler sites in the United States and elsewhere in order to obtain a global perspective of British colonial occupation. This work also serves as an introduction to the archaeology of contact between settlers and African farming communities, and the scope for further work is considerable.

Work at many excavations in Cape Town (for example Paradijs and Bree Street) extends into the British period and the nineteenth century. The inventory studies of Malan and the ceramic studies of Klose were undertaken specifically to enable comparison between the VOC and British periods, and they therefore extend into that century. However, the major nineteenth-century work at the Cape is an ongoing public archaeology project involving research on the part of the city known as District Six. The area was declared a slum by the apartheid government in the 1960s, and its inhabitants were forcibly removed to suburbs further from the city center. Buildings were bulldozed, and District Six became a wasteland.

The archaeology of District Six is now the major focus of the Research Unit for the Archaeology of Cape Town (RESUNACT), established by Martin Hall in order to investigate the nineteenth and twentieth centuries. Public archaeology is an important feature of RESUNACT, which incorporates a special schools program that is aimed at including teachers and pupils in fieldwork projects. It must, however, be pointed out that this is not an innovation. From the beginning of the Paradijs project, interested members of the public, especially those attending the University of Cape Town's summer school lectures, were encouraged to participate in the excavation, and a schools project

was also organized by senior students who took groups of pupils, especially those from disadvantaged communities, to a variety of sites during weekends and holidays.

At present, a new school curriculum, which will include archaeology, is being introduced. In order to thoroughly prepare teachers, students, and scholars for this study, Hall established the Multimedia Education Group. At the same time, the project moves archaeology at the University of Cape Town firmly into the twenty-first century, as the focus is very much on the creative and interactive use of computer-generated information as a teaching aid. Hall's theoretical work, too, is already well ensconced within the ambit of the new millennium as he ponders the possibilities as well as the pitfalls the expansion of the Internet offers. Seeing this expansion as a kind of "virtual colonization," he suggests that it might subject less-advantaged communities to the same kind of indignities they suffered during the period of real colonial expansion by the advantaged nations (Hall 1999).

One must conclude that a great deal has been accomplished considering the relatively late and slow start, the limited research funding available, and the small number of professional archaeologists in South Africa compared to Europe and the United States. But an abundance of work remains to be done, especially in the northern and eastern regions of the country, where mission stations, the Boer War, industrial archaeology, and indigenous African-European contact offer vast potential for historical archaeologists. The archaeology of the Great Trek, which began in 1835, also remains largely unexplored. The discovery of diamonds and gold during the late nineteenth century, the ensuing vigorous growth of towns, and the development of a vast mining industry have thus far yielded only one ongoing historical archaeology project: the systematic survey of an explosives factory at Modderfontein. One mission station, at Schoemansdal, has been excavated and restored as a museum.

As far as contact archaeology is concerned, the work of Simon Hall must be mentioned. Working at the interface between Iron Age and historical archaeology, Hall uses principles from both types of archaeology to understand the effects of European contact on African tribalism, ethnicity, and identity. The marrying of the two sets of principles promises to yield interesting results.

Yvonne Brink

See also Africa, South, Prehistory; Australia, Historical

References

Baker, H. 1900. "Introduction." In *Old Colonial Houses of the Cape of Good Hope*. Ed. A. Trotter. London: Batsford.

Brink, Y. 1997. "Figuring the Cultural Landscape: Land, Identity, and Material Culture at the Cape in the Eighteenth Century." *South African Archaeological Bulletin* 52, no. 166: 105–112.

Cox, G., and J. Sealy. 1997. "Investigating Identity and Life Histories: Isotopic Analysis and Historical Documentation of Slave Skeletons Found on the Cape Town Foreshore, South Africa." *International Journal of Historical Archaeology* 1, no. 3: 207–224.

Hall, M. 1991. "High and Low in the Townscapes of Dutch South America and South Africa: The Dialectics of Material Culture." *Social Dynamics* 17, no. 2: 1–75.

———. 1999. "Virtual Colonization." *Journal of Material Culture* 4, no. 1: 39–55.

Hall, M., D. Halkett, P. Huigen van Beek, and J. Klose. 1990. "A Stone Wall out of the Earth that Thundering Cannon Cannot Destroy? Bastion and Moat at the Castle, Cape Town." *Social Dynamics* 16, no. 1: 2–37.

Hall, M., and A. Markell. 1993. "Introduction: Historical Archaeology in the Western Cape." *South African Archaeological Bulletin* (Goodwin Series) 7: 3–7.

Malan, A. 1998. "Beneath the Surface, behind the Doors: Historical Archaeology of Households in Mid-eighteenth Century Cape Town." *Social Dynamics* 24, no. 1: 88–118.

Markell, A. 1993. "Building on the Past: The Architecture and Archaeology of Vergelegen." *South African Archaeological Bulletin* (Goodwin Series) 7: 71–83.

Schrire, C., K. Cruz-Uribe, and J. Klose. 1993. "The Site History of the Historical Site at Oudepost I, Cape." *South African Archaeological Bulletin* (Goodwin Series) 7: 21–32.

Sealy, J., A. Morris, R. Armstrong, A. Markell, and C. Schrire. 1993. "An Historic Skeleton from the Slave Lodge at Vergelegen." *South African Archaeological Bulletin* (Goodwin Series) 7: 84–91.

Walton, J. 1965. *Homesteads and Villages of South Africa*. Pretoria: Van Schaik.

Werz, B. 1993. "Maritime Archaeological Project, Table Bay: Aspects of the First Field Season." *South African Archaeological Bulletin* (Goodwin Series) 7: 33–39.

Winer, M., and J. Deetz. 1990. "The Transformation of British Culture in the Eastern Cape, 1820–1860." *Social Dynamics* 16, no. 1: 55–75.

Africa, South, Prehistory

When the first world prehistories came to be written in the mid-nineteenth century, traces of Stone Age peoples were known from Europe, Egypt, and southernmost Africa. The prehistory of the rest of the globe was then largely terra incognita. The fact that there were stone artifacts recorded from the ends of the African continent should have been reason enough to expect that an important part of the human story was played out on that continent, but it has taken more than a century of observation for that idea to be amply confirmed. Much of the information on the prehistory of southern Africa considered here comes from the Republic of South Africa, but reference is made to the independent states of Lesotho, Swaziland, Namibia, Botswana, Zimbabwe, and Mozambique, countries that share common boundaries with the Republic of South Africa. Proximity means there have been strong links in the development of archaeology in this part of the continent.

South Africa is an elevated subcontinent of plateaus, escarpments, and mountains where surface soil mantles tend to be thin. It lies mainly south of the African woodland savannah and has a significant extratropical area. The vegetation cover is shrub and grassland with thicket and open woodland in the more tropical areas; there are only relict patches of Afro-alpine forest. Archaeological exposures are generally good, and the landscape is littered with traces of the presence of prehistoric peoples as befits a region that has seen changing populations over some 2 million years.

Discovering a Prehistoric Past

It was the remarkable wealth of stone artifacts in South Africa and a Victorian yen for collect-

South African Prehistoric Sites

ing curiosities that gave the initial impetus to archaeological studies in the subcontinent. Thomas Holden Bowker is credited with being the first person to recognize and make a collection of stone artifacts. The year was 1858, and the location was in the sand dunes near the mouth of the Great Fish River in Eastern Cape Province (Hewitt 1955). In 1866, a collection of forty-one of those artifacts was donated to the Royal Artillery Museum in Woolwich, London, where the items were kept for almost 100 years before being returned to South Africa; they are now part of the collections of the Albany Museum in Grahamstown.

Bowker may have been aware that artifacts of stone preceded those made of iron because he assumed they were not made by present-day people, like the Xhosa, who were metalwork-ers. It seems to have been the regular triangular shape of the pieces that forced his recognition that they were artificially made, and his immediate conclusion was that they served as spear points. They are a series of middle–Stone Age blades and points. The importance of Bowker's observation was that once stone artifacts had been recognized, they were recorded at surface sites in many different parts of the country by Victorian collectors.

The active collectors were professional people like teachers, clergy, lawyers, and medical doctors. Later, they were joined by geologists as the country was opened up to prospecting for diamonds and other minerals. These were schooled observers, aware of their environment and motivated to learn about the land, the diversity of its peoples, and its history. The ability to recognize stone artifacts gave this educated elite knowledge of the past from a time before written history began, and, in some sense, through their knowledge they controlled that unwritten precolonial past.

The Zimbabwe-type structures apart, there are few monumental archaeological features in the South African landscape that draw attention and demand interpretation. Instead, numerous shell middens were encountered along the coast in positions far above the reach of the sea, and yet it took many years of debate to resolve whether these piles of shell were natural or owing to the activities of people. The shell midden controversy (Goodwin 1935) can be traced back to the exchange between two early travelers—the Englishman John Barrow and the Swedish naturalist Henry Lichtenstein—at the beginning of the nineteenth century. Neither seem to have been aware of Van Riebeeck's journal, which was written at the time when the Dutch East India Company founded a refreshment station at the Cape in 1652, in which Van Riebeeck referred to people he called "Strandlopers" who were harvesting shellfish and other marine resources for food.

In the mid-nineteenth century, the same debate was taken up in the pages of the *Cape Monthly Magazine,* but by this time it was known that the heaps contained not only shellfish but also animal bones and even human burials and that the piles were food remains discarded at living sites. There are still numerous shell midden deposits along the coast, but they are under threat from the continuing development of resort towns.

In the last decades of the nineteenth century, there were attempts by Dunn, Gooch, Stow, and others to write archaeologies of South Africa. Stow's book, *The Native Races of South Africa* (1905), published more than twenty years after it was written, is a good example of the state of the knowledge, and in its time, it was a magnificent piece of scholarship. The book takes the view that until recent times, the San (bushmen) had been stone toolmakers and that they represented a people long resident in southern Africa. Other peoples were seen as being later immigrants. At the time Stow was writing,

there were folk memories of stone toolmaking groups of San (Kannemeyer 1890), and recent genetic research (Soodyall and Jenkins 1992) has amply confirmed the antiquity of the San genotype. Shrouded in mystery were the people who may have preceded "the bushmen."

A feature of the book is a map that is a classic example of the migration model. The map is a mass of arrows showing waves of migrations from eastern Africa of San painter and sculptor "tribes," who were responsible for the rock art; of Khoekhoe (or Khoikhoi, known as Hottentots to white settlers) herders; and of different siNtu- (Bantu-)speaking agricultural groups migrating into southern Africa. By assuming that the social, political, and linguistic divisions had gone unchanged, Stow projected the ethnic diversity that was understood in his own times into the past. That projection is too simplistic as individuals and communities interact and social groupings are and were in a state of continuous change or transformation. However, the importance of Stow's work cannot be underrated. His was a first attempt to explain the peopling of southern Africa. Migration models, although not as extreme as Stow's, have remained a popular form of explanation in South African archaeology, particularly in the study of the "spread" of early farming communities.

Stow is also remembered as a pioneer recorder of rock art. He was not the first to make field copies, as several of the early travelers had reported and made copies of rock paintings and engravings. Barrow (1801), for example, on a visit to the Graaff-Reinet area in the early nineteenth century, commented that the paintings were so fresh that they must have been made very recently. Rock art became known as "bushman paintings" and stone artifacts as "bushman implements."

Without any reliable estimates of the time scale of precolonial history or knowledge of "prebushman" peoples, archaeology could not develop. Many of the finds of stone artifacts occurred on the surface, not deeply buried, which was taken to indicate that they were relatively recent and that most, if not all, artifacts were of the same age. Comparisons could be made with the deeply buried and undoubtedly ancient stone artifacts, which were associated with extinct kinds of animals found in Europe. Penning (1886), a geologist of Stow's generation, appreciated that surface finds were not necessarily recent in age. The land surfaces of southern Africa had not been glaciated in the Ice Age, as had happened in Europe, and therefore they were not covered with glacial debris. In a region not affected by glaciation, artifacts occurring on the surface may still be tens and even hundreds of thousands of years old.

Perhaps the clearest statement on how old artifacts in the South African landscape might be came from L. Péringuey, a French-trained entomologist. Péringuey's work took him to the vineyards around Stellenbosch where Acheuean artifacts are regularly plowed out of the ground. Such artifacts were also known to occur in great quantities in the gravels mined for diamonds along the Vaal River and had been found as far afield as Swaziland and Victoria Falls in Zimbabwe. Péringuey recognized that similar kinds of stone artifacts were known from the oldest deposits in France and claimed that the stone artifacts from Stellenbosch were as old as the most ancient in Europe (Péringuey 1900). At the turn of the century it was a revolutionary idea that people may have had as long a history of living in Africa as in Europe.

Péringuey became the director of the South African Museum, and after the turn of the twentieth century, with the growth of museums in South Africa, he and other museum directors were active in promoting archaeological studies. The museums became the storehouses for collections, and the close association between archaeology and museums has continued to the present. One of Péringuey's counterparts, J. Hewitt, a zoologist and director of the Albany Museum in Grahamstown from 1910 to 1954, spent weekends and holidays investigating coastal shell middens and excavated a number of rock shelters. His most important excavations in the 1920s and 1930s were on three farms: Wilton near Alicedale, Howiesons Poort near Grahamstown, and Melkhoutboom, which is inland from Port Elizabeth. These were among the first systematic excavations undertaken in South Africa. Although trained as natural scientists and not as archaeologists, researchers like Hewitt brought a new rigor to the fledgling subject of archaeology.

Beginnings of Professional Studies

The first South African to be trained as an archaeologist was Astley John Hilary Goodwin. Born in Pietermaritzburg in 1900, Goodwin studied archaeology under Miles Burkitt and Alfred Haddon at Cambridge University and returned to South Africa in 1923 (J. Deacon 1990; Schrire, Deacon, Hall, and Lewis-Williams 1986). He gave himself the task of making archaeology a more systematic study. The museum collections had been accumulated by casual rather than systematic collecting, and they represented a body of information that needed to be put in order. In a series of writings in the 1920s, Goodwin developed and publicized his ideas. The culmination was the publication of the *Stone Age Cultures of South Africa,* written in collaboration with Clarence van Riet Lowe (Goodwin and van Riet Lowe 1929). The concept of the book owed much to Goodwin, and van Riet Lowe supplied the information on the archaeology of the interior of the country that he had gathered while working as an engineer engaged in building bridges.

That publication had a lasting influence on the development of archaeology in South Africa. In it, the authors proposed a three-stage division of the Stone Age into the earlier, middle, and later Stone Ages. The earlier Stone Age was characterized by large bifacial (flaked over both faces) artifacts with Acheulean hand-axes being the diagnostic form. The middle Stone Age was characterized by the use of prepared or Levallois-type cores to produce triangular or parallel-sided flakes. The definition of the later Stone Age suggested a technology designed to produce microlithic tools and blades but stressed the association with the San, rock art, and burials. The later Stone Age, therefore, was the link with historical times.

The three Stone Ages proposed were properly technological stages much like CHRISTIAN JÜRGENSEN THOMSEN's three-age system or the three-fold division of the Paleolithic adopted in Europe in the nineteenth century. Goodwin

(1958) in particular took pains to avoid adopting a Euro-biased terminology that would imply far-flung correlations that could not be demonstrated. It is not possible to force South African Paleolithic prehistory into the tripartite European divisions, not the least because there is no equivalent of the Upper Paleolithic represented in sub-Saharan Africa. The later Stone Age of southern Africa is Epipaleolithic, not Upper Paleolithic, in character.

A further legacy of the Goodwin and van Riet Lowe publication is the terms derived from the names of places where type or reference collections were found. The type site name is conventionally used as a label to identify similar artifacts at other sites, the underlying assumption being that differences in artifacts denoted peoples of different cultures, languages, or tribes. It is now known that much of the variability in the stone artifacts had to do with time-successive innovations and that at any one time, similar artifacts were made over much of southern Africa. The archaeological record, for the most part, is too coarse to distinguish social or linguistic groupings. Some labels continue to be used as an archaeological convenience, and considerable effort has been expended in redefining such terms and understanding what implications they carry.

Goodwin and van Riet Lowe had no means of establishing anything other than the relative ages of the stages they recognized from the somewhat meager stratigraphic information at their disposal. At least collections and archaeological sites could be ordered in a gross chronological sense. The later Stone Age was thought to date to the last 2,000 years, with the middle Stone Age extending back perhaps a further 2,000 years. It was not until the advent of radiocarbon dating in the 1950s that more precise estimates of age ranges could be obtained. The radiocarbon revolution when combined with other dating techniques has shown that the guessed ages of these pioneers were out by a factor of at least ten. Thus, 21,000 years is a better estimate for the duration of the later Stone Age than their guess of 2,000 years, while the middle Stone Age may have begun as much as 250,000 years ago.

The two men were the dominant figures in South African archaeology from the 1920s to the 1950s. Goodwin carried out extensive field-work in Western Cape Province in the 1930s, notably at the site of Oakhurst (Goodwin 1938) and Cape St. Blaize Cave (Goodwin and Malan 1935) at Mossel Bay. These excavations were aimed at investigating the divisions of the middle and later Stone Ages. After the interruption of World War II, Goodwin devoted himself more to the promotion of archaeology through the founding of the South African Archaeological Society in 1946 and editing the *South African Archaeological Bulletin,* the main publication of the society. This journal published material on the archaeology of different regions in sub-Saharan Africa.

Van Riet Lowe became director of the Archaeological Survey in South Africa and, apart from being the spokesperson for archaeological concerns in the country, he made a major contribution through his studies of the Acheulean gravel deposits of the Vaal River (van Riet Lowe 1952). He died in 1957, a year after his retirement, and Goodwin died in 1959. In two short years, South African archaeology lost its two leading authorities.

Coming of Age

The Archaeological Survey in South Africa was disbanded in 1962, and one of Goodwin's former students who had worked in the survey, B. D. Malan, became secretary of the Historical Monuments Commission, a forerunner of the National Monument Council and the present South African Heritage Resources Agency. Another of Goodwin's students, R. J. Mason, became the founding staff member of a new Department of Archaeology at the University of the Witwatersrand. In 1960, Goodwin's teaching position at the University of Cape Town was filled by R. R. Inskeep, who was initially responsible for training a number of students to fill new posts as they became available.

The economic boom of the 1960s saw archaeology, worldwide, enter a growth phase, and the same was true in South Africa. New posts were created in museums and universities, and from a complement of some 6 professionals

Large-scale excavation at Boomplaas Cave, 1970s. Workers are excavating the Khoekhoe stockpost levels; 2,000-year-old Later Stone Age storage pit horizon is exposed in the foreground. (H. Deacon).

in 1960, the number had grown to more than 100 by the end of the twentieth century. In South Africa, in addition to the Universities of Cape Town and Witwatersrand, archaeological courses are now offered at the Universities of Pretoria and Fort Hare—and until recently, Stellenbosch. Universities in Botswana, Zimbabwe, and Mozambique also offer archaeological training and are centers for research. The economic downturn in the 1990s has not been adequately compensated by an increase in opportunities in cultural resource and heritage management, and there is reduced employment for new graduates.

Part of coming of age was the adoption of new theoretical orientations. Archaeology generally was moving from a primary concern with documenting and ordering artifacts into periods to constructing histories of cultures. Heralded as "the new archaeology," the paradigm of the 1960s was the processual movement, so-called because of the concern with the processes leading to the cultural changes in the past. This movement reflected a positivist approach in the natural and human sciences and had the benefit

that archaeologists became more rigorously scientific in practice and more theoretically aware.

The positivist approach also provoked the criticism that explanations were too deterministic and did not take human agencies sufficiently into account. This criticism spawned a competing postprocessualist theoretical movement, which has taken a more relativist position, arguing that the past is created out of the present and there cannot be a single authoritative past. It has been a concern of archaeologists in South Africa that constructions of the past have been manipulated to disadvantage and undervalue the role of some groups and minorities lacking a written history. Although influenced by theoretical advances elsewhere and other disciplines, archaeology in South Africa has made significant contributions to the discipline's development.

The long human occupation of the subcontinent and the high archaeological visibility of the prehistoric sites have made a number of fields a focus for research. These include the study of human origins, both the origins of humankind and the origins of modern humans; the study of the history of the San and recent hunter-gatherers;

the study of the spread of agriculture, both Khoekhoe pastoralism and the settlement of mixed farming communities; and a field outside the scope of this article, the study of the colonial period, the last 350 years.

Human Origins

It has been established since the 1960s that some sedimentary units in two of the best-known sites, Sterkfontein (Kuman 1994) and Swartkrans (Clark 1993), include undoubted Oldowan and Acheulean artifacts and bone tools. These can be dated by the associated faunas to 2 million years old and are among the oldest dated archaeological occurrences. It has been suggested that the number of burned pieces of bone discovered at Sterkfontein (Brain and Sillen 1988) in deposits that may date to about a million years ago may be early evidence of the antiquity of fire-minding if not of fire-making. After half a century of research, these caverns continue to be a focus of archaeological attention as they continue to provide new evidence of early human behavior.

There are few, if any, acceptable Oldowan-aged sites other than the solution cavern occurrences. However, there is a very strong presence of Acheulean biface makers known throughout the subcontinent, and these would date to between more than 1 million years ago and some 300,000 years ago. They are evidence of the establishment of significant human populations on the subcontinent. As a result of alluvial diamond diggings, the Vaal River terraces and gravels north of Kimberley became known as a prolific source of Acheulean artifacts. Systematic research initiated in the 1930s by van Riet Lowe (Söhnge, Visser, and van Riet Lowe 1937; van Riet Lowe 1952) established Canteen Koppie near Barkly West and Riverview Estates near Windsorton as two of the main sites. Expectations that five or more substages of what Goodwin and van Riet Lowe (1929) defined as the Stellenbosch (Acheulean) culture could be recognized on the principle that bifaces took on more refined forms through time have proved too simplistic (H. J. Deacon 1975). The collections were selected from mining dumps and excavated samples (Beaumont 1999; Mason

1988), and more stratigraphic and dating controls became available only later.

Cornelia in Free State Province and Elandsfontein in Western Cape Province are some of the few Acheulean sites that have provided adequate faunal samples, but in neither case can the fauna be directly associated with the artifacts. A date in the range 400,000–700,000 years ago can be ascribed to these faunas (Klein and Cruz-Uribe 1991), and at Elandsfontein, the Saldanha calvarium, which is morphologically similar to the Kabwe skull from Zambia, was recovered in 1952.

Most Acheulean sites are open stations, and other than the solution cavern occurrences, only three cave sites are known to have been occupied in this time range: Cave of Hearths, Montagu Cave, and Wonderwerk. A human mandible was recovered during 1952 excavations at the Cave of Hearths (Mason 1988) as well as a limited fauna, younger than that from Cornelia. Montagu Cave was reexcavated in 1964 (Keller 1973) and produced large artifact samples of Acheulean and younger age but no fauna. Wonderwerk, a large, deep tunnel-like cave but with some seven meters of deposits of different ages, was again disturbed by guano mining, and it includes important Acheulean horizons (Beaumont 1999). Acheulean sites have proved very difficult to study because of poor preservation of context and associations, which has limited progress in developing hypotheses about the meaning of the Acheulean occurrences.

Since the 1960s, Acheulean studies have emphasized the evidence for activity variation in the relative proportions of large, heavy bifacial tools to small flake tools in separate lake margin occurrences in East Africa. In such situations, the context was assumed to be one of little disturbance. As research has progressed, this assumption has not proved justified, and it is apparent the patterning is more readily explained by the selective transport of different sizes and masses of artifacts (Isaac 1977). Most South African open-air Acheulean sites are in valleys and on their margins, and although these areas have been geomorphologically active there has not been same degree of winnowing of artifact sizes and there is little or no evidence for activity variation. It is the valley and pan, or lake-margin, situation of the Acheulean sites that is the most impressive characteristic, which suggests a degree of terrain specialization, or stenotopia. In this respect, there is a major contrast with the behavior of later modern peoples who occupied all available niches in the landscape (H. J. Deacon 1998).

If the earlier Stone Age Acheulean populations represent archaic people, the middle Stone Age represents modern people. The Fauresmith (an outdated description of what were later classified as Acheulean hand axes) included in the earlier Stone Age by Goodwin and van Riet Lowe (1929) was defined as a small biface industry accompanied by points and blades produced from small prepared cores. These cores are smaller than the Victoria West or proto-Levallois prepared cores (van Riet Lowe 1945) that were made in the Acheulean period (100,000 years ago) to produce large biface blanks. In this sense, the Fauresmith has been seen as transitional between the earlier and middle Stone Ages and was placed in the first intermediate period (Clark 1959). Recorded mainly from open-air stations in Free State and Northern Provinces, the Fauresmith is still poorly defined but may date to more than 200,000 years ago. An early modern human skull (*Homo helmei*), found in 1932 at Florisbad north of Bloemfontein, dated to some 250,000 years ago (Grün et al. 1996), and associated with essentially modern fauna, may relate to this period. The time range represented by the Fauresmith is crucial to the further understanding of modern human origins.

The middle Stone Age is represented in many cave sequences and open stations. Lacking any good idea of the dating of the sites, Goodwin and van Riet Lowe (1929) defined a number of variations or industries and assumed they were artifacts made by different peoples. Thus, names like Mossel Bay, Still Bay, and Howiesons Poort came into the literature. Scholars had to wait for advances in dating techniques, not only radiocarbon but also alternative dating techniques like uranium disequilibrium dating and luminescence dating, before they could obtain relatively precise measures of the ages of the middle–Stone Age substages that were proposed. A key sequence is that at Klasies River, first excavated in the 1960s (Singer and Wymer 1982). This site, on the southern coast of South Africa, was occupied from the beginning of the late Pleistocene period, 115,000 years ago, and shows the use of marine resources like shellfish and seals from that time and the presence of anatomically modern humans (H. J. Deacon 1995).

Contrary to the expectations of Goodwin and van Riet Lowe (1929) and later researchers (Clark 1959), Howiesons Poort, characterized by distinctive backed tools, was found to be in the middle of the sequence and not at the end. It did not represent a transitional substage to the later Stone Age in which backed tools again occurred. The lesson to be learned was that there was no simple typological evolution between the middle and later Stone Ages. The establishment of the stratigraphic position of Howiesons Poort in the Klasies River sequence (Wurz 1999) has been important because Howiesons Poort is a distinctive horizon marker that can be identified in many middle–Stone Age sequences in southern Africa, which allows typological and chronometric correlations to be made. The dating of Howiesons Poort centers on 70,000 years and postdates the Still Bay with its bifacial points and the Mossel Bay with its thick platformed Levallois-type points.

Molecular biological studies published in the 1980s (Stoneking 1993) led to the formulation of the out-of-Africa hypothesis and focused attention on evidence for modern human origins in Africa. Sites with significant human remains, like Klasies River and the less-well-dated Border Cave in KwaZulu-Natal (Beaumont 1980), assumed particular importance. An apparent anomaly is that early modern human remains in Africa are associated with middle–Stone Age artifacts, whereas in Eurasia in the same time range a different species, or deme, the Neanderthals, considered to be nonmodern in their behavior, are associated with similar middle Paleolithic-Mousterian artifacts. This has led to the proposition that early modern humans in Africa were anatomically but not behaviorally modern (Klein 1995). This proposition, called the later modern behavior hypothesis, equates modern behavior with the level of symbolic expression evident some 40,000 years ago with the spread of the Upper Paleolithic into western Europe.

The alternative, earlier modern behavior hypothesis recognizes that behavior is context specific and sees the Upper Palaeolithic as a regional phenomenon not represented in sub-Saharan Africa. It holds that by the beginning of the late Pleistocene (H. J. Deacon 1998), evidence concerning the organization of living space, the arbitrary changes in styles of artifact designs, and the use of colored pigments at middle–Stone Age sites in Africa indicates a capacity for modern symbolic communication. This is part of an ongoing debate that is taking the study of the origins and dispersal of modern humans out of regional contexts and making it global in compass.

Recent Stone Age Ancestors

Southern Africa is one of the few areas of the globe where there are extant communities of hunter-gatherers, the San. Systematic studies of San language and ethnography were initiated in the 1870s by Wilhelm Bleek (Lewis-Williams 2000) and continued after his death by his sister-in-law, Lucy Lloyd (Bleek and Lloyd 1911), and his daughter, Dorothea. After the turn of the century, interest in San ethnography continued, but within South Africa there had been an almost total disruption of traditional San societies. However, San communities continued to exist in Namibia and Botswana (D. F. Bleek 1928), and it was in those countries that there was a revival of research stimulated in the 1950s by the Marshall family (L. Marshall 1976; T. E. Marshall 1959) and later by researchers associated with the University of Harvard and other overseas institutions.

The Bleek and Lloyd historical records and the corpus of more recent ethnographic research continue to provide a rich source of analogies for later–Stone Age studies. Goodwin and van Riet Lowe (1929) appreciated a direct link between the historical San and the later Stone Age but struggled to explain the relationship between the major Wilton and Smithfield cultures they recognized and perceived similarities between the Wilton and the Capsian of North Africa.

Goodwin (1938) had laid the basis for later–Stone Age research through his excavations at Oakhurst, but this work was not followed up with a new phase of excavations until after the 1950s. Holocene Wilton and Smithfield sites could be dated by radiocarbon at the Council for Scientific and Industrial Research facility in Pretoria, which was started by J. C. Vogel. This facility played a large part, not only in ordering Stone Age sites but also in dating the advent of agriculture. Chronologies showed that the cultures Goodwin and van Riet Lowe had assumed to be geographically and culturally distinct entities were better explained in a temporal sequence of innovations and changes in San technology (J. Deacon 1974). Radiocarbon dating has also resolved the age of the youngest middle–Stone Age occurrence to 22,000 years at Strathalan (Opperman and Heydenrych 1990) and the oldest later Stone Age to 21,000 at Boomplaas (H. J. Deacon 1995). The latter age estimate is close to that for the earliest Epipaleolithic industries throughout the continent, which suggests that there was indeed some basis for Goodwin and van Riet Lowe's concern with similar industries found in North Africa.

The continuity between the later Stone Age and the ethnographic present is very impressive with items like ostrich eggshell containers and tortoise-shell bowls still being made as they were 15,000 years ago. This continuity finds no better demonstration than in the use of historical ethnography like the Bleek and Lloyd records to understand the metaphors expressed in the rock art. Although the art has long been trivialized as childlike drawings and engravings to do with hunting magic, myths, and legends, research since the 1960s (Lewis-Williams 1981; Vinnicombe 1976) has highlighted the symbolic significance of depictions like those of the eland and has shown that the art is essentially shamanic and religious. There are more than 10,000 rock-art sites known in South Africa alone, and many more have been recorded in Namibia, Botswana, Zimbabwe, and Mozambique. Southern African rock art covers the area where San click-language speakers were known or can be suggested to have been present. An outlier of rock art with similar metaphors occurs in central Tanzania where click languages are also spoken.

Herders and Farmers

Within the last 2,000 years, herding economies have developed in the more arid, western part of the subcontinent and mixed agriculture, in the wetter, eastern half. Historically, herding communities were Khoekhoe speakers, and the largest extant community is the 100,000-strong Nama in Namaqualand and southern Namibia. The identification of sheep remains associated with bag-shaped pottery at Die Kelders in southern Namibia (Schweitzer 1974) showed that it was possible to investigate the history of Khoekhoe settlement through archaeology. A stock post was identified at Boomplaas where age profiles of the animals indicate that stock raising was intensive (H. J. Deacon 1995). A main kraal, or settlement, was identified at Kasteelberg (Smith 1992) in which the remains included not only sheep but cattle that ethnography suggests were ritually slaughtered. Khoekhoen and San interaction was recorded historically, but with the fluid nature of economic and social groupings, it has proved difficult to document them archaeologically.

The Zimbabwe-type settlements attracted early interest not the least because of their association with gold artifacts. However, the first serious archaeological investigation of the ruins of GREAT ZIMBABWE was undertaken by GERTRUDE CATON-THOMPSON (1931), and she was able to show that the settlement was medieval in age based on its porcelain imports. This find was followed by extensive excavations at the Iron Age sites (eleventh to twelfth centuries A.D) of K2 and Mapungubwe (Fouché 1937) in the Limpopo Valley of the Northern Transvaal in South Africa. Although pioneers like Schofield (1948) continued to study the pottery finds from early farming settlements, such studies only achieved formal recognition after World War. This recognition came through the proposal of the term *Iron Age* (Summers 1951) as distinguished from the Stone Age. With this recognition came the appreciation that the unwritten history of many extant communities in

southern Africa was accessible only through archaeology (Mason 1989). Early farming communities contained metalworkers and miners as well as stock farmers; cultivators of millet, sorghum, and other crops; and the manufacturers of regionally and temporally distinctive styles of pottery. Iron technology was a prerequisite for their expansion as it enabled them to bring new fields under cultivation.

The Iron Age of southern Africa is part of the wider phenomenon of the expansion of siNtu, or Bantu, language speakers (Vansina 1995) in equatorial, eastern, and southern Africa. Since D. W. Phillipson's (1977) synthesis, the main debates have been when and by what pathways or "streams" different movements of peoples into southern Africa may have taken place, which underscores the popularity of migration models (Huffman 1989). With large parts of subequatorial Africa underresearched and given that range expansion rather than purposeful migration was involved, the models remain relatively general in their resolution of past events.

The best attested expansion was down the eastern coast, and radiocarbon dating has shown that the distinctive pottery at the site of Silver Leaves in Mapumalanga, dated to A.D. 350, is similar to that which appeared on the Tanzanian coast at Kwale a scant 150 years earlier. Other expansions traced through pottery styles and radiocarbon chronologies appear to have been along a route through Malawi into Zimbabwe and through a western corridor from Angola and Botswana into South Africa. The southernmost limit of the coalescence of these expansions was near modern East London in the Natal province of South Africa, a limit imposed by edaphic and climatic factors.

Radiocarbon dating and the seriation of pottery styles have shown there were a number of expansions and contractions in the agricultural settlement of the subcontinent that are explicable in terms of climatic forcing and socioeconomic conditions. Largely as a consequence of prosperity brought about through trade with the east coast, progressively more-complex hierarchical societies emerged in the Limpopo Valley (Hall 1987). The best-known sites remain K2 and Mapungubwe, but it is only recently that

Klasies River main site—the Middle Stone Age sequence that has provided much evidence on the origins and behavior of early modern humans in Africa (H. Deacon)

their significance as precursors to Great Zimbabwe have been appreciated.

Great Zimbabwe (A.D. 1250–1450) emerged as the capital of a state (Huffman 1981), an African kingdom similar those that flourished in other parts of sub-Saharan Africa in the last 2,000 years as world trade expanded. Portuguese competition for the Indian Ocean trade routes and internal conflicts fragmented the original Zimbabwe state into several lesser states, which survived into historical times. This fact allows for confidence in linking the Zimbabwe state to Shona language speakers. The histories of the Sotho and Nguni language speakers are less clear, but through tracing traditional decorative motifs in pottery, it can be shown that they were present in southern Africa from the early part of the last millennium (ca. 1000 A.D.). Linking prehistory to the very short period of recorded history remains a goal of researchers.

Perspective

From Victorian antiquarianism, prehistoric archaeological studies have developed in stages. The very visible surface trail of stone artifacts in the landscape encouraged an interest in the peopling of the subcontinent. Beginning in the 1930s, discoveries of the australopithecine remains preserved in solution caverns in dolomites provided a window of opportunity to explore the prehuman ancestry that RAYMOND DART suggested for the Taung child. True human populations making Acheulean artifacts more than 1 million years old are widely represented although progress in the study of these populations has been slow because preservation of remains other than stone is rare and the occurrences are difficult to sample and date. The roots of modern humans now appear to be in the middle Pleistocene in Africa (Howell 1999), which makes the later Acheulean and the Fauresmith of developing interest. The finds of early modern human remains and associated evidence for the emergence of symbolic behavior in beginning late Pleistocene, middle–Stone Age sites like Klasies River have questioned the conventional wisdom that the first evidence of such behavior is in the Upper Paleolithic in Eurasia.

The occurrence of long-sequence cave and rock-shelter sites has made it possible for considerable advances in the study of the middle and later Stone Ages, and a wealth of historical and ethnographic data have aided in these studies. An accessible part of this Stone Age record is the rock art, which, with well in excess of 15,000 sites, is a considerable cultural resource for heritage management. Not only are there surviving San communities, but the descendants of Khoekhoe herders and Iron Age farmers make up the main population of the subcontinent. As archaeology in southern Africa enters the new millennium, it is poised to make a greater contribution to educating communities about their unwritten and largely forgotten past.

H. J. Deacon

Acknowledgments

This entry is a contribution made within the University of Stellenbosch research project The Origins of Modern Humans, *Homo Sapiens,* in Africa. I thank Tim Murray for his encouragement to prepare the chapter.

See also Africa, South, Historical; Lithic Analysis; Rock Art

References

Barrow, J. 1801. *An Account of Travels into the Interior of Southern Africa in the Years 1797 and 1798.* London: T. Cadell Jun. and W. Davies.

Beaumont, P. B. 1980. "On the Age of the Border Cave Hominids 1–5." *Palaeontologia Africana* 23: 21–33.

———. 1999. *INQUA Excursion B7 Northern Cape.* Kimberley: McGregor Museum.

Bleek, D. F. 1928. *The Naron, a Bushman Tribe of the Central Kalahari.* Cambridge: Cambridge University Press.

Bleek, W. H. I., and L. C. Lloyd. 1911. *Specimens of Bushman Folklore.* London: George Allen.

Brain, C. K., and A. Sillen. 1988. "Evidence from the Swartkrans Cave for the Earliest Use of Fire." *Nature* 336: 464–466.

Caton-Thompson, G. 1931. *The Zimbabwe Culture: Ruins and Reactions.* Oxford: Clarendon Press.

Clark, J. D. 1959. *The Prehistory of Southern Africa.* Harmondsworth, UK: Penguin.

———. 1993. "Stone Artifact Assemblages from Members 1–3, Swartkrans Cave." In *Swartkrans: A Cave's Chronicle of Early Man,* 167–194. Ed. C. K. Brain. Monograph no. 8. Pretoria: Transvaal Museum.

Deacon, H. J. 1975. "Demography, Subsistence, and Culture during the Acheulian in Southern Africa." In *After the Australopithecines*, 543–569. Ed. K. W. Butzer and G. Ll. Isaac. The Hague: Mouton.

———. 1995. "Two Late Pleistocene-Holocene Archaeological Depositories from the Southern Cape, South Africa." *South African Archaeological Bulletin* 50: 121–131.

———. 1998. "Elandsfontein and Klasies River Revisited." In *A Master of His Craft: Papers in Stone Age Archaeology Presented to John Wymer*, 23–28. Ed. N. M. Ashton, F. Healy, and P. B. Pettitt. Oxford: Oxbow Books.

Deacon, J. 1974. "Patterning in the Radiocarbon Dates for the Wilton/Smithfield Complex in South Africa." *South African Archaeological Bulletin* 29: 3–18.

———. 1990. "Weaving the Fabric of Stone Age Research in Southern Africa." In *A History of African Archaeology*, 39–58. Ed. P. Robertshaw. London: James Currey.

Fouché, L. 1937. *Mapungubwe: Ancient Bantu Civilization on the Limpopo*. Cambridge: Cambridge University Press.

Goodwin, A. J. H. 1935. "A Commentary on the History and Present Position of South African Prehistory, with Full Bibliography." *Bantu Studies* 9: 291–417.

———. 1938. "Archaeology of the Oakhurst Shelter, George." *Transactions of the Royal Society of South Africa* 25: 229–324.

———. 1958. "Formative Years of Our Prehistoric Terminology." *South African Archaeological Bulletin* 13: 25–33.

Goodwin, A. J. H., and B. D. Malan. 1935. "Archaeology of Cape St. Blaize Cave and Raised Beach, Mossel Bay." *Annals of the South African Museum* 24: 111–140.

Goodwin, A. J. H., and C. Van Riet Lowe. 1929. "The Stone Age Cultures of South Africa." *Annals of the South African Museum* 27: 1–289.

Grün, R., J. S. Brink, N. A. Spooner, L. Taylor, C. B. Stringer, R. G. Fransiscus, and A. S. Murray. 1996. "Direct Dating of Florisbad Hominid." *Nature* 382: 500–501.

Hall, M. L. 1987. *The Changing Past: Farmers, Kings, and Traders in Southern Africa, 200–1860*. Cape Town: David Philip.

Hewitt, J. 1955. "Further Light on the Bowker Implements." *South African Archaeological Bulletin* 10: 94–95.

Howell, F. C. 1999. "Paleo-demes, Species, Clades, and Extinctions in the Pleistocene Hominin Record." *Journal of Anthropological Research* 55: 191–243.

Huffman, T. N. 1981. "Snakes, Birds: Expressive Space at Great Zimbabwe." *African Studies* 40: 131–150.

———. 1989. *Iron Age Migrations*. Johannesburg: Witwatersrand University Press.

Isaac, G. Ll. 1977. *Olorgesailie: Archaeological Studies of a Middle Pleistocene Lake Basin in Kenya*. Chicago: University of Chicago Press.

Kannemeyer, D. R. 1890. "Stone Implements, with a Description of Bushman Stone Implements and Relics: Their Names, Uses, Mode of Manufacture, and Occurrence." *Cape Illustrated Magazine* 1: 120–130.

Keller, C. M. 1973. "Montagu Cave in Prehistory: A Descriptive Analysis." *University of California Anthropological Records* 28: 1–98.

Klein, R. G. 1995. "Anatomy, Behaviour, and Modern Human Origins." *Journal of World Prehistory* 9: 167–198.

Klein, R. G., and K. Cruz-Uribe. 1991. "The Bovids from Elandsfontein, South Africa, and Their Implications for the Age, Palaeoenvironment, and Origins of the Site." *African Archaeological Review* 9: 21–79.

Kuman, K. 1994. "The Archaeology of Sterkfontein: Past and Present." *Journal of Human Evolution* 27: 471–495.

Lewis-Williams, J. D. 1981. *Believing and Seeing: Symbolic Meanings in Southern San Rock Paintings*. London: Academic Press.

———. 2000. *Stories that Float from Afar*. Cape Town: David Philip.

Marshall, L. 1976. *The !Kung of Nyae Nyae*. Cambridge, MA: Harvard University Press.

Marshall, T. E. 1959. *The Harmless People*. Harmondsworth, UK: Penguin.

Mason, R. J. 1988. *Cave of Hearths, Makapansgat, Transvaal*. Archaeological Research Unit Occasional Paper no. 21. Johannesburg: University of the Witwatersrand.

———. 1989. *South African Archaeology 1922–1988*. Archaeological Research Unit Occasional Paper no. 22. Johannesburg: University of the Witwatersrand.

Opperman, H., and B. Heydenrych. 1990. "A 22,000 Year Old Stone Age Camp Site with Plant Food Remains from the North-Eastern Cape." *South African Archaeological Bulletin* 45: 93–99.

Penning, W. H. 1886. "Notes on a Few Stone Implements Found in South Africa." *Journal of the Anthropological Institute* 16: 68–70.

Péringuey, L. 1900. "Notes on Stone Implements of Palaeolithic (Old Stone Age) Type Found at Stellenbosch and Vicinity." *Proceedings of the South African Philosophical Society* 11: xxiv–xxv.

Phillipson, D. W. 1977. "The Spread of Bantu Languages." *Scientific American* 236: 106–114.

Schofield, J. F. 1948. *Primitive Pottery: An Introduction to South African Ceramics.* Cape Town: South African Archaeological Society.

Schrire, C., J. Deacon, M. Hall, and D. Lewis-Williams. 1986. "Burkitt's Milestone." *Antiquity* 60: 123–131.

Schweitzer, F. R. 1974. "Archaeological Evidence for Sheep at the Cape." *South African Archaeological Bulletin* 29: 75–82.

Singer, R., and J. J. Wymer. 1982. *The Middle Stone Age at Klasies River Mouth in South Africa.* Chicago: University of Chicago Press.

Smith, A. B. 1992. *Pastoralism in Africa: Origins and Development.* London: Hurst and Company.

Söhnge, P. G., D. J. L. Visser, and C. Van Riet Lowe. 1937. *The Geology and Archaeology of the Vaal River Basin.* Geological Survey Memoir 35. Pretoria: Government Printer.

Soodyall, H., and T. Jenkins. 1992. "Mitochondrial DNA Polymorphisms in Khoisan Populations from Southern Africa." *Annals of Human Genetics* 56: 315–324.

Stoneking, M. 1993. "DNA and Recent Human Evolution." *Evolutionary Anthropology* 2: 60–73.

Stow, G. W. 1905. *The Native Races of South Africa.* London: Swan.

Summers, R. 1951. "Iron Age Cultures in Southern Rhodesia." *South African Journal of Science* 47: 95–107.

van Riet Lowe, C. 1945. "The Evolution of the Levallois Technique in South Africa." *Man* 45: 37–51.

———. 1952. "The Vaal River Chronology: An Up-to-Date Summary." *South African Archaeological Bulletin* 7: 135–149.

Vansina, J. 1995. "New Linguistic Evidence and 'the Bantu Expansion.'" *Journal of African History* 36: 173–195.

Vinnicombe, P. 1976. *People of the Eland: Rock Paintings of the Drakensberg Bushmen as a Reflection of Their Life and Thought.* Pietermaritzburg: University of Natal Press.

Wurz, S. 1999. "The Howiesons Poort at Klasies River—An Argument for Symbolic Behaviour." *South African Archaeological Bulletin* 54, no. 69: 38–50.

Africa, Sudanic Kingdoms

Between A.D. 800 and A.D. 1500, the important kingdoms of Ghana, Kawkaw (Gao), Takrur, and Mali flourished in the Sudanic zone of West Africa between Lake Chad and the Atlantic Ocean. Repeatedly mentioned and described in varying degrees of detail by Arab chroniclers of the period, the capitals and major entrepôts of these polities have attracted considerable archaeological attention, much of which has been conducted in an historicist mode with archaeology serving mainly to identify the towns and trading posts described in the Arab texts. Archaeological data were sought to embellish or fill out textual accounts; they were rarely used to address questions beyond those already raised by text content or analysis. Because the core areas of the kingdoms lay mainly within the former French West Sudan, the influence of French scholars on the trajectory of research in this century has been considerable. Since the 1970s, however, scholars trained outside the French system, including Dutch, Swiss, Germans, Norwegians, British, and Americans, have increasingly made important contributions.

The Colonial Period (1900–1960s)

For the first half of the twentieth century, archaeological undertakings relevant to the Sahelian kingdoms were pursued by French civil servants and military personnel. There was no professionalization of archaeology analogous to that in England, where scholars of the caliber of MORTIMER WHEELER and GERTRUDE CATON-THOMPSON mounted important excavations at sites such as Mohenjo Daro and GREAT ZIMBABWE. Rather, in French West Sudan, curious administrators and officers who lacked any formal training were offered a variety of opportunities to investigate highly visible archaeological sites. As with the explorers who set out to map the course of the Niger River in the nineteenth century, some of these officials had a gift for systematically describing what they saw along the way but most did not.

Lieutenant Louis Desplagnes had not only a gift for detailed observation and reportage but also a passion for archaeology and ethnology. In his richly detailed *Le plateau central nigérien*

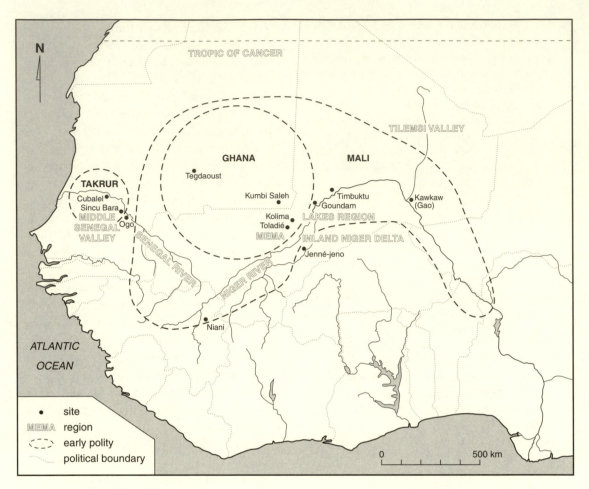

Sudanic Kingdoms of West Africa

(1907), Desplagnes presented sketches and photographs of archaeological material, tombs, dwellings, people, modes of transport, and the various environments to be found in the area of the Niger Bend. He conducted excavations at two impressive tumuli near Goundam, where he was posted, drawing attention to the similarity of the burial ritual to that practiced by Sudanic chiefs at the time of the kingdom of Ghana, as described by al-Bakri in the eleventh century (Mauny 1961, 95–97). He described in considerable detail what he observed as he excavated and the objects he found, and his descriptions were accompanied by drawings.

It would be more than thirty years before French West Sudan again saw that level of quality in excavation and description. In the interim, many sites significant to an understanding of the regional context of the emergence of

the kingdom of Ghana were hacked at by bored soldiers, administrators, civil servants, and journalists looking for excitement. Clerisse, for example, who managed to undermine or topple most of the dozens of phalliforme megaliths at Tondidaro within a space of a few weeks (Mauny 1961, 131–134). Huge occupation tells, such as Kolima, were ruthlessly trenched for intact pots and valuable goods. Even the well-intentioned Bonnel de Mezières, in his earnest quest to find the capital of Ghana, managed to plow through five houses, six tumuli, and eighteen tombs at the tell of Koumbi Saleh in March 1914, concluding "contrary to my hopes, I have learned nothing from these excavations and have not been able to affirm that Koumbi Saleh was the capital of Ghana" (Bonnel de Mezières grave 1923, 255).

Fascination with locating the capitals of the

great Sudanic kingdoms owed much to the work of Maurice Delafosse, governor-general of the French colonies of West Africa, who was trained in Oriental languages. His *Haut-Sénégal-Niger* (1912) integrated classical and Arab historical sources along with local written and oral histories to create a narrative about the history and development of the peoples of the French West Sudan. It was Delafosse's Arabicist lens that focused attention on places mentioned in texts and attributed all cultural and political achievements in the West Sudan to influences from the north. Within this diffusionist perspective, it made perfect sense to toss out all material of local manufacture recovered during excavation and concentrate on imports and inscriptions, and the various excavations in the quest of the capitals of Ghana and Mali prior to 1940 all reflected this point of view. Delafosse's influence was pervasive for several decades (De Barros 1990, 158–162; Holl 1990, 298–300).

With the arrival of Raymond Mauny in 1938 at the newly created Institut Français de l'Afrique Noire (IFAN) in Dakar, the approach to proto-history in the western Sudan became more systematic. Although trained as a lawyer and an administrator, Mauny had a gift for observation and a habit of meticulous recording similar to that of Desplagnes. Mauny's interests were wide ranging, but he was particularly attracted to the trans-Saharan trade and the great Sudanic kingdoms. His monumental synthesis of all known archaeological and historical information relevant to West African proto-history, *Tableau géographique de l'Ouest Africain au Moyen Age* (1961), remains indispensable today.

Mauny did, however, effectively "medievalize" the western Sudan by regarding it largely as an "exclusive economic and cultural dependent of the Islamic world, principally the Arabo-Berber North African sphere" (Mauny 1961, 15). This construction of a West African Middle Ages profoundly influenced the development of the archaeology of the Sudanic kingdoms by transferring the preoccupation with architecture, trade, and text from European/Arab medieval history and archaeology to West Africa. Mauny's excavations at Koumbi Saleh and Gao set the pattern for French excavations well into

the 1970s: a focus on prominent architectural units (stone or fired-brick houses, mosques, tombs), detailed publication of inscriptions (funerary stelae, glass denerals) and imports, but a relatively cursory description of other classes of material. The local context and content of these kingdoms had not yet appeared as a topic of interest. Furthermore, excavation methodology was conceived of in fairly broad terms, making the reconstruction of finely tuned chronological or depositional sequences difficult.

Yet Mauny's multidisciplinary vision for archaeology—combining geography, oral and written sources, and field research—and his pioneering use of techniques such as aerial photography and radiocarbon dating pointed the way to the future of research on the Sudanic kingdoms. In addition, he was an archivist par excellence, extracting from people throughout French West Sudan observations and reports on things archaeological and historical. The IFAN archives in Dakar remain an important resource, although their quality declined precipitously after Mauny's departure.

On the cusp of independence, a new generation of French researchers began work at Sahelian sites including Koumbi Saleh and Tegdaoust (the latter thought to be the entrepôt of Awdaghost mentioned by eleventh-century Arab chronicles and linked to Ghana). Jean Devisse, a medieval historian from the Sorbonne, and his team sought to verify on the ground the caravan routes described by the Arab authors. They mobilized large-scale resources to excavate hundreds of square meters of stone-built foundation down to a depth of seven or more meters (Devisse 1983; Polet 1985; Robert-Chaleix 1989; Vanacker 1979), and they excavated houses, mosques, and tombs. Trucks removed tons of material for later study. True to the historically framed objectives of the research, a limited subset of the material has received the bulk of the systematic study and publication to date: architecture, coins, glass denerals, North African oil lamps, imported pottery, and metals. Detailed investigation of the subsistence economy or domestic pottery production has generally not been undertaken. Ironically enough, for all the resources expended on the excavations at the two sites, no material was recovered that would permit positive identification of them as the sites of Awdaghost or the capital of Ghana described by early chroniclers. The strong case for these identifications is archaeological rather than epigraphic in nature.

Among the major questions that remain unanswered is the nature of the settlement system at Koumbi Saleh and Tegdaoust. The "city-centric" approach of the Devisse team, which mainly focused on the central area of stone-built ruins, involved little systematic investigation of sites in the hinterland of these two towns. We thus do not know if Koumbi Saleh and Tegdaoust existed essentially as ports of call, supported by trade and local agriculture but largely isolated from other sites of appreciable size, or whether they functioned as part of a well-integrated network of villages and hamlets. Bonnel de Mezières (1923) commented on the dense zone of archaeological material that extended around Koumbi Saleh in a zone thirty-five kilometers in diameter. Because there is no pottery sequence for the region, it is impossible to know which of the sites in this zone were contemporaneous with Koumbi Saleh at various points in its evolution. Thus, we know little of the developing settlement system, which is fundamental to any reconstruction of the nature of the Ghana polity.

The emphasis on the medieval paradigm on North African artifacts and influences has also left us remarkably uninformed as to the Sudanic aspects of the Ghana polity. Al-Bakri's information establishes firmly, however, the very sub-Saharan nature of the kingdom. In his description of the pagan cults of Ghana we readily recognize the forest shrines, fetishes, and sorcery that are widespread in the Mande religion and elsewhere in West Africa.

French archaeological activity in the middle Senegal Valley (MSV), in the area of the early kingdoms of Takrur and Sila mentioned by al-Bakri, was relatively rare during the colonial period and most often took the form of casual surface reconnaissance. The unsystematic collection of a small number of appealing artifacts from surface walking or small-scale sondages was a common method of fieldwork into the 1980s. The animating spirit of these collections, registered with minimal notes or accompanying observations at IFAN in Dakar, was strongly antiquarian.

Internationalization (1970s Onward)

The general site inventory accomplished between 1971 and 1973 under the leadership of Charles Becker (a historian by training) was an important step toward a more systematic approach to archaeology in the MSV (Martin and Becker 1974, 1984). Contemporaneous with the inventory by Martin and Becker were large-scale excavations undertaken by the IFAN physical anthropologist Guy Thilmans and IFAN research associate Annie Ravisé at Sincu Bara. Important not only for highly significant finds of brass and silver artifacts, the excavations also ushered in an era of modern archaeology in the Senegal Valley. The excavation report includes specialized analyses of pollen, sediments, metals and slags, and animal bone, and the spectacular brass and silver artifacts, which suggest that Sincu Bara functioned as an elite site within the Takrur or Sila polity, are thoroughly described. Pottery did not receive equal attention, however, so the establishment of a basic pottery sequence for the region was relegated to a future time. Other important excavations in the MSV were conducted by Bruno Chavane (1985) in the mid-1970s.

With an increasing internationalization of archaeology in the western Sudan after the late 1970s, new paradigms, perspectives, and methodologies were applied to research on the Sudanic kingdoms. Partly as the result of the participation of Americans familiar with research paradigms in MESOAMERICA and MESOPOTAMIA, a diachronic and regional perspective on the origins and development of complex societies was introduced along with methodologies appropriate to those concerns (McIntosh and McIntosh 1984). The fundamental building blocks of this approach are the establishment of detailed chronological sequences through controlled stratigraphic excavation and a detailed study of domestic pottery assemblages, systematic site survey and surface investigation using explicit sampling strategies, and establishment of basic time-space systematics. The explanatory framework emphasizes processes of endogenous change instead of diffusion and migration. This approach has been applied at several locales along the middle Niger in Soninke-speaking zones that are linked in oral traditions to the Ghana kingdom as well as along the MSV in the general area thought to correspond to the Takrur polity. This work has revealed some basic aspects of the development of society and economy in the first millennium A.D. at a time prior to, and overlapping with, the emergence of historically documented regional polities in the eighth or ninth (Ghana) and eleventh (Takrur) centuries.

Southeast of Koumbi Saleh, in the Mema and adjacent inland Niger delta, research has demonstrated that settlements in favorable areas grew rapidly in the middle part of the first millennium under improved hydrologic and climatic conditions. Occupation mounds such as Toladié in the Mema reached eighty hectares before being abandoned, apparently owing to increasing dryness in the twelfth or thirteenth century (Togola 1996). The growth of occupation mounds has also been documented further east at Tango Maare Jaabel. Jenné-jeno in the inland delta achieved its maximum size of thirty-three hectares before A.D. 900 after being founded ca. 200 B.C. Jenné-jeno's expansion was linked to the development throughout the first millennium of local trade networks in iron, stone, and staple commodities along the Niger River and adjacent regions (McIntosh and McIntosh 1993). This research, plus Norwegian work on the first-millennium iron-smelting industry in the Mema (Håland 1980), and Dutch research on other sites in the upper inland Niger delta or Inland Niger Delta (IND) (Bedaux et al. 1978; van der Waals, Schmidt, and Dembelé 1993), has reoriented interest toward understanding the nature of indigenous societies in the western Sudan, their development through time, and the changes they sustained subsequent to the establishment of the trans-Saharan trade. French and Malian archaeologists have produced important work in this perspective on the occupation mounds of the lakes region in the lower inland Niger delta (Raimbault and Sanogo 1991), and there has also been an attempt to establish an integrated culture historical framework for the entire middle Niger south of Timbuktu in the first and second millennia A.D. (McIntosh, S. K., 1995, 360–372).

Along the central sector of the MSV, a research program very similar to the IND project was conducted by American and Senegalese researchers in 1990–1993 with the goal of recovering broadly comparable data sets on the organization and economy of societies in the two great floodplains of the western Sudan (McIntosh, McIntosh, and Bocoum 1992). In the MSV, the trajectory during the first millennium differed significantly from the rapid growth of occupation mound clusters encountered in the IND. In the former, sites appear to have remained small, undifferentiated, and homogeneous throughout the first millennium, experiencing rapid growth and change only after the appearance of artifacts related to the trans-Saharan trade in the ninth or tenth century A.D. The earliest brass and glass imports at the sites of Cubalel, Ogo, and Sincu Bara are associated with pottery imitating decorative motifs popular at Tegdaoust. Earlier reconstructions, in which sophisticated brass metallurgy and hierarchical political organization were thought to be present in the MSV from the fifth century A.D. (Thilmans and Ravisé 1980), are now known to be erroneous, the result of mixed and disturbed deposits (McIntosh and Bocoum 2000). It now appears likely that societies along the middle Senegal experienced major and extremely rapid transformation in scale and complexity in the tenth century. Historical evidence for the existence of towns and regional polities on the middle Senegal in the mid-eleventh century is provided by al-Bakri, who described the town of Takrur as well as the kingdom of Sila. One hundred years later, the historian al-Idrisi included Sila among the domains of the powerful Takrur king who traded gold and slaves with the north. New radiocarbon dates on over a dozen of the more than 40,000 iron-smelting furnaces documented at sites on both sides of the middle Senegal cluster in the early second millennium, which suggests that iron production may have been integral to the political and commercial activities of the Takrur polity (Robert-Chaleix and Sognane 1983; Robert-Chaleix 1994).

For the other two great polities of the western Sudan, Gao (known to Arab authors as Kawkaw) and Mali, our knowledge remains largely historical. The two archaeological sites known at Gao are the old town (Gao ancien), north of the existing town, and Gao Sané, several kilometers to the east on the opposite side of a channel (which likely flowed perennially in the late first millennium) leading north to the Tilemsi Valley. Numerous brick structures are visible on the surface of both sites, some of which were excavated by Colin Flight of the University of Birmingham to reveal a confusing sequence of building and razing episodes (Insoll 1996 provides a very useful summary). Tim Insoll's archaeological work in 1994 included excavations at both Gao ancien and Gao Sané. Although very limited in scale, his excavations have provided concrete details on the appearance of trans-Saharan trade goods, including ceramics and glass, in the tenth or early eleventh century and insights into the process of Islamization. Gao apparently was a part of trade networks extending to North Africa and Spain.

In the thirteenth century, all the regions discussed above became consolidated within the hegemony of the Empire of Mali, and little archaeological information is available for Mali. The Polish research project at Niani in Guinea (Filopowiak 1979) is noteworthy for its regional perspective, even though claims that the site was the capital of Mali visited by Ibn Battuta in the fourteenth century are problematic. There is, in fact, little compelling evidence from the excavations for occupation deposits dating to this period (McIntosh and McIntosh 1984). Excavations in the Arab Quarter, for example, produced mostly material dated to the seventh to eleventh centuries A.D. and a notable lack of imported goods.

However, from that material we can get a glimpse of Mali society during the period of small villages and petty chiefdoms described by eleventh- and twelfth-century Arab authors in the area called Malal. In this regard, Filopo-

wiak's surface survey of fifty sites (iron-smelting sites, funerary tumuli, small villages) located within a four-square-kilometer area around Niani offers the potential for understanding an evolving settlement system. Of particular interest are small stone tumuli with rock-cut shaft-and-chamber collective graves similar to graves in the southwestern part of modern Mali, which indicate strong first-millennium cultural connections within this whole area that became the political heartland of the Empire of Mali in the thirteenth century. Unfortunately, the systematic study and description of the Niani pottery necessary to establish the chronological relationships of these hinterland sites has not yet been accomplished.

Conclusions

From a colonial, medievalist paradigm concerned mainly with recovering objects, inscriptions, and architecture that testified to outside influences at work in the empires of western Sudan, archaeology has moved since the 1970s to documenting local contexts and components of change. The opening of archaeology in the former French West Sudan to broad international collaboration has resulted in a variety of more regionally based research projects concerned with the establishment of the basic chronological sequences and site inventory data that are the foundation of all sustainable archaeological interpretation. As comparative regional data on settlement systems become available for the first time from different parts of western Sudan, important theoretical issues for archaeology as a whole emerge from the diversity of trajectories leading to the social complexity that may be detected there (McIntosh, S., 1999a, 1999b, 1999c). As a consequence, the empires of western Sudan, which have been largely marginal to mainstream archaeological theorizing about the rise of complexity until now, may in the future play a more prominent role.

Susan Keech McIntosh

See also Africa, Francophone; Jenné and Jenné-Jeno; Maghreb

References

Bedaux, R., T. S. Constandse-Westermann, L. Hacquebord, A. G. Lange, and J. D. van der

Waals. 1978. "Recherches archéologiques dans le delta intérieur du Niger." *Palaeohistoria* 20: 91–220.

Bonnel de Mezières, M. 1923. "Recherches sur l'emplacement de Ghana et Takrur." *Memoires Académie des Inscriptions et Belles-Lettres* 13, no. 1: 227–273.

Chavane, B. 1985. *Villages de l'ancien Tekrour.* Paris: Editions Karthala.

Connah, Graham. 1987. *African Civilizations.* Cambridge: Cambridge University Press.

DeBarros, P. 1990. "Changing Paradigms, Goals, and Methods in the Archaeology of Francophone West Africa." In *A History of Archaeology in Africa,* 155–172. Ed. P. Robertshaw. London: Thames and Hudson.

Delafosse, M. 1912. *Haut-Sénégal-Niger.* 2 vols. Paris: E. Larose.

Desplagnes, L. 1907. *Le plateau central nigérien: Une mission archéologique et ethnographique au Soudan français.* Paris: E. Larose.

Devisse, J., Robert, D. Devisse, and Robert S. Devisse. 1983. *Tegdaoust III: Recherches sur Aoudaghost. Campagnes, 1960–1965.* Paris: ADPF.

Filopowiak, W. 1979. *Études archéologiques sur la capitale médiévale du Mali.* Szczecin, Poland: Museum Narodowe w Sczczecinie.

Håland, R. 1980. "Man's Role in the Changing Habitat of Méma during the Old Kingdom of Ghana." *Norwegian Archaeological Review* 13, no. 1: 31–46.

Holl, A. 1990. "West African Archaeology: Colonialism and Nationalism." In *A History of Archaeology in Africa,* 296–308. Ed. P. Robertshaw. London: Thames and Hudson.

Insoll, T. 1996. *Islam, Archaeology, and History: Gao Region (Mali) c. A.D. 900–1250.* International Series no. 647. Oxford: British Archaeological Reports.

Levtzion, N. 1973. *Ancient Ghana and Mali.* London: Methuen.

MacDonald, K., R. H. MacDonald, and T. Togola. 1998. "Tango Maare Diabel: Excavations at a First Millennium A.D. Malian Town." Paper presented at the fourteenth biennial meeting of the Society of Africanist Archaeologists, Syracuse, NY, 20–24 May 1998.

McIntosh, S. 1994. "Changing Perceptions of West Africa's Past." *Journal of Archaeological Research* 2, no. 2: 165–198.

———. 1999a. "Floodplains and the Development of Complex Society: Comparative Perspectives from the West African Semi-arid Tropics." In *Complex Polities in the Ancient Tropical World.* Ed. E. Bacus. Arlington, VA: American Anthropological Association.

———. 1999b. "Modeling Political Organization in Large-scale Settlement Clusters: A Case Study from the Inland Niger Delta, Mali." In *Beyond Chiefdoms: Pathways to Complexity in Africa.* Ed. S. McIntosh. Cambridge: Cambridge University Press.

———. 1999c. "Pathways to Complexity: An African Perspective." In *Beyond Chiefdoms: Pathways to Complexity in Africa.* Ed. S. McIntosh. Cambridge: Cambridge University Press.

McIntosh, S., ed. 1995. *Excavations at Jenne-jeno, Hambarketolo, and Kaniana (Inland Niger Delta, Mali): The 1981 Season.* Berkeley: University of California Press.

McIntosh, S., and H. Bocoum. 2000. "New Perspectives on Sincu Bara, a First Millennium Site in the Senegal Valley." *African Archaeological Review* 17.

McIntosh, S., and R. McIntosh. 1984. "The Early City in West Africa: Towards an Understanding." *African Archaeological Review* 2: 73–98.

———. 1993. "Cities without Citadels: Understanding West African Urbanism." In *The Archaeology of Africa: Foods Metals and Towns,* 622–641. Ed. T. Shaw et al. London: Unwin Hyman.

McIntosh, S., R. McIntosh, and H. Bocoum. 1992. "The Middle Senegal Valley Project: Preliminary Results from the 1990–91 Field Season." *Nyame Akuma* 38: 47–61.

Martin, V., and Ch. Becker. 1974. "Vestiges protohistoriques et occupation humaine au Senegal." *Annales de Demographie Historique,* 403–429.

———. 1984. *Inventaire des sites protohistoriques de la Senegambie.* Kaolack, Senegal: C.N.R.S.

Mauny, R. 1961. *Tableau géographique de l'Ouest Africain au moyen age d'après les sources écrites, la tradition orale, et l'archéologie.* Mémoire de l'IFAN. Dakar: IFAN.

Polet, J. 1985. *Tegdaoust IV: Fouille d'un quartier de Tegdaoust. Urbanisation, architecture, utilisation, de l'espace construite.* Paris: ADPF.

Raimbault, and K. Sanogo, eds. 1991. *Recherches archéologiques au Mali.* Paris: Editions Karthala.

Robert-Chaleix, D. 1989. *Tegdaoust V: Une concession médiévale à Tegdaoust. Implantation, evolution d'une unité d'habitation.* Paris: ADPF.

———. 1994 "Metallurgie du fer dans la Moyenne Vallée du Sénégal: Les bas fourneaux de Silla." *Journal des Africanistes* 64, no. 2: 113–127.

Robert-Chaleix, D., and M. Sognane. 1983. "Une industrie métallurgique ancienne sur la rive mauritanienne du fleuve Sénégal." In *Métallurgies anciennes: Nouvelles contributions,* 45–62. Ed. N. Echard. Mémoire de la Société des Africanistes no. 9. Paris.

Thilmans, G., and A. Ravise. 1980. *Protohistoire du Senegal: Sintiou-Bara et les sites du fleuve.* Memoires, no. 91. Dakar: IFAN.

Togola, T. 1996. "Iron Age Occupation in the Méma Region, Mali." *African Archaeological Review* 13, no. 2: 91–110.

van der Waals, D., A. Schmidt, and M. Dembelé. 1993. "Prospections de sites archéologiques dans le delta intérieure du Niger." In *Vallées du Niger,* 218–232. Ed. J. Devisse. Paris: Editions de la réunion des musées nationaux.

Vanacker, C. 1979. *Tegdaoust II: Fouille d'un quartier artisanal.* Paris: Arts et Metiers Graphiques.

Africa, Swahili Coast of

See Swahili Coast of Africa

Akrotiri-Aetokremnos

Until the excavations by Alan Simmons at Akrotiri-Aetokremnos, there was no evidence of any pre-Neolithic occupation of CYPRUS. This small, collapsed rock shelter on the south coast of the island contains deposits of stone tools and animal bones representing a relatively short period, approximately 10,000 B.C. A large proportion of the bones are of the pygmy hippopotamus, which became extinct at the end of the Pleistocene period. It is possible that human predation was a factor in this extinction. Although the site has been important in establishing an early date for Mediterranean island colonization, it is still difficult to use this single site as the basis for developing more general models of the processes involved.

David Frankel

References

Simmons, A. H. 1991. "Humans, Island Colonisation, and Pleistocene Extinctions in the Mediterranean: The View from Akrotiri-Aetokremnos Cyprus." *Antiquity* 65: 857–869.

Albright, William Foxwell (1891–1971)

The son of an American Wesleyan missionary couple, Albright spent his childhood in Chile. While working as a high school teacher in South Dakota, he taught himself Hebrew and Akkadian, eventually winning a scholarship to Johns Hopkins University. Albright became one of the most eminent Orientalists of the twentieth century and was known as the father of biblical archaeology. He directed the American School of Oriental Research in Jerusalem from 1920 to 1929, and again between 1933 and 1936. Albright established the modern discipline of biblical archeology, in which ancient Near Eastern archaeological material was used to elucidate scholarly understanding of the Bible. He was to dominate this field from the early 1920s until the 1960s. His protégé, G. Ernest Wright of Harvard University, carried on the Albright tradition by blending the "biblical theology" movement of the 1950s through the 1970s with "biblical archaeology."

Between the two world wars many of the American excavations in Palestine were at biblical sites and were staffed by Protestant seminarians and clergymen, who were supported by funds raised by churches. These included Albright's own excavations at Tell en-Nasbeh (1926–1935), at Beth-shemesh (1928–1933), and at many smaller sites. Albright also excavated Tell el-Fûl (1922), Bethel (1934), and Tell Beit Mirsim (1926–1932), from which he established a pottery chronology for Western Palestine. Albright was Chairman of the Oriental Seminary at Johns Hopkins, and from 1930 to 1968 he edited the *Bulletin of the American Schools of Oriental Research.* It was in this latter role that he recognized and publicised the great discoveries of the Ugaritic tablets (1929–1930) and the Dead Sea Scrolls (1947 on).

Tim Murray

See also American Schools of Oriental Research; Dead Sea Scrolls; Israel; Syro-Palestinian and Biblical Archaeology

Ulisse Aldrovandi (Ann Ronan Picture Library)

Aldrovandi, Ulisse (1522–1605)

A scholar of tremendous range with a focus on natural history and an interest in antiquarianism. Aldrovandi taught medicine at the University of Bologna in Italy in the late sixteenth century. Among his many researches was the natural history of "ceraunia," thought to be thunderbolts but actually worked flints and stone tools, which he discussed at considerable length in his *Musaeum Metallicum* (1648). Although another scholar at the time, MICHELE MERCATI, was persuaded that many of these stones had been shaped by human beings, Aldrovandi preferred to account for them as the result of natural geological processes.

Tim Murray

See also Lithic Analysis
References
Schnapp, Alain. 1997. *The Discovery of the Past* (translated from the French by Ian Kinnes and Gillian Varndell). New York: Harry N. Abrams, 1997.

Alesia

Alesia is located at Alise-Saint-Reine in the department of Côte d'Or in France. There were two battles of Alesia. The first, against Julius Caesar, was by a large Gaulish tribal coalition led by Vercingetorix in 52 B.C., and it resulted in the defeat of the latter. The other, which is still taking place today, began in 1850 when scholars began debating the exact location of the famous siege of Alesia, at either Alise on Mount Quxois in Burgundy or Alaise in the department of Franche-Comté, the two most favored sites for this great event. However, tradition also provided the scholars with another site to dispute, the village of Alise-Saint-Reine, which had replaced a Gaulish *oppidum* (fortified town) with a Gallo-Roman town and which, in fact, is the real site of Alesia. In the ninth century A.D., scholars had recorded this link, but it had been forgotten by the Middle Ages. In 1838, a military officer making a relief map of the site of Alise was struck by its coincidental resemblance to Caesar's description of Alesia. Several years later, the people of Franche-Comté, supported by the relief map and the analysis of Caesar's troop movements, debated this claim and proposed Alise as the alternative.

With the encouragement of Napoleon III, soundings were made around Alise between 1861 and 1865, and they revealed the traces of pickax diggings made during a Roman, Gaulish, or German siege. The siege pits corresponded to Caesar's general descriptions, and the many remains of arms and coins dated the battle. Pits were dug alongside the basic *oppidum* and confirmed the existence of a Roman settlement, and a "Gaulish wall" was excavated, but it could have been built after the conquest.

In the years from 1950 to 1990, the corpus of coins, ranging from bronze forgeries of the golden statere of Vercingetorix to coins used during the nineteenth century A.D., was analyzed. Aerial prospecting revealed many traces of the pits, contours, and camps installed by Caesar around the citadel. Excavations by a Franco-German team made Alise, for the scientific world at least, a special reference site for dating other contemporaneous sites and for the study of Roman army camps. The traces of the pits and camps were validated by excavations in the nineteenth century and Caesar's written descriptions. The pits were laid out on the site exactly as he had described them, and a rigorous study of movable artifacts confirmed their origins and dates. One of the Gaulish walls of the *oppidum* was built before the siege, and the archaeological proof of that fact is incontrovertible.

The hill of Alesia is attached to the chalky Auxis range by only a narrow pass. It resembles a plateau, with a ninety-hectare surface surrounded by steep cliffs, and the impression from the Laumes Plain is much less grand than Caesar's description of it as being as high and great as Sienna's. Rather it is similar to the Puy d'Issolud (Vayrac, Lot), and resembles Uxellodunum, which Caesar put under siege in 51 B.C. The rampart was very little enlarged, because the cliffs discouraged direct attack. However, it is on the plain, as Caesar himself noted elsewhere, that the traces of battle can be best found.

The identification of the site of this battle gave archaeologists a fixed location point for an absolutely certain and essential chronology for the history of weapons, armaments, and coinage. Some of the coins did not have dates, only rare inscriptions of the name of chiefdoms, and only their weights and the alloy compositions enabled them to be classified. The presence of money in Alesia attests to its circulation in 52 B.C., and at this point it is enough to find a monetary series. As Vercingetorix called on the troops from all across Gaul to come to his rescue, Alesia must be considered a reference site for regions that were far away but participated in the uprising.

Caesar's genius was exemplified not only in the conduct of the war's operations, which caused the surrender of the Gaulish coalition, but also in his political exploitation of the situation. In 52 B.C., not only were the so-called conquered cities in revolt but also the great tribes of Bituriges, Arvernes, and all of their allies led by the Heduens. After many months of indecisive fighting, Vercingetorix called for another army to come and help him, but it never reached him; it was unable to penetrate Caesar's defense.

Caesar went into battle at the most decisive moment of the war, and the siege of Uxellodunum the following year was the consequence of this. Contemporaries echo their general's description of this secondary *oppidum* as a key site for a "Gaulish nation," which was of their invention and for their glory. The kings, the emperors, and later the school of the Third Republic changed the rebellion of the Gaulic tribes into the first manifestation of the resistance of a French nation to an enemy. The hexagon shape of FRANCE can be justified in two ways: the space was defined by natural frontiers—the Rhine River, the Alps, and the Pyrenees Mountains; in time, it was the coalition of Gaulish peoples around Vercingetorix, who founded a modern French nation at Alesia.

It took more than 100 years of archaeological research to prove that the written record of history was, in part, Caesarian propaganda.

Oliver Buchsenschutz

References

Le Gall, J. 1963. *Alesia: Archéologie et Histoire*. Paris: Fayard.

Reddé, M., and S. Von Schurnbein. 1993. "Fouilles et recherches nouvelles sur les travaux du siège d'Alésia. Paris." *Comptes Rendus Académie des Inscriptions et Belles-Lettres*.

Reddé, M., et al. 1995. "Fouilles et recherches nouvelles sur les travaux de Cesar devant Alésia, 1991–1994." *Aus Bericht der Römisch-Germanischen Komission* 76, 73–158.

Schnapp, A., and O. Buchsenschutz. 1993. "Alésia." In *Les Lieux de mémoire*, 272–315. Ed. P. Nora. Paris: Gallimard.

Altamira

Altimira is the name of a cave in Santander Province, northern SPAIN, where Don Marcelino Sanz de Sautuola, a local landowner, discovered Paleolithic paintings and engravings in 1879. The ceiling of the cave is particularly famous as it is decorated with an array of polychrome bison figures. Unfortunately, Sautuola's claims for the art's antiquity were rejected by the archaeological establishment for twenty years as a result of several factors—among them, he was an unknown amateur, no Paleolithic art had previously been found outside France, and the animal figures looked too fresh and sophisticated to be genuinely ancient.

Paleolithic cave painting from Altamira (Ann Ronan Picture Library)

Altamira contains a wealth of other paintings and engravings, including "masks" and quadrilateral signs like those of the cave of El Castillo in the same region. The two caves also contain identical multiple-line engravings of deer, both on the walls and on shoulder-blade bone of animal remains found in the cave, and some of these bones have been radiocarbon dated to 13,550 B.C. Altamira's art probably spans a period from about 20,000 to 14,000 years ago. Charcoal from black figures in different parts of the cave has produced direct dates from 16,480 to 14,650 years ago.

The ceiling is clearly a complex palimpsest of figures from different phases, but scholars from Sanz de Sautuola onward have believed that the polychrome bison were produced in one episode or even by a single artist. However, charcoal in some of the ceiling's bison has yielded radiocarbon results from 14,820 to 13,130 years ago, which, if valid, suggests that the figures may not constitute a single homogeneous composition after all.

Paul Bahn

See also Rock Art Studies

American Academy in Rome

The American Academy in Rome is the U.S. center in Rome for scholars, architects, artists, and musicians and incorporates a School of Classical Studies. Originally two separate schools—the American School of Architecture in Rome, founded in 1894 by Charles Follen McKim, and the American School of Classical Studies in Rome, established in 1895 by the

ARCHAEOLOGICAL INSTITUTE OF AMERICA (AIA)— the American Academy in Rome (AAR) became a single institution in 1912.

The architectural school had taken the French Academy in the grand Villa Medici in Rome as its model, and McKim had envisioned it as a center for architects to study the noble buildings of ancient Rome. Its first home was, however, anything but imperial, consisting of eight rented rooms in the Palazzo Torlonia. The classical school was the second such school the AIA founded, and its model was the American School of Classical Studies in Athens, established in 1882, also in emulation of older European institutions. The Rome classical school, too, began life in rented quarters—in the Villa Aurora on the Pincio Hill.

The two American schools in Rome moved from their separate quarters to a new building on the Janiculum Hill in 1914. This main building, together with the neighboring Villa Aurelia (a 1909 bequest to the architectural school) and several other buildings, is the home of the AAR to this day, and the complex houses a research library, art studios, music rooms, exhibition galleries, and residential and dining facilities. The American Academy in Rome is unique among the many foreign schools in that city because of its status as a privately funded organization and its diverse Rome Prize fellowship program that brings together archaeologists, philologists, historians, art historians, architects, painters, sculptors, and musicians to form a vibrant intellectual and artistic community.

Unlike its sister institution in Greece, the American School of Classical Studies in Rome was unable to undertake any excavations in Italy for half a century after its foundation. Its members consequently confined their activities to the study of architecture, topography, inscriptions, and classical statuary. Among the noteworthy studies produced during the AAR's early years were Esther Van Deman's on Roman construction techniques and Samuel Ball Platner's on Roman topography.

It was not until after World War II that a more receptive attitude in Italy toward foreign excavation permitted members of the AAR to begin major fieldwork. In 1948, under the direction of

Frank E. Brown, a U.S. team began to uncover the remains of the Republican colony of Cosa on the coast northwest of Rome, focusing on the temples of the Capitolium, the civic buildings of the Forum, and some private houses. Publications of the excavations have appeared in several volumes of the *Memoirs of the American Academy in Rome*. The academy donated the site and its museum to Italy in 1981. In Rome itself, the AAR has excavated in the Regia and the Atrium Vestae in the Forum Romanum and, most recently, on the slope of the Palatine Hill.

Fred S. Kleiner

References

Dyson, S. L. 1998. *Ancient Marbles to American Shores: Classical Archaeology in the United States*. Philadelphia: University of Pennsylvania Press.

Kopff, E. C. 1996. "American Academy in Rome." In *An Encyclopedia of the History of Classical Archaeology*, 41–43. Ed. N. T. de Grummond. Westport, CT: Greenwood Press.

Valentine, L., and A. Valentine. 1973. *The American Academy in Rome, 1894–1969*. Charlottesville: University of Virginia Press.

Yegül, F. 1991. *Gentlemen of Instinct and Breeding: Architecture at the American Academy in Rome, 1894–1940*. New York: Oxford University Press.

American Antiquity

American Antiquity is the quarterly journal of the Society for American Archaeology (SAA), and it includes articles on the archaeology of North and South America and archaeological method and theory worldwide. The SAA was founded in 1934 to promote communication within the professional archaeological community and between professional and avocational archaeologists through various means, including a journal. In 1937, Carl E. Guthe proposed the name *American Antiquity* for the journal, following the lead of the English journal *Antiquity*.

All members in the society receive *American Antiquity*, and funding for its publication comes primarily from dues paid to the society. Prior to 1958, authors paid for some or all of the cost of illustrations. Until 1993, a single nominee for editor was selected for a four-year term (shortened to three years in 1978) by the society's nominating committee and was "elected" by the membership. Now, as a result of a change in the bylaws, the editor is selected by the SAA executive board and is no longer a voting member of that governing body.

The early editors managed the journal from their institutional office with editorial assistance from spouses, students, and assistant editors representing different geographical areas or archaeological specialties. As the workload increased, associate editors were added for different sections of the journal. In 1989, a full-time managing editor took over many of the production tasks.

Review of articles submitted was in the hands of the editor and the assistant editors until 1969 when peer review of each submission by two people was instituted. The number of reviewers for each manuscript was increased to four in 1989. Prior to peer review, the acceptance rate of article submissions was 65–90 percent, and at times editors were desperate for copy. After peer review began, a change that coincided with a period of tremendous growth in the society, the acceptance rate fell below 50 percent.

The general character of the journal's contents has remained fairly uniform even though the organization has changed. The principal purpose of the journal from the beginning was to present research articles, and these make up the majority of each issue. Although issue contents are usually determined by what is submitted, occasional special issues are designed with a particular geographic or topical focus. The twenty-fifth and fiftieth anniversaries of the SAA were occasions for special issues of historical interest.

In the early issues, a correspondence section was included to provide a forum for brief comments by amateurs, but as it worked out, professional archaeologists dominated that section along with the others. A facts and comments section was added in 1938. The notes and news section continued the annual archaeological fieldwork summary compiled by the National Research Council's Committee on State Archaeological Surveys and published in *American Anthropologist* until 1932. That section, which became current research in 1962, provided up-to-date summaries of archaeological research in the Americas and for a brief period (1973–1976), the Old World. The section was dropped in 1994 because of space constraints.

The book review section, always important for membership participation and reader interest, includes books from all areas of the world. An important section published annually is the report of the society's business meeting, including committee reports. Until 1974, this section also included titles of papers given at the annual meeting.

As membership in the SAA has always been dominated by citizens of the United States, articles in *American Antiquity* have had a strong focus on America north of Mexico, even though there have been occasional complaints from the membership about the number of Mesoamerican articles. Steps to internationalize the journal include publication of a few articles in Spanish in the 1940s, inclusion of translated Russian articles in the early 1960s, institution of an annual review of Old World archaeology in 1978 (discontinued in 1990), and publication of Spanish abstracts for articles beginning in 1989. In the late 1980s, the demand for a journal specifically devoted to Middle and South America was strong enough that the society created *Latin American Antiquity*, which is available to SAA members at an additional charge. This journal began publication in 1990, and since then, *American Antiquity* has focused more on articles on archaeology in the United States and Canada and on archaeological method and theory. As foreign membership and subscription increased in the 1970s, particularly in Europe, *American Antiquity* became the medium by which the state of American archaeology is judged.

The contents of *American Antiquity* provide a fairly good measure of the interests and theoretical orientations of professional archaeologists in the United States, but the journal does not reflect the work of Americanists in other countries nearly as well. In one study of the journal's contents for the first fifty years, articles on excavation, material culture, and culture process were found to account for 60 percent or more of the articles until the last half of the 1960s. Since that time, the number of articles

devoted to these three areas has declined, and articles on floral and faunal remains and analytical methods have increased to give a more balanced coverage of archaeological topics.

In another study that looks at the trends in articles emphasizing data, method, or theory for the first forty years of the journal, articles emphasizing data consistently made up 60 percent or more of the total published until the term of the last editor in the sample, Edwin N. Wilmsen, when the proportion dropped to one-third. Interestingly, this dramatic shift also occurred at the time when peer review was introduced. Articles on method consistently represented around 20 percent of the articles until the 1960s when they began to increase, reaching 50 percent by the early 1970s. Articles on theory were always 10 percent or less except during the terms of the earliest and latest editors, when they reached 15 percent.

Archival materials relating to *American Antiquity* are housed in the National Anthropological Archives of the National Museum of Natural History of the Smithsonian Institution. Materials over ten years old are available to researchers except for confidential files, such as referee comments, which are restricted for fifty years.

Andrew L. Christenson

American Journal of Archaeology

The *American Journal of Archaeology* is the official journal of the ARCHAEOLOGICAL INSTITUTE OF AMERICA (AIA). In January 1885, fewer than six years after the formation of that institute, Arthur Lincoln Frothingham, Jr., published the first issue of the *American Journal of Archaeology for the Study of the Monuments of Antiquity and of the Middle Ages*. The new journal was to be "the official organ of the Archaeological Institute of America," and its stated goal was "to further the interests for which the Institute was founded."

Twelve years later, the young periodical, now simply called the *American Journal of Archaeology (AJA)*, marked the inauguration of its second series by placing the institute's seal on its title page and adopting as its subtitle, "the Journal of the Archaeological Institute of America." The rationale for the second series was to bring "greater unity and uniformity" to the institute's diverse publications. Henceforth, *AJA* would be the sole venue for the publication of articles on the fieldwork and research conducted by the AIA's new American schools of classical studies established in 1882 in Athens and in 1895 in Rome. Although *AJA* no longer has a monopoly on AIA research (the American School in Athens, for example, has published its own journal, *Hesperia,* since 1932), more than a century later the second series continues to appear in quarterly fascicles. *AJA* remains the AIA's official journal and publishes each April the abstracts of the papers presented at the institute's annual meeting in December; the citations of the AIA's awards for scholarship, teaching, and service; and the texts of important resolutions of the AIA's governing council.

Although the original mission of *AJA* was to "treat all branches of Archaeology and Art— Oriental, Classical, Early Christian, Mediaeval, and American," the archaeology of the AIA's own continent never gained a strong foothold in the journal, and scholars of medieval art preferred to publish their research in art history publications rather than archaeological journals. From the beginning, *AJA,* like the AIA itself, reflected its founders' preoccupation with the classical world, especially Greece. The defined scope of *AJA* today is "the art and archaeology of ancient Europe and the Mediterranean world, including the Near East and Egypt, from prehistoric to late antique times." In recent years, although retaining its focus on Greece and Rome, *AJA* has published articles on all periods of Old World art and archaeology as well as newsletters on fieldwork in Cyprus, Iraq, Israel, Jordan, Sardinia, Syria, and Turkey. Other regular features have been a series of critical reviews of Aegean prehistory, book reviews, obituaries, and the proceedings of the AIA's annual meetings.

In conformity with an AIA 1973 resolution opposing the illicit international trade in antiquities and the despoliation of archaeological sites, *AJA*'s editorial policy precludes "the announcement or initial scholarly presentation of any object in a private or public collection acquired after 30 December 1973, unless the object was part of a previously existing collection

or has been legally exported from the country of origin."

Fred S. Kleiner

References

Donohue, A. A. 1985. "One Hundred Years of the *American Journal of Archaeology:* An Archival History." *American Journal of Archaeology* 89: 3–30.

Dyson, S. L. 1985. "Two Paths to the Past: A Comparative Study of the Last Fifty Years of *American Antiquity* and the *American Journal of Archaeology.*" *American Antiquity* 50: 452–463.

———. 1998. *Ancient Marbles to American Shore: Classical Archaeology in the United States.* Philadelphia: University of Pennsylvania Press.

Kleiner, F. S. 1990. "On the Publication of Recent Acquisitions of Antiquities." *American Journal of Archaeology* 94: 525–527.

———. 1996. "The *American Journal of Archaeology* and the Archaeological Institute of America." *American Journal of Archaeology* 100: 1–4.

American School of Classical Studies at Athens

The American School of Classical Studies at Athens, the largest foreign research center in Greece, is dedicated to the study of Greek archaeology, history, and culture. Founded in 1882 by the ARCHAEOLOGICAL INSTITUTE OF AMERICA (AIA), the American School of Classical Studies at Athens (ASCSA) was conceived as a place where U.S. scholars could study classical Greek monuments at first hand. In establishing a research center in Greece, the AIA was following the lead of France, whose school in Athens had opened in 1846, and of Germany, which had inaugurated the Athenian branch of the Deutsches Archäologisches Institut in 1874. But unlike its European counterparts, the ASCSA, like the AIA itself, was (and still is) a privately funded organization dependent on college and university support as well as the generosity of individuals and foundations.

The ASCSA began in rented quarters near the Arch of Hadrian, but two years later the Greek government donated land for a permanent home on the south slope of Mt. Lykabettos adjacent to the plot previously given to the British School of Archaeology. The Americans moved into their newly constructed Main

Building in 1888, which was enlarged in 1913–1916, 1958–1959, and 1992. Construction of a residential/dining facility, Loring Hall, took place in 1930.

In 1922, Joannes Gennadius, a prominent Greek diplomat, offered to donate his extensive personal library on the history and culture of Greece to the ASCSA if the school would build a separate building to house it and make the collection available to researchers of any nationality. A gift from the Carnegie Foundation made possible construction of the Gennadeion, a neoclassical marble structure, which opened in 1926. It houses not only rare books but also Edward Lear landscapes of Greece and archival material on the archaeologist Heinrich Schliemann.

Immediately after its foundation, the ASCSA launched a program of excavation and publication—even before the school began construction of its permanent headquarters. The first major ASCSA site was the Argive Heraion, excavated between 1892 and 1895. The school's two largest continuing excavations are at Corinth and in the Athenian Agora, but members of the school have explored Greek sites that span a very wide range, both chronologically and geographically, including Franchthi Cave, Lerna, Olynthos, Messenia, Nemea, Samothrace, Keos, and Kommos.

Work began in Corinth in 1896, and the excavation of a major ancient Greek city lent prestige to the fourteen-year-old U.S. institution. The French and Germans had earlier secured permits to excavate at Delphi (the Americans had also wanted a permit to excavate there but had failed to obtain one) and Olympia, respectively. Excavation in the historic Plaka district of Athens to uncover the classical Agora started in 1931. Reconstruction of the Stoa of Attalos to serve as the excavation headquarters; a museum was begun in 1953 and completed in 1956.

The ASCSA initially published reports of its fieldwork in the *American Journal of Archaeology,* but the opening of the Agora excavations prompted the school to create its own journal, *Hesperia,* in 1932. The ASCSA also publishes a multivolume series for each of its major excavations, monographs on diverse topics, site guides, and a series of inexpensive *Picture Books*

for the general public. The school offers a formal curriculum as well as research fellowships for graduate students during the academic year and a summer program for both students and teachers. It is the official liaison between more than 150 affiliated North American colleges and universities and the Greek Ministry of Culture, which grants all fieldwork permits.

Fred S. Kleiner

References

Dyson, S. L. 1998. *Ancient Marbles to American Shores: Classical Archaeology in the United States.* Philadelphia: University of Pennsylvania Press.

Hoff, M. 1996. "American School of Classical Studies at Athens." In *An Encyclopedia of the History of Classical Archaeology,* 44–45. Ed. N. T. de Grummond. Westport, CT: Greenwood Press.

Lord, L. E. 1947. *A History of the American School of Classical Studies at Athens 1882–1942: An Intercollegiate Project.* Cambridge, MA: Harvard University Press.

Meritt, L. S. 1984. *History of the American School of Classical Studies at Athens, 1939–1980.* Princeton, NJ: American School of Classical Studies at Athens.

Norton, C. E. 1903. "The Founding of the School at Athens." *American Journal of Archaeology* 7: 351–356.

American Schools of Oriental Research

The American Schools of Oriental Research (ASOR) is the principal North American research organization for the study of the ancient Near East. Founded in 1900 under the aegis of the Archaeological Institute of America (AIA), the Society of Biblical Literature, and the American Oriental Society, the ASOR is a consortium of approximately 140 North American colleges, universities, museums, seminaries, and libraries. Its administrative offices are currently on the campus of Boston University and are housed in the same building as the AIA's national headquarters.

Like its AIA siblings, the American School of Classical Studies in Athens and the American Academy in Rome, ASOR is a privately funded rather than a government-funded institution. ASOR has three permanent research centers abroad: the W. F. Albright Institute of Archaeological Research (AIAR) in Jerusalem; the American Center of Oriental Research (ACOR) in Amman, Jordan; and the Cyprus American Archaeological Research Institute (CAARI) in Nicosia. These centers sponsor scores of field projects in the Middle East.

ASOR publishes the *Bulletin of the American Schools of Oriental Research* (the first issue appeared in 1919), the *Journal of Cuneiform Studies* (begun in 1947), *Biblical Archaeologist* (a popular journal launched in 1938), and several monograph series. ASOR celebrated its centennial on 15 April 2000 with a conference at the Smithsonian Institution in Washington, D.C., entitled "Footsteps in the Dust: A Century of ASOR Discoveries in the Ancient Near East."

ASOR established its first overseas research center in 1900 in Jerusalem. The AIAR's present home, just north of the old walled city, opened in 1925. Originally called the American School of Oriental Research, the AIAR assumed its present name in 1970 in honor of WILLIAM FOXWELL ALBRIGHT, a pioneer in the scientific excavation of sites in Palestine and a longtime director of the school. The building, which was enlarged in 1930 and renovated in 1985, houses a research library, laboratories, and residential and dining facilities for fellows and visitors. The AIAR sponsors seminars, workshops, and lectures and currently coordinates the excavation, surveying, and publication of approximately twenty archaeological sites, chief among them Ashkelon, Caesarea, Sepphoris, and Tel Miqne-Ekron.

ASOR's Jordanian center was born in 1968 after the Six-Day War in June 1967 between Israel and the Arab world brought an end to AIAR work in the Hashemite Kingdom. The Jordanian government regarded the new branch of ASOR, originally called the American Research Center in Amman, as an exiled operation of the Jerusalem school. Reflecting the new political reality of the Middle East, in 1970 the Amman Committee of ASOR became a separate corporate entity and assumed its present name (the Jerusalem school took on its new name at the same time). ACOR is now the largest research institute in Amman and is the liaison between the Jordanian Department of Antiquities and North American excavators and researchers.

ACOR's present headquarters, constructed in 1984–1986, are in a five-story structure located near the University of Jordan and the British and German archaeological institutes. The building houses a research library, offices, workrooms, a lecture hall, a conservation laboratory, and residential and dining facilities. ACOR currently coordinates about thirty excavations, surveys, or publication projects covering several millennia of the history of Jordan. Among the most notable sites are 'Ain Ghazal, Petra, Aqaba/Ayla, and the Citadel of Amman.

The newest of ASOR's research centers, CAARI, founded in 1978, is the only foreign organization in Cyprus dedicated to archaeological study, and it opens its doors to visitors from all over the world. CAARI's headquarters, a remodeled two-story residence built in the 1930s, is in central Nicosia near the Cyprus Museum. Like the AIA institutions in Jerusalem and Amman, CAARI houses a research library, laboratory, workrooms, and residential quarters; sponsors lectures and symposia; and offers research fellowships. As the liaison between the Cypriot Department of Antiquities and North American scholars, CAARI facilitates numerous American field and research projects on the island from prehistory through the classical, Byzantine, Venetian, and Ottoman periods.

Fred S. Kleiner

References

ACOR: The First 25 Years. The American Center of Oriental Research: 1968–1993. 1993. Amman, Jordan: ACOR.

Davis, T. W. 1989. "A History of American Archaeology on Cyprus." *Biblical Archaeologist* 163–169.

King, P. J. 1983. *American Archaeology in the Mideast: A History of the American Schools of Oriental Research*. Philadelphia: American Schools of Oriental Research.

Andersson, Johan Gunnar (1874–1960)

The first major archaeological fieldwork in CHINA was carried out by Western scientists attached to the Geological Survey of China established in Beijing in 1916. J. G. Andersson was a fossil hunter and explorer who spent long periods in China, where he became fascinated with stories of "dragon bones," which were highly valued by the Chinese for their magical and pharmaceutical uses. In 1921, the search for fossils led Andersson to Zhoukoudian Cave, in Hebei province near Beijing, which was a giant fissure in a limestone cliff filled with fossil animal bones. Excavation revealed a major Chinese Paleolithic site, containing human skeletal material in the same levels as crude stone tools, animal bones, and traces of thick hearths. Zhoukoudian was excavated under the direction of Canadian anatomist Davidson Black. The first skull cap of *Homo erectus,* known initially as Peking Man or Sinanthropus, was excavated by Chinese archaeologist PEI WENZHONG in 1929. The site has yielded the only large population of *Homo erectus,* with fragments of more than forty individuals of the species worldwide. Most of the bones were lost during World War II.

Tim Murray

References

Andersson, J. G. 1934. *Children of the Yellow Earth: Studies in Prehistoric China.* New York: Macmillan.

Antiquity

In 1925, O. G. S. CRAWFORD, then age thirty-nine, had the idea of a new archaeological publication to serve the very lively and active group, the then-young generation of archaeologists working in England. Existing journals smoldered on, but they neither flamed nor gave light. Unusually, Crawford did not seek a publisher, for he wanted a completely free hand to say and to publish whatever he liked. Instead, he set up *Antiquity* as his own enterprise with money borrowed from a friend.

Sending a prospectus to 20,000 names and addresses, he soon had over 600 subscribers, and the venture was launched as a quarterly journal in 1927. Reports on the Glozel affair, the faking of Neolithic writing in eastern France, helped energize the new venture, and in 1928, the journal published the first scholarly report of LEONARD WOOLLEY's excavation of the royal tombs at UR in MESOPOTAMIA.

In rereading the early articles published in *Antiquity,* the journal's distinctive character is evident. In each number, Crawford wrote a lively editorial with snippets of news, comment, and reports of passing events and curiosities with an archaeological aspect; as he said, "Try living on a desert island with a book of verse and no loaf of bread—or *Antiquity* without a jug of wine!" (Crawford 1955, 177). His own interests in aerial photography are evident, and the field reports start from the focal area in the classic landscapes of southern Britain, especially its chalk land. Crawford's broader interests are also revealed in the coverage of Africa; there is, for example, pioneering work in the field that would now be called "ethnoarchaeology." Great names of the next generation, like CHRISTOPHER HAWKES and STUART PIGGOTT, are conspicuous. Names from the Americas are largely absent.

The first number of the tenth volume, for March 1936, shows the pattern in its 128 pages: editorial, six long reports ("The Coming of Iron," "Pit and Pit-dwellings in Southeast Europe," "Roman Barrows," "Easter Island," "Anglo-Saxon Vine-Scroll Ornament," and "Cyclopean Walls at Tarragona"), ten short reports and a pair of air photographs, book notes, and twenty-two book reviews. Of one book, Crawford commented, "We are surprised that the Oxford University Press should sponsor such a shocking piece of work as this." The diversity is important, and the range of subjects in each of the year's other three numbers is equally diverse.

Crawford edited *Antiquity* largely on his own, and when he died in 1957 it was found that no provision had been made for a successor. GLYN DANIEL was persuaded to take it on, in tandem with his wife, Ruth Daniel, as production editor, and he published his first issue early in 1958. In order to safeguard the future of the journal, £5,000 was gathered from well-wishers to buy the publication, and a nonprofit organization, Antiquity Trust, was created to own it in perpetuity.

Like Crawford, Daniel had a good eye for news and the telling of anecdotes, and his Cambridge, television, and book-editing contacts made for a continuing broad vision. The makeup of a typical Daniel issue, the first number of the fortieth volume, for March 1976, is as follows: editorial, six long reports ("Prehistoric Archaeology in Thailand," "The Origins of Writing in the Near East," "The Destruction of the Palace of Knossos," "Ugarit," "The Ezero Mound in Bulgaria," and "The Vix Mound"), eleven short reports including an air-photographic report, and twelve book reviews.

During the long Daniel era, which lasted until 1986, it became harder for *Antiquity* to maintain its established role. The "general readers," people with a broad interest in archaeology among many other things, seemed to be disappearing (if they had ever existed), and the publication could no longer be part journal, part popular magazine. About half of the circulation of *Antiquity* went to libraries, mostly in universities, and the balance to individuals who were often in some way in the business of archaeology. The world of archaeology continued to expand in every way, but *Antiquity* did not. Production costs reduced it to three thinner issues a year instead of four, so it began to have too few pages to cover that larger world with any fullness.

I was appointed editor in 1987 in succession to the Daniels, again in partnership with the editor's spouse, Anne Chippindale. *Antiquity* was switched to the then-new printing technology of desk-top production. In 1988, it was again published quarterly with a total of about 1,000 pages a year. The content has remained the same—a personal editorial, research reports of varied length, and a strong review section—and so has the commitment to lively and novel work, to rapid publication, and to good presentation. Various devices have been created with its review editors, first Timothy Taylor and then Cyprian Broodbank, to cover new publications well in the review section, it being quite impossible to keep up with *all* that is new.

Archaeology is becoming more specialized and more subdivided, as other sciences have before it. Nearly all the general journals of science have disappeared, leaving only *Nature* and *Science*—the two heavyweights—and I think the same will be true in archaeology. *Antiquity* has been able to cover a broad field of archaeology only by becoming larger. As I envisaged it, inside each larger number of *Antiquity* there is a

smaller number, different for each single reader, of those contributions that are of telling interest. [Editorial note: Christopher Chippindale was editor of *Antiquity* until the end of 1997.]

Christopher Chippindale

References
Crawford, O. G. S. 1955. *Said and Done: The Autobiography of an Archaeologist*. London: Phoenix House.

Anyang

Anyang is one of the most significant sites of the Shang dynasty in CHINA (approximately thirteenth century B.C.). Excavated by archaeologist LI CHI between 1928 and 1937, Anyang comprises a royal cemetery of massive shaft graves and a diversity of major public buildings, residences, and workshops. Anyang has been a major source of information about Shang material culture and burial practices, and the scale of the remains has been thought to demonstrate that the site was the capital of late Shang China.

Tim Murray

Arabian Peninsula

The Arabian peninsula is an area in which archaeological research has always been conditioned by a host of political, economic, religious, and social factors over which individual researchers have had little or no influence. The relative isolation of the region until recently has meant that the constraints affecting archaeology have remained obscure to all but those actually engaged in fieldwork there. Indeed, Arabia is, generally speaking, obscure in most people's imaginations—a land of harsh climatic conditions, ultraconservative religious movements, and oil; a land without the obvious heritage of Persia, MESOPOTAMIA, or Egypt; a land in which little of archaeological interest or value is thought to exist. The experience of the last few decades in particular has proved these assumptions wrong, but few people are aware of the reasons why it took so long for this change in awareness to occur.

Histories of Arabian exploration abound. The pre-twentieth-century exploration of the peninsula is well summarized by F. Hommel (1903) and DAVID G. HOGARTH (1904), but for the first half of the twentieth century, A. Grohmann (1963) is the only comprehensive survey yet published. Quite obviously, there is a difference between exploration and archaeology. The heroic accounts of the often dangerous expeditions to Yemen led by Joseph Halévy in 1869, Eduard Glaser in 1884–1894, and Count Landberg in 1898; of the journeys to Madain Salih, al-'Ula, and Tayma in the Hejaz (northwestern Arabia) undertaken by Charles Doughty in 1876–1878, Julius Euting in 1884, Charles Huber in 1884, and the Dominican fathers A. J. Jaussen and R. Savignac from 1907 to 1910; and of the unparalleled survey of central Arabia conducted by G. and J. Ryckmans, Captain P. Lippens, and H. St. J. B. Philby in 1951 do not, properly speaking, belong to the history of Arabian archaeology. These investigations were primarily epigraphic ones, for the early "penetration of Arabia," to use Hogarth's phrase, was largely the work of scholars of Semitic languages seeking to throw new light on the Bible.

Nineteenth-century scholars, many of whom were products of the German comparative philological method, looked to the newly discovered inscriptions of southern and northwestern Arabia for answers to Old Testament riddles. As Hommel wrote in 1903: "The queen of Sheba proved Solomon with hard questions, all of which in his wisdom he answered her. Now we who study the Old Testament, reversing the process, go to the wonderland of that queen with a multitude of inquiries, to many of which it has already given us a satisfactory reply. For the fact that we now have such comparatively clear views on all these points is due chiefly to the results of epigraphical researches in Arabia during the nineteenth century" (751).

When Hommel and Hogarth praised the intrepidness of the likes of Halévy and Glaser, they did so with good reason. More than one would-be explorer of Yemen lost his life in the attempt, and political conditions throughout most of the Arabian peninsula during the nineteenth century, with the possible exceptions of Bahrain and Oman, were indeed anarchic by any standard. Ottoman influence was only slight in

Yemen and al-Hasa, today's eastern province of Saudi Arabia; inner Arabia was lawless and outside the sphere of the great powers; and diplomatic representation was nonexistent in all but a few ports of call in the Arabian Gulf. Thus, in contrast to Mesopotamia, IRAN, TURKEY, Syria, and Egypt, where more-stable political conditions permitted the undertaking of archaeological excavations by British, French, and eventually American and German missions in the late nineteenth and early twentieth centuries, the Arabian peninsula was virtually untouched until after World War II. With this general background in mind, let us turn now to a closer examination of the individual subregions of the Arabian peninsula, since the history of archaeological research in each has followed a unique trajectory.

Yemen

Despite the fact that the first southern Arabian inscriptions were copied as early as 1810 by the German schoolteacher Ulrich Jasper Seetzen, Yemen's archaeological heritage has only been slowly revealed since that time. Tribal conflict in Yemen has long been endemic, which had precluded field research on anything but a very restricted scale.

Excavations at al-Huqqa in 1928 by C. Rathjens and H. von Wissmann were the first ever conducted in Yemen, and helped by the British political presence in Aden, GERTRUDE CATON-THOMPSON and R. A. B. Hamilton worked in the Hadhramaut in 1937–1938. World War II interrupted the fieldwork, and there was little activity until 1951–1952, when the American explorer and later oil baron, Wendell Phillips, launched his American Foundation for the Study of Man (AFSM) expeditions to Timna (capital of the kingdom of Qataban), Hajar Bin Humaid (a major stratified prehistoric site), Marib (capital of the kingdom of Sheba), and Khor Rori (a southern Arabian colony founded on the coast of Dhofar in what is now Oman. The work at Marib ended abruptly when relations broke down between the team's epigrapher, Father A. Jamme, and the local governor and the Americans were forced to flee Yemen after a series of incidents involving harassment, intimidation at gunpoint, and temporary confinement by the military.

Although sporadic discoveries were reported in the decades following 1952, it was not until 1974 that a French mission, working at Shabwa, capital of the kingdom of Hadhramaut, resumed regular excavations, which have continued, off and on, to this day. By the late 1970s, a research station of the German Archaeological Institute (DEUTSCHES ARCHÄOLOGISCHES INSTITUT) had been established in Sanaa, the capital of Yemen, and in the early 1980s, an important Italian expedition began working on Bronze Age remains in the country. At about the same time the AFSM resumed work in the Wadi al-Jubah under the direction of J. Sauer. Several years later, a Soviet team, working in what was then the communist People's Democratic Republic of Yemen, established a mission with excavations both at Qana on the coast and Raybun in the Hadhramaut.

At the time of writing, tribal conflicts had once again curtailed work by Italian, French, and German scholars in the northern part of Yemen where the political authority of the central government is weak. The 1990 political unification of the two Yemens also brought tensions to the surface between authorities who had formerly been responsible for antiquities in each state, which exacerbated an already difficult situation.

Bahrain, Kuwait, Qatar, and the United Arab Emirates

A primitive attempt to excavate several burial mounds on Bahrain in 1879 by Captain E. L. Durand was the first archaeological excavation of any kind on the Arabian peninsula. Durand was followed by a series of amateurs, including Mr. and Mrs. T. Bent (1889), A. Jouannin (1903), Captain F. B. Prideaux (1906), Major C. K. Daly (1921–1926), and E. J. H. Mackay (1925). In the early 1950s, T. G. Bibby, an employee in Bahrain of the Iraq Petroleum Company, developed an interest in the mystery of the more than 100,000 burial mounds that dot the northern portion of the main island. Bibby contacted his old friend, the Danish prehistorian P. V. Glob. Bibby, who had worked with Glob in Norway and had himself married a

Dane, proposed that a Danish team come to work on Bahrain. At the same time, R. H. Dyson of the University of Pennsylvania made a similar proposal to the emir of Bahrain, who consulted his British adviser, Sir Charles Belgrave, as to how best to proceed. Belgrave chose to toss a coin, and the Danes won.

That was the beginning of what grew into the largest foreign expedition ever mounted by Denmark. Glob put separate teams to work in the 1950s and 1960s not only at the great mound of Qalat al-Bahrain but on Bronze Age and Hellenistic settlements on Failaka (Kuwait), prehistoric sites in Qatar, and third-millennium graves and habitation sites (Umm an-Nar, Hili, Qattarah) in what were then the Trucial States (now the United Arab Emirates). An entire generation of Danish archaeologists participated in the Gulf expeditions, including H. H. Andersen, K. Frifelt, K. Jeppesen, H. Kapel, P. Kjærum, and P. Mortensen. Frifelt subsequently went on to conduct her own fieldwork at Bat in Oman while several of the others are or have been involved in the publication of the massive amount of material generated by the dozens of excavations and surveys conducted by the expedition. Publication of these results has been a major problem, however, partly because most of the people involved went on to assume posts dealing with Danish prehistory that gave them neither the time nor the institutional context in which to adequately digest and analyze the results of the fieldwork.

Since the end of the Danish expedition in 1965, much excavation has been conducted by French scholars such as M. Kervran and P. Lombard, and during the 1990s, a British expedition at Saar has been uncovering a large settlement of the early second millennium. Bahrain is also exceptional for the high level of involvement on the part of local nationals. The Department of Antiquities has conducted salvage excavations at literally thousands of graves threatened by development during the fifteen years before 2000.

Unable to continue her work in Iran after the 1966 excavations at Bampur, the British archaeologist B. de Cardi began survey work in Ras al-Khaimah, the northernmost of what was then the Trucial States, in 1968. This was followed in

1973 by the visit of a team of Iraqi archaeologists on a goodwill mission to the newly created United Arab Emirates (UAE). The Iraqis conducted soundings at a host of important sites, including Tell Abraq, ed-Dur, Mleiha, Julfar, and al-Qusais. Excavation activity remained sporadic, however, until the mid-1980s when teams from Belgium, Great Britain, Denmark, France, Germany, Japan, and Switzerland began to focus their efforts on a wide range of prehistoric and early historic sites. More recently, Australian and Spanish teams have also begun work in the UAE.

The reasons behind this flurry of activity, which continues to this day, are varied. Many of the scholars involved had formerly worked in Iran or Iraq, areas no longer accessible for political reasons. The comparative ease of working in the UAE, the high level of support given to foreign teams by local governments, the relatively unbureaucratic nature of the enterprise when compared to conditions in many other countries in western Asia, and the inherent interest of the archaeological problems being investigated have all contributed to a burgeoning of archaeological research in southeastern Arabia.

Archaeology in Kuwait, initially dominated by the Danish expedition, was later pursued by the American T. H. Carter and, from 1983 to 1988, by a French mission led by J.-F. Salles. Interrupted by the Gulf War, French excavations have now resumed on several of the smaller offshore islands.

Archaeology in Oman, on the other hand, has had quite a different history. Following the expulsion of Wendell Phillips's team from Yemen, the AFSM turned its sights on Oman where R. Cleveland initiated excavations at Sohar in 1958. Prior to that time, the region had been only sporadically explored during the mid-nineteenth and early twentieth centuries. It was not until Sultan Qaboos deposed his father Sultan Taimur in 1970 that the country moved from a state of medieval isolation to one of comparative wealth as its oil resources were exploited.

The creation of a Ministry of Heritage and Culture was an early, enlightened move on the part of the new ruler, as was the appointment of the late Andrew Williamson from Oxford, an expert in the archaeology and economic history of medieval Iran, as the ministry's archaeological adviser. Williamson invited archaeologists from Harvard University to undertake the first systematic surveys and test excavations in Oman, and other scholars, including B. de Cardi and M. Tosi, soon initiated new projects.

In spite of the death of Williamson in 1975, when the Land Rover he was in (with a military escort) hit a landmine in Dhofar (where the communist-backed guerrillas supporting the separation of Dhofar Province from the Sultanate of Oman had only recently been suppressed), archaeological exploration by foreign teams flourished in the 1970s and early 1980s, not least because of the care and support provided by the Italian archaeologist P. Costa, who succeeded Williamson as archaeological adviser. A major focus of work by a team led by G. Weisgerber from the German mining museum in Bochum has been the investigation of copper metallurgy in the Oman mountains and the identification of Oman with the copper supply area known in Mesopotamian cuneiform sources as *Magan*. Italian surveys and excavations by M. Tosi and P. Biagi have focused on maritime adaptation in coastal Oman.

Saudi Arabia

Territorially speaking, the Kingdom of Saudi Arabia occupies the largest portion of the Arabian peninsula, but paradoxically, archaeological exploration there has lagged far behind what has been achieved in most of the other countries on the peninsula. The earliest explorations in the Hejaz brought to light important epigraphic finds, many of which are to be found today in the LOUVRE in Paris (since most of the early explorers were French) and Istanbul (because the Hejaz was, nominally at least, part of the Ottoman Empire). However, the fanaticism and xenophobia of the population, most of whom belonged to the Wahhabi sect of Islamic fundamentalists, meant that exploration was very limited throughout the early twentieth century, and individuals who were able to travel freely throughout Saudi Arabia, such as H. St. J. B. Philby, a close friend of the founder of the kingdom, Abdul Aziz Ibn Saud, were rare. A major influx of American oilmen and their families began in the 1930s, however, and over the years many employees of Arabian American Oil Company (ARAMCO) made important surface finds that were communicated to scholars in Europe and America.

It was not until 1968 though that the first archaeological excavations were sanctioned in the kingdom. In that one year, T. G. Bibby was granted permission to work at Thaj, a large Hellenistic city in northeastern Arabia; P. J. Parr led a survey team to the Hejaz; and G. van Beek undertook a survey and soundings at Najran near the Saudi-Yemeni border. A Society of History and Archaeology was established in the history department at the University of Riyadh (now King Saud University) in 1969 (the present Department of Archaeology and Museology dates only to 1978), and in 1972, A. R. Al-Ansary, a specialist in pre-Islamic Arabian epigraphy and a student of the Leeds Semitist B. S. J. Isserlin, initiated excavations at the late pre-Islamic site of Qaryat al-Fau in the interior of Saudi Arabia where generations of Saudi nationals have gained field experience in Arabian archaeology.

A. H. Masry, a Saudi national who earned his Ph.D. under ROBERT MCCORMICK ADAMS and ROBERT J. BRAIDWOOD at the University of Chicago, returned to Riyadh in 1973 as director of antiquities, and three years later, he launched an ambitious program of survey and test excavation around the country. Known as the Comprehensive Survey of the Kingdom of Saudi Arabia, the project aimed at surveying the country, making surface collections, identifying sites of particular importance for future investigation and protection, and laying the groundwork for a network of provincial museums. The comprehensive survey continued until the mid-1980s and was followed by select excavations at sites such as Thaj and Tayma. Many Saudi nationals who had gained their initial training in Riyadh with Al-Ansary and later field experience in the Department of Antiquities and Museums were sent abroad during this period to do postgraduate study in the United States and Great Britain. The drop in oil revenues during the late 1980s, the ensuing budget deficit in Saudi Arabia, and the departure of Masry to a nonarchaeological post in London led to stagnation in archaeological research in Saudi Arabia.

Retrospect and Prospect

The fact that, for political reasons, little fieldwork was possible in the Arabian peninsula during the nineteenth and early twentieth centuries has meant that, relative to the surrounding regions, much less was known of this area until recently. Since the 1950s, however, there has been a steady stream of foreign teams working in all of the countries of the peninsula. Obviously, the rate of progress depends very much on foreign and local funding sources and political stability. Tribal wars in Yemen and the 1990 Gulf War are examples of political events that have halted or severely curtailed archaeological research on the Arabian peninsula.

The institutional framework of the archaeology being carried out by foreign teams varies greatly. Many expeditions owe their existence to the interests of one scholar who builds up a team of colleagues and brings funding from his or her nation's public and private funding agencies. The French work in the Gulf states has been more of a coordinated effort on the part of the National Center of Scientific Research (CNRS), and Yemen is the only country on the peninsula with permanent, foreign research "schools" (French, German, and American). It is apparent that in the case of such schools, archaeological research is viewed as part and parcel of an overarching policy of cultural exchange between the country sponsoring the foreign teams and the host nation. In such a situation, archaeology, benefiting from government funding, is used as an arm of foreign (cultural) policy. The presence of a team from a given foreign country in a particular Arab state is viewed as beneficial by the foreign power, as its presence helps to spread goodwill, heighten awareness of that country, contribute to local heritage interests, and ultimately, sell the products of that country in a foreign market.

With the exception of the extraordinary efforts made by the Bahraini Department of Antiquities to excavate graves threatened by the construction of new urban areas, it cannot be said that the large number of foreign missions working on the Arabian peninsula has been matched by a corresponding number of local ones. National museums exist in all countries of the peninsula, but degrees of awareness of archaeology, heritage, and history vary greatly from country to country. Journals for the dissemination of archaeological research exist in Oman (*Journal of Oman Studies*) and Saudi Arabia (*Atlal*), and in varying degrees, antiquities laws have been passed and departments of antiquities have been set up and empowered to protect local sites and monuments. Finding bright and competent nationals to pursue careers in archaeology has been difficult, however, for in many of the countries of the peninsula the monetary rewards to be won in business by a bright student so far surpass what one can expect to earn and achieve as a civil servant that few of the best and brightest have been attracted to a career in archaeology.

The neocolonial aspect of foreign teams exploiting the past of a host country is only part of the truth, however, for in many cases the attitude taken toward archaeologists is the same as that taken toward petroleum engineers or any other foreign technical specialist. If non-Arabs from the West have the particular expertise needed to investigate the past that is lacking locally, then there is no harm in letting such work be done by them. Moreover, in all of the countries of the peninsula there is a certain population of nonlocal Arab archaeologists working on a contract basis for the universities and antiquities departments, which often includes scholars with advanced degrees from universities in the West. Just as American or British engineers seek lucrative employment in the tax-free Gulf states, so, too, do archaeologists from the Sudan, Egypt, India, Pakistan, Iraq, Jordan, Lebanon, and Syria for whom the language and culture of the Arabian states is no barrier to the pursuit of their profession. In some rare cases, such as Oman, however, programs to nationalize the workforce have tended to push foreign "experts" out of certain jobs, including archaeological advisory ones, which has affected Arab and Asian archaeologists as well as Western ones.

D. T. Potts

References

Al-Ansary, A. R. 1982. *Qaryat al-Fau: A Portrait of Pre-Islamic Civilisation in Saudi Arabia.* London: Croom Helm.

Bibby, T. G. 1969. *Looking for Dilmun.* New York: Knopf.

Grohmann, A. 1963. *Arabien.* Munich: Beck.

Hogarth, D. G. 1904. *The Penetration of Arabia.* London: Lawrence and Bullen.

Hommel, F. 1903. "Explorations in Arabia." In *Explorations in Bible Lands during the 19th Century.* Ed. H. V. Hilprecht. Philadelphia: A. J. Holman.

Phillips, W. 1955. *Qataban and Sheba.* New York: Harcourt, Brace and Company.

Potts, D. T. 1990. *The Arabian Gulf in Antiquity.* Oxford: Clarendon Press.

Arambourg, Camille (1888–1969)

Born in Paris, Camille Arambourg graduated as an agricultural engineer and became interested in paleontology when he discovered fossil fish while working at improving the water supply of his parents' vineyard in Algeria. He fought in the Dardanelles and in Macedonia during World War I, and afterward his interest in fossils led him to undertake further studies in geology.

In 1920, Arambourg became professor of geology at l'Institut Agricole d'Alger where he worked for the next ten years. During that time he also studied in Paris under MARCELLIN BOULE at the Muséum National d'Histoire Naturelle. In 1932–1933, he led an expedition to the Omo Valley in Ethiopia where he collected Pleistocene vertebrate fossils and made a detailed study of the geology of the region. In 1938, he succeeded Boule at the museum and moved to Paris.

After World War II, Arambourg returned to work in North Africa. In 1947–1948, he excavated at Saint Arnaud (now Ain Hanech) in northern Algeria, and along with other fossils located in this early Pleistocene site, Arambourg found worked, spheroid stone tools, the first to be found in North Africa. In 1954–1955, he excavated at Ternifine near Mascara in northwestern Algeria, and there he found fragments of three hominid mandibles, a parietal bone in association with Acheulean bifaces, Clactonian-like stone tools, and a rich variety of extinct mammalian bones. Based on this evidence, Arambourg argued that the Acheulean stone toolmakers had been "pithecanthropoid" hominids, a theory that was reinforced by a similar discovery at a Moroccan site in 1955. Arambourg also argued that these North African remains were similar to the bones found at the site of Choukoutien (now Zhoukoudian) in China, and, indeed, these mandibles, and those from Zhoukoudianzhen are now recognized as belonging to *Homo erectus.*

Arambourg also excavated the cave of Tamar Hat in Algeria. The only Ibero-maurusian sequence excavated to bedrock, it has been dated at ca. 20,600 B.P. The cave was used as a camp for hunting Barbary sheep, and its three meters of deposit indicated that it had been used and reused by people for nearly 5,000 years.

Arambourg was seventy when he retired from the museum, but he remained actively involved in research until his death. Between 1967 and 1969, he led the French team of the International Palaeontological Research Expedition to the Omo Valley in Ethiopia, and during the first field season, Arambourg and his colleague Yves Coppens found an Austalopithecine mandible. The Omo research expedition was a complex paleoanthropological project, and its results became a keystone in understanding the chronology of African prehistory.

Arambourg's monograph on North African vertebrate paleontology was published posthumously in two parts in 1970 and 1979. He was president of the Societé Geologique de France and the Societé Prehistorique Francaise, he received the Gaudry Prize in 1959, and he was elected to the Academie des Sciences in 1961.

Tim Murray

See also France; Maghreb

Archaeological Heritage Management

The concepts of antiquities, monuments, and heritage are relatively recent innovations. An awareness of the special qualities of structures and artifacts produced by earlier peoples and generations developed slowly and sporadically over a long period in various parts of the world. The deliberate collection of artifacts from earlier periods was observed in CHINA during the Han dynasty in the first century B.C. (Schnapp 1993), and there were conscious efforts by Roman emperors, notably Hadrian (A.D. 117–138), to protect and conserve notable struc-

tures from past epochs, such as dynastic Egypt and classical GREECE. It is arguable, however, whether such activities can be interpreted as conscious attempts at heritage management. In both cases, collectors may well have been motivated by a mixture of religious, philosophical, political, and aesthetic objectives.

The systematic study of relics from the past and deliberate actions designed to ensure their conservation may be deemed (in Europe at least) to have begun with the Renaissance and the reintroduction of the values of classical antiquity. Rome was where the values encapsulated in the remains of its imperial past were first identified and where conscious efforts were made to conserve them starting in the latter part of the fifteenth century. The artist Raphael (Raffaello Sanzio, 1483–1520) was instructed by Pope Leo X in 1515 to carry out a survey of the monuments of the city of Rome (Jokilehto 1999, 32 ff.) and was given the resounding title of "prefect of marbles and stones." In a report produced four years later, Raphael set out in meticulous detail the requirements of such a survey, which was carried out by other papal functionaries. From this time onward, the buildings of imperial Rome and the marble statuary and facings that decorated them no longer served solely as a quarry for bedecking palaces and churches (or, worse, as a source of materials for lime kilns).

Meanwhile, in northern Europe, a second movement was developing that was to lay the foundations of modern heritage management. The systematic study and recording of antiquities, both portable and monumental, diffused northward through the work of French antiquaries such as Nicolas-Claude Fabri de Peiresc (1580–1637). As such work moved into lands that had been little, if at all, influenced by Roman culture, the quest for information shifted to the landscape—in particular, the many field monuments such as earthworks and stone settings—that were still to be found in profusion at that time. Attention was also directed toward early buildings such as castles, monasteries, and churches whose origins owed nothing to classical models. In England, John Leland (1506?–1552) was appointed to the post of king's antiquary by Henry VIII in 1533, and his peregrinations around the country produced a paradigm for future investigations. Of those who followed Leland, the most influential was WILLIAM CAMDEN (1551–1623), and his monumental work *Britannia,* published in 1586, was the first general guide to the antiquities of a single country. Its subjects ranged from prehistoric stone circles (notably Stonehenge) to Roman ruins (such as the forts of "the Saxon shore") to Saxon work preserved in later churches.

In Great Britain, Camden's work was continued by diligent field antiquarians such as Robert Plot (1640–1696) and EDWARD LHWYD (1660–1708) in Wales and JOHN AUBREY (1626–1697) and WILLIAM STUKELEY (1687–1765) in England. Elsewhere in northern Europe similar studies were being carried out by peripatetic scholars. In Denmark, OLE WORM, or Olaus Wormius (1588–1654), published several works on the antiquities of that country in which he sought to establish direct links between monuments and history. He was influential in the composition of a royal decree that was sent in 1626 to all Danish clergy requesting them to report on all the historical remains in their parishes. JOHAN BURE, or Johannes Bureus (1568–1652), spent much of his long life touring his native land of Sweden studying antiquities, in particular, runic inscriptions. Bure became the first holder of the post of royal antiquary. It was in Sweden that the first university chair of antiquities was created, at the University of Uppsala in 1662.

Elsewhere in Europe, similar studies were being undertaken by scholars who adopted the title of "antiquary." In France, the major figure was the Benedictine priest BERNARD DE MONTFAUCON (1655–1741), whose initial paleographic and philological studies led him to the study of antiquities and culminated in his seminal book, *L'antiquité expliquée et représentée en figures* (1719). His work inspired other French antiquaries to begin the systematic survey of the historic landscape. In the last volume of his *Recueil d'antiquités égyptiennes, étrusques, grecques, et gauloises* (1767), another major figure, Anne Claude Philippe de Turbières de Grimoard de Pestels de Lévis, COMTE DE CAYLUS, published detailed surveys of many prehistoric and Gallo-Roman field monuments in France.

In the eighteenth century, there were attempts by European scholars to analyze and classify the whole of nature and human life. The work of the encyclopedists and of Carolus Linnaeus (Carl von Linné, 1707–1778) had a profound influence on antiquarian studies, and the most significant impact was probably that exercised on CHRISTIAN JÜRGENSEN THOMSEN (1788–1865). When he was appointed the first curator of the Danish National Museum 1816, he was called upon to prepare some rational form of presentation for the many thousands of ancient artifacts in that heterogeneous "cabinet of curiosities," and to do so, he derived the THREE-AGE SYSTEM (Stone, Bronze, and Iron Ages), which laid the foundations for modern prehistoric studies.

The Development of Legislation

In 1666, four years after Olof Verelius became the first professor of antiquities at Sweden's Uppsala University, he was appointed royal antiquary. The first result of this appointment was the promulgation of a royal proclamation that declared all field monuments in the Swedish kingdom (which at that time included Finland) were the property of the crown, which undertook to protect and preserve them. The decree also imposed strict controls over all forms of intervention on such monuments. Three years later, a second royal proclamation extended this protection and control to all "portable" antiquities, which similarly became crown property. There are two interesting features in this pioneer legislation. First, while the ownership of monuments and artefacts was vested in the crown, their protection and preservation was in the name of the Swedish people, as part of their heritage. Second, antiquities were deemed to be protected even before they were discovered; thus, protection was accorded to them from the moment of their discovery.

It was another seventy years before another European state introduced similar heritage protection legislation. The discovery of the buried cities of HERCULANEUM and POMPEII led Charles IV, the Bourbon king of Naples, to assert in 1738 royal ownership of all buried materials and sites in his kingdom. This relatively simple statute was to form the basis of protection legislation for the whole of the Italian peninsula after unification in 1870, along with a papal law of 1802 that regulated "the preservation of monuments and of works of art" (d'Agostino 1984).

The antiquarian and archaeological developments of the eighteenth century continued at an increasing rate during the nineteenth century. Systematic field surveys in various parts of the world, such as Britain, DENMARK, Germany, and India, combined with an awareness of the adverse impact of the improvements resulting from late-eighteenth-century agrarian improvements and reforms, led to the progressive enactment of protection legislation. A Danish declaration of 1807 (Klindt-Jensen, 1975; Kristiansen, 1984) established statutory protection of major monuments in Denmark on the Swedish model. A number of German states also enacted heritage protection legislation in the first half of the nineteenth century—Mecklenburg in 1804, Bavaria in 1812, Prussia (which was to serve as the basis for German legislation after 1870) in 1815, Hesse-Darmstadt in 1818, Württemberg in 1828, and Baden in 1837. The Austro-Hungarian Empire enacted its first heritage protection law in 1850.

Within four years of gaining independence from Ottoman Turkey, GREECE enacted its first monuments protection legislation (1834), and it was based on the fundamental premise that "all objects of antiquity in Greece, being the productions of the ancestors of the Hellenic people, are regarded as the common national possession of all Hellenes." The first British Ancient Monuments Protection Act was not promulgated until 1882, although there was protective legislation in force in India as early as 1863. There was no adequate protection in France until 1913, whereas legislation was enacted in JAPAN in 1897 and in the United States in 1904.

In the countries that emerged after the struggles for independence in Latin America during the first half of the nineteenth century, the pre-Hispanic cultures were potent symbols of cultural identity, and their protection became a priority for the emerging legislatures. MEXICO achieved independence in 1821, and in 1825 the first law controlling the country's archaeological heritage was passed. PERU freed itself from Spanish rule in 1822, and in the same year a supreme decree was published that forbade any trade in ancient relics.

By the outbreak of World War I in 1914, there was some form of antiquities protection legislation in almost every European country (with the notable exception of BELGIUM) and in most of the major countries around the world. In addition, the colonial powers had introduced legislation in many of their overseas territories or extended the application of their metropolitan statutes to their colonies. In the new nations that emerged after 1918, similar legislation was introduced soon after their constitutions had been approved, generally on the basis of the statutes of the major countries from which they had been formed.

During the interwar period, heritage legislative protection in a number of countries was progressively amended and expanded. For example, new antiquities laws were introduced in Denmark, Greece, and the United Kingdom in the 1930s, and two major laws covering the protection of the cultural and natural heritage, both of them still in force, were promulgated in Italy just before the outbreak of World War II. In Japan, the 1897 law, which had covered only ancient temples and shrines, was extended to all "national treasures" in 1929. The legislative protection of the cultural heritage in Peru stems from a basic law passed in 1929, while that of Bolivia was established by law in 1927.

With the creation of the Soviet Union and the introduction of a socialist constitution, state ownership of all cultural property was asserted in a fundamental law enacted in October 1918. This provided the model for the antiquities legislation of all the countries of the socialist bloc of central and eastern Europe that was formed after the end of World War II, as well as the legislation of other socialist countries such as the People's Republic of China and Cuba.

As the colonial territories of Africa and Asia successively achieved independence from their European overlords, they introduced protective legislation, often modeled on that of the colonial powers. Thus, there is a consistency to be observed in the legislation of former British colonies, based on what became known as "the Westminster model constitution," and British legislation in India served as the basis for the formulation of improved protection of the cultural heritage of that newly independent country.

Over the second half of the twentieth century, there was progressive extension and improvement of heritage legislation. Every year was marked by new or amended laws being passed by national legislatures in at least one country in the world. In addition, work began within the framework of the League of Nations in the interwar years that led to the drafting and adoption in the 1970s of international conventions, under the aegis of the United Nations Educational, Scientific, and Cultural Organization (UNESCO), designed to protect and preserve the cultural heritage. Similar conventions have also been prepared at the regional level, notably by the Council of Europe.

Managers

Legislation is effective only if provision is made for its implementation and for the enforcement of penalties when it is transgressed. The earliest recorded appointments of what today would be known as "heritage managers" were made by Renaissance popes, as in the case of Raphael. There was a continuous policy of restoration and conservation of ancient monuments in Rome, supervised by different commissions and executed by distinguished artists and architects such as Antonio Canova (1757–1822). Similar provisions applied in other cities and states of pre-unification Italy, such as Naples.

A number of European countries followed the same pattern in the late-eighteenth and early-nineteenth centuries. In most cases, this began with the appointment of a voluntary commission of experts drawn from the academies and universities and employing architects and conservators on specific contracts. However, these bodies found themselves requiring the services of full-time professional officials as interest in and concern for antiquities grew. The role of architects in the development of heritage management was an important one. In Germany, Karl-Friedrich Schinkel (1781–1841) played a crucial role in the preservation of

monuments in the territories of the kingdom of Prussia. He proposed the establishment of a formal organization for this work, but it was not until two years after his death that the first conservator of artistic monuments was appointed. France had anticipated such an appointment, the post of inspector-general of historical monuments in France being created by Louis-Philippe shortly after his accession in 1830. The first such inspector was Ludovic Vitet (1802–1873), and he was succeeded in 1834 by Prosper Mérimée (1803–1870), better known as the author of *Carmen* but notable for his intervention to save the Roman and medieval defenses of Carcassonne in southern France.

German conservators such as Schinkel and, in particular, the Bavarian Leo von Klenze (1784–1864) provided professional advice to the new Greek state after 1830. The first general conservator was Kiriakos Pittakis (1798–1863), and he was assisted by Danish and German architects. In Russia, an Imperial Archaeological Commission was set up in 1859, and soon afterward the country's first full-time inspector was appointed.

The Scandinavian tradition began with the appointment of Verelius as royal antiquary in 1666. The monuments service grew steadily, and from the nineteenth century onward, it made extensive use of the talents of the leisured, educated middle class (clergymen, teachers, retired army officers) for the surveying and recording activities that spread over the entire country. Denmark did not follow suit until the first decade of the nineteenth century, but work there developed very rapidly, not only in the evolution of museology but also in systematic field survey. JENS JACOB WORSAAE (1821–1885), who had worked with Thomsen (whom he succeeded in 1865) at the National Museum, was appointed inspector-general of antiquities in Denmark by the king in 1847, and he traveled over the entire country in the years that followed recording monuments of all kinds. He built up a professional staff from 1865 onward, and in 1873 began the systematic survey of all the field monuments in Denmark, with voluntary assistance. This work was to continue for some fifty years, and the field reports, now housed in the National Museum in Copenhagen, constitute an incomparable record of the state of the cultural heritage in this small country before the advent of modern agricultural techniques and population growth.

When the Ancient Monuments Protection Act came into force in the United Kingdom in 1883, the first inspector of ancient monuments was the redoubtable Major-General AUGUSTUS HENRY PITT RIVERS (1827–1900), considered by many to be the founder of modern scientific archaeological excavation techniques. Like Worsaae, Pitt Rivers traveled the length and breadth of Britain recording and designating protected monuments. He had no funds beyond a token government salary, but he made use of his own great wealth to employ a small team of surveyors and excavators.

After the death of Pitt Rivers, the post of inspector of ancient monuments was vacant for a decade. However, in 1908 three new bodies were set up in England, Scotland, and Wales, and they were charged with the survey of monuments in their respective countries and with the preparation of detailed inventories. It was intended that the work of these bodies, the royal commissions for ancient and historical monuments, would be complete in twenty-five years. However, at the end of the twentieth century, the commissions in Scotland and Wales were continuing their work, and when the English royal commission was merged with English Heritage, the state agency responsible for monument protection in England, in 1999, its survey and inventory work was still little more than half complete.

The same year that Pitt Rivers died, the government of India set up the Archaeological Survey of India, and JOHN MARSHALL (1876–1958) was appointed as its director-general. The survey became fully professionalized in 1906 and undertook responsibility for all aspects of heritage management, including conservation, excavation, epigraphy, museums, and publishing. The regional structure created by Marshall largely survives intact.

In ITALY, the General Directorate of Excavations and Museums was established in 1872. This organization evolved in 1891 into the General Directorate of Antiquities and Fine Arts, with regional superintendents for archaeology, architecture, museums, and fine arts, a system that has lasted to the present day. The superintendents are responsible for the protection of all monuments within their specialities situated in their areas.

A number of separate entities responsible for museums and monuments were set up in MEXICO, and these came together in 1939 to form the National Institute for Anthropology and History (Instituto Nacional de Antropología e Historia, INAH), which is responsible for ensuring the application of the strong national heritage legislation. Other heritage organizations, based on the model of Mexico's INAH, have been set up in most Latin American countries.

Throughout the first half of the twentieth century, monuments or antiquities services responsible for archaeological and historical heritage management grew slowly. Although the term *heritage management* is relatively recent, it is generally recognized that it covers survey and inventory, excavation, application of protection legislation, interaction with land-use planners, management of protected sites and monuments, and general promotion and presentation as well as museums in a number of countries. Most of these activities were carried out by existing agencies at the beginning of World War II, albeit in a somewhat leisurely, static way. The term *cultural resource management,* with the dynamic element contained in its final word, was first used in the United States in the 1970s alongside an alternative, *public archaeology.* However, these terms are gradually giving way to the use of "archaeological heritage management," which translates more easily from English into other languages.

After World War II, the rate of expansion of activities of this kind increased almost exponentially. Postwar reconstruction and the impact of social and economic development, not least in developing countries, that followed reconstruction placed severe demands on the limited professional services that were available to preserve or record rapidly vanishing heritages. J. Reichstein (1984, 38) has listed five acute and nine chronic threats to archaeological heritage, including urban renewal, pipeline projects, open-cast mineral working, deep plowing, illegal excavations, drainage of wetlands, military training, and uncontrolled tree growth. This was the period, beginning in the late 1950s, of "rescue archaeology," with its dramatic overtones.

The conventional professional services were overwhelmed by the tasks that confronted them, and different strategies emerged. In some cases, the professional bodies were considerably enlarged, as in Japan and Sweden, so as to be able to undertake the work demanded of them from their own resources. In others, more modest enlargement was accompanied by the extensive use of archaeological contractors (universities, museums, private professional groups), as in the United Kingdom and Germany and, more recently, in Italy and Sweden. It is noteworthy that systems of this kind are becoming increasingly common, not only for rescue excavations but also for inventory and physical conservation. In the United States, where there has never been a centralized monuments service, this work has been undertaken almost entirely by private agencies following the passage of the 1974 Archaeological and Historic Preservation Act, which required funds to be allocated for archaeological mitigation in all projects on federally owned land or projects financed by the federal government.

Solutions to the problems of archaeological heritage management vary according to the constitutional structures of different countries. In federal states, such as Australia, CANADA, and Germany, responsibility for heritage management is largely devolved down to the state or province level. In a sense, the same is also the case in the United Kingdom, where there are separate services for England, Scotland, Wales, and Northern Ireland. In certain countries with centralized governments, such as the People's Republic of China, Italy, and SPAIN, there is a central supervisory body responsible for overall policymaking and the disbursement of central government funds, but executive control rests with provincial administrations or, in the case of Italy, regional superintendents. Finally, there are those countries, which make up the majority, in which heritage management is the responsibil-

ity of a centralized agency. However, a movement toward decentralization is becoming increasingly apparent, and in the United Kingdom, the management of protected monuments is now being transferred to local authorities; currently, there are proposals to introduce a similar system in Mexico.

Henry Cleere

See also Individual countries
References
Cleere, H., ed. 1984. *Approaches to the Archaeological Heritage.* Cambridge: Cambridge University Press.
———. 1996. *Archaeological Heritage Management in the Modern World.* London: Routledge.
d'Agostino, B. 1984. "Italy." In *Approaches to the Archaeological Heritage,* 73–81. Ed. H. Cleere. Cambridge: Cambridge University Press.
Daniel, G. 1981. *A Short History of Archaeology.* London: Thames and Hudson.
Jokilehto, J. 1999. *A History of Architectural Conservation.* Oxford: Butterworth-Heinemann.
Klindt-Jensen, O. 1975. *A History of Scandinavian Archaeology.* London: Thames and Hudson.
Kristiansen, K. 1984. "Denmark." In *Approaches to the Archaeological Heritage,* 21–36. Ed. H. Cleere. Cambridge: Cambridge University Press.
Reichstein, J. 1984. "Federal Republic of Germany." In *Approaches to the Archaeological Heritage,* 37–47. Ed. H. Cleere. Cambridge: Cambridge University Press.
Schnapp, A. 1993. *La conquête du passé.* Paris: Carré. English translation, *The Conquest of the Past.* London: BM Publications, 1996.

Archaeological Institute of America

The Archaeological Institute of America (AIA) is the oldest and largest archaeological organization in North America. Founded in 1879 in Boston, Massachusetts, by Charles Eliot Norton and eleven other Bostonians, the AIA quickly formed additional chapters in New York, Baltimore, and Philadelphia and, by the end of the century, in the Midwest as well. A chapter opened in Los Angeles, California, in 1903. Today, the AIA has more than 100 local societies throughout the United States and Canada and more than 11,000 members on several continents. In 1994, the Archaeological Institute of

America/Institut Archéologique d'Amérique was incorporated in Canada as an independent affiliate of the AIA in the United States.

The original goal of the nineteenth-century organization was to support archaeological excavation and publication both at home and abroad, but Old World archaeology, especially classical archaeology, has always played a dominant role in the AIA. Although the institute founded a School of American Archaeology in 1907 (today the School of American Research in Santa Fe, New Mexico), the first archaeological schools the AIA created—and still its principal affiliated organizations—were the AMERICAN SCHOOL OF CLASSICAL STUDIES AT ATHENS, founded in 1882, and the American School of Classical Studies in Rome, established in 1895, now a division of the American Academy in Rome. The AIA is also the "parent" of the AMERICAN SCHOOLS OF ORIENTAL RESEARCH, founded in 1900, which oversees three archaeological schools in Jerusalem; Amman, JORDAN; and Nicosia, CYPRUS.

The AIA's first excavations took place between 1881 and 1883 at Assos in northwestern TURKEY, with the cosponsorship of the recently established Boston Museum of Fine Arts. (In one of the last agreements of its kind, the Turkish government granted the Boston museum permission to export one-third of the excavated finds to help build its collections of classical art.) After the AIA opened research schools abroad, almost all subsequent U.S. excavations in the Mediterranean and Mideast have been conducted under the auspices of AIA's affiliates or individual universities rather than the institute itself.

Consistent with its founders' belief in the importance of publication as well as exploration, the AIA inaugurated the AMERICAN JOURNAL OF ARCHAEOLOGY (AJA) in 1885. A magazine aimed at a much larger popular audience, Art and Archaeology, appeared in 1914 but ceased publication two decades later. In 1948, the AIA launched a successor magazine, Archaeology, which currently appears bimonthly and has a circulation exceeding 200,000. Unlike AJA, which is a journal of Old World archaeology, Archaeology is global in scope. Between 1948 and

1973, the AIA also published a series of monographs in cooperation with the College Art Association, and in the 1990s, the institute initiated a new publication series consisting of both monographs and colloquium proceedings. The AIA also oversees the publication of the American volumes of the Corpus Vasorum Antiquorum.

Other than its status as a privately funded nonprofit organization, one of the distinctive features of the AIA that separates it from many other national archaeological societies is that it counts thousands of laypeople among its members. Central to its public outreach effort is its national lecture program, begun formally in 1896 although the institute had sponsored a lecture series by Rodolfo Lanciani a decade earlier. Currently, the AIA sends three lecturers annually to each of its local societies. The institute also holds an annual meeting at different cities throughout the United States and Canada at which scholars present the results of their fieldwork or research projects.

Fred S. Kleiner

References

Dow, S. 1980. "A Century of Humane Archaeology." *Archaeology* (May–June): 42–51.

Dyson, S. L. 1998. *Ancient Marbles to American Shores: Classical Archaeology in the United States.* Philadelphia: University of Pennsylvania Press.

Sheftel, P. S.1979. "The Archaeological Institute of America 1879–1979: A Centennial Review." *American Journal of Archaeology* 83: 3–17.

———. 1996. "Archaeological Institute of America." In *An Encyclopedia of the History of Classical Archaeology,* 61–63. Ed. N. T. de Grummond. Westport, CT: Greenwood Press.

Thompson, H. A. 1980. "In Pursuit of the Past: The American Role, 1879–1979." *American Journal of Archaeology* 84: 263–270.

Archaeometry

Although the term *archaeometry* is of fairly recent origin, it is now used to cover an important field of archaeological research, one that has its own journals, major symposium sessions, and research centers. The term *archaeometry* was coined by the British archaeologist CHRISTOPHER HAWKES to name the bulletin of the Research Laboratory for Archaeology and the History of

Art at Oxford University, which began publication in 1958. Yet archaeometry is now more than just the name of a journal; it is a field of study. Indeed, the discipline of archaeometry was practiced for many years before it was actually named. In a historical review on scientific measurement in archaeology, Stuart Fleming (1982), of the Museum Applied Center for Archaeology at the University of Pennsylvania, places the origin of archaeometry in the late 1920s when an astronomer, ANDREW ELLICOT DOUGLASS, from the University of Arizona pioneered the dating technique of dendrochronology.

Although the journal was not initially explicit about what archaeometry was, its articles were restricted to the hard sciences, i.e., they were based in physics and chemistry. To understand the history of archaeometry is to understand the major developments within the hard sciences in answering archaeological questions. Archaeological geology, for instance, has a long history. In the early nineteenth century, CHARLES LYELL's *Principles of Geology* gave time depth to the world, which early European archaeologists used to incorporate their models of human antiquity and theories of evolution. Geology thus gave the means for associating flint tools with fossil mammals and the relative dating of the ice ages.

Occasional examples of the application of chemistry and physics in answering questions about the past can be found throughout the nineteenth and early twentieth centuries, yet the true development of archaeometry can be traced to later in the twentieth century and is intertwined with two developments. The first concerns archaeologists' seeking answers to specific problems that were a product of the theoretical developments within the discipline. The second is tied to advances in science and technology. Two approaches are presented here: the use of characterization studies in identifying trade and exchange and the use of dating techniques in determining time depth. The post–World War II developments in nuclear science have been crucial in both instances.

Characterization Studies

Advances in science and technology have made the sourcing and characterization of many ar-

chaeological materials that provide evidence for the physical identification of their movement easily available. These advances have gone hand in hand with a shift in archaeological theory in which archaeologists began to see the usefulness of using trade and exchange in modeling the distribution of materials over space and in explaining changes in societies over time.

The identification of traded archaeological material is not a recent phenomenon. Perhaps the most famous early study was by Anna Shepard, who in the 1930s and 1940s postulated the exchange of pottery over wide areas of the U.S. Southwest by analyzing mineral inclusions in thin sections to pinpoint the origins of such minerals (Shepard 1965). Chemical techniques to identify the elemental composition of archaeological materials as a means of characterization are also not new. Neutron activation analysis was applied to coins from the Louvre in 1952, and in 1957, oriental ceramics were analyzed using the nondestructive methods of X-ray fluorescence spectrometry (XRF) and X-ray diffraction (XRD) analysis (Young and Whitmore 1957). Access to these techniques, however, was restricted and costly.

A major advance in the chemical analysis of archaeological material came from the initiative of Robert Oppenheimer. On 8 March 1956, he assembled a group of archaeologists and chemists at the Institute of Advanced Studies, Princeton, to discuss the possibility of applying methods of nuclear research to the study of archaeology (Sayre and Dodson 1957). As a result of this meeting, work was undertaken at two laboratories, the Brookhaven National Laboratory in the United States and the Research Laboratory for Archaeology and the History of Art in Oxford, England. Techniques deployed included neutron activation analysis (NAA) and spectrographic methods.

Those studies were reasonably successful in being able to separate pottery wares from Asia Minor, GREECE, and ITALY or different factories of Samian ware, and the studies laid the foundations for chemical analyses in the next three decades, in which thousands of analyses using varying techniques were carried out on many types of objects including pottery, stone (obsid-

A variety of archaeometric techniques could be used to characterize these wine cups and containers from a newly discovered storeroom. (Gamma)

ian, marble, chert, volcanic rocks), amber, and metals, including coins. Apart from NAA, XRF, XRD, and spectrographic methods, techniques currently in use include proton-induced X-ray emission and proton-induced gamma ray emission (PIXE-PIGME), inductively coupled plasma emission spectrometry (ICP), lead isotope analysis, and electron microscopy. Major changes in the instrumentation of these techniques have meant that more elements can be analyzed with higher precision. The choice of technique depends on the availability to the archaeologist and the cost.

The need for characterization studies is the result of a reorientation in the ways archaeologists have perceived how trade and exchange have operated in the past. The realization that migrationist/invasion models could not adequately explain the distribution of material across the landscape, or changes in societies over time, led archaeologists to look at other mechanisms. By studying trade and exchange, the intention was to reconstruct the economies and organizations of past societies and their changes over time. Access to and control over

prestige goods through trade and exchange were seen as the prime movers for change leading to ranked societies.

Dating Techniques

Colin Renfrew (1982, 94) pointed out that DAT-ING is the most fundamental archaeometric technique available to archaeologists. Two of the most important techniques that revolutionized archaeology are dendrochronology and radiocarbon dating. Today, many techniques are used in dating, including luminescence, fission track, potassium argon, fluorine and nitrogen dating, obsidian hydration dating, and amino racemisation analysis on bone. When these techniques were developed, archaeologists were ready to apply them.

Dendrochronology

Dendrochronology was pioneered in the beginning of the twentieth century by the astronomer A. E. Douglass. The Laboratory of Tree-ring Research at the University of Arizona was set up shortly afterward, and a few more laboratories added forty years later. Toward the beginning of the twenty-first century, there were over 100 tree ring programs (Dean 1997, 33). The technique entails the use of tree growth rings for dating and studying climatic variations in the past. Although Douglass had been researching tree growth rings since the beginning of the twentieth century, it was in the 1920s that he applied the technique to archaeology by constructing a chronology for Pueblo ruins of the U.S. Southwest. A tree adds a ring (xylem growth) each year, so by counting the number of rings one can obtain an estimate of age. The thickness of the ring is dependent on climatic variations: wet years produce thick rings; dry years, thin rings. Ring patterns from different species of trees are compared and cross-dated with known age samples to form a baseline with which to compare older samples, thus building up a sequence of tree ring growth back into the past.

The Radiocarbon Revolution

One of the most important archaeometric techniques is radiocarbon dating, one of a number of techniques that use radioactive decay. It was pioneered by WILLARD LIBBY, then of the University of Chicago, in the late 1940s and is based on the premise that all living organisms have an uptake of radiocarbon (carbon–14) that ceases when they die. As carbon–14 is unstable, it decays at a half-life of what Libby thought was 5,568 years. By measuring the amount of radioactive carbon of organic matter in an archaeological sample (charcoal, bone, or shell) of known age and comparing it to the radiocarbon in living matter, Libby was able to estimate the time lapse since the organism died.

Radiocarbon dating has undergone many changes since its advent, in particular with regard to refinement in the calculation of the half-life, the development of a calibration curve to give calendar years, and in the techniques for measuring the amount of carbon–14 in a sample. Accelerator mass spectrometry (AMS), for instance, is a relatively new method that determines the amount of carbon–14 in a sample by measuring the atoms directly. Although more expensive than the conventional C-14 dating, this method can utilize much smaller samples.

The importance of radiocarbon dating for both chemistry and archaeology cannot be overestimated. Libby was awarded the Nobel Prize for Chemistry in 1960, and laboratories were set up at the University of Pennsylvania in 1951 and in various centers in Europe soon after the one at Chicago. For the first time, chronologies could be established for areas where conventional dating techniques were difficult to apply. The human time depth of areas such as Australia, Southeast Asia, and the Pacific was recognized for the first time, and a "revolution" occurred in dating Europe's prehistory, which had been previously based on cross-dating to objects of known age. For a full discussion on the radiocarbon revolution on European and U.S. archaeology see Renfrew (1976) and G. Marlowe (1999), respectively.

Luminescence Dating

Although first suggested in the mid-1950s and there was an application to archaeological pottery in the 1960s, it has only been since 1970 that thermoluminescence dating (TL) has been applied routinely in archaeology with levels of precision of plus or minus 10 percent. Major developments occurred after dedicated laboratories were set up, such as that by Michael Aitken at Oxford University during the 1960s, and a book on the technique and its application to archaeology was published in 1979 (Fleming 1979).

The advantage of TL is that it dates the artifact itself. TL has been used to date archaeological materials that have mineral grains, such as quartz and feldspar, and have been exposed to heating: pottery, flint, burned stone, earth ovens, etc. TL is based on the assumption that energy from long-term exposure to ionizing radiation is built up or trapped over time in the lattice of crystals. When heated above 500 degrees centigrade, this stored energy is released in the form of emitted light called thermoluminescence, and the TL clock reset back to zero. The measurement of TL emitted can indicate the time elapsed since the last firing.

Major advances have occurred since the development of the technique, including the use of optical dating (OD). Rather than dating min-

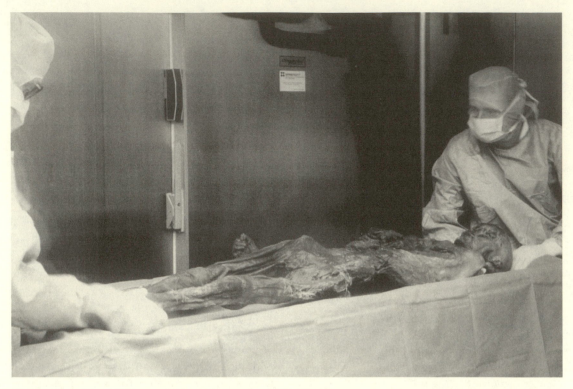

The discovery of the 5,000-year-old frozen "ice man" in 1991 afforded a unique opportunity for the application of biological techniques to an archaeological find. (Gamma)

erals that have been exposed to heat, OD measures exposure to light, that is, the stored energy released by an exposure to a beam of light, for instance, blue/green light or infrared radiation (see Aitken 1997, 183). Optically stimulated luminescence (OSL) is defined by Aitken as "commonly used as an umbrella term that includes both types of stimulation as well as use of other wavelengths" (Aitken 1997, 183).

Optical dating, like thermoluminescence, allows the dating of sediments. The dating of sediment became possible in the 1980s, with the dating of unburned sediment extending the chronology of Australia (Roberts, Jones, and Smith 1990).

Future Directions in Archaeometry

Advances in science have given archaeologists unique insights into the social and economic development of societies through identifying trade and exchange, and they have given chronological depth to the discipline. These advances have been supported by the development of institutional laboratories. The collaboration between

archaeology and physics was to bear fruit in the 1950s with the establishment of the Oxford Research Laboratory for Archaeology and Art, which arose out of the collaboration between an archaeologist (Christopher Hawkes, professor of European archaeology) and a physicist (Lord Charwell, professor of physics). Other early laboratories include the Applied Science Center for Archaeology at the UNIVERSITY OF PENNSYLVANIA MUSEUM OF ARCHAEOLOGY and the BRITISH MUSEUM. These laboratories set the standards for interlaboratory comparisons, and meeting places were arranged to ensure open dialogue among the practitioners. Subsequently, a series of conferences arose, including the International Symposium on Archaeometry, which is held every two years (the thirty-second symposium was held in 2000).

Since 1980, there has been a proliferation of journals, societies, and news groups covering the many different types of applications of science to archaeology. Since the success of the journal *Archaeometry,* other journals have been started, including *Journal of Archaeological Sci-*

ences, which began in 1974; *MASCA Journal,* of the Museum of Applied Science Center for Archaeology at the University of Pennsylvania; *Archaeo-Physika;* and *SAS (Society of Archaeological Sciences) Research Notes,* which began in 1977. These publications have extended the term *archaeometry* from its restricted application to just the hard sciences to include biological sciences, earth sciences, and mathematics.

It is hard to picture archaeology without the use of radiocarbon and other scientific techniques of dating to construct chronologies or physico-chemical techniques to identify the movement of materials in building models of trade or exchange. This is the value of archaeometry to archaeology, and it is reflected in the growing literature on the subject, the increase in the number of institutions undertaking archaeometry, the number of journals dedicated to the topic, and the conferences organized each year to present new advances. But who sets the agenda for archaeometry and what is its future? The answer depends, of course, on the players, who are made up of two sets of professionals: the scientists and the archaeologists.

The interplay between the two sets of players is best seen in the proceedings of a 1981 round-table forum, sponsored by the Conservation-Analytical Laboratory of the Smithsonian Institution and held in conjunction with the twenty-first Symposium for Archaeometry at the Brookhaven National Laboratory, New York. The forum was titled "Future Directions in Archaeometry," with archaeometry defined as "the application and interpretation of natural science data in archaeological and art historical studies" (Olin 1982, 19). This narrow definition of archaeometry reflected the players who set the agenda. The physicists and chemists think of archaeologists as the customers and themselves as providing the service. Archaeometry conferences were thus seen by Renfrew as divided into techniques and run by self-named "archaeometrists"—i.e., physicists or chemists—not archaeologists.

To redress this imbalance, archaeologists have directed the discussion back to the purpose of the discipline and why archaeologists use these techniques—what is the archaeological question asked? Renfrew (1982) puts archaeometry as a subset of the archaeological sciences, which, in turn, are a subset of human history. Indeed, as Rhys Jones (1982) has urged, the research aim of archaeometry must also be the elucidation and testing of archaeological questions.

Thus, a name initially coined for a university journal is now either a discipline representing the interface between the natural and physical sciences and archaeology or a forum for the selling and application of natural and physical science services by self-identified archaeometrists. The future of archaeometry, however, lies in the development of a "new breed" of people who cross the traditional boundaries of archaeology and science.

A major direction for archaeometry lies in both the establishment of archaeometry courses, in which archaeologists are taught the rudiments of the techniques they are using and helping to develop, and the development of archaeometry-based laboratories, in which techniques can be dedicated to solving archaeological questions. Carbon dating, for instance, is an excellent example, for archaeologists must have a comprehensive understanding of how the method works, including the calibrations and other adjustments used (oceanic reservoir effect, etc.), and its limitations and potential. The same applies to the chemical characterization of pottery or obsidian using a multitude of techniques. With agencies such as the U.S. National Science Foundation and the British Science Council providing funding for archaeometric projects, the future of archaeometry lies in archaeology-led projects in which science can provide some of the answers. Any major future advances in archaeometry must lie with developments in archaeological thought and the development of new scientific techniques to answer new archaeological questions.

Glenn Summerhayes

References

Aitken, M. J. 1997. "Luminescence Dating." In *Advances in Archaeological and Museum Science.* Vol. 2, *Chronometric Dating in Archaeology,* 183–216. Ed. R. E. Taylor and M. J. Aitken. New York: Plenum Press.

Dean, J. S. 1997. "Dendrochronology." In *Advances in Archaeological and Museum Science*. Vol. 2, *Chronometric Dating in Archaeology,* 31–64. Ed. R. E. Taylor and M. J. Aitken. New York: Plenum Press.

Fleming, S. 1979. *Themoluminescence Techniques in Archaeology.* Oxford: Clarendon Press.

———. 1982. "Scientific Measurement in Archaeology." In *Archaeometry: An Australasian Perspective,* 7–21. Ed. W. Ambrose and P. Duerden. Canberra: Department of Prehistory, Research School of Pacific Studies, Australian National University.

Jones, R. 1982. "Ions and Eons: Some Thoughts on Archaeological Science and Scientific Archaeology. In *Archaeometry: An Australasian Perspective,* 22–35. Ed. W. Ambrose and P. Duerden. Canberra: Department of Prehistory, Research School of Pacific Studies, Australian National University.

Marlowe, G. 1999. "Year One: Radiocarbon Dating and American Archaeology, 1947–1948." *American Antiquity* 64: 9–32.

Olin, J. S. 1982. "Introduction." In *Future Directions in Archaeometry: A Round Table,* 19–22. Ed. J. S. Olin. Washington, DC: Smithsonian Institution.

Renfrew, C. 1976. *Before Civilization: The Radiocarbon Revolution and Prehistoric Europe.* Harmondsworth, UK: Penguin Books.

———. 1982. "Interfacing Problems in Archaeological Sciences." In *Future Directions in Archaeometry: A Round Table,* 93–99. Ed. J. S. Olin. Washington, DC: Smithsonian Institution.

Roberts, R. G., R. Jones, and M. A. Smith. 1990. "Thermoluminescence Dating of a 50,000-Years-Old Occupation Site in Northern Australia." *Nature* 345: 153–156.

Sayre, E., and R. Dodson. 1957. "Neutron Activation Study of Mediterranean Potsherds." *American Journal of Archaeology* 61: 35–41

Shepard, A. 1965. "Rio Grande Glaze-Paint Pottery: A Test of Petrographic Analysis." In *Ceramics and Man.* Ed. F. Matson. Publications in Anthropology no. 41. New York: Viking Fund.

Young, W., and F. Whitmore. 1957. "Analysis of Oriental Ceramics by Non-destructive Methods." *Far Eastern Ceramic Bulletin* 9: 1–27.

Argentina
The Early Nineteenth Century

The quest for knowledge of our past is one of the most universal human preoccupations, but it is not necessarily the first priority of a nation, state, or people. For this reason, in Argentina (as in many other countries) it is difficult to pinpoint the particular moment in time when archaeological inquiry began. Travelers, pioneers, and colonizers left important references and data about this huge South American country beginning in the early sixteenth century when the Spanish first arrived on its shores, looking for a maritime passage between the Atlantic and Pacific Oceans. After Argentina gained its independence from Spain in 1816, many of its intellectuals began to be influenced by the great European naturalists of the nineteenth century, not only through their books but also through their visits to the country.

Under this naturalist boom the Argentine government established the Museo Nacional in 1864, which was the foundation of archaeological research there. The museum comprised an archaeological section where researchers such as Burmeister, F. P. Moreno, F. Ameghino, J. B. Ambrosetti, E. Boman, Outes, Casanova, and Gallardo began Argentine archaeology. They were influenced by Charles Darwin, Alexander von Humboldt, and William Wallace and also by the Argentine historical movement known as the Generación de 1880. Scholars such as F. Ameghino, F. P. Moreno, and R. Lista explored Argentina and collected different kinds of scientific information, including archaeological evidence.

The results of this research were initially circulated within a small academic milieu—among the staff at the Museo Nacional and the Sociedad Científica Argentina, for example. It was not until the creation of the Museo de Ciencias Naturales at the Universidad de La Plata (ULP) in 1880 and the Museo Etnográfico at the Universidad de Buenos Aires (UBA) in 1904 that archaeology was inserted into the curriculum of some history courses.

This first Argentine archaeology was characterized by a historical perspective and the meticulous description of collected artifacts. Important museum collections were established as a result of different expeditions, and most of the archaeological materials were gathered from exploratory excavations or exposed surfaces. The interpretations of the collections were based on linguistics, ethnography, and ethnohistory, focusing on the relationship between the known native populations and the recovered archaeological artifacts. Archaeology was regarded as part of the natural sciences, but two different influences affected it: the first and most common was the naturalist influence, as expressed in the works of Moreno and Burmeister (which in turn influenced Lista, Roth, and Pico), and the second was the evolutionary influence, as seen in the work of the Ameghino brothers and Ambrosetti. Between these two perspectives were the works of people such as S. Lafone Quevedo, Zeballos, Rusconi, Montes, and Vignati. Patagonia, the Argentine northwest, and the Pampas were the regions most explored during the nineteenth century, primarily by researchers who lived in Buenos Aires and La Plata. There were few local researchers in other cities, with the exception of A. Quiroga in Catamarca.

The last thirty years of the nineteenth century were important for the development of Argentine archaeology because they established the regionalization of future work. During these years travelers, naturalists, and explorers were able to conduct research because leaders of the Generación de 1880 were establishing and maintaining territories and boundaries to support their political and economic interests. In Patagonia, for instance, Argentina disputed the frontier with CHILE, which necessitated constant territorial reconnaissance; inhabited by hunter-gatherers, Patagonia was regarded as a land of savagery. In the northwest region, the Argentine government was trying to establish certain industries, including the sugar industry, and it needed the cooperation of local workers; the social structures of the northwest, given the Inca influence and the significant and large Creole population there, were easy to incorporate into the Argentine economy. (The difference between these two regions—a very real one from both anthropological and archaeological points of view—became the basis of the stereotype that has been perpetuated over time.) The Pampas—the land of gauchos and *estancias* (large rural holdings)—was far away from frontier problems and Creole populations, and it, too, was easily incorporated into the Argentine economy. These three regions would be the sub-

jects of major archaeological investigations in the twentieth century.

The First Half of the Twentieth Century
The first decades of the twentieth century were significant because of the number of foreign researchers at work in Argentina's northwest region, among them R. Lehmann Nitsche, Boman, and E. Nordensköld. The Museo de La Plata held the most important archaeological collections, including one from F. P. Moreno. In 1911 the Instituto Geográfico Argentino, which had supplied more funds for archaeological projects than any other institution, disappeared, and the Sociedad Científica Argentina began to support archaeological investigations. The University of Buenos Aires and the University of La Plata also started to fund archaeological research and expeditions, the most important of which were those of UBA's Museo Etnográfico and ULP's Museo de Ciencias Naturales specifically in the northwest region. In addition, significant private support for archaeology came from individuals, such as B. Muñiz Barreto. During these years Argentina began to participate in and be recognized by the rest of the scientific world, and it hosted two international congresses of Americanists, one in 1910 at Buenos Aires and the other in 1932 at La Plata. At both congresses significant discussions were devoted to the archaeology of Patagonia and the northwest.

Even as archaeological investigations of the Pampas comparatively decreased, more archaeological expeditions headed to the northwest region than to any other area of Argentina in the first decades of the twentieth century—including those by Ambrosetti (see photo, page 108), Weiser, Lehmann Nitsche, MAX UHLE, and Gerling. Meanwhile, the first chronological frameworks for Argentine archaeology began to appear: for the northwest by Ulhe, Boman, and Ambrosetti; for Patagonia by JUNIUS BIRD; and for the Pampas by the Ameghino brothers. Archaeology was still only taught in single courses at the Universities of Buenos Aires and La Plata, and the naturalist influence on archaeology slowly waned, with historical and ethnohistorical explanations becoming more popular. In the 1930s Imbelloni was the first archaeologist to

Section of the Pucará de Tilcara, Jujuy (Photo by Noel Montoya)

use the methods of the Vienna school. In 1936 the Sociedad Argentina de Antropología was created, with only ten members; Outes served as its first president. This society arranged a number of important scientific meetings—the Semana de Antropología—for the discussion of anthropology and archaeology.

During the economic depression of the 1930s, and throughout World War II, archaeology and prehistory courses were given at other universities such as Rosario, Cuyo, Tucumán, and Córdoba, resulting in a significant increase in the number of researchers and research projects. In addition, archaeological investigations of whole new areas were launched—in the Mesopotamia regions by Serrano and de Aparicio and in Cuyo by Canals Frau and Semper. However, most of the fieldwork was still done in the northwest; the least was done in the Pampas and Patagonia.

The Second Half of the Twentieth Century
During the post–World War II period Argentine archaeology flourished. This was the consequence of the work of Wendell C. Bennett and A. R. González in the northwest and the arrival

in Buenos Aires of O. Menghin. After 1955, with the advent of radiocarbon dating, more-regional explanations of archaeological variation were discussed. Between 1950 and 1960 both the University of Buenos Aires and the University of La Plata began to teach anthropology and to specialize in archaeology, definitively incorporating both in an Argentine university degree. Other universities followed their example over the next decades.

The work of González and Menghin characterized Argentine archaeology after the 1960s. González, working in the northwest, and Menghin, working first in the Pampas and later in Patagonia, resolved the theoretical framework for each region, and their studies were followed up by other archaeologists, such as Cigliano, Bórmida, Schobinger, and Lafon. However, they also represented two opposing traditions and schools of thought: González the North American culture-history school and Menghin the Vienna school. Both of them established general regional chronologies that would be used for the next forty years.

The Argentine national government became

Excavations at Imiwaia, Beagle Channel, Tierra del Fuego (Photo by Luis Orquera)

the sole supporter of archaeological investigations through the universities and CONICET, the government agency that controlled research funding in science and technology, after 1958. During the 1960s the first generations of Argentine anthropologists and archaeologists graduated from local universities and spread their disciplines into new regions, but the northwest and Patagonia remained the most popular places for research.

The military coups d'état in 1966 and 1976 significantly disrupted academic life and archaeological fieldwork, and many archaeologists were forced to leave Argentina. This emigration particularly affected archaeology in the northwest region. In contrast, Patagonia has experienced an archaeolological boom since the early 1970s, due to the long-term projects of Gradín, Aschero, and Aguerre in Cueva de las Manos; Sanguinetti at the Río Gallegos basin; and Orquera and Piana at the Beagle Channel, Tierra del Fuego (see photo above). In the northwest region, hunter-gatherer archaeology became more popular, but Raffino continued to study complex societies, and the Pampas still had few archaeological teams

working in it. Paradoxically, only after archaeology had been pursued in the country for more than 100 years was the first Argentine National Congress of Archaeology organized; it was held in in the city of Rosario in 1970.

At the turn of the twenty-first century, Argentine archaeology is divided by theoretical approaches, political opinions, regional interests, and academic issues. Under these conditions North American "New Archaeology" has provided a more neutral perspective, which has allowed the latest generation of Argentine archaeologists to continue working. First employed by archaeologists at the University of La Plata, New Archaeology began to play a major role in Argentina in the 1980s. North American processual archaeology was established across all regions of Argentina by different archaeologists —Politis in the Pampas, Borrero in Patagonia, and Yacobaccio and Olivera in the northwest. Due to a more neutral political perspective, a generational turnover, and the return of democracy in 1983, processual archaeology was very well received in Argentina. Its impact can be seen in the significant number of papers associated with the need to build middle-range theory and in the amount of work related to formation processes (taphonomy), faunal analysis, and regional studies.

The rebirth of democracy at a national level has led to the return of the exiled archaeologists who emigrated in 1976, the creation of new careers in archaeology at other universities, and more opportunities for research. The Argentine National Congress of Archaeology now meets regularly and more frequently than in the past—every two to three years—and a number of important regional meetings address specific topics. Northwest regional studies have begun to flourish once again, and the Pampas has been definitively incorporated into archaeological discussions, as have the Sierras Centrales, Cuyo, and the Mesopotamian regions. New research areas in Patagonia have also been incorporated. Unfortunately, however, some parts of Argentina, such as the Chaco, remain almost archaeologically unknown today.

After the 1980s it became common for Argentine archaeologists to pursue postdoctoral work overseas—especially in the United States and the United Kingdom—and Argentine archaeologists now routinely attend international congresses and meetings, not only submitting papers but also organizing symposiums. In addition, a number of Argentine students have taken postgraduate courses in North American and European universities since 1995.

Argentine Archaeology Today

As a normal consequence of the maturing of Argentine archaeology, there are few debates today pitting the northwest against Patagonia or processual against more traditional archaeology. Theoretically and methodologically speaking, Argentine archaeology now comprises a variety of perspectives: the evolutionist approach (Lanata, Borrero); social theory in all its different aspects (Nielsen, Acuto, Lazzari, Zarankin); postprocessual archaeology (Haber); historical archaeology (Senatore, Bárcena); urban archaeology (Weissel); underwater archaeology (Elkin); and heritage and conservation (Endere and Curtoni). There is also an increase in contract archaeology. The chronological frame-

works of the northwest from the 1960s are being rebuilt and extended not only by members of younger generations of archaeologists, such as Ratto and Muscio, but also by older and more established members of the field, such as Pérez Gollán and Tarragó. Finally, the Asociación de Arqueológos Profesionales de la República Argentina (AAPRA) was founded in 1998, and J. Rodriguez was elected as its first president.

José Luis Lanata

See also Bolivia; Brazil

References

Fernández, Jorge. 1982. *Historia de la arqueología Argentina.* Mendoza: Asociación Cuyana de Antropología.

González, Alberto R. 1985. "Cincuenta años de arqueología del Noroeste Argentino (1930–1980): Apuntes de un casi testigo y algo de protagonista." *American Antiquity* 50: 505–517.

Orquera, Luis A. n.d. "Historia de las investigaciones arqueológicas en Pampa, Patagonia y Tierra del Fuego." Ms.

Politis, Gustavo. 1995. "The Socio-Politics of the Development of Archaeology in Hispanic South America." In *Theory in Archaeology. A World Perspective,* 197–228. Ed. P. Ucko. London and New York: Routledge.

Ashmolean Museum

Opening on 24 May 1683, the Ashmolean Museum in Oxford, England, was originally based on the private collection of Elias Ashmole (1617–1692), which was presented to the University of Oxford. At the core of Ashmole's gift was a collection originally assembled by John Tradescant the elder (died 1638) and his son John Tradescant (1608–1662).

The first curator of the Asmolean Museum was Robert Plot, an antiquary of distinction. Unusually, from the start the Ashmolean was open to the public and had clear research and teaching (as well as display) functions. The fortunes of the museum waxed and waned over the next 150 years with the natural history side of the collections assuming greater importance than the human antiquities.

However, from the mid-nineteenth century onward, the character of the Ashmolean Museum changed to the form we know today, com-

Ashmolean Museum (Ancient Art and Architecture Collection Ltd.)

prising significant collections of antiquities derived from archaeological excavation and collection. Many famous collections have been presented to the Ashmolean, an example being SIR RICHARD COLT HOARE's donation of "the Douglas collection" of Anglo-Saxon antiquities in 1827. The museum has also benefited from the activities of its keepers, the most famous of whom was SIR ARTHUR EVANS. Under Evans, the Ashmolean once again rationalized its exhibits, expanded, and moved into new premises in Beaumont Street in Oxford. These changes have ensured that the Ashmolean remains one of the most significant archaeological museums in the world, and the research of its staff allows it to remain at the cutting edge of world archaeology.

Tim Murray

References
Ovenell, R. F. 1986. *The Ashmolean Museum 1683–1894.* Oxford: Clarendon Press.

Atwater, Caleb (1778–1867)

An early American antiquary and amateur archaeologist who was born in North Adams, Massachussets. Atwater received a B.A. from Williams College and became a Presbyterian minister; he later studied and practiced law in New York City. After moving his legal practice to Circleville, Ohio, in 1815 to practice law, he used his spare time to study and record local earthworks and antiquities. The American Antiquarian Society (established in 1812) published his *Descriptions of the Antiquities Discovered in the State of Ohio and Other Western States* (1820) in the first volume of their transactions.

The earth mounds discovered west of the Appalachian Mountains contained artifacts made of pottery, shell, and native copper, and they challenged the widespread belief that native American Indians were too primitive and inferior to create such "sophisticated" artifacts and complex structures. Indeed at that time the bulk of observers could not accept that the ancestors of native American Indians were capable of such building feats, and their origins of the earth mounds became the focus of an ongoing debate. Some antiquarians and members of the public argued that they were built by Vikings or other Europeans, or by the ancestors of Mexicans who later moved south. Other scholars proposed that indigenous Americans had destroyed the civilization that built the mounds, and used this as part of a justification to in turn destroy them. Atwater had his own theory about their origin, arguing that the mounds had been constructed by Hindus who had migrated from India, via Ohio, to Mexico. Notwithstanding these now discredited hypotheses, Atwater's study contained valuable descriptions of the earthmounds, which were later destroyed.

Atwater became an active local politician, and in 1829 he was appointed by President Jackson to help negotiate a treaty with the Winnebago and other Indians at Prairie du Chien in what is now Wisconsin. In 1833 he published an account of this process and his travels, which included his earlier study on antiquities in *The Writings of Caleb Atwater*. In 1838 he published *A History of the State of Ohio, Natural and Civil,* one of the earliest histories of the state.

Tim Murray

See also Jefferson, Thomas; United States of America, Prehistoric Archaeology

Aubrey, John (1626–1697)

John Aubrey was born and grew up near Malmesbury, Wiltshire, England, where Neolithic remains cover the countryside. The son of local gentry, Aubrey was a close friend of the philosopher Thomas Hobbes and attended Trinity College, Oxford, where he indulged his passion for learning and his insatiable curiosity for all things old.

The formative influence on Aubrey's early career was WILLIAM DUGDALE's *Antiquities of Warwickshire* (1656), which inspired him to begin a similar survey of Wiltshire. Most of the material he collected for his "Wiltshire Antiquities" could be classified as local history and his compilations were for the most part fairly conventional and in the tradition of Dugdale.

The unconventional material in his collections related to ancient stone monuments and earthworks, to which he was powerfully attracted. His familiarity with Wiltshire had made him aware of the large number of standing stones, tumuli, and barrows scattered across the country, and his

John Aubrey (Ann Ronan Picture Library)

imagination was stirred by his attempts to guess the origin and purpose of these monuments. Stonehenge had always fascinated him, but he himself discovered the even larger Neolithic monumental complex at AVEBURY in 1649, when he was out hunting. The nucleus of Avebury was largely known as an ancient site, but Aubrey was the first to recognize the full extent of the monument and to appreciate that it was not a camp but some kind of ceremonial site, the scheme of which had been obscured by the growth of the village on the spot. He identified the circle of megaliths for the first time as a man-made construction and he returned many times to map the complex and reflect on its significance. He traced the bank and fosse, proving that it was not part of a defensive system. He identified the first section of the great avenue and suspected it had a ceremonial function. He was able to reconstruct a secondary circle of stones within the greater circle. He also tried to locate the complex within the landscape, by noting the old approach roads and the relationship of Avebury to Silbury Hill and to neighboring barrows.

As his interest in the explication of ancient monuments grew he abandoned "Wiltshire Antiquities" and began a new manuscript devoted entirely to the investigation of fieldworks and entitled *Monumenta Britannica,* which developed into the most original and enterprising study of British prehistoric remains in the seventeenth century. Aubrey was the first person to seriously assert that these remains—stone circles, barrows, and hill-forts——were the work of the ancient Britons. Previously learned opinion had assigned them variously to the Romans, the Saxons, or the Danes. Aubrey's belief that stone monuments were raised by the ancient Britons was thus a conceptual breakthrough. By observation and by information from correspondents, he gathered details of stone circles, megaliths, barrows, tumuli, hill-forts, camps, ramparts, and ditches from all over the British Isles, and it gradually became clear to him that a common primitive culture had once covered the whole region. Moreover, since their monuments lay in so many places beyond the perimeter of Roman, Saxon, or Danish occupations, they must antedate any of those settlements.

In compiling *Monumenta Britannica* Aubrey was assembling the first book in English that could be seriously regarded as an archaeological treatise. His concern was principally with the field monuments themselves. He described them in great detail, measured them, and often provided competent sketches as illustrations; he looked closely at the material remains of a vanished culture, made comparisons with similar structures to determine that there were definite categories of monuments, and tried by observations and reflection to deduce the function of stone circles, standing stones, mounds, and earthworks.

A further section of *Monumenta Britannica* was devoted to notes on Roman remains in Britain, based on Aubrey's own investigations or on reports from correspondents. Besides familiar details of Verulamium, York, Colchester, Chester, and other well-known sites, there was a wealth of information about Roman discoveries in London, many of them the result of the rebuilding of the city after the Great Fire of 1666. The most rewarding result of Aubrey's considerable familiarity with Roman Britain was the map he drew of the southwest region, showing the Roman and British settlements, camps, and hill-forts and the roads and tracks connecting them.

John Aubrey was elected a member of the Royal Society in 1663. Soon afterward he presented a paper on Avebury, the first occasion on which an antiquarian subject was discussed at the society. In fact, since no similar paper had been offered to the SOCIETY OF ANTIQUARIES OF LONDON earlier in the century, Aubrey was effectively the first to present a true archaeological paper in England.

His wandering life after his bankruptcy in 1671 and the gradual dispersal of his private library thereafter affected his ability to work consistently; the perennial disorder of his manuscript collections grew worse. All he ever brought to publication were his *Miscellanies* in 1695. After 1667 Aubrey collaborated for many years with Anthony Wood, the Oxford antiquary, in accumulating biographical details of notable Englishmen and of Oxford writers in particular for Wood's monumental biographical register, *Athenae Oxoniences,* published in 1691 and 1692. Aubrey's own collection of biographical sketches became the chief vehicle of his fame in the twentieth century under the title of *Brief Lives.* Aubrey wrote several other works, all of which remained in manuscript during his lifetime. *Monumenta Britannica* has never been printed in its entirety, the confused and overwritten condition of the manuscript being the main obstacle to its publication. In the last phase of his life Aubrey became closely associated with the younger generation of antiquaries then emerging in Oxford. The benefits of Aubrey's work began to appear in public and his papers were consulted by those scholars who Oxford antiquary Edmund Gibson recruited to revise and enlarge WILLIAM CAMDEN's *Britannica* in the 1690s. The eighteenth-century antiquary WILLIAM STUKELEY used Aubrey's remarks on stone circles to develop his own elaborate theories about them.

Graham Parry

See also Britain, Prehistoric Archaeology; Britain, Roman

References

For references, see *Encyclopedia of Archaeology: The Great Archaeologists, Vol. 2,* ed. Tim Murray (Santa Barbara, CA: ABC-CLIO, 1999), pp. 15–26.

Australia, Historical

Formal British settlement of Australia did not begin until 1788, with the establishment of the convict colony at Sydney, but there is a much longer history of European exploration, which began with the Dutch in the seventeenth century. Along the north coast of Australia there was also an extensive trading system with fishermen from Southeast Asia that dates to at least the eighteenth century (McKnight 1976). European settlement began in earnest in the nineteenth century, and the archaeological record of colonization has been shaped by the influences of global economies and industrial technologies, which were by then well established. Since the 1970s terrestrial and maritime archaeologists have begun to investigate this material record, and vital and dynamic fields of research have emerged. The archaeology of the postcontact period is typically called "historical archaeology," although "contact archaeology" and "Aboriginal historical archaeology" are also used to describe the archaeology of the Aboriginal people during the same period.

The origins of historical archaeology in Australia date to the 1960s and the first excavations of European settler sites. At the Australian National University in Canberra, Jim Allen (Allen 1969) undertook Ph.D. research on Port Essington, in the Northern Territory, while Campbell McKnight (1976) studied the Macassan trepang industry (sea slug harvesting) that flourished in the same region, also for a Ph.D. At the University of Sydney, Judy Birmingham (1976) carried out excavations at James King's pottery at Irrawang, New South Wales, and at the Tasmanian Aboriginal settlement of Wybalenna on Flinders Island. At the University of New England, Graham Connah began the study of the pastoral establishment of Winterbourne (Connah, Rowland, et al. 1978). In Melbourne, Bill Culican from the University of Melbourne excavated the Fossil Beach cement works on the Mornington peninsula (Culican and Taylor 1972). During the same decade, sport divers in Western Australia discovered the wreck sites of Dutch East India Company ships, among them the *Batavia* and the *Vergulde Draeck* (Green 1973, 1989), and maritime archaeology in Australia began.

Ian Jack (1985, 153–156) attributes the emergence of historical archaeology at this time to two developments. One was an increasing interest in what he terms *local history* within university history departments and the attendant interest in its surviving physical remains. The second development came from within departments teaching classical and Near Eastern archaeology where a need was identified for a less costly means of training students in excavation methods than the traditional practice of taking them to sites overseas. Thus, one of the important forces shaping historical archaeology in Australia was, from the outset, its institutional home in departments of prehistory, classical, and Near Eastern archaeology.

As those departments were themselves closely modeled on British university systems, anthropology was not as great an influence in Australian historical archaeology as it was in the United States. In addition to those with a training in archaeology, other early practitioners came from a variety of backgrounds, including history, geography, architectural history, and engineering. All of these scholarly traditions influenced the field, and the wide-ranging and multidisciplinary nature of historical archaeology in Australia was thus established from the beginning. In 1971, the Australian (now Australasian) Society for Historical Archaeology (ASHA) was formed, and it was followed in 1982 by the Australian Institute of Maritime Archaeology (AIMA).

The field grew rapidly during the 1970s, led by scholars at the University of Sydney and the University of New England and as a result of the emergence of cultural heritage management. By 1983 and the publication of the first issue of ASHA's journal *Australian Journal of Historical Archaeology* (later *Australasian Historical Archaeology*), Jane Wesson (Wesson 1983, 1984) was able to compile a bibliography of more than 450 entries. Many of these studies were necessarily descriptive, as researchers attempted to define the nature of material record of Australia's settler society.

Other scholars, however, were already seeking to understand local sites within wider historical and archaeological contexts. Allen (1973)

ARAFURA SEA　　　　　　　TORRES STRAIT

Port Essington　　　　　• *Pandora*

Darwin

NORTHERN

TERRITORY

QUEENSLAND

WESTERN

AUSTRALIA

SOUTH

AUSTRALIA

Batavia

NEW SOUTH WALES

Winterbourne
Armidale•

Vergulde　•
Draeck　■Perth

Irrawang•
Sydney■

Adelaide

Canberra■

VICTORIA

N

■Melbourne

Fossil Beach

Sydney Cove　　**Wybalenna**

TASMANIA　　　　　**Burghley**
　　　　　　　　　　　Ross

0　　　　　1000 km

Hobart

Australian Historical Archaeological Sites

argued that the remains of the settlement at Port Essington could best be understood, not as a failed attempt at colonization, but as a successful, if short-term, display of British military presence in the region that achieved a number of strategic imperial functions. Birmingham's (1976) study of James King's Irrawang pottery emphasized that the ready availability of cheap, industrial wares imported from Great Britain reduced the viability of any local craft tradition and that King, who was not a potter himself, succeeded because of his skills as an entrepreneurial industrialist rather than as a craftsman. In his study of the great house at Winterbourne (Connah, Rowland, et

al. 1978), Connah was able to demonstrate the various English antecedents for local building traditions and also to document the taphonomic processes by which the house was first built and then later dismantled, a process that itself shed light on the changing structure of pastoral work.

Published studies have predominantly dealt with site-based excavations and surveys. Artifact studies have not been as numerous, and on the whole, the systematic analysis of Australian assemblages has not reached its full potential (Lawrence 1999). However, a series of preliminary articles initially published in the ASHA *Newsletter* did establish important groundwork for such an analysis, and there have also been other detailed studies of some kinds of artifacts. Michael Pearson has contributed thorough research on a number of areas, including ships' tanks (Pearson 1992) and whaling tools (Pearson 1983). Robert Varman (1979, 1980) has undertaken to work on building materials while Marjorie Graham (1979) has produced several general overviews of Australian pottery. James Boow's (1992) work on the Australian glass industry is an excellent resource, and Mark Staniforth and Mike Nash (1998) have published an exhaustive study of Chinese export porcelain from the 1791 wreck of the *Sydney Cove*.

The first, and so far only, broad synthesis of research in Australian historical archaeology appeared in 1988. *The Archaeology of Australia's History* (Connah 1988) provides a comprehensive guide to the scope and nature of work done up to that time. The establishment of a regular journal in 1983 provided scholars with a forum in which to present their work and stimulated the beginnings of theoretical awareness in the field. One reason for the slow development of this area of research was the narrow academic base (until 1987 historical archaeology was taught regularly at only two universities) and the recent establishment of teaching programs. However, during the 1980s, the maturation of the first generation of students trained in historical archaeology was the occasion for more-thoughtful reflection on the nature of the discipline, its achievements to date, and its aims and potential. The discussion was inaugurated in the first volume of the *Australian Journal of Historical Archaeology* and rapidly came to focus on questions at the heart of historical archaeology's place in the humanities as scholars sought to determine which of history, anthropology, and archaeology was the most appropriate source of methodological and theoretical approaches.

Graham Connah (1983) and Vincent Megaw (1984) pointed to the need for greater problem orientation in research if the field were to contribute to the understanding of the human past, but they stopped short of advocating specific kinds of problems. In 1983, Birmingham and Denis Jeans (1983) took problem orientation one step further by proposing a model that at-

tempted to explain various aspects of the archaeology of Australian colonization within the same integrative framework. Damaris Bairstow (1984a, 1984b) accepted the need to contribute to a greater understanding of the human past but rejected the hypothetico-deductive methods of "the new archaeology" that had so far been proposed and instead argued for inductive reasoning based on the particularities of individual sites and circumstances—a more "historical" approach. Tim Murray (1985) and Murray and Allen (1986) in turn responded by asserting the embeddedness of historical archaeological theory within archaeological theory building as a whole and the need to look to theoretical developments in anthropology, sociology, and history.

The 1980s also saw the entrenchment of cultural heritage management (CHM) as the major impetus behind work on historical sites. In addition to providing employment for historical archaeologists, this type of management also stimulated the growth of new areas of research. In particular, it shifted attention from the bush, where rural sites and industries were accessible to academic researchers with limited budgets, to the cities, where rapid urban development exposed a plethora of sites that required mitigation work. Rescue work was most established in Sydney, although such work also took place in the other capital cities.

Foremost among the early Sydney sites was that of First Government House, ruins of which were uncovered during development work in 1983 (Proudfoot, Bickford, et al. 1991). Another important venue was the harborside neighborhood of the Rocks, home to the convict settlers of the First Fleet. The Rocks grew into a vibrant inner-city working-class area before being condemned as a slum at the turn of the twentieth century. Flagged for redevelopment in the 1970s, a coalition of community groups was instrumental in preserving the area as a distinct heritage precinct, one in which numerous archaeological studies have subsequently been carried out (Gojak 1995; Gojak and Iacono 1993; Lydon 1993).

Urban archaeology became an important forum for theoretical and methodological development (Bairstow 1991; Birmingham 1990). Grace

The excavated shepherd's hut at Burghley, northwest Tasmania, built in 1827 (Courtesy of Tim Murray)

Karskens and Thorpe (1992) proposed a series of broad integrative research questions for addressing the archaeology of Sydney, and the questions were taken up by the Sydney Cove Authority and Godden Mackay Logan Heritage Consultants in the innovative and highly successful Cumberland/Gloucester Streets project (Karskens 1996, 1997, 1999). Similar collaborative work between archaeologists and historians developed in Melbourne around the assemblages from the inner-city site of Little Lon (Mayne and Lawrence 1998; Murray and Mayne forthcoming).

At the same time, cultural heritage management concerns were requiring thematic studies geared toward the creation of heritage inventories, which continued to stimulate work in rural areas. Included were studies of the mining, whaling, and pastoral industries (Bell 1987; Kostoglou and McCarthy 1991; Pearson 1983). Research also continued in other areas of long-standing interest, such as industrial archaeology (Jack and Cremin 1994), rural elites (Connah 1986; Wilson 1988), and the Chinese (Bell 1993; Gaughwin 1993; McCarthy 1988). Work

was carried out on a number of major convict sites, including the Great North Road between Sydney and Newcastle (Karskens 1984); Hyde Park Barracks in Sydney; and Port Arthur, Tasmania (Davies and Buckley 1987; Egloff 1984). Most research has emphasized male convicts, but historians and archaeologists have begun to explore the experiences of female convicts (Casella 1996, 1997).

Contact archaeology also began to attract more attention as researchers investigated the maintenance of Aboriginal culture despite the trauma of postcontact dislocation (Birmingham 1992; Colley and Bickford 1996; Mulvaney 1989). In the 1990s, research broadened to include a variety of postcontact sites, from traditional rock shelters and shell middens containing artifacts of European origin (Colley 1997) to sites such as Burghley, Tasmania, which was abandoned by English-speaking shepherds but reoccupied by Aboriginal people (Murray 1993), to pastoral stations where Aboriginal men worked as stockmen and Aboriginal women worked as housemaids, cooks, and nannies.

Maritime archaeologists carried out excavations of several wrecks around the Australian coast in the 1980s and early 1990s. This research built on the skills and frameworks developed during earlier excavation of the Dutch VOC (Verenigde Oostindische Compagnie, Dutch East India Company) wrecks in Western Australia carried out by the Western Australian Maritime Museum in the 1970s (Hosty and Stuart 1994). Underwater archaeologists trained in Western Australia began to investigate more recent wrecks, including the *Sydney Cove,* which sank in 1791 while on a voyage to supply the infant colony at Sydney (Nash 1997; Strachan 1986), and the *Pandora,* which sank off Queensland's Great Barrier Reef while returning to England with some of the *Bounty* mutineers (Gestner 1991). Other important studies include the work done on the *James Matthews* in Western Australia and the *William Salthouse* in Melbourne, both of which were bringing supplies (Staniforth 1987, 1995). The *Hive,* a convict transport wrecked off the New South Wales coast (Nutley 1995), and the *Litherland,* a whaling ship cum coastal trader that sank in Bass Strait (Nash 1990), have also been investigated.

In the 1990s, debate continued about the future of historical archaeology in Australia (Connah 1998; Egloff 1994; Mackay and Karskens 1999). Although the decline of historical archaeology in the traditional strongholds of the Universities of Sydney and New England was cause for concern, at the same time historical archaeology was also able to claim a truly nationwide distribution. New appointments at Flinders University in Adelaide, James Cook University in Townsville, the Northern Territory University in Darwin, and the University of Western Australia in Perth, in addition to existing appointments at La Trobe University in Melbourne, meant that for the first time programs in historical archaeology were being taught at the university level around the country. In addition, a spate of doctoral dissertations effectively doubled the number of practitioners with Ph.D.s in historical archaeology, and there are sufficient numbers presently completing their Ph.D. to double that number again in the next few years. The fact that practitioners are increasingly seeking postgraduate qualifications suggests that the theoretical sophistication of research carried out, both inside the academy and in public archaeology, will continue to develop.

The impact of this third generation of historical archaeologists in Australia is gradually being felt. Four major monographs, the first of their kind to find commercial publishers, have recently been published, making work available to a broader audience within Australia and overseas. This work, and other studies also being undertaken, draw from a wide range of theoretical approaches. Resistance theory and feminist approaches shaped the study of the female convict site of Ross Factory (Casella 1996, 1997), while postcolonial theory has been influential in shaping studies such as Jane Lydon's nuanced analysis of the Chinese in the Rocks (Lydon 1999) and Tracey Ireland's (Ireland forthcoming) study of historical archaeology and Australian identity. Other studies have made use of the fine-grained historical ethnographic approach pioneered by Rhys Isaac and Greg Dening (Karskens 1999; Lawrence 2000). H. Burke's (1999) analysis of architectural form in Armidale, New South Wales, represents the most fully articulated application of Marxist theory yet seen in Australian historical archaeology. In his 1994 review of the field, Brian Egloff (1994) argued that for historical archaeology to continue, it needed to demonstrate its engagement with issues of concern to issues of general concern. Although the field in Australia is still developing, there are signs that wider relevance is being sought and that the field will continue to increase in strength and diversity.

Susan Lawrence

See also Australia, Prehistoric; New Zealand, Historical Archaeology; United States of America, Prehistoric Archaeology

References
Allen, J. 1969. "Archaeology and the History of Port Essington." *Research School of Pacific Studies.* Ph.D. dissertation, Australian National University.
———. 1973. "The Archaeology of Nineteenth-Century British Imperialism: An Australian Case Study." *World Archaeology* 5, no. 1: 44–60.
Bairstow, D. 1984a. "Historical Archaeology at the Crossroads: An Appraisal of Theoretical Considerations." *Australian Archaeology* 18: 32–39.
———. 1984b. "The Swiss Family Robinson

Model: A Comment and Appraisal." *Australian Journal of Historical Archaeology* 2: 3–6.

———. 1991. "Urban Archaeology: American Theory, Australian Practice." *Australian Archaeology* 33: 52–58.

Bell, P. 1987. *Gold, Iron, and Steam: The Industrial Archaeology of the Palmer Goldfield.* Townsville, Queensland: James Cook University.

———. 1993. "Chinese Ovens on Mining Settlement Sites in Australia." In *Histories of the Chinese in Australasia and the South Pacific: Proceedings of an International Public Conference Held at the Museum of Chinese Australian History Melbourne, 8–10 October 1993,* 213–229. Ed. P. MacGregor. Melbourne: Museum of Chinese Australian History.

Birmingham, J. 1976. "The Archaeological Contribution to History: Some Australian Case Studies." *World Archaeology* 7, no. 3: 306–317.

———. 1990. "A Decade of Diggings: Deconstructing Urban Archaeology." *Australian Journal of Historical Archaeology* 8: 13–22.

———. 1992. *Wybalenna: The Archaeology of Cultural Accommodation in Nineteenth Century Tasmania.* Sydney: Australian Society for Historical Archaeology.

Birmingham, J., and D. Jeans. 1983. "The Swiss Family Robinson and the Archaeology of Colonisations." *Australian Journal of Historical Archaeology* 1: 3–14.

Boow, J. 1992. *Early Australian Commercial Glass: Manufacturing Processes.* Sydney: Department of Planning, New South Wales.

Burke, H. 1999. *Meaning and Ideology in Historical Archaeology: Style, Social Identity, and Capitalism in an Australian Town.* New York: Kluwer Academic/Plenum Publishers.

Casella, E. 1996. "'One or Two Globular Lamps Made of Glass': Archaeology and the Cultural Landscapes of Tasmanian Convictism." In *Australian Archaeology 1995: Proceedings of the 1995 Australian Archaeological Association Annual Conference,* 257–264. Ed. S. Ulm, I. Lilley, and A. Ross. St. Lucia, Queensland: Anthropology Museum, University of Queensland.

———. 1997. "'A Large and Efficient Establishment': Preliminary Report on Fieldwork at the Ross Female Factory." *Australasian Historical Archaeology* 15: 79–89.

Colley, S. 1997. "A Pre-and Post-Contact Aboriginal Shell Midden at Disaster Bay, New South Wales South Coast." *Australian Archaeology* 45: 1–20.

Colley, S., and A. Bickford. 1996. "'Real' Aborigines and 'Real' Archaeology: Aboriginal Places and Australian Historical Archaeology." *World Archaeological Bulletin* 7: 5–21.

Connah, G. 1983. "Stamp-collecting or Increasing Understanding? The Dilemma of Historical Archaeology." *Australian Journal of Historical Archaeology* 1: 15–21.

———. 1986. "Historical Reality, Archaeological Reality: Excavations at Regentville, Penrith, NSW, 1985." *Australian Journal of Historical Archaeology* 4: 29–42.

———. 1988. *"Of the Hut I Builded": The Archaeology of Australia's History.* Cambridge: Cambridge University Press.

———. 1998. "Pattern and Purpose in Historical Archaeology." *Australasian Historical Archaeology* 16: 3–7.

Connah, G., M. Rowland, et al. 1978. *Captain Richards' House at Winterbourne: A Study in Historical Archaeology.* Armidale, New South Wales: Department of Prehistory and Archaeology, University of New England.

Culican, W., and J. Taylor. 1972. *Fossil Beach Cement Works, Mornington, Victoria: An Essay in Industrial Archaeology.* Deception Bay, Queensland: Refulgence Publishers.

Davies, M., and K. Buckley. 1987. *Archaeological Procedures Manual: Port Arthur Conservation and Development Project.* Hobart: Department of Lands, Parks, and Wildlife.

Egloff, B. 1984. "Cultural Resource Management, a View from Port Arthur Historic Site." *Australian Journal of Historical Archaeology* 2.

———. 1994. "From Swiss Family Robinson to Sir Russell Drysdale: Towards Changing the Tone of Historical Archaeology in Australia." *Australian Archaeology* 39: 1–9.

Gaughwin, D. 1993. "Chinese Settlement Sites in North East Tasmania: An Archaeological View." In *Histories of the Chinese in Australasia and the South Pacific: Proceedings of an International Public Conference Held at the Museum of Chinese Australian History Melbourne, 8–10 October 1993,* 230–248. Ed. P. MacGregor. Melbourne: Museum of Chinese Australian History.

Gestner, P. 1991. *Pandora: An Archaeological Perspective.* Brisbane: Queensland Museum.

Gojak, D. 1995. "Clay Tobacco Pipes from Cadman's Cottage, Sydney, Australia." *Society for Clay Pipe Research Newsletter* 48: 11–19.

Gojak, D., and N. Iacono. 1993. "The Archaeology and History of the Sydney Sailors Home, the

Rocks, Sydney." *Bulletin of the Australian Institute for Maritime Archaeology* 17, no. 1: 27–32.

Graham, M. 1979. *Australian Pottery of the Nineteenth and Early Twentieth Century.* Sydney: David Ell Press.

Green, J. 1973. "The Wreck of the Dutch East Indiaman the *Vergulde Draeck, 1656*." *International Journal of Nautical Archaeology* 2, no. 2: 267–289.

———. 1989. *The Loss of the Verenigde Oostindische Compagnie Retourschip* Batavia, *Western Australia, 1629: An Excavation Report and Catalogue of Artefacts.* Oxford: B.A.R.

Hosty, K., and I. Stuart. 1994. "Maritime Archaeology over the Last Twenty Years." *Australian Archaeology* 39: 9–18.

Ireland, T. Forthcoming. "Historical Archaeology and Australian Identity." In *Recent Work in Historical Archaeology in Australia and New Zealand.* Ed. S. Lawrence and G. Karskens. Society for Historical Archaeology.

Jack, R. I. 1985. "The Archaeology of Colonial Australia." In *Comparative Studies in the Archaeology of Colonialism,* 153–176. Ed. S. L. Dyson. Oxford: British Archaeological Reports S233.

Jack, R. I., and A. Cremin. 1994. *Australia's Age of Iron.* London and Sydney: Oxford University Press in association with Sydney University Press.

Karskens, G. 1984. "The Convict Road Station Site at Wiseman's Ferry: An Historical and Archaeological Investigation." *Australian Journal of Historical Archaeology* 2: 17–26.

———. 1996. *Cumberland / Gloucester Streets Site: Archaeological Investigation.* Vol. 2, *Main Report.* Sydney: Sydney Cove Authority.

———. 1997. "Crossing Over: Archaeology and History at the Cumberland / Gloucester Street Site, the Rocks, 1994–1996." *Public History Review* 5–6: 30–49.

———. 1999. *Inside the Rocks: The Archaeology of a Neighbourhood.* Sydney: Hale and Iremonger.

Karskens, G., and W. Thorpe, 1992. "History and Archaeology in Sydney: Towards Integration and Interpretation." *Journal of the Royal Australian Historical Society* 78, nos. 3–4: 52–75.

Kostoglou, P., and J. McCarthy. 1991. *Whaling and Sealing Sites in South Australia.* South Australian Maritime Archaeology Series no. 2. Special Publications no. 6. Adelaide: Department of Environment and Planning and Australian Institute for Maritime Archaeology.

Lawrence, S. 1999. "The Role of Material Culture in Australasian Archaeology." *Australasian Historical Archaeology* 16: 8–15.

———. 2000. *Dolly's Creek: An Archaeology of a Victorian Gold Rush Community.* Melbourne: Melbourne University Press.

Lydon, J. 1993. "Archaeology in the Rocks, Sydney, 1979–1993: From Old Sydney Gaol to Mrs. Lewis's Boarding House." *Australasian Historical Archaeology* 11: 33–42.

———. 1999. *Many Inventions: The Chinese in the Rocks 1890–1930.* Clayton, Victoria: Department of History, Monash University.

McCarthy, J. 1988. "The New Gold Mountain: Chinese Trade Networks in Northern Australia." In *Archaeology and Colonisation: Australia in the World Context.* Ed. J. Birmingham, D. Bairstow, and A. Wilson. Sydney: Australian Society for Historical Archaeology.

Mackay, R., and G. Karskens. 1999. "Historical Archaeology in Australia: Historical or Hysterical? Crisis or Creative Awakening?" *Australasian Historical Archaeology* 17: 110–115.

McKnight, C. 1976. *The Voyage to Marege: Macassan Trepangers in Northern Australia.* Melbourne: Melbourne University Press.

Mayne, A., and S. Lawrence. 1998. "An Ethnography of Place: Imagining 'Little Lon.'" *Journal of Australian Studies* 57: 93–107.

Megaw, J. V. S. 1984. "The Archaeology of Rubbish or Rubbishing Archaeology: Backward Looks and Forward Glances." *Australian Journal of Historical Archaeology* 2: 7–13.

Mulvaney, J. 1989. *Encounters in Place: Outsiders and Aboriginal Australians 1606–1985.* St. Lucia: University of Queensland Press.

Murray, T. 1985. "Historical Archaeology Losing its Way: Bairstow at the Theoretical Crossroads." *Australian Archaeology* 20: 121–132.

———. 1993. "The Childhood of William Lanne: Contact Archaeology and Aboriginality in Tasmania." *Antiquity* 67, no. 256: 504–519.

Murray, T., and J. Allen. 1986. "Theory and the Development of Historical Archaeology in Australia." *Archaeology in Oceania* 21: 85–93.

Murray, T., and A. Mayne. Forthcoming "(Re) Constructing a Lost Community: 'Little Lon,' Melbourne, Australia." In *Recent Work in Historical Archaeology in Australia and New Zealand.* Ed. S. Lawrence and G. Karskens. Society for Historical Archaeology.

Nash, M. 1990. "Survey of the Historic Ship *Litherland* (1834–1853)." *Bulletin of the Australian Institute for Maritime Archaeology* 14, no. 1.

———. 1997. *Cargo for the Colony: The Wreck of the Merchant Ship* Sydney Cove. Sydney: Braxus Press.

Nutley, D. 1995. "More than a Shipwreck: The Convict Ship *Hive,* Aboriginal and European Contact Site." Paper presented at joint conference of the Australasian Society for Historical Archaeology and the Australian Institute for Maritime Archaeology, Hobart.

Pearson, M. 1983. "The Technology of Whaling in Australian Waters in the 19th Century." *Australian Journal of Historical Archaeology* 1: 40–55.

———. 1984. "The Excavation of the Mount Wood Woolscour, Tibooburra, N.S.W." *Australian Journal of Historical Archaeology* 2: 38–50.

———. 1992. "From Ship to the Bush: Ship Tanks in Australia." *Australasian Historical Archaeology* 10: 24–29.

Staniforth, M. 1987. "The Casks from the Wreck of the *William Salthouse.*" *Australian Journal of Historical Archaeology* 5: 21–28.

———. 1995. *Dependent Colonies: The Importation of Material Culture into the Australian Colonies (1788–1850).* Underwater Archaeology Proceedings, SHA Conference 1995. Society for Historical Archaeology.

Staniforth, M., and M. Nash. 1998. *Chinese Export Porcelain from the Wreck of the* Sydney Cove *(1797).* Australian Institute for Maritime Archaeology.

Strachan, S. 1986. *The History and Archaeology of the* Sydney Cove *Shipwreck (1797): A Resource for Future Site Work.* Occasional Papers in Prehistory no. 5. Canberra: Australian National University.

Varman, R. 1979. *The Marseilles or French Pattern Tile in Australia.* Sydney: Australian Society for Historical Archaeology.

———. 1980. "The Nail as a Criterion for the Dating of Building and Building Sites (Late 18th Century to 1900)." *ASHA Bulletin* 10, no. 1.

Wesson, J. 1983. "A First Bibliography of Historical Archaeology in Australia." *Australian Journal of Historical Archaeology* 1: 22–34.

———. 1984. "A First Bibliography of Historical Archaeology in Australia Continued." *Australian Journal of Historical Archaeology* 2: 13–16.

Wilson, A. 1988. "A Failed Colonial Squire: Sir John Jamison at Regentville." In *Archaeology and Colonisation: Australia in the World Context.* Ed. J. Birmingham, D. Bairstow, and A. Wilson. Sydney: Australian Society for Historical Archaeology.

Australia, Prehistoric

The practice of archaeology in Australia has always been conditioned by two major factors: by ideas that European Australians have had about the nature and history of Aboriginal society and by the fact that European Australians have maintained a close and abiding interest in the history of European civilization. For the greater part of the last 200 years, archaeology in Australia has generally meant archaeology done by Australians in the Mediterranean and the Middle East, as part of a more general inquiry into the history of civilization and (more particularly) the archaeology of the Bible. This area remains a significant focus for archaeological activity by Australians, with courses in ancient history, art history, classics, and Near Eastern studies being offered at many Australian universities and with considerable funds being provided by the Australian government to support field research in ITALY, GREECE, CYPRUS, Egypt, TURKEY, JORDAN, and Syria.

Since the 1960s, however, there has been a tremendous growth of interest in the archaeology of Aboriginal Australia and in the historical archaeology of European settlement. During this period university departments teaching Australian archaeology have been established, legislation protecting the archaeological heritage of black and white Australians has been passed by state and federal departments, major government agencies (such as the Australian Heritage Commission) have been established to administer such legislation, thousands of sites have been located, recorded, and excavated, and Australian archaeology has acquired international prominence. By far the majority of Australian archaeologists work in this field, and it has now become clear that their discoveries have revolutionized white people's understanding of Aboriginal society in Australia. The implications of that improved understanding (particularly a growing acceptance of the value of Aboriginal Australia and of the need to restore self-determination to the traditional owners of the continent) have become powerful elements in contemporary Australian politics and society.

In this entry these two branches of Australian archaeology are discussed separately because,

Australian Prehistoric Archaeological Sites

notwithstanding the fact that they are frequently taught at the same universities (with students taking courses in both areas), there has been remarkably little professional contact between the two fields until recent times. This is partly explained by the real differences in technique and approach that exist between them, but these differences are just as great in the archaeology of Africa, Southeast Asia, and the Pacific, where many Australians also work. A more complete explanation would encompass an understanding

of the cultural and institutional contexts of the two fields and of their very different histories.

The Archaeology of European Civilization

Australians of European ancestry have long been interested in the history of European civilization. Although formal courses in the art and archaeology of the Mediterranean did not begin at the University of Sydney until 1946, the Nicholson Museum (the core collection of which was given to the university in 1860) became a focus for students of Classical antiquity before that time. In 1948 the Department of Archaeology was established, and the professor Dale Trendall (Australia's most eminent classical scholar) was joined by J. R. B. Stewart (who would become a professor) to expand offerings in the archaeology of Cyprus and the Middle East. Since then the teaching of classical and Middle Eastern archaeology has flourished, especially at the University of Sydney but also at the Universities of Melbourne, La Trobe, Macquarie, Monash, New England, Queensland, and Tasmania and at the Australian National University (ANU). Field research has been undertaken in Greece at Zagora on the island of Andros, at Torone in the Chalkidiki, and at Koukos near Sykia. Australian teams have also worked at Pompeii and I Fani in Italy, at Teleilat Ghassul and Pella in Jordan, and in Egypt, Cyprus, Turkey, the Persian Gulf, and Syria. Universities and the great state galleries and museums have not been the only sources of funding and inspiration for research into the archaeology of the Middle East. Indeed, one private foundation, the Australian Institute of Archaeology in Melbourne (founded in 1946 with a focus on using archaeology to prove the literal truth of the Bible) has made significant financial contributions to research and the education of the general public. The vigor of this field of archaeology is reflected in the recent founding of the journal *Mediterranean Archaeology* as a vehicle for the publication of research undertaken in Australia and elsewhere. Perhaps most significant was the foundation of the Australian Archaeological Institute at Athens. Begun in 1981 by Alexander Cambitoglou, then professor of Classical archaeology at Sydney University, the institute has developed into a significant force for the promotion of classical scholarship and has branches in all the states of Australia.

The Archaeology of Australia

Although the archaeology of Australia has only recently been taught in Australian universities, an interest in the archaeology of the region began with the European conquest of the continent in 1788. Detailed studies of Aboriginal life and customs were undertaken for a wide variety of purposes, but questions of origin and antiquity were always prominent. Where had the Aborigines come from? How long had they been in Australia? Were the inhabitants of Tasmania and the Aborigines of the mainland really the same people? What lessons could Europeans learn from the Aborigines?

It was soon recognized that the conquest of Australia would have disastrous consequences for the traditional landowners, as dispossession was frequently followed by death due to social dislocation, disease, and frontier violence. These factors underscored the conventional wisdom about "strong" races overcoming the "weak" and led to the widespread acceptance of the inevitability that traditional Aboriginal society would die out. This popular understanding gave further impetus to those hoping to record examples of the most savage (and hence most primitive) of all the human races, before all evidence of the "childhood of humanity" disappeared from view. Thus, from the first, an understanding of the antiquity of Aboriginal Australia and the need to document traditional societies under great stress became part of the same process. Archaeology, ethnography, and anthropology have had an enduring relationship in Australia ever since.

The sense that Australian Aborigines were a "people without history" stemmed from the fact that for the greater part of the nineteenth century European observers could not imagine a people more primitive than contemporary Aborigines. This meant either that Aboriginal society had remained fixed and unchanged since the initial colonization of Australia or that it had experienced periods of growth and stasis and degeneration over the centuries. In either case the contemporary inhabitants (particularly the Tasmanians) were believed to be the best examples of what Europeans had looked and behaved like long ago. Thus an important early stimulus to archaeological inquires was the sense that Europeans were documenting their own history in their studies of Australia. Yet there were always inconsistencies in this approach, especially when it was recognized that the real social and cultural differences between Aboriginal societies at contact were magnified by differences in

The entry to the cave site of Nunamira occupied during the last ice age in southwest Tasmania (Courtesy of Richard Cosgrove)

the physical features of Aboriginal populations. A further complication was the fact that this identified cultural variation included stone technologies that crossed both the Paleolithic (Old Stone Age) and the Neolithic (New Stone Age). Lastly, by the end of the nineteenth century, largely as a result of work undertaken by Australian geologists and paleontologists such as Edgeworth David, it was more widely appreciated that the physical geography of Australia had been far from static. Ice ages had carved glaciers, the sea levels had fallen and risen, and the climate of the continent had changed dramatically. The Aboriginal people of Australia were not fixed in time, but where had their history gone?

Although there had been a long tradition of private inquiries into Aboriginal culture—as manifested in collections of artifacts, in the proceedings of mainstream scientific societies such as the State Royal Societies, and in more low-key gatherings of naturalists and antiquarians—the sophisticated and systematic investigation into the archaeology of Australia did not really begin until the 1920s. The work of NORMAN TINDALE in south Australia and FRED MCCARTHY, first in New South Wales and later across the continent and into Southeast Asia, created a platform of data and interpretation that (although very much a reflection of contemporary cultural values) both identified and explained cultural change in precontact Aboriginal society. In concert with other researchers (such as D. S. Davidson), McCarthy and Tindale went on to produce foundational analyses of Aboriginal art and material culture that, though they had little impact on Australian society prior to the 1960s, made possible the phenomenal advances of professionally trained archaeologists since the early 1970s.

The recent history of Australian archaeology has been characterized by a rapid increase in the numbers of archaeologists, the expanding range of working environments (from universities and museums to private consultancies, government agencies, and Aboriginal organizations), the vast increase in government and private funds being applied to archaeological investigations, and the increasing importance attached by Australians to the archaeology of their country. Beginning with the appointment of JOHN MULVANEY to the History Department at Melbourne University in 1953 and greatly strengthened by appointments made to the Anthropology and Prehistory Departments at Sydney and ANU shortly afterward, the archaeology of Aboriginal Australia has become a very significant element in Australian culture. Since 1970, thousands of sites have been recorded and excavated, and our understanding of the human history of the continent has been transformed. Sites such as Lake Mungo have been placed on the World Heritage register, and the presence of significant cultural remains in Kakadu National Park and southwest Tasmania contributed to their World Heritage listings as well. Australians now understand that the Aboriginal history of their country exceeds 40,000 years and is marked by great cultural change and variety. Australian archaeology is taught in every mainland state and territory today, and it plugs into an increasingly complex infrastructure of government agencies created to administer heritage legislation and promote an understanding of Aboriginal Australia (such as the Australian Institute of Aboriginal and Torres Straits Islander Studies, founded in 1961). During this period Aboriginal people have reasserted their rights and interests in the investigation and management of their heritage. As a result Australian archaeologists of the modern era are more aware that they are investigating not the relics of a dead or dying society but the history of a living one. The implications of this fundamental change of focus have been very significant indeed.

Oceania, Asia, and the Archaeology of Contact

During this same period Australian archaeologists also paid increasing attention to the islands adjacent to the tropical coastlines. Although a great deal of the focus has been on Papua New Guinea and Melanesia, Australians have worked (and continue to work) in Timor, Indonesia, and Southeast Asia. Research initiatives, such as the Lapita Homeland Project organized by Jim Allen, first professor of archaeology at La Trobe University in Melbourne, were based on a perception that understanding the history of oceanic exploration and settlement required the assembly of an international team of researchers. Much the same thinking has supported a more consistent push by Australian-based researchers into China and south Asia.

Although there has long been a strong focus on establishing the antiquity of human occupation in Australia, the 1990s also witnessed a rapid expansion in contact archaeology, a branch of the general discipline that deals with the archaeology of Aboriginal Australia during the phase of initial contact by Europeans, Macassans, and, in some cases, Chinese. It is widely recognized that contact archaeology's subject matter can be more general than this—for example, it might cover longer periods of interaction between Aboriginal people and others at places such as mission stations as well as pastoral and industrial enterprises. Again the question of what constitutes contact is quite vexed because it is now understood that items of European material culture were entering Aboriginal societies well in advance of actual European exploration or settlement. This type of "wave effect" certainly applies to disease, for Aboriginal populations (particularly in the southeast of the continent) were already seriously jeopardized by the introduction of exotic viral and bacterial infections.

Interest in contact archaeology is increasing among archaeologists, but it has long been a significant inquiry for Aboriginal people. Although some see it as the archaeology of the "end" of traditional Aboriginal society and the beginning of European Australia, others are beginning to realize that contact studies might allow us to examine the archaeology of present-day Aboriginal Australia—particularly of Aboriginal communities that have been established since the middle of the nineteenth century. It is frequently difficult to identify Aboriginal people in the absence of identifiably Aboriginal material culture (such as stone tools), but archaeologists are developing approaches that integrate oral histories, archaeological investigation, and documentary evidence (such as maps, company records, private diaries, and the records of government departments) to overcome this "invisibility" factor.

The benefits of this new approach have been seen in our enhanced understanding of how Aboriginality has changed and developed in institutional environments such as the Lake Condah Mission (Victoria) and Wybalenna (Flinders Island). Contact sites associated with less-structured contexts, such as Macassan trepanging (sea slug harvesting) sites (northern Territory) or stock camps such as Burghley (Tasmania), are also being investigated.

Past, Present, and Future?

Understandings of the nature and significance of the human history of Australia have long had great influence beyond the shores of the island continent. In the nineteenth century (and well into the twentieth century), reports of the customs, technologies, and societies of indigenous Australians played a vital role in the development of anthropology and archaeology. Indigenous Australia was considered to be one of the great laboratories of "primitive" human beings. With the great expansion of archaeological research beginning in the 1960s, Australians came to understand the scale and richness of the history of Australia before the European invasion in the late eighteenth century. These developments also attracted the attention of archaeologists (particularly in the United States and the United Kingdom) who were keen to conduct ethno-archaeological studies among contemporary indigenous Australians. The primary purpose of these studies was to pursue inquiries about prehistoric society, technology, and human ecology on the world scale. These studies attracted considerable interest among local archaeologists, but by far the bulk of their attention was (and still is) firmly focused on establishing the antiquity of human beings on the continent and documenting the changing relationships between people and environment. The benefits deriving from this foundational work are undeniable, but they have led to a sense of theoretical stagnation within a discipline concentrated on absolute dating technologies as well as a decline in the impact of archaeology on Australian society. Thus, although the archaeology of Australia continues to pose great methodological and theoretical challenges to the field, the struggle to broaden the focus of research beyond a concentration on antiquity and human ecology is perhaps the greatest challenge of all.

Tim Murray

See also Australia, Historical; Golson, Jack; McCarthy, Fred; Papua New Guinea and Melanesia; Polynesia

References

For Mediterranean archaeology, see R. Sinclair, ed., *Past Present and Future: Ancient World Studies in Australia* (1990); R. S. Merrilees, *Living with Egypt's Past in Australia* (Melbourne: Museum of Victoria, 1990). For Australian archaeology, see Tom Griffiths, *Hunters and Collectors: The Antiquarian Imagination in Australia* (Cambridge: Cambridge University Press, 1996); D. J. Mulvaney, "The Australian Aborigines, 1606–1929: Opinion and Fieldwork, Parts I and II" (1957), *Historical Studies: Australia and New Zealand* 8: 131–151 and 297–314, and "A Sense of Making History: Australian Aboriginal Studies, 1961–1986" (1986), *Australian Aboriginal Studies*, no. 2: 48–56; T. Murray and J. P. White, "Cambridge in the Bush? Archaeology in Australia and New Guinea" (1981), *World Archaeology* 13, 2: 255–263; J. Golson, "Old Guards and New Waves: Reflections on Antipodean Archaeology, 1954–1975" (1986), *Archaeology in Oceania* 21: 2–12; and I. McBryde, "Australia's Once and Future Archaeology" (1986), *Archaeology in Oceania* 21: 13–28. For general discussions of relationships between archaeologists and Aboriginal people and of issues of heritage management, see T. Murray, "The Discourse of Australian Prehistoric Archaeology" (1992), in B. Attwood, ed., *Power, Knowledge, and Aborigines*, 1–19; I. McBryde, ed., *Who Owns the Past?* (Melbourne: Oxford University Press, 1985); H. Creamer, "Aboriginal Perceptions of the Past: The Implications for Cultural Resource Management in Australia" (1989), in P. Gathercole and D. Lowenthal, eds., *The Politics of the Past* (London: Unwin Hyman), 130–140; I.

Davidson, "Archaeologists and Aborigines" (1992), *Australian Journal of Anthropology* 2: 247–258; and J. Flood "'Tread Softly for You Tread on My Bones': The Development of Cultural Resource Management in Australia," (1989), in H. Cleere, ed., *Archaeological Heritage Management in the Modern World* (London: Unwin Hyman), 79–101.

The standard work on Australian prehistoric archaeology is D. J. Mulvaney and J. Kamminga, *The Prehistory of Australia,* 3d ed. (St. Leonards, NSW: Allen and Unwin, 1999). A useful collection of significant papers is T. Murray, ed., *Archaeology of Aboriginal Australia* (St. Leonards, NSW: Allen and Unwin,1998).

Austria

General Structure

Archaeology in Austria is carried out within two academic disciplines: classical archaeology and pre- and proto-history. The investigation of the Stone, Bronze, and Iron Ages is the domain of prehistory; the archaeology of the provinces of Raetia, Noricum, and Pannonia, in part coeval with the area of modern Austria is the domain of classical archaeology. Prehistorians study all of the areas north of the Danube, i.e., those that lay beyond the limits of the Roman Empire, in the Roman imperial period, migration period, and early Middle Ages. Generally speaking, medieval and historical archaeological research in Austria today is conducted more by prehistorians and less often by classical archaeologists. An exception to this rule is provided by the archaeological investigation of churches and urban centers, which is mainly conducted by classical archaeologists. The study of the epigraphic finds, so important for Roman provincial history, is the domain of ancient history, and ancient coins found in the country are the province of numismatists. In Austria, provincial Roman archaeology is not an independent discipline.

The Prescientific Period

One of the first scholars interested in antiquities in Austria was Thomas Ebendorfer von Haselbach (1387–1464), who founded the discipline of history at the University of Vienna. Other scholars in the humanist tradition linked to the court of Emperor Maximilian I included Konrad Celtis and Johannes Cuspinian; later there were Carolus Clusius and Wolfgang Lazius, the latter the first scholar to publish on the Roman monuments of Vienna and to inspire a corpus of ancient coins. The first collections began at this time, and the imperial collection in Vienna and the antiquarian collection in Ambras Castle in the Tirol should be noted. The most important find of this period is the Jüngling of Magdalensberg ("youth" or "young man of Magdalensberg"), which was discovered in state of Carinthia (German, Kärnten) in 1502.

During the Baroque era, the research of Johann Dominikus Prunner in Zollfeld (Carinthia) and the excavations of Maximilian III in Carnuntum took place. In the eighteenth century, the Münz- und Antikenkabinett (Cabinet of Coin and Antiquities) was established; today, they are departments of the Kunthistorischen Museum Wien (Viennese Museum of Art). Johann Josef Hilarius Eckhel, who took over the directorship of this collection in 1774, was also appointed to the chair of Altertümer und historischen Hilfsmittel (Antiquities and Historical Sources) at the University of Vienna.

Beginning in the middle of the eighteenth century, the collection of archaeological finds intensified—for example, Franz Steinkogler of Hallstatt collected Roman objects that have remained in the Mathematischen Turm (Mathematical Tower) of the Kremsmünster Monastery. In the early nineteenth century, reports of finds began to increase, and regional museums were founded, beginning with the Joanneum in Graz (1811), followed by the Ferdinandeum in Innsbruck (1823) and the Oberösterreichische Landesmuseum (Upper Austrian Regional Museum, 1833).

Among the scientific organizations founded in this period, the Geschichtsverein für Kärnten (Kärnten Historical Society), established in 1843, is particularly important. Not only does it publish one of the oldest and most important regional scholarly journals, *Carinthia,* but it also undertook the earliest excavations at Magdalensberg. In 1840, Johann Gabriel Seidl, an employee of the Münz- und Antikenkabinett, began to compile a collection of all notices of finds and their publications. In this way, *Carinthia* came to be the most important scientific journal for Austrian archaeology.

Provincial Roman Archaeology

Most of the scholarly institutions concerned with classical archaeology were founded during the second half of the nineteenth century. In 1869, Alexander Conze was appointed to the newly established Lehrkanzel für Klassische Archäologie (Chair of Classical Archaeology) at the University of Vienna, and together with Otto Hirschfeld (holder of the Lehrkanzel für römische Geschichte, Altertumskunde, und Epigraphik [Chair of Roman History, Archaeology, and Epigraphy]) he founded the Archäologisch-epigraphische Seminar (Archaeological-Epigraphic Institute) in 1876. Conze was followed in the Chair of Classical Archaeology by Otto Benndorf, Emil Reisch, Camillo Praschniker, Otto Walter, Fritz Eichler, Hedwig Kenner, and Jürgen Borchhardt.

Other institutions founded in Vienna included the Archäologisch-philologische Gesellschaft (Archaeological-Philological Society) at the University of Vienna. Established in 1889, today it is known as Eranos Vindobonensis, as well as the Kommission zur Erforschung des römischen Limes (Commission for the Study of the Roman Limes). Limes are the boundaries of Roman defense and influence. Established by the Academy of Sciences in 1889 as a result of a proposal from Friedrich von Kenner, the commission publishes the series *Der römische Limes in Österreich (RLÖ)* [The Roman Limes in Austria]. At the instigation of Otto Benndorf, the Österreichische Archäologische Institut (Austrian Archaeological Institute) was founded in 1898. Benndorf's successors as director included Robert von Schneider, Emil Reisch, Camillo Praschniker, Rudolf Egger, Josef Keil, Otto Walter, Fritz Eichler, Hermann Vetters, and Gerhard Langmann. The institute not only organizes numerous excavations, it also publishes excavation reports on Roman provincial sites in the supplements of its *Jahreshefte* [Yearbooks].

The Institute für Klassische Archäologie (Institute of Classical Archaeology) of the University of Graz was founded in 1895 (the first professor in 1890 was Wilhelm Gurlitt, followed by Rudolf Heberdey, Arnold Schober, Erna Diez, and Hanns-Thuri Lorenz), and the Institute für Klassische Archäologie of the University of Innsbruck was begun in 1899 (professors since World War II were Alfons Wotschitzky, Bernhard Neuss, and Elisabeth Walde). Both of these institutes concentrated on the art history aspects of classical archaeology in the Roman provinces. Studies of funerary monuments and bronzes were particularly stressed. More recently, settlement studies and research on Roman villas have been carried out. Provincial Roman archaeology has been represented at the University of Salzburg since the 1970s in the Institut für Alte Geschichte (Institute of Ancient History) where Norbert Heger, Kurt Genser, and Erwin M. Ruprechtsberger have been active in the field.

In addition to the national institutions already named, regional ones have carried out the bulk of the fieldwork in the field of provincial Roman archaeology in Austria. It is impossible to name all of the regional and city museums, associations, institutes, and their members who have been involved in this work (for more information see Niegl 1980). Most of the significant cities of Austria Romana, including Carnuntum, Vindobona, Solva, Teurnia, Virunum, Aguntum, Lauriacum, Lentia, Iuvavum, Veldidena, and Brigantium, have been investigated, though only rarely have architectural remains been preserved. Exceptions include the Archäologische Park Carnuntum (Carnuntum Archaeological Park), adjacent to the Museum Carnuntinum (established 1904) as well as the site displays created by Gernot Piccottini at Magdalensberg and by Wilhelm Alzinger at Aguntum.

Of the many archaeologists involved in such work, some of the outstanding ones who were active in the early twentieth century were Maximilian Groller von Mildensee, Friedrich von Kenner, Wilhelm Kubitschek, Rudolf Egger, Erich Swoboda, Arnold Schober, Rudolf Noll, and Hedwig Kenner. The focus of their work was, in addition to art history problems, early Christian monuments and the Roman *limes*. In his book on the provincial capital Carnuntum (reprinted three times), Erich Swoboda, professor of ancient history at the University of Graz, combined the results of archaeological field-work with provincial Roman history. Treatments of grave and votive inscriptions were undertaken by ancient historians beginning with Otto Hirschfeld and Eugen Bormann who worked on *Corpus inscriptionum latinarum* III with Theodor Mommsen. Today, this tradition is carried on by Ekkehard Weber and Manfred Hainzmann. The numerous publications of Fritz Lochner-Hüttenbach are also noteworthy.

Supraregional, monographic studies of small finds are rare. Ceramic research was initiated by August Schörgendorfer and Éva Bónis (Hungary), and *terra sigillata* (red ware pottery) studies were begun by Paul Karnitsch (Austria). Lamps were first systematically studied by Franz Miltner (Austria); *fibulae* (broaches) by Ilona Kovrig (Hungary) and Jochen Garbsch (Germany); bronzes by Robert Fleischer (Austria); bronze vessels by Aladar Radnóti (Hungary); and bricks by Alfred Neumann (Austria). These subjects are researched today by numerous archaeologists working in various parts of Austria. The bibliography in the journal *Pro Austria Romana* gives a good overview of this material. The *Kärntner Museumsschriften* [Kärnten Museum Series] and *Der römische Limes in Österreich* [The Roman *limes* in Austria] are two important series in which individual categories of finds are treated in monograph-length studies.

Research Foci since 1960

The establishment in 1966 by the Austrian Academy of Sciences of the Kommission für das Corpus der Skulpturen der Römischen Welt (CSIR, Commission for the Corpus of Sculpture in the Roman World) is an initiative in which many archaeologists, both from the regional museums and from the Federal Monuments Authority (Bundesdenkmalamt), participate. In 1969, a second chair in Klassische Archäologie mit besonderer Berücksichtigung der Feldarchäologie (Classical Archaeology with Particular Attention to Field Archaeology) was established. First occupied by Vetters, it has also been led by Fritz Krinzinger. Since 1978, the Numismatische Kommission der Österreichischen Akademie der Wissenschaften (Numismatic Commission of the Austrian Academy of Sciences), under the direction of the late Robert Göbl, has published *Die Fundmünzen der römischen Zeit in Österreich* [Numismatic Finds of the Roman Period in Austria]. Thus, for the systematic cataloging of individual categories of material, the various commissions established by the Austrian Academy of Sciences since the 1960s have been of enormous value, particularly since old groups of finds have been restudied in their entirety and published in a new, improved format.

Today, archaeological research in Carinthia is particularly noteworthy, e.g., Piccottini's investigations of traces of early Roman settlement at Magdalensberg and Franz Glaser's work on early Christian churches at Hemmaberg and a late antique bishopric in Teurnia. Such research projects, carried out systematically over a number of years with the results regularly published, are a hallmark of Austrian archaeology.

Another area of research focus is the Roman *limes*. In recent decades Herma Stiglitz and Hannsjörg Ubl have undertaken numerous excavations, although final publications for most of their sites have yet to appear. As a result it is difficult to get an overview of the excavations of Carnuntum, the most important Roman city in Austria, particularly as excavations have been carried out at numerous locales and only rarely published in a coordinated way. Around Carnuntum the damage done by illicit excavators working with metal detectors is clear, as are the problems created by so much uncoordinated fieldwork. Thus, one must conclude that the fragmentation of the research efforts of a relatively small number of investigators among such a large group of institutions and publications is an unfortunate characteristic of provincial Roman archaeology in Austria. The journal *Pro Austria Romana*, founded by Rudolf Noll in 1951, and the annual Österreichische Archäologentage (Austrian Archaeologists Meetings), which began in 1983, have been helpful in facilitating the exchange of up-to-date information. The most important major congress in recent years was the 14. Internationale Limeskongreß (Fourteenth International Limes Congress) held in Carnuntum in 1986 (proceedings published in *RLÖ* in 1990).

Prehistory

Prehistoric research in Austria began slightly later than classical archaeology. The foundations of prehistoric inquiry were laid down by Moritz Hoernes around 1860, albeit not in an academic context. In 1870, the Anthropologische Gesellschaft in Wien (Anthropological Society of Vienna) was founded under the leadership of Ferdinand Freiherr von Andrian-Werburg, and the subjects of prehistory, ethnography, ethnology, and physical anthropology all found a common home there. A prehistoric collection was displayed in the Anthropologisch-ethnographischen Abteilung (Department of Anthropology and Ethnography) of the Naturhistorischen Hofmuseum (Imperial Museum of Natural History), founded in 1889. In 1878, the Prähistorische Commission (Prehistoric Commission) of the Kaiser was founded by the Akademie der Wissenschaften (Imperial Academy of Sciences), under the chairmanship Ferdinand von Hochstetter.

In 1889, Hoernes described Eduard Freiherr von Sacken and Ferdinand von Hochstetter as the two prongs of prehistoric research in Austria, and the division between theoreticians (Sacken) and practitioners (Hochstetter), so typical of Austrian prehistory, was already apparent. Hoernes received the first lectureship in prehistoric archaeology at the University of Vienna in 1893; in 1899, he was appointed to an extraordinary position, albeit in geography; and in 1911, he was given an established chair. Thus, the prehistoric research institutions, which remain important to this day, were all established in Vienna in the second half of the nineteenth century.

Hoernes's study of classical archaeology, his work in the Natural History Museum, and his association with the Anthropological Society laid the foundation for the three research interests that are prominent in his major publications: prehistory as an historical discipline (*Die Urgeschichte des Menschen nach dem heutigen Stand der Wissenschaft* [Prehistory of Mankind in the Light of Current Research], 1892); prehistoric archaeology in the sense of an art history of the remote past (*Urgeschichte der bildenden Kunst in Europa* [Prehistory of the Fine Arts in Europe],

1898); and prehistory as an anthropological discipline with links to physical anthropology and ethnology (*Natur und Urgeschichte des Menschen* [Nature and Prehistory of Mankind], 1909). Hoernes was, first and foremost, a compiler, but in his later years he was also a teacher.

Following Hoernes, Oswald Menghin thought of prehistoric archaeology as a branch of universal history. His close connection with the Viennese school of ethnology, which was deeply influenced by the culture area *(Kulturkreis)* theories of Father Wilhelm Schmidt, influenced Menghin's view of history, which is made clear in his major work *Die Welgeschichte der Steinzeit* [World History of the Stone Age]. The geographical breadth of Menghin's lectures attracted many foreign students as well, and this breadth, which extended well beyond the confines of Austria, is clearly reflected in the Wiener Prähistorische Gesellschaft (Viennese Prehistory Society, which emerged in 1914 from the Anthropological Society and returned to it after 1945) and its journal, *Wiener Prähistorische Zeitschrift* [Viennese Journal of Prehistory].

In 1945, after World War II, Richard Pittioni became the new professor at the University of Vienna. In his *Urgeschichte des österreichischen Raumes* [Prehistory of the Austrian Region], Pittioni elaborated a systematic view of Austrian prehistory, the roots of which were first published in 1937. This work was last revised in 1980. Methodological questions were of particular interest for both Menghin and Pittioni. In this regard, the position of prehistory within a family tree of the sciences was of particular interest, as was its relationship to related disciplines and to complementary natural sciences. In addition, Pittioni was responsible for a sophisticated terminology. On the other hand, his use of parallels between prehistoric find complexes and sociological entities seems too mechanical now, and his overall presentation of prehistory seems too schematic.

J. Ramsauer's excavations in the cemetery at Hallstatt between 1846 and 1863 mark the beginning of scientific excavations in Austria, and Ferdinand von Hochstetter's work was also significant. At the request of the Academy of Sciences, Hochstetter introduced lake-dwelling research into Austria (originally pioneered in SWITZERLAND) in 1864 and continued the excavations at Hallstatt. His student Josef Szombathy was also an active excavator, and Matthäus Much was an important contemporary—it was he who discovered and first excavated a great number of prehistoric sites. Although Much's interpretations can no longer be maintained, his collection still forms the core of the study collection of the Institut für Ur- und Frühgeschichte (Institute of Pre- and Proto-history) of the University of Vienna (founded in 1917 and renamed many times). Szombathy was followed as director of the Prähistorischen Abteilung (Department of Prehistory) by Josef Bayer, who conducted numerous important excavations in lower Austria and was in many ways the opposite of Oswald Menghin.

At about the same time, the Bundesdenkmalamt (Federal Monuments Authority) began regular rescue excavations at archaeological sites threatened by destruction. The work of Julius Caspart, who had already begun photogrammetric documentation in the 1930s, is a good example of the excavation techniques of this era, and building on his experiences in Switzerland, Fritz Felgenhauer became particularly active in rescue excavation after World War II. Most of the leading prehistorians of today gained practical excavation experience via the Urgeschichtlichen Arbeitsgemeinschaft (Prehistoric Working Group), which was founded in 1950 as a part of the Anthropological Society and today is known as the Österreichische Gesellschaft für Ur- und Frühgeschichte (Austrian Society of Pre- and Proto-history). In 1964, F. Felgenhauer became extraordinary professor at the University of Vienna and ordinary professor in 1973. He was succeeded in 1992 by Andreas Lippert.

In addition to the University of Vienna, the University of Innsbruck has also taught pre- and proto-history since 1940, and Gero von Merhart was employed there as a lecturer as early as 1923–1927. After Kurt Willvonseder held the extraordinary professorship there for several months, Leonhard Franz was appointed to an ordinary professorship in 1942, and a separate institute was established. Franz was followed by

Karl Kromer in 1967 and then by Konrad Spindler. In addition, an extraordinary professorship, to which Osmund Menghin was appointed, came into being in 1970. During this period, two prehistorians in regional museums received their habilitations, or doctorates, Walter Modrijan in Graz (1966), who became honorary professor of pre- and proto-history at the University of Salzburg in 1971, and Elmar Vonbank in Innsbruck (1967). In 1976, Ämilian Kloiber was appointed to a professorship in burial archaeology at the University of Graz.

During the 1950s, Paleolithic research in Austria reached a high point under F. Felgenhauer. In the 1960s, international standards of archaeological research, marked by interdisciplinary inquiry involving diverse earth and biological sciences, could not be achieved, and it was not until the 1980s that new research began—for example, that by Gernot Rabeder (continued by George Kyrle and his followers' tradition of cave research in Austria) and Christine Neugebauer-Maresch. The Neolithic period has been increasingly investigated by Elisabeth Ruttkays, who has built on the results achieved by Pittioni. Ruttkays has been followed by Eva Lenneis and Neugebauer-Maresch. Interdisciplinary projects of the sort found elsewhere in the world, for example, research on the domestication and exploitation of plants and animals, have only been conducted on a very modest scale. Thanks to the intensive use of aerial photography, numerous Neolithic ditchworks (Kreisgrabenanlagen) have been discovered, and since the 1980s, these have been investigated systematically by Gerhard Trnka.

Bronze Age finds from the Salzkammergut damp-ground settlements/waterlogged sites (Feuchtbodensiedlungen), originally published by Much and Willvonseder have now been restudied in the context of smaller projects led by Ruttkays to compare them with material from northern Italy and southern Germany. Underwater archaeological research is being carried out by Hans Offenberger. The early and middle Bronze Ages have been investigated by Horst Adler, who carried out the first analysis of associated types in a cemetery at Linz, as well as Zoja Benkovsky and Johannes-Wolfgang Neuge-

Four-thousand-year-old body discovered in an Austrian glacier (Gamma)

bauer. For the late Bronze Age (Urnfeld period), the cemetery studies of Clemens Eibner and the long-term settlement excavations of F. Felgenhauer and Herwig Friesinger are particularly noteworthy.

Research into the early Iron Age (Hallstatt period) has concentrated on the eponymous site of Hallstatt. New excavations begun there by Karl Kromer in the 1960s were taken over by Fritz Eckart Barth and continue to this day. The excavations of the prehistoric salt mines of Hallstatt are not only unique in Austria but constitute an important research focus of mining archaeology in a broader European context. Two research projects are of particular importance for the late Iron Age (LA TÈNE period): the excavations of Dürrnberg bei Hallein in Salzburg and Magdalensberg in Kärnten. *Die Kelten in Österreich* [The Celts in Austria] by Gerhard Dobesch, professor at the Institute of Ancient History in Vienna, brings together all of the ancient sources for this period and forms the foundation for the historical interpretation of the relevant archaeological remains.

In general, it can be said that settlement archaeology has been most prominent since the 1960s, whether studies of specific settlement areas (e.g., Stillfried), valley systems (e.g., the Kamp, Inn, and Danube Valleys), or larger regions (e.g., the Bischofshofen area). Thematic investigations, such as the mining study of the Grauwacken area and the establishment by Franz Hampl of an open-air museum in Asparn on the Zaya River in the 1960s (opened in 1970), are also important. Similarly, the development of modern archaeological techniques, particularly aerial photography, has been significant. The large-scale investigations of the numerous prehistoric cemeteries and settlements of the Traisental (lower Austria) have opened up entirely new perspectives. For the first time, large cemeteries have been excavated and salvaged, and beginning in 1981, Neugebauer has been in charge of some ongoing, year-round salvage excavations.

Proto-history
In 1940, Eduard Beninger became the first Austrian to write a doctoral thesis dealing with

proto-history, and he was followed by Herbert Mitscha-Märheim, Herwig Friesinger, and Falk Daim. Proto-history was still not recognized as a separate discipline as late as 1952, as is shown by the fact that Mitscha-Märheim's *venia legendi* (right-to-lecture qualification) from the University of Vienna included the awkward title "non-Roman archaeology of the first millennium in Central Europe." In 1949, a Conseil du Haute Moyen-Age (Council of the High Middle Ages) was formed in Linz, and members included, among others, Wilhelm Albert R. von Jenny, Rudolf Egger, Erich Zollner, and Mitscha-Märheim.

Thanks to the systematic study of Germanic, Avar, and Slavic finds by Friesinger and students of Mitscha-Märheim (who succeeded to the chair formerly held by Pittioni in 1978), the state of proto-history publications is relatively good. Peter Stadler's studies on the seriation of Avar cemeteries have broken new ground, methodologically speaking, in terms of both chronology and spatial analysis. A series edited by Daim entitled *Studien zur Archäologie der Awaren* [Studies in the Archaeology of the Avars] publishes work by many colleagues in countries east of Austria. Close cooperation with the Institut für österreichische Geschichtsforschung (Institute of Austrian Historiography) has been particularly stimulating and has led to important discussions of ethnogenesis as well as to academic conferences in neighboring countries, including the regular symposia on *Ausgewählten Problemen der Frühgeschichte* [Selected Problems of Protohistory].

One of the first articles on medieval ceramics was by Beninger (Beninger 1958), and for this reason he can be considered a pioneer in the field of medieval archaeology. Later scholars active in this area included Hertha Ladenbauer-Orel, for city and church excavations; F. Felgenhauer, who founded an archive for medieval archaeology; and Pittioni, who in 1976 proposed the creation of a Kommission für Mittelalter-Archäologie (Commission for Medieval Archaeology) within the Prehistoric Commission of the Austrian Academy of Sciences. In 1989, Sabine Felgenhauer completed a doctorate in medieval archaeology, and in 1992, Daim

was appointed to an extraordinary professorship in proto-history and medieval archaeology at the Institute of Pre- and Protohistory of the University of Vienna.

The roots of the archaeology of the modern era go back to the terms *Industriearchäologie* ("industrial archaeology") and *Gasthausarchäologie* ("inn" or "hotel archaeology") introduced by Pittioni in 1968 and 1969, respectively. Thereafter, rescue excavations took place in advance of major building projects in, for example, Salzburg and Vienna. In 1989, Spindler's activities in this regard were recognized institutionally with the establishment of an Abteilung für Mittelalterarchäologie und Neuzeitliche Archäologie (Department of Medieval and Modern Archaeology) in the Institute of Pre- and Protohistory. Methodologically speaking, "modern" archaeology remains closely linked to medieval archaeology. Industrial archaeological investigations have been particularly important along the Steirisch rail line, and practitioners in this field have recently investigated battlefields and remains of World War II. The significance of such sites was discussed at a symposium convened in 1990, but most participants were sceptical of their worth.

Protection of Monuments

With respect to archaeological excavation and the protection of sites and finds, the highest civic authority in Austria is the Bundesdenkmalamt, which succeeded the Zentralkommission zur Erforschung und Erhaltung der kunst- und historischen Denkmale (Imperial Central Commission for the Investigation and Preservation of Historical and Artistic Monuments). The role of the Department of Sites is to make determinations regarding the protection of endangered sites and monuments as well as to organize and carry out salvage excavations in Austria. However, because of a general policy of not using consultants, the personnel of the department are often overworked. Other duties, consistent with those of monuments authorities elsewhere, include the maintenance of a country-wide registry of all archaeological sites as well as assistance with conservation and restoration projects. Normally regional archaeologists (e.g.,

Fritz Moosleitner in Salzburg, Diether Kramer in Steiermark, and Karl Kaus in Burgenland) collaborate with the Bundesdenkmalamt on salvage excavations, but the ultimate responsibility for these excavations rests with the Department of Sites within the Bundesdenkmalamt.

Education

Today, there are two institutes of pre- and proto-history and four institutes of classical archaeology in Austria. Pre- and proto-history are taught at the Universities of Vienna and Innsbruck, and classical archaeology is offered at the Universities of Vienna, Salzburg, Graz, and Innsbruck. In addition, archaeology is taught in the Institute of Ancient History at the University of Salzburg. Roughly half of the lecturers are not employed by the universities but teach in addition to their regular work in museums or the Bundesdenkmalamt.

Archaeology in Austria Today

The fragmentation of archaeology into different academic disciplines has led to the frequent absence of fruitful, positive discussion. Moreover, it has made it much more difficult to gain a synthetic view of the country's past. To date, interdisciplinary research institutes with particular thematic concentrations have not been established, and the fact that most projects, financed by grants, are funded only over the short term hardly helps matters. Even sensational new finds, such as the Bronze Age Ice Man discovered in 1991, fail to improve the situation.

Compared to similar institutions in other countries the Austrian Bundesdenkmalamt functions poorly. The general regard in which archaeology is held in Austria is low, and the legal foundations of the relevant legislation concerning sites and monuments are often divorced from reality. Fulfilling the requirements of the existing laws is almost impossible, and the cooperation between regional and federal offices required by the archaeological research increases the difficulties of compliance.

Moreover, a publicly available register of all protected sites and monuments, and clear signs in the landscape to point them out to visitors, are lacking, so the public is scarcely aware that certain sites are, in fact, protected. The Österreichisches Nationalkomitee zur Koordination und Beratung im Bereich der archäologischen Forschung Österreichs (Austrian National Committee for Coordination and Advice on Archaeological Research in Austria), an advisory council, has as its main task a long overdue review and reorganization of the structures in place. Coordination of all federal, regional, and local offices; amateur investigators; and folk museums and a definition of their jurisdictions and responsibilities, along with the identification of opportunities for cooperation in the protection of monuments and the prosecution of research, would be highly desirable.

Otto H. Urban; translated by Dan Potts

See also Czech Republic; German Prehistoric
　　Archaeology; Slovenia
References
Betz, A., and E. Weber. 1990. *Aus Osterreichs romischer Vergangenheit, Osterr.* Vienna: Bundesverlag.
Dobesch, G. 1980. *Die Kelten in Osterreich nach den altesten Berichten der Antike.* Vienna: Bohlaus Nachf.
Ehrenberger, K. 1962. "Georg Kyrtes Wirken als Spelaologe und fur die Spelaologie." *Die Hohle* 13: 33–39.
Felgenhauer, F. 1965. "Zur Geschichte des Faches 'Urgeschichte' an der Universitat Wien." In *Studien zur Geschichte der Universitat Wien* 3: 7–27. Graz and Cologne: Bohlaus Nachf.
———. 1971. "Stand und Aufgaben der Mittelalterarchaologie in Osterreich, Burgen-und Siedlungsarchaologie des Mittelalters." *Veroffentl. D. Osterr. Arbeitsgem. F. Ur-u. Fruhgesch.* 5: 18–21.
Friesinger, H., and B. Vacha. 1987. *Die vielen Vater Osterreichs.* Vienna: Compress.
Genser, K. 1986. *Der osterreichische Donaulimes in der Romerzeit. Der romische Limes in Osterreich* 33. Vienna: Verlag der Österreichischen Akademie der Wissensschaften.
Hoernes, M. 1889–1890. "Die Prahistorie in Osterreich." *Archiv fur Anthropologe.* 18: 289–295, 346–360; 19: 101–110.
———. 1892. *Die Urgeschichte des Menschen nach dem heutigen Stand der Wissenschaft.* Vienna: Hartleben.
———. 1898. *Urgeschichte der bildenden Kunst in Europa.* Vienna: Holzhausen. 2d ed., Vienna: Schroll, 1915.

The Cove in Avebury, England (Corel)

————. 1909. *Natur und Urgeschichte des Menschen.* Vienna: Hartlelen.

Jakubovitsch, H. 1991. "Die Forschungsgeschichte des Faches Ur- und Fruhgeschichte." Dissertation, University of Vienna.

Kandler, M., and H. Vetters. 1986. *Der romische Limes in Osterreich.* Vienna: OAW.

Kenner, H., G. Dobesch, and E. Kirsten. 1977. *Hundert Jahre Institut fur Alte Geschichte, Archaologie und Epigraphik der Universitat Wien 1876–1976.* Vienna: Eigenverlag.

Lippert, A., ed. 1985. *Reclams Archaologiefuhrer Osterreich und Sudtirol.* Stuttgart: Reclam.

Menghin, Osmund. 1974. "Leonhard Franz und das Institut fur Vor- und Fruhgeschichte der Universitat Innsbruck." *Innsbr. Beitr. Z Kulturwiss.*

Menghin, Oswald. 1957. "Urgeschichtliche Grundfragen." *Historia Mundi* 1: 229–258.

Niegl, M. A. 1980. *Die archaologische Erforschung der Romerzeit in Osterreich.* Denkschr., phil-hist. Kl. D. Oster. Acad. D. Wiss. 141.

Pittioni, R. 1954. *Urgeschichte des osterreichischen Raumes.* Vienna: Deuticke.

————. 1976. "Aufgaben und Moglichkeiten der Kommission fur Burgenforschung und Mittelalter-Archaologie." *Anz. Phil.-hist. Kl. Oster. Akad. Wiss.* 113: 339 ff.

Swoboda, E. 1958. *Carnuntum.* 3d ed. Graz and Cologne: Bohlaus Nachf.

Urban, O. H. 1989. *Wegweiser in die Urgeschichte Osterreichs, Osterr.* Vienna: Bundersverlag.

Vetters, H. 1973. *75 Jahre Osterreichisches-Archaologisches Institut.* Vienna: Eigenverlag.

————. 1977. "Austria." In *European Towns: Their Archaeology and Early History,* 261–290. Ed. M. W. Barley. London: Academic Press.

————. 1989. "Archaologie in Osterreich 1945–1985." *Rom. Hist. Mitt.* 31: 41–52.

Avebury

Located in southern England, the site of Avebury comprises a large enclosure that features extensive earthworks and arrangements of standing stones of the late Neolithic age. First brought to prominence by the patient recording work of WILLIAM STUKELEY in the eighteenth century, the site has been much damaged, and many of the standing stones have been buried or broken up. Stukeley's map is therefore invaluable, and its accuracy has been confirmed by excavation and nondisturbing REMOTE SENSING techniques such as aerial photography. Avebury and the slightly later site of Stonehenge have often been compared as they both stand at the center of large landscapes featuring earthworks and other associated sites. Located in the Avebury landscape are the West Kennet Long Barrow, Windmill Hill (both earlier than the mon-

Lord Avebury, from an 1884 print (Ann Ronan Picture Library)

ument itself), and Silbury Hill (roughly contemporaneous with Avebury).

Tim Murray

References

Burl, Aubrey. 1979. *Prehistoric Avebury*. New Haven: Yale University Press.

Avebury, Lord (Sir John Lubbock, 1834–1913)

Best known to archaeologists as the author of *Prehistoric Times* (which went through seven editions from 1865 to 1913), Sir John Lubbock was also prodigiously talented in other areas. Born into a titled family (his father was a baronet), Lubbock went to Eton and then entered the family banking business. However, in common with many people of his social standing in England, Lubbock spent his time away from banking engaged in a wide range of scientific pursuits. In this respect he was following in the footsteps of his father, who was an amateur astronomer and a friend of Charles Darwin. Lubbock's views on natural history (and eventually on human evolution) were strongly influenced by Darwin. Equally, Lubbock's position as an influential Victorian scientist (he held offices in the Royal Society, the British Association for the Advancement of Science, the Geological Society of London, and the Linnaean Society, among others) was of great value to Darwin when the time came to promote public acceptance of his account of the evolution of life on earth.

Notwithstanding his activities as a banker, member of Parliament, vice-chancellor of the University of London, and keen student of insects and wildflowers, Lubbock's enduring fame results from his central role in the foundation of prehistoric archaeology in Great Britain. Through the publication of *Prehistoric Times* and a later work, *The Origins of Civilization* (1870), Lubbock set much of the agenda for the emerging science of prehistoric archaeology. His keen interest in the antiquity of human beings, his classification of the Stone Age into Paleolithic (old Stone Age) and Neolithic (new Stone Age), and his firm belief that the purpose of archaeology (and anthropology) was to demonstrate the essential unity of human beings did much to establish the public face of prehistoric archaeology as a legitimate scientific pursuit. This work bore fruit in 1882 when, as a member of Parliament for the University of London, Lubbock's long years of advocacy paid off with the passage of the first Ancient Monuments Protection Act, a measure designed to preserve the physical remains of the prehistory of Britain.

After the passage of this Act, Lubbock's fascination with prehistoric archaeology had to compete more directly with his other research in natural history, but he continued to serve as a senior member of the core anthropological and archaeological societies in Britain and to carry on a voluminous correspondence with scholars from all over the world. Lubbock's advocacy of the THREE-AGE SYSTEM was instrumental in its ac-

ceptance in England, but subsequent research indicates that his translation of Swedish archaeologist SVEN NILSSON's *The Primitive Inhabitants of Scandinavia* (1868) stressed an evolutionary message that was somewhat at odds with the original text. There is no modern biography of Lubbock.

Tim Murray

See also Britain, Prehistoric Archaeology

Aztecs

"Aztecs" is the name popularly used today to label the people of central MEXICO that Hernán Cortés conquered in 1521. Actually, "the Aztecs" never used the term to describe themselves; rather, they were Nahuatl-speaking peoples divided into about twenty different ethnic groups. The most famous of these groups, and the preeminent one when the Spaniards arrived in Mexico, were the Mexica, whose capital was TENOCHTITLÁN.

An Aztec calendar stone (North Wind Picture Archives)

The Mexica arrived in the basin of Mexico (where Mexico City stands today) probably some time during the thirteenth century A.D. According to their own legends, they arrived as an impoverished, uncouth group into a region that was already fairly fully occupied by a series of kingdoms. They were despised as barbarians by the existing inhabitants: their only skill was an aptitude for warfare under the strong influence of their patron god of war, Huitzilopochtli.

Gradually, the Mexica grew stronger. They settled their capital, Tenochtitlán, some time around A.D. 1325. In 1428, they and several allies overthrew the Tepanecs of Azcapotzalco, the most powerful kingdom in the basin of Mexico at the time. In one sudden move, the Mexica had become the most-powerful group in ancient Mexico. With their main allies, the Texcoco and the Tlacopan, the Mexica formed a so-called triple alliance that proceeded to expand its territory aggressively throughout central Mexico; they were still doing so when the Spaniards arrived in 1519.

The Mexica controlled what has often been called "the Aztec empire." In fact, the "empire" was a collection of subjugated groups and kingdoms held together by a combination of force and intimidation. A major aspect of this subjugation was tribute. If a town or region submitted voluntarily to the Mexica might, the amount of tribute that it would have to pay annually might be quite light; regions captured in war or rebellious towns would be assessed a far more onerous amount. There are detailed surviving accounts of the tribute that poured into Tenochtitlán each year: the tribute was one of the things the Spaniards were most interested in as they wished to continue the process for their benefit.

The Mexica are perhaps best known for the savage warfare they waged and for their practice of human sacrifice (things they had in common with all the other peoples of ancient Mexico). But they were also great engineers, architects, artists, and poets. The Spaniards could barely believe the beauty of the Mexica capital, Tenochtitlán, when they entered it and were astounded by the great artistry of the Mexica in paint, wood, ceramic, stone, and silver and gold (almost all of which the Spanish nevertheless melted down into ingots).

"Who could defeat Tenochtitlán, who could shake the foundation of heaven," says one Mexica poem. In fact, the Mexica were conquered rather easily by the Spaniards and a host of native allies. After a siege of several months, Cortés and his troops entered Tenochtitlán on 13 August 1521, signaling the end of the Mexica empire. Nevertheless, the Mexica, "the Aztecs," live on, and there are still over 1 million people in Mexico today who speak the Aztec language, Nahuatl.

Peter Mathews

References
Smith, M. E. 1996. *The Aztecs: A History.* Oxford: Blackwell.

Babylonian Civilization

Although sharing roots with other Mesopotamian civilizations, such as the Sumerian and the Assyrian, the Babylonian civilization derived from the city of Babylon, a major city in southern MESOPOTAMIA (now Iraq). Much of what we know about the history of the Babylonian civilization comes from the analysis of cuneiform texts that have been preserved among the ruins of palaces, temples, and administrative buildings. Monuments and other items of material culture have been used to give further texture to information derived from the excavation of cities and from surveys of the landscape of the region.

The empire of Hammurabi (1792–1750 B.C.) marks the emergence of Babylon as the major cultural and political center of the region as a result of warfare and later economic reorganization. The empire barely survived Hammurabi's reign, however. The decline of the old Babylonian kingdom after Hammurabi was most likely the result of a complex interplay of political and environmental factors, the latter directly related to the changing behavior of the Euphrates River as a source of water for irrigation. After Babylon was attacked by the Hittites in 1595 B.C., the political picture becomes hazy until the mid-fifteenth century B.C. when the Kassites seized control of Babylon. Although

Fragment from an early Babylonian royal stela (Ann Ronan Picture Library)

there is ample evidence for political upheavals both before and after the Kassite period, it is also clear that the language and other cultural institutions that lay at the heart of the Babylonian civilization continued to prosper. The political instability of Babylon was further increased by the growing power of the Assyrian empire, and on more than one occasion the city was occupied by Assyrian kings or their nominees.

That situation persisted until the end of the seventh century B.C., when the Babylonians (in league with the Medes) turned the tables on the Assyrians and destroyed them. This change of fortunes ushered in the neo-Babylonian empire under Nebuchadnezzar II (604–562 B.C.), which included a major restoration and expansion of Babylon, the most famous features of which were the Ishtar Gate and the Hanging Gardens.

However the neo-Babylonian empire was as short-lived as Babylon, and the territory fell victim to the Persians under Cyrus II (559–530 B.C.). The gods and religious customs and the language of Babylon lay at the heart of its civilization, but in the long term, loss of political independence meant that its distinctive form lost out after an eventful 1,200-year history.

Tim Murray

See also Iran; Layard, Sir Austen Henry; Rawlinson, Sir Henry Creswicke
References
Lloyd, S. 1978. *Foundations in the Dust: A Story of Mesopotamia Exploration.* New York: AMS Press.

Bahrain
See Arabian Peninsula

Ban Chiang
Jointly excavated by the University of Pennsylvania and the Thai Department of Fine Arts in the 1970s, Ban Chiang, a major site in northeastern Thailand, essentially set the framework of a regional chronology. Although the dating of the site (via radiometric means) remains somewhat controversial, there is little doubt that the long sequence of occupation (from about 3600 B.C. to A.D. 500) makes it an ideal place to explore the cultural history of the region.

The value of Ban Chiang is further enhanced by the richness of the site, which boasts evidence of early rice cultivation (once thought to predate that in China but now believed to postdate it), early bronze technology, and a diversity of ceramic, metal, and shell objects. Aside from the long cultural sequence (which spans technological developments from the Stone Age through the Bronze Age to the Iron Age), one of the reasons for the richness and diversity of the cultural remains found at Ban Chiang is that there is evidence of ordinary habitations as well as graves.

Tim Murray

See also Cambodia
References
Higham, C. 1989. *The Archaeology of Mainland South East Asia.* Cambridge: Cambridge University Press.

Banerji, Rakal Das (1885–1930)
R. D. Banerji worked for the Archaeological Survey of India in the second and third decades of the twentieth century and became, after his early retirement from the survey in 1925, a professor of Indology at Banaras Hindu University. He specialized in several fields of ancient Indian studies—sculpture and architecture, numismatics, epigraphy, and palaeography and archaeological field investigations—and he was the first archaeologist to conduct excavations at the Indus Valley site of Mohenjo Daro, which had been noticed both by him and by D. R. Bhandarkar, a contemporary officer in the survey.

Banerji also excavated the eighth-century A.D. Buddhist stupa and monastic site of Paharpur in modern Bangladesh in 1924. In the field of sculpture and architecture, his contribution lay in the publication of *The Temple of Siva at Bhumara* (1924), *Basreliefs of Badami* (1928), and *Eastern Indian School of Mediaeval Sculpture* (1933). The publication of the last volume may be said to have cohesively established the existence of a distinct school of sculpture in eastern India which demonstrated the impact of the state of Orissa on the architecture of the region.

In the field of numismatics, Banerji wrote a large number of papers, which were mostly published in the Calcutta Asiatic Society journals and proceedings. He edited a large number of inscriptions for *Epigraphia Indica* (see vols. 15, 16, 18, 19), and the range of his edited inscriptions was chronologically and geographically wide. His mastery of the primary sources of ancient India led him to a study of its political history, and one of his books on the subject is *The Age of the Imperial Guptas* (1933). He wrote extensively in his mother tongue, Bengali, even writing a large number of historical novels with themes selected from ancient India.

Dilip Chakrabarti

See also Indus Civilization; South Asia

Banpo

Excavated between 1954 and 1957, the Neolithic village of Banpo is a short drive from Xi'an, the capital of Shaanxi Province in central CHINA. Banpo has great significance in the history of Chinese archaeology for several reasons. First, the well-preserved remains of houses, ditches, and burials and the large number of artifacts that were found during excavation make this a type site for the Yangshao phase of the early Chinese Neolithic period (about 5000 B.C. to 4000 B.C.).

Second, the site was interpreted as providing clear evidence of the existence of a matrilineal society during the Neolithic period, an interpretation that accorded very well with the analysis of precapitalist societies put forward by Friedrich Engels (ca. 1884) in his *Origins of the Family, Private Property, and the State* and subsequent Marxist ideological interpretations encouraged by the Chinese Communist Party. Third, the site was transformed into a major museum based around a building that completely enclosed a large portion of it, including different types of houses and burials. This major museum, which recently had a tourist village constructed adjacent to it, continues to play a significant role in informing the Chinese people about life in Neolithic China.

Tim Murray

References

Chang, K.-C. 1986. *The Archaeology of Ancient China*. 4th ed., revised and enlarged. New Haven, CT: Yale University Press.

Bay Springs Mill, Mississippi

In 1836, one George Gresham built a water-powered sawmill and gristmill on Mackeys Creek in northeastern Mississippi, and in 1852, the Bay Springs Union Factory was built at the same location to spin cotton and wool raised locally. Unlike most textile mills of the period, the Bay Springs Mill spun yarn that local families knitted into socks and wove into cloth for themselves and for sale. The development of power looms in New England had largely made this kind of symbiosis impractical by 1820, but at Bay Springs this relic of the early years of industrialization continued operating until 1885 when the mill burned.

In 1979, a team of researchers led by William H. Adams investigated the mill and surrounding community, including a general store, a Masonic lodge, a barracks, nine farmhouses, six millworkers' houses, and two other mill buildings. Much of the original equipment remained on the site, and Steven D. Smith, Timothy B. Riordan, and Albert F. Bartovics analyzed the archaeological remains. The historical geographer Howard Adkins researched the documentary history of this community, and the folklorists David F. Barton and Stephen Poyser interviewed over sixty people—their recordings are in the Library of Congress, the Mississippi Department of Archives and History, and the Indiana University Folklore Archives. The community approach used at SILCOTT, WASHINGTON, and WAVERLY PLANTATION was used at Bay Springs as well to provide a broader historical context for the material recovered. The study of commodity flows by Riordan and Adams provides a model for quantifying material culture within the context of the national market.

W. H. Adams

Beazley, Sir John Davidson (1885–1970)

Beazley was born in Glasgow, the son of a member of the Arts and Crafts movement, so it is perhaps not surprising that he was to be fascinated by craftsmen and artists for most of his life. He attended Balliol and Christ Church Colleges at Oxford, where he later became Lincoln professor of archaeology. Beazley was a fine classical scholar and an excellent teacher, but his major interests were Greek art and Attic vase-painting. Vase-painting, because of its quality and the fact it had survived when all other forms of painting in ancient GREECE did not, made it particularly important to the history of art. Beazley's work on vase painting was to revolutionize the disciplines of art history and archaeology.

By the early twentieth century the collections of Greek pottery formed by SIR WILLIAM HAMILTON and other aristocratic antiquarians during the early nineteenth century had found their way into museums across Europe. German scholars such as Hartwig, Hauser, and Furtwangler had noted that some pots carried short inscriptions, including what appeared to be "signatures" or short texts giving the name of an artist, followed by a verb, as in "made or painted by," which allowed a typology based on signed works to be created. German scholars applied this typology only to those pots that were signed and were diagnostic of a particular style or technique.

Beazley broadened this method to include the whole corpus of Attic pottery. By identifying the unconscious details of individual artists—such as painted features and elements—he was able to add unsigned pieces to the rest of the corpus of signed ones—and so tens of thousands of Attic red-figure and black-figure pottery could be grouped as the works of individual artists. Beazley's method has been described as identifying the "hands" of the painters and potters of Athens, and these additional identifications supplemented the names of craftsmen that appeared on the pottery. Thus he was able to transform the hitherto chaotic study of vase-painting into an organized field of study, similar to other documented schools of painting. He went on to successfully apply his method to Etruscan, Corinthian, Eastern Greek, and South Italian pottery.

Tim Murray

See also Britain, Classical Archaeology

Beidha

Excavated by English archaeologist Diana Kirkbride between 1958 and 1967, Beidha is a significant Natufian and prepottery Neolithic site in southern JORDAN. Excavation revealed changes in domestic architecture and provided evidence of the early cultivation of barley and emmer wheat (prior to the development of a domesticated morphology for these plants). Beidha also exhibited evidence of long-distance trade in obsidian, the origins of which are at Anatolia in central TURKEY.

Tim Murray

See also Syro-Palestinian and Biblical Archaeology

Belgium

The state of Belgium was founded in 1830. Within its small territory (30,513 square kilometers), it comprises two major language groups, which has been an important factor in the country's recent political history. Since 1980, Belgium has been a federal state divided into three regions, each with substantial autonomy. The Flemish region, which occupies the northern part of the country, consists of sandy lowlands bordering the North Sea and part of the central Belgian loam belt covering a range of low foothills. The linguistic border between the Flemish- and French-speaking populations runs across these hills from east to west. Brussels is a separate bilingual region.

To the south, there are Cretaceous limestone formations dissected by the Sambre and Meuse Rivers. From there, the land rises to the Ardennes uplands with a maximum altitude of just below 700 meters above sea level. Belgium was the first country on the European continent to go through a process of industrialization early in the nineteenth century, and this industrialization entailed major infrastructural and mining activities. The country's geographical features, political developments, and economic prosperity have all been influential in the development of archaeology in Belgium.

The leading role of Belgian naturalists and geologists in the establishment of prehistory during the later nineteenth century is well known. Earlier, however, historians had been

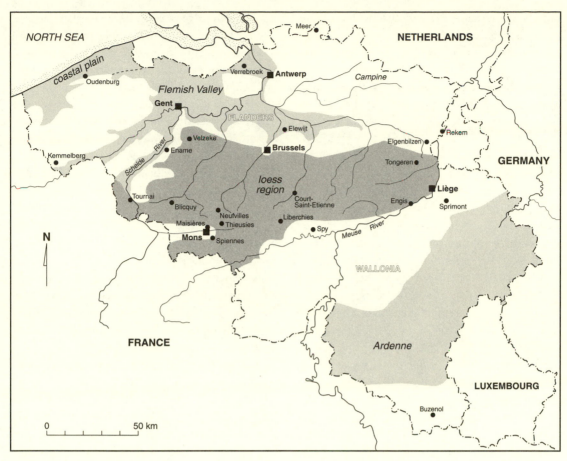

Archaeological Sites in Belgium

using archaeological evidence relating to the late-protohistoric and early-historic periods. Although occasional chance discoveries had been made in the seventeenth and eighteenth centuries, e.g., the tomb of the Merovingian king Childeric at Tournai in 1653 and the Celtic burial chamber at Eigenbilzen in 1781, an incipient archaeological interest emerged in the late eighteenth and early nineteenth centuries. Such activities were stimulated by the Imperial Academy of Brussels and later by the Royal Academy, which was founded in 1816 during the short-lived reign of the Dutch king William I.

The name *Belgium* came from the Roman province of Belgica, which was established in northern Gaul after Julius Caesar's conquest in 59–52 B.C. It was divided into a number of *civitates* (regions) inhabited by the Belgae, a people of Germano-Celtic origin who had crossed the Rhine in the last centuries B.C. Early historians such as Caussin, De Bast, Dewez, and Heylen

(writing in Latin) were interested in tribal territories, their main centers, and the Celtic origin of modern cities. Problems like these were addressed using such evidence as the distribution of coin treasures. Tongeren, capital of the Civitas Tungrorum and Belgium's main Roman center, received particular attention.

In the years after 1830, nationalist motives made archaeology a recognized discipline. It figured as an independent section within the Class of Letters of the Royal Academy, and in 1835, it was among the obligatory fields of instruction at the four universities. Private historical and archaeological societies were also established. The most important of these were the Royal Academy of Archaeology at Antwerp and the Archaeological Society of Brussels. Most fieldwork was done by members of the societies, who were often members of the clergy or nobility. The historic roots of the different language groups, or "races" in the current terminology, were major preoccupations. Numerous protohistoric burial sites as well as Roman villa complexes on the Campagna Romana, the fertile loess belt of central Belgium, were unearthed during the second half of the century. Several hoards of bronzes were found, and in the first years of the twentieth century, at the Royal Museum for Art and History, Jacobsen undertook chemical analyses of these in order to determine their production centers.

Completely separate from that milieu, the first prehistoric sites were investigated in the karstic caves of the Meuse and some of its tributaries and in the region of Mons. PHILIPPE CHARLES SCHMERLING, a professor of zoology at the University of Liège, found human fossil bones, including a Neanderthal child skull as it later appeared, in 1830 at the cave of Engis. Observing the association of these fossils with extinct mammal bones and their similar physical appearance, he came to believe in the antiquity of man. Having almost by accident become involved, Schmerling was truly a precursor of the science of prehistory. In his own opinion, the human fossils were not essential in establishing human antiquity as is indicated by this oft-cited phrase: "Therefore, their [stone and bone tools] presence is very important. Even if I had not found human bones in a condition suggesting that they belong to the antediluvian era, the existence of man would have been proven by the presence of these worked bones and stone tools." He agonized over the way in which human bones and other faunal remains might have become associated and wondered if the latter would not have been reworked from older deposits. Schmerling stood alone in holding this theory, and his importance was only acknowledged much later.

However, from the 1860s onward, the intellectual climate changed radically. Prehistory not only became an acceptable science, it also became a matter of national prestige. Research into the antiquity of man was of great interest in neighboring countries, and the academy would not have Belgium's potential unexploited. At its request, the government appointed geologist Edouard Dupont in 1863 to explore the Meuse caves. At the age of twenty-two Dupont under-

took this massive task, which he worked on until 1869. His first problem was the establishment of a regional relative chronology. On the assumption that both the formation of the caves and the deposition of the lowermost sediments within them were contemporaneous with progressive river incision, altitude above the present water level became a chronological marker for human occupation in the caves. In all later accounts of Dupont's work, this principle is singled out as a major flaw, and some critics go so far as to have Dupont extend his assumption to the complete sediment fill and to wrongly deny him any knowledge of the principle of superposition. But clearly, Dupont showed a most explicit concern with superimposed depositional units and the occupation levels (sols d'habitat) within them. In his thinking about both the science of prehistory (or ethnography, in his own terminology) and its methods, he was exceptional.

During the same period, industrial activities in the basin of the Haine, a tributary of the Scheldt River, led to the discovery of a number of open-air Paleolithic sites and of Neolithic flint mine shafts at Spiennes. Over a number of years, the question of the eoliths and Tertiary man was argued in Belgium as it was in neighboring countries. Until the mid-twentieth century, Rutot would remain an ardent defender of eoliths and Tertiary man, although Dupont had already expressed his doubts on the subject.

Early Belgian prehistory was the work of anthropologists, naturalists, geologists, and engineers and was not considered to belong to the realm of archaeology. This view came about because the field methods were entirely different and material culture typologies were much less of a concern than in national archaeology. The fields grew closer when the Archaeological and Historic Federation of Belgium was established at the initiative of the Royal Academy for Archaeology in 1884, and the discovery of two Neanderthal fossils at Spy by De Puydt and Lohest, both from the University of Liège, was announced at the federation's second national congress. Study of the fossils by Fraipont established widespread acceptance of the Neanderthal species. In a review publication of scientific developments in Belgium on the seventy-fifth anniversary of the federation,

A mammoth tusk from the Upper Paleolithic level at the site of Maisieres (Royal Belgian Institute for Natural Sciences)

the two research fields were treated together in the section entitled "anthropological and archaeological sciences."

Notwithstanding the affiliation of archaeology (now including prehistory) with history, its impact on academic historiography was negligible. In the five editions between 1900 and 1928 of the first volume of his monumental *History of Belgium,* the leading historian Henri Pirenne spent half a page on the prehistoric period. In his discussion of Celtic tribes and the early Roman occupation, almost no reference was made to archaeological evidence except for a few illustrations of archaeological finds. At the universities, archaeology had lost its initial importance through numerous educational reforms during the course of the nineteenth century, and it had disappeared as a legal academic discipline. Universities were entitled, however, to organize scientific programs freely, and some took the opportunity to create programs for classical archaeology and the history of art. At the University of Brussels at the end of the century there were courses on medieval archaeology and European prehistory.

An official structure for archaeological field research was created with the establishment of a State Service for Excavations in 1903 within the Department of National Antiquities at the Royal Museum of Art and History in Brussels. Fieldwork increased rapidly, and during the next twenty-five years, an impressive number of sites, mostly Neolithic and later, filled the archaeological distribution map. This work remained restricted to a documentary level and served essentially to enhance museum collections. There was little concern for interpretation and synthesis, and the archaeological profession remained exclusively francophone.

Even though Belgium officially became a bilingual country in 1898, French remained the language of effective power as the south was the politically and economically dominant region. Flanders struggled for its cultural identity and for education in its own language. It was only shortly after World War I that the University of Ghent became the first institution of higher education teaching in Flemish, and the academy remained exclusively francophone until 1938.

Although a chair of prehistory had been established at the University of Liège in 1926, departments of national archaeology were not created at Ghent and bilingual Louvain until the end of the 1940s. The new branches were integrated into existing institutes for archaeology and the history of art, and it was only at Ghent that there was also a connection to the Department of History.

Between the two world wars, field research generally began reaching a level comparable to that in neighboring countries. Jacques Breuer, director of the State Service for Excavations and trained in the Netherlands, introduced the open-area and quadrant methods of excavation and created the journal *Archéologie* to provide rapid publication of field data. There was, however, one fundamental obstacle to archaeology's development—the absence of legislation to regulate the protection and excavation of sites. As late as 1972, Jozef Mertens, research director under Breuer, could proclaim with a sense of irony that Belgium was one of the few countries in the world without illegal archaeological activities, and it would stay that way for another two decades. The handful of professional archaeologists working for the State Service and at universities and self-educated amateurs were unable to cope with professional looters, development projects, and growing population density. At Court-Saint-Etienne, only a few of the original sixty or more large Hallstatt burial mounds remained intact for archaeological investigation, and during large-scale construction activities in Brussels in the 1950s, which cut through the city's medieval center, not a single archaeological site or artifact was reported.

The three decades after World War II were very productive in terms of both fieldwork and interpretation. Syntheses of variable quality were published for different periods, and in those published on more recent periods, the origin of the language frontier was always an issue. At Ghent, the historian Hubert Van De Weerd formed the first generation of Flemish archaeologists, and one of these, Sigfried J. De Laet, was appointed to the Chair of National Pre- and Protohistory. Jozef R. Mertens, research director at the State Service for Excava-

tions under Breuer, was appointed to the university in Louvain. Jean de Heinzelin resumed the Museum of Natural History's historic interest in Paleolithic prehistory, and the museum's excavation of the Upper Paleolithic open-air site at Maisières is a landmark for its detailed stratigraphic recording and elaborate paleoenvironmental reconstructions. All of these researchers were convinced of the discipline's need to both rethink its aims and utilize new methods, particularly those for environmental reconstruction.

In an impressive fieldwork record ranging from Iron Age to medieval sites, Mertens changed the nature of provincial Roman archaeology, redefining it as a social geography involving such issues as settlement systems, land partitioning, and transportation networks. De Laet was concerned with the nature of archaeology in general and was well aware of the changes in this respect that were taking place internationally. He is the only Belgian archaeologist to have published a major theoretical reflection, in which he expressed severe criticisms of traditional archaeology, its unwarranted ethnic interpretations, and the danger of possible political misuse. At the same time, however, he was strongly opposed to the nomothetic (positivist search for the laws of human history) aims of the new archaeology and to anthropological archaeology.

The State Service for Excavations, still attached to the Royal Museum for Art and History, became an independent scientific institution in 1963, and a parallel National Centre for Archaeological Research was established for documentation. During the 1960s, the latter published exhaustive inventories of archaeological sites in Belgium, and De Laet created the journal *Helinium* to publish contributions on the archaeology of Belgium, the Netherlands, and Luxembourg. Some of Belgium's most important sites were excavated during this period: Roman settlements such as the *vici* of Liberchies, Blicqui, Elewijt, and Velzeke and the fortified site at Oudenburg on the North Sea coast; LA TÈNE oppida (fortified cities) at the Kemmelberg and Buzenol sites and a number of protohistoric burial sites in the Campine region; and

Middle Neolithic enclosures at Thieusies and Neufvilles in central Belgium. Middle and Upper Paleolithic collections from cave sites were reanalyzed. New sites were excavated in the Haine basin, which gave Paleolithic research new impetus. At the Late Paleolithic site of Meer, detailed excavation and recording procedures were supplemented by refitting and microwear analyses of stone tools to infer the spatial organization of the site. This study gained international renown.

In retrospect, the 1960s appear to have been a turning point for Belgian archaeology. On its way to becoming a mature research discipline, it would, in the next decades, lose connection to a field rapidly passing through stages of epistemological upheaval. The embodiment of archaeology with theory and the severing of its ties with history was met with resistance in Belgium as in the rest of continental Europe. One unfortunate consequence was that an increasingly important part of the field's identity was not acknowledged in university programs, which is an important reason for Belgium's disconnection from the mainstream. A scientific discipline ultimately thrives on education, which involves transmitting the scientific discipline's state of the art, if only to enable disagreement. The academic establishment of a national archaeology rising from fieldwork on mundane archaeological records might have challenged the traditional structures of education when archaeology was an ill-defined and a subordinate field among classical culture studies, yet that relict of an outdated culture-historic perspective was maintained even after the 1960s.

Unable to take issue with some of the major developments in the field, archaeology did not do well from an organizational point of view either. A 1986 census established the ratio of professional national archaeologists per million inhabitants at three to one, one of the lowest figures in the European Community. As a consequence of institutional reforms in Belgium, the funding of archaeological research gradually became the responsibility of regional governments. In 1989, the National Service of Excavations ceased to exist and was replaced by the Institute for Archaeological Heritage on the Flemish side and the Direction of Excavations in the Walloon (French-speaking) region.

Contacts are maintained across the linguistic border, and joint projects are occasionally carried out, but generally, the archaeology of both regions has taken off in different directions. Wallonia was quick to implement archaeological legislation and to accordingly provide a bureaucratic structure. In 1980, Belgium's oldest site (recently suggested to be 1 million years old) was discovered at Sprimont, in eastern Belgium, and immediate protective measures ensured its long-term research. Systematic programs, on the early Neolithic occupation of the loess belt and on Iron Age fortifications for instance, were initiated, and increased financial means resulted in a major project of urban archaeology at Place Saint Lambert in Liège, the first of its kind in Belgium.

The Flemish parliament did not pass a law regulating the management and exploitation of the archaeological heritage of the northern part of the country until 1993, and it is still not supported by an effective organizational framework. Although there are major developments in heritage management policies in the rest of Western Europe, Flanders is lagging behind. Often divided by internal struggle, the profession has failed to create an awareness of archaeological heritage among the public and its representatives beyond that of a folklore interest level. Mostly small-scale projects by temporarily employed individuals have maintained fieldwork at the same level since the 1980s.

In 2000, some sound and longer-term projects were established. Using different analytical methods, spatial organization, and dynamic site formation, the Federmesser site of Rekem has been reconstructed in astonishing detail, and at Verrebroek, a large-scale subsurface survey and a subsequent open-area excavation are revealing an early Mesolithic settlement in an alluvial context. With regard to increasing the awareness of archaeology the public, the medieval site of Ename has been made popular by means of on-site virtual computer reconstructions. These are examples of what the future of archaeology in Belgium can be, and in this respect, the recently installed Flemish Archaeological Council, an independent mediator between all parties involved in archaeology, has a crucial part to play.

Phillip van Peer

See also France; Netherlands

References

Barlet, J., J. Barthélémy, R. Brulet, P, Gilissen, and A. Ledent. 1993. *L'Archéologie en région wallonne.* Dossier de la Commission Royale des Monuments, Sites et Fouilles, vol. 1. Division des Monuments, Sites et Fouilles, Jambes.

Cahen, D., and P. Haesaerts. 1984. *Peuples chasseurs de la Belgique préhistorique dans leur cadre naturel.* Brussels: Patrimoine de l'Institut Royal des Sciences Naturelles de Belgique.

Cahen, D., L. H. Keeley, and F. Van Noten. 1979. "Stone Tools, Toolkits, and Human Behaviour." *Current Anthropology* 20: 661–683.

De Laet, S. J. 1957. *Archaeology and Its Problems.* London: Phoenix House.

———. 1982. *La Belgique d'avant les Romains.* Wetteren: Universa.

De Puydt, M., and M. Lohest. 1887. "L'homme contemporain du mammouth à spy (Namur)." *Annales de la Fédération archéologique et historique de Belgique* 2: 207–235.

Dupont, E. 1874. "Théorie des ages de la Pierre en Belgique." *Bulletin de la Société d'Anthropologie de Bruxelles,* 2d series, 9: 728–761.

Fraipont, J., and A. de Loë. 1908. "Les sciences anthropologiques et archéologiques." In *Le mouvement scientifique en Belgique 1830–1905,* 2:141–183. Ed. C. Van Overbergh. Brussels: Société Belge de Librairie.

Haesaerts, P., and J. de Heinzelin. 1979. "Le site paléolithique de Maisières-Canal." *Dissertationes archaeologicae Gandenses,* vol. 19.

Mariën, M. E. 1951. "Coup d'oeuil sur l'étude de l'Age du Bronze en Belgique." *Handelingen van de Koninklijke Maatschappij voor Geschiedenis en Oudheidkunde van Gent* 5: 215–224.

Mertens, J. R. 1985. "L'archéologie gallo-romaine en Belgique: Quelques réflexions." *Les etudes classiques* 53: 25–31.

Otte, M. 1983. "Esquisse du Paléolithique belge." *L'Anthropologie* 87: 291–332.

Rutot, A. 1918. *La Préhistoire, Première partie: Introduction à l'étude de la préhistoire de la Belgique.* Brussels: Les Naturalistes Belges.

Sacassyn-della Santa, E. 1946. *La Belgique préhistorique.* Collection nationale, 6th series, vol. 69. Brussels: Office de Publicité.

Schmerling, P. C. 1834. *Recherches sur les ossements fossiles découverts dans les cavernes de la province de Liège.* 3 vols. Liège: Collardin.

Wankenne, A. 1979. *La Belgique au temps de Rome.* Namur: Presses Universitaires de Namur.

Belize

Belize, until 1973 the Crown Colony of British Honduras, is the only part of the Americas within the British Empire in which an ancient civilization flourished. Located on the eastern side of the Yucatán Peninsula bordering MEXICO and GUATEMALA, it occupies part of the area in which the preclassic, classic, and postclassic Maya culture thrived from the first millennium B.C. until the Spanish conquest in the sixteenth century A.D., a span of over 2,500 years. The presence of Maya ruins, the absence of other archaeological remains, and the British colonial history of Belize, which set it apart politically and culturally from its hispanophone neighbors, all governed a distinctive progress of archaeological investigation in the nineteenth and twentieth centuries.

The history of Maya archaeology generally can be divided into five successive periods (Hammond 1983b). During the first two of these—*the era of the Spanish travelers* (1524–1759) and *the era of the Spanish explorers* (1759–1840)—Belize remained little settled and archaeologically unnoted. Two Americans, JOHN LLOYD STEPHENS and FREDERICK CATHERWOOD, passed through Belize in October 1839 on their first expedition to visit MAYA sites in Central America and Yucatán, but their visit did not encourage archaeological interest in this small nation. Nor was interest sparked when Patrick Walker, the colony's secretary, led an expedition from Belize hoping to forestall Stephens at the ruins of PALENQUE on the far side of the Maya lowlands.

During the succeeding *period of the major scholars* (1840–1924), little attention was paid to archaeology in Belize until the end of the nineteenth century, although Belize City was the port of entry for traffic into the Peten, Guatemala's northern rain forest department where many of the most noted Maya cities stand. Even the pub-

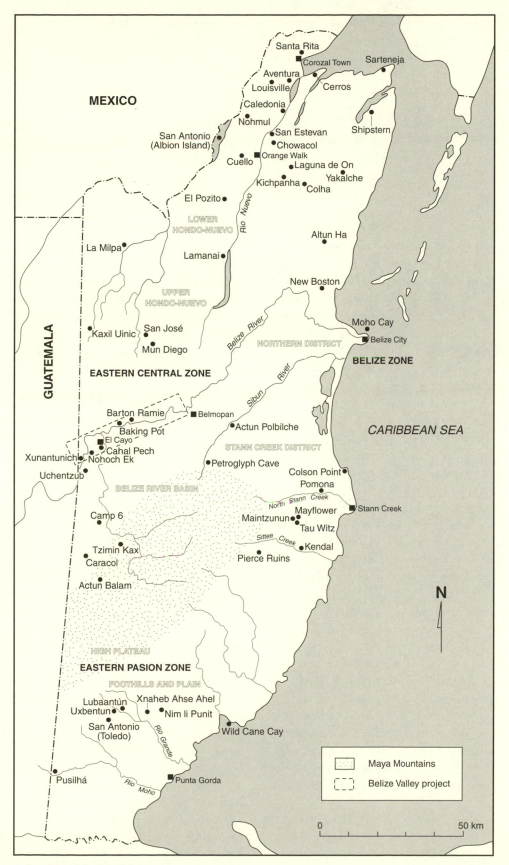

Santa Rita

Corozal Town

Sarteneja

Aventura

MEXICO

Louisville

Cerros

Caledonia

Nohmul

Shipstern

San Antonio
(Albion Island)

San Estevan

Chowacol

Cuello

Orange Walk

Laguna de On

Kichpanha

Yakalche

Colha

El Pozito

LOWER
HONDO-NUEVO

Rio Nuevo

Altun Ha

La Milpa

Lamanai

UPPER
HONDO-NUEVO

New Boston

Belize River

Moho Cay

GUATEMALA

Kaxil Uinic

San José

Mun Diego

EASTERN CENTRAL ZONE

NORTHERN DISTRICT

Belize City

Sibun River

BELIZE ZONE

Barton Ramie

Belmopan

Actun Polbilche

CARIBBEAN SEA

Baking Pot

El Cayo

Cahal Pech

STANN CREEK DISTRICT

Xunantunich

Nohoch Ek

Petroglyph Cave

Colson Point

Uchentzub

BELIZE RIVER BASIN

Pomona

North Stann *Creek*

Mayflower

Camp 6

Maintzunun

Stann Creek

Tau Witz

Tzimin Kax

Sittee Creek

Kendal

Caracol

Pierce Ruins

Actun Balam

N

HIGH PLATEAU

EASTERN PASION ZONE

FOOTHILLS AND PLAIN

Lubaantún

Xnaheb Ahse Ahel

Uxbentun

Nim li Punit

San Antonio
(Toledo)

Rio Grande

Wild Cane Cay

Maya Mountains

Pusilhá

Belize Valley project

Rio Moho

Punta Gorda

0   50 km

Archaeological Sites in Belize

lication in London of Alfred Maudslay's great *Biologia Centrali-Americana: Archaeology* (1889–1902), which showed in detail how impressive the sites of TIKAL, Palenque, Quirigua, Copan, and CHICHÉN ITZÁ were, apparently had no impact on British Honduras, although the sites of Lubaantun and Xunantunich were known and reported in the local press toward the end of the century.

The first important investigation in the colony was carried out in 1896 by Thomas Gann, an Anglo-Irish physician posted to the colony in 1893 and initially stationed at Corozal Town, close to the Mexican border in the north. The mounds of Santa Rita lay on the outskirts of Corozal and were even then being mined for building stone. Gann's curiosity was aroused, and he began a career of amateur digging that continued until shortly before his death in 1938. His methods were crude, and his laborers were often left unsupervised for days at a time, but his records are the only ones extant for many sites, especially around Corozal, that are now vanished. His initial work at Santa Rita was done with care and included the recording of a set of polychrome murals in the "International Style of the Late Postclassic" (Robertson 1970); these were published by the SOCIETY OF ANTIQUARIES OF LONDON and again by the SMITHSONIAN INSTITUTION (Gann 1900), and Gann's tracings have proved both accurate and of enduring value.

Gann also developed a descriptive typology for Maya mounds, distinguishing house-platforms, courtyard groups, and temple-pyramids; he explored the ruins of Lubaantun in the south of Belize, Xunantunich in the far west, Laguna de On in the north, Wild Cane Cay, and other coastal islands, and in the 1930s he worked at Nohmul and finally at Louisville. His reports on these sites (including a series of five or six popular books—see the bibliography in Hammond 1983b, as well as Pendergast 1993a), though not of professional quality, led to subsequent scholarly investigation of all of them, and he was noted for encouraging archaeologists to visit the colony.

Among the expeditions stimulated by Gann's initial discoveries were those to Lubaantun by R. E. Merwin in 1915 (which resulted in the identification of the first classic period ballcourt in the southern lowlands) and those of the BRITISH MUSEUM under T. A. Joyce in 1926 and 1927. In the latter year J. ERIC S. THOMPSON joined the museum staff, carried out useful stratigraphic tests, and disproved most of Joyce's treasured notions on the great age and architectural uniqueness of the Lubaantun ruins. The discovery of Pusilhà, with its numerous well-preserved stelae that were removed to London, diverted the museum's attention from 1928 to 1930, after which formal British involvement in the archaeology of British Honduras was suspended for four decades.

The British Museum expeditions were among the first of the *institutional period* (1924–1970), during which Maya archaeology was dominated by the Carnegie Institution of Washington's Division of Historical Research, under the direction of SYLVANUS G. MORLEY and then ALFRED V. KIDDER. Carnegie personnel working on numerous projects in the Peten, especially the long-term excavations at Uaxactun, gained access through Belize, but the only Carnegie work carried out in the colony was done by Eric Thompson. Having investigated the small center of Tzimin Kax in the Maya Mountains for the Field Museum of Chicago, Thompson was recruited by Kidder and continued his important work at San José, intended as a study of a "typical" small Maya site to balance the major Carnegie projects at Uaxactun and Chichén Itzá. Thompson (1939) brought in Anna O. Shepard to carry out paste analyses of pottery—a pioneering application of archaeological science perhaps stimulated by the broadband approach employed by the Carnegie Institution in Yucatán.

When World War II caused a temporary cessation of major Maya projects, less than a dozen sites in Belize had been professionally investigated, and no local administration of archaeology existed even though good legislation had been passed in 1924. After the war Hamilton Anderson, a colonial civil servant who had carried out the initial exploration of Caracol in 1938 and been the governor's informal adviser on archaeology became Belize's first archaeological commissioner in 1957. Anderson invited

Mayan temple ruins, Xanantunich, Cayo, Belize (Spectrum Colour Library)

Maya specialists from U.S. universities to work in Belize: Linton Satterthwaite from the University of Pennsylvania began work at Caracol in 1951, followed by GORDON WILLEY of Harvard, who worked in the Belize Valley in 1953. Willey had already done innovative settlement-pattern work in PERU, and he now brought the idea of regional archaeology to Belize, at the same time moving away from the major sites to examine rural residences. Most of his work was focused on Barton Ramie, an arbitrarily cleared zone of valley bottom located downstream from Xunantunich; at this site a substantial sample of house-platforms were tested and some excavated totally, and a ceramic chronology from around 600 B.C. to A.D. 1000 was elucidated. The final publication (Willey et al. 1965) developed a model of Maya settlement dynamics that underpinned numerous other projects across the lowlands in the ensuing decades. The Barton Ramie site, like so many others in Belize, was later destroyed by bulldozing to make way for agricultural development.

William R. Bullard Jr., a member of Willey's team, joined the Royal Ontario Museum in Toronto, CANADA, and initiated a program of field research that was scheduled to begin in 1961 at the large site of Lamanai. Hurricane damage and a loss of communications instead led Bullard to study Baking Pot, the major center close to Barton Ramie, and then San Estevan in northern Belize. His successor at the Royal Ontario Museum, David M. Pendergast, took up Anderson's invitation to work at Altun Ha, closer to Belize City; between 1964 and 1970 the modest ruins yielded a series of spectacular burials and finds (Pendergast 1979–1990). These efforts culminated in 1968 with the discovery of the largest Maya jade known, in the form of a head of the Sun God. This, more than anything else, changed perceptions of the eastern lowlands as a cultural backwater, distant from the innovative developments in Peten and Yucatán.

The *problem-oriented period* (1970 to the present) began under the combined influence of the processualist New Archaeology and major funding from the National Science Foundation in the United States. Both joined research designs with a predefined set of expectations; exploration on the Carnegie model, to acquire knowledge and build interpretation from it, was no longer fashionable or fundable. In Belize a new and comprehensive antiquities law was enacted in 1971, allowing the archaeological commissioner to demand a justifiable research design. Joseph O. Palacio became the first Belizean commissioner in 1972, and the practice of allocating half of the excavated material to foreign institutions in return for their investment of research funds (a practice begun by Anderson on the basis of successful schemes elsewhere) was eventually reconsidered. The practice was eventually phased out entirely in the 1990s, leading several major museums to redeploy their research funds.

Fieldwork in Belize included renewed efforts at Lubaantun, which placed the site within a regional context and studied its ecological and economic aspects (Hammond 1975). This work was followed by the Corozal Project (CP), an explicitly regional study of 3,500 square kilometers in northern Belize that located, mapped, and tested sites of all sizes and periods to investigate long-term landscape history. Sites discovered by the Corozal Project included Cuello, a preclassic settlement dating to 1200 B.C. (although initially thought to be much older—see Hammond 1991), and Colha, a major chert-tool production site that also dated to the preclassic era. CP excavations there and at Nohmul, Santa Rita, Corozal, and San Estevan engendered successive projects by a variety of former CP staff members and others interested in investigating different aspects of the postclassic, settlement patterns, lithic studies, and urban genesis. CP results also stimulated independent projects on drained-field agriculture at Pulltrouser Swamp (Turner and Harrison 1983) and on possible Archaic occupation of the Maya lowlands. Other investigators examined drained-field complexes on the Rio Hondo and the late-preclassic site of Cerros, where the plan of a preclassic community was elucidated for the first time and elaborate polychrome stucco masks were uncovered on several temples (Robertson and Freidel 1986).

Northern Belize was saturated with archaeologists, but the Royal Ontario Museum's long-term project at Lamanai from 1974 to 1984 (see Pendergast 1981) was on a scale that dwarfed any other work. This was succeeded in 1985 by the equally ambitious surveys and excavations at Caracol that are still ongoing (see, e.g., Chase and Chase 1994), and, from 1992 onward, a large-scale investigation of La Milpa. Complementary investigation of dozens of smaller sites in the biological reserve around La Milpa, linking to earlier work immediately west across the frontier into Guatemala around Rio Azul, and recent surveys in southeastern Campeche, immediately north into Mexico, have created the largest database for ancient Maya landscape and settlement archaeology to date.

The Belize Valley has also seen a concentration of work, with major projects at Xunantunich, Cahal Pech, Buenavista del Cayo, Blackman Eddy, and other sites: the hills flanking the valley, largely ignored in Willey's survey, proved to have been heavily populated and home to a number of important and early centers. Transects from the valley floor northward, extending to the new site of El Pilar (itself part of a transfrontier park established in concert with Guatemala), have linked the limestone uplands where La Milpa and San José lie with the corridor of the river valley and routes west into Peten. To the south, cave studies in the Maya Mountains, begun on an ad hoc basis by Anderson and Pendergast from the 1950s onward, were advanced by the recruitment of speleologists (cave explorers), who penetrated deep caves and found extensive Maya utilization there dating to the late-preclassic period. Such use, originally thought to be just for collecting *zuhuy ha* (virgin water) for rituals, has now been shown to be part of a concern with the chthonic realm that permeated Maya society at all levels. Recent work in the Xibun Valley by Patricia A. McAnany has integrated surface settlement history with the history of cave use.

The first systematic surveys east of the Maya Mountains were carried out in the Stann Creek District by Elizabeth Graham (1994), archaeological commissioner from 1977 to 1979, and the unexplored southeastern valleys of the massif in Toledo District were penetrated by Peter S. Dunham in the 1990s. At the same time, the more accessible lowlands of Toledo were restudied in several projects, including renewed work at Pusilhà, Nim li punit, and Wild Cane Cay.

Work in Toledo was coeval with the rise of a movement for greater political autonomy among the Mopan and Kekchi inhabitants of the region, which impacted on archaeology in both positive and negative ways.

In the late 1990s European Union funds were used to carry out major restoration at both Lubaantun and Nim li punit, as one facet of tourism development for national as well as local benefit. Similar restoration had been done at Altun Ha and Xunantunich in earlier decades; the latter site has seen renewed work, and major developments have begun at Caracol and are planned for Lamanai. All of this is part of the *Ruta Maya* (the Mayan Route) program of cooperation between the five countries of the Maya area, by which Belize is belatedly benefiting from the economic impact of low-volume, high-value eco- and archaeotourism. Archaeology is also widely used in Belizean schools as part of nation-building education: in this ethnically diverse country, a significant proportion of the population has Maya blood. Sites of the contact period in the sixteenth century have been excavated at Lamanai and, notably, at Tipu (Pendergast 1993b), and a historical archaeology of the colonial period has begun (Finamore 1994). A national museum spanning the Maya and colonial periods has been planned for many years in the capital, Belmopan; it may now be built in Belize City, the epicenter of tourism and the nation's largest population center.

Archaeology in Belize, almost entirely confined to Gann's activities until the beginning of the institutional period in 1924, developed slowly in the middle fifty years of the twentieth century but accelerated after 1975. During those years a large-scale investigation of the country's three major Maya sites (Caracol, La Milpa, and Lamanai) began, and numerous regional and smaller-site projects were completed. Unlike Mexico, where an indigenous school of archaeological practice developed soon after the revolution of 1910 under the influence of MANUEL GAMIO, or GUATEMALA, where an intense interest in colonial history spilled over into archaeological work by Guatemalans of European ancestry, Belize had too small a population to pursue archaeological projects in

a similar fashion. It also had a colonial government attuned to a policy of benign neglect. As a result, virtually all archaeological research in Belize has been conducted by outsiders; apart from a short episode of British Museum interest in the 1920s, the colonial power left things to others. Institutions in the United States (primarily the University of Pennsylvania, Harvard, Rutgers, the University of Texas, and Boston University) and in Canada (the Royal Ontario Museum) have dominated research in Belize. Given the relatively informal administration of the archaeological commissioner's office and the absence of political problems like those affecting neighboring countries, Belize has proved attractive to researchers over the past quarter century—so attractive, in fact, that it has ceased to be considered a backwater and become one of the most intensively investigated and productive areas for Maya research.

Norman Hammond

See also Maya Civilization; Maya Epigraphy

References

Chase, Diane Z., and Arlen F. Chase, eds. 1994. *Studies in the Archaeology of Caracol, Belize.* Pre-Columbian Art Research Institute, Monograph 7. San Francisco.

Finamore, Daniel R. 1994. "Sailors and Slaves on the Wood-Cutting Frontier: Archaeology of the British Bay Settlement, Belize." Ph.D. dissertation, Boston University.

Gann, Thomas. 1900. "Mounds in Northern Honduras." *Bureau of American Ethnology, Smithsonian Institution, 19th Annual Report, for 1897–98.* Part 2: 661–692. Washington, DC: Smithsonian Institution.

Graham, Elizabeth. 1994. *The Highlands of the Lowlands: Environment and Archaeology in the Stann Creek District, Belize, Central America.* Madison, WI: Prehistory Press.

Hammond, Norman. 1975. *Lubaantun: A Classic Maya Realm.* Monographs of the Peabody Museum, Harvard University, 2. Cambridge, MA.

———. 1983a. "Lords of the Jungle: A Prosopography of Maya Archaeology." In *Civilizations of the Ancient Americas: Studies in Honor of Gordon R. Willey,* 3–32. Ed. R. M. Leventhal and A. L. Kolata. Cambridge, MA: Peabody Museum Press and Albuquerque: University of New Mexico Press.

———. 1983b. "The Development of Belizean Archaeology." *Antiquity* 57: 19–27.

Hammond, Norman, ed. 1991. *Cuello: An Early Maya Community in Belize.* Cambridge: Cambridge University Press.

Pendergast, David M. 1979–1990. *Excavations at Altun Ha, Belize, 1964–1970.* Vols. 1–3. Toronto: Royal Ontario Museum.

———. 1981. "Lamanai, Belize: Summary of Excavation Results, 1974–1980." *Journal of Field Archaeology* 8: 29–53.

———. 1993a. "The Center and the Edge: Archaeology in Belize, 1809–1992." *Journal of World Prehistory* 7: 1–33.

———. 1993b. "Worlds in Collision: The Maya/Spanish Encounter in Sixteenth and Seventeenth Century Belize." *Proceedings of the British Academy* 81: 105–143.

Robertson, Donald. 1970. "The International Style of the Late Postclassic." *Verhandlungen des XXXVIII Amerikanistenkongresses* 2: 77–88. Munich.

Robertson, Robin, and David A. Freidel, eds. 1986. *Archaeology at Cerros, Belize, Central America.* Vol. 1, *An Interim Report.* Dallas, TX: Southern Methodist University Press.

Thompson, J. Eric S. 1939. *Excavations at San José, British Honduras.* Carnegie Institution of Washington Publication 506. Washington, DC.

Turner, B. L., II, and Peter D. Harrison, eds. 1983. *Pulltrouser Swamp: Ancient Maya Habitat, Agriculture, and Settlement in Northern Belize.* Austin: University of Texas Press.

Willey, Gordon R., William R. Bullard Jr., John B. Glass, and James C. Gifford. 1965. *Prehistoric Maya Settlements in the Belize Valley.* Papers of the Peabody Museum, Harvard University, 54. Cambridge, MA.

Bell, Gertrude Margaret Lowthian (1868–1926)

Born in County Durham, the daughter of Sir Thomas Hugh Bell, a local industrialist, Gertrude Bell was among the first female students at Oxford at Lady Margaret Hall. She graduated in 1888 at the age of twenty with first class honors in modern history, the first woman to attain this level at the university.

Bell began her long relationship with the countries of the Near East when she first visited her diplomat uncle and aunt, Sir Frank and Lady

Gertrude Bell (Hulton Getty)

Lascelles, in Tehran, Iran. She learned Persian and later published a verse translation of Persian poetry. However it was in 1899, when Bell spent some time in Jerusalem learning Arabic and visiting Petra and Palmyra, that she really became interested in desert travel and archaeology. Bell's love of alpine mountaineering occupied her for the next five years, as she explored the Engelhorner mountains and ascended the Matterhorn from the Italian side.

In 1905 Bell traveled from Jerusalem, through Syria and Cilicia, to Konya in central Turkey. She became a self-taught and competent field archaeologist and in 1907, with Sir W. M. Ramsay, explored the Hittite and Byzantine site of Bin-Bir-Kilisse. In 1909 she traveled down the Euphrates from Aleppo and returned by way of Baghdad and Mosul in Iraq. She explored Ukhaidir, a huge Abbasid Palace, in 1911. All of these travels resulted in popular publications. Bell then set out to explore central Arabia, where only one other European woman had been. Starting from Damascus she traveled to Hail but was not allowed to travel any further and was kept as an honored prisoner until she had no alternative but to go back to Baghdad.

In 1914 with the outbreak of war Bell joined the Red Cross and worked in Boulogne, France. In 1915 she was sent back to London to reorganize Red Cross headquarters. In the same year when the Arabs rebelled against Turkish rule Bell was drafted into the War Office's Arab Intelligence Bureau and moved to Cairo. Her task was to collect and summarize information about the Bedouin tribes and sheikhs of northern Arabia whose rebellion against Turkey was supported by the British. She was later attached to the military intelligence staff of the Mesopotamian Expeditionary Force and became political officer and Oriental secretary to Sir Percy Cox. Her special knowledge of Arab politics, her prewar friendships with Arab leaders, and her linguistic abilities were valuable to successful liaisons between the British and the rebelling desert tribes. Bell moved to Baghdad in 1917, after its capture, and she continued to act as an adviser in a civil capacity, as chief political officer, completing an administrative review of MESOPOTAMIA in 1920. She and Sir Percy Cox, then high commissioner in Mesopotamia, strongly supported the election of Saud Emir Feisal and the creation of a new Arab government in Iraq.

While she continued to work as political secretary, Bell was made Iraq's Director of Antiquities, responsible for all archaeological excavations and for establishing an antiquities service and a national museum at Baghdad. The museum was inaugurated in 1923 and moved into its new building in 1926. Bell was looking for a permanent director of antiquities so that she could return to England after her ten years of service in Iraq, when she died in Baghdad. She was buried in the English cemetery in Baghdad and in 1927, at the suggestion of King Feisal, a wing of the Baghdad Museum was named for her.

Tim Murray

References
Winstone, H. W. V. 1978. *Gertrude Bell*. London: Cape.

Belzoni, Giovanni Battista (1778–1823)

When Napoleon invaded Egypt he took with him dozens of scholars and scientists to explore and record its ancient monuments. The twenty-four volume *Description d'Egypt* published in 1809 introduced Europe to ancient Egyptian civilization, provoking enormous interest both popular and museological, which led to the development of a lucrative market for Egyptian antiquities. Napoleon's army and his agent Drovetti had already plundered many antiquities when the British consul-general in Cairo, the former portrait painter Henry Salt, hired Giovanni Belzoni to ensure Britain's share. The Italian Belzoni had been a strong man in a circus before he began to collect antiquities on Salt's behalf, and his collecting techniques reflected this background. There was nothing scientific or careful about his removal of artifacts. Indeed it was his strength and his abilities to use levers and pulleys that enabled Belzoni to transport the monumental granite head of Rameses II from Thebes, and Rameses III's sarcophagus from the Valley of the Kings, back to England. In October 1817 Belzoni discovered the tomb of Seti I, the most richly decorated of all Egyptian royal tombs in the Valley of the Kings. Because it could not be transported as a whole Belzoni spent a great deal of time and effort recording the details of the wall paintings of the tomb for posterity.

Belzoni returned to England in 1819 and was taken up by London society. In 1821 he opened the Egyptian Hall in the BRITISH MUSEUM. He died in Benin in West Africa in 1823 on an expedition to find the source of the River Niger.

Tim Murray

See also Egypt, Dynastic; French Archaeology in Egypt and the Middle East

References
Belzoni, G. B. 1820. *Narrative of the Operations and Recent Discoveries with the Pyramids, Temples, Tombs, and Excavations, in Egypt and Nubia*. London.

Giovanni Battista Belzoni examines the ruins of the temple at Karnak in this ca. 1860 engraving. (Ann Ronan Picture Library)

Bernal Garcia, Ignacio (1910–1992)

Born in Paris, France, the son of a wealthy landowning Mexican family, Ignacio Bernal Garcia first studied law before transferring to study anthropology at the National Institute of Anthropology and the National Autonomous University of Mexico (UNAM), from which he received a Ph.D. and an LL.D. in 1949.

Bernal is best known for his work at the great sites of MONTE ALBÁN, Dainzu, and others in the southern highland Mexican state of Oaxaca and for excavations and restorations at TEOTIHUACÁN. He was professor of archaeology at both UNAM from 1948 and at Mexico City College from 1950 to 1962. He was director of anthropology at the University of the Americas from 1948 to 1959 and the National School of Anthropology and History from 1950 to 1955 and director of the National Museum of Anthropology from 1962 to 1968. He also worked for the United Nations Educational, Scientific, and Cultural Organization (UNESCO) during the 1950s in the areas of international and prehistoric monument protection and education.

Tim Murray

See also Mexico

Bersu, Gerhard (1889–1964)

A German archaeologist and Director of the Romisch-Germanischen Kommission in Frankfurt, a key German archaeological institution, Bersu was removed by the Nazis in 1935 for refusing to adhere to National Socialist ideology. He emigrated to Britain, where he introduced Continental methods of excavation to English archaeologists. These included the open area excavation of settlement sites, which comprised the stripping of large areas to reveal the plans of buildings and other structures and the spatial and chronological relations between them.

These methods were used in the now-classic excavations at the Iron Age farm of Little Woodbury in Wiltshire from 1938 to 1939. Little Woodbury was an oval ditched enclosure in which potholes were found. Occupied from 400 to 200 B.C., it contained one large round house, a small circular structure, four post gran-

aries, and storage pits.

During the Second World War, Bersu excavated Iron Age houses on the Isle of Man during his internment there as a German citizen. From 1947 to 1950 he was professor of archaeology at the Royal Irish Academy, Dublin. In 1950 he returned to Frankfurt.

Tim Murray

See also German Prehistoric Archaeology
References
Evans, C. 1989. "Archaeology and Modern Times: Bersu's Little Woodbury, 1938 and 1939." *Antiquity* 63: 436–450.

Beyer, Henry Otley (1883–1966)

In the history of Philippine archaeology the name Henry Otley Beyer is prominent. A pioneer in Philippine anthropological research, Beyer was one of the first scholars to explore the beginnings of Philippine society and culture. By organizing the enormous amount of archaeological data he collected during his years of active work in the PHILIPPINES, he launched the search for explanations regarding the peopling of the archipelago and the cultural relationships that existed between Filipinos and their Southeast Asian neighbors.

Beyer was born into a pioneering German-American family in Edgewood, Iowa, on July 13, 1883. Even as a young boy he was noted to have the interests of a naturalist, and he enjoyed spending time by himself in the woods near the farm where he grew up.

Majoring in chemistry and geology, Beyer graduated from the University of Denver in 1904. During archaeological fieldwork in the summer he probed the remains of the Indians of the Southwest. This apparently was his first exposure to archaeology and he also worked on the collection of artifacts from the ruins. In 1910 he went to Harvard on a scholarship, completing a one-year graduate program in anthropology.

Beyer was first introduced to the Philippine culture when he visited the 1904 Louisiana Purchase Centennial Exposition in Saint Louis, Missouri. The exposition included an exhibit on Philippine ethnic groups that featured complete houses with Philippine occupants wearing traditional costumes.

In August 1905, at the age of twenty-two, Beyer arrived in Manila. This was the start of over five decades of productive work on Philippine culture and society. The head of the United States Bureau of Education, David P. Barrows, who held a Ph.D. in anthropology, employed Beyer to work as a schoolteacher among the Ifugao in the mountains of northern Luzon. The young teacher became so absorbed in the people and lifestyle of the province that he married the daughter of an Ifugao chief.

In 1914 Beyer was appointed to the professorial chair of anthropology and ethnology at the University of the Philippines. He continued to occupy that position until his retirement and was the founder and first chairman of the school's Department of Anthropology.

His first writings on the Philippines date to 1921. He was prolific as an ethnographer, producing a 150-volume work entitled *The Philippine Ethnographic Series,* a collation of his research that later included data from the central and southern Philippines and covered 150 ethnolinguistic groups in all.

Early in 1926 Beyer took part in his first archaeological fieldwork in the Philippines, the result of an accidental discovery of major prehistoric sites at Novaliches during the construction of a dam for Manila's water supply. His ensuing investigation was the beginning of an important archaeological survey, which, after five years of work, resulted in the identification of 120 sites and a collection of almost half a million artifacts. Beyer turned down an offer to join the Anthropology Department at Harvard University because of the importance of the Novaliches sites to Philippine prehistory.

During the Japanese occupation of the Philippines, from 1941 to 1945, Beyer was placed under conditional internment, but the Japanese allowed him to continue writing. He was able to complete two important publications, *Outline Review of Philippine Archaeology by Islands and Provinces* and *Philippine and East Asian Archaeology, and Its Relation to the Origin of the Pacific Islands Population* (Beyer 1947, 1948). These major works are invaluable references and are still used by contemporary archaeologists working in the Philippines.

Archaeological research in the Philippines until the 1950s was almost completely monopolized by Beyer. A private person who worked alone, he was extremely independent. He avoided publicity and was not well known outside Southeast Asia until after his two postwar publications appeared. With countless informants all over the country, he was able to organize the archipelago's archaeological finds and sites and artifacts, and he proposed a localized cultural chronology (Old Stone Age, New Stone Age, Iron Age, Porcelain Age, and so forth). As the only professional researcher interested in the archipelago's prehistory, he accumulated numerous artifacts.

Many anthropologists working in Southeast Asia were his close friends, including Austrian scholar Robert Heine-Geldern and P. V. Stein Callenfels. As a group, they were all drawn into the regional history of Southeast Asia, and this common interest initiated the Far Eastern Prehistory Congresses held in Hanoi in 1932, Manila in 1935, and Singapore in 1938, which proved useful for comparing data and material from across Asia.

Numerous honors were accorded him by various institutions for his untiring efforts and interest in Philippine prehistory and culture. These include special awards from two Philippine presidents and honorary doctorate degrees from three Philippine universities—Silliman in 1959, the Ateneo de Manila in 1961, and the University of the Philippines in 1964. He was also honored by a scholarly symposium in 1965 on his eighty-second birthday.

Henry Otley Beyer died one year later, on December 31, 1966. He was buried, as he requested, in an Ifugao death house in Banaue, Ifugao, in the mountains of northern Luzon.

Wilfredo P. Ronquillo

See also Island Southeast Asia
References
Ang, G. R. 1968. "Dr H. Otley Beyer: Pioneer in Philippine Anthropology." In *Dr H. Otley Beyer, Dean of Philippine Anthropology.* Ed. R. Rahmann and G. R. Ang. Cebu City, Philippines: San Carlos Publications, University of San Carlos.

Beyer, H. O. 1947. "Outline Review of Philippine Archaeology by Islands and Provinces." *Philippine Journal of Science* 77, 3 and 4: 205–374.

————. 1948. *Philippine and East Asian Archaeology, and Its Relation to the Origin of the Pacific Islands Population*. National Research Council of the Philippines, Bulletin 29, Quezon City. Manila.

Lynch, F. 1967. "Henry Otley Beyer, 1883–1966." *Philippine Studies* 15, 1: 3–18.

Solheim, W. G. 1971. "Henry Otley Beyer." In *Asian Perspectives* 12. Ed. W. G. Solheim II. University of Hawaii Press.

Biblical Archaeology

See Albright, William Foxwell; Mesopotamia; Syro-Palestinian and Biblical Archaeology

Bibracte

Bibracte is located at Mont Beuvray in the commune of Saint-Leger-sous-Beuvray in the French department of Saône-et-Loire. The *oppidium* (fortified town) of Bibracte, the city of Greater Gaul that witnessed the return of Julius Caesar on many occasions, was the capital of the tribe known as Heduens, who lived west of what is now the region of Burgundy. The Heduens were allies of the Romans and defected to Caesar at the beginning of the revolt of 52 B.C. It was in Bibracte that Vercingetorix pleaded his case for a union of tribes against Caesar, it was in Bibracte that Caesar compiled most of his book on Greater Gaul during the winter of 52–51 B.C., and it was close to this city that the Helvetians had fought their battles in 58 B.C. at the beginning of the rebellion.

By the fifteenth century A.D., it was traditional to locate Bibracte on Mont Beuvray, but scholars of the eighteenth century, anxious to claim greatest antiquity for the town of Autun, refuted that location. However in 1851, a young wine merchant, Jean-Gabriel Bulliot, began to reexamine all of the evidence through with a survey of the area and its archaeological evidence. It took him fifteen years, and the moral and financial encouragement of Emperor Napoleon III, to justify his thesis to his scholarly adversaries—Bibracte was on Mont Beuvray. The archaeological research was pieced together between 1867 and 1895, the year his nephew archaeologist JOSEPH DÉCHELETTE, the celebrated author of the *Manuel d'archéologie,* took over the project and continued his uncle's work until 1907. The research on Bibracte played a large role in the development of archaeological methods in France and in what became known as Iron Age studies: "the Beuvraisian" was for a long time the name given to the last phase of the late LA TÈNE period, 140–30 B.C.

Mont Beuvray, which stands out from the southern Morvan Mountains, is more than 800 meters in altitude and comprises three hills whose rounded slopes are joined by gentle plateau. Covered by fir tree forests, it was still partly cultivated and partly planted with beech and chestnut trees as late as the 1950s. The substrata, disturbed by numerous tectonic movements, is essentially composed of rhyolites. Bulliot located a rampart five kilometers long that ran in part along the upper reaches of the slopes and delimited a surface area of approximately 135 hectares. Recent research has identified a second line of defense, even older, that encircled an area of 200 hectares.

Bulliot noted the first rampart in 1867, but it was not until 1868, after the publication of research concerning the fort of Murcens, located in Cras in the department of Lot, by E. Castagne that Bulliot began to establish links between his structure of beams and rocks and "the Gaulish wall" written about by Caesar during the siege of Bourges (Avaricum) in 52 B.C. (*Bello gallico* 7.23). The extent of this wall, with its beams fixed into each other by long iron pieces, and the development of monumental gateways marked the impetus to establish, for the first time in the Celtic world, an urban area or town, not just a hill fort, that was distinct from the surrounding country.

Bulliot insisted that the original occupations of this built-up area would have included parts of the town that were devoted to artisans working in iron, bronze, and enameling. There would have been a residential quarter grouping the houses of the rich together, which would have been constructed from local materials but would have used Roman plans and building techniques. Part of the plateau would have been taken up by a market and sanctuaries. If this urban plan is taken at face value today, then the idea of living conditions, which reflect the workings of a real town, from the end of the second century B.C. become characteristic of the late La Tène period, and subsequently the reply to F. Braudel's question, "Was there really a type of Gaulish town before the Roman conquest?" would be yes.

The archaeological remains were reexamined in 1984, supported by a research center that was welcomed by university teams from all over Europe because the site of Mont Beuvray had remained an important point of reference for all Celtic specialists. The large numbers and variety of artifacts attracted numismatists, epigraphers, and ceramologists, and the stratigraphy, as an open-area site, was the source of much useful archaeological research. The first results focused on what had developed essentially between the second and the first centuries B.C., between the La Tène C (II) and the Roman stratigraphic horizons, wedged before the camps of the German limes (fortified frontier). Neither the buildings, nor the phases of construction, nor the events of the years 58–52 B.C. could be read at the site, but dendrochronology provided some sort of precision in dating, with the identifiable phases in combination with all the variables covering a period of about twenty years.

The remains of the Porte du Rebout revealed at least four principal phases of construction between 90 and 10 B.C. The first phase of this gate was more than twenty meters in size, gigantic in comparison to similar gates found at more modern Celtic *oppida*. The gate's northern access consisted of a passage forty meters in depth. During subsequent phases, its size was reduced, and the Gaulish wall was replaced by wooden foundations and earthen embankments. The fortification, with its role as much monumental as defensive, would have necessitated thousands of hours of work, dozens of tons of iron, and thousands of cubic meters of wood.

Bulliot had already assigned a significance and luxury to the houses of the rich residential quarter, which rivaled the houses of POMPEII. One of the houses covered 3,000 square meters, and its atrium and peristyle were Roman in style. The remains revealed five successive building stages and floors, all built during the first century B.C., and the original wooden construction was little by little transformed into a stone mansion.

Trade and the craft industry evolved more quickly than architecture. Artisan production soon became mass production, for example, in the fabrication of fibulae (metal pieces); materials, shapes, and molds were modified to ensure greater productivity. We can follow the evolution of the supply of wine, from different parts of ITALY and SPAIN, thanks to the innumerable amphorae at the site.

It is this process of acculturation that is being followed today at Bibracte. The sanctuary, the lanes, and the tombs will all reveal, in a very short time, how they were transformed from an *oppidum,* a concept that was perhaps completely new in the second century B.C., into a veritable Roman town. It was the generosity of the Emperor Augustus, when he allowed the creation of the town of Autun-Augustodum to be built from the remains of Bibracte in about 15 B.C., that ruined the site and eventually led to this archaeological project of the late twentieth century.

Oliver Buchsenschutz

See also Alesia; Celts
References
Buchsenschutz, O., I. B. M. Ralston, and J.-P. Guillaumet. 1999. *Les remparts de Bibracte.* Bibracte 2, 250 p. Glux-en-Glenne: Centre Archéologique Européen du Mont Beuvray.
Goudineau, C., and C. Peyre. 1993. *Bibracte et les Eduens: A la découverte d'un peuple gaulois.* Paris: Errance.
Guillaumet, J.-P. 1996. *Bibracte, bibliographie et plans anciens.* Danièle Bertin et Eric Melot, no. 57. Paris : Editions de la Maison des Sciences de L'homme.
Richard, H., and O. Buchsenschutz, eds. 1997. *L'environnement du Mont Beuvray.* Glux-en-Glenne: Centre Archéologique Européen.

Binford, Lewis R. (1929–)

One of the most influential archaeologists of the twentieth century, Lewis R. Binford was born in Norfolk, Virginia. After high school he attended Virginia Polytechnic Institute (1948–1952), and following a stint with the U.S. Army in Korea he gained a B.A. in anthropology from the University of North Carolina (1957). Moving to the University of Michigan, Binford received his M.A. in 1958 and his Ph.D. in 1964. Although Binford was at this stage primarily a student of North American prehistoric archaeology, his interest in world prehistory and general archaeological method and theory was already apparent.

Between 1961 and 1965, Binford taught in the Department of Anthropology at the University of Chicago, a period in which he took the first steps toward defining an original position on the relationships between archaeology and anthropology. During these years, Binford's focus on the nature of the archaeological record, on ethnoarchaeology, on the use (and abuse) of inference and analogy in archaeology, and on understanding variability in lithic assemblages made him the center of changes sweeping the practice of archaeology in North America. Although these changes would be later thought of as "the new archaeology," or processual archaeology, and attract a large following, it is clear that Binford was following a research agenda of research of a breadth and significance that was not widely understood.

In 1966, he left Chicago for the Department of Anthropology at the University of California, Santa Barbara, and soon after moved to the Department of Anthropology at the University of California, Los Angeles. It was during this period that Binford's fame as the progenitor of the "new" archaeology first gained widespread attention, especially in 1968 with the publication of *New Perspectives in Archaeology,* a book of essays by the most significant of the new archaeologists, which he edited with his wife, Sally Binford. In 1968, Binford moved to the Department of Anthropology, University of New Mexico, staying there until he became the distinguished professor of anthropology at Southern Methodist University in Dallas, Texas, in 1991.

After 1968, Binford continued to develop his ideas about the nature of the archaeological record and the role of the archaeologist as anthropologist. He has published numerous books and articles, given conference addresses, seminar presentations, and been an invited speaker

at many of the major archaeological departments around the globe. Although his focus has tended to be on the prehistoric record, Binford has undertaken significant ethnoarchaeological field research in Alaska and observed similar studies in Australia. He has also pursued fundamental research into site formation processes and taphonomy as well as continuing his interests in assemblage variability and the origins of humanity. A noted speaker and fierce debater, Binford has collected volumes of his essays, which are made more interesting still by frequent asides and vignettes of his personal history. Binford remains a strong opponent of those who seek to move archaeology away from a concern with science.

For an archaeologist of his undoubted influence and significance, Binford has been granted few honors by the members of his profession. He received an honorary doctorate from the University of Southampton in the 1980s, and in 2000, the University of Leiden in the Netherlands conferred a doctorate on him.

Tim Murray

See also United States of America, Prehistoric Archaeology

References

For references, see *Encyclopedia of Archaeology: The Great Archaeologists,Vol. 2,* ed. Tim Murray (Santa Barbara, CA: ABC-CLIO, 1999), 811–834.

Bird, Junius Bouton (1907–1982)

Born in Rye, New York, Bird became an accomplished sailor and outdoorsman at an early age and sailed to the Arctic several times, where he undertook his first research in Greenland and Labrador. A pioneer of radiocarbon dating methods and the study and conservation of textiles, Bird worked as an archaeologist at the American Museum of Natural History in New York City for fifty years.

Between 1936 and 1937 Bird excavated Fell's Cave and other sites in Chilean Patagonia, where he found human artifacts in association with extinct fauna, establishing the antiquity of the Paleo-Indian occupation of South America. In 1941 Bird excavated a long prehistoric sequence in the Atacama region in northern

CHILE. From 1946 to 1947 he worked in PERU, as part of the VIRÚ VALLEY survey, where he excavated the mound at Huaca Prieta. Data from this excavation not only proved the existence of pre-ceramic cultures on the Peruvian coast, but also established textiles as the major form of expression of ancient Andean culture. Bird continued to work at smaller sites in South America, but in his final years he worked in PANAMA.

Bird received the Viking Fund Medal and the Order of the Sun of Peru. He was president of the Society of American Archaeology and chairman of the Anthropology Section of the New York Academy of Sciences. He received an honorary doctorate from Wesleyan University in 1958.

Tim Murray

Biskupin

The site of Biskupin is located in Bydgoszcz Province in northwestern POLAND. It is an early–Iron Age fortified settlement belonging to the late Lusatian culture and dates to approximately 750–550 B.C. Biskupin is the country's best known archaeological site both within Poland and outside of it.

The settlement at Biskupin was situated on an island, defended by timber breakwaters, and fortified by ramparts of timber compartments filled with earth and stones. The earth embankments were usually built on a foundation of beams and secured by vertical piles. The gateways to the settlement were an important part of fortifications, and the main feature of each was an approach that was lined on both sides by massive palisade walls and was probably covered on the top.

The settlement inside was constructed according to a plan, with a regular network of streets and communication tracks. The main arterial road was the street leading around the ramparts, and there were eleven parallel streets perpendicular to the arterial road. There was a small square near each of the gateways. The settlement consisted of 104–106 rectangular tim-

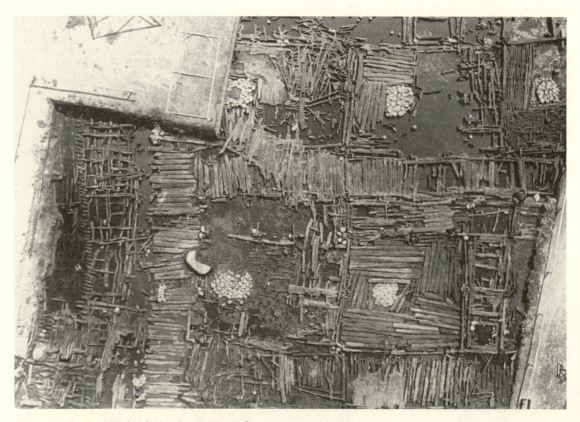

Biskupin (Klaudyna Kucharska/Archivum Fotograficzne Meseum Archeologicznego)

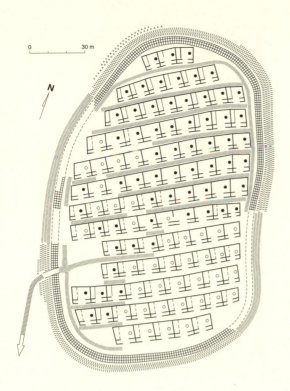

Plan of Biskupin

ber houses laid out on a regular street system, and they may have housed up to 1,000 people. Each house interior was divided into two parts with the entrance fulfilling economic functions. Two phases of occupation have been distinguished, and 75 percent of the site has been excavated thus far.

The fortified settlement of Biskupin was found in 1933 and excavation began in 1934. Fieldwork was directed by JÓZEF KOSTRZEWSKI and Zdzislaw Rajewski with the participation of Wojciech Kocka, Tadeusz Wieczorowski, Feliks Wydra, and Jozef Szubert. Excavations were carried out in the years 1934–1939, and when they resumed in 1946 after World War II, they continued until the 1960s. Various specialists from complementary disciplines participated: soil and geological studies (Feliks Terlikowski, Jozef Czekalski, Karol Paulo), palynological analyses (Adam Paszewski, Julian Witold Rafalski), archaeozoological studies (Edward Lubicz-Niezabitowski), botanical and dendrological studies (Bronislaw Jaron, Tadeusz Dominik), ethnographic research of the Biskupin architecture (Stanislaw Poniatowski), and others.

Photographic documentation of the site was very important. Wojciech Kocka developed the technique of taking pictures from a small balloon, and there were very successful attempts to produce color photographs as early as 1939. Research at Biskupin marked enormous progress in Polish archaeological studies. It was truly comprehensive, owing to the fruitful cooperation with specialists from other disciplines. This cooperation was characterized by real partnership, and it led to the development of new methods of excavation. The large scale of the research was also significant. After World War II, Biskupin was the place where practical courses on excavation methods for students of archaeology, history, and the history of art were organized. As a result, the great majority of students of that time gained their archaeological experiences in Biskupin.

Biskupin is now a well-known archaeological open-air museum. It was, and still is, an important center for experimental archaeology, especially in building, tillage, food preparation, stone and flint work, antler and bone work, wood and wool work, clay processing, and the obtaining of tar.

Arkadiusz Marciniak

References
Rajewski, Zdzislaw. 1959. *Biskupin: Polish Excavations* [translation by Leopold Widymski]. Warsaw: Polonia.

Blegen, Carl William (1887–1971)

Born in Minneapolis, Minnesota, Blegen excavated at Korakou, Prosymna, and Pylos in GREECE, but he is best known for his extensive excavations at Troy. Blegen was professor of classical archaeology at the University of Cincinnati, Ohio (1927–1957). As secretary of the AMERICAN SCHOOL OF CLASSICAL STUDIES AT ATHENS, Blegen, along with Alan Wace, director of the British School in Athens, devised a chronology for mainland Greece for the Early, Middle, and Late Helladic periods through the pottery sequence from their excavation of the prehistoric site of Korakou in Corinthia (1915–1916). Blegen and Wace were convinced that although Minoan in origin Mycenean civilization was not the result of the conquest of mainland Greece, as argued by SIR ARTHUR EVANS, but was a combination of Minoan civilization with another civilization on the mainland.

To elucidate the relationship between Mycenean and Minoan civilization Wace began excavating Mycenae in 1921 (and finished, after many interruptions, in 1955) while Blegen investigated Troy, which he regarded as a key Aegean and Anatolian site. Between 1932 and 1938 Blegen tested sections of the mound that had not been touched by HEINRICH SCHLIEMANN and WILHELM DORPFELD, finding that the previously identified nine cities of Troy only represented two or more phases in the Bronze Age out of a total of forty-six phases. He attributed Homer's Troy to the major period VIIa (ca. 1250 B.C.) because there was strong evidence that the city was destroyed by war.

In 1939 Blegen returned to mainland Greece to find the Mycenean capital of Messinia, which Homer had said belonged to "King Nester of Pylos." He excavated the hilltop of Espano Englianos and found a Mycenean palace, the excavation of which was not completed until 1966. The palace of Pylos was much better preserved and more carefully excavated than those at Mycenae or Tiryns, even if it was not as large. While its layout and decoration were similar to those of Minoan palaces, it was more fundamentally like Greek Mycenean palaces. In this architectural analysis Blegen had accurately defined the extent of Minoan influence on Mycenean Greece. Of equal importance were hundreds of clay tablets inscribed with early European script and dating from ca. 1250 B.C. discovered by Blegen at Pylos. Blegen's account of the history of Pylos received important confirmation when MICHAEL VENTRIS deciphered Linear B in 1951.

Tim Murray

See also Linear A/Linear B

Boğazköy

Boğazköy is the site of the ancient city of Hattusha, the capital of the Hittites. Located in north-central Anatolia (TURKEY), Boğazköy was first discovered in 1834 by French archaeologist Charles Felix Marie Texier, who also recorded bas relief carvings of humans and animals and some unusual hieroglyphs. The site was further described on several occasions during the late-nineteenth century, but it was not until 1906 when Hugo Winckler (an Assyriologist) began to excavate that a great archive of cuneiform tablets was uncovered. Some of these were in Hittite, but a sufficiently large number were in Akkadian, an ancient language that had already been deciphered. Excavation by German teams at Boğazköy has continued and has revealed much about Hittite history.

Tim Murray

Bolivia
Colonial Period (1530–1824)

After the discovery of the New World, the Spanish colonial system was established in a large part of the Americas, including what is now Bolivia. During this period, early Spanish chroniclers started to describe the customs, traditions, and monuments of native cultures.

An extensive array of documents was produced, such as the early chronicles and descriptions by both Spaniards and Creoles, legal and litigant documents, and administrative censuses for taxes. Such efforts have had a variety of purposes: they provide the information needed to "adapt" the native socioeconomic institutions into the colonial system; to "civilize" and christianize the Indians; to claim ancient rights pertaining to land, wealth, and status in favor of native elites; or to denounce the abuses of Indians on the part of the Spanish authorities and *encomenderos*. Because of the varied nature of such documents, each provides a different perspective on the impact that the colonial system had on native Bolivian populations. These documents are also of great anthropological value for understanding complex cultural variability in the Andes and for an accurate combination of the archaeological and ethnohistorical disciplines in the reconstruction of the prehistoric Bolivian past.

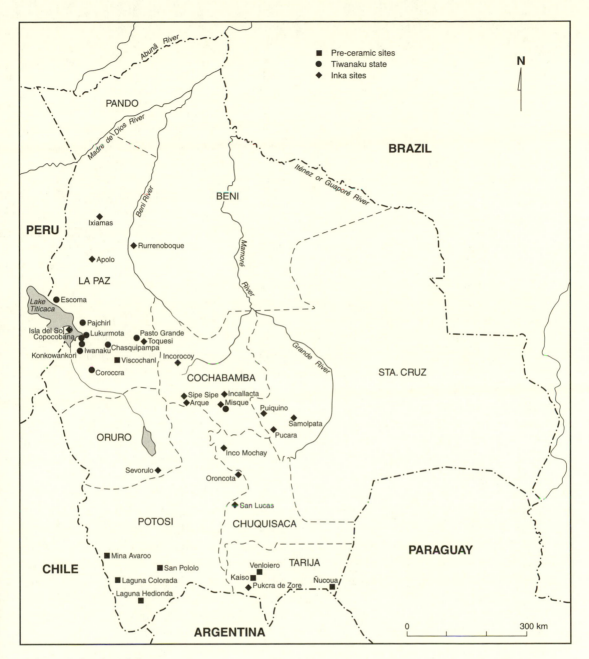

Pre-ceramic sites
Tiwanaku state
Inka sites

N

PANDO

Abuná River

BRAZIL

Madre de Dios River

Beni River

BENI

Iténez or Guaporé River

PERU

◆ Ixiamas

◆ Rurrenoboque

◆ Apolo

LA PAZ

Mamoré River

Lake Titicaca

● Escoma

● Pajchirl

Isla del Sol ◆
Copocobana

● Lukurmota   ● Pasto Grande
◆ Toquesi
■ Chasquipampa

Konkowankori   ● Iwanaku   ◆ Incorocoy
■ Viscochanl

● Coroccra

COCHABAMBA

◆ Sipe Sipe   ◆ Incallacta
◆ Arque   ● Misque

● Puiquino

Grande River

STA. CRUZ

◆ Samolpata
◆ Pucara

● Inco Mochay

ORURO

● Sevorulo

◆ Oroncota

◆ San Lucas

POTOSI

CHUQUISACA

PARAGUAY

■ Mina Avaroo

■ San Pololo   Venloiero
■ Kaiso   TARIJA
■ Laguna Colorada   ◆ Pukcra de Zore   Ñucoua ■

CHILE

■ Laguna Hedionda

0   300 km

ARGENTINA

Bolivian Archaeological Sites

The Republican Period (1825–1890)

The consolidation of Bolivia as a state brought with it a series of changes in the way native antiquities were perceived. Still with a colonialist approach, a new interest emerged in ancient cultures and native groups. During the first part of this period, foreign scholars visited Bolivia with a renewed interest in ethnography, ancient monuments, natural sciences, zoology, and botany. Their focus was mostly descriptive, and the value of their documents lies in the extensive descriptive information provided. The most important scholars visiting Bolivia at this time included Alcides D'Orbigny (1839), a French naturalist whose main goal in the 1830s was to compile information about the diversity of the human races in South America; Johan J. Tschudi (1851), a German naturalist who described the early native monuments around 1838–1842; and Francis de Castelnau (1851), who argued that Tiwanaku was an influential predecessor of the Inca empire. Ephraim George Squier (1870), a U.S. diplomat appointed to Lima, PERU, in the 1860s, stands out for his detailed description and mapping of Tiwanaku and other important archaeological sites (Albarracín-Jordan 1999; Ponce Sanginés 1995).

On the local level, the consolidation of Bolivia as a nation state was coupled with the need of emerging Creole elites to develop their own sense of identity, one that was different from that of colonial Spain but still divorced from the oppressed Indian populations. Additionally, the increasing visits of foreign explorers involved with diplomatic affairs renewed the interest of the Bolivian government in its ancient monuments. For example, the Bolivian president José Ballivian ordered nonsystematic excavations in Tiwanaku with only the goal of collecting archaeological pieces for the local museum in the city of La Paz (Ponce Sanginés 1995). The perception that archaeology was simply part of art history, involved with the recollection and collection of aesthetic artifacts, was part of a broader tendency in the first stages of archaeology before its consolidation as a science. During this period, and even later, most of the archaeological work in Bolivia was restricted to the collection of artifacts and description of archaeological monuments.

The Beginnings of Archaeology (1890–1952)

During the last decade of the nineteenth century and the first half of the twentieth, the beginnings of Bolivian archaeology emerged with a more scientific approach. These first efforts were by foreign researchers visiting Bolivia, most of them part of research programs promoted by international museums. The goal of these scholars was, not just scientific inquiry, but in some cases, to acquire archaeological collections for exhibition in foreign museums. This practice of acquiring collections of artifacts from developing countries for display in the

home country's museums was part of the colonial approach to archaeology and typical of those times. On a national level, this was the period of intensive exploitation and export of tin and the advent of liberalism and modernism into the Bolivian political arena.

Adolph Bandelier, an archaeologist working in the American Museum of Natural History in New York City, visited different places in Peru and Bolivia during 1892–1897. From Bolivia, Bandelier (1910) provided important descriptions, maps, and collected indigenous myths of origin from the Island of the Sun, the Island of the Moon, and Tiwanaku (the mythical centers of origin of the Inca empire). He also collected archaeological objects that were later transported to the American Museum of Natural History.

Erland Nordenskiöld, a Swedish scholar, also conducted several scientific expeditions with an archaeological and ethnographical focus in different areas of Bolivian territory during 1901–1914. His work was conducted not only in the Bolivian highlands, but he was also one of the first to provide firsthand information about the intermediate valleys and Amazonian tropics. He described the variety of ethnic groups inhabiting those areas, and he also carried out excavations at several habitation mounds in the lowlands (Trinidad), at sites located in the valleys of Cochabamba (Mizque, Caballero, Saipina), and in Santa Cruz. He provided the first relative chronologies and detailed artifact inventories, and he identified previously unknown archaeological cultures. His extensive work was published in 1953.

The work of Arthur Posnansky (1904–1940) also stands out. As a naval engineer from Vienna who was impressed by the ruins of Tiwanaku, Posnansky (1945) produced detailed maps of the monuments and structures in Tiwanaku. He also speculated that this ancient culture was the cradle of American humans and that Tiwanaku was on the shores of an ancient lake.

In 1903, a multidisciplinary French expedition directed by Georges de Crèqui-Montfort made the first excavations in Tiwanaku. Several areas of Tiwanaku were excavated such as the pyramid of Akapana, the semi-sunken temple of

Aerial photograph of Tiwanaku (Marilyn Bridges)

Kalasasaya, and Putuni. However, written material documenting these findings remains scarce, and part of the excavated material was transported to the Musée de l'Homme in Paris (Ponce Sanginés 1995).

From 1932 to 1934, Wendell C. Bennett from the Museum of Natural History, New York City, made a series of excavations and test pits around Tiwanaku, Lukurmata, Pajchiri, and Chiripa in the Bolivian highlands and other prehistoric sites in the Cochabamba valleys such as Arani. Bennett's main contribution was to establish a relative chronology based on stylistic ceramic changes over time, and his chronology is still the basis for modern archaeological studies. The excavations, coordinated with the Bolivian National Museum, provided a great number of finds that were later transported to the Museum of Natural History in New York City (Bennett 1934, 1936; Ponce Sanginés 1995).

Starting in 1940 and continuing for several years, the Argentine Dick E. Ibarra Grasso undertook small-scale excavations and artifact collection in different Bolivian regions, and he was

one of the first to identify a number of local archaeological cultures in Bolivian valleys such Mojocoya, Tupuraya, Nazcoide-Omereque, Yampara, Yura, and Uruquilla. He also provided a relative chronology and local sequence for these archaeological cultures, and the materials he collected constituted the bases for regional museums throughout Bolivia (Ibarra Grasso and Querejazu Lewis 1986).

During 1938, the Swedish archaeologist Stig Rydén from the Ethnographic Museum of Göteborg conducted a series of excavations in Tiwanaku and Wankani. He confirmed Bennett's chronological sequence, identified Tiwanaku's domestic ceramic assemblage, and recognized post-Tiwanaku cultural components in the highlands. During 1951–1952, Rydén conducted excavations in the intermediate valleys of La Paz (Muñecas, Bautista Saavedra), in the Cochabamba valleys (Tupuraya) and in Oruro (Cayhuasi), collecting and providing detailed artifact inventories of the local cultural components of these areas, including the post-Tiwanaku funerary towers *(chullpas)* from the late intermediate period and Inca remains (Rydén 1952, 1957). During 1958, a German, Heinz Walter, conducted excavations in the regions of Mizque-Lakatambo (Cochabamba) and Icla-Chullpamoko (Chuquisaca) to investigate the chronology and stylistic distribution of local ceramic styles (Walter 1968).

In 1955, the American archaeologist ALFRED KIDDER from the Museum of Pennsylvania visited Bolivia and studied the ruins of Chiripa, the cultural predecessor of Tiwanaku during the formative period. He excavated the ceremonial mound of Chiripa, along with Gregorio Cordero, a Bolivian archaeologist working at the National Museum of Tiwanaku (Kidder 1956). Unfortunately, little information about these excavations was published. Between 1974 and 1975, David Browman also focused his efforts on the excavation of Chiripa, providing a new interpretation of the origins and formation of Tiwanaku as the capital of a multiethnic confederation and highlighting the role of llama caravans in the economic and political integration of the Bolivian highlands and valleys (Browman 1981).

There was almost an absence of Bolivian archaeologists excavating or generating theoretical interpretations during this period. Among the few and most important ones were Maks Portugal Zamora and Gregorio Cordero Miranda, both of whom were involved in the direction of the National Museum of Tiwanaku. Portugal Zamora (1957) excavated different archaeological sites such as Chiripa and others in the highlands while Cordero Miranda (1955, 1978) focused his research in Tiwanaku and excavating different areas, including the Pumapunku pyramid. However, most of their investigations were neither documented nor published, which is a loss for Bolivian archaeology.

Another significant feature of this period is the near absence of Bolivians participating in international archaeological projects. When Bolivians did participate, their role was secondary. There are three main reasons for this situation: first, Bolivian archaeology was not as yet institutionalized; second, Bolivian researchers did not have a clear vision about the role of archaeology as a scientific discipline; and third, the economic support of archaeology by the Bolivian state was minimal.

Institutionalization and the Rise of National Archaeology

The nationalist revolution in 1952 had a great impact on the way Bolivian archaeology was organized and structured at the government level. One of the goals of the new revolutionary government was to reinforce the image of a unified nationhood by creating a sense of national identity. In this process, the construction of a glorious past became an important element, and archaeology gained the support of the emerging elites. In 1958, the Center of Archaeological Investigations in Tiwanaku (CIAT) was created under the direction of the Ministry of Education, and its main goal was to conduct extensive research and archaeological excavations in Tiwanaku.

The creation of CIAT constituted the first systematic effort of the Bolivian state toward the institutionalization of archaeological research. Starting in 1957, under the direction of Carlos Ponce Sanginés and the sponsorship of the Bolivian government, different areas of Tiwanaku such as Kalasasaya and Akapana were extensively excavated, preserved, and restored, constituting what is today one of the most important sites of Bolivian patrimony. As a result of these excavations, Ponce formulated an evolutionary sequence for Tiwanaku, based on radiocarbon dating, as follows: (1) Hamlet Tiwanaku, B.C. 1590–A.D. 43; (2) Urban Tiwanaku, A.D. 43–667; and (3) Imperial Tiwanaku, A.D. 667–1050. It is clear that Tiwanaku was not just a ceremonial center, as previously suggested (Bennett 1934), but an extensive urban center and the capital of an expansive empire (Ponce Sanginés 1981). Ponce's ideas and interpretation remain pivotal for the understanding of the Tiwanaku polity, and they were spread widely through a series of publications.

In 1975, the National Institute of Archaeology (INAR) was established as the main government organization in charge of executing, organizing, sponsoring, and regulating archaeological research in all of Bolivia. Ponce Sanginés, its main promoter and first director, organized a series archaeological projects in

The Gateway of the Sun, Tiwanaku (Wolfgang Kaehler / Corbis)

different Bolivian regions and created diverse regional centers for archaeological research. Among these were the Regional Museum of Aukapata (1973), the Centers of Archaeological Investigations in Samaipata-Santa Cruz (1974), and the Center of Archaeological Research in Copacabana (1978) (Ponce Sanginés 1995). In contrast to the previous period, most archaeological research was conducted by Bolivians. Among those who stand out are Max Portugal Ortiz, Juan Faldín, José Estévez, and Oswaldo Rivera S. Portugal.

Portugal Ortiz (1992) defined the Pa-Ajanu lithic sculpture style, discussed its connection with other formative cultures in Peru (Pucara), and augmented the inventory of Tiwanaku and Amazonian-related archaeological sites. Juan Faldín worked with the Mollo culture in Iskanwaya (in the mesothermal valleys) and refined the artifact inventory of the culture. José Estévez carried out excavations at Lukurmata (a secondary site of Tiwanaku) and Pasto Grande

(in the Bolivian Yungas), and in collaboration with Marc Bermann, he investigated Wankarani, a formative highland culture. Oswaldo Rivera Sundt, along with Alan Kolata, worked in the rehabilitation of ancient agricultural raised fields in modern Aymara communities. Jorge Arellano also excavated different areas of Iskanwaya, defined the sources of the lithic materials of the Pumapunku pyramid, and conducted research at southern Bolivian Paleolithic sites.

In 1985, a new generation of Bolivian archaeologists, such as Eduardo Pareja and Javier Escalante, began working on research projects sponsored by INAR. This increase in archaeological research has focused on the highlands and on different excavations and surveys conducted by university museums throughout the country. The Institute of Anthropologic Research and the Archaeological Museum from the San Simón University (Cochabamba) and the Archaeological Museum of San Francisco Xavier (Chuquisaca) have coparticipated in a series of archaeological projects and have promoted the protection of the prehistoric cultural heritage in those regions. Added to these efforts, the creation of the Department of Anthropology and Archaeology at the University of San Andrés in La Paz in 1984 provided a firm base for the education of a new generation of Bolivian archaeologists.

Current Archaeological Research

Since the 1980s, new multinational and multidisciplinary projects have been conducted in Bolivia. The Wilajawira archaeological project, under the direction of Alan Kolata and Oswaldo Rivera Sundt, has revealed the importance of raised fields in the Tiwanaku agricultural economy, the centralized structure of the Tiwanaku state (with a quadripartite hierarchical system), and the nature of urbanism in the Tiwanaku core (Kolata 1989, 1993).

The International Seminar of Archaeological Excavations in Tiwanaku, a part of the Wilajawira project directed by Kolata and Ponce Sanginés, developed a number of specifically oriented research areas such as paleoethnobotany and diet analysis (Lennstrom, Hastorf, and Wright 1991), settlement pattern studies (Albarracín-Jordán 1990; Mathews 1992), household and domestic archaeology (Bermann 1994; Janusek 1994), craft specialization (Rivera Casanovas 1994), public architecture (Couture 1992; Manzanilla and Woodard 1992; Rivera Sundt 1989; Sampeck 1991), physical anthropology and demography (Blom 1999), paleozoology (Webster 1993), and ceramic analysis (Alconini 1995; Sutherland 1991). Undoubtedly, the Wilajawira archaeological project constituted the largest multinational effort, produced a great body of information about Tiwanaku, and set the foundation for a multidisciplinary approach to Bolivian archaeology.

Other multinational and multidisciplinary projects have been conducted in the highlands. Since 1992, Christine Hastorf, head of the Taraco archaeological project, has been conducting an extensive investigation of the site of Chiripa, a pre-Tiwanaku polity that arose during the formative period near the shores of Lake Titicaca. The most important contributions of this project were the excavation and exposure of the ceremonial core of Chiripa, comprising a series of terraced platforms, specialized architecture, and burial and domestic areas around a semi-sunken temple. The project has also refined the chronological sequence of the site, conducted regional studies, and paleobotanical analysis (Hastorf et al. 1996). Another large-scale project was the Iwawe archaeological project, which was directed by William H. Isbell and Juan Albarracín-Jordán between 1995 and 1998 in the Iwawe region near Lake Titicaca. This work clarified our understanding of the formative period and the origins of Tiwanaku before it became a state (Isbell 1993). Charles Stanish and others have conducted extensive excavations and settlement studies at the Island of the Sun, Lake Titicaca (Stanish et al. 1996).

Small-scale projects, with Bolivian participation, have also been conducted in the Bolivian highlands. These include the Yaya-Mama archaeological project, coordinated by Karen Mohr Chavez, Sergio Chavez, and Eduardo Pareja in the region of Copacabana and adjacent areas since 1993, which seeks to understand the role played by religion in the unification of the various polities around the lake before the emergence of Tiwanaku. A new approach to archaeology has been implemented by Sergio Chavez in his promotion of the participation of local indigenous Aymara communities in different stages of archaeological research, part of a strategy to make them active participants in the reconstruction and reappropriation of their own cultural past.

Other regions of Bolivia were also subjected to similar multinational and multidisciplinary projects in the decade 1990–2000. Albert Meyers (1997), from the University of Bonn, and a German-Bolivian team have extensively excavated, conserved, and restored different areas of Samaipata, an Inca complex with one of the largest carved rocks in South America located at the margins of the sub-Andean piedmont before the rise of the Amazonian savannas. Other small-scale binational projects have been conducted in these tropical areas. In Beni, Clark Erickson, along with Bolivian and American archaeologists, has documented the landscape,

Incallajta Inca complex in the Cochabamba valleys (from Werner Guttentag, Incallajta y la Conquista Incaica del Collasuyu *[La Paz-Cochabamba: Los Amigos del Libro, 1998])*

spatial distribution, variability, and chronology of the extensive raised fields on the Moxos tropical savannas. This work was based on initial observations made by William Denevan in the 1960s about this prehistoric agricultural technique on the Moxos plains, and similar work has been conducted by Marcos Michel on the Beni plains. Heiko Prümers and his team have excavated a series of occupational mounds in the tropical savannas of Santa Cruz and Beni in order to identify different archaeological cultures and provide a chronological sequence for the region (Prümers and Winkler 1997).

In the southern highlands of Potosí, Patrice Lecoq (1997), in cooperation with the Archaeological Museum of Cochabamba and INAR, has conducted extensive surveys and settlement studies related to Altiplanic post-Tiwanaku cultures during the late intermediate and Inca periods in the inter-Salar region of Uyuni-Coypasa (Potosí and Oruro). In the intermediate Cochabamba valleys, János Gyarmati and András Varga (1999) have documented and excavated different areas of Incarracay, an important

Inca installation in the valleys, and Cotapachi, an extensive Inca storage area. Donald Brockington (1995) has studied and documented the formative period in the southeastern Cochabamba valleys, and Marianne Vetters and Alvaro Higueras (1994) have explored different areas of these multiethnic valleys to understand the settlement pattern distribution and type of interaction established between local populations and Tiwanaku.

In the southern valleys, efforts to identify and document local prehistoric manifestations are being conducted by the Bolivians in the region inhabited by the Uruquillas (Rivera Casanovas 1998) and in the regions of Oroncota and Monteagudo inhabited by the Yamparas, Incas, and Chiriguanos (Alconini M. 1998). Martti Pärssinen has worked in Chuquisaca, in regions also inhabited by the Yamparas, in order to define the nature of the Inca impact by combining ethnohistorical and archaeological sources. Additionally, John Janusek has conducted studies related to settlement pattern and prehistoric household economy in the region of

Icla (Chuquisaca), and Axel Nielsen has worked in the southern Bolivian region on ethnoarchaeological research related to the economy of llama caravans. On the national level, the Department of Anthropology and Archaeology at the Mayor University of San Andrés has been promoting small-scale projects and research dissertations throughout Bolivia.

The last decades have witnessed a growth in Bolivian archaeology as a scientific discipline. Not only is more research being conducted, but its nature is more multidisciplinary and its focus has expanded from the highlands into the valleys and Amazonian regions. New theoretical paradigms, methodologies, and techniques are now being applied to archaeological data by both Bolivian and foreign archaeologists. The execution of bilateral and binational research projects, although still being consolidated, offers an opportunity of mutual enrichment under the protection of the national archaeological patrimony on both domestic and international levels. New international laws reinforcing the protection of archaeological, historic, and native heritage, and tied to the institutionalization of Bolivian archaeology, have contributed to the growth of public awareness about the importance of research projects involving national and foreign scholars and native populations. However, in comparison with other countries in Latin America, such as MEXICO and Peru, archaeology in Bolivia is still in the process of consolidation and maturation.

Sonia Alconini

See also Inca

References

Albarracín-Jordán, Juan V. 1999. *The Archaeology of Tiwanaku: The Myths, History, and Science of an Ancient Andean Civilization.* La Paz: Edición del Autor.

Albarracín-Jordan, Juan V., and James E. Mathews. 1990. *Asentamientos prehispánicos del Valle de Tiwanaku.* Vol. 1. La Paz: Producciones Cima.

Alconini M., Sonia. 1991. "Algunas reflexiones sobre la formación de la arqueología en Bolivia." *Etnología: Boletín del Museo Nacional de Etnografía y Folklore* no. 19.

———. 1995. *Rito, símbolo, e historia en la Pirámide de Akapana, Tiwanaku: Un análisis de cerámica ceremonial prehispánica.* La Paz: Editorial Acción.

———. 1998. *Frontera Inka en el Chaco: Una aproximación a la interacción Inka con los Guaraní-Chiriguanos.* Informe de trabajo de campo no publicado 1996 presentado a la Secretaría Nacional de Cultura y la Dirección Nacional de Arqueología y Anthropología.

Bandelier, Adolph Francis. 1910. *The Islands of Titicaca and Koati.* Ed. Hispanic Society of America, New York: The Hispanic Society of America.

Bennett, Wendell Clark. 1934. *Excavations at Tiahuanaco.* Anthropological Papers 34, 14. New York: American Museum of Natural History.

———. 1936. *Excavations in Bolivia.* Anthropological Papers 35, 3. New York: American Museum of Natural History.

Bermann, Mar. 1994. *Lukrmata: Household Archaeology in Prehispanic Bolivia.* Princeton, NJ: Princeton University Press.

Blom, Deborah Eileen. 1999. "Tiwanaku Regional Interaction and Social Identity: A Bioarchaeological Approach." Ph.D. dissertation, Department of Anthropology, University of Chicago.

Brockington, Donald. 1995. *Estudios arqueológicos del periodo formativo en el sur-este de Cochabamba, 1988–1989.* Cochabamba, Bolivia: Instituto de Investigaciones Antropológicas y Museo Arqueológico, Universidad Mayor de San Simón, Instituto Antropológico y Museo.

Browman, David L. 1981. "New Light on Andean Tiwanaku." *American Scientist* 69: 408–419.

Castelnau, Francis de. 1851. *Expéditions dans les parties centrales de l'Amérique du Sud: Historie du voyage.* Vol. 3. Paris: P. Bertrand.

Cordero Miranda, Gregorio. 1955. "Informe de las excavaciones de dos pozos en Tihuanacu." Unpublished document, 29 July. La Paz.

———. 1978. "Informe preliminar acerca de las excavaciones en Pumapunku." Instituto Nacional de Arqueología unpublished document N. 33/78. Presented to the "Segunda reunión de las jornadas peruano bolivianas de estudio científico del altiplano boliviano y del sur del Peru." La Paz.

Couture, Nicole Claire. 1992. "Excavations at Mollo Kontu, Tiwanaku." Master's thesis, Department of Anthropology, University of Chicago.

Créqui-Montfort, Georges de. 1905. "Exploración científica en Bolivia." *Boletín de la Sociedad Geográfica de La Paz.* La Paz: Romero.

D'Orbigny, Alcides. 1839. *L'homme americain.* Vol. 1. Paris: Chez Pitois-Levrault.

Erickson, Clark L. 1999. "Neo-environmental Determinism and Agrarian 'Collapse' in Andean Prehistory." *Antiquity* 73, no. 281: 634–642.

Gyarmati, János, and András Varga. 1999. *The Chacaras of War: An Inka State Estate in the Cochabamba Valley, Bolivia.* Budapest: Museum of Ethnography.

Hastorf, Christine, Matthew Bandy, Deborah Blom, Emily Dean, Melissa Goodman, David Kojan, Mario Montaño Aragón, José Luis Paz, David Steadman, Lee Steadman, and William Whitehead. 1996. "Proyecto arqueológico Taraco: Excavaciones de 1996 en Chiripa, Bolivia." Unpublished document presented to the Dirección de la Secretaría Nacional de Cultura-Instituto Nacional de Arqueología and the University of California, Berkeley.

Higueras, Alvaro. 1994. "Tiwanaku Interaction and Human/Land Relationships in Cochabamba, Bolivia." Unpublished paper presented at the thirteenth annual Northeast Conference on Andean Archaeology and Ethnohistory, 15–16 October, Ithaca, NY.

Ibarra Grasso, Dick Edgar, and Roy Querejazu Lewis. 1986. *30.0000 años de prehistoria en Bolivia.* La Paz–Cochabamba, Bolivia: Los Amigos del Libro Werner Guttentag.

Isbell, William H. 1993. "Iwawi Cermic Style Project." Unpublished proposal funded by the National Science Foundation.

Janusek, John W. 1994. "State and Local Power in a Prehispanic Andean Polity: Changing Patters of Urban Residence in Tiwanaku and Lukurmata, Bolivia." Ph.D. dissertation, Department of Anthropology, University of Chicago.

Kidder, Alfred V. 1956. "Digging in the Titicaca Basin." *University Museum Bulletin, University of Pennsylvania* 20, no. 3.

Kolata, Alan. 1989. "The Agricultural Foundations of the Tiwanaku State: A View from the Heartland. *American Antiquity* 51: 748–762.

———. 1993. *The Tiwanaku: Portrait of an Andean Civilization.* Cambridge: Blackwell.

Lecoq, Patrice. 1997. *Patrón de asentamiento, estilos cerámicos, y grupos etnicos: El ejemplo de la región intersalar en Bolivia.* Ed. Thérèse Boysse-Cassagne. Saberes in Memorias en Los Andes: In Memoriam Thierry Saignes. Lima: IHEAL-IFEA.

Lennstrom, Heidy, Christine Hastorf, and Melanie Wright. 1991. "Tiwanaku Akapana Mound Flotation Samples." Unpublished n. 21 report from the Archaeo-Botanic Laboratory, University of Minnesota.

Manzanilla, Linda, and Eric Woodard. 1992. *Akapana: Una pirámide en el centro del mundo.* Mexico City: Instituto de Investigaciones Antropológicas, Universidad Nacional Autónoma.

Mathews, James E. 1992. "Prehispanic Settlement and Agriculture in the Middle Tiwanaku Valley, Bolivia." Ph.D. dissertation, Department of Anthropology, University of Chicago.

Meyers, Albert. 1997. *Informe de labores sobre las campañas arqueológicas llevadas a cabo en los años de 1994–1996 en el sitio llamado:"El Fuerte de Samaipata."* Bonn: Junio.

Michel L., Marcos, and Claudia Rivera C. 1993–1995. "La práctica de la arqueología en Bolivia." *Instituto Panamericano de Geografía e Historia: Revista de Arqueología Americana* 8 (July–December 1993 and January–June 1995).

Nordenskiöld, Erland. 1953. *Investigaciones arqueológicas en la región fronteriza de Peru y Bolivia.* Trans. Carlos Ponce Sanginés and Stig Rydén. La Paz: Biblioteca Paceña.

Pärssinnen, Martti. 1997. *Investigaciones arqueológicas con ayuda de fuentes históricas: Experiencias en Cajamarca, Pacasa, y Yampara.* Ed. Thérèse Boysse-Cassagne. Saberes in Memorias en Los Andes: In Memoriam Thierry Saignes. Lima: IHEAL-IFEA.

Ponce Sanginés, Carlos. 1981. *Tiwanaku: Espacio tiempo y cultura; ensayo de síntesis arqueológica.* 4th ed. La Paz and Cochabamba: Los Amigos del Libro editorial.

———. 1995. *Tiwanaku: 200 años de investigaciones arqueológicas.* La Paz: Producciones Cima.

Portugal Ortiz, Max. 1992. "Aspectos de la cultura Chiripa." *Textos Antropológicos* 3: 9–26.

Portugal Zamora, Maks. 1957. "Arqueología de La Paz." *Arqueología Boliviana* 341–401.

Posnansky, Arthur. 1945. *Tihuanacu: Cuna del hombre americano.* 2 vols. New York: J. J. Austin.

Prümers, Heiko, and Wilma Winkler. 1997. *Excavaciones arqueológicas en las tierras bajas Bolivianas: Primer informe del proyecto grigotá.* Beiträge zue Allgemeinen und vergleichenden archäologie, vol. 17. Bonn: Kommission für Allgemeine und Vegleichende Archäologie des Deutschen Archäologischen Instituts.

Rivera Casanovas, Claudia. 1994. "Ch'iji Jawira: Evidencias sobre la producción de cerámica en Tiwanaku." Licenciature thesis, Carreras Department of Anthropology and Archaeology, University Mayor de San Andrés.

———. 1998. "Settlement Patterns and Regional

Interaction in the Cinty Valley, Chuquisaca, Bolivia." Unpublished paper presented to the sixty-third annual meeting of the Society of American Archaeology, Seattle, Washington.

Rivera Sundt, Oswaldo. 1989. Resultados de la excavación en el centro ceremonial de lukurmata. Vol. 2, *Arqueología de Lukurmata.* La Paz: Producciones Puma Punku.

Rydén, Stig. 1952. "Chullpa Pampa: A Pre-Tihuanacu Archaeological Site in the Cochabamba Region, a Preliminary Report." *Ethnos* 1–4: 39–50.

———. 1957. *Andean Excavations, I: The Tihuanaco Era East of Lake Titicaca.* Monograph series. Stockholm: Ethnographical Museum of Sweden.

Sampeck, Kathryn E. 1991. "Excavations at Putuni, Tiwanaku, Bolivia." M.A. thesis, Faculty of Social Sciences, University of Chicago.

Squier, E. George. 1870. "The Primeval Monuments of Peru Compared with Those in Other Parts of the World." *American Naturalist* 4: 3–19.

Stanish, Charles, Brian Bauer, Oswaldo River, Javier Escalante, and Matt Seddon. 1996. "Report of Proyecto tiksi Kjarka on the Island of the Sun, Bolivia, 1994–1995." Unpublished document.

Sutherland, Cheryl Ann. 1991. "Methodological Stylistic and Functional Ceramic Analysis: The Surface Collection at Akapana-East Tiwanaku." M.A. thesis, Department of Anthropology, Faculty of Social Sciences, University of Chicago.

Tschudi, Johan J. 1963. *Peru: Reiseskizzen aus den Jahren 1838–1842.* Graz: Akademische Druck.

Walter, Heinz. 1968. *Archäologische Studien in den Kordilleren Boliviens II: Beitrage zur Archäologie Boliviens.* Baessler-Archiv, Beitrage zur volkerkunde. Berlin: Verlag Von Dietrich Reimer.

Webster, Ann DeMuth. 1993. "The Role of South American Camelid in the Development of the Tiwanaku State." Ph.D. dissertation, Department of Anthropology, University of Chicago.

Bonampak'

A classic Maya site in Chiapas in southern MEXICO, Bonampak' is most famous for the well-preserved murals adorning the interior walls of its principal temple. For decades the temple had been a place of worship by the Lacandon Maya, who today inhabit the region, but the murals became known to the outside world only in 1946.

Bonampak' was the capital city of one of the many small kingdoms that formed the map of the Maya world during the Maya classic period (A.D. 250–900). It alternated between peaceful and bellicose relations with its neighbors, and like many other kingdoms during the classic period was at times dominant and at other times subservient in the hierarchy of kingdoms in the complex political geography of the times. The most famous king of Bonampak' was Yajaw-Chan-Muwa:n, who was responsible for most of the carved monuments that survive at the site. Yajaw-Chan-Muwa:n, who was related by marriage to the royal family of Yaxchilan that lived in a neighboring kingdom, became king of Bonampak' in A.D. 776, toward the end of the capital's history. In one of his carved stelae (Bonampak' Stela 2), he portrays himself about to let blood from his genitals, flanked by his wife (a princess of Yaxchilan) and his mother.

Yajaw-Chan-Muwa:n also built and decorated Structure 1 of Bonampak', which contains the famous murals. These murals are among the best preserved in Mesoamerica and give a fascinating glimpse into classic Maya ritual, warfare, and courtly life. The murals cover the surfaces of all three rooms of the temple. The first room portrays an elaborate procession at the Bonampak' court, in which the key event is the public presentation of the young son of Yajaw-Chan-Muwa:n as the heir apparent to the throne of the kingdom. In the second room is the depiction of a pitched battle in which Yajaw-Chan-Muwa:n and his allies are victorious. Over the doorway of this room, the captives—destined for sacrifice—are displayed before Yajaw-Chan-Muwa:n. The murals in the third room show the victory dance of the triumphant Bonampak' lords while a captive is being sacrificed and members of the court are engaged in letting their own blood.

These wonderful murals were intended to be a lasting record of the ceremonies surrounding the designation of Yajaw-Chan-Muwa:n's son as heir to the throne. The irony is that the young boy portrayed in the murals almost certainly never became king, for, apparently, the site was abandoned before he ever came of age, and

A view from the back, toward the entrance, Temple of Murals, Bonampak' (Ann Ronan Picture Library)

there are indications that the murals were never quite completed.

Peter Mathews

See also Maya Civilization

Bordes, François (1919–1981)

One of the most influential Paleolithic archaeologists of the twentieth century, François Bordes was most famous for his standard Mousterian stone tool typology. He created the typology during the 1950s and refined it over the next decades until it gained enormous influence in the classification of Mousterian materials in Europe and southwestern Asia.

Bordes's great area of influence was in the heartland of French Paleolithic archaeology, southwestern FRANCE, including the Périgord region, and is best expressed by his classic excavation of the sites of Combe Grenal and Pech de l'Azé. Bordes's great advance on previous classifications was in his use of statistical analysis for very large assemblages, which allows the archaeologist to plot changing distribution of artifact types between sites and over time. Bordes also argued that his system allowed the archaeologist to identify the existence of distinct tribes during the Mousterian period in southwestern France, his logic being that distinct toolmaking traditions were the expression of distinct tribal ethnicities. This argument was strongly contested by American archaeologist LEWIS BINFORD (among others), who contended that the variability that Bordes had identified was more likely the product of the different functions the tools were used to perform, different raw materials, different stages in a total production process for tools (reduction sequence), or different time periods. Notwithstanding these arguments, many archaeologists would readily accept the assertion that Paleolithic archaeology was transformed by Bordes's vision. In his spare time, Bordes wrote science-fiction stories and cultivated an interest in cartooning.

Tim Murray

See also Lithic Analysis

References

For references, see Encyclopedia of Archaeology: The Great Archaeologists, Vol. 2, ed. Tim Murray (Santa Barbara, CA: ABC-CLIO, 1999), pp. 773–774.

Botta, Paul Emile (1802–1870)

The son of distinguished Italian historian Carlo Botta, Paul Emile Botta was physician to Pasha Mohammed Ali of Egypt. In 1833 Botta was appointed French consul in Alexandria and in 1840 he was transferred to Mosul in northern Iraq with instructions to find and excavate the biblical city of NINEVEH.

Botta began excavating at Quyunjik, which was believed to be Nineveh, in 1842 but found little to interest him in his initial excavations. There appeared to be more of archaeological interest at nearby Khorsabad, and in 1843 Botta moved his excavations to this site, where he unearthed the palace of Sargon II (721–705 B.C.). With the support of the French government, and with 300 workmen, Botta dug Khorsabad for two years, acquiring magnificent bas-reliefs, artifacts such as four-meter-high winged bulls with human heads, and many cuneiform tablets, which were displayed at the LOUVRE in Paris in 1846. Botta's discoveries caused huge interest in Paris—equivalent to the excitement engendered by Napoleon's Egyptian expedition.

Botta and artist Eugene Flandin published the Monument du Nineve, a four-volume record and illustration of the site, between 1846 and 1850. The Paris revolution of 1848 put an end to French work in Mesopotamia, and in 1851 Botta was dismissed in political disgrace. He was transferred to minor diplomatic posts in Jerusalem, Tripoli, and Syria. He died in Lebanon in 1870.

Tim Murray

See also French Archaeology in Egypt and the Middle East; Mesopotamia

Boucher de Perthes, Jacques (1788–1868)

A French customs official, an amateur antiquary, and a provincial man of letters, Boucher de Perthes has been sometimes described as the founder of the discipline of prehistory because of his discovery of ancient bifacially flaked stone tools in the gravels of the Somme River in northern France, tools that he attributed to "antediluvian" (pre-flood) human beings.

As president of a regional learned society he began his career in prehistory at the age of 49, assisting his friend Dr. Casimir Picard, who was compiling an archaeological survey of the Somme Valley. He continued this work after Picard died. In 1837 during an excavation underneath the town walls of Abbeville, Boucher de Perthes found stone tools in the same stratigraphic levels as animal remains and pottery. While these artifacts became part of the Natural History Museum's collection, they were not recognized by the scientific establishment as being made by humans, and were classified as geological and paleontological—of natural rather than human scientific interest.

Boucher de Perthes also excavated at Menchcourt-les-Abbeville, a site formerly dug by Georges Cuvier, which was full of fossil elephant and rhino bones. Here he found not only stone tools but also polished pebble stone axes. Boucher de Perthes believed that if the tools and the bones were found in the same undisturbed stratigraphic unit then they were likely to be of the same age. In 1842 he retrieved a bifaced stone tool from these units and he continued to find and collect stone tools from numerous local railway cuttings, canal building sites, and quarries. Boucher de Perthes begun to write up his discoveries in what was to become the first part of Antiquités celtiques et antédiluviennes, in which he argued for the great age of the stone tools he had discovered. In this highly idiosyncratic work Boucher de Perthes advocated the need for methodological conventions of description and analysis that he felt would distinguish a science of archaeology, while at the same time arguing that his stone tools had been made by Celts who lived before the biblical flood. While he was not without supporters, the French scientific estab-

Jacques Boucher de Perthes (Science Photo Library)

lishment, through the Académie des Sciences, flatly rejected his claims in 1846.

Ten years later Boucher de Perthes experienced a kind of rehabilitation. In 1858 the Geological Society of London, largely prompted by the great HUGH FALCONER, visited Abbeville to examine his evidence and to compare it with material found in England. In 1859 the Royal Society of London upheld that "flint implements were the product of the conception and work of man," and that they were associated with numerous extinct animals. In 1859 Albert Gaudry, the French Natural History Museum's paleontologist, defended Boucher de Perthes's findings to the Académie des Sciences, and this time that learned establishment recognized the antiquity of mankind and the evidence for it. Charles Darwin's *Origin of Species* was published that same year.

Tim Murray

References

Van Riper, A. Bowdoin. 1993. *Men among the Mammoths: Victorian Science and the Discovery of Human Prehistory.* Chicago: University of Chicago Press.

Boule, Marcellin (1861–1942)

Marcellin Boule was born on 1 January 1861 at Motsalvy, in the French province of Cantal and was introduced to the natural sciences in his youth by the local pharmacist, Jean-Baptiste Rames, who was also an amateur geologist. Boule studied first in Toulouse and took degrees in natural science and geology. While there, he met the prehistorians and cave art specialists EMILE CARTAILHAC and Louis Lartet, and they introduced him to paleoanthropology and prehistory. In 1886, he won a scholarship to Paris to study, and there his chief mentors were Ferdinand Fouque, a geologist at the College de France who introduced him to petrography, and Albert Gaudry, a paleontologist at the Muséum National d'Histoire Naturelle. In 1892, Boule became Gaudry's assistant at the museum and succeeded him as professor of paleontology in 1903, a position he held to his retirement in 1936.

Boule received the Chevalier de la Légion d'Honneur for his reorganization of the museum's paleontology gallery, which was opened in 1898. He was one of the founders and editor (1893–1930) of the distinguished journal *L'Anthropologie*. Boule was the unrivaled leader of French paleontology in the first third of the twentieth century, receiving the Huxley Medal from the Royal Institute of Anthropology of Great Britain and Ireland and the Wollaston Medal from the Geological Society of London. He taught and inspired many French paleontologists.

Two major works stand out from his prolific output. The first is the study of the La Chapelle-aux-Saints skeleton, in which Boule was able to explain his ideas on paleontology by proposing an original identification and reconstruction of Neanderthal man. He insisted that Neanderthals could not be ancestral to modern man, that they were a genuine fossil with no descendants. He was to use the same argument later about *Homo erectus,* the pithecanthopines discovered in Indonesia and China. He believed that there was a yet-to-be-found hominoid ancestor from which modern humans had descended.

The second major work is his popular book *Les hommes fossiles, eléments de paléontologie humaine* (1921), which summarized his thinking about human ancestry for the general public. Albert I, prince of Monaco, was so impressed by this book that he founded the Institut de Paléontologie Humaine in Paris in 1914. The first organization for specialized research in the field, Boule was the Institute's first director when it opened in 1920.

Boule believed that the function of paleoanthropology was to revitalize prehistory by giving it the status of a "historical science," one that was indispensable to the study of the earliest humans. In the context of late-nineteenth-century prehistory, Boule's contribution was innovative. Using Quaternary geology, paleontology, and archaeology, Boule provided an alternative method to the study of prehistory. His method replaced the predominant one elucidated by GABRIEL DE MORTILLET, one that was based exclusively on the classification of artifacts manufactured by humans. Boule argued that stone tools could only be used as chronological data if they were a proven part of geology and paleontology.

Nathalie Richard; translated by Judith Braid

See also France

References

For references, see *Encyclopedia of Archaeology: The Great Archaeologists, Vol. 1,* ed. Tim Murray (Santa Barbara, CA: ABC-CLIO, 1999), p. 273.

Boxgrove

In West Sussex (United Kingdom), 12 kilometers inland from the current shoreline of the English Channel, lies the parish of Boxgrove, where Middle Pleistocene sediments have been exposed in quarries along the southern margin of the hills of the South Downs. From the beginning of the twentieth century onward, similar deposits in the region were reported to yield archaeological finds. Research by the British Geological Survey in the 1970s demonstrated the occurrence of archaeological materials within the deposits at Boxgrove, and a survey and trial excavation undertaken by Mark Roberts in 1983 established the presence of a rich archaeological horizon. Funding by English Heritage enabled further research in 1984, and in 1985 the Boxgrove Lower Palaeolithic Project was set up by the Institute of Archaeology, part of University College London.

Excavations carried out until 1996 under the direction of Mark Roberts and Simon Parfitt have revealed extensive lithic scatters comprising large amounts of debitage (debris made by stone tools), numerous hand-axes, and some cores and flake tools. Moreover, the site complex has yielded one of the most diverse vertebrate faunas from a Lower Paleolithic context in Europe. The assemblages have been dated on the basis of mammalian biostratigraphy to the last temperate stage of the Cromerian Complex, tentatively correlated with Oxygen Isotope Stage 13 (524,000–478,000). Although later dates have been proposed on the basis of other data, such as the calcareous nannofossils, Boxgrove occupies a prime position in the ongoing debate about the earliest occupation of northern Europe. A robust hominid tibia found at Boxgrove in 1993 has been assigned to *Homo* spp., with possible further reference to *Homo* cf. *heidelbergensis* on temporal and geographic grounds.

Geologic study suggests that the archaeological remains were deposited within a markedly changing environment. Under decreasing marine influence the area developed from a beach setting, through a lagoonal setting in which artifacts were left on intertidal mudflats, and into a more terrestrial setting that later became inundated with freshwater. The excellent preservation of artifacts in the lagoonal silts and their exposure over relatively large areas have earned Boxgrove the description of "a Middle Pleistocene PINCEVENT," as have the detailed excavation and documentation procedures applied.

The assemblages recovered at Boxgrove are interpreted in terms of the procurement and processing of animal and lithic resources by hominids. Large mammal bone fragments with cut marks and percussion damage suggest meat and marrow exploitation. Use-wear on a small number of hand-axes is interpreted to stem from contact with meat and hide. All the lithic artifacts are made of locally available flint, and refitting data suggest that lithics in varying stages of reduction were transported. Other finds include an antler hammer with splinters of flint embedded in the striking surface and a horse scapula with damage suggested to be the result of a projectile impact.

Seleucia, south of Baghdad. Robert Braidwood participated in an ongoing excavation here, which eventually uncovered four levels of occupation. (© Arthur Thevenant/CORBIS)

The excellent preservation and documentation of archaeological data from Boxgrove have fueled expectations that assemblage studies will yield new insights into hominid behavior. Different data sets have been compiled to suggest that the hominids who left their artifacts at Boxgrove hunted large game, cooperated with each other, planned ahead, and used spoken language. Although these characteristics would not be unbecoming to those thought to be among the earliest colonizers of northern Europe, they remain contested. As research continues, the data from Boxgrove may prove particularly informative for the potential of and the limits to archaeological interpretation.

Josara De Lange

References

Roberts, M. B., and S. A. Parfitt. 1999. *Boxgrove. A Middle Pleistocene Hominid Site at Eartham Quarry, Boxgrove, West Sussex.* English Heritage Archaeological Report 17. London.

Roberts, M. B., S. A. Parfitt, and M. I. Pope. In press. *The Archaeology of the Middle Pleistocene Hominid Site at Boxgrove, West Sussex, UK: Excavations, 1990–1996.* English Heritage Monograph Series. London.

Roberts, M. B., S. A. Parfitt, M. I. Pope, and F. F. Wenban-Smith. 1997. "Boxgrove, West Sussex: Rescue Excavations of a Lower Palaeolithic Landsurface (Boxgrove Project B, 1989–91)." *Proceedings of the Prehistoric Society* 63, 303–358.

Braidwood, Robert John (1907–)

Robert Braidwood, born in Detroit, Michigan, in 1907, first studied to be an architect but returned to university in 1930 to study art history and anthropology because of the adverse effects of the Great Depression on the building industry. He traveled to Iraq in 1930–1931 to participate in the excavation of Seleucia, and this trip marked the beginning of his long interest in and significant contributions to Near Eastern archaeology. Braidwood worked briefly in Illinois and New Mexico, but all the rest of his fieldwork was under the aegis of the University of Chicago's ORIENTAL INSTITUTE: Syria, 1933–1938; Iraq, 1947–

1948, 1950–1951, and 1954–1955; IRAN, 1959–1960; and TURKEY, 1963 until the mid-1990s.

During the 1930s, Braidwood participated in Amuq expeditions in Syria directed by HENRI FRANKFORT, who became professor of Near Eastern archaeology at the Oriental Institute and was the head of Braidwood's dissertation committee. In 1945, Braidwood became the first specialist in prehistory to hold a full-time position at the institute (as well as a joint appointment in the University of Chicago's Department of Anthropology). He held both positions until 1978 when he became emeritus professor of Old World prehistory at the institute and emeritus professor of anthropology.

Braidwood's name is most closely associated with a major transition in the human past—the origins of food production in the Near East—and with the site of JARMO in northern Iraq, for many years the oldest village of farmers and herders known anywhere in the world. Braidwood's contribution, in the 1950s and 1960s, to the archaeology of agricultural origins and to archaeology more generally was primarily methodological, conceiving and implementing interdisciplinary staffs at the fieldwork level. He initiated a highly productive research trajectory that has claimed the attention of several generations of archaeologists and natural scientists. The interdisciplinary investigations he pioneered in Iraq and Iran became models for elucidating agricultural transitions and have also been acknowledged as the best means to delineate regional culture-historical sequences.

Members of Braidwood's project teams also intitiated two other important firsts in Near Eastern field archaeology: systematic ethnographic observations for archaeological purposes and the recovery of pollen from deeply stratified wet contexts. Much of what Braidwood pioneered is now central to archaeological research design, and he was a powerful force in world archaeology for at least three decades.

Patty Jo Watson

See also Mesopotamia

References

For references, see *Encyclopedia of Archaeology: The Great Archaeologists, Vol. 2,* ed. Tim Murray (Santa Barbara, CA: ABC-CLIO, 1999), pp. 503–505.

Brazil
Periods in the History of Archaeology

The history of archaeology in Brazil has been divided into phases following different criteria. Most authors consider that archaeology should have its own disciplinary history, untied to the overall political history of the country. André Prous (1992) identified five periods and Alfredo Mendonça de Souza (1991) followed the same disciplinary history approach but proposed only four periods.

The history of archaeology in Brazil should not, however, be considered independent from Brazilian history. Because the development of archaeology's practice, theory, and methodology depends directly on the sociopolitical conditions in a given country, it is possible to relate the social practice of archaeology and political changes. As with any intellectual endeavor, archaeological activities are the result of social conditions and relations prevailing in different periods. Thus, we can say that archaeology in Brazil went through seven phases: the colonial period (1500–1822); the Brazilian Empire (1822–1889); the early republic (1889–1920s); an intermediate period (1920s–1940s); the inception of university research (1950–1964); the military period and the constitution of an archaeological establishment (1964–1985); and democracy and a pluralist archaeology (1985 onward).

The Colonial Period (1500–1822)

There are few references in colonial sources to archaeological sites, though Fernão Cardim (1925) referred to shellmounds, known in Brazil by their Tupi name *sambaquis,* and Feliciano Coelho's soldiers, as early as 1598, mentioned rock inscriptions (Prous 1992, 5). However, travelers and writers such as Yves d'Euvreux (1985), Gabriel Soares (1944), G. Carvajal (1942), Father Anchieta (1988), André Thevet (1944), and Hans Staden (1930) described native inhabitants and their culture, furnishing a good deal of data on Indian material culture. Thanks to these sources, it is possible to study native settlements while taking into full account the historical evidence relating to the following areas: the East Amazon basin area (Porro 1992; Taylor 1992; Erikson 1992;

Wright 1992); the North Amazon region (Farage and Santilli 1992; Menéndez 1992; Amoroso 1992); the South Amazon area (Perrone-Moisés 1992; Franchetto 1992; Lopes da Silva 1992); the northeast (Paraíso 1992; Dantas, Sampaio, and Carvalho 1992); the southwest (S. Carvalho 1992); the south (Monteiro 1992; Kern 1982); and the entire country (Fausto 1992). Evidence provided by these documents include written descriptions as well as drawings and paintings that are very useful in the analysis of material remains; Hans Staden's drawings are perhaps the best example of this kind of early evidence. But the use of all this early evidence necessitates an awareness of the bias of the early authors. U. Fleischmann and M. R. Assunção (1991) studied the documents, emphasizing that the authors were not describing but interpreting native customs according to both their own ideologies and their own interests. This means that colonial sources, iconography, and written documents alike, although very useful, must be interpreted within their social context. They are overwhelmingly biased against Native Americans, Africans, and even poor Europeans, and thus they must be studied carefully by archaeologists.

The Brazilian Empire (1822–1889)

Peter Wilhelm Lund, born in Copenhagen in 1801, is considered to be the first scholar to describe Brazilian prehistory. He went to Brazil as early as 1825, staying for three years and returning in 1833. Lund established a paleontological laboratory in the village of Lagoa Santa, in Minas Gerais Province, where he found human and animal fossils. The Brazilian emperor Peter II, under the influence of classical German education, went in person to Lagoa Santa to visit the Danish scholar. Between 1834 and 1844 Lund surveyed some 800 caves and found fossils thousands of years old. He collected a great deal of material and studied a variety of extinct fauna. At Sumidouro Lake he found human bones associated with extinct animals. Paleontologists who followed Georges Cuvier, such as his pupil Lund, believed there had been a universal biblical deluge and that the association of human remains with extinct animals meant that men had lived in the New World before the deluge. Although Lund was not sure that Cuvier's universal deluge theory was useful for the Americas, he was a Christian, and he did not choose to challenge current ideas, preferring instead to isolate himself and avoid controversial attitudes. Lund was a leading pioneer in his field, and his position illustrated the tensions arising from undertaking scientific archaeological work in Brazil. Dogma and supposedly established truths, when challenged by evidence, tended to prevail and force people to comply.

At the same time, the National Museum, thanks to Charles Wiener (1876), pioneered the studies of lithic material, and the Canadian Charles Friedrich Hartt (1871, 1872, 1874, 1876, 1885) explored the Amazon basin, a region also studied by D. S. Ferreira Penna (1876) and J. Barbosa Rodrigues (1876, 1892). Karl Rath (1871) studied shellmounds, and the German scholar Fritz Mueller was employed by the National Museum as natural and human material collector. The activities of all these researchers were an outgrowth of the enlightened character of the Brazilian royal court. During the second half of the nineteenth century, thanks to Emperor Peter II and his European outlook, there was official sponsorship of fields such as paleontology and ethnology. Ladislau Neto (1876, 1885a, 1885b), as director of the National Museum, was perhaps the first Brazilian to explicitly study and write about archaeology as such. Neto sought out Native Americans and was very much in touch with international academic standards. His exchange of letters with the French scholar Ernst Renan is a prime example of the good communications existing between these early Brazilian and European scientists. It is clear that, from its inception, archaeology in Brazil was linked to both foreign influence and state patronage.

The Early Republic (1889–1920s)

Archaeology during the early republican period continued to be dominated by people attached to museums. With the growing importance of the State of São Paulo within the federation of Brazilian states and as a result of its economic hegemony, there was cultural shift in the country from the court in Rio de Janeiro to the new Paulista elite. This shift explains the role the Paulista Museum played in the field from the beginning of the twentieth century. To be sure, there were people studying elsewhere, such as the Swiss Emílio Goeldi (1897–1898, 1900), who explored the Amazon basin from his post at the Museu do Pará (now known as the Museu Paraense Emílio Goeldi), or Alberto Loefgren (1893, 1903), who studied shellmounds from São Paulo and Rio de Janeiro, as did Ricardo Krone (1902, 1909, 1910, 1914, 1918). However, long-standing archaeological activities were in São Paulo. The German scholar Hermann von Ihering (1895, 1902, 1904, 1907, 1911) became director of the Paulista Museum in 1895 and was in charge until 1916, when he was dismissed for political reasons (Losano 1992, 99). Although Ihering was a racist and even defended the extermination of native Indians in Brazil, and although he opposed the idea that shellmounds were evidence of prehistoric human settlements, he should be considered as the first conservative ideologist of Brazilian archaeology. It is interesting to note that he was, at the same time, out of touch with modern research in Europe and a political reactionary. The conservative establishment born in the 1960s would inherit this outlook.

Teodoro Sampaio (1916, 1918, 1922) was perhaps the best example of this generation of pioneer scholars, none of them professional archaeologists. His general paper entitled "Brazilian Archaeology" (1922) and believed wholeheartedly that rock scratches should be interpreted as hieroglyphic writing.

The Formative Period (1920–1949)

Important changes occurred in Brazil during this period, particularly in terms of political, social, and cultural upheavals. Rebellions, revolutions, and dictatorship went hand in hand with cultural transformation. Modernism and later fascist and communist ideas fostered discussions on democracy in intellectual circles. From that point on intellectuals would address the peoples' interests, and even as the masses were the subject of intellectual discourse, they were also

its ultimate audience. The establishment of the first university in Brazil in the early 1930s, São Paulo State University (USP), was a direct result of this new situation. As a side effect archaeologists began to take the public into account and tried for the first time to carry out taxonomic scientific analysis.

This period thus witnessed two new developments in archaeology: the study of artifact collections and the publication of manuals. Anibal Mattos continued the tradition of earlier periods but produced scholarly manuals, especially on material from the State of Minas Gerais. Mattos's *Brazilian Prehistory Handbook* (1938) is still worth reading, particularly his introductory assessment of the disputes between different practitioners. Angyone Costa (1935, 1936, 1984) produced the first overall introductions to Brazilian archaeology and prehistory. Frederico Barata (1944, 1950, 1952) wrote the first introduction to prehistoric art in Brazil. The Argentinean Antônio Serrano (1937, 1938, 1940, 1946) studied Brazilian collections of artifacts and thus established a new field in Brazilian archaeology. This whole period before the introduction of archaeology into the Brazilian academic world (that is, prior to the 1950s) is usually dismissed by students of the history of Brazilian archaeology. But the significance of the publication of the first manuals and the inception of collection studies should not be underestimated, considering that archaeology in Brazil continues to lag behind that of other Latin American countries in both these areas. Consequently, this formative period should be reinterpreted as an important landmark. If there is a lack of handbooks and collection studies later on, notably after 1964, the reasons should be sought not in the period from the 1920s to the 1950s but rather in the military clampdown on the academic world in the 1960s and 1970s.

The Inception of University Research (1950–1964)

After World War II Brazil enjoyed its longest democratic period. The participation of Brazilian soldiers in the Allied fight against fascism in Europe (1942–1945) established the basis for the overthrow of the Brazilian dictatorship (which held power from 1937 to 1945). Democracy meant the introduction of broader concerns with intellectual discourse and the spread of the university and other learning institutions throughout the country. Furthermore, industrialization, especially in south Brazil, made relatively large funds available for cultural activities.

It was in this context that academic or scholarly archaeology was created by the leading Brazilian humanist Paulo Duarte. Thanks to his friendship with Paul Rivet, director of the Musée de l'Homme in Paris, and complementing his own struggle for human rights in Brazil, Duarte created the Prehistory Commission at USP in 1952. An outstanding Brazilian intellectual, he was able to change long-standing features of Brazilian archaeology—its tendency to be parochial, racist, and out of touch, in the tradition of Ihering and others. Duarte was not a museum director pretending to be a scholar, as was the case of directors before and after him. Rather, he was an intellectual and human rights activist who struggled to introduce ethical principles into the very act of creating archaeology as an academic discipline. Duarte also worked politically to craft legislation to protect Brazilian heritage, and thanks to his efforts, the Brazilian Parliament enacted a federal bill (approved as Bill 3924 in 1961) protecting prehistoric assets (Duarte 1958). He studied shell-mounds (1952, 1955, 1968, 1969) and encouraged French archaeologists Joseph Emperaire and Annette Laming-Emperaire (1975).

The Military Period and the Constitution of an Archaeological Establishment (1964–1985)

On April 1, 1964, there was a military coup in Brazil, and the armed forces held power until March 15, 1985. Twenty years of authoritarian rule meant that all kinds of human rights abuses were committed. From 1964 until 1968 political repression involved the suppression of formal liberties. After 1968 the military introduced more violent practices, such as expulsion, detention without trial, torture, and murder. Within academia, suppression meant censorship first and expulsion later. The very

slow process of relaxing this repression began in the late 1970s and continued until 1985.

In archaeological terms, the main contributors to the discipline during this period were two Americans, Clifford Evans and Betty Meggers (1947, 1954). Although they had excavated at the mouth of the Amazon River as early as 1949 and had produced papers before 1964, it was only after the military coup of April 1964 that Evans and Meggers were able to set up a network that would result in the development of an archaeological establishment.

Duarte's scholarly archaeology project was mildly opposed by people in power at first, so between 1964 to 1969 he was deprived of funding (the most subtle but effective weapon). Cuts in university budgets in general affected, first and foremost, the human and social sciences, and in the case of archaeology budgetary restrictions were a very powerful way of hindering development. This passive strategy changed as the military begun to use force to rule the country and subdue intellectual opposition in general. The new and violent approach of the authorities was evidenced by the official support of death squads in the late 1960s, introducing Brazilians to the disgusting concept of "missing people" (i.e., people who were arrested and executed secretly because of their political beliefs). Intellectual life underwent radical changes. In the words of Octávio Ianni (1978):

> For those who controlled state power from the 1964 coup, there was and there is, in 1978, a need to control, to marginalize, to curb or to suppress dissident voices. The cultural policy in Brazil in the period 1964–1978 divides intellectuals in three categories. There is an encouraged or protected intellectual production; it is the official one. For people in power, this is the only sound production. Then, there is the tolerated overlooked production. Finally, there is the forbidden, censored one.

The archaeological establishment created by the military followed the official line, using Ianni's terms, and Brazilian archaeology was once again in the hands of museum directors and other bureaucratic officials. Perhaps the best (or worst) example involved Paulo Duarte.

He was expelled from the university in 1969 and was succeeded by an official appointed by the authorities and considered to be a reliable bureaucrat. Duarte died years later while still in internal exile, and his successor continues to be regarded as a leading museum director.

From 1965 to 1971 Evans and Meggers, from the SMITHSONIAN INSTITUTION in the United States, set up the National Archaeological Research Project (PRONAPA), bringing together the Paraense Museum Emílio Goeldi, Brazilian Heritage, and most of the archaeological practitioners from the south and northeast regions. In addition to training a new generation of Brazilian field-workers, PRONAPA conducted surveys and tests throughout the country. During the 1970s the following archaeological centers were created in São Paulo State (only the largest are mentioned here):

- The Prehistory Institute (IPH). Founded in 1952 by Paulo Duarte as the Prehistory Commission, it continued to be active until 1989, when it became part of the new Archaeological and Ethnological Museum (MAE-USP). From 1952 until 1989, some 100 papers by sixty authors were produced by or indirectly related to the IPH.
- The Paulista Museum. Until 1989 there was a prehistory section in this museum, active in excavations in the western part of the state. This section joined the IPH to form the new MAE-USP.
- The Archaeological and Ethnological Museum of São Paulo State University. From the 1970s on there was a section on Brazilian prehistory in this museum. Since 1989 all prehistoric archaeology in the university's museums is carried out in the new MAE-USP.

Prominent archaeological centers were also established in other states:

- The Emílio Goeldi Paraense Museum (MPEG), Pará State
- The Archaeological Studies Section (NEA), Federal University at Pernambuco State (UFPE)
- The Anthropological Museum, Federal University at Santa Catarina State
- The Estácio de Sá University, Rio de Janeiro

- The Federal University at Rio de Janeiro State
- The Brazilian Archaeology Institute, Rio de Janeiro
- The Natural History Museum, Federal University at Minas Gerais State (UFMG)
- The National Museum of Rio de Janeiro, Federal University at Rio de Janeiro State
- The American Man Museum, Piauí State
- The Anthropological Museum, Federal University at Goiás State
- The Anchieta's Archaeological Research Institute, São Leopoldo, Rio Grande do Sul State

Graduate courses on archaeology were created at some universities, notably, at São Paulo State University and the Federal University at Pernambuco State. In 1980 the archaeological establishment was able to set up the conservative Society for Brazilian Archaeology (SAB). The main journals created from the 1960s were:

- *Revista de Pré-História* (published by IPH-USP until 1989)
- *Dédalo* (published by MAE-USP until 1989)
- *Revista do Museu de Arqueologia e Etnologia* (from 1991)
- *Clio* (published by UFPE)
- *Pesquisa* (published by the Instituto Anchietano de Pesquisas Arqueológicas, São Leopoldo, Rio Grande do Sul)
- *Revista do Museu Paulista* (until 1989)
- *Arquivos do Museu de História Natural* (published by UFMG)
- *Revista de Arqueologia* (published by the National Research Center)

Heritage management has been developing in Brazil for a long time, but it was only in the 1930s that official bills were enacted in relation to the protection of monuments. In 1937 the Historic and Artistic National Heritage Service (Serviço do Patrimônio Histórico e Artístico Nacional) was established. This office changed its name several times (e.g., to Secretaria do Patrimônio Histórico Artístico Nacional and then Fundação Nacional Pró-Memória) and is presently known as the Instituto Brasileiro de Patrimônio Cultural (Brazilian Heritage). It has a national department in Brasilia and regional sections in each state of the country. The national office in Brasilia is the controlling department, and the regional offices usually are run by political appointees, sometimes aided by archaeologists, architects, and other scholars, who are mostly underpaid and unable to enforce technical decisions. Officially, all excavators should ask for authorization from the Brazilian Heritage regional office, but most fieldwork, even that carried out by staff from universities and museums, is not recorded by Brazilian Heritage. Among other reasons, this is because the bureaucratic character of this office inhibits archaeologists. Some states have their own state heritage foundations, the most effective probably being the São Paulo State Heritage (Conselho de Defesa do Patrimônio Histórico, Arqueológico, Artístico e Turístico do Estado de São Paulo). Brazilian and state heritage offices are under direct political influence and are thus subject to very acute changes from time to time (usually after a change of government). IBPC, for example, became extinct in 1990 as a result of the new government and was reinstated some months later. The offices occasionally produce books and journals, but unfortunately, such works are mostly used for political propaganda. Journals such as *Revista do Patrimônio Histórico e Artístico Nacional* are not regularly published, and useful books (e.g., Arantes 1984) are seldom published. More recently some major cities, among them São Paulo, Rio de Janeiro, and Porto Alegre, introduced their own local heritage offices but again their activities are overly dependent on political parties and loyalties.

The development of historical archaeology is a good example of the way in which political and scientific trends have affected the history of archaeology in Brazil. The study of historical material culture has been carried out by three kinds of practitioners: nonarchaeologists, nonacademic field-workers, and archaeologists working in scholarly institutions. Until the 1960s colonial and postcolonial artifacts, buildings, and monuments were studied by architects and art historians (e.g., Arroyo 1954). However, it was only from the 1960s that architects, art historians, and heritage managers developed a scholarly approach. Architects were at the forefront of the interest in historical buildings; good examples of literature in this area include

papers by Yves Bruand (1966) on the colonial buildings in Minas Gerais State, by Benedito Lima de Toledo (1966, 1981) on the road between São Paulo and Santos. These works were mostly descriptive and concerned with the restoration of monuments.

Two books perhaps best illustrate the achievements and limitations of the architectural trend. Nestor Goulart Reis (1970) attempted to study Brazilian historical heritage by "emphasizing the importance of our artistic and historical heritage for the proposition of creative cultural activities" (Reis 1970, 11). His survey of Brazilian houses, trying to track their origins and social functions in different periods, is an interesting starting point for the study of housing from colonial times until the present. Luis Saia (1972) studied housing in the State of São Paulo and tried to relate architectural features to specific social groups, such as the *bandeirantes* (pioneers) who were interpreted as feudal in character (Saia 1972, 132). The weakness of all these works is the scholars' lack of interest in collecting a large sample of artifacts (in this case, buildings), which could substantiate their impressionistic analyses.

Some art historians were also approaching material culture with the same disregard for actual evidence. Enrico Schaeffer (1965), studying colonial painting, and Oliveira Ribeiro (1968), analyzing pottery statues of Catholic saints, considered it more important to quote the existence of "hundreds of copies" (Ribeiro 1968, 25) than to actually collect, publish, and study them! It is true that the detailed material study of artifacts is the specific task of archaeologists, and as such, this disregard for the actual artifacts is not surprising. But the importance of the contribution of archaeology should be recognized.

Some very useful studies can be considered as para-archaeological or as hermeneutic tools for archaeology. A case in point is the work of Maria Isaura Pereira de Queiroz (1969, 1974), who, in two seminal studies on slums and the perception of space, was able to provide archaeologists with real insights, albeit via sociological and thus nonarchaeological analysis. Similar insights were provided in studies on immigrant housing (Segawa 1989), on national identity and colonial art (Oliveira 1989), on blacks as represented in paintings (Lima 1988), and on statues and ideology (Doberstein 1992). Furthermore, during the dictatorship years (1964 to 1985), when the archaeological establishment was either allied with the military or silent, the struggle for human rights was carried on by the Brazilian Committee for Art History and its leader, Paulo Ferreira Santos (Vasconcelos 1989, 174–183). It is amazing that at the same time, professional archaeologists were working "in collaboration with the Brazilian Army," in the words of Paulo Zanettini and Miriam Cazzetta (1993, 6), as in the case of the fieldwork at the colonial military site near Recife (M. Albuquerque 1969). Recent examples of architectural and art historical contributions to the study of historical material culture appear in papers by W. Pfeiffer (1992) on religious architecture and by Tirapoli (1992) on seventeenth-century art at Minas Gerais, both of which were published in *Les dossiers de l'archéologie*. The protection of the earliest Jewish synagogue in the Americas, established in 1641 at Recife (in the northeast), has been led by a journalist, Leonardo Dantas Silva (1993). And last but not least, the study of the mass graves of the missing people has been carried out by the physician Eric Stover for the Physicians for Human Rights and Human Rights Watch (Stover 1991). For both scientific and political reasons, then, we cannot underestimate the importance of the contributions of architects, art historians, and other scholars to the inception and development of historical material culture studies.

The presence of the second group of practitioners—nonacademic field-workers—is the direct result of the development of private archaeological entrepreneurs since the late 1960s. State corporations and some large private companies blossomed during the heyday of the Brazilian "economic miracle" and were able to fund private fieldwork to carry out specific archaeological tasks. Nonacademic field-workers also came to the fore when crews working on large developments (such as huge dams, urban refashioning, or road construction) had to rescue archaeological material before beginning their projects. However, most of this fieldwork

is and will remain unpublished. Funds were not used to study the material, and in general, there was no estimating of and funding for the storage of collected artifacts. Some professional archaeologists worked under these conditions, mainly because of the poor pay they received in museums and heritage offices, but they were unable to shun the constraints of these rescue activities. Another negative side effect of the situation was that field-workers were chosen not for their merits but because of personal and/or familial ties with corporate managers. With field-workers being paid as friends, receiving in two months more than a Ph.D. scholar receives in two years of scientific work in any academic post, it is easy to understand the stress that this situation causes, exacerbating differences between scholars and market-oriented field-workers.

Professional archaeologists, working in academic institutions such as universities, museums, and heritage institutions, form the third group of people dealing with historical material culture. Some professional archaeologists have been excavating historical sites using a descriptive approach. But many field seasons produce no written reports, and others result only in unpublished descriptive accounts. The more active field-workers are Marcos Albuquerque (1971, 1980, 1991) in the northeast, Margarida Davina Andreatta (1981–1982, 1986) in São Paulo, Maria da Conceição Beltrão (Neme, Beltrão, and Niemeyer 1992) at Bahia and Rio de Janeiro, and Ulysses Pernambucano de Mello (1975, 1976, 1983) in the northeast. Young graduate students are also active, among them Paulo Tadeu de Souza Albuquerque (1991) at Vila Flor (in the northeast), Miriam Cazzetta (1991), and Paulo Zanettini (1986, 1990). Archaeologists dealing with heritage management have also been publishing papers on urban archaeology (Vogel and Mello 1984) and on historical archaeology and heritage (Vianna 1992). The first introductory handbook on historical archaeology was written by Charles E. Orser Jr. and translated by Pedro Paulo A. Funari in 1992. This is a landmark, giving practicing students access to an up-to-date manual on the field (Orser 1992b).

The scholarly study of historical sites in Brazil has been particularly seminal in the two areas of African material culture and Jesuit missions. Carlos Magno Guimarães has been studying Maroon (fugitive slave) settlements in Minas Gerais for more than a decade, and he has examined written documents and archaeological material. Other scholarly archaeological research on runaway slaves started in 1992 at the Palmares *quilombo,* the largest maroon settlement, which blossomed during almost all of the seventeenth century (Funari 1991a; Orser 1992a). The study of African material culture is important both scientifically and socially, as these scholarly enterprises can address the problem of the struggle for freedom by ordinary people. The archaeological study of the Jesuit missions in the south of Brazil has been going on for years and is now the best example of what scholarly historical archaeology has achieved in Brazil. Arno Alvarez Kern (1982, 1984, 1985, 1987, 1988, 1989, 1991a, 1991b) has been directing fieldwork at different Jesuit mission towns. He established a field school for students and has trained many undergraduate and graduate pupils, typically using written documents and material culture. In addition, papers and books on the mission sites have been regularly published, which is unusual and worthy of particular praise.

In Brazilian archaeology in general during this period, no handbook was produced, and the overwhelming majority of papers were excavation or survey reports, often in the form of master's theses or Ph.D. dissertations. These works usually dealt with a single site or even a single fieldwork season, as the titles of two dissertations—"Archaeological Excavations at Corondo Site, 1978 Season" (E. Carvalho 1984) and "Rescue Archaeology at Tucurui Region" (Costa 1983).

Current Trends (1985 Onward)

"I know enough history to realize that great crises move slowly, and such poor little chaps as ourselves can only take pride in our resignation." Marc Bloch's words (in Fink 1991, 54) describe the feelings of Brazilian intellectuals who survived the long ordeal of military rule. By the late 1970s Brazilian humanities scholars and so-

cial scientists were able to reintroduce free and uncensored discussion to academia, and as a result Brazilian scholarship in history, anthropology, and sociology became both scientifically structured inside the country and more widely recognized abroad through different interpretive schools and trends. This has been a much tougher task for archaeology for many reasons, not least of all because the archaeological establishment, impervious to change, continued to control funds for fieldwork. Walter A. Neves (1988, 205) emphasized that "no law, no political determination, no governmental aims or potential competence can stand up to the academic corporativism." Even foreign researchers such as Anna Roosevelt (1991, 106–107) had problems publishing evidence and interpretations contradicting established truths. Others, among them Denis Vialou and Vilhena Vialou, were the targets of different attacks by local patrons, despite the fact that they authored many papers on Brazilian prehistory that were published abroad.

Brazilians continue to be victims of human rights abuses, massacres by security forces (Margolis 1992), and death squad activities. However, the restoration of civilian rule in 1985 has meant that freedom of expression, if nothing else, is once again viable. It has become possible to develop some unconventional approaches, and the publication of an issue of *Les dossiers d'archéologie* on Brazil (March 1992) bears witness to the renewed blooming of Brazilian archaeology. The first interpretive handbook on archaeology written by a Brazilian came out in the late 1980s (Funari 1988). In addition, Prous (1992) has published a 605-page description of archaeological activities in Brazil, and summarizing papers have also been published (e.g., Prous 1987).

The History of Archaeological Theory in Brazil

Brazilian archaeology's theoretical trends have depended directly on the overall, changing political background. The early historical and humanist approach of the years between 1950 and 1964, under direct European influence (cf. the case of the other social sciences, as described in Pereira de Queiroz [1989]), was overturned by the empiricism imposed by the North Americans Evans and Meggers. Their environmental determinism and their emphasis on empirical fieldwork, however, did not produce a generation of ecological determinists. As the archaeological establishment was being set up in the late 1960s and 1970s under military rule, Brazilian archaeologists who were trained to become empiricists and ecological determinists were not interested in fulfilling their role as defenders of a specific scientific approach. Because there were no checks on their activities and power, we cannot say that, as a group, the Brazilian archaeologists educated by Meggers were recognized as respected empiricists and determinists outside the country and by international standards. Unarticulated fieldwork, the absence of corpora, and poor classification were accompanied by a poor development of ecological models.

The restoration of civilian rule in 1985 was bound to introduce radical changes to this picture. Once again, European influences were at the root of a new upsurge of interest in the application of historical and social theories to archaeology and material culture studies. The first papers on archaeological theory written by Brazilians were produced in the late 1980s and early 1990s (Funari 1989; Kern 1991a, 1991b). Today, a younger generation of students are regularly reading such authors as LEWIS R. BINFORD, Courbin, J. J. F. DEETZ, Gardin, Hodder, Shanks, Tilley, and B. Trigger. Although the archaeological establishment continues along its conservative, antitheoretical track, young scholars are increasingly venturing into theoretical readings and previously unexplored research areas. A case in point is the master's thesis by the young archaeologist Leila Maria Serafim Pacheco (1992, 5), "directly under the influence of the English-language archaeological theory produced in the 1980s," as she puts it. English-language titles represent 58 percent of all quoted works (36 of 62), and there is no doubt that the so-called postprocessual approaches dominating British and North American archaeologies are becoming increasingly popular in Brazil. The work of Eduardo Góes Neves, a young archaeologist at the Ethnological and Archaeological Museum, is a good example of this theoretical trend among Brazilian prehistory scholars. Nonetheless, there is still a preference for processual (or at least noncritical) approaches and for authors such as Carl Moberg, James Deetz (mostly his prehistory works), and Lewis Binford (E. Neves 1989). There is a new focus on reading the work of social scientists and historians. Arno Alvarez Kern and Adriana Schmid Dias recently published an inspiring paper entitled "Remarks on the relationship between archaeology and history of ancient societies," which dealt with four main theoretical subjects: material culture; material culture and archaeology; artifacts and history; and archaeology and the knowledge of ancient societies. In this paper there was an eclectic use of different authors and approaches, as the authors put together Annales School historians (such as Fernand Braudel and Marc Bloch), neopositivist historians (such as Paul Veyne), classical and traditional archaeologists (such as Renée Ginouves and MORTIMER WHEELER), and, among others, Jean-Marie Pesez, Alexandr Mongait, and Richard Bucaille. In this case, there was no reference to postprocessual archaeology, and although the explicit goal of the article was to emphasize the necessary links between archaeology and history, the authors concluded that the "New Archaeology" (processual archaeology), despite unspecified attacks or drawbacks, was a breath of fresh air.

Another recent and interesting theoretical trend in Brazil is the study of the epistemology of archaeological reasoning. Haiganuch Sarian (1989) has paid attention to the archaeological interpretation of pottery in terms of both practical and methodological analyses. Although a descriptive approach to artifacts still prevails in Brazilian archaeology, pottery studies are increasingly influenced by analytical scholars. Norberto Luiz Guarinello (1989), for example, represents a young generation of scholars who (under the influence of theoreticians Michael Rowlands and Andrea Carandini, among others) are interested in discussing such questions as the relationship between written documents and material culture and how archaeology can be used to study general subjects like imperialism and exploitation. It is important to emphasize that these young archaeologists lecture at some of the most influential academic institutions and are thus bound to educate and influence a new generation of theoretically minded scholars. Lecturers at the Universities of São Paulo (H. Sarian, N. L. Guarinello), Campinas (P. P. A. Funari), and Rio Grande do Sul (A. A. Kern) have been very active in promoting the study of archaeological theory and method, and as a result theoretical lectures, once very rare, are increasingly popular. And this is the case not only in large cities, such as Rio de Janeiro, but also in small towns, such as Taquara (in Rio Grande do Sul State) or Assis (in São Paulo State).

Pedro Paulo A. Funari

References

Albuquerque, M. 1969. "O sítio arqueológico PE 13-Ln—Um sítio de contato inter-étnico: Nota prévia, Anais do II Simpósio de Arqueologia da Area do Prata, Pesquisas." *Antropologia* 20: 79–89.

———. 1971. *O sítio arqueológico PE 16-Cp.* Recife: UFPE.

———. 1980. "Escavaçoes arqueológicas realizadas na igreja quinhentista de Nossa Senhora da Divina Graça, em Olinda." *Clio* 3: 89–90.

———. 1991. "Perspectivas da arqueologia histórica no Brasil." *Resumos da VI Reunião Científica da Sociedade de Arqueologia Brasileira, Rio de Janeiro,* 32–33.

Albuquerque, P. T. S. 1991. "A faiança portuguesa dos séculos XVI ao XIX em Vila Flor, Rio Grande do Norte." Master's thesis, Recife.

Amoroso, M. R. 1992. "Corsários no caminho fluvial: Os mura do Rio Madeira." In *História dos Índios no Brasil,* 297–310. Ed. M Carneiro da Cunha. São Paulo: Cia das Letras.

Andreatta, M. D. 1981–1982. "Arqueologia histórica no município de São Paulo." *Revista do Museu Paulista, São Paulo* 28: 174–177.

———. 1986. "A Casa do Grito, Ipiranga." *Revista do Arquivo Municipal* 197: 151–172.

Arantes, A. A. 1984. *Produzindo o passado: Estratégias de construção do patrimônio cultural.* São Paulo: Brasiliense.

Arroyo, L. 1954. *Igrejas de São Paulo.* Rio de Janeiro: José Olympio.

Barata, F. 1944. "Os maravilhosos cachimbos de Santarém." *Estudos Brasileiros* 7, 13: 37–39.

———. 1950. *A arte oleira dos Tapajó.* Belém: Instituto de Anropologia e Etnologia do Pará.

———. 1952. *As artes plásticas no Brasil: Arqueologia.* Rio de Janeiro: Larragoiti.

Barbosa Rodrigues, J. 1876. *Antiguidades do Amazonas: Ensaios de ciência por diversos amadores,* 19–125. Rio de Janeiro: Brown.

———. 1892. "Antiguidades do Amazonas." *Vellosia* 2: 1–40.

Bruand, Y. 1966. "Rarroco e rococó na arquitetura de Minas Gerais." *Dédalo* 3: 13–33.

Cardim, F. 1925. *Tratado da terra e gente do Brasil* [1583]. Rio de Janeiro.

Carvajal. G. 1942. *Relación del nuevo descubrimiento del famoso Rio Grande* [1542]. Quito: Biblioteca Amazonas.

Carvalho, E. T. 1984. "Escavaçoes arqueológicas no sítio Corondo—Missão de 1978." Ph.D. dissertation, São Paulo State University.

Carvalho, S. M. S. 1992. "Chaco: Encruzilhada de povos e "melting pot" cultural, suas relaçoes com a bacia do Paraná e o sul mato-grossense." In *História dos Índios no Brasil,* 457–474. Ed. M. Carneiro da Cunha. São Paulo: Cia das Letras.

Cazzetta, M. 1991. "Arqueologia e planejamento urbano, I congreso Latino-americano sobre cultura arquitetônica e urbanística, Porto Alegre." Typescript.

Costa, A. 1935. *Civilizaciones pré-colombianas brasilenas.* Buenos Aires.

———. 1936. *Arqueologia Geral.* São Paulo: Cia Nacional.

———. 1984. *Introdução à Arqueologia Brasileira.* São Paulo: Cia Nacional.

Costa, F. H. J. C. A. 1983. "Projeto Baixo Tocantins: Salvamento arqueológico na região do Tucurui." Ph.D. dissertation, São Paulo State University.

D'évreux, Y. 1985. *Voyage du nord au nord du Brésil: Fait en 1613 et 1614.* Paris: Payot.

Dantas, B. G., J. A. L. Sampaio, and M. R. G. de Carvalho. 1992. "Os povos indígenas no nordeste brasileiro: Um esboço histórico." In *História dos Índios no Brasil,* 431–456. Ed. M. Carneiro da Cunha. São Paulo: Cia das Letras.

Doberstein, A. W. 1992. *Estatuária e ideologia.* Porto Alegre: Secretaria Municipal de Cultura.

Duarte, P. 1952. "Sambaquis do Brasil." *Anhembi* 6, 17: 205–211.

———. 1955. "Comentários à sessão de estudos de sambaquis." In *Anais do XXXI Congreso Internacional de Americanistas,* 2: 613–618. Ed. H. Baldus.

———. 1958. "Defesa do patrimônio arqueológico do Brasil" *Anhembi* 30: 543–551.

———. 1968. *O sambaqui visto através de alguns sambaquis.* São Paulo: IPH-USP.

———. 1969. *Estudos de pré-história geral e Brasileira.* São Paulo: IPH-USP.

Erikson, Ph. 1992. "Uma singular pluralidade: A etno-história pano." In *História dos Índios no Brasil,* 239–252. Ed. M. Carneiro da Cunha. São Paulo: Cia das Letras.

Farage, N., and P. Santilli. 1992. "Estado de sítio: Territórios e identidades no vale do Rio Branco." In *História dos Índios no Brasil,* 267–280. Ed. M. Carneiro da Cunha. São Paulo: Cia das Letras.

Fausto, C. 1992. "Fragmentos da história e cultura Tupinambá: Da etnologia como instrumento crítico de conhecimento etno-histórico." In *História dos Índios no Brasil,* 381–396. Ed. M. Carneiro da Cunha. São Paulo: Cia das Letras.

Ferreira Penna, D. S. 1876. "Breve notícia sobre os sambaquis do Pará." *Arquivos do Museu Nacional do Rio de Janeiro* 1: 85–99.

Fink, C. 1991. *Marc Bloch: A Life in History.* Cambridge: CANTO.

Fleischmann, U., and M. R. Assunção. 1991. "Os Tupinambá: Realidade e ficcçãõ nos relatos quinhentistas." *Revista Brasileira de História* 10, 21: 125–145 (originally in P. Waldmann and G. Elwert, eds., *Ethnizitaet im Wandel, Saarbrucken,* Fort Lauderdale, FL: Breitenbach Verlag, 1989).

Franchetto, B. 1992. "O aparecimento dos caraíba: Para uma história kuikuro e alto xinguana." In *História dos Índios no Brasil* 339–356. Ed. M. Carneiro da Cunha. São Paulo: Cia das Letras.

Funari, P. P. A. 1988. *Arqueologia.* São Paulo.

———. 1989. "Reflexões sobre a mais recente teoria arqueológica." *Revista de Pré-História* 7: 203–209.

———. 1991a. "A arqueologia e a cultura africana nas Américas." *Estudos Ibero-Americanos,* PUCRS, 17, 2: 61–71.

———. 1991b. "Education through Archaeology in Brazil: A Bumpy but Exciting Road." *Ciência e Cultura* (Journal of the Brazilian Association for the Advancement of Science), 43: 15–16.

Goeldi, E. 1897–1898. "Estado atual dos conhecimentos sobre os índios do Brasil." *Boletim do Museu Paraense* 2: 1–4.

———. 1900. *Excavaçõoes arqueológicas em 1895 executadas pelo Museu Paraense no Litoral da Guiana entre o Oiapoque e o Amazonas.* Paris.

———. 1905. "Escavaçõoes arqueológicas em 1895." *Memórias do Museu Goeldi.*

Guarinello, N. L. 1989. "Resenha crítica." *Revista de Pré-História* 7: 212–214.

Guimarães, C. M. 1992. "Esclavage, quilombos et archéologie." *Les Dossiers d'Archéologie* 169: 67.

Hartt, C. F. 1871. "The Ancient Indian Pottery of Marajó." *American Naturalist* 5.

———. 1872. "On the Occurrence of Face Urns in Brazil." *American Naturalist* 6.

———. 1874. "Preliminary Report of the Morgan Expedition 1870–71: Report of the Reconnaissance of the Lower Tapajós." *Bulletin of Cornell University* 1.

———. 1876. "Nota sobre algumas tangas de barro cozido dos antigos indígenas da Ilha de Marajó." *Aquivos do Museu Nacional do Rio de Janeiro* 1.

———. 1885. "Contribuição para a etnologia do Vale do Amazonas." *Aquivos do Museu Nacional do Rio de Janeiro* 6.

Ianni, O. 1978. "O estado e a organização da cultura." *Encontros da Civilização Brasileira* 1: 216–241.

Ihering, H. von. 1895. "A civilização pré-histórica do Brasil meridional." *Revista do Museu Paulista* 1.

———. 1902. "Natterer e Langsdorff." *Revista do Museu Paulista* 5.

———. 1904. "A arqueologia comparativa do Brasil." *Revista do Museu Paulista* 6.

———. 1907. "A antropologia do Estado de São Paulo." *Revista do Museu Paulista* 7.

———. 1911. "Fósseis de São José do Rio Preto." *Revista do Museu Paulista* 8.

Kern, A. A. 1982. *Missões: Uma utopia política.* Porto Alegre: Mercado Aberto.

———. 1984. "O processo histórico platino no século XVII: Da aldeia guarani ao povoado missioneiro, folia histórica del nordeste." *Resistencia* 6: 11–31.

———. 1985. "A importãncia da pesquisa arqueológica na universidade." *Revista do CEPA* 12, 14: 5–11.

———. 1987. "Problemas teórico-metodológicos relativos à análise do processo histórico missioneiro." *Anais da VI Reuniào da Sociedade Brasileira de Pesquisa Histórica, São Paulo,* 5–11.

———. 1988. "Arqueologia histórica missioneira." *Anais, Simpósio Nacional de Estudos Missioneiros* 7: 184–194.

———. 1989. "Escavaçõoes arqueológicas na missão Jesuítico-Guarani de São Lourenço." *Estudos Ibero-Americanos* 15, 1: 111–133.

———. 1991a. "Abordagens teóricas em arque-ologia." Typescript. Porto Alegre.

———. 1991b. "Sociedade barroca e missoes guaranis: Do cofronto à complementaridade." *Actas, Primeiro Congresso Internacional do Barroco,* 445–465. Oporto: Universidade do Porto.

Kern, A. A., and A. S. Dias. 1990. "A propósito das relaçœs entre arqueologia e história no estudo das sociedades antigas." *Anais do IV Simpósio de História Antiga e I Ciclo Internacional de História Antiga Oriental,* 119–129. Porto Alegre: UFRGS.

Krone, R. 1902. "Contribuiçœs para a etnografia Paulista." *Revista do Instituto Histórico e Gográfico de São Paulo* 7.

———. 1909. "Estudo sobre as cavernas do vale do Ribeira." *Arquivo do Museu Nacional do Rio de Janeiro* 15.

———. 1910. *O ídolo antropomorfo de Iguape: Sua relação com os sambaquis e a pré-história brasileira.* Iguape.

———. 1914. *Informaçœs etnográficas do vale do Rio Ribeira do Iguape.* São Paulo.

———. 1918. "Notas de pré-história Paulista." *Revista do Museu Nacional do Rio de Janeiro* 10.

Laming-Emperaire, A. 1975. "Problemes de préhistoire brésilienne." *Annales: économies, Sociétés, Civilisations* 5: 1229–1260.

Lima, Y. S. 1988. "A presença do negro na coleção de artes visuais Mário de Andrade." *Revista do Instituto de Estudos Brasileiros* 28: 117–137.

Loefgren, A. 1893. "Contribuiçœs para a arqueologia paulista: Os sambaquis." *Boletim da Comissão Geográfica e Geológica do Estado de São Paulo* 9.

———. 1903. "Os sambaquis." *Revista do Instituto Histórico e Geográfico de São Paulo* 7.

Lopes da Silva, A. 1992. "Dois séculos e meio de história xavante." In *História dos Índios no Brasil,* 357–380. Ed. M. Carneiro da Cunha. São Paulo: Cia das Letras.

Losano, M. G. 1992. "Hermann vo Ihering, um precursor da ecologia no Brasil." *Revista USP* 13: 88–99.

Mattos, A. 1938. *Pre-história Brasileira.* São Paulo: Cia Ed. Nacional (Brasiliana n.137).

Meggers, B. J. 1947. "The Beal-steers Collection of Pottery from Marajó Island, Brazil." *Papers of the Michigan Academy of Science, Arts and Letters* 31, 3: 193–213.

———. 1954. "Envirnomental Limitations on the Development of Culture." *American Anthropologist* 56: 801–824.

Mello, U. P. 1975. "Arqueologia histórica, pesquisa histórica e restauração de monumentos." *Revista Pernambucana de Desenvolvimento* 2, 1: 13–17.

———. 1976. "O galeão sacramento (1668), um naufrágio do seculo XVII e os resultados de uma pesquisa arqueológica submarina na Bahia." *Navigator,* 13.

———. 1983. *O Forte das Cinco Pontas.* Recife: FCCR.

Mendonça de Souza, A. 1991. *História da arqueologia Brasileira.* Instituto Anchietano de Pesquisas, Antropologia no. 46. São Leopoldo.

Menéndez, M. A. 1992. "A área Madeira-Tapajós: Situação de contato e relaçœs entre colonizador e indígenas." In *História dos Índios no Brasil,* 281–296. Ed. M. Carneiro da Cunha. São Paulo: Cia das Letras.

Monteiro, J. M. 1992. "Os Guarani e a história do Brasil Meridional: Séculos XVI-XVII." In *História dos Índios no Brasil,* 475–500. Ed. M. Carneiro da Cunha. São Paulo: Cia das Letras.

Neme, S., M. Beltrão, and H. Niemeyer. 1992. "Historical Archaeology Features of Project Central." Typescript.

Neto, L. 1876. "Apontamentos sobre os Tembetás." *Arquivos do Museu Nacional do Rio de Janeiro* 1.

———. 1885a. "Investigaçœs sobre a arqueologia brasileira." *Arquivos do Museu Nacional do Rio de Janeiro* 6.

———. 1885b. Lettre à Mr. Ernest Renan à propos de l'inscription phénicienne apocryphe. Rio de Janeiro.

Neves, E. G. 1989. "Resenhas." *Revista de Pré-História* 7: 210–212, 214–216.

Neves, W. A. 1988. "Arqueologia brasileira: Algumas consideraçœs." *Boletim do Museu Paraense Emílio Goeldi* 4, 2: 200–205.

Oliveira, M. A. R. 1989. "O conceito de identidade nacional na arte mineira do peRiodo colonial." *Revista do Instituto de Estudos Brasileiros* 30: 117–128.

Orser, C. E. 1992a. *In Search of Zumbi.* Normal: Illinois State University.

———. 1992b. *Introdução à arqueologia histórica.* Belo Horizonte: Oficina de Livros.

Pacheco, L. M. S. 1992. "Informação e contexto: Uma análise arqueológica." Master's thesis, Federal University at Rio de Janeiro.

Paraíso, M. H. B. 1992. "Os botocudos e sua trajetória." In *História dos Índios no Brasil,* 413–430. Ed. M. Carneiro da Cunha. São Paulo: Cia das Letras.

Pereira de Queiroz, M. I. 1989. "Desenvolvimento das ciências sociais na América Latina e a contribuição européia: O caso brasileiro." *Ciência e Cultura* 41, 4: 378–388.

Perrone-Moisés, B. 1992. "Índios livre e índios escravos: Os princípios da legislação indigenista do peRiodo colonial (séculos XVI a XVIII)." In *História dos Índios no Brasil,* 115–132. Ed. M. Carneiro da Cunha. São Paulo: Cia das Letras.

Pfeiffer, W. 1992. "L'architecture religieuse." *Les Dossiers d'Archéologie* 169: 36–39.

Porro, A. 1992. "História indígena do alto e médio Amazonas: Séculos XVI a XVIII." In *História dos Índios no Brasil,* 175–196. Ed. M. Carneiro da Cunha. São Paulo: Cia das Letras.

Prous, A. 1987. "O Brasil antigo visto pela arqueologia." *Revista do Departamento de História da Universidade Federal de Minas Gerais* 4: 100–115.

———. 1992. *Arqueologia Brasileira.* Brasília: Editora da UnB.

Queiroz, M. I. P. 1969. "Favelas urbanas, favelas rurais." *Revista do Instituto de Estudos Brasileiros* 7: 81–99.

———. 1974. "O sitiante tradicional e a percepção do espaço." *Revista do Instituto de Estudos Brasileiros* 15: 79–98.

Rath, C. F. 1871. "Notícia etnológica sobre um povo que já habitou as costas do Brasil bem como o interior, antes do dilúvio universal." *Revista do Instituto Histórico e Geográfico Brasileiro* 34.

Reis, N. G. 1970. *Quadro da arquitetura Brasileira.* São Paulo: Perspectiva.

Ribeiro, O. 1968. "Santos de barro paulista no século XVII." *Revista do Instituto de Estudos Brasileiros* 4: 15–30.

Ribeiro, P. A. M. 1978. "A arte rupestre no sul do Brasil." *CEPA* 7: 1–27.

Rohr, J. A. 1969. "Petrógrafos da ilha de Santa Catarina e ilhas adjacentes." *Pesquisas* 19: 1–30.

Roosevelt, A. C. 1989. *Lost Civilizations on the Lower Amazon in Natural History.* New York.

———. 1991. "Determinismo ecológico na interpretação do desenvolvimento social indígena da Amazônia." In *Origens, adapataçœs e diversidade biológica do homem nativo da Amazônia,* 103–141. Ed. W. A. Neves. Belém: Museu Emílio Goeldi.

———. 1992. "Arqueologia Amazônica" In *História dos Índios no Brasil,* 53–86. Ed. M. Carneiro da Cunha. São Paulo: Cia das Letras.

Saia, L. 1972. *Morada Paulista.* São Paulo: Perspectiva.

Sampaio, T. 1916. "Dois artefatos indígenas do Museu Arqueológico do Instituto Geográfico e Histórico da Bahia." *Revista do Instituto Geográfico e Histórico da Bahia* 42.

———. 1918. "Inscriçœs lapidares indígenas no vale do Paraguaçu." *Anais do Quinto Congresso Brasileiro de Geografia,* vol. 2. Bahia.

———. 1922. "Arqueologia Brasileira." *Dicionário Histórico, Geográfico e Etnológico do Brasil.* Rio de Janeiro.

Sarian, H. 1989. "Resenha." *Revista de Pré-História* 7: 216–219.

Schaeffer, E. 1965. "Albert Eckhout e a pintura colonial brasileira." *Dédalo* 1: 47–74.

Segawa, H. 1989. "Arquitetura de hospedarias de imigrantes." *Revista do Instituto de Estudos Brasileiros* 30: 23–42.

Serrano, A. 1937. "Arqueologia Brasileira: Subsídios para a arqueologia do Brasil meridional." *Revista do Arquivo Municipal de São Paulo* 36.

———. 1938. "La ceramica de Santarem." *Revista Geográfica Americana* 9.

———. 1940. "Los sambaquis y otros ensayos de arqueologia brasilena." *Anais do Terceiro Congresso Rio-Grandense de História e Geografia, Porto Alegre.*

———. 1946. "The Sambaquis of the Brazilian Coast." *Handbook of South American Indians,* 3. Washington, DC.

Silva, L. D. 1993 "A primeira sinagoga das Américas." *D. O. Leitura* 12, 136: 16.

Soares, G. 1944. *Tratado descritivo do Brasil em 1587.* São Paulo: Biblioteca Histórica Brasileira.

Staden, H. 1930. *Viagem ao Brasil.* Rio de Janeiro: Associação Brasileira do Livro.

Stover, E. 1991. *Em busca dos desaparecidos. A vala comum no Cemitério Dom Bosco.* São Paulo: USP.

Taunay, A. E. 1924–1950. *História geral das bandeiras Paulistas.* São Paulo.

Taylor, A. C. 1992. "História pre-colombiana da alta Amazônia." In *História dos Índios no Brasil,* 213–238. Ed. M. Carneiro da Cunha. São Paulo: Cia das Letras.

Thevet, A. 1944. *Singularidades da França Antártica, a que outros chamam América* [1575]. São Paulo: Cia Nacional.

Toledo, B. L. 1966. "O caminho do mar." *Revista do Instituto de Estudos Brasileiros* 1: 37–54.

———. 1981. *O real corpo de engenheiros na Capitania de São Paulo.* São Paulo: João Fortes Engenharia.

Vaconcelos, A. C. 1989. "A presença de Paulo Ferreira Santos." *Revista do Instituto de Estudos Brasileiros* 30: 167–187.

Vianna, H. 1992. "Arqueologia e patrimônio municipal: Repensando funçœs e possibilidades." *Cadernos do Patrimônio Cultural* 2, 2: 57–64.

Vogel, A., and M. A. S. Mello. 1984. "Sistemas

construídos e memória social: Uma arqueologia urbana?" *Revista de Arqueologia* 2, 2: 46–50.

Wiener, C. 1876. "Estudo sobre os sambaquis do sul do Brasil." *Arquivos do Museu Nacional do Rio de Janeiro* 1.

Wright, R. M. 1992. "História indígena do noroeste da Amazônia: Hipóteses e perspectivas." In *História dos Índios no Brasil*, 253–266. Ed. M. Carneiro da Cunha. São Paulo: Cia das Letras.

Zanettini, P. E., and M. Cazzetta. 1993. "Arqueologia histórica no Brasil: Ela existe mas você desconhece." Typescript. São Paulo.

Zanettini, P. E. 1986. "Pequeno roteiro para classificação de louças em pesquisas arqueológicas de sítios históricos." *Arqueologia* 5: 117–130.

———.1990. "Calçada do Lorena: O primeiro caminho para o mar." *Memória, São Paulo (Eletropaulo)* 9, 3: 30–35.

Breuil, Abbé Henri (1877–1961)

Born in Mortain in the Department of Manche in FRANCE, Henri Breuil trained as a priest and was ordained in 1900. His interest in paleontology began during his priestly education, but his career as a prehistorian took off later under the influence of the archaeologists EMILE CARTAILHAC, Louis Capitan, and DENIS PEYRONY. Between 1901 and 1905, Breuil helped Capitan and Peyrony investigate several major prehistoric sites and caves in the Dordogne region of France, such as Les Combarelles and Font-de-Gaume, and he accompanied Cartailhac on his cave explorations, including the one to ALTAMIRA in SPAIN.

In 1905, on the basis of his experience and his resulting publications, Breuil became a professor at the Catholic University of Fribourg, and in 1910 he went to Paris to become professor of prehistoric ethnography at the Institut de Paléontologie Humaine. From 1929 until 1947, Breuil was the first professor of prehistory at the Collège de France.

Breuil reclassified the artifact sequences and chronology of the Paleolithic period, and his scheme of successive cultural periods still forms, with some revisions, the current framework for the interpretation of European prehistory. Breuil not only added several new Paleolithic stages—the Clactonian, Levalloisian, and Tayacian—but also refined the Chellean period into the Acheulean, which then progressed and was transformed into the Mousterian. He also revised the chronology of the upper Paleolithic period, arguing for the significant impact of Aurignacian cultures on Mousterian traditions and establishing that the Aurignacian preceded the Solutrean; he also divided the Magdalenean into six phases based on changes in tool types.

Breuil's explorations of cave art continued as well. In 1906, he and Cartailhac explored the cave of Niaux in the Ariège, and much later, he was the first to enter the cave of LASCAUX after its discovery by schoolboys in 1940. He was recognized as the international expert on Paleolithic cave art, and with each new discovery, he became the arbiter of authenticity. He visited, recorded, and reproduced cave art and cave decorations, not just in western Europe, but in Africa, the Sahara, Abyssinia, Asia Minor, and CHINA. Breuil saw in this art not only the fruit of artistic spontaneity but also a communal religious and magical expression testifying to collective interests linked to the way of life of the great hunters of prehistory. Breuil was the first prehistorian to explore and decipher this art, and he also established the chronological and methodological bases for its study.

Breuil worked briefly in China at Zhoukoudian in the early 1930s and after World War II in southwestern Africa and Rhodesia (now Zimbabwe). He received many awards and honors, including being elected to the Institut de France in 1938 and receiving the Huxley Medal from the Royal Anthropological Institute in 1941.

Claudine Cohen

See also Lithic Analysis
References
For references, see *Encyclopedia of Archaeology: The Great Archaeologists, Vol. 1*, ed. Tim Murray (Santa Barbara, CA: ABC-CLIO, 1999), p. 312.

Britain, Classical Archaeology

The British, so precocious in the study of the prehistory of their own islands (Daniel 1967, 34–47), were at first, by Continental standards, slow and amateurish in their contributions to the study of classical archaeology. To this day, the primacy of prehistory in British archaeological studies is a constant source of surprise to scholars from other European countries.

In keeping with this amateur tradition, it was the scholarly diplomat SIR WILLIAM HAMILTON (1731–1803) who became the first British figure of any note in Mediterranean studies. During a thirty-six-year tour of duty in Naples, he built up a large collection of Greek pottery from Italian sites and published information about it. Hamilton was notable among his contemporaries for his realization that much of his pottery must be of Greek, not Etruscan, manufacture. Though at first he still located the centers of production among the Greek colonies of southern Italy, a later consideration of the small quantities of material then known from GREECE itself led him to modify his view. Hamilton was also responsible for inaugurating the very high evaluation of Greek painted pottery, both figuratively, as a field of study, and literally, in terms of the market value of actual specimens; both have lasted to our own times. By contrast, his overriding aim, to use his collection to influence contemporary design, was to prove less durable.

In the period before the Greek War of Independence (1821–1830), and at times even after it, travel in Greece outside of Athens was hazardous. It is true that in 1751 the SOCIETY OF DILETTANTI had sent the architects James Stuart and Nicholas Revett to Athens to record the standing remains of ancient architecture. This mission was executed to a very high standard of precision and accuracy and, in due time, was to bring into being a whole new branch of the discipline. But that was only in the following century, when their lead was followed by professionals of various nationalities, and the venture was for the time being an isolated one.

In general, Greece remained a country to be studied primarily through ancient texts, and it was only in ITALY that scholars could acquire firsthand experience of classical landscapes. Thus, Hamilton was also an early and frequent visitor to the excavations at POMPEII and HERCULANEUM, where an unmatched insight into Roman life was being gradually built up. But an independent tradition of British fieldwork in classical lands was slow to arrive. Its origins, and its almost total separation from the connoisseurship represented by Hamilton's researches, may best be found in a very different and much more characteristically British tradition, that of the enterprising, educated traveler.

From as early as the 1670s, isolated British travelers had been writing accounts of their journeys through Greece and southern Italy, but such activity was raised to a higher plane by the arrival of William Martin Leake (1777–1860), a captain of artillery who resided in Greece and Asia Minor from 1799 to 1815 as an agent of the British government. Leake's voluminous accounts of his travels are informed not only by his familiarity with the ancient texts but also by a practical eye for the date and nature of the visible remains, including inscriptions, and by an unusual sensitivity to the contemporary landscape. The claim advanced in his epitaph, "He rescued the early history of Greece from obscurity and the modern from misrepresentation," is hardly an exaggeration.

Leake's stay in Greece also witnessed the onset of two other movements, each of long-term importance for Greece, for Great Britain and other European powers, and specifically for archaeology. First, there was the arrival of a wave of representatives of the northern European elite who used the opportunity of the closing years of Ottoman rule in Greece to appropriate, for themselves or for their governments, a choice selection of sculptural and architectural antiquities before an independent Greece could call a halt to the practice. Second, there were the first harbingers of the philhellene movement, whose members strove to bring that independence about. The two most prominent members of these respective groups were, not surprisingly, also bitter enemies: Thomas Bruce, the seventh earl of Elgin, and Lord Byron. From the point of view of future British participation in Greek archaeology, it was the former group's activity that turned out to be the more relevant because of the degree to which it raised public consciousness of what Greek art might have to offer. The main countries to benefit were Britain, which got the Parthenon marbles and the Bassai frieze, and Bavaria, which obtained the Aigina pediments.

Those events coincided with an independent change in modern perceptions of the classical world in which the Greeks rapidly overtook the Romans in general esteem and in their standing as founders of European civilization, and admiration for Greek architecture became almost as widespread as that for Greek sculpture. There was a clear progression from the activities of LORD ELGIN, who disposed ruthlessly of architectural features that obstructed his access to sculptures, to those of C. R. Cockerell, who, only a decade later, lovingly recorded the architecture of Aigina and Bassai and for the most part left it in situ.

The philhellene movement, after the fulfillment of its primary mission of bringing about Greek independence, did not bear any immediate fruit for its main participants in terms of involvement in archaeological fieldwork in Greece. Instead, ironically, attention was next directed to the part of the ancient Greek world that remained under Ottoman rule—western Asia Minor. A similar policy of appropriating the choicer finds continued. British political influence, which in the new Greece had major rivals, was here supreme, and here, too, there were the footsteps of Leake and other travelers to point the way. In 1842, Sir Charles Fellows went to Xanthos under the aegis of a British naval expedition and removed the greater part of the Nereid Monument to London. But the dominant personality in this area was the curiously isolated figure of Sir Charles Newton (1816–1894), who spent much of the 1850s in Ionia as a British consul working at Knidos, Halicarnassus, and elsewhere. A notable result of his work was the acquisition of the frieze of the Mausoleum of Halicarnassus for the BRITISH MUSEUM, as important a possession for the fourth century B.C. as the Elgin Marbles had been for the fifth. Though his activities at first sight remind one more of Elgin than of Stuart and Revett or Cockerell, Newton has some claim to be regarded as the true founder of British classical field archaeology in that he envisaged the potential for archaeology as an independent source of knowledge for the ancient world.

Hitherto, deference to the ancient written sources had been the guiding principal of all serious practitioners, in Britain and elsewhere. This had been the prime legacy of the founding father of the whole discipline a century earlier, the German art historian JOHAN JOACHIM WINCKELMANN (Morris 1994). As the junior partner of traditional classics, classical archaeology had a fairly humble role but an apparently secure one, which even had incidental advantages (the participation of women, for example, was less strongly discouraged, and after 1900, an increasing number of women were able to take advantage of this fact). But Newton was more interested in evolutionary change in art than in illustrating texts or capturing a timeless ideal of perfection. The large collection of painted pottery that he donated to the British Museum was, for him, a potential independent source for the study of Greek society, religion, and everyday life rather than a reflection of the texts or an exemplification of classical beauty. Yet one senses that he died a disappointed man, probably in part because of the major change of direction in British archaeology of the Greek world that he had lived to see, and which was equally deprecated by much younger leading figures in the discipline.

The importance of the prehistoric discoveries by HEINRICH SCHLIEMANN in the Aegean, from 1870 onward, was perhaps more favorably received among the educated public in Britain than in his native Germany or elsewhere, especially after they received the accolade of Prime Minister Gladstone's patronage. When the British, slow and parsimonious to the last, eventually established a school of art and history in Athens in 1886 (years after the French, Germans, and Americans), the tide of prehistoric Aegean archaeology was already running fast, and it was to dominate the activity of the new school for the next century and more.

By 1896, the British had embarked on their first major prehistoric excavation at Phylakopi on the island of Melos, and in 1900, this work was rapidly eclipsed by the sensational discoveries of ARTHUR EVANS (1850–1941) at KNOSSOS on Crete. Meanwhile, A. J. B. Wace (1879–1957) had already become active in the exploration of prehistoric Thessaly, and after World War I, he began the long-term excavation of a third great Bronze Age site, Mycenae. Other prehistoric sites of the first rank were investigated at Palaikastro in eastern Crete and Thermi on the island of Lesbos. All of these sites except Thermi have seen recent British work—Knossos and Mycenae intermittently ever since the British connection was established.

That concentrated direction of effort has no counterpart in the activities of the other foreign missions, whose work in Greece either preceded the British (France, Germany, the United States) or followed it fairly soon afterward (Italy, Austria, Denmark, Sweden, and more recently, a number of other countries in Europe and the British Commonwealth), nor in the activities of the Greeks themselves. Such a long-standing tradition calls for some specific explanation, and there is a hint of one in the early British preoccupation with prehistory noted earlier, in which case its roots lie very deep indeed and this will not be the last illustration of it. Meanwhile, we should note the early and lasting involvement of the Athens school in Cypriot archaeology, which lasted through and beyond the British occupation of that island between 1878 and 1960.

For the other nations involved in Greek archaeology, the late nineteenth and early twentieth centuries were the time of the great sanctuary projects (i.e., major centers of religion) with their uniquely rich yields of works of art. The German operations at Olympia, long postponed, began in 1875. The equally continuous French connection with Delphi dates from 1894, and their connection with Delos began in 1904. The Greeks began a systematic exploration of the preclassical levels on the Athenian Acropolis in 1882, the Americans began work at the Argive Heraion in 1894, and the Danes started at Lindos in 1904. Other major long-term undertakings followed later. The only partial British counterparts were the much briefer campaigns at the Artemision of EPHESUS in 1904–1905 and at the Artemis Orthia sanctuary at Sparta between 1906 and 1910. There was no return to either site, and almost the only major British excavation of a classical Greek settlement to date has been that at Megalopolis (1890–1893).

There thus arose a most fundamental divergence between the implicit aims behind the setting up of a permanent British school in Greece and its main outcome. Art and connoisseurship, even at the end of the nineteenth century, were still uppermost in the minds of those who had encouraged the venture, and they were to be the justification and reward for involvement in Greek archaeology. In the account of a great meeting, primarily for the purpose of fund-raising, that the Athens school persuaded the Prince of Wales to chair at St. James's Palace in 1895, it is the artists who stand out from the dazzling list of dignitaries present—Leighton, Millais, Poynter, Alma-Tadema, and other members of the Royal Academy who are now forgotten. The interest is clear, and it was indeed to be satisfied, but in a different way and by scholars who had little connection with fieldwork or the new school. Throughout the twentieth century, the mantle of Hamilton was worn, with varying degrees of distinction, by British students of Greek painted pottery and, more intermittently, of Greek sculpture and architecture. Their achievement, in this as in other branches of classical studies, was steadily eclipsed by German scholars until the heyday of the greatest of these scholars, Adolf Furtwängler, in the final decade of the century.

But an era of British resurgence was eventually to dawn. By applying to Greek pottery methods first developed in the study of Renaissance painting, J. D. BEAZLEY (1885–1970), the greatest of all students of vase painting, transformed the subject itself and gave it a place in the main discourse of art history. Single-handedly, he attributed many thousands of vases to individual painters for the first time, providing a substitute for the lost masterpieces of the great names in Greek sculpture, which, as was only now becoming clear, were in the vast majority of cases lost forever. He thereby gave a further lease on life to another branch of classical archaeology—one that, for all the discoveries in Aegean prehistory, remains closer to the heart of the subject in public perception. He was also important in founding a following whose work extended across a wide field of Greek art. His two successors in the Lincoln Chair at Oxford, Bernard Ashmole (1894–1989) and Martin Robertson (1914–), were each in their time to be considered as being among the outstanding exponents of Greek art history. Humfry Payne (1902–1936), despite his early death, was another.

The archaeology of Italy and of the Roman Empire in general had followed an almost entirely separate course, in British though hardly in Continental scholarship, and was practiced not merely by different individuals but by quite different kinds of archaeologists. In Britain, the study of Roman art languished while the investigation of remains in the field held sway. We may begin with Roman Britain itself. From the time of WILLIAM CAMDEN's survey of Hadrian's Wall in 1599, it was taken for granted that Roman-British remains lay within the purview of the antiquaries who studied the prehistory of Britain. Of all the famous British prehistorians, from pioneers like WILLIAM STUKELEY to moderns like MORTIMER WHEELER, some involvement with Roman-British archaeology was a common feature, and a standing army of gifted amateurs provided specialization in their own localities. The artistic quality of the finds offered few attractions for the aesthetic approach, and the surviving documentary sources were too thin to provide much opening for textual learning. A separate tradition had grown up, and a measure of its achievement is that, to this day, Britannia remains from most points of view the most thoroughly studied province of the Roman Empire.

In Rome itself, the establishment of a British school of archaeology occurred only in 1901 (seventy-two years after the opening of a corresponding German-based institution). From the start, a new note was detectable, businesslike and unfussy, and it can be seen in the inaugural numbers of the respective periodicals of the two schools. Ironically, it was in Rome that formal provision was to be made for practicing artists. Whereas the launch of the Athens school celebrated the participation of royalty, the church, and the arts, the Rome Papers begin with a fifteen-line note from the chairman, stating only, "The title of this volume sufficiently indicates its character."

The dominant personality of the early years was Thomas Ashby (1874–1931), the school's director for nearly twenty years and in whose work we see the reemergence of another long-established British tradition, topographical survey. The characteristics of that tradition were hardihood and rapid movement, for the aim was to traverse a whole region, preferably on foot, registering all surviving ancient features of any note and recording them in sketches or, by Ashby's time, in photographs.

That kind of work was enthusiastically taken up in Greece, too, especially in Crete and northern Greece, as a host of subsequent papers in the Athens annual volume testifies. But in the work of the Rome school, with less competition from grand excavations, it has continued to hold a special place—it will suffice here to mention the ground-breaking work in the territory of southern Etruria led by J. B. Ward-Perkins from 1950 to 1974. The mention of Etruria also recalls the long-standing British enthusiasm for the Villanovan and Etruscan archaeology of Iron Age Italy, which far antedates the lifetimes of its two best-known British exponents, George Dennis (1814–1898) and David Randall-McIver (1873–1945).

The intervention of two world wars brought substantial interruptions to British archaeological work in the Mediterranean but not major changes. When one consults periodicals or university syllabi of, say, 1960, there is a greater resemblance to those of 1900 than to those of even a few years later. There were minor shifts of emphasis, however, and one that is worth noting is the extension of interest, after World War II, to the proto-history of the early Iron Age in Greece, between about 1100 and 800 B.C., which was to become as much of a British specialty as full prehistory. Another feature of this period was the gradual expansion of British fieldwork into new provinces of the Roman Empire, beginning with Libya and extending later to Tunisia, Spain, France, Bulgaria, and Dalmatia. But greater change, in the fields of method and content, was on the way.

The birth of a self-consciously theoretical approach in archaeology—aptly named by one of its pioneers as "the loss of innocence"—came about in fields far removed in time and space from the ancient Mediterranean. But it did take place above all in the Anglo-Saxon countries, and it was to be expected that in due course it would affect British archaeology in the Mediterranean. By the 1970s, the impact was clearly visible and rather abrupt, as different questions began to be asked and different priorities advanced. For the classical archaeologist, this followed closely on another, more traumatic change, the equally sudden eclipse of classics as the supreme discipline in the humanities. It was no longer enough to color in the black-and-white picture book of text-based classics; every discipline was faced by demands to justify its existence, and archaeology began to formulate answers that could be used in the classical field as well. A much wider range of environmental evidence began to be studied alongside the artifacts, quantification and scientific aids began to appear, and new approaches in the field were proposed as alternatives to both the expansive excavation of the early era and the speculative soundings of more recent years.

The most obvious, intensive regional survey, developed easily from the long British tradition of regional topographical study. As in the work of Leake and Ashby, there was an emphasis on the rural rather than the urban aspect of ancient life and on the lateral extension of the classical cultures rather than the highest pinnacles of their achievement. What was new was the aim of neutrality and objectivity on the part of teams of field-walkers in assessing the landscape instead of aiming for the known or visible features of ancient origin, searching the whole landscape for the previously invisible. In this regard, they enjoyed the same advantage that had attracted the excavators a century before—the unique artifactual richness of the Mediterranean past.

Just as the buried structures and their contents had yielded work for whole generations of catalogers and analysts, so the Mediterranean environment, with its 5,000 years of more or less continuous agriculture, proved to have left on the surface of the landscape a quite unexpected wealth of discarded artifacts. These were undeserving of individual study but collectively very informative about past exploitation of the soil. Ancient city sites, if they had been fortunate enough not to remain centers of habitation, had left huge "shadows" of pottery, stone,

and tile on the surface. Thus, a technique that had been pioneered for archaeologically impoverished landscapes in other parts of the world was transplanted to the terrain of Italy, Greece, and a number of other Mediterranean countries with outstanding success. Regions, rather than parts of an individual site, became the targets for investigation. Since such a technique is wasteful if it concentrates on a single period, an interesting by-product has been the resurgence of interest in periods that had been relatively neglected in traditional fieldwork, including the Hellenistic and especially the late Roman and early medieval periods.

Intensive survey is merely one tangible outcome of the new, theoretically conscious approach in Mediterranean archaeology. But in every area of activity, from the new style of small-scale, problem-oriented excavation to the generalized social or environmental analysis, there has been change of such rapidity that it belies the tradition-bound reputation of classical archaeology.

Certain lasting characteristics can nevertheless be seen in the British approach over the past two centuries. A constant theme, and ostensibly a purely negative one, has been the chronic reference to the shortage of funding by comparison with the other industrially advanced nations. Some of the consequences of this indeed appear negative, the most obvious being the absence of official, century-long excavations at notable classical sites and the resulting excavation reports that run to thirty or forty volumes. Yet the long-term effects are not necessarily unfavorable. If the indefatigable topographers of earlier years had been tied down to major site publications, they would hardly have ventured on their journeys; if the Artemis Orthia excavation at Sparta had yielded lavish works of art and architecture, and continued for forty years instead of four, the pioneering stratigraphic observations that so distinguish it among the early sanctuary projects might never have been made. The common thread running through the past two centuries has been one of cautious innovation, and there has been the serendipity that often rewards the pursuit of the unfashionable.

Anthony Snodgrass

References

Daniel, G. 1967. *The Origins and Growth of Archaeology.* Harmondsworth, UK: Penguin.

Morris, I. 1994. "Archaeologies of Greece." In *Classical Greece: Ancient Histories and Modern Archaeologies,* 8–47. Ed. I. Morris. Cambridge: Cambridge University Press.

Britain, Prehistoric Archaeology

Scholars writing about the prehistoric archaeology of Britain have played a central role in the development of archaeology in the Anglo-Saxon world. Given this fact, it is remarkable that no substantial, book-length history of British archaeology has yet been written. This observation is even more striking when we consider that archaeologists such as GLYN DANIEL (1943, 1964, 1967, 1971, 1975, 1976, 1981) and STUART PIGGOTT, not to mention VERE GORDON CHILDE, J. G. D. CLARK, and DAVID CLARKE, have made such significant contributions to the historiography of archaeology generally.

Of course, there are studies of specific episodes or periods in the history of archaeology in Britain. Graham Parry (1995), Piggott (1975, 1976, 1978, 1981, 1985), and Michael Hunter (1975) have written illuminatingly about the history of antiquarianism, particularly about the work of WILLIAM STUKELEY, WILLIAM CAMDEN, JOHN AUBREY, and others. Barry Marsden (1984) has produced an often amusing (and richly detailed) account of the activities of antiquaries and archaeologists during the nineteenth century. Analyses of the role of archaeologists such as LORD AVEBURY (Sir John Lubbock) and AUGUSTUS PITT RIVERS in the passage of heritage-preservation legislation in the nineteenth century (Chapman 1989a; Chippindale 1983; Murray 1990) have appeared alongside detailed discussions of the discovery of high human antiquity (Grayson 1983; Murray 1997; Van Riper 1996). In addition, more specific discussions of changing perceptions of sites such as Stonehenge (Chippindale 1985), the historiographic significance of sites such as the Glastonbury Lake Village (Coles, Goodall, and Minnitt 1992) and Little Woodbury (excavated by GERHARD BERSU) (Evans 1989), or the

history of British Paleolithic archaeology (Davis and Charles 1999; Roberts 1999; Roe 1981a; Spencer 1990) have provided much-needed context to broader considerations. And notable archaeologists have been encouraged to indulge in autobiography (see, for example, Daniel and Chippindale 1989), complementing a growing list of biographies and biographical essays (particularly those of Gordon Childe, Pitt Rivers, SIR FLINDERS PETRIE, GERTRUDE BELL, and T. E. Lawrence, as well as the entries in both volumes of *The Great Archaeologists,* ed. Tim Murray, 1999).

At a larger scale historians of science such as P. Levine (1986) have explored the professionalization of British archaeology within the context of British history. And some general histories of archaeology, including those written by G. E. Daniel (1975) and B. G. Trigger (1987), in the course of reconstructing the origins and growth of archaeology and the archaeological perspective, have provided an outline of the history of prehistoric archaeology in Britain. These overviews have to some extent been matched by the introductory chapters to surveys of British prehistoric archaeology, such as those by T. Darvill (1987, 13–27), J. Hunter and I. Ralston (1999), I. Longworth and J. Cherry (1986), C. Renfrew (1972), and D. Roe (1981b).

Notwithstanding the importance of these general overviews, however, our understanding of the context of archaeology and archaeological knowledge in British society is still quite rudimentary. A great deal of fundamental research into all aspects of that history remains to be done. In recent years some attention has been given to the need to study the histories of county and metropolitan archaeological societies (particularly those founded in the nineteenth century), and considerable encouragement has been given to efforts to explore the lives of the less famous British archaeologists (especially women—see, for example, M. Diaz-Andreu and M. L. S. Sorensen 1998). But there is still a very long way to go.

This state of affairs is all the more curious when we consider the major role played by British archaeology (and archaeologists) in the development of archaeological theory in the last

N

ATLANTIC
OCEAN

NORTH SEA

Skara Brae

Oronsay

Mount Sandel

Cass'ny Hawin

Star Carr

IRISH
SEA

IRELAND

Pontnewydd Cave   Creswell

Flag Fen   High Lodge

Avebury
Silbury Hill   Haddenham
West Kennet
Windmill Hill   Wayland's Smithy   Sutton Hoo
Clacton
Paviland Cave   Yiewsley

Aveline's Hole & Gough's Cave   Baker's Hole
& Swanscombe   Oldbury

Sweet Track

Maiden Castle   Boxgrove

CELTIC SEA   Stonehenge
                                     Woodhenge

0   200 km

Kent's Cavern
& Windmill Cave   Hengistbury Head

Prehistoric Archaeological Sites in Britain

thirty-five years of the twentieth century. In his highly original and influential *Analytical Archaeology* (1968), David Clarke sought to explain why archaeology in general (but British archaeology in particular) needed to change by means of a short but potent history of archaeology. A sense of the importance of the history of archaeology also underwrote Trigger's spirited defense of historical perspectives in archaeology. But since the rise of theoretical archaeology as a recognizable field of archaeological endeavor in Britain in the early 1970s, few theoretical archaeologists have paid much attention to the history of their discipline either as a source of inspiration or as the basis for understanding the social, cultural, and political contexts of archaeological research (Champion [1991] and Pinsky and Wylie [1990] being among the exceptions). An ignorance of the history of British prehistoric archaeology has been used to explain why so much of the processual as well as the postprocessual archaeological program in Britain (as elsewhere) has the flavor of "old wine in new skins."

The lack of fundamental research (and the fact that British prehistoric archaeologists still seem to need persuading about the value of an understanding of disciplinary history to their own work) has had some straightforward consequences. One of the most obvious of these is the perpetuation of ideas about that history that have largely gone unexamined—ideas that underwrote preceding theoretical frameworks, many of which are no longer fashionable. In the rare cases in which conventional historical accounts have been scrutinized (such as in the work of the antiquarians or in the discovery of high human antiquity), clear shortcomings in them have been identified. There is every reason to expect that if detailed explorations were to be undertaken—of, for instance, the application of the THREE-AGE SYSTEM to British archaeology, the development of the culture concept in the late nineteenth century, the funding of British archaeological research in the twentieth century, or the rapid and successful development of popular archaeology programs on television—new insights could be gained into the nature and significance of British prehistoric archaeology.

However, there can be no doubt about the daunting scale of the task. To produce a worthwhile historical synthesis, one has to take into account the fact that British prehistoric archaeology is a large and complex entity, made up of many producers and consumers of archaeological knowledge who intersect with the discipline through a wide range of institutional, social, political, and cultural contexts. The difficulty of the task is increased by two related factors. First, the practice of British prehistoric archaeology has had global implications ever since Lubbock published *Prehistoric Times* in 1865. Much of the methodological and theoretical contour of prehistoric archaeology has been shaped by people based in Britain or working on British materials. By the same token the interpretation of British prehistory has relied on inferences drawn from all over the world. Second, each temporal division of British prehistoric archaeology (Paleolithic, Neolithic, Bronze Age, and Iron Age) has its own traditions and rhythms, and it is uncommon for archaeologists to understand and appreciate these matters in all prehistoric periods.

The history of British archaeology can be found in a large number of entries in this encyclopedia dealing with specific sites, people, periods, and types of archaeology. The entry on the archaeology of Roman Britain links with other entries on archaeology in medieval Europe, industrial archaeology, and the contribution of British archaeology to the archaeology of the classical world, as well as entries on major museums (such as the BRITISH MUSEUM and the ASHMOLEAN) and major societies (the SOCIETY OF ANTIQUARIES OF LONDON, the SOCIETY OF ANTIQUARIES OF SCOTLAND, the ROYAL ARCHAEOLOGICAL INSTITUTE, the EGYPT EXPLORATION SOCIETY, and so forth). Although this list is by no means complete (for example, there is no entry on the Prehistoric Society, though this is well discussed in the literature—see Smith [1999]), these entries, in conjunction with those on major journals such as *Antiquity* and *World Archaeology,* can give readers a stronger sense of the institutional fabric of British archaeology. This sense can also be enhanced by the biographies of significant archaeologists that are included throughout the five volumes of the encyclopedia.

The fact that no single entry can encompass all the richness and complexity of British prehistoric archaeology (let alone British archaeology in general) heightens our awareness of the gaps that exist in our understanding of that history. As is the case in most western countries, British archaeology is also a complex social institution that does not necessarily always display a high degree of institutional coherence. Some of the most important elements of that institution include: heritage legislation passed by the British Parliament (and the agencies that have been created to administer it, such as English Heritage); the policies and practices of local government and the heritage-management industry; university departments that train professional archaeologists, whose members undertake research designed to expand the frontiers of knowledge and understanding; archaeologists (either freelance or employed by government or nongovernment agencies) who are directly involved in the management of archaeological heritage; archaeological societies (both local and national) whose members (be they amateur or professional) are actively engaged in exploring the archaeology of Britain and communicating its importance to others; television stations, publishers, tourism operators, and others who "market" the archaeology of Britain for commercial gain; and members of the general public who visit sites, have their rights to use land encumbered, protest the destruction of archaeological heritage, or simply live in rich archaeological landscapes. Tracing the evolution of such an important social, political, and cultural force since the days of John Leland and William Camden is well beyond the scope of this entry.

This overview will, however, provide a brief and very general narrative of that evolution, isolating several themes that are generally considered to be historically significant. As mentioned earlier, one of the consequences of the lack of research into that history was the perpetuation of questionable perspectives, and in the following passages this shortcoming will be explored through one case study dealing with the relationships between British prehistoric archaeology, ethnology, and physical anthropology in the mid-nineteenth century. This highly specific and detailed case study stands in sharp distinction to the generalizations of the rest of the text, which incorporates a conventional reading of the evolution of British prehistoric archaeology and a brief recounting of some of the more notable circumstances of the postwar era that are considered to be the subject of commonsense understandings.

It is perhaps predictable that the history of British prehistoric archaeology reaches back into the sixteenth and seventeenth centuries—the time of the antiquaries such as William Camden and John Speed and well before the creation of prehistoric archaeology as a distinct discipline. It is a commonplace of the history of British archaeology that we can find the origins of the discipline in the questions and methods of the antiquaries and natural historians. Their questions related to the history of Britain prior to Roman times—Who were the occupants? Who created the ruins in the British landscape at places such as Stonehenge and AVEBURY?—and have inspired British prehistoric archaeology ever since. Indeed, the theme of establishing a connection between past and present, of making the physical remains of the past play a role in the history of Britain (thus becoming intelligible and worth preserving), is the central feature of British prehistoric archaeology. Other themes flow directly from this sense of making history: the relationship between the British Isles and the rest of Europe; the relationship between the early history of the British Isles and the contemporary indigenous communities found at the margins of the British Empire; the close relationship between prehistoric archaeology and what was to become anthropology in the late nineteenth century; and the central role to be played by prehistoric archaeology in imagining the British nation—either as a succession of conquests or as an accretion of cultural and ethnic diversities.

These themes have provided the cognitive underpinning of technical and methodological developments from the early landscape studies of the antiquarians to the science-based analyses of archaeological data that have featured so prominently in British prehistoric archaeology since the 1950s. They have also been significant in the development of theory in British prehistoric archaeology, but though it is important to stress the reality of continuity, it is also very true that the interpretation of those themes has shifted dramatically over the last 500 years. Changing patterns of interpretation and explanation have influenced the ways in which archaeologists have sought to pursue research and to make sense of their findings.

Parry (1995), Piggott (1976), and others have clearly established that the long history of British antiquarianism prior to the 1830s was based on the gradual acceptance that what we would now call archaeological data (sites, monuments, landscapes, material culture) had the

The ancient stone monument Stonehenge in England (Corel)

capacity to assist in the writing of prehistory. Much antiquarian scholarship was based on close analysis of the works of the classical authors, which were considered to have much the same status as eyewitness testimony. But there was also an increasing element of material analysis—involving coins, inscriptions, and other artifacts that had been accumulated by antiquaries in "cabinets of curiosities." These collections, which were sometimes vast (as in the case of Sir Robert Bruce Cotton), were a significant resource for the antiquaries; they also formed the core of the collections in many museums, such as the Ashmolean and the British Museum.

The rigorous analysis of material culture was a vital source of direct information about the prehistoric past, but this was equally true of field studies on monuments (through recording rather than excavation). Notable early exponents of such work were John Aubrey, WILLIAM DUGDALE, EDWARD LHWYD, and Robert Plot, who amassed records of hundreds of sites of "pre-Roman" age during the seventeenth cen-

tury. This tradition was ably carried on in the eighteenth century, most prominently by Stukeley, whose long career in the field was crowned by his careful excavations at Stonehenge. The realignment of British antiquarian interest from a concentration on the analysis of literary sources, coins, and field surveys to the inclusion of site excavations (particularly mounds and barrows) is the most significant innovation of the eighteenth century (along with the foundation of the Society of Antiquaries of London in 1718). Something of an excavation mania gripped British antiquarian circles from the mid-eighteenth century until well into the nineteenth. Most notable among the early excavators was the Reverend Bryan Fausett (1720–1776), who focused on Saxon tumuli and is reported to have excavated over 750 of them. There can be little doubt that Fausett's enthusiasm was not matched by his skill, and the damage done through his uncontrolled excavation was incalculable. Nonetheless, he was an ardent collector and an untiring propagandist for British antiquity. Fausett's passion was shared rather more usefully by the enigmatic James Douglas (1753–1819), whose *Nenia Britannica* (1793) was a thorough and at times brilliant discussion of the burial customs of "ancient Britons."

Generations of systematic (and frequently unsystematic) fieldwork had, by the end of the eighteenth century, created a crisis in British antiquarian circles. Although a great deal of material culture had been excavated, swelling the collections of antiquaries and providing the foundations for the collections of new museums, its usefulness for writing history was severely curtailed by what seemed to be insuperable problems with establishing chronology. Many of the more careful observers (especially those with field experience in either excavation or survey) well understood that everything could not be the same age and that there was variation within and between sites and artifact types, but things basically came to a grinding halt at that point. Naturally, this did not stop antiquaries from continuing their researches. Indeed, in many ways the problem became even more acute through the systematic work of RICHARD COLT HOARE, WILLIAM CUNNINGTON, and others; in *Ancient Wiltshire* (1810–1821), for instance, Colt Hoare took pains to limit his interpretations to the physical data he had at hand—interpretations that were consequently confined to admitting his inability to write the history of prehistoric Wiltshire.

It is well known that the solution to Colt Hoare's problems—the three-age system—had already been worked out in Scandinavia by C. J. THOMSEN and JENS JACOB WORSAAE. Although Thomsen's great work was not translated into English until 1848 (as the *Guide to Northern Archaeology*) and Worsaae's was not issued in English until 1849 (as *The Primeval Antiquities of Denmark*), some British antiquaries were *au fait* with the system before then. Nonetheless, the three-age system received a mixed welcome in Britain and from institutions such as the British Museum. Thomas Wright, who regarded himself as one of the leading British antiquaries, would have none of it, but Sir John Lubbock enthusiastically embraced it as a major step forward. Throughout the rest of the period (and continuing for the remainder of the nineteenth century) differences of opinion about the value of the three-age system (or perhaps more spectacularly the discovery of high human antiquity) were aired in a wide variety of scientific and antiquarian associations. The case study that follows focuses on the British Archaeological Association (BAA) and the Royal Archaeological Institute (RAI), but the same kinds of issues were the meat and drink of debate and dispute in similar associations in Britain (and, of course, elsewhere in Europe).

Certainly, excavation continued right across Britain, but the goals of such work became increasingly diverse as the problems with chronology, so apparent in the efforts of Colt Hoare and his predecessors, were gradually resolved by adjusting the three-age system to more closely fit regional realities in British prehistoric archaeology. One example of this growing diversity was the work of John Thurnam (1810–1873), whose primary interest was in the skeletal remains found in barrows and tumuli. Thurnam (later in partnership with J. B. Davis [1801–1881]) sought to use these remains to write the racial history of Britain, a goal that he and Davis believed they had achieved with the publication of *Crania Britannica* (1856–1865). Others, such as Thomas Bateman (1787–1835), Charles Roach Smith (1807–1890), and the indefatigable Canon William Greenwell (1820–1918), continued to dig barrows at a fast pace and with rather broader interests in mind. Greenwell's *British Barrows* (1877) represented the high tide of antiquarian activity in a world where the kind of prehistoric archaeology undertaken had clear cultural and political implications. It is testimony to the three-age system that the resolution of chronological problems, however imperfect it was, could release such passion and creativity among those writing the prehistory of Britain.

Case Study: Institutions and Disciplinary Identity in the Mid-Nineteenth Century

This analysis of the early years of the British Archaeological Association and the Royal Archaeological Institute should be read in conjunction with the entry, "Royal Archaeological Institute," by Martin Millett in this encyclopedia. Here, the reasons for their foundation with regard to their dual role—the advancement of archaeological research through the publication of the work of British and Scandinavian antiquaries and the advocacy of conservation—will be addressed. These were linked by promoting the reliability of archaeological knowledge and the understanding of their unique nature as a source of information about human prehistory.

No full-scale study of the BAA has been written (but see Chapman 1989b). The RAI has fared rather better (see Millett's entry in this encyclopedia). The BAA was formed in 1844, with a membership largely drawn from the Society of Antiquaries of London. The BAA prospectus clearly outlined the connections to that more "senior" society and hinted at the reasons for a separate foundation: "The object of this Association is to investigate, preserve, and illustrate all ancient Monuments of the History, Manners, Customs, and Arts of our forefathers, and in furtherance of the principles with which the Society of Antiquaries of London was established, to render available the researches of a numerous class of lovers of Antiquity, who are unconnected with that institution."

The "Introduction" to the first volume of the *Archaeological Journal* (in 1845) stressed the need to encourage intelligent research into British antiquities and vigilant care for their preservation. The two objectives were seen to be complementary. The author, the antiquary Albert Way (1805–1874), reiterated the basic principle, enshrined in the Society of Antiquaries, that ancient memorials of an important national character were not solely confined to those of the classical world. Way made an explicit appeal to the potential "scientificness" of archaeology through a comparison with geology, a discipline that he considered a science because it turned the incomprehensible into fact. In his view archaeology could, in the light of the three-age system, do likewise. The plea to science was also important from the perspective of conservation. Way clearly believed that the new science of archaeology could imbue the monuments with rationally assessable meaning and value, and the BAA was to capitalize on this prospect by coordinating attempts to preserve them.

Way was also quite explicit about the reasons for establishing a group separate from the Society of Antiquaries. The first reason was that the society's charter did not make specific reference to concerted attempts at preservation. The second was that the society was based in London, thereby denying most of the provincial middle class the opportunity to attend its meetings. The BAA was promoted as the group that would fill these gaps and more effectively respond to the advancement of extended interest in Archaic researches. The anonymous review of Worsaae's *Denmark's Olden Times* (1844), which appeared in the second volume of the *Archaeological Journal* (Anonymous 1846), summed up the association's view of how prehistoric archaeology should be written if it were to assist in the preservation of monuments. The reviewer noted government support for the Danish National Museum. He further observed that a firm case had been made for the national and historical importance of archaeological data by means of Worsaae's account of climatic and ecological change, the archaeological data themselves, and the use of ethnographic analogy in their interpretation. Significantly, the reviewer also made an explicit appeal to the racial aspects of Worsaae's prehistory, emphasizing that the English would also see value in the work because it added to the history of the German race. Finally, the reviewer, unlike most others, stressed the significance of the third section of Worsaae's work, in which the author had considered the meaning and value of the archaeological resources and argued for strong links between formal professional notions of value and popularly accepted justifications for their preservation.

The interests of the RAI, which had by this time split from the BAA, and the establishment of a language and a purpose for the discipline of archaeology developed right through the period prior to the discoveries made by JOHN EVANS and HUGH FALCONER at BRIXHAM CAVE. J. M. K.'s "Introduction" to the sixth volume of the *Archaeological Journal* (1849) stressed that archaeologists were collectors with a definite purpose and method: "The higher purpose at which we ought to strive is the record of human development—the History of Man imagined in the History of one collection of men" (1849, 3).

This not entirely comfortable reconciliation of the differences between universal history and historicism became a frequent subject of debate within archaeology through the nineteenth century and into the twentieth. Was it possible to glimpse the general through the analysis of the particular? Was the prehistory of Europe the only sure guide to reconstructing the chain of human development? By 1850 some self-congratulations were thought to be due. The "Introduction" to volume 7 of the *Archaeological Journal* (1850) was a retrospective on the history of archaeological research, which naturally concluded that great progress had been made. Prior to 1850 an interest in archaeology had been deemed "mere learned but unprofitable trifling" (1850, 1). Archaeology had, therefore, been sneered at, if not completely ignored, until recent years. The anonymous author evidently believed that this view was not unfounded because in his assessment, the "sole interest of archaeology was to collect scraps of antiquity without selection, order or application" (1850, 4). It was thus pure dilettantism. This was a harsh judgment on those who had collected antiquities as exemplars of taste and who certainly did so with criteria of selection. It was also a thinly veiled attack on the Society of Antiquaries. By 1850 the rules of the game had changed dramatically.

No longer was collection for the cultivation of taste enough of a purpose, when the reasons for collection were themselves the subject of debate. Although the preceding centuries had seen the methods of Camden and Speed developed by Aubrey and even by Stukeley to the stage at which archaeological data were widely considered to be important and meaningful in the writing of British history, additional measures of practical value were incorporated in the nineteenth century. For the members of the RAI (and many within the Society of Antiquaries), the purpose of collection had to include a relevance to contemporary problems—and there were no more relevant problems than race and nationalism. The author of the 1850 *Archaeological Journal* Introduction obviously had this in mind. The purpose of collection, he asserted, should be to link the objects with the history of national descent and to promote "sentiments of national attachment" (1850, 5–6).

In keeping with the general attitude of the RAI, the emphasis was on providing justifications for preservation, through the process of "illustration":

> The study of the habits which have belonged to different ages of social life, will induce the consideration of the intricacies of race, and in this the philosopher and the antiquary will be usefully combined. Archaeology will then assume a still more dignified station among the objects of mind, and will justly be recognized as a necessary and most valuable auxiliary in the elucidation of the interesting speculations that are now being developed in connection with ethnological inquiries (1850, 6).

This new basis for archaeology, fostered by Worsaae but also confirmed by the racial and linguistic theorists, was to provide the ultimate justification for the preservation of the monuments. In so doing, it also exposed archaeology to debates concerning human nature and the nature and meaning of human history that, despite decades if not centuries of disputation, remained firmly at the level of polemic. No one perspective had been able to convincingly demolish all the others. Archaeology was called into the fray precisely because all sides agreed that it might well provide an important empirical justification for their views (a justification that was sorely lacking).

The framework in which British prehistoric archaeology had been practiced over the preceding 200 years thus changed as a result of pressures external to the recovery and analysis of the record itself. Accordingly, the monuments had begun to undergo a subtle change in meaning that was still historical and still ethnographic (in the sense that they could be interpreted through the classical and Amerindian ethnographies), but they had now also become firmly national and racial.

The reconciliation between universal history and romantic historicism mentioned earlier was indeed an uncomfortable one because it presupposed links to other disciplines such as ethnology and philology, and the generalizations that those disciplines made were primarily drawn from nonarchaeological data. The links with these disciplines therefore required that the generalizations be reformulated or translated into archaeological terms, a process that increased the reliance of archaeologists on interpretative theory that was itself ungrounded in archaeology, as it was in the other disciplines. Charles Newton's "On the Study of Archaeology" (1851) was a case in point. The account opened with the claim that the subject matter of archaeology was oral, written, and monumental. Newton emphasized the oral, claiming that through this source of evidence archaeologists had the chance to reconstruct language, manners, and customs (a concern of the antiquaries since Camden and Speed had demolished GEOFFREY OF MONMOUTH's "history," which had been developed by Lhwyd): "These obsolete and rare forms of speech are to the philologist what the extinct Fauna and Floras of the primeval world are to the comparative anatomist and the botanist" (1851, 3). The conscious appeal to links between such classificatory sciences and archaeology was a feature of the period. Archaeology would become scientific by comparison.

Following the leaders of romantic philology, Walter Scott and Jacob Grimm, Newton appealed to the peasants (read *Volk*) as the true source of important themes with which to reconstruct the prehistoric past: "The peasant's mind reflects what has been rather than what is. It revolves in the same circle as the more cultivated mind of the nation, but at a much slower rate. On the great dial-plate of time, one is the hourhand while the other is the minutehand" (1851, 4).

The prime determinant of archaeological interpretation was to be philological because mind was represented in the symbolic acts, manners, and customs that had survived from the deep past in the customs of the peasantry. This viewpoint clearly circumscribed the applicability of Amerindian ethnography. The object of reconstructing national prehistory was to emphasize the inhabitants of the nation itself, and national differences rather than broad similarities were stressed.

E. Oldfield's "Introductory Address" of 1852 considered these issues as well but from the perspective of conservationism, a view more clearly linked with the traditional concerns of the RAI. A tension within the institute, rooted in the conflict between romantic and utilitarian philosophies, began to surface here, mirroring that within British society in general. Once again, there was a pause for self-congratulations: "Within no very distant period the study of antiquities has passed in popular esteem, from contempt to comparative honour" (Oldfield 1852, 1). This, according to Oldfield, had not been accomplished by means of the romantic approach of reverence for the past or its sensibility to the impressions of romance. Rather, the key was the practical and utilitarian nature of the discipline, brought about through an improvement in method:

> Whilst the remains of former times were collected and treasured for their own sake, than for the illustration they afforded history, social manners, or art, the antiquary was considered a worshipper of what was essentially unreal, and therefore had little claim for the sympathy and support from others. His researches have risen in estimation, as they have been animated by a more comprehensive spirit, and directed a more instructive end: whilst the very effort which has elevated Archaeology to the dignity of a science, has at the same time, by exhibiting the past in a more lively relationship with the present, given to the study more general interest (Oldfield 1852, 1).

In other words, for archaeology to continue to claim the public's attention and provide a socially acceptable context of meaning and value for the archaeological information that the discipline's scholars (or antiquaries) sought to preserve, the relevance of the past to the present had to be established. To be taken seriously, archaeology not only had to adopt the methods of other sciences but also had to contribute to the great issues of the day, just as ethnology and philology did. However, the discipline was not to be completely at the whim of contemporary concerns: "An honourable position has thus been gained. To maintain it, the student of antiquities must struggle,—not against the 'spirit of the age,' still less against rival sciences,—but against that which can alone permanently degrade any science, an unphilosophic or sterile system" (Oldfield 1852, 1).

The appeal to system was one way for archaeologists to find their way through the mass of conflicting positions that had been developed from the crucial issues of the day. Needless to say, such an appeal to the corrective and rational powers of empiricism was more often honored in the breach than the observance, precisely because the issues were critical ones about which all educated people had to form opinions and because the positions that could have been adopted were frequently undeveloped beyond perspective and polemic.

Oldfield proceeded to outline the position of British prehistoric archaeology relative to other disciplines. For him, this archaeology had three major uses. First, it purveyed facts to other disciplines, with the test of archaeological efficiency being the value of the evidence to these disciplines. Second, it provided illustrations of personal life among English ancestors—who they were and what they did, thought, and felt. The methodology here was to start with the most complete case (usually folkloric studies) and argue from the known to the unknown. Third, prehistoric archaeology could use the evidence of other disciplines to improve this reconstruction. An example of the first use was easy to find:

> In those branches of ideal and ornamental design which are known distinctively as the "Fine Arts," the best models are to be found in the Past; not from any inherent superiority in the genius or taste of preceding ages, but simply because in that which is not in its nature progressive, but the independent offspring of independent intellects, the competition of all Time has naturally vanquished the efforts of a single generation. To discover, select and preserve such models, and render them available for aesthetic teaching, is the honourable tribute of Archaeology to Art (Oldfield 1852, 3).

The value of archaeological data clearly stretched beyond the immediate needs of the discipline and was further exemplified by the discoveries at NINEVEH, which Oldfield referred to as the "California of Archaeology" (1852, 4). However, not all antiquarians or archaeologists were swayed by either Newton or Oldfield, and remnants of an older framework for interpreting and explaining archaeological data were still to be found, especially in a classic paper by A. H. Rhind in the tenth volume of the *Archaeological Journal* (1853). Rhind's interpretation of the so-called Pict's House was primarily based on literary evidence, in this case Pennant's tours of north Scotland, where he had observed the inhabitants living underground in conditions of great squalor. These more current "folkloric" observations, allied with material derived from Diodorus Siculus, allowed Rhind to claim that the Pict's House had a much more recent antiquity than that given it by DANIEL WILSON. Yet much of Wilson's work *was* acceptable to Rhind. Though he may have offered a critique of a particular ascription from the literary evidence, Rhind had no intention of disputing Wilson's method or the broad sweep of his results. For Rhind at least, if not for others, the three-age system and its attendant methodology were not open to question.

> It must, however, be noted that ancient though they undoubtedly are, there nevertheless seems to be a tendency among archaeologists to ascribe them a more remote antiquity than the existing data warrant. Wilson, for instance, incorporated them in the first section of his recent, excellent work, *The Prehistoric Annals of Scotland,* implying that they date from the earliest ages of permanent human occupancy, and Munch of Christiana, in a letter addressed to a correspondent in Orkney and published in a northern journal (*John O'Groats Journal,* May 30, 1851), expressly declared that these buildings belong to the stone-period, or to that mysterious people of the stone-period whose nationality is not yet ascertained (in Rhind 1853, 223).

There was still some problem squaring archaeological and ethnographic authorities with older literary ones, and Rhind considered it dangerous to dispense with knowledge gained from this other source. Citing Tacitus and Diodorus Siculus and the fact that no stone artifacts had been found in the Pict's House, Rhind concluded that they were recent enough to be "in harmony with archaeological data and the statements of the earliest authors, who offered us a glimpse of the internal condition of our own country" (1853, 223). Rhind may not have considered the temporal limitations of ethnographic analogy, the eternally frozen ethnographic present for archaeology, but he did understand that if archaeologists aspired to know the manners and customs of people from the remote past and to explain the archaeological data themselves, then they had to use ethnographic analogy. He further emphasized the importance of national differences in the remote past in his assessment of the three-age system, "On the History of the Systematic Classification of Primeval Relics" (Rhind 1856).

Rhind spoke of the one great stride that separated the old order from the new—the constitution of archaeology as an inductive science with a diversity of theory incident to a speculative inquiry—and concluded: "Here, then, is a change which, as is sometimes insisted upon, is no less salient than the annals of any intellectual pursuit have recorded—a change implying a total revolution of an important inquiry" (1856, 210). However, in gaining this systematization, British prehistoric archaeology also gained a diverse range of interpretative and explanatory theory from ethnology, philology, and comparative human anatomy, which placed even greater pressure on the archaeological data because it became clear that those data could be interpreted in a variety of ways. Archaeology became involved in the clash between monogenism and polygenism, as well as the long-running conflict between universal history and historicism.

This involvement entailed significant consequences that archaeologists have had to live with to this day. Shifts in the general framework for understanding human nature, which had provided the spur to the recognition of the value of archaeological data for writing a rational history of the remote human past, also established concepts and categories within prehistoric archaeology that its practitioners found increasingly difficult to reformulate in terms of the data at hand. In the mid-nineteenth century

there was every danger that the search for an intelligible human past would bring archaeology under the sway of other disciplines such as ethnology, philology, and comparative human anatomy, whose practitioners regarded archaeological data as contingent, useful supporting information. The real question was whether prehistoric archaeology could exist as more than a concatenation of techniques designed to wrest historical or ethnological data from archaeological data.

This danger was exemplified in a paper by J. Barnard Davis (the associate of the great barrow digger Thurnam) entitled "On Some of the Bearings of Ethnology upon Archaeological Science" (1856), in which the concept of race (and its links to nation and history) was used in a synthetic role. Davis thought that although comparative philology would be useful (1856, 316), it alone was not enough to make headway because "Man, in his origin, his relations and alliances in all their extent, constitute a series of complex and difficult subjects of inquiry" (1856, 316). Ethnology, based on an understanding of the laws governing the variety of the human physical form, was considered by Davis to be the surest guide to the formation of a science of archaeology, but he felt that this could only be achieved within an empiricist framework. If archaeology ignored the scientific laws of racial formation, it would never attain the status of a science: "This must first of all require fixed and well-defined principles before it can deserve the name of a science. It must first before all be ascertained by a close and thorough investigation of different races of people, that they have and do observe something like definite laws in their origin, developments, alliances, and mutations, before ethnology itself can have any firm ground to stand on" (1856, 316–317).

Davis, an ardent polygenist, argued that race was immutable. He also held that mental and moral qualities were both immutable and racially distinct. Moreover, racial differences existed between Caucasians, Negroes, and Chinese, as well as among Caucasians themselves. Thus, the Celts and Anglo-Saxons not only behaved differently, they were also different in physical character. Davis perforce had to come out against hybridity of the races, an article of faith in the polygenist camp. Finally, he contended, civilization was for given races only. The data of archaeology, to Davis's mind at least, formed an important basis from which to mount an argument against the reality of monogenism, despite the arguments of James Cowles Prichard and others: "It is scarcely necessary to allude to the most extraordinary doctrine that the discovery of stone weapons and implements in every quarter of the globe, is a valid evidence that the very same race, a nation of workers in stone, has been spread over all these vastly separated countries. Such incredible hypothesis is by no means necessary to account for this fact" (Davis 1856, 324).

Instead of the monogenist hypothesis, Davis offered the fact that, within very broad bounds, humans have similar physical structures and bodily needs. Yet notwithstanding these similarities, the use of stone occurred during different periods and to different extents. On this basis Davis considered the term *stone-period* or *stone-age* to be incorrect (an objection frequently voiced by Rhind and others but not necessarily for the same reasons). Davis's conclusion was that archaeology had to become ethnology and contribute to the debates that were conducted under its aegis. The first step toward a useful contribution was for archaeologists to do more ethnology, particularly within the British Isles, where racial differences were thought to be marked.

Narrative: 1860–1900

During the forty years between the acceptance of high human antiquity (in 1859) and the end of the nineteenth century, British prehistoric archaeology became widely accepted as a science. By that most delicate of measures—the passage of legislation to protect ancient monuments, which limited the private rights of individuals and established government agencies to bring that legislation into effect (see Murray 1990)—the science of prehistoric archaeology had gained popular and scholarly recognition as an important Victorian scientific and cultural endeavor. As mentioned, serious debate had taken place before this period about the nature of prehistoric archaeology, and the issues raised by

Davis and others mentioned in the case study continued to plague practitioners until the 1870s. It is important to note that the fights between the proponents of ethnology, anthropology, archaic anthropology, and prehistoric archaeology (which were just some of the many diverse positions taken up by people with an interest in the prehistory of Britain) were primarily waged at the level of institutions and societies. Although relationships between the British Archaeological Association and the Royal Archaeological Institute were far from cordial, they had nothing of the viciousness that characterized the exchanges between the Ethnological and Anthropological Societies of London and between the members of the British Association for the Advancement of Science (see Stocking 1971).

Despite the significance of the application of the three-age system to British prehistoric archaeology after Thomsen's and Worsaae's works were translated, it was the discovery of high human antiquity that seized the imagination of the scientific world. D. K. Grayson (1983) and A. Bowdoin Van Riper (1996) have discussed this history in considerable detail, and much has also been written about the role played by Sir John Lubbock (and his *Prehistoric Times* [1865]) and E. B. Tylor (and his *Researches into the Early History of Man* [1865] and *Primitive Culture* [1870]) in the creation of what Trigger called "evolutionary archaeology." But the dominance of evolutionary theory in British prehistoric archaeology was always tempered by the needs of history—particularly the racial history of the British Isles. Attempts to square British history with the three-age system would be made by generations of barrow diggers such as Canon Greenwell, John Thurnam, Charles Roach Smith, and Thomas Bateman (who was among the first to apply the principles of the system in Britain in his *Vestiges of the Antiquities of Derbyshire* [1848]). Yet there was never universal approbation of that concept or of the idea that the British past could unproblematically serve Lubbock's or Tylor's universal models of human history. Certainly, the canny observer Daniel Wilson well understood the difference and forswore the more serious of Lubbock's overgeneralizations. But again, although much of the period after 1860 was devoted to an elaboration of the three-age system and its subdivisions (both in Britain and in France), such elaborations inevitably led to an appreciation of difference and variety, as well as change, in both prehistoric Britain and its Continental neighbors.

This recognition of variety (and of the reality of history) became all the more obvious as truly systematic attempts to describe the artifacts of British prehistory increasingly came to the fore, an outcome that also rested on the gradual improvement in excavation strategy and techniques that had been fostered at Brixham Cave but greatly enhanced by the work of Pitt Rivers, especially at Cranborne Chase (1887). Building on the traditions of Fausett, Roach Smith, and others, Sir John Evans, in two remarkable books (*Ancient Stone Implements: Weapons and Ornaments of Great Britain* [1872] and *Ancient Bronze Implements* [1881]), developed the typology of such artifacts to the level at which the patterns of chronology and distribution raised significant historical questions. Although British prehistory was devoid of an absolute chronology for all but the later phases of the Iron Age, sufficient information existed for Boyd Dawkins and other workers to set the British Paleolithic within a Continental sequence (a task also completed by GABRIEL DE MORTILLET in France) and for OSCAR MONTELIUS's European chronology to be applied to Britain. The essence of that chronology and of those sequences was that British prehistory was a kind of afterthought to the great forces of moving populations and changing climates that characterized Europe. But there were always bits that failed to fit, as ARTHUR EVANS was able to demonstrate in his celebrated analysis of the cemetery at Aylesford in Kent (1890). The task of comprehending the prehistory of Britain as a problem in itself was to occupy archaeologists for the next half century, as the dual inheritances of evolutionary universalist archaeology and the historicism of the three-age system played themselves out in what was later proven to be an illusory temporal environment. The absence of absolute chronology and the essentially circular interpretive logic that flowed from the relative chronologies of Montelius and de Mortillet would heighten the concentration on simple historicist explanations for cultural change at the very time when prehistoric archaeology (certainly as espoused by Gordon Childe) required more.

Evans was, of course, quite right about the significance of the evidence from Aylesford. What British prehistoric archaeologists urgently needed to do was to write history, to make the classifications of Montelius and others relate in real historical terms to the patterns being noted in the field. But prehistoric archaeology (as a part of anthropology) was far from alone in this concern with history and historicism. Although from the 1880s onward perceptions of human diversity made a forceful return to the ranks of anthropological theory, this diversity was clearly to be located in ethnic and cultural, rather than purely physical, differences. The explanations for diversity and similarity would increasingly be sought in cultural-historical factors, instead of the doctrine of independent inventions and the psychic unity of humankind. Real historical forces acting on real (different) groups of people, past and present, could explain the peculiar differences between human beings far more convincingly than generalized uniformitarian forces. Anthropology and prehistoric archaeology, previously focused on providing evidence of the evolution of human beings and their societies and cultures, now became more firmly linked to a less encompassing task—writing the ethnic histories of European nations.

Narrative: 1901–1960

Often described in histories of British archaeology as the phase of culture-history in which archaeologists further honed their excavation skills and used their abilities in artifact analysis and the creation of typologies to create histories of British prehistoric "cultures," the first sixty years of the twentieth century saw both continuity and change. There was continuity in the sense that the typological studies and Continental prehistories of Montelius, de Mortillet, and others provided an essential starting point. And there was change also in the sense that serious debate about the relationships between archaeological and anthropological knowledge tended

An archaeologist cleans one of several skeletons revealed at Maiden Castle, near Dorchester, during an excavation supervised by Mortimer Wheeler. (Hulton Deutsch Collection / Corbis)

(with the exception of the works of Gordon Childe and J. G. D. Clark) to fade from view.

However, change was uneven across all fields of prehistoric archaeology. For example, although a great deal of argument continued to be caused by the eolith controversy and its eventual links to the Piltdown forgery (see Spencer 1990), amateur Paleolithic archaeologists continued to scour the countryside for old sites. More-senior figures (such as Miles Burkitt) were engaged less in fieldwork than in continuing to refine tool typologies and chronologies on a global scale, but others retained a strong commitment to field study. (Among the latter group was DOROTHY GARROD, the first female professor of archaeology in Britain, who was beginning foundational work in France at that point—work that fully prepared her for her great field research in the Near East [see Davis and Charles 1999].) During this period the primary locations for change within the study of British prehistoric archaeology were in the later

periods—J. G. D. Clark's brilliantly innovative studies of the Mesolithic, Stuart Piggott's *Neolithic Cultures of the British Isles* (1954), and CHRISTOPHER HAWKES's penetrating studies of Iron Age Britain.

Change and development also occurred on the technical and methodological sides of prehistoric archaeology, most notably in the work of the Fenland Research Committee (established in 1932), which conducted foundational research into the reconstruction of ancient British landscapes and environments. Excavation techniques were also developed on the basis of those inherited from Pitt Rivers and Flinders Petrie—especially by Sir MORTIMER WHEELER at Maiden Castle and elsewhere and by Gerhard Bersu (see Evans 1989). Wheeler and Glyn Daniel were especially responsible for enhancing public understanding of the prehistoric archaeology of Britain by communicating with visitors to sites and developing television programs such as *Animal, Vegetable and Mineral,* which was aired by the British Broadcasting Corporation (BBC) to mass audiences. The global reach of British prehistoric archaeology was also extended by the foundation of the Institute of Archaeology in London (in which Wheeler was particularly influential and Gordon Childe served as the first director). Students from all over the world studied there, learning the techniques that would be used to undertake foundational work in countries as diverse as China and India. A further extension of interest was achieved with the foundation of the journal ANTIQUITY by O. G. S. CRAWFORD and the transformation of the Prehistoric Society of East Anglia into, simply, the Prehistoric Society.

Notwithstanding the significance of these developments, the period is most notable for the work of Gordon Childe and J. G. D. Clark. Between 1925 and 1956 Childe literally transformed archaeology in the Anglo-Saxon world (and beyond) through a series of classic publications that greatly enhanced both the professional and the public understanding of British prehistory in particular and archaeology in general. But Childe certainly stood on the shoulders of giants, and during his long career he also profited much from the work of those he had strongly influenced (including Piggott and Hawkes). The tradition of rigorous analysis of artifacts from Neolithic, Bronze Age, and Iron Age contexts that provided Childe with much of his British information was developed and enhanced during this period. Renfrew (1972, 12) has rightly identified LORD ABERCROMBY's *Bronze Age of Pottery of Great Britain and Ireland* (1912) as an early example of the British archaeologists' exploration of the spatial distribution of material culture types (the real potential of which was established by Crawford in *Man and His Past*). But it was Gordon Childe's development of the concept of the archaeological culture that provided the core interpretive perspective needed to make such culture-histories plausible. Childe demonstrated the potential of this new way of seeing in *The Dawn of European Civilization* (1925) and elaborated it in *The Bronze Age* (1930) and subsequent publications. Renfrew (1972) has also stressed that in the 1930s British prehistoric archaeologists were able to

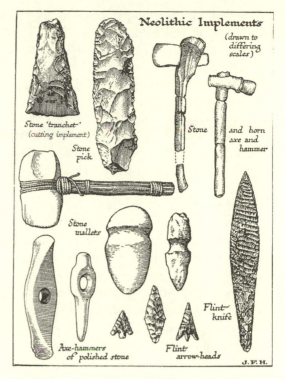

Neolithic implements, drawn to differing scales (Ann Ronan Picture Library)

consider the spatial organization of culture in terms of human geography—as expounded by Sir Cyril Fox in his pathbreaking "regional prehistory" entitled *The Personality of Britain* (1932)—and that this was also a major influence on their practice.

Historians of archaeology (particularly Trigger [1987]) have seen the years between the late 1930s and the advent of radiometric dating in the late 1950s as a long period during which Childe's account of the archaeological culture and the project of culture-history was elaborated. There is merit in this assessment of the period in which change in later British prehistory was almost always explained as the outcome of migrations, invasions, or diffusions—certainly of forces that (along with climate change) lay external to the societies whose histories Childe and others were trying to understand. There is little doubt that Childean archaeology dominated the theoretical landscape of British prehistoric archaeology throughout this period, but there were significant tensions between Childe's culture-history and the detailed economic and ecological approaches to understanding the archaeology of the Mesolithic that were being developed by J. G. D. Clark.

Clearly, Childe and Clark had widely differing views about politics, but in emphasizing these differences, scholars have tended to gloss over more significant similarities in theories and goals. Beginning with *The Mesolithic Age in Britain* (1932) and culminating in his highly influential work at the site of Star Carr (published in 1954) and in *Prehistoric Europe: The Economic Basis* (1952), Clark elaborated an archaeology that required its practitioners to extend their competence to contextual factors. He reminded British prehistorians of the basic disciplinary commitment to understanding *how* prehistoric societies actually functioned, rather than just contenting themselves with charting the distributions of artifact types and culture areas. In this focus on the need to understand society, he was closer to Childe than many others of his time.

Childe's and Clark's advocacy of the principles of social archaeology would bear fruit in coming decades. There is little doubt that the crowning theoretical achievement of British prehistoric archaeology during the first sixty years of the twentieth century (despite most practitioners' lack of interest in this field) was a broadening and deepening of the relationships between history, archaeology, and anthropology. For the majority of archaeologists who focused on issues of typology and chronology, the world was about to change, and social archaeology was to provide a new reason for being.

Narrative: 1961 to the Present

Renfrew (1972) has rightly observed that the cracks in the interpretive consensus of culture-history and typology (brought about by the economic prehistory of J. G. D. Clark) were greatly enlarged by the application of radiocarbon dating to British prehistory. Radiocarbon dates first became available in the late 1950s, and it was soon clear that there were serious disparities between the dates arrived at through conventional typological study (previously the mainstay of British prehistoric archaeology, no matter the period) and those being produced by radiometric means. The first significant impact was on the Neolithic period—famously at the site of Dur-

rington Walls, where the radiocarbon dates were much older than those established by the excavator Stuart Piggott (then the doyen of British Neolithic studies) on the basis of typological analysis. From this point on no part of British prehistory was immune, although it is fair to say that the major impacts were felt by archaeologists working in the Neolithic, Bronze, and Iron Ages. Renfrew (1972) neatly summarized this history as not just being about dates but as fostering a fundamental shift in the direction of European prehistory as well. For example, new dates from Wessex and other places made it clear that cultural elements such as megalithic tombs (once thought to have been diffused from the south of the European landmass) could now be argued to have had a local origin.

> It has become clear that no-one is seriously arguing for strong and significant Aegean influence upon the early bronze age of Britain, whether or not there may have been some contacts between the two regions. No-one today would *explain* the developments of the British early bronze age in these terms. . . . The Wessex-Mycenae link is no longer regarded, as it was by Evans and Childe, as a lynch-pin for British chronology, nor are the accompanying diffusionist arguments accepted any longer (Renfrew 1974, 33).

Archaeologists had to find new models of British prehistory to account for what now seemed better understood by exploring the internal dynamics of prehistoric societies and seeking explanations for change that emphasized cultural processes, in addition to diffusion through invasion and migration. But there was a significant sense of continuity here as well, as previous work on environmental reconstruction and prehistoric human ecology played an important part in J. G. D. Clark's demolition of the invasion hypothesis in 1966. It is always risky to point to specific dates as watersheds, but Renfrew's assessment of the importance of radiometric dating in the development of British prehistoric archaeology after 1966 was very close to the mark.

Although Clark had essentially "created" world prehistory in 1961 by applying radiometric-dating technologies on a global scale, the great flowering of British theoretical archaeology in the latter part of the twentieth century was underwritten by the clear demonstration that interpretive frameworks could no longer satisfactorily explain prehistoric Britain. Archaeologists had once spent their lives elaborating typologies (largely for the purpose of establishing relative chronologies); now, radiometric dating provided a release from all that and an opportunity to take up Gordon Childe's challenge to seek an understanding of the nature of prehistoric societies and their particular histories. The challenge was being experienced by archaeologists all over the world, and what was happening in Britain influenced and was in turn influenced by what was happening elsewhere (particularly in the United States). This expansion of interpretive and explanatory horizons (in terms of both the sense of problem and the community of scholars working on it) quickly demonstrated that archaeologists could disagree about almost all of the issues involved in understanding prehistoric societies. The pathway that eventually led through all of the varieties of archaeology that have since been explored in an effort to resolve those disagreements (occasionally referred to by an alphabet soup of adjectives—analytical, behavioral, cultural ecological, demographic, economic . . . processual and postprocessual, etc.) was opened up in the process.

British prehistoric archaeologists have also played a major role in the development of scientific applications to archaeology. Reference has already been made to the early work of the Fenland Research Committee and its impact on the development of Clark's economic archaeology, and the period since 1960 has seen a massive development in this aspect of British prehistoric archaeology. From ERIC HIGGS's development of paleoeconomy through the British Academy Major Research Project on the Early History of Agriculture (1967–1976)—in which faunal analysis and environmental reconstruction played a vital role in understanding prehistoric resources—to new methodologies for surveying and sampling sites, new analyses of artifacts, and new approaches to forensic archaeology, British prehistoric archaeology has made a valuable contribution to world archaeology (see Brothwell and Higgs 1962 as a very early example of this). It is worth noting that the Science Based Archaeology Committee (1975–1995) both promoted and underwrote much of this research, which will stand as one of the major legacies of British prehistoric archaeology during this period.

The social and cultural context of British archaeology also underwent massive changes after the 1960s. In Britain, as in other countries, the "applied" side of archaeology has since risen to prominence—archaeological heritage management, the interpretation of sites for cultural tourism (Jorvik is just one of a great many examples), the rapid growth in popular archaeological publishing, and specialist television coverage on programs such as *Meet the Ancestors* and *The Time Team,* which are broadcast all over the world. By the same token, the global reach of British prehistoric archaeology in professional circles is most closely associated with the activities of major British publishers, such as Cambridge University Press and Routledge, which have made it possible for the post-1960s generations of British archaeologists to be heard. Many of the archaeologists produced in this phase—as university archaeology departments grew in size and number (there are now about thirty)—found work in the heritage-management industry, which is by far the biggest source of funds for excavation and analysis in Britain, just as it is elsewhere. Others staffed the new and expanded university departments or left to fill academic posts in other countries (see Clark 1989), and the remainder swelled the ranks of a British public already strongly committed to supporting British prehistoric archaeology by participating in amateur societies, visiting sites, and maintaining a knowledgeable interest in the past.

At the beginning of the twenty-first century British prehistoric archaeologists continue to train budding professionals from all over the world. British journals such as *Antiquity, Proceedings of the Prehistoric Society,* and *World Archaeology* continue to assist in perpetuating the idea of world prehistory, and organizations such as the Theoretical Archaeology Group and the WORLD ARCHAEOLOGICAL CONGRESS (both founded in Britain during this period) play a valuable part in fostering discussion and debate in an increasingly diverse discipline.

Conclusion

One goal of this all too brief discussion of the history of British prehistoric archaeology was to determine whether the great diversity of the discipline's past and its contemporary practice could be effectively synthesized through the identification of overarching themes and issues. This synthesis (and others, such as Renfrew 1974) has been only partially successful, primarily because there is still so much that we do not know about the specifics of that history. Certainly, in those areas in which detailed research has been carried out, a complex and frequently counterintuitive history has been revealed. Given the fact that British prehistoric archaeologists have long had considerable impact on practices outside of Britain (particularly in the Anglo-Saxon world), a deeper understanding of the discipline's social and cultural history is important for archaeologists across the globe.

Tim Murray

See also Britain, Classical Archaeology; Britain, Roman Historiography; Layard, Sir Austen Henry

References

Anonymous. 1846. "Review of *Denmark's Olden Times,* by J. J. A. Worsaae." *Archaeological Journal* 2: 291–292.

Brothwell, D., and E. S. Higgs. 1962. *Science in Archaeology: A Comprehensive Survey of Progress and Research.* London: Thames and Hudson.

Champion, T. 1991. "Theoretical Archaeology in Britain." In *Archaeological Theory in Europe: The Last Three Decades,* 129–160. Ed. I. Hodder. London: Routledge.

Chapman, W. 1989a. "The Organisational Context in the History of Archaeology: Pitt Rivers and Other British Archaeologists in the 1860s." *Antiquaries Journal* 69: 23–42.

———. 1989b. "Towards an Institutional History of Archaeology: British Archaeologists and Allied Interests in the 1860s." In *Tracing Archaeology's Past: The Historiography of Archaeology.* Ed. A. L. Christenson. Carbondale: University of Southern Illinois Press.

Chippindale, C. 1983. "Stonehenge, General Pitt Rivers, and the First Ancient Monuments Act." *Archaeological Review from Cambridge* 2: 59–65.

———. 1985. *Stonehenge Complete.* London: Thames and Hudson.

Clark, J. Grahame. D. 1989. *Prehistory at Cambridge and Beyond.* Cambridge and New York: Cambridge University Press.

Coles, J., A. Goodall, and S. Minnitt. 1992. *Arthur Bulleid and the Glastonbury Lake Village, 1892–1992.* Somerset County Museum Services.

Daniel, G. E. 1943. *The Three Ages: An Essay on Archaeological Method.* Cambridge and New York: Cambridge University Press.

———. 1964. *The Idea of Prehistory.* Harmondsworth, England: Pelican Books.

———. 1967. *The Origins and Growth of Archaeology.* Harmondsworth, England: Pelican Books.

———. 1971. "From Worsaae to Childe: The Models of Prehistory." *Proceedings of the Prehistoric Society* 37: 140–153.

———. 1975. *One Hundred and Fifty Years of Archaeology* (2d ed. of *One Hundred Years of Archaeology*). London: Duckworth.

———. 1976. "Stone, Bronze and Iron." In *To Illustrate the Monuments: Essays on Archaeology Presented to Stuart Piggott on the Occasion of His Sixty-Fifth Birthday,* 35–42. Ed. J. V. S. Megaw. London: Thames and Hudson.

———. 1981. "Introduction: The Necessity for an Historical Approach to Archaeology." In *Towards a History of Archaeology,* 9–13. Ed. G. E. Daniel. London: Thames and Hudson.

Daniel, G. E., and C. Chippindale, eds. 1989. *The Pastmasters: Eleven Modern Pioneers of Archaeology.* London: Thames and Hudson.

Darvill, T. 1987. *Prehistoric Britain.* London: Batsford.

Davis, J. B. 1856. "On Some of the Bearings of Ethnology upon Archaeological Science." *Archaeological Journal* 13: 315–327.

Davis, W., and R. Charles, eds. 1999. *Dorothy Garrod and the Progress of the Palaeolithic: Studies in the Prehistoric Archaeology of Near East and Europe.* Oxford: Oxbow.

Diaz-Andreu, M., and M. L. S. Sorensen, eds. 1998. *Excavating Women: A History of Women in European Archaeology.* London: Routledge.

Evans, C. 1989. "Archaeology and Modern Times: Bersu's Woodbury 1938 and 1939." *Antiquity* 63: 436–450.

Grayson, D. K. 1983. *The Establishment of Human Antiquity.* New York: Academic Press.

Hunter, J., and Ian Ralston, eds. 1999. *The Archaeology of Britain. An Introduction from the Upper*

Palaeolithic to the Industrial Revolution. London: Routledge.

Hunter, M. 1975. *John Aubrey and the Realm of Learning.* London: Duckworth.

Levine, P. 1986. *The Amateur and the Professional: Antiquarians, Historians and Archaeologists in Victorian England, 1836–1886.* Cambridge: Cambridge University Press.

Longworth, I., and J. Cherry, eds. 1986. *Archaeology in Britain since 1945: New Directions.* London: British Museum.

Marsden, Barry M. 1984. *Pioneers of Prehistory: Leaders and Landmarks in English Archaeology (1500–1900).* Ormskirk and Northridge, UK: Hesketh.

Murray, Tim. 1990. "The History, Philosophy and Sociology of Archaeology: The Case of the Ancient Monuments Protection Act (1882)." In *Critical Directions in Contemporary Archaeology,* 55–67. Ed. V. Pinsky and A. Wylie. Cambridge: Cambridge University Press.

———. 1997. "Dynamic Modelling and New Social Theory of the Mid-to-Long Term." In *Time, Process, and Structured Transformation,* 449–463. Ed. S. van der Leeuw and James McGlade. London: Routledge.

Murray, Tim, ed. 1999. *Encyclopedia of Archaeology: The Great Archaeologists,* 2 vols. Santa Barbara, CA: ABC-CLIO.

Newton, C. 1851. "On the Study of Archaeology." *Archaeological Journal* 8: 1–26.

Oldfield, E. 1852. "Introductory Address." *Archaeological Journal* 9: 1–6.

Parry, G. 1995. *The Trophies of Time: English Antiquarians of the Seventeenth Century.* Oxford and New York: Oxford University Press.

Piggott, S. 1975. *The Druids.* London: Thames and Hudson.

———. 1976. *Ruins in a Landscape: Essays in Antiquarianism.* Edinburgh: Edinburgh University Press.

———. 1978. *Antiquity Depicted: Aspects of Archaeological Illustration.* London: Thames and Hudson.

———. 1981. "'Vast Perennial Memorials': The First Antiquaries Look at Megaliths." In *Antiquity and Man,* 19–25. Ed. J. D. Evans, B. Cunliffe, and C. Renfrew. London: Thames and Hudson.

———. 1985. *William Stukeley: An Eighteenth Century Antiquary,* 2d ed. rev. London: Thames and Hudson.

Pinsky, V., and A. Wylie, eds. 1990. *Critical Directions in Contemporary Archaeology.* Cambridge: Cambridge University Press.

Renfrew, C., ed. 1972. *British Prehistory: A New Outline.* London: Duckworth.

Rhind, A. H. 1853. "Notice of the Exploration of a 'Pict's House,' at Kettleburn, in the County of Caithness." *Archaeological Journal* 10: 212–223.

———. 1856. "On the History of the Systematic Classification of Primeval Relics." *Archaeological Journal* 13: 209–315.

Roberts, M. 1999. "A History of Research in the Boxgrove Area." In *Boxgrove: A Middle Pleistocene Hominid Site at Eartham Quarry, Boxgrove, West Sussex,* 8–15. Archaeological Report no. 17. Ed. M. Roberts and S. Parfitt. London: English Heritage.

Roe, D. 1981a. "Amateurs and Archaeologists: Some Early Contributions to British Palaeolithic Studies." In *Antiquity and Man: Essays in Honour of Glyn Daniel,* 214–220. Ed. J. D. Evans, B. Cunliffe, and C. Renfrew. London: Thames and Hudson.

———. 1981b. *The Lower and Middle Palaeolithic Periods in Britain.* London: Routledge and Kegan Paul.

Smith, P. J. 1999. "'The Coup': How Did the Prehistoric Society of East Anglia Become the Prehistoric Society?" *Proceedings of the Prehistoric Society* 65: 465–470.

Spencer, F. 1990. *Piltdown: A Scientific Forgery.* London: Natural History Museum Press and Oxford University Press.

Stocking, G. W., Jr. 1971. "What's in a Name? The Origins of the Royal Anthropological Institute (1837–71)." *Man,* n.s., 6: 369–390.

Trigger, B. G. 1987. *A History of Archaeological Thought.* Cambridge: Cambridge University Press.

Tylor, E. B. 1865. *Researches into the Early History of Man.* London: John Murray.

———. 1870. *Primitive Culture.* London: John Murray.

Van Riper, A. Bowdoin. 1996. *Men among the Mammoths: Victorian Science and the Discovery of Human Prehistory.* Chicago: University of Chicago Press.

Britain, Roman

The study of Roman Britain has its origins in the very earliest stages of archaeology in Great Britain. The people who were interested in the past in the sixteenth and seventeenth centuries invariably had a classical education, so there was a tendency to seek physical monuments illustrative of the classical texts that mentioned Roman

Britain. There was particular interest in items such as coins and inscriptions, which themselves provided texts that could be read and interpreted to supplement the meager classical sources.

The documentation of the Roman occupation of Britain also led to the widespread, if generally misguided, popular trend to identify visible earthwork sites generally as "Roman camps" or, in particular, as a "Caesar's camp." Although some of the speculations of the early writers like WILLIAM CAMDEN (1551–1623) or WILLIAM STUKELEY (1687–1765) are now difficult to reconcile with the evidence, others produced syntheses of information of enduring value. Of particular note is the volume by John Horsley (ca. 1684–1732) entitled *Britannia Romana* (1732) as it first put the study of Hadrian's Wall on a systematic footing. Equally, the cartographic work undertaken by General William Roy (1726–1790), the founder of the Ordnance Survey who mapped the length of both Hadrian's Wall and the Antonine Wall, provided detailed scale plans of the forts that are truly remarkable. This survey, published after Roy's death as *The Military Antiquities of the Romans in Northern Britain* (1793), is perhaps the earliest example of a full-scale geographical treatment of a major monument. It certainly illustrates a continuing tradition of modern soldiers taking an active interest in the archaeology of the Roman army.

The eighteenth-century growth of interest in the classical world was stimulated by an increasing trend to travel to Italy and beyond. Ideas brought back from "the grand tour" encouraged a widespread gentlemanly interest in the antiquities of Britain, including the continuing trend to attempt to rediscover sites named in ancient texts.

With the restrictions on travel imposed by the Napoleonic Wars, this interest increasingly turned to the active exploration of sites connected with the Roman occupation of Britain. As in Italy, some of this work resulted in lavish publications, and notable examples of such work include the accounts by Samuel Lysons (1763–1819) of the villas at Woodchester, Gloucestershire (*An Account of the Roman Antiqui-*

ties Discovered at Woodchester, 1797), and Bignor, Sussex (*Reliquiae britannico-romanae,* 1817), and Edmund Artis's (1789–1847) *The Durobrivae of Antoninus Identified and Illustrated in a Series of Plates Exhibiting the Excavated Remains of That Roman Station in the Vicinity of Castor, Northants* (1828). Projects like these commonly concentrated upon items such as mosaics that had an immediate artistic appeal, but the accounts are equally perceptive in their comments about the sites and their histories. Equally, publication through the medium of communications to the SOCIETY OF ANTIQUARIES OF LONDON in *Archaeologia* also records the systematic exploration of major monuments, for instance, Gage's report on the spectacular finds from the early Roman tumuli in the Bartlow Hills in Essex (*Archaeologia* 25 and 26, 1834 and 1836).

Antiquarian work undoubtedly raised awareness of antiquities in Britain, and a steady stream of sites and objects were reported upon. Through the nineteenth century the increased pace of development led to a more widespread and less exclusively aristocratic interest, as is shown by the popular growth of the new national and county archaeological societies. The work of individuals like Charles Roach Smith (1807–1890) in London led to a systematic recording of antiquities that were found during development. Similarly, the increased network of interested individuals and local societies encouraged the reporting and publication of finds in a range of new journals and the development of systematic initiatives to explore sites. These projects were often the initiative of individuals or small groups supported with cash raised by public appeal.

Some of the earliest systematic explorations of Roman forts and town sites represent this aspect of Victorian scholarship. For instance, Thomas Wright worked at Wroxeter in the 1850s and 1860s, and Charles Roach Smith dug at a series of fort sites in the southeastern part of the country, including Richborough, Lymme, and Reculver. Similar work was undertaken on Hadrian's Wall with a particularly significant contribution being made by John Clayton (1792–1890). In 1849, John Collingwood Bruce (1805–1892) organized the first of ten yearly "pilgrimages" to the wall, and subsequently published his synthesis of research, *The Roman Wall* (1851). Later editions of this work, published as *The Handbook to the Roman Wall*, remain a main source for the study of that frontier.

The culmination of this phase in the exploration of Roman Britain consisted of several excavations that sought to provide information about sites on a hitherto unimagined scale. Best known of these projects was that undertaken under the aegis of the Society of Antiquaries of London on the Roman town at Silchester in Hampshire between 1890 and 1910. Here the whole of the area within the Roman walls was trenched, and a sequence of annual reports, published in *Archaeologia*, provided an unparalleled view of the plan of a whole Romano-British town. Although in retrospect the quality of the excavations can be seen to have been poor, Silchester remains one of only a handful of towns in the Roman Empire for which we have a clear idea of the entire plan. Similar major campaigns of excavations looked at the Roman towns at Caerwent in South Wales (1899–1913) and Wroxeter, Shropshire (1912–1914), while work at Corbridge, Northumberland (1906–1914), examined a substantial part of a military town in the hinterland of Hadrian's Wall.

This upsurge in interest produced an enormous amount of evidence, but the potential for addressing broad historical questions was limited by the rather fragmentary nature of the work and the scattered publications. The first real steps toward synthesis came in the work of Francis Haverfield (1860–1919). Based at Oxford, where he was appointed to the Camden Chair of Ancient History in 1907, he worked very much in the German tradition, that of his mentor Theodor Mommsen. With enormous energy, Haverfield set about the process of drawing together the evidence from Roman Britain and attempting to make sense of it.

He first became an editor of the *Corpus inscriptionum latinarum* in 1888, publishing the addenda to Volume 7 on Britain in 1892. Haverfield also provided the descriptions of the Roman antiquities for the early volumes of the *Victoria County History*, published to celebrate the reign of Queen Victoria. In this way, he developed an unparalleled knowledge of the details of local evidence, and that knowledge was complemented by his broader understanding of the Roman Empire. His reflections on the development of the province were first published in a lecture to the British Academy in 1905, which appeared in that body's *Proceedings* in 1906 and subsequently as a book, *The Romanization of Roman Britain* (1912), which went through a series of editions. This work was supplemented by his Ford lectures, *The Roman Occupation of Britain*, which were eventually published in 1924. The enduring value of these works was to provide a clear framework for interpreting the material evidence of archaeology in relation to the broader structure of the Roman Empire, a framework that remained influential for well over fifty years. Haverfield was also one of those responsible for founding the Society for the Promotion of Roman Studies in 1910, an organization that has continued to take a lead in the subject ever since.

After World War I, the traditions of large-scale site clearance that had epitomized the Edwardian era continued, but with a reduced momentum. The major campaign at Richborough (1922–1938) exemplifies this trend. The period also saw the emergence of two other types of excavation. First, there was a series of much more focused campaigns of research. Some, such as those undertaken by SIR MORTIMER WHEELER and his wife, Tessa Wheeler, at sites in Wales and then Verulamium (1930–1934), were designed to pay new attention to the detail of stratigraphy and dating and were undertaken with the firm idea of writing new history. By contrast, the scale of work undertaken by scholars investigating the history of Hadrian's Wall was much more modest but designed to elucidate the history of the frontier through careful excavations. At Durham University, F. Gerald Simpson and, later, Eric Birley and Ian Richmond were key members of this group. Their excavations and studies of the inscriptions from the wall led to the development of a specialized and focused study of the frontier in particular and the Roman army in general.

By contrast, development pressures also led to the exploration of sites that were threatened with destruction. Notable early examples of this type of work were the excavations prior to the construction of the Colchester by-pass in 1930–1935, which provided the context for C. F. C. HAWKES and M. R. Hull's classic investigation of the late–Iron Age *oppidum* (fortified town) at Camulodunum. Such rescue work set the stage for the latter part of the century.

The systematization of knowledge in this period allowed the first authoritative modern historical account of the Roman Britain to be written by R. G. Collingwood, whose work *Roman Britain and the English Settlements* in the Oxford History of England series appeared in 1936. Although some of the details of this volume have been heavily criticized, its creative style and its general form, combining as it does historical narrative with thematic treatments of cultural history, have been emulated ever since. Collingwood was Waynfleet Professor of Metaphysical Philosophy at Oxford, and his clear-thinking approach certainly set much of the agenda for Roman British studies for over half a century. He was also influential in the process of systematically cataloging all the Roman inscriptions from Britain. His *Roman Inscriptions of Britain* (continued after his death by others) has been fundamental for subsequent research.

The model of compiling authoritative *corpora,* or extended works, was emulated in other spheres during the second half of the twentieth century. A. R. Birley brought into print *The Fasti of Roman Britain* (1981), a valuable compilation of information about individuals known from historical and epigraphic sources that had been begun by his father, Eric Birley. A. L. F. Rivet and C. Smith published *The Place-names of Roman Britain* in 1979, and information on sculptural material is still being published in the British volumes of the *Corpus Signorum Imperii Romani* series, the first volume of which appeared in 1977. In addition to these texts has been the publication of two authoritative maps of Roman Britain produced by the Ordnance Survey in 1956 and 1978. With the appearance of these works of reference, the systematic study of Roman Britain has become much more soundly based. In the period after World War II there was a major shift in the character of the excava-

tions. The destruction of major urban sites caused by the wartime bombing meant that the limited resources for excavation were directed mostly toward the examination of these partially destroyed town centers. The major Roman settlements that were consequently the subject of excavation were London (including Southwark), Canterbury, and Exeter.

In London, W. F. Grimes's relatively small-scale work provided vital new evidence that formed the basis of a new understanding of the development of the city. His spectacular discovery of the remains of the Temple of Mithras in 1954 also brought the destruction of archaeological sites by redevelopment to the attention of the public for the first time. In Canterbury, S. S. Frere developed the skill of deep stratigraphic excavation under difficult circumstances. However, it was his subsequent excavations in the 1950s and 1960s at Verulamium that transformed the understanding of Romano-British towns. For the first time, the careful analysis of a major urban site was combined with an intellectual rigor to provide a detailed account of the early development of a town. Elsewhere, the threat of development led to a wide range of excavations on an increasing diversity of sites. However, resources and excavators' energies were not always put into postexcavation work, with the result that few of the major rescue projects of the 1950s and 1960s were fully published.

Nevertheless, there was an energy behind much of the archaeological work in the 1960s as witnessed by the range of published archaeological conferences and more general works of synthesis. Outstanding among these was S. S. Frere's *Britannia: A History of Roman Britain,* first published in 1967. This book drew on the full range of historical, epigraphic, and archaeological sources to produce a firmly argued account of the history and development of the province. Frere's work exemplifies the culmination of the tradition of using archaeological sources to write a narrative history of Roman Britain. Although innumerable others have followed this model, no other work has the same stature. Frere was also instrumental in founding the journal *Britannia,* a journal devoted to the study of Roman Britain that first appeared in 1970.

A well-preserved Roman mosaic floor uncovered on the site of the ancient Verulamium in England during an excavation led by Shepard Frere, 1958 (Hulton Deutsch Collection / Corbis)

In many senses, the period around 1970 marks a watershed in the development of the study of Roman Britain, for since that date, a much broader variety of approaches to the subject has emerged and there has been less interest in writing narrow narrative histories. This diversification is partly a reflection of broader changes in British archaeology and partly a symbol of changed approaches to the classical world. There has been a general move toward professional excavation, with the growth of permanent excavation teams who deploy a full variety of techniques and investigate sites of all periods, not just Roman sites.

Changes in educational background of those who study Roman archaeology have also had a profound impact. Before the 1960s, most people came to the subject from classics or history, but after the growth of universities in the 1960s, most now offer degrees in archaeology. This change led to the diversification of approaches, with the people working on Roman Britain being interested in a wider variety of subjects like agriculture, environment, food, and trade as well as the traditional themes of art history and historical events. Different universities teaching archaeology have had varying approaches, so individual teachers and some major excavations created informal networks that have been of enduring influence. The groups who worked on the major excavations at Verulamium, Cirencester, Winchester, and Corbridge created one such set of networks. Others can be traced to the students who attended university at Durham, Cardiff, the Institute of Archaeology in London, and Manchester during the 1960s and 1970s.

On one level, the period since 1970 has seen

a staggering increase in the amount of evidence available. Large-scale aerial photographic work revealed literally thousands of new sites with a wide range of different forms, and excavations in advance of gravel extraction and road building revolutionized our understanding of the diversity of rural settlement forms, showing that unpretentious farmsteads were far more typical than the more showy villas. Equally, fieldwork in areas like the fens of East Anglia illustrated how nucleated villages were dominant in some regions. Major large-scale excavations in advance of urban redevelopment at places like London, Lincoln, and Colchester have greatly enhanced knowledge of the patterns of urban development while also providing entirely new insights into the conditions of life, the diet of the inhabitants, and their changing productive and trading economies. In particular, the excavation of well-preserved waterlogged material at sites in London, YORK, and Carlisle has added a new dimension to the material available.

The investigation of religious sites at Bath, Uley, and Hayling Island provided entirely new understandings of religious rituals. Such new understanding was especially the result of the discovery at Bath of a large number of *defixiones* (or inscriptions), which record "contracts" made between believers and the goddess of the spring. Although the bulk of the new information came from excavations away from the frontiers, there has been one exception, for at Vindolanda in the hinterland behind Hadrian's Wall, excavations uncovered the well-preserved archive of a fort dating to around A.D. 100. The deciphering of the ink texts on these wooden writing tablets provided insight into the life and organization of a unit of the Roman army that is only paralleled by finds in Roman Egypt.

The information from excavations conducted in advance of development has been complemented by information drawn from pure research. Some of this work has continued the tradition of research excavation, and through this medium, sites like the palace at Fishbourne have become better known. There has been a growth in field survey and artifact research, the latter incorporating a geographical dimension and producing a series of studies of manufacture and distribution of pottery and other artifacts that contribute to our understanding of the economy of the province. The widespread deployment of metal detectors in the hands of amateur treasure hunters has also resulted in a series of spectacular finds, most notably the hoard of fourth-century Christian silver plate found at Water Newton, Cambridgeshire, in 1975.

Along with the growth in information, the last decades of the twentieth century saw wide debate about the nature of social change within the Roman province. The idea that social change, or Romanization, was almost certainly brought about by Rome's "civilizing mission" was dominant until the 1970s. There was then a shift toward explanations that sought to explain the success of Rome's conquest through its creation of an identity of interest with the indigenous leaders. Most recently, some people have laid greater stress on the resistance of indigenous peoples to Roman power and the emergence of a diverse range of societies that sought to subvert it. The characteristics of research at the end of the twentieth century were a diversity of approach and a willingness both to contest accepted ideas and to present new interpretations.

Martin Millett

See also Britain, Classical Archaeology; Britain, Prehistoric Archaeology

References

Birley, E. 1961. *Research on Hadrian's Wall*. Kendal, England: T. Wilson.

Freeman, P. W. M. 1997. "Momsen to Haverfield: The Origins of Studies of Romanization in Late 19th Century Britain." In *Dialogues in Roman Imperialism,* 27–20. Ed. D. J. Mattingly. Portsmouth, RI: JRA.

Frere, S. S. 1987. *Roman Britain since Haverfield and Richmond: A Lecture Delivered at All Souls College, 23 October 1987*. Oxford.

Hobley, B. 1975. "Charles Roach Smith (1807–90): Pioneer Rescue Archaeologist." *London Archaeologist* 2: 328–333.

Jones, R. F. J. 1987. "The Archaeologists of Roman Britain." *Bulletin of the University of London Institute of Archaeology* 24: 85–98.

MacDonald, G. 1924. Biographical notice. In *The Roman Occupation of Britain*. Ed. F. Haverfield and G. MacDonald. Oxford: The Clarendon Press.

British Museum

Founded by act of the British Parliament in 1753, the British Museum is widely regarded as having one of the greatest collection of antiquities anywhere in the world. As is true for many great museums, such as the ASHMOLEAN in Oxford and the LOUVRE in Paris, the British Museum was founded on the private collections of individuals, in this case Sir Hans Sloane and Sir Robert Bruce Cotton. In its early years, the British Museum was favored by monarchy. In 1757, King George II presented the Royal Library to the museum, and the library of George III was transferred there in 1828.

Notwithstanding the very great importance of the British Museum as a library, the fortunes of its collections of antiquities are of perhaps greater importance. These were also supplemented by royal patronage. For example, George III presented the Rosetta Stone after its capture from the French in Egypt (1799). Parliament has also been a benefactor, especially in the celebrated case of the Parthenon marbles purchased from LORD ELGIN in 1816.

The British Museum has since acquired antiquities from all parts of the world, but it is especially strong in British antiquities and those derived from Egypt, western Asia, Greece, and Rome. Major pieces such as the material from NIMRUD, NINEVEH, and Khorsabad (building on the collections and excavations of SIR AUSTEN HENRY LAYARD), the magnificent artifacts excavated by SIR LEONARD WOOLLEY at UR, and elements of the mausoleum of Halicarnassus and the Temple of Artemis at EPHESUS were acquired through the efforts of private collectors. The EGYPT EXPLORATION SOCIETY was also a major source of Egyptian antiquities from the late-nineteenth century until the beginning of the World War II.

Notwithstanding the mechanics of assembling such great collections, the British Museum has also played a major role in pure archaeological research. Throughout the twentieth century, research by British Museum staff members has added considerably to our knowledge of archaeology on the global scale.

Tim Murray

See also Belzoni, Giovanni Battista; Egypt, Dynastic; Hamilton, William; Mesopotamia

Brixham Cave

Located on the Devonshire coast of England, Brixham Cave was discovered in 1858. The story of its excavation and the role the discoveries made there played in the history of archaeology is an enduring one. Owing to the great skills and energy of early archaeologists HUGH FALCONER and WILLIAM PENGELLY, it was possible to raise funds and the support of some of the most eminent British scientists of the day (such as CHARLES LYELL, Richard Owen, and JOSEPH PRESTWICH) to undertake a systematic excavation of the cave. Falconer understood clearly that maintaining tight stratigraphic control was crucial to securing plausible evidence of the coexistence of ancient human beings and extinct animals, and such control was achieved thanks to innovations in excavation techniques made by Pengelly and Prestwich.

The site was excavated between 1858 and 1859, and a body of evidence was produced that, although initially convincing only Falconer and Pengelly (along with a few others), when viewed along with the evidence from French archaeologist JACQUES BOUCHER DE PERTHES's excavations in the Somme Valley became the first widely accepted evidence of an even greater human antiquity.

Tim Murray

See also Britain, Prehistoric Archaeology
References
van Riper, A. Bowdoin. 1995. *Men among the Mammoths: Victorian Science and the Discovery of Human Prehistory.* Chicago: University of Chicago Press.

Brodar, Srecko (1893–1987)

A pioneer of Paleolithic archaeology in SLOVENIA, Srecko Brodar first studied natural sciences in Vienna. He graduated from the University of Zagreb in 1920, and received his Ph.D. from Ljubljana University in 1939. In 1946 he became a professor at Ljubljana University, director of the Institute of Archaeology at the Slovenian Academy of Arts and Sciences, and member of the International Quaternary Association and the INTERNATIONAL UNION OF PREHISTORIC AND PROTOHISTORIC SCIENCES (UISPP).

Brodar was the first trained Paleolithic archaeologist in Slovenia. He began his archaeological career in 1928 with the excavation of the Upper Paleolithic cave site of POTOČKA ZIJALKA in the Karavanke mountains in northern Slovenia. The results of his research on this site greatly influenced the interpretation of the process of Wurm glaciation in alpine areas. Prior to the outbreak of World War II, Brodar discovered five new Paleolithic sites in Slovenia and demonstrated the connection between the Paleolithic cultures of the eastern alpine region with Paleolithic settlements on the Slovenian Pannonian Plain and in northwestern Italy.

After the war, Brodar's research focused on the Karst area of southwestern Slovenia, especially on the multiperiod Paleolithic and prehistoric site of Betalov Spodmol near Postojna. Brodar also discovered the first Mesolithic settlements in Slovenia, such as the Spehovka cave. He substantially contributed to the development of Paleolithic studies in the other republics of the former Yugoslavia, especially in Serbia and Bosnia and Herzegovina.

Drasko Josipovic

References

Brodar, S. 1938. "Das Palaolithikum in Jugoslawien." *Quartar* 1: 140–172.

———. 1956. "Ein Beitrag zum Karstpalaolithikum im Nordwesten Jugoslawiens." In *Actes du IV INQUA Congres* (Roma-Pisa 1953), 737–742.

Brześć Kujawski

The site of Brześć Kujawski, located in the Polish province of Wloclawek, comprises a group of settlements and inhumation cemeteries located in the black-earth region of Kuiavia in central POLAND. The site belongs either to the Brześć Kujawski group of the Lengyel culture, according to Konrad Jazdzewski's classification (Jazdzewski 1938, 6), or to the late Band Pottery culture, according to the classification of Lech Czerniak (Czerniak 1994, 66). The best known site, site 4, is a large settlement site with fifty-one trapezoidal long houses from a few phases of occupation along with outbuildings, objects, and human graves. On the basis of this material, the Brześć Kujawski group of the Lengyel culture was distinguished.

From 700 pits, 1,800 postholes, fifty-five human graves, and twenty hearths were excavated. Trapezoidal houses, up to forty meters in length and not smaller than thirteen meters, were also located. The long axis of the houses was oriented north and south with a slight northwest tilt. The interior of these houses was divided into three parts. The external pillars, which were construction elements of the walls, were situated in ditches. The walls were constructed from both whole tree trunks and logs split lengthways. The split logs were set upright in the trench, alternating with the flat side facing outward so that the interior and exterior walls were smooth. The houses were associated with a variety of features found in the immediate area. Adult burials have been found in storage pits near the long houses, and other burials have been found in graves and pits in the settlement. Some of the graves are typical inhumation graves mainly containing dress ornaments and copper grave goods. The settlement and the graves are contemporary, but the majority of the graves date from the late phase of the settlement.

The settlement is situated on the bank of a lake. During the occupation of the site, which lasted more than 200 years, the houses were destroyed and rebuilt many times, and some estimates suggest that houses were rebuilt eleven times. The many phases of occupation are indicated by overlapping house plans. The causes of the frequent rebuilding are thought to be the result of a rotational system or as a consequence of natural destruction, such as fire. The settlement usually consisted of forty-nine long houses, and household cluster was the archaeological manifestation of a fundamental socioeconomic unit of the Brześć Kujawski group. The settlement is related to a set of smaller camps in the neighborhood.

The settlement of Brześć Kujawski was excavated before World War II. The initiators of the excavation were Konrad Jazdzewski and Stanislaw Madajski, who carried out large-scale excavations

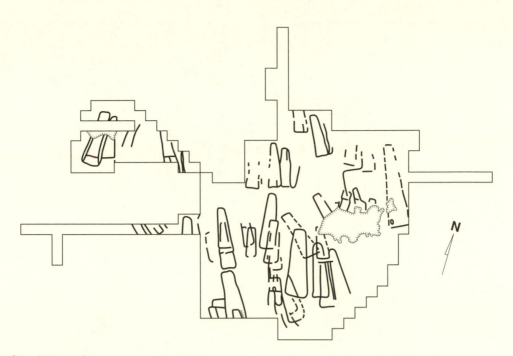

Plan of Brześć Kujawski

of settlements of cultures of southern origin in the Brześć Kujawski region from 1934 to 1939. The excavations in Brześć Kujawski were carried out later by Maria Chmielewski and Waldemar Chmielewski in the 1950s and by Ryszard Grygiel and Peter I. Bogucki in the 1970s and 1980s.

Arkadiusz Marciniak

Buckland, William (1784–1856)

English geologist, Anglican priest, and professor of mineralogy at Oxford University, William Buckland believed that universal catastrophes had wiped out species and that God had created new ones to take their place. Buckland studied the chronology and stratigraphy of caves, and along with the French geologist Georges Cuvier explored the association between fossil humans and the remains of extinct animals. Evidence of the increasing complexity of plant and animal life in successive geological strata was viewed by Buckland as the result of separate and individual acts of creation and not as a developmental sequence. He believed that God and not the natural world was responsible for evolution.

In 1823 Buckland published his *Reliquiae diluvianae,* listing all the then-known finds of fossil human and faunal remains. He concluded that human bones were not as old as the animal bones with which they were found because they were intrusions, the result of geological processes, faults, or tectonic movements. For over twenty years his views dominated the scientific establishment, until those of geologist CHARLES LYELL, and the antiquaries and archaeologists who had burgeoning evidence of human antiquity, superseded them.

Tim Murray

See also Boucher de Perthes, J.; Britain, Prehistoric; Prestwich, J.

Bulgaria

For objective historical reasons, the beginning of Bulgarian archaeology has been traced back no earlier than the last decades of the nineteenth century. During the sixteenth to the nineteenth centuries, many European travelers who passed through the Ottoman Empire described various antiquities in Bulgarian lands. Thus, in 1868, the French scholar A. Dumont traveled in southern Bulgaria, then under Ottoman rule, and later published his reports (Dumont 1892). However, it would be some years

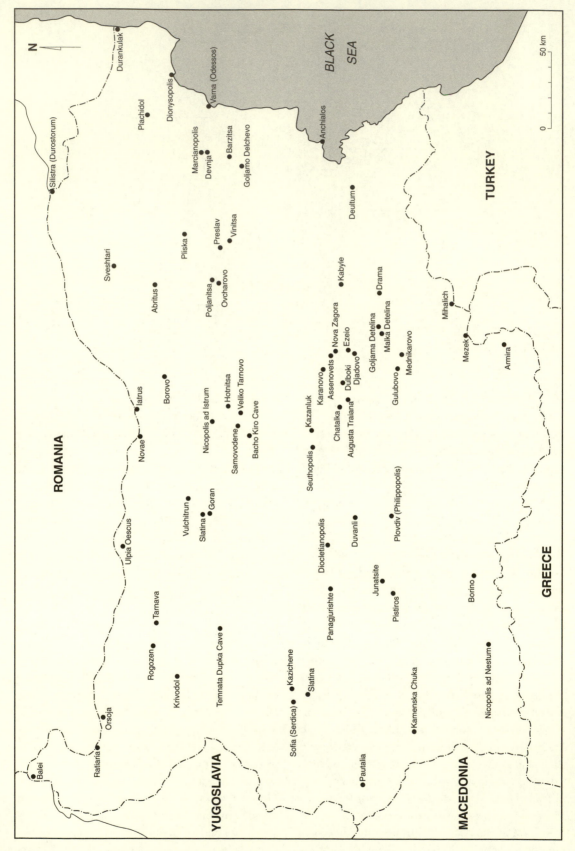

Bulgarian Archaeological Sites

N

BLACK SEA

ROMANIA

TURKEY

YUGOSLAVIA

MACEDONIA

GREECE

50 km

Durankulak

Silistra (Durostorum)

Plachidol

Dionysopolis

Varna (Odessos)

Marcianopolis

Devnja

Barzitsa

Goljamo Delchevo

Anchialos

Deultum

Pliska

Preslav

Vinitsa

Sveshtari

Abritus

Poljanitsa

Ovcharovo

Kabyle

Drama

Mihalich

Nova Zagora

Assenovets

Ezeio

Goljama Detelina

Malka Detelina

Mezek

Karanovo

Mednikarovo

Armira

Iatrus

Borovo

Hotnitsa

Seuthopolis

Kazanluk

Chatalka

Duboki

Djadovo

Gulubovo

Novae

Nicopolis ad Istrum

Samovodene

Veliko Tarnovo

Bacho Kiro Cave

Augusta Traiana

Vulchitrun

Slatina

Goran

Diocletianopolis

Duvanli

Plovdiv (Philippopolis)

Ulpia Oescus

Panagjurishte

Junatsite

Pistiros

Tarnava

Borino

Rogozen

Kazichene

Slatina

Krivodol

Temnata Dupka Cave

Sofia (Serdica)

Kamenska Chuka

Nicopolis ad Nestum

Ratiaria

Orsoja

Balei

Pautalia

after Bulgaria was emancipated in 1878 before the pioneers of Bulgarian archaeology started excavating sites and studying diverse ancient and mediaeval artifacts. The pioneers were usually Bulgarian enthusiasts whose experience in archaeology was acquired in the course of their work; therefore, it was the Czech scholars C. Jireček, V. Dobrusky, and H. and K. Škorpil who initiated real archaeology in Bulgaria and published the first archaeological studies (Dobrusky 1896, 1897; Jireček 1877, 1881; H. Škorpil 1894; H. Škorpil and K. Škorpil 1896).

In the period 1879–1900, several local archaeological societies were established in the country, and in 1901, the Bulgarian Archaeological Society was constituted as a center of archaeological studies. Although some small collections of archaeological materials already existed in the mid-nineteenth century, the first museum collection was founded in 1878 at the public library in Sofia, and it was set up as the National Archaeological Museum in 1892. In 1880, another important archaeological museum was established in Plovdiv, and in 1891, a course in Greek and Roman archaeology started at Sofia University St. Kliment Ohridski, the oldest Bulgarian university established in 1888.

The first archaeological excavations began in 1884 in Veliko Tarnovo, the last medieval Bulgarian capital. The special interest of scholars in the history of the medieval kingdom was completely reasonable in light of the establishment of the new Bulgarian State and, in 1899–1900, excavations of the other medieval Bulgarian capital, Pliska, were organized (K. Škorpil 1905). In 1898, the French scholar P. Jerôme started prehistoric research by drilling excavations in southern Bulgaria (Jerôme 1901), and H. and K. Škorpil published their survey on Thracian burial mounds in Bulgarian lands (H. Škorpil and K. Škorpil 1898). From 1904 to 1909, V. Dobrusky conducted excavations in the Roman provincial towns of Ulpia Oescus and Nicopolis ad Istrum.

During the first half of the twentieth century, a number of Bulgarian archaeologists who had studied abroad started working in their home country, and consequently, different European schools stimulated the development of Bulgarian archaeology. Important preliminary information was accumulated, numerous sites were registered, various finds were collected and studied, some important archaeological excavations were organized, and diverse studies were published, both in Bulgarian periodicals and abroad. In 1920, the Bulgarian Archaeological Institute was established, the most important archaeological institution even today, and some local museums were founded, becoming important centers for regional archaeological research.

In the early twentieth century, R. Popov organized excavations in different prehistoric sites in Bulgaria and studied Thracian materials of the first millennium B.C. (Popov 1912, 1928, 1930). A. Chilingirov excavated some prehistoric tells, and B. Djakovich worked in Thracian and ancient archaeology. Very important were the researches of G. Kazarow (1916, 1930, 1936, 1938) and D. Detschew (1976), who studied in detail the history, linguistics, and archaeology of ancient Thrace during the Iron Age and the Roman period. At the same time, B. Filow began his studies on the Roman period (Filow 1906, 1931); he established Thracian archaeology as well and later excavated one of the most remarkable Thracian burial sites (Filow 1917, 1934a, 1937). Filow was interested in Middle Ages Bulgarian art and published important studies in that area as well (Filow 1919, 1934b). Important research continued at medieval sites, with A. Protič studying medieval architecture (Protič 1924), and J. Gospodinov excavated at Presale, the second Bulgarian capital (Gospodinov 1914).

After World War I, a new generation of Bulgarian archaeologists began studying different topics. As a result of field surveys, V. Mika registered a number of prehistoric sites and undertook limited excavation of several tells (Mikov 1933, 1939); he also studied the mortuary practices of the ancient Thracians (Mikov 1942, 1954). P. Detev registered prehistoric sites and organized some excavation works. I. Velkov excavated a number of sites and did important research on ancient Thrace (Velkov 1930, 1931) and the medieval period (Velkov 1939). D. P. Dimitrov investigated the Roman period and published some important studies (Dimitrov 1937, 1942). K. Mijatev continued researching Pliska, Preslav, and Veliko Tarnovo and wrote key publications on the architecture and art of the Bulgarian kingdom during the Middle Ages (Mijatev 1932, 1936, 1965). V. Ivanova (1922–1925) and A. Rashenov (1932) manifested special interest in Christian archaeology and studied early and medieval churches.

Some foreign scholars also worked in Bulgaria in this period: the U.S. archaeologist J. H. Gaul generalized and systematized prehistoric research in Bulgaria (Gaul 1948), the Turkish scholar A. M. Mansel investigated Thracian tombs (Mansel 1943), the Italian archaeologist A. Frova organized excavations in the Roman town of Ulpia Oescus (Frova 1948), the Hungarian scholar G. Fehér studied the proto-Bulgarians (Fehér 1931), and the French scholar A. Grabar examined religious paintings of medieval Bulgaria (Grabar 1928).

After World War II, Bulgaria was occupied by the Soviet army, and a Communist dictatorship was established in the country. In 1945, the great Bulgarian archaeologist B. Filow was assassinated, and over the following decades, Communist ideology and total party control ruled not only everyday life but also the sciences and humanities. Achievements in prewar Bulgarian archaeology were neglected or rejected, contacts with western scholars and institutions were restricted and even forbidden, and only a few Bulgarian archaeologists were permitted to maintain international relations.

At the same time, a lot of new building work provoked archaeological rescue endeavors. The government supported the excavation of numerous archaeological sites, and many materials were collected and studied. Although mistakes were often made as a result of taking the theses of Soviet science for granted, many Bulgarian archaeologists managed to follow the traditions of prewar archaeology in Bulgaria.

In the 1960s, archaeological excavations and studies intensified, and during the 1970s, scientific contact with the West became possible for more scholars, although such contact was strictly controlled by the Communist Party. As a result, several important international field projects for studying prehistoric and ancient sites in Bulgaria began during the 1970s and 1980s, various international congresses and conferences were held, and impressive collections of ancient Bulgarian art treasures were exhibited in some world-famous museums in the West.

At the same time, many Bulgarian archaeologists learned more about the achievements of their western colleagues, adopted modern interdisciplinary methodology for field excavation and the study of materials, and examined many diverse questions of archaeology (e.g., chronology and periods, cultural interrelations and interactions, processes of ethnic formation, cult and religion, architecture, art, etc.), although many other topics remained underdeveloped. The main weak points of Bulgarian archaeology of the time were some nationalistic trends toward interpreting the past, which was typical of archaeological studies in the other Balkan countries as well, and a lack of adequate publications on the great number of finds and sites that were investigated. Unfortunately, the results and materials from intensive fieldwork often remained unpublished or only partially published, the archaeological data usually being interpreted rather than clearly represented, and the number of final complete publications was too small.

In 1989, the Communist regime in Bulgaria collapsed, and Bulgaria began a difficult transformation toward democracy. The new political situation in the 1990s enabled many Bulgarian archaeologists, especially younger scholars, to freely establish contacts with scholars and institutions in the West, to study abroad, to participate in conferences and symposia, and to publish materials from Bulgaria in international periodicals. The main challenges for Bulgarian archaeologists in the present economic situation are a lack of enough financial resources for further excavations and a strong need for the great amount of data and materials from past fieldwork to be published. Another priority of Bulgarian archaeology now is further international cooperation and joint archaeological projects.

Currently, the Bulgarian Archaeological Institute in Sofia supervises archaeological excavations in Bulgaria. Many students studied archaeology at the Sofia University St. Kliment Ohridski and the Veliko Tarnovo University St. Cyril and St. Methodius, both of which are important centers for archaeological study. The

National Archaeological Museum and the National Museum of History, both located in Sofia, have the most significant collections of antiquities, but many other historical and archaeological museums in the country also contain important collections. The main periodicals being currently published are *Archeologija* (in Bulgarian with French abstracts), *Archaeologia Bulgarica* (mainly in English with some papers in French or German), and *Archaeological Novelties* (bilingual in English and Bulgarian), and several regional annual volumes (in Bulgarian) are also published by local museums, although with some breaks.

Research on the Paleolithic period (ca. 130,000–15,000 B.C.) in Bulgaria began about 1950 and by the end of the 1970s, more than thirty caves and open settlements had been studied through excavation and drilling. The most important Paleolithic sites investigated during the last years are the Bacho Kiro cave, a Middle Paleolithic site excavated by a Bulgarian-Polish team (Kozlowski 1982), and another synchronous site, the Temnata Dupka cave, where Bulgarian, Polish, and French scholars have worked together (Kozlowski, Laville, Sirakov, and Ginter 1992). The best-investigated regions in Bulgaria now are the west and central Balkan Mountains and the western Rhodope Mountains, and various sites that date from the Paleolithic and Mesolithic periods (ca. 15,000–6300 or 6100 B.C.) are known so far (Bailey and Panayotov 1995).

Study of the Neolithic (6300 or 6100–4900 or 4850 B.C.) and the Eneolithic (4900 or 4850–4100 or 3800 B.C.) periods and the transition period (3850–3200 B.C.) in Bulgaria have produced significant results. The Karanovo tell has been the most important site for Bulgarian prehistory, and now excavations are being resumed by a Bulgarian-Austrian team (Hiller and Nikolov 1997). On the basis of the excavation results, the Karanovo chronology system was introduced: Karanovo I-IV, Neolithic; Karanovo V-VI, Eneolithic; and Karanovo VII, early Bronze Age (Georgiev 1961).

More than 500 prehistoric tells (from the Neolithic, Eneolithic, and Bronze Age) are registered in Bulgaria today; around 10 percent of them are being investigated, and several sites have been completely excavated. Some of the most important Neolithic sites are located at Samovodene, Slatina, Ovcharovo, and Hotnitsa; for the Eneolithic period, important sites are Ovcharovo, Poljanitsa, Vinitsa, Durankulak, Goljamo Delchevo, and Krivodol. These tells have thick cultural layers and create the background for the study of both periods. A number of cemeteries located near the settlements are also being investigated, the most important being the Varna cemetery, which has an impressive wealth of material (gold, copper, bone, and pottery) and clearly shows the social ranking in the Eneolithic society (Fol and Lichardus 1988). Special attention has also been paid to the copper metalwork from the Eneolithic period (Todorova 1981). The results of intensive excavation works gave the opportunity for publishing some general studies and articles devoted to the problems of the Neolithic, Eneolithic, and transition periods in Bulgaria (Bailey and Panayotov 1995; Leshtakov 1997; Nikolov 1998; Nikolova 1999; Stefanovich, Todorova, and Hauptmann 1998; Todorova 1979; Todorova and Vaissov 1993).

Investigations of the Bronze Age (divided in three periods: early, 3500 or 3200–2100 B.C.; middle, 2100–1600 or 1500 B.C.; and late, 1600 or 1500–1100 or 1050 B.C.) in Bulgaria have significantly increased since 1970. Owing to the gradual adoption of the stratigraphic method in archaeological excavations, the relative chronology of the Bronze Age was established. Moreover, materials threw additional light upon the problems of synchronization between Europe and northwestern Asia Minor by clarifying the chronological position of the Bronze Age in Troy in relation to European prehistory. Some of the most important settlement sites (usually multilayer tells that were inhabited in earlier periods) are located at Ezero, Junatsite, Djadovo (excavated by a Bulgarian-Japanese team), and Drama (investigated by a Bulgarian-German expedition). Other sites that have produced important results are near Gulubovo, Mihalich, Balei, Assenovets, and Kamenska Chuka at Blagoevgrad, the last excavated by a Bulgarian-American team.

Along with settlement investigations, the study of mortuary practices has been signifi-

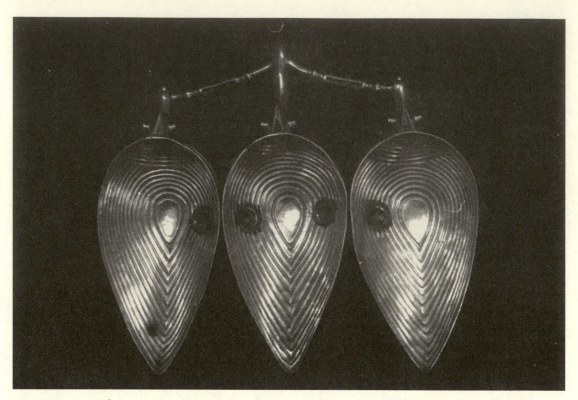

Gold libation vessel from the Vulchitrun treasure, Late Bronze Age (Courtesy of Nilola Theodossiev)

cantly developed. The great number of early–Bronze Age tumuli allowed a certain analysis of the Pit-Grave culture to be made (Panayotov 1989), and important late–Bronze Age flat and tumular necropolises were excavated near Orsoja, Nova Zagora, and Borino. Moreover, both historical and epigraphic (Linear B texts) records and the archaeological data show that during the late Bronze Age, the present Bulgarian lands were already inhabited by Thracian tribes. Special studies pay attention to Bronze Age chronology, periods, and culture (Bailey and Panayotov 1995; Bonev 1988; Katinčarov 1975; Leshtakov 1997; Nikolova 1999; Panayotov 1988; Stefanovich, Todorova, and Hauptmann 1998), and also the bronze metalwork (Chernych 1978). One of the most important finds from the late Bronze Age is the Vulchitrun treasure, a ritual set of thirteen gold items 12.425 kilograms in weight (*Ancient Gold* 1998; Venedikov 1987).

Study of the Iron Age (divided in two periods: early, 1050 or 1000–550 or 450 B.C., and late, 550 or 450 B.C.–late first century B.C. or

early first century A.D.) has produced most important results concerning the cultural and historical development of ancient Thrace (part of modern Bulgaria). Some fortresses, open settlements, and sanctuaries from the early Iron Age have been investigated, and the mortuary practices show significant diversity: both flat graves and tumuli with inhumation and cremation burials were used while numerous rock-cut tombs and megalithic dolmens were built in southeastern Thrace. The introduction of iron metallurgy caused social and economic changes, and bronze was used mainly in the production of jewelry and cult figurines. Several rich finds like the Barzitsa treasure and the Kazichene hoard reflected the economic advance of the Thracian aristocracy.

Some general studies and articles on the early Iron Age have been published (Archibald 1998; Bailey and Panayotov 1995; Gergova 1987; Stefanovich, Todorova, and Hauptmann 1998; Stoyanov 1997; Tončeva 1980). From the sixth century B.C. onward, interrelations among Thrace, ancient Greece, and Anatolia intensi-

Part of the paintings in the tholos chamber of the Kazanluk tomb, late fourth–early third centuries B.C. (Courtesy of Nikola Theodossiev)

fied, and the first Thracian tribal states ruled by local kings emerged in the late sixth–first half of the fifth century B.C. The strong interactions caused a change of culture, and during the late-classical and Hellenistic ages, the Thracian aristocracy adopted diverse achievements from Greece and Anatolia, while many Greeks lived in colonies along the Thracian coasts and inland (Archibald 1998). Several regions of Thrace were influenced by the LA TÈNE culture, too, when CELTS settled there in the early third century B.C. (Domaradzki 1984; Theodossiev 2000). Various sanctuaries, open settlements, fortresses, *emporia* (trading posts), and towns were excavated, the most important among them being Seuthopolis, Kabyle, Philippopolis, and Pistiros, the last being investigated by Bulgarian, British, Czech, and French scholars (Archibald 1998; Dimitrov and Chichikova 1978).

Diversity in funerary customs increased during the late Iron Age (Kitov 1994), and some rich tumuli, like those at Duvanli and Dulboki, have been unearthed (Archibald 1998; Filow

1934a). At the same time, numerous monumental beehive tholoi (rectangular or barrel-vaulted tombs) were built under mounds for aristocratic burials, the most famous ones being located at Kazanluk (Mikov 1954), Sveshtari (Fol, Chichikova, Ivanov, and Teofilov 1986), and Mezek (Filow 1937; Mansel 1943). About ten hoards consisting of gold and silver vessels of local origin or imports are also spectacular, such as the treasures from Panagjurishte, Rogozen, and Borovo (*Ancient Gold* 1998; Archibald 1998; Čončev 1956; Cook 1989). The rich materials from the late Iron Age enable many scholars to publish important general studies on the period (Archibald 1998; Fol and Marazov 1977; Gergova 1996; Getov 1995; Hoddinott 1981; Kull 1997; Theodossiev 2000; Venedikov and Gerasimov 1975).

The Roman period in Bulgaria has been thoroughly investigated since the late nineteenth century. During the first century A.D., the Roman Empire imposed full control upon the Thracian lands, and two provinces—Moesia and Thracia—were established. The Romans con-

Sixth-century basilica at the foot of the fortress at Spasovitsa (Hulton Getty)

structed an excellent road network and built a number of provincial towns that became important centers of the Romanizing process and the new syncretic culture, inspired by citizens of different ethnic origin.

Ulpia Oescus was an important town established in the early second century A.D., which existed until late antiquity. Archaeological excavations in progress have revealed the town's significant architecture: a strong fortification system, the forum and some nearby temples, a civil basilica, etc. (Ivanov and Ivanov 1998). Another remarkable town that existed from the early second to the beginning of the seventh century A.D. was Nicopolis ad Istrum, now being investigated by a Bulgarian-British team, and some of its architectural complexes and buildings are being studied, like the fortifications, the forum, an odeon, the city council, a civil basilica, a bath, the palaestra, etc. (Ivanov and Ivanov 1994; Poulter 1995). A joint Bulgarian-German expedition currently excavates Iatrus, a late-

Roman and early-Byzantine castle, and the fieldwork has already produced important results (Iatrus–Krivina 1995).

Other significant Roman and late-antiquity towns in present-day Bulgaria were Ratiaria, Novae, Abritus, Marcianopolis, Durostorum, Dionysopolis, Odessos, Anchialos, Serdica, Pautalia, Nicopolis ad Nestum, Diocletianopolis, Philippopolis, Augusta Traiana, and Deultum, all of them with monumental architecture and rich necropolises (Ivanov 1967; Velkov 1977). Some rural villas, like those at Chatalka (Nicolov 1976) and Armira (Mladenova 1991), became centers of the local Thracian aristocracy and achieved economic advances during the Roman period. At the same time, cult monuments show clearly the strong religious syncretism of the first few centuries A.D. (Kazarow 1936; Tacheva-Hitova 1983), although a Thracian hero seems to have remained a widely worshiped deity (Gočeva and Oppermann 1979– 1984; Kazarow 1938).

The great number of impressive materials from the Roman period enable scholars to work on different topics like sculpture, funerary reliefs, jewelry, and gems (Končev 1959; Dimitrov 1937, 1942; Dimitrova-Milčeva 1980; Ruseva-Slokoska 1991). Moreover, some monuments, like the mosaic from Ulpia Oescus (Ivanov 1954) and the painted tomb in Silistra (Dimitrov 1962), are real masterpieces of Roman and late-antiquity art.

Certain topics are of great importance for medieval Bulgarian archaeology. Thus, data for an early Bulgarian and Slavic presence was especially looked for, and some settlements and necropolises were investigated (Beshevliev 1981; Stanchev 1958; Vazharova 1976, 1986). Other important studies have been devoted to the formation of the medieval Bulgarian nation and culture after the Bulgarian kingdom was established in A.D. 681 (Beshevliev 1981; Filow 1919; Grabar 1928; Mavrodinov 1959, 1966; Mijatev 1936; Vaklinov 1977). Excavations in the medieval Bulgarian capitals have also produced significant results (Mijatev 1932, 1965; Rashev and Georgiev 1996; Totev 1993; Vaklinov 1977). Problems like the chronology and character of the medieval buildings have been stated in a new way, although the suggested hypotheses have sometimes been politically influenced.

Pliska was the first Bulgarian capital (ca. 681–893), and it existed as a town until the second half of the eleventh century. The outwork fortifications consisted of ditches and banks that enclosed about twenty-three square kilometers. A stone wall built in the beginning of the ninth century surrounded the inner town. The area between the outerworks and the inner town was occupied by settlements with semidug dwellings, workshops, and civil complexes. After the baptism of Bulgarians in A.D. 864–865, a lot of churches were built in Pliska, the most significant being a huge monastery complex, which included a great basilica. The central part of the inner town was occupied by a palace that was built on the foundations of an earlier enormous building, a shrine rebuilt in a church, a brick wall that enclosed the court areas, several baths, etc. There were also water supply and drainage systems as well as secret subways. All these remains reveal a complicated chronology with several building periods.

Preslav was the second capital (893–971) of the Bulgarian kingdom. The outer stone wall surrounded an area of three and half square kilometers, and in its center, the inner town included the court complex, episcopal complex, civic buildings, workshops, a shrine from the precapital period, water supply and drainage systems, etc. The complicated chronology shows several building periods. A number of monasteries were scattered within and outside the fortified area with various workshops for all kinds of art: ceramics, sculpture, bone carving, mosaic, and so on.

After a period of about two centuries when Bulgaria was under Byzantine rule, the Bulgarian kingdom was restored, and Veliko Tarnovo became the last medieval capital (1186–1393). This town was built on two hills—Tsarevets and Trapezica—and the surrounding area. Tsarevets had its own fortress with one main entrance. The patriarch church and the palace of the kings were built on Tsarevets together with houses and workshops of the common population, churches, and monasteries. Trapezica has not been as well studied, but the ruins of seventeen churches are known. In the late fourteenth century, Bulgaria fell under the Ottoman rule.

Nikola Theodossiev, Roumjana Koleva, and Borislav Borislavov

See also Celts; Czech Republic; La Tène; Medieval Archaeology

References

Ancient Gold, the Wealth of the Thracians: Treasures from the Republic of Bulgaria. 1998. New York.

Archibald, Z. H. 1998. *The Odrysian Kingdom of Thrace: Orpheus Unmasked.* New York: Oxford University Press.

Bailey, D. W., and I. Panayotov, eds. 1995. *Prehistoric Bulgaria.* Monographs in World Archaeology no. 22. Madison, WI: Prehistory Press.

Beshevliev, V. 1981. *Purvobulgarite: bit i kultura.* Sofia: Izd-vo Nauka i izkustvo.

Bonev, A. 1988. *Trakija i Aegejskijat svjat prez vtorata polovina na II hiljadoletie pr.n.e.* Razkopki i Prouchvanija no. 20. Sofia.

Chernych, E. 1978. *Gornoe delo i metallurgija v drevnejshei Bolgarii.* Sofia.

Končev, D. 1956. *Der Goldschatz von Panagjuriˇste.* Prague.

———.1959. "Monuments de la sculpture romaine en Bulgarie méridionale." *Collection Latomus* 39: 1–44.

Cook, B. F., ed. 1989. *The Rogozen Treasure: Papers of the Anglo-Bulgarian Conference, 12 March 1987.* London.

Detschew, D. 1976. *Die thrakischen Sprachreste.* Vienna.

Dimitrov, D. P. 1937. "Römische Grabsteine in Bulgarien (Vortrag)." *Archäologischer Anzeiger* 52: 310–335.

———. 1942. *Nadgrobnite plochi ot rimsko vreme v Severna Bulgaria.* Sofia.

———. 1962. "Le système décoratif et la date des peintures murales du tombeau antique de Silistra." *Cahiers Archéologiques* 12: 35–52.

Dimitrov, D. P., and M. Chichikova. 1978. *The Thracian City of Seuthopolis.* British Archaeological Reports, Supplementary Series no. 38. Oxford.

Dimitrova-Milčeva, A. 1980. *Antike Gemmen und Kameen aus dem Archäologischen Nationalmuseum in Sofia.* Sofia.

Dobrusky, V. 1896. "Grabstele des Anaxandros aus Apollonia am Pontus." *Archäologischer Anzeiger* 11: 136–138.

———. 1897. "Inscriptions et monuments figurés

de la Thrace." *Bulletin de Correspodance Hellénique* 21: 118–140.

Domaradzki, M. 1984. *Keltite na Balkanskija poluostrov (IV-I)*. Sofia.

Dumont, A. 1892. "Rapport sur un voyage archéologique en Thrace." In *Mélanges d'archéologie et d'épigraphie,* 186–287. Ed. A Dumont. Paris.

Fehér, G. 1931. *Les monuments de la culture protobulgare et leurs relations hongroises*. Budapest.

Filow, B. 1906. *Die Legionen der Provinz Moesia von Augustus bis auf Diokletian*. Leipzig.

———. 1917. "Denkmäler der thrakischen Kunst." *Mitteilungen des Deutschen Archäologischen Instituts, Römische Abteilung* 32: 21–73.

———. 1919. *Early Bulgarian Art*. Berne: P. Haupt.

———. 1931. *Rimskoto vladichestvo v Bulgaria*. Varna.

———. 1934a. *Die Grabhügelnekropole bei Duvanlij in Südbulgarien*. Sofia: Staatsdruckerei.

———. 1934b. *Les miniatures de l'évangile du roi Jean Alexandre à Londres*. Sofia.

———. 1937. "The Beehive Tombs of Mezek." *Antiquity* 11: 300–304.

Fol, A., and I. Marazov. 1977. *Thrace and the Thracians*. London: Cassell.

Fol, A., M. Chichikova, T. Ivanov, and T. Teofilov. 1986. *The Thracian Tomb near the Village of Sveshtari*. Sofia: Svyat Publishers.

Fol, A., and J. Lichardus, eds. 1988. *Macht, Herrschaft, und Gold: Das Gräberfeld von Varna (Bulgarien) und die Anfänge einer neuen europäischen Zivilisation*. Catalog. Saarbrücken: Moderne Galerie des Saarland-Museums.

Frova, A. 1948. "Lo scavo della missione archeologica italiana in Bulgaria ad Oescus." *Bolletino dell'Istituto Nazionale di Archeologia e Storia dell'Arte* 11: 73–114.

Gaul, J. H. 1948. *The Neolithic Period in Bulgaria: Early Food-Producing Cultures of Eastern Europe*. American School of Prehistoric Research, Bulletin no. 16.

Georgiev, G. I. 1961. "Kulturgruppen der Jungsstein- und der Kupferzeit in der Ebene von Thrazien (Sud-Bulgarien)." In *L'Europe à la fin de l'âge de la pierre,* 45–100. Actes du Symposium consacré aux problèmes du Néolithique européen. Prague.

Georgieva, S., and V. Velkov. 1974. *Bibliographie de l'archéologie Bulgare (1879–1966)*. Sofia: BAN.

Gergova, D. 1987. *Früh- und ältereisenzeitliche Fibeln in Bulgarien*. Prähistorische Bronzefunde 14, 7. Munich: Beck.

———. 1996. *Obredat na obezsmartjavaneto v drevna Trakija*. Sofia: Izd-vo "Agató."

Getov, L. 1995. *Amphori i amphorni pechati ot Kabyle (IV-II v.pr.n.e.)*. Sofia: Univ. izd-vo "Sv. Kliment Okhridski,"

Gočeva, Z., and M. Oppermann. 1979–1984. *Corpus cultus equitis Thracii*. 2 vols. Leiden.

Gospodinov, J. 1914. "Razkopki v Patlejna." *Izvestija na Bulgarskoto Arheologichesko Druzhestvo* 4: 113–128.

Grabar, A. 1928. *La peinture religieuse en Bulgarie*. Paris: P. Geuthner

Hiller, S., and V. Nikolov. 1997. *Karanovo: Die Ausgrabungen im Südsektor 1984–1992*. Salzburg.

Hoddinott, R. 1981. *The Thracians*. London: Thames and Hudson.

Ivanov, T. 1954. *Rimskata mozajka ot Ulpia Oescus*. Sofia.

———. 1967. "Gradoustrojstvoto prez rimskata i kasnoantichnata epoha v Bulgaria." *Arheologija* 9, no. 4: 10–29.

Ivanov, T., and R. Ivanov. 1994. *Nicopolis ad Istrum*. Vol. 1. Sofia.

———. 1998. *Ulpia Oescus*. Vol. 1. Sofia.

Ivanova, V. 1922–1925. "Stari carkvi i manastiri v bulgarskite zemi." *Godishnik na Narodnija Arheologicheski Muzej* 5: 429–582.

Jerôme, P. 1901. "L'époque néolitique dans la vallée du Tonsus (Thrace)." *Revue Archéologique* 1: 328–349.

Jireček, C. 1877. *Die Heerstraße von Belgrad nach Konstantinopel und die Balkanpässe: Eine historisch-geographische Studie*. Prague.

———. 1881. "Beiträge zur antiken Geographie und Epigraphik von Bulgarien und Rumelien." *Monatsberichte der kgl. Akademie der Wissenschaften in Berlin, Sitzung von 12.V.,* 434–469.

Katinčarov, R. 1975. "Traits caractéristiques de la civilisation de l'âge du bronze ancien et moyen en Bulgarie." *Acta Archaeologica Carpathica* 15: 85–110.

Kazarow, G. 1916. *Beiträge zur Kulturgeschichte der Thraker*. Sarajevo.

———. 1930: "Thrace." In *Cambridge Ancient History,* 8:534–560, 781–783. Ed. A. E. Astin. Cambridge: Cambridge University Press.

———. 1936. "Thrakische Religion." In *Pauly-Wissowa Real-Encyclopädie der klassischen Altertumswissenschaft,* 6A, col. 472–551.

———. 1938. *Die Denkmäler des Thrakischen Reitergottes in Bulgarien*. Budapest.

Kitov, G. 1994. "The Thracian Mounds." *Bulletin of the Ancient Orient Museum* (Tokyo) 15: 121–147.

Kozlowski, J. K., ed. 1982. *Excavation in the Bacho Kiro Cave (Bulgaria), Final Report*. Warsaw.

Kozlowski, J. K., J. H. Laville, N. Sirakov, and B. Ginter. 1992. *Temnata Dupka Cave: Excavations in Karlukovo Karst Area Bulgaria*. Vol.1, pt. 1. Cracow.

Kull, B. 1997. "Tod und Apotheose: Zur Ikonographie in Grab und Kunst der jüngeren Eisenzeit an der unteren Donau und ihrer Bedeutung für die Interpretation von 'Prunkgräbern.'" *Bericht der Römisch-Germanischen Kommission* 78: 197–466.

Leshtakov, K., ed. 1997. *Maritsa Project*. Vol. 1. Sofia.

Mansel, A. M. 1943. *Die Kuppelgraeber von Kirklareli in Thrakien*. Ankara.

Mavrodinov, N. 1959. *Starobulgarskoto izkustvo: Izkustvoto na parvoto bulgarsko tsarstvo*. Sofia.

———. 1966. *Starobulgarskoto izkustvo XI-XIII vek*. Sofia.

Mijatev, K. 1932. *Kraglata tsarkva v Preslav*. Sofia.

———. 1936. *Preslavskata keramika*. Sofia.

———. 1965. *Arhitekturata na srednovekovna Bulgaria*. Sofia.

Mikov, V. 1933. *Predistoricheski selishta i nahodki v Bulgaria*. Sofia.

———. 1939. "Karanovo (Bulgaria)." *Antiquity* 13: 345–349.

———. 1942. "Proizhod na nadgrobnite mogili v Bulgaria." *Godishnik na Narodnija Arheologicheski Muzei* 7: 15–31.

———. 1954. *Le tombeau antique près de Kazanlak*. Sofia.

Mladenova, J. 1991. *Antichnata vila Armira krai Ivajlovgrad*. Sofia.

Nicolov, D. 1976. *The Roman Villa at Chatalka, Bulgaria*. British Archaeological Reports, Supplementary Series no. 17. Oxford.

Nikolov, V. 1998. *Prouchvanija vurhu neolitnata keramika v Trakia*. Sofia.

Nikolova, L. 1999. *The Balkans in Later Prehistory*. British Archaeological Reports, International Series no. 791. Oxford.

Panayotov, I. 1988. "Studies on the Bronze Age in the Bulgarian Lands (Historiographic Notes)." *Thracia* 8: 157–175.

———. 1989. *Yamnata kultura v bulgarskite zemi*. Razkopki I Prouchvanija no. 21. Sofia.

Popov, R. 1912. "Beiträge zur Vorgeschichte Bulgariens." *Prähistorische Zeitschrift* 4: 88–113.

———. 1928–1930. *Kultura i zhivot na predistoricheskija chovek v Bulgaria*. 2 vols. Sofia.

Poulter, A. 1995. *Nicopolis ad Istrum: A Roman, Late Roman, and Early Byzantine City*. London.: Society for the Promotion of Roman Studies.

Protič, A. 1924. *L'architecture religieuse bulgare*. Sofia.

Rashenov, A. 1932. *Mesemvrijskite tsarkvi*. Sofia.

Rashev, R., and P. Georgiev. 1996. *Pliska: Patevoditel*. Sofia.

Ruseva-Slokoska, L. 1991. *Roman Jewellery*. Sofia.

Škorpil, H. 1894. "Antike Inschriften aus Bulgarien." *Archäologisch-epigraphische Mitteilungen* 17: 170–224.

Škorpil, H., and K. Škorpil. 1896. "Altbulgarische Inscriften." *Archäologisch-epigraphische Mitteilungen* 19: 237–248.

———. 1898. *Mogili*. Plovdiv.

Škorpil, K. 1905. "Aboba-Pliska." *Izvestija Russkogo Arheologicheskogo Instituta v Konstantinople* 10.

Stanchev, S. 1958. *Nekropolat do Novi Pazar*. Sofia.

Stefanovich, M., H. Todorova, and H. Hauptmann, eds. 1998. *James Harvey Gaul: In memoriam*. Sofia.

Stoyanov, T. 1997. *Early Iron Age Tumular Necropolis: Sboryanovo I*. Sofia.

Tacheva-Hitova, M. 1983. *Eastern Cults in Moesia Inferior and Thracia (5th Century B.C.–4th Century A.D.)*. Leiden.

Theodossiev, N. 2000. *North-Western Thrace from the 5th to the 1st Centuries B.C.* British Archaeological Reports, International Series. Oxford.

Todorova, H. 1979. *The Eneolithic Period in Bulgaria*. British Archaeological Reports, International Series no. 49. Oxford.

———. 1981. *Die kupferzeitlichen Äxte und Beile in Bulgarien*. Prähistorische Bronzefunde 9, 14. Munich.

Todorova, H., and I. Vaissov. 1993. *Novokamennata epocha v Bulgaria*. Sofia.

Tončeva, G. 1980. *Chronologie du Hallstatt ancien dans la Bulgarie de nord-est*. Studia Thracica no. 5. Sofia.

Totev, T. 1993. *Veliki Preslav: Patevoditel*. Varna.

Vaklinov, S. 1977. *Formirane na starobulgarskata kultura*. Sofia.

Vazharova, Zh. 1976. *Slavjani i prabulgari po danni na nekropolite VI-XI vek na teritorijata na Bulgarija*. Sofia.

———. 1986. *Srednovekovnoto selishte s. Garvan, Silistrenski okr.* Sofia.

Velkov, I. 1930. "Grabhügelfunde aus Duvanlij in Südbulgarien." *Jahrbuch des Deutschen Archäologischen Instituts* 45: 280–322.

———. 1931. "Grabfund von Maltepe." *Archäologischer Anzeiger* 46: 418–422.

———. 1939. "Pliska." *Antiquity* 13: 293–303.

Velkov, V. 1977. *Cities in Thrace and Dacia in Late Antiquity (Studies and Materials)*. Amsterdam.

Venedikov, I. 1987. *The Vulchitrun Treasure*. Sofia.

Venedikov, I., and T. Gerasimov. 1975. *Thracian Art Treasures*. Sofia.

von Bunsen, Christian Karl Josias (1791–1860)

Educated at various German universities in modern, ancient, and original languages; theology; and law, Bunsen joined his mentor Barthold Niebuhr in Rome during the early nineteenth century where Niebuhr was Prussian minister to the Vatican. Bunsen succeeded to this post in 1824 and, with his English wife, made their residence the center of a German cultural milieu in Rome.

Bunsen was also interested in archaeology and art, and during his years in Rome his residence also became a meeting place for artists, archaeologists, and scholars from every country. The sculptor Thorwaldsen, the philosopher Chateaubriand, JEAN-FRANÇOIS CHAMPOLLION, and Leopardi were visitors. Archaeologists such as F. G. Welcker, professor at Bonn and one of the most renowned philologists of the time, Heinrich Panofka, and Eduard Gerhard congregated around Bunsen.

Gerhard was to become the lifetime administrator of the Instituto di Corrispondenza Archeologica (which later became the DEUTSCHES ARCHÄOLOGISCHES INSTITUT). The institute was Bunsen's initiative, conceived as an international organization, whose main task was to improve the knowledge of antiquities among archaeologists and art historians. There was so much being discovered about the past at this time that the institute was responsible for producing a formidable range of regular publications on notable archaeological discoveries. Scholars, collectors, and archaeologists contributed to its publications in the areas of method (academic philology); aesthetics, in the style of JOHANN JOACHIM WINCKELMANN; and the discoveries of the Grand Tour. These publications created a kind of living encyclopedia of archaeology covering all categories and specialties, such as museum catalogues, topographic description, epigraphy, ceramic studies, and iconography.

Bunsen left Rome in 1838. He was Prussian minister to Switzerland until 1841 and then he was minister to England, the most important diplomatic post at the time. He worked hard to improve international relations between Prussia and England, which were strained by the Schleswig-Holstein issue. He also tried to bring Prussia into the alliance against Russia during the Crimean War, and as a result of this he was recalled to Prussia in 1854.

Tim Murray

See also German Classical Archaeology

Bure, Johan (1568–1652)

The son of a pastor in Uppsala, SWEDEN, Bure received a strict classical education. In addition to learning Greek and Latin, Bure taught himself Hebrew. In 1602 he became tutor to Crown Prince Gustavus Adolphus, future king of Sweden, who was one of the great politicians and military leaders of the seventeenth century.

The interest in the antiquities of Rome and Greece that occurred in the more southern parts of Europe and England was matched by an interest in Nordic monuments and antiquities in those countries further to the north. In these countries the history of antiquarianism and that of nationalism are difficult to separate. In the seventeenth century Sweden/Norway and Denmark/Finland were political rivals each with two double monarchies. They were determined to justify their ambitions in Europe by recalling the triumphs of their past. At about the same time antiquaries throughout Europe began to systematically record the monuments and antiquities of their countries and regions and nowhere was this more advanced than in Scandinavia. The decipherment of runes allowed for the reading of the earliest records of the northern kingdoms, and the extensive field surveys revealed monuments that were quickly interpreted as being something to be proud of.

At the court Bure began to decipher Nordic

runes, a script used on the monuments, memorial stones, and artifacts throughout northern Europe, and he was one of the first to collect and systematically analyze these ancient inscriptions. He established a runic alphabet and transcription rules, he proposed a dating system, and he began a collection of Swedish inscriptions. From 1599 Bure and two assistants went on topographic and archaeological surveys, carefully recording and illustrating monuments and ancient examples of runic epigraphy. Bure transformed the antiquarian tour into a systematic study, completing the first professional archaeological survey. He is regarded as one of the founders of landscape archaeology.

Bure's travels and collections were strongly supported by the king of Sweden and in 1630 Gustav Adolphus published a statute protecting Swedish antiquities. Sweden was the first state in the world to not only endow an archaeological service but also to legislate to protect its heritage. As important, for the first time here was evidence and proof of a past that was neither Roman nor Greek and that was recognized as being worthy of protection and study in its own right.

Tim Murray

References
Schnapp, A. 1996. *The Discovery of the Past.* London: British Museum Press.

Bylany
See Czech Republic

Cambodia

The spectacular ruin of Angkor Wat is an enduring icon of Cambodian archaeology and a powerful symbol of national identity. Europeans "discovered" this ruin in the mid-nineteenth century and ultimately attributed it to the ancestors of ethnic Khmers who live in Cambodia today. Cambodia was part of an area historically known as Indochina, a colonial entity controlled by the French from the mid-nineteenth to mid-twentieth centuries. Since French colonial archaeologists who worked in Cambodia also worked in other areas of Indochina, understanding the history of Cambodian archaeology requires some knowledge of the history of archaeology throughout Indochina, including work in the neighboring countries of Vietnam and Laos.

Indochinese archaeology began in earnest during the mid-nineteenth century and reached its apex in the first half of the twentieth century. During this time archaeology was a distinctly colonialist endeavor that was embedded in a broader *mission civilisatrice* (civilizing mission). Archaeology, epigraphy, and art history were undertaken by a host of colonial officials and administrators who believed that research on the cultures and history of this new French colony served as one means of gaining—and maintaining—colonial control over the region.

Since 1850 Cambodian archaeology has been characterized by two parallel archaeological traditions: one rooted in the humanities and the other in the natural sciences. The historical tradition focuses on the ancient civilizations of the region and combines architectural, art-historical, and epigraphic approaches with archaeological methods to study developments since the beginning of the Roman Empire (ca. 500 B.C.–A.D. 1432). The prehistoric tradition, drawing extensively from a geological background, studies the period before about 500 B.C. and has focused most of its attention on Holocene developments that culminated in the Bronze Age.

The Indochinese peninsula, which would ultimately become Vietnam, Cambodia, and Laos, attracted French commercial and missionary interests by the mid-nineteenth century. Despite great resistance by the Vietnamese, the French raised its flags in the southern and northern capitals (Saigon and Hanoi, respectively) by 1873. Cambodia, under a weak sovereign, acceded to the French in 1864, and the feuding kingdoms of Laos were unified between 1885 and 1899. Through military power and fueled by commercial interest, French Indochina was born.

The Impact of Nineteenth-Century Expeditions on European Knowledge of Cambodia's Past

Several important expeditions were undertaken through the new French Indochina during the mid- and late nineteenth centuries to chart its territory, document the resources of the region, and seek potential trade routes to link the colony with markets in southern China. From 1858 to 1861 the French explorer and naturalist Henri Mouhot undertook three natural history expeditions that covered regions of Thailand, Laos, and Cambodia. Mouhot described the customs of the peoples he met during these travels, and in his January 1860 visit to northwestern Cambodia, he encountered the crumbling ruins of Angkor Wat. Mouhot died of a fever near Luang Prabang, Laos, in 1861. Two years later his

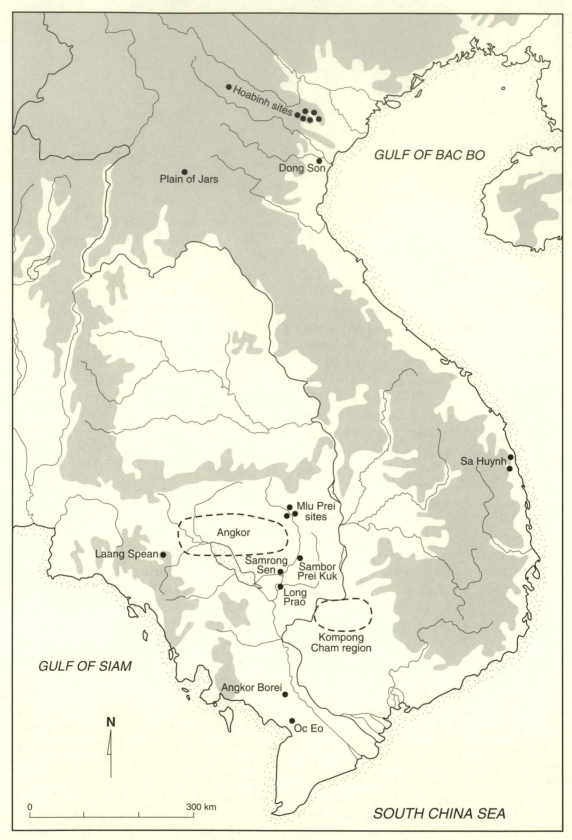

GULF OF BAC BO

Hoabinh sites

Dong Son

Plain of Jars

Sa Huynh

Mlu Prei
sites

Angkor

Laang Spean

Samrong
Sen

Sambor
Prei Kuk

Long
Prao

Kompong
Cham region

GULF OF SIAM

N

Angkor Borei

Oc Eo

SOUTH CHINA SEA

0   300 km

Archaeological Sites in Indochina

Major temple group, Angkor Wat (Courtesy of Miriam Stark)

descriptions of Angkor were published in serial format in *Tour du Monde* in Europe.

Other nineteenth-century expeditions also shed light on Cambodia's archaeological legacy. One of these was the Mekong Exploration Commission's expedition from Saigon up the Mekong River to southern China in 1866, headed by Francis Garnier and Capt. Doudart de Lagrée. Its goals were to find a navigable route from Cochin China to Yunnan and to explore commercial possibilities in the tea and silk markets of southern China. However, the Mekong expedition also included a ten-day survey of the Angkor region. Expedition members copied ancient Khmer inscriptions and took stone sculptures back to FRANCE.

One expedition member, Louis Delaporte, pursued his interest in Angkor by heading the Mission d'Explorations des Monuments Khmers (Mission to explore the Khmer Monuments) in 1873 to document ancient monuments in northwestern Cambodia. His efforts produced scale drawings of Khmer monuments and sculptures and generated evocative illustrations of the Angkorian ruins that captured the European imagination in the Paris Exhibition of 1878. In 1885 Auguste Pavie was appointed by the Cochin Chinese government to establish telegraph lines between southern Vietnam and northwestern Cambodia. Pavie's archaeological research at Angkor and his imaginative essays surrounding this monument proclaimed the glory of this lost civilization, and he contrasted the current (sordid) conditions of the Cambodians with their glorious and vanished past.

We now know that Cambodians had never entirely abandoned the crumbling ruins of Angkor and that the Cambodian state continued (even if in diminished form) until and throughout the French colonial period. We also know that foreigners, both Asian and European, had visited the ruins for centuries before the French; historical and scientific research now suggests that many of Pavie's ideas regarding the Angkorian past lack scientific substance. Yet it was through French expeditions such as those of Mouhot, de Lagrée, and Pavie that images of a glorious and vanished Cambodian past were lodged in the minds of Europeans, whose countries were then colonizing most of Southeast Asia.

Cambodian Archaeology through Nineteenth-Century Research

Investigations also began at archaeological sites throughout the colony during this period. The earliest of these endeavors were carried out by army and naval officers, administrators, and missionaries who lacked formal training in archaeology. They concentrated their efforts in Vietnam (particularly in the north) and in northwestern Cambodia and studied art history, epigraphy, and archaeology. Most work focused on the period that began with the Roman Empire and ended in the European Middle Ages; in Indochina this period is characterized by monumental Khmer and Cham architecture. From 1879 to 1885 Etienne Aymonier undertook his exhaustive study of archaeological sites and Khmer inscriptions throughout Cambodia. Visits to the Cambodian site of Samrong Sen, together with archaeological work conducted there by several notables (e.g., Noulet, Fuchs, Moura, EMILE CARTAILHAC), yielded bronze weapons and tools and established the notion of an Indochinese Bronze Age. In 1886 Gustave Dumoutier and Paul Bert arrived in Hanoi and launched the first systematic archaeological and historical research in Vietnam.

The end of the nineteenth century witnessed a turning point in colonial research on Indochina's archaeological past. This shift was marked by Gen. Paul Doumer's establishment, on December 15, 1898, of a permanent archaeological mission in Indochina. This institution was to be under the control of the Académie des Inscriptions et Belles-Lettres, and its mission was to coordinate all historical, epigraphical, art-historical, and archaeological research in the region. The governor-general then created the Geological Service of Indochina in 1899, headed by Henri Mansuy and M. Lantenois. Most prehistoric archaeological research during the colonial period was done through this institution. In 1901 Louis Finot was appointed the first director of the permanent archaeological mission, which was then renamed the École Française d' Extrême Orient (EFEO).

Louis Finot earned degrees in law and literature before he began his research on Sanskrit and assumed the directorship of EFEO, the institution that would become the premier organization to focus on Indochina's cultural heritage for the rest of the colonial period. Interestingly, few of the early and important EFEO archaeologists had technical training in the field: Lunet de Lajonquière was a military officer, Henri Mansuy had no formal college degree, Louis Bezacier and Henri Parmentier were architects, and Louis Malleret went to Indochina as a language teacher. The field of Southeast Asian studies was so underdeveloped in Europe at the time that even those with professional training (such as Victor Goloubew, whose background lay in art history) had little familiarity with the region before their arrival.

EFEO's explicit goal was to conserve and restore the ruined Khmer and Cham monuments of Indochina; safeguarding monuments that would otherwise be destroyed involved not only their study but also their restoration or conservation. In 1907 France signed a treaty with Siam (Thailand) that assured the return of three western provinces of Cambodia containing Angkor and its associated monuments. In 1908 EFEO launched its systematic program to conserve and restore the monuments of Khmer (and, to a far lesser extent, Cham). EFEO founding directors Louis Finot and Alfred Foucher also established the Service Archéologique as one arm of the institution.

Understanding the history of archaeological research in Cambodia requires a dual focus on developments in both prehistoric and historical archaeology. Colonial archaeological research in these two realms began in earnest in the second decade of the twentieth century and continued vigorously until the outbreak of World War II. The effective end of EFEO archaeological service occurred in 1945, and the French withdrawal from Vietnam in 1954 resulted in the transfer of authority from France to the newly independent countries of Cambodia, Vietnam, and Laos. In Cambodia the period before World War II was the golden age of archaeology; field research ceased altogether by the early 1970s. Archaeological work in Laos also faltered after this time. Vietnam, however, quickly established institutes of archaeology in the north (in Ha Noi) and in the south (in Ho Chi Minh City) and pursued a vigorous program of archaeological research, with a strengthened focus on prehistoric archaeology.

Prehistoric Archaeology in Indochina: 1901–1970

Intellectual influences on prehistoric archaeology derived from the natural sciences, with a strong emphasis on geology and paleontology. The earliest prehistoric archaeological research was undertaken in the late nineteenth century at sites such as Samrong Sen. It was only with the establishment of the Geological Service of Indochina that technical experts (Henri Mansuy, Madeleine Colani, Etienne Patte, Max de Pirey, J. Fromaget, Edmond Saurin) began to grapple with the region's prehistory. The first and most important of these scholars was Mansuy, who helped establish the Geological Service in 1899. His archaeological work at Samrong Sen and Long Prao comprised a small part of his impressive corpus of field research on Pleistocene and Holocene sites in Cambodia, Upper Laos, and northern Vietnam.

In the next three decades prehistoric archaeologists visited and excavated sites throughout Indochina whose occupational period ran from the Paleolithic (Pleistocene) to the Iron Age. The early to middle Holocene was one of the first periods to receive systematic archaeological attention. In the 1920s Madeleine Colani's reconnaissance of caves and rock shelters in northern Vietnam identified a Mesolithic-like tool tradition of early-Holocene age. Named after Hoa Binh Province (in Vietnam) where these sites were originally found, Hoabinhian sites were found in Upper Laos and northern Vietnam. From 1966 to 1968 Roland and Cecile Mourer excavated the Hoabinhian of Laang Spean in northwestern Cambodia in what represents the most systematic prehistoric archaeological work in Cambodia yet published. Vietnamese research on the Hoabinhian since 1960 is too voluminous to report here.

Work by Henri Mansuy in the caves of northern Vietnam, particularly in the mountain range of Bac Son, recovered stone tools and human remains from a late-Hoabinhian/early-Neolithic cultural manifestation that is now called the Bacsonian tradition. The general paucity of "Neolithic" research in Cambodia remains problematic. Bernard-Philippe Groslier's excavations in 1959 at four monuments in the Angkor region uncovered "Neolithic" adzes but did not investigate this time period. During the 1950s and 1960s both Louis Malleret and Groslier worked in eastern Cambodia (in Kompong Cham Province) at circular earthwork sites; work in the 1990s at these sites has produced dates that begin—but do not terminate—in the Neolithic period (i.e., ca. 4000 B.P.).

The next breakthrough in Indochina's prehistoric archaeology focused first on the Iron Age and then on the Bronze Age. In 1909 M. Vinet published the first report of earthenware jar burials in the region of Sa Huynh. Fifteen years later Henri Parmentier published results of archaeological work that included illustrations of jar burials containing cremations, beads, and iron tools recovered from the site of Sa Huynh (in Quang Ngai Province, central Vietnam). In 1934, using results of excavations in the region, Madeleine Colani proposed the term *Sa Huynh culture* for one manifestation of Indochina's Iron Age.

Ancient bronze drums from Southeast Asia were the subject of comparative study by Franz Heger in 1902. In 1924 tax collector L. Pajot reported bronze artifacts that a fisherman found in a riverbank along the Ma River in northern Vietnam. Subsequent EFEO excavations recovered several graves, remains of pile houses, and bronze artifacts, which Victor Goloubew published in 1929. Olov Janse's excavations at Dong Son from 1934 to 1939 recovered bronze drums in stratigraphic context. In 1935 Madeleine Colani reported the recovery of molds for casting bronze tools as part of the megalith culture from Upper Laos, now known as the Plain of Jars.

In Cambodia systematic excavations of Bronze Age sites were restricted to Mansuy's work (published in 1902 and 1921) at Samrong Sen and to

Paul Lévy's work in the late 1930s at three sites in the Mlu Prei region (in Kompong Thom Province). Most bronze objects ascribed to Samrong Sen lack provenance, but Mansuy's work recovered stone adzes, bronze objects, and human remains. Lévy's excavations at Mlu Prei recovered earthenware pottery, bronze tools, and at least one sandstone mold used to cast bronze axes and sickles.

Work by J. Fromaget and Edmond Saurin established the existence of a Paleolithic tradition in the caves and rock shelters of Upper Laos in 1934. Excavations there recovered a middle-Pleistocene animal assemblage and fragments of human bone. That work, together with Saurin's subsequent work on Pleistocene gravel terraces in northeastern Cambodia and Russian archaeologist Pavel Boriskovsky's in northern Vietnam, argued for a Paleolithic "pebble tool" culture in Indochina. The evidence for a Cambodian Paleolithic, offered by Saurin in the mid-1960s, is particularly equivocal, but most archaeologists now believe that humans occupied Indochina during the Pleistocene.

The foregoing summary of prehistoric archaeology in Indochina highlights some of the major developments from 1901 to 1970. A huge number of prehistoric archaeological sites were discovered and excavated during this time. Colonial archaeology made significant contributions, and Vietnamese archaeologists have made great strides in our understanding of Indochina's prehistory. To explain key developments in the prehistoric sequence, colonial archaeologists working throughout Southeast Asia at the time offered a variety of diffusion and migration models, rather than independent invention. It is perhaps intriguing that the adoption of radiocarbon-dating techniques in Indochinese archaeology coincided with the emergence of indigenous archaeologists and the appearance of alternative models that emphasized local development rather than importation from beyond the region.

Historical Archaeology in Indochina: 1901–1970

It might well be said that the history of colonial archaeology in Indochina is the history of Angkorian archaeology. The EFEO's mission was the documentation and protection of archaeological sites, and several scholars made significant contributions to our knowledge of Cham archaeology, notably Henri Parmentier, J.-Y. Claeys, and Louis Bezacier. Nonetheless, Angkor occupied the heart and soul of EFEO, and much of that organization's research focused on the Angkorian and pre-Angkorian periods. The abundance of EFEO research cannot be summarized here; sections that follow use selected examples of archaeological work to illustrate general trends.

The collection of monuments that is often glossed as "Angkor" is found immediately north of the Tonle Sap Lake in northwestern Cambodia. The primary goal of work at Angkor was the conservation of the monuments, and the Conservation d'Angkor was created in 1908 after Siam returned Cambodia's three western provinces. In Phnom Penh, Georges Groslier established the Musée Albert Sarraut in 1920, under the patronage of King Sisowat and (French) Résident Supérior Baudoin. Renamed the National Museum of Cambodia, the institution serves as the repository for Khmer sculptures, inscriptions, and other Cambodian antiquities. The Archaeological Park of Angkor was established in 1926. Henri Marchal and Maurice Glaize, two of Angkor's conservators between 1916 and 1953, introduced the method called "anastylosis" from Dutch conservators in Java. EFEO conservation involved more than engineering and consolidation: it also involved epigraphic research to assign ages to the monuments, compiling archaeological maps (using ground and aerial techniques) to study the construction sequence in different areas, and archaeological work in connection with restoration.

Archaeological research was also undertaken through EFEO activities that involved the location, mapping, and dating of monuments. One aspect of the organization's early mission—documentation—involved a general reconnaissance of archaeological sites to supplement earlier reconnaissance by Etienne Aymonier. Lunet de Lajonquière undertook an archaeological survey from 1900 to 1908 that identified the geographic limits of the Khmer Empire. At its peak the empire extended west into central and

Bas relief from the Temple of Angkor depicting gods (Gamma)

northeast Thailand, north into Laos, east into Vietnam, and south into the Mekong Delta. Within the Angkor region many scholars used inscriptions, architectural and sculptural analysis, and (to a lesser degree) archaeological work to establish a chronology of the monuments. Most notable among these scholars were Georges Coedès, Jean Boisselier, and Pierre Dupont. By the time that France gave judicial powers and technical responsibilities to countries in its former colony in 1951, EFEO had identified 1,256 monuments: 780 in Cambodia, 401 in Vietnam, and 75 in Laos.

Although much effort was devoted to developing the time and space systematics of Angkor, some EFEO archaeological research also explored politics and economics in the Khmer Empire. Victor Goloubew's pioneering use of aerial photography in the 1930s identified road networks radiating out from Angkor and mapped the limits of the expansion by Jayavarman VII, the last of the great Khmer kings, in the twelfth and thirteenth centuries. In 1979 Bernard-Philippe Groslier's "hydraulic city" model, using agricultural and hydrological systems visible in aerial photographs, suggested demographic and ecological limits of the system and reasons for its ultimate demise.

A second focus of EFEO research was the documentation of the pre-Angkorian period of Cambodia and the ancient kingdom of Champa in Vietnam. Henri Parmentier's Cham project, from 1900 to 1904, centered on brick monuments in Cambodia and Vietnam. He contended that many were Cham, but others (and particularly those in the Mekong Delta) represented a pre-Angkorian architectural tradition. Georges Trouvé's conservation efforts at the site of Ak Yom from 1932 to 1935 revealed that the earliest construction of the monument occurred during the seventh century A.D. In 1936 Victor Goloubew used aerial photographic techniques to study the pre-Angkorian site of Banteay Prei Nokor. Such work on the pre-Angkorian period greatly piqued other scholars' interest in that era, which they pursued throughout Indochina.

Systematic archaeological excavations gained importance in the 1940s. From 1942 to 1945 Malleret investigated the pre-Angkorian "Funan" occupation of the Mekong Delta in his ex-

Bas relief of an archer, Angkor Wat (Gamma)

cavations at Oc Eo. From 1952 to 1953 Groslier directed archaeological excavations at the Royal Palace that uncovered a cemetery of cremated remains. In the 1950s both Malleret and Groslier investigated prehistoric circular earthwork sites in eastern Cambodia.

After achieving independence in the 1950s, the three countries of Indochina pursued archaeological work to varying degrees. In Vietnam archaeology served nationalistic interests, and efforts were concentrated on finding the roots of Vietnamese civilization. After 1954 the states of North and South Vietnam established the institutes of archaeology in Hanoi and Ho Chi Minh City, respectively. Archaeological work continued unabated in Vietnam throughout the Vietnam War, although research slowed in both Cambodia and Laos during this time. Conservation activities at Angkor went on, as did the historical and epigraphical research that laid the foundations for archaeological interpretations of the monuments.

Cambodian Archaeology since 1970

A bleak period in Cambodian archaeology began in 1970 with the onset of civil war in the country. All archaeological research activities ceased, and the next five years were plagued by political instability that ultimately forced the closure of the Conservation d'Angkor in 1972, the end of its work in 1973, and the departure of its staff. The Khmer Rouge used Angkor to recall former glory and spared the ruins from the destruction that they wrought on Buddhist temples throughout the country. Angkor was completely abandoned until the end of the Pol Pot regime in 1978, and forces of nature undid much of the clearing work that the EFEO had undertaken to protect the monuments from destruction.

Most of Cambodia's trained archaeologists and technical experts perished between 1975 and 1978 as a result of the Khmer Rouge plan to eliminate the educated elements of society. With the entry of Vietnamese soldiers in 1979 as part of Vietnam's occupation of Cambodia, Angkor's antiquities were pillaged, and Angkorian artifacts (sculpture, architectural elements, other artifacts) flooded the international antiquities market. Only one international team, from India, dared return to Angkor Wat soon after 1979, when fighting between the Vietnamese and the Khmer Rouge continued in the region.

With the Vietnamese withdrawal and the process of reconstruction after 1989, Cambo-

Part of the moat at the vast Angkor Wat temple complex (Hulton Getty)

dian archaeology has witnessed a slow but promising resurgence that began with conservation activities in the Angkor region. Such work has been difficult because fighting between government troops and the Khmer Rouge continued in parts of northern Cambodia for most of the 1990s. Cambodia's legacy of land mines, poor infrastructure, and inadequate transportation routes have also slowed archaeological work of all kinds. Yet the Angkorian past—and Cambodia's cultural heritage—remains an important symbol of nationalism and Khmer ethnic identity. In fact, national pride is a major catalyst behind efforts to resume archaeological work throughout the country and train students in archaeological and conservation techniques.

Much of the archaeological research in Cambodia since 1995 has taken place in collaboration with the Ministry of Culture and Fine Arts, which is responsible for training students in the archaeology department at the Royal University of Fine Arts (RUFA). One example involves the study of the circular earthwork sites of Kompong Cham by international teams of German, Japanese, and U.S. archaeologists working with

RUFA students and faculty members. Their research documents variability in the earthwork sites in order to draw comparisons with sites on the Vietnamese side of the border and develop a chronology of the settlements that were first built around 4000 B.P. Collaborative work at Angkor Borei (in Takeo Province) since 1995 has involved the University of Hawaii's East-West Center and the Royal University of Fine Arts. Research by the Lower Mekong Archaeological Project has established the settlement of this large site in the middle of the first millennium B.C. and has begun to chronicle the region's settlement history before the rise of settlements in Vietnam such as Oc Eo.

New archaeological research directions have also been evident in and around Angkor since the mid-1990s, most obviously in the many applications of remote-sensing data to archaeological questions. The use of remote-sensing data was appealing for several reasons: it offered an alternative to field survey in an area made unsafe, until recently, by land mines, and it also had broad geographic scope. Archaeologists have used remote-sensing data to identify dozens of pre-

Angkorian and possibly prehistoric sites in the region and to document the growth of urban settlement there. Several studies have challenged Groslier's hydraulic city model by analyzing the nature and availability of arable and irrigable land with respect to the giant reservoirs (*baray*) that Bernard-Philippe Groslier believed were used to channel water to fields.

A number of important conservation and restoration projects have begun or resumed at Angkor since 1989. Foremost among the countries sponsoring such efforts is Japan; its United Nations Educational, Scientific, and Cultural Organization (UNESCO) Japanese Trust Fund (Japanese Government Team for Safeguarding Angkor, or JSA) is supporting work at Angkor Wat and Angkor Thom. In addition, Sophia University is conducting research at Banteay Kdei, and EFEO has resumed its work in Angkor Thom after a twenty-year hiatus. Other ongoing projects around Angkor include those sponsored by Hungary, Indonesia, Italy, and the United States (World Monuments Fund). The governmental organization Autorité pour la Protection du Site et l'Aménagement de la Région d'Angkor (APSARA) was created in 1995 to assume responsibility for managing the Angkor area.

Angkor Wat—and Cambodia's archaeological sites in general—are sources of pride, and Cambodians support efforts to study and protect their ancient heritage. Perhaps the most distinctive features of the archaeological work pursued in Cambodia since 1989, be it research or conservation, are its collaborative nature and its commitment to training future generations of Khmer archaeologists. From the late nineteenth century to the mid-twentieth century, colonial-period archaeologists made impressive contributions to our understanding of Indochina's archaeological past. With classroom, field, and professional training programs now in place, the history of Cambodian archaeology in the next century promises to include many contributions by indigenous archaeologists who are studying their own archaeological heritage.

Miriam Stark

References

Bezacier, Louis. 1959. *L'archéologie au Viêt-nam d'après les travaux de L'École Française d'Extrême Orient.* Saigon: France-Asie.

Coedès, Georges. 1951. "Études Indochinoises." *Bulletin de la Société des Études Indochinoises,* n.s., 26, 4: 437–462.

Glover, Ian. 1999. "Letting the Past Serve the Present—Some Contemporary Uses of Archaeology in Viet Nam." *Antiquity* 73: 594–602.

Grousset, René. 1951. "Figures d'Orientalistes." *Bulletin de la Société des Études Indochinoises,* n.s. 26, 4: 413–426.

Higham, Charles. 1996. *The Bronze Age of Southeast Asia.* Cambridge: Cambridge University Press.

Malleret, Louis. 1969. "Histoire abrégée de l'archéologie Indochinoise jusqu'à 1950." *Asian Perspectives* 12: 43–68.

Mourer, Roland. 1994. "Contribution a l'étude de la préhistoire du Cambodge." In *Récherches nouvelles sur le Cambodge,* 143–187. Ed. F. Bizot. Paris: L'École Française d'Extrême Orient.

Saurin, Edmond. 1969. "Les recherches préhistoriques au Cambodge, Laos, et Viet Nam (1877–1966)." *Asian Perspectives* 12: 27–41.

Worman, Eugene C., Jr. 1949. "Samrong Sen and the Reconstruction of Prehistory in Indochina." *Southwestern Journal of Anthropology* 5, 4: 318–329.

Camden, William (1551–1623)

Born in London the son of a painter, William Camden attended St. Paul's School, where he received an excellent classical training, and then proceeded to Oxford. In 1575, he became a master at Westminster School in London, where he taught for the rest of his life.

Camden was the founder of antiquarian studies in England through his immensely influential book *Britannia,* which was first published in 1586, and he brought a wide range of skills to the elucidation of the remote past of his country. Well read in Greek and Roman literature, he was familiar with all the references to Britain made by the ancient historians, geographers, and poets. He was an eminent topographer and had a pronounced interest in coins and inscriptions. He was expert in genealogies and the his-

William Camden (Hulton Getty)

tory of significant families and knowledgeable about the office and ceremonies of state. He became the historian of his own age, writing an important account of the reigns of Elizabeth I and James I, so that by the end of his own life he was not only the master of British antiquity but also the interpreter of the modern political scene.

Britannia broke with the mythologies of British history by taking advantage of the existence of a wide range of well-edited classical texts, the product of a century of humanist scholarship. Camden was persuaded that the people who occupied Britain at the time of the Roman invasions were closely related to the Gauls, whom he was able to identify as a Celtic people. He also examined the origins of the Picts and the Scots. To solve problems of origins and relationships, Camden employed etymology. Already proficient in Greek and Latin, he learned Welsh and studied Anglo-Saxon. He was also particularly attentive to the coinage of the Britons in the first century A.D. But it was the

relating of history to landscape that was the permanent achievement of *Britiannia*. The body of the book took the form of a "perambulation" through the counties of Britain, with Camden offering a many-layered account of each particular region. Camden made a number of field trips to examine monuments and to gather information—he saw more of Britain at first hand than any previous observer.

Six editions of *Britannia* were published between 1586 and 1607, an English translation appeared in 1610 and 1637, and another Latin edition was published in Frankfurt in 1590. The appearance of *Britannia* in 1586 might well have prompted the formation of the SOCIETY OF ANTIQUARIES OF LONDON, which began to meet in that year. It certainly encouraged the growth of antiquarian studies in provincial centers by stimulating local curiosity about the regional past.

Camden enjoyed the friendship of a wide circle of European humanist scholars, such as Scaliger, Ortelius, Lipsius, Hondius, Casaubon, Peiresc, Hotman, and de Thou. Largely through his contacts, English antiquaries of the Jacobean age were linked to their European counterparts.

Graham Parry

References

For references, see *Encyclopedia of Archaeology: The Great Archaeologists, Vol. 1,* ed. Tim Murray (Santa Barbara, CA: ABC-CLIO, 1999), p. 13.

Canada

The border between Canada and the United States slices arbitrarily across North America, and European colonization began north of the border almost as early as to the south. Yet, for climatic and geological reasons, European settlement progressed more slowly in Canada, and the bulk of the country's population remained concentrated near the border. The surface area of Canada is larger than that of the United States, but Canada is only about one-tenth as populous. Because of this and related political factors, archaeology has developed in Canada more slowly and somewhat differently than it has in the United States.

Antiquarian Beginnings

It is recorded that Indian stone tools were dug up in the course of construction work in southern QUEBEC at various times during the seventeenth century. In 1700, workmen unearthed some magnificent ground slate projectile points at Bécancour. These finds, now known to date from the Archaic period (3000–2000 B.C.), were preserved at the Ursuline convent in nearby Trois-Rivières and constitute Canada's oldest archaeological collection.

In the first half of the nineteenth century, farmers and other interested British colonists in southern Ontario and the Maritimes began to assemble private collections of Indian artifacts. Relic hunters also pillaged Indian burial sites to recover such materials. Only brief accounts of these activities were recorded in local newspapers and British journals.

The most sustained archaeological work of this period was initiated by two Jesuit priests soon after members of that order returned to Quebec in 1842. Father Jean-Pierre Chazelle identified the stone ruins of two seventeenth-century Jesuit missions in southern Ontario, and following in his footsteps, first Father Felix Martin and then Professor Joseph-Charles Tache of the University of Laval explored the Huron Indian sites around these missions. Apart from this work, there was little concern with archaeology in French-speaking Quebec. Unlike English Canadian farmers, French Canadian ones were uninterested in the artifacts they unearthed in the course of their farming operations.

After 1853, two leading Canadian scholars studied and wrote about archaeology. DANIEL WILSON, a Scottish archaeologist who eventually became president of the University of Toronto, and John William Dawson, a Nova Scotian geologist who was principal of McGill University in Montreal. Both did archaeological work in Canada in the 1850s and early 1860s, and Wilson asserted that his ambition was to become "a Canadian antiquary." Yet both men's interests soon became more broadly anthropological. Despite their many anthropological publications that incorporated archaeological data, neither of these eminent scholars made a tangible contribution to the development of archaeology in Canada.

Throughout the nineteenth century, Canadians remained largely preoccupied with practical matters, and it was expected that gifted individuals would apply their talents to public life. Pursuits such as archaeology were not viewed as suitable full-time occupations for men of ability. Academics were few in number and so deeply involved in political and religious controversies that they had little time for archaeology.

Even so, in the second half of the nineteenth century, natural history, literary, and historical societies were founded, or became more active, in Montreal, Toronto, Halifax, and St. John, New Brunswick. These societies played a major role in drawing their members' attention to archaeological developments in Europe and the United States, and their journals made possible the publication of archaeological research. In 1863, members of the Nova Scotian Institute of Natural Science were inspired to excavate local shell mounds by the Swiss archaeologist Adolf Morlot's report of Danish shell-mound investigations published in the widely distributed *Annual Report of the Smithsonian Institution* for 1860. In 1884, the Natural History Society of New Brunswick published George Matthew's account of a stratified shell midden at Bocabec, New Brunswick; the best excavation carried out by a Canadian in the nineteenth century. Although numerous studies of the archaeology of the Maritime Provinces were published locally in the late nineteenth century, no specifically archaeological positions were established in universities or museums in that part of Canada. In Quebec, only a small number of archaeological studies were published, mainly by English-speaking residents of Montreal. A few brief notes on archaeological finds appeared in *Le Naturaliste Canadien* in the 1880s.

Developments of more lasting importance for Canadian archaeology centered on the Canadian Institute (later the Royal Canadian Institute) founded in Toronto in 1849 by provincial land surveyors and other professionals wishing to promote the advancement of the natural sciences and the arts. In 1852, the institute issued a circular drafted by Sandford Fleming, civil engineer and future inventor of standard time, urging the reporting of Indian sites that

Steep cliffs stand at the area of Head-Smashed-in Buffalo Jump in Alberta, Canada. Here Native Americans hunted and killed buffalo by driving the panic-stricken beasts over the cliff edge, producing a huge buffalo graveyard. (Paul A. Souders/Corbis)

were thought likely to be found in large numbers as a result of the building of railway lines. Daniel Wilson contributed numerous general articles about Canadian and European archaeology to the institute's *Canadian Journal,* which was founded in 1852, including a plea for the formation of a collection of prehistoric crania.

In 1884, William Boyle, a Scottish-born schoolteacher and bookstore owner, became the archaeological curator at the Canadian Institute Museum and incorporated his own extensive collection of Indian artifacts into that institution. In 1887, he received a small salary from funds supplied by the Ontario government, which made him the first professional archaeologist in Canada. The same year Boyle began editing the *Annual Archaeological Report* for Ontario, which continued to be published until 1928. This was Canada's first archaeological journal. When Boyle died in 1911, the archaeological material he had collected, and which had been moved to the Ontario Provincial Museum

in 1897, consisted of 32,000 artifacts from across southern Ontario. Boyle classified these finds according to provenience, material, and assumed use. He developed a close working relationship with the professional archaeologists at the Smithsonian Institution in Washington, D.C., and trained a small group of amateur archaeologists to carry out investigations across Ontario. The most successful of these was Andrew Hunter, who recorded 637 sites in Simcoe County (the location of the Jesuits' seventeenth-century Huron missions), assigning them, according to the presence or absence of European goods, to either prehistoric or historical times.

European settlement and archaeology began considerably later west of Ontario. The first burial mounds were recorded in Manitoba in 1867, and in the 1880s and 1890s, there was growing interest in these mounds on the part of local amateur archaeologists and visiting scientists who generally interpreted them in terms of

American opinions about the Mound Builders. Farther west, archaeological material was collected in the 1890s by geologists and surveyors from eastern Canada, many of them working for the Geological Survey of Canada. At this time, resident amateur archaeologists also began to study the Indian burials, middens, and the rock art of British Columbia.

Canadian archaeologists generally viewed Indians in the same way U.S. evolutionary anthropologists did: as peoples whose cultures were very primitive and therefore prehistorically must have been similar to what they were like at the time of European discovery. As a result, these archaeologists saw no need to try to work out elaborate chronologies. In Canada, the successful government efforts, after the Indians ceased to be useful allies against the United States, to move them as quietly as possible onto reserves or to more remote parts of the country meant that Indians did not loom large in the experience or imagination of most Euro-Canadians. In the United States, as prolonged and violent confrontations with aboriginal peoples came to an end, Indians were appropriated by their conquerors as romantic symbols of republican freedom, a theme that had little appeal for Canadians. As a result of these developments, there was far less pressure on governments in Canada than there was in the United States to devote public funds to prehistoric archaeological research.

The little interest that Canadians had in prehistoric archaeology waned in the early twentieth century. It was virtually extinct in the Maritimes by 1919, partly as a consequence of the economic decline of that region, and there was also diminishing interest in Manitoba, British Columbia, and Ontario as the broader concern to study Canada's past that had arisen following confederation in 1867 subsided. No provincial government provided the means for training archaeologists or employment for them. Even the position of provincial archaeologist in Ontario lapsed after Boyle's mediocre successor died in 1933.

In 1897, the Jesup North Pacific Expedition of the American Museum of Natural History began archaeological work in coastal British Co-

lumbia. This was the first of many foreign (mainly U.S. and Scandinavian) expeditions that carried out archaeological research in Canada, and in particular, they added to an understanding of Arctic prehistory. Although some of these expeditions provided Canadian archaeologists with opportunities to do fieldwork, others contributed nothing to the institutional development of Canadian archaeology and even retarded it by removing artifacts from Canada. Although such incursions into southern Canada had largely ceased the end of the century foreign expeditions continue to be authorized in northern Canada.

The Belated Development of Prehistoric Archaeology

A new phase in Canadian archaeology began in 1910 when the Geological Survey of Canada established an Anthropology Division. For many years, scientists attached to the survey had been collecting archaeological and ethnological material in western Canada, and pressure from a small number of Canadian amateur anthropologists and from the British Association for the Advancement of Science finally resulted in the allocation of government funds to this unit. Its first director was Edward Sapir, a young U.S. linguistic anthropologist who had studied with Franz Boas at Columbia University in New York City. Within two years, Sapir had hired Harlan Smith, a middle-aged U.S. archaeologist who had worked for the Jesup Expedition in British Columbia, and William Wintemberg, an amateur archaeologist from Ontario who had assisted Boyle. Working together in Ontario and Nova Scotia, Smith taught Wintemberg how to excavate and write site reports, with an emphasis on the functional interpretation of artifacts. Thereafter, despite frail health, Wintemberg carried out surveys and excavations in Newfoundland (not yet part of Canada), New Brunswick, and on the prairies while Smith continued to concentrate on British Columbia.

Wintemberg's most important research was done in southern Ontario, where he worked out a rough chronology of Iroquoian cultural development. Yet, so great was his isolation from mainstream U.S. archaeology, it was only shortly before his death in 1941 that he became aware of the culture-historical approach that had been developing in the United States since 1914. He is credited with stimulating the development of amateur archaeology in Saskatchewan, where the Saskatoon Archaeological Society was founded in 1935 and the Regina Archaeological Society was founded in 1943. In Ontario, Wintemberg inspired Wilfrid Jury to become a self-trained archaeologist in the Boyle tradition.

In the United States, during the Great Depression of the 1930s, federal relief agencies looking for ways to create temporary jobs supported a vast program of archaeological research that enabled archaeologists to work out detailed cultural chronologies for large areas of the country. This data base laid the foundations for the development of processual archaeology in the 1960s. In Canada, the underfunding of archaeological research continued through the first half of the twentieth century. Part of the problem was the low priority assigned to archaeological research by Diamond Jenness, the New Zealand-born ethnologist who, in 1925, succeeded Sapir as director of the Anthropology Division. Although Jenness had identified the prehistoric Dorset culture of northern Canada on the basis of archaeological collections in Ottawa and had excavated in Alaska, he maintained that it was more important to record the vanishing cultures and languages of contemporary aboriginal peoples than it was to excavate prehistoric remains, which he mistakenly believed would be safe in the ground for centuries. Even if the Canadian government had been willing and constitutionally able to sponsor archaeological research on a large scale during the 1930s, there would not have been enough archaeologists in Canada to direct such work. As a consequence, when a map entitled "Archaeological Areas of North America" was published in 1947, most of Canada had no areas marked on it.

The period following World War II was one of rapidly growing population and unprecedented economic prosperity that lasted into the 1970s. Slowly at first and then with explosive rapidity in the 1960s, government and university administrators sought to enhance their power and influence and to meet the growing expectations of various segments of the Canadian public by expanding the structures they controlled. As a result, many archaeologists were appointed to research and teaching positions across Canada. In the mid-1950s, fewer than 10 archaeologists were employed in Canada; by 1976, there were over 140.

The first prehistoric archaeology course taught at a Canadian university was offered by Phileo Nash in the Anthropology Department at the University of Toronto in 1938. The first enduring program to train archaeologists began in that department following the appointment, in 1947, of Norman Emerson, a Chicago-trained Canadian who mainly researched Iroquoian prehistory. In 1949, Charles Borden, a professor of German who had become interested in prehistoric archaeology, began offering courses at the University of British Columbia. In 1960, William J. Mayer-Oakes, an American who had taught at the University of Toronto, began an archaeological teaching and research program at the University of Manitoba, and in the same year, archaeology courses were offered at the University of Montreal.

The Glenbow Foundation began sponsoring archaeological research in Alberta beginning in 1955, which aroused interest in archaeology in that province. In 1963, Alan Bryan and Ruth Gruhn started to teach prehistoric archaeology at the University of Alberta, and in the following year, Richard S. MacNeish and Richard Forbis founded the first Department of Archaeology in North America at the University of Calgary. That department was to specialize in New World archaeology, for MacNeish and Forbis were convinced that archaeology had become a discipline with enough knowledge of its own to justify specialized training. A second archaeology department was started in 1971 at Simon Fraser University in British Columbia as a result of an acrimonious breakup of a larger social science unit. During the 1960s, archaeology was also taught in anthropology departments across Canada.

Until the 1960s, there were no coherent programs to train archaeology graduate students in Canada. Many Canadians interested in archaeology studied at U.S. universities, especially the University of Chicago, Yale University, and the University of Wisconsin. As academic positions opened up in Canada, many of these individuals returned, but there were not enough Canadians with doctorates to fill all the new positions. There was therefore an influx of a large number of U.S. archaeologists into Canada, and many of them continued to hold key university positions for many years. Calgary provided the majority of Canadian-trained archaeological Ph.D.s beginning in the late 1960s, along with the University of Toronto and, later, Simon Fraser University. At first, most of these graduates were able to secure academic positions, but ironically, by the mid-1970s, when graduate programs in prehistoric archaeology were in place in universities across Canada, few academic positions were available for the archaeologists trained by those programs.

The largest single employer of prehistoric archaeologists after 1945 continued to be the Archaeology Division of the National Museum of Canada, which had separated from the Geological Survey of Canada in 1920. These archaeologists played an active role in carrying out fieldwork across Canada, and the division further encouraged research by means of a contracting system started when William E. Taylor, Jr., was director. Between 1960 and the mid-1970s, the division poured over $1 million into some 250 projects, many cosponsored by universities. Thus, the National Museum played an important role in stimulating the study of Canadian archaeology. Unfortunately, funds for this operation were severely curtailed as a result of government cutbacks in 1969, and by the mid-1970s, the activities of the division's archaeologists were generally confined to federal lands (all of the Northwest and Yukon Territories, airports, harbors, etc.), which meant that alternative funding had to be found for archaeology on lands under provincial jurisdiction.

In 1967, the National Museums of Canada Corporation established a National Museum of Man, with William E. Taylor, Jr., as its director. In 1971, the Archaeological Survey of Canada was established within this museum to oversee the preservation of archaeological sites on federal lands, encourage research into Canadian prehistory, and inform the public about archaeological findings. One of the survey's most important creations was the publication the Mercury Series, which, beginning in 1972, distributed free copies of significant theses, conference papers, and research reports dealing with Canadian archaeology until it, too, fell victim to cutbacks.

The most important task facing Canadian archaeologists after 1945 was to construct cultural chronologies for the whole country. This was a severe challenge, since many areas were remote from research institutions, difficult to travel in, and could be studied only during short summer seasons. The National Museum was active in encouraging and funding research, and archaeologists employed there, such as Richard S. MacNeish, James V. Wright, and William Taylor, played a major role in constructing cultural sequences across northern Canada. Archaeologists employed in universities and museums in southern Canada began to elaborate the cultural chronologies of their respective regions as well as working in the north.

There was also growing public interest in archaeology, which led to the establishment of provincial archaeological societies. The Ontario Archaeological Society was founded in 1950, and others were established in Alberta, Manitoba, Saskatchewan, Quebec, and British Columbia between 1960 and 1966. In 1968, the Canadian Archaeological Association was founded. Modeled on the Society for American Archaeology, this association sought to embrace the interests and concerns of everyone who was investigating the archaeology of Canada. Its journal, the *Canadian Journal of Archaeology / Journal Canadien d'Archéologie,* publishes articles on all aspects of Canadian archaeology but primarily those relating to prehistory.

By the 1970s, cultural chronologies for most areas of Canada had been at least provisionally sketched out. The principal chronological question that remained unanswered was whether human beings had lived in any part of Canada prior to the end of the last Ice Age. Despite the great effort invested in the research that William Irving and Richard Morlan carried out in the Old Crow region of the Yukon and in other studies, no satisfactory resolution of this problem has been achieved.

As chronologies for more recent periods were better understood, archaeologists began to seek a more detailed understanding of the factors that accounted for change over time. In some fields, such as the study of Iroquoian prehistory, where Canadian archaeologists initiated extensive site surveys and began to excavate entire habitation sites, both the scale and the quality of archaeological research came to surpass what was being done in adjacent parts of the United States.

A survey carried out by Roy Carlson in 1973 indicated that the most widely shared interest of archaeologists working in Canada was the study of cultural history, and an analysis of the *Canadian Journal of Archaeology* reveals that 67 percent of the articles published in that journal between 1988 and 1992 dealt with culture history while about 40 percent exhibited an interest in ecology. The preoccupation with recovering primary data and building cultural chronologies tended to insulate Canadian archaeology from the impact that processual archaeology had in the United States during the 1960s. Most U.S. archaeologists who found employment in Canada and Canadians who had studied in the United States had received their training prior to the rise of processual archaeology, and some were inclined to be hostile or indifferent to the new movement; others embraced it.

In general, however, the demands of archaeological research in Canada and the agenda set by the National Museum tended to dilute the impact of the movement. Many Canadian archaeologists became genuinely interested in the ecological approaches advocated by processual archaeology, but most of them rejected its antihistoricism, extreme positivism, and privileging of a deductive methodology. This espousal of an eclectic, middle-of-the-road approach appears to have been more than a result of the late development of archaeological research in Canada or of the proverbial Canadian penchant for compromise. Theorists such as Gordon Lowther, Alison Wylie, Marsha Hanen, Jane Kelley, and Bruce Trigger have formulated philosophical underpinnings for such an approach that involve a blend of relativism and empiricism, which appears to be increasingly marketable abroad as postmodern trends impact on archaeology everywhere.

A major challenge confronting archaeologists working in Canada today is to establish effective working relations with indigenous peoples, who are increasingly determined to control their cultural heritage and securing the legal right to do so. Many native people object on religious grounds to the excavation of burial sites and places where their ancestors lived. Others see archaeology as enhancing an understanding of aboriginal history and culture. The Canadian Archaeological Association is seeking to develop cooperative agreements and principles of conduct to govern relations between archaeologists and the indigenous peoples. On the whole, such discussions have been productive, although it is clear that archaeology is going to have to change to address issues of major concern to aboriginal people. These issues generally relate to the recent past and favor a combination of archaeology, ethnology, and oral history that recent generations of ecologically inclined archaeologists have tended to ignore. A more contentious legal issue is whether public ownership of the archaeological record is vested in the government or belongs to native peoples.

Historical Archaeology

Historical archaeology, which is concerned primarily with sites relating to European settlement in Canada, began in the 1890s when Chazelle relocated the two Jesuit mission sites in southern Ontario. For a long time there was little more than an interest in identifying the locations of buildings and major events associated with the early colonization of eastern Canada. In 1919, the federal government created the Historic Sites and Monuments Board, which commemorated but did not have the power to protect such sites. The first scientific excavation of a historical site was carried out between 1941 and 1943 by Kenneth Kidd of the Royal Ontario Museum at the larger and earlier of the Jesuit mission sites that Chazelle had identified. The excavation of this site was completed between 1947 and 1951 by Wilfrid Jury, after which Sainte-Marie Among the Hurons was reconstructed as a tourist attraction by the Ontario government. Kidd's monograph on that site was a milestone in the early development of historical archaeology in North America.

Historical archaeology tended to interest the Canadian public more than prehistoric archaeology, and governments viewed the reconstruction of historical sites as a way to encourage tourism, especially in poorer areas of the country. In 1961, the federal government established the Canadian Historic Sites Service (now the Archaeology Division of the Canadian Parks Service) with John Rick as senior archaeologist. This service was intended to encourage the excavation of historic sites as well as their reconstruction for historical and recreational purposes. Among the numerous projects that provided cultural images for Euro-Canadians were the excavation and rebuilding of the French fortress of Louisbourg in Nova Scotia and the Viking settlement at L'Anse aux Meadows in Newfoundland. Between 1962 and 1966, six research positions were added to the service and large amounts of contract funding were made available by the federal government. In more recent years, there has also been growing interest in industrial archaeology, which is supported by conservation groups.

For a long time, the Historic Sites Service and the Archaeological Survey of Canada tended to divide the work according to whether sites dated from the historical or prehistoric periods. Because of the specialized skills required to carry out historical archaeology, many of the original archaeologists attached to the Historic Sites Service were recruited from abroad. They had little interest in prehistoric archaeology and initially had few connections with the existing archaeological community. After the merger with Parks Canada, a growing number of Historic Sites Service archaeologists were knowledgeable about prehistoric as well as historical archaeology. The archaeology departments at Calgary and Simon Fraser Universities were generally more willing to train historical archaeologists than were anthropology departments, which remained focused on prehistoric

archaeology, but Canada still does not have a major center for educating historical archaeologists. Individuals who were trained in prehistoric archaeology but have done major work on historical sites include the late Walter Kenyon of the Royal Ontario Museum and James Tuck at Memorial University of Newfoundland. The Canadian Parks Service issues its own publications dealing with historical archaeology, and relatively few articles on this subject appear in the *Canadian Journal of Archaeology*.

Heritage Management

The oldest heritage legislation in Canada is the British Columbia Historic Objects Preservation Act of 1925, which was designed primarily to prohibit the removal of rock carvings and other aboriginal artifacts from that province. Between 1954 and 1980, expanding provincial government bureaucracies, following the examples of other countries, passed heritage acts to provide legal protection for cultural resources and allocated funds to conserve and manage them. The powers granted to regulatory bodies included requiring assessments of archaeological potential in advance of land use, licensing archaeological activities, and the obligatory reporting of the findings of archaeological research. The implementation of the legislation varied according to the strength of the provincial legislation, the will of the provincial governments to enforce it, and the highly variable resources of the different provinces.

Federal antiquities legislation, though not integrated in a single body of law applying to all contexts, is incorporated within several acts, the principal ones being the Canada Environmental Assessment Act and the Canadian Cultural Property Export and Import Act. The drafting of comprehensive legislation has been impeded by interdepartmental jurisdictional disputes and by the refusal of some aboriginal peoples to acknowledge government ownership of archaeological remains.

The growth of archaeological resource management provided two new categories of employment for archaeologists. A significant number of civil service posts were created within government departments to deal with a mixture of administrative and salvage activities. Much of the fieldwork and report writing associated with resource management now is done through contracting, which has led archaeologists to establish private consulting firms for this purpose. Since the early 1980s, as employment in universities, museums, and governments has become hard to find, these firms have provided most of the jobs available to young archaeologists. At present, cultural resource archaeologists generally are better funded and are carrying out more excavations in Canada than are university and museum archaeologists.

Archaeology Abroad

Early in the twentieth century, a few Canadians began to do archaeological work abroad. The most famous was the Peking-based physician Davidson Black, who in 1927 identified *Sinanthropus pekinensis* (Peking Man) and was involved in the excavations at Zhoukoudien until his death in 1934. The Canadian School of Prehistoric Research, a privately funded institution founded in 1925 by the geologist Henry Ami, carried out Paleolithic excavations in France into the 1930s. Amice Calverley, who began to work for the EGYPT EXPLORATION SOCIETY in 1927, copied the reliefs of the Temple of Seti I at Abydos and published them between 1933 and 1959.

The person who had the greatest impact on Canadian archaeology done abroad was Charles Currelley, who excavated in Egypt for the Egypt Exploration Fund from 1902 to 1907, originally as an assistant to W. M. F. PETRIE, before becoming the first director of the Royal Ontario Museum of Archaeology when it was established in Toronto in 1912. This museum, which absorbed the old Ontario Provincial Museum, was to become a major center for archaeological research both within Ontario and outside Canada. Homer Thompson, who held appointments at both the University of Toronto and the Royal Ontario Museum beginning in 1933, was a key member of the AMERICAN SCHOOL OF CLASSICAL STUDIES' project to excavate and restore the Agora in Athens. A. D. Tushingham, who moved from Queen's University to the Royal Ontario Museum in 1955, remains active in biblical archaeology.

Since 1945, archaeologists employed at the Royal Ontario Museum have excavated in IRAN, Iraq, GREECE, Egypt, the Sudan, BELIZE, and other countries. Some of the excavations have been carried out in collaboration with other institutions, and Royal Ontario Museum archaeologists have participated in research organized by other groups. Often work has continued at the same site or in the same region for many years. This research, together with studies of the vast Chinese collections assembled during Currelley's directorship, has made the Royal Ontario Museum Canada's most important center for archaeology abroad. It has also played an important role in encouraging the development of classical, Near Eastern, and Egyptian archaeology at the University of Toronto.

Since 1960, a substantial number of archaeologists who do research abroad have found employment across Canada in university departments of anthropology, archaeology, classics, history, Near Eastern studies, art history, and religion. By the mid-1970s, these archaeologists outnumbered university-based archaeologists studying Canada by more than two to one. In 1961, the federal government supplied funding for a Canadian expedition, led by Philip Smith, that carried out prehistoric research as part of the UNESCO Campaign to Save the Monuments of NUBIA. Since then, research abroad has been greatly facilitated by federal government funds supplied through the Canada Council and the Social Sciences and Humanities Research Council of Canada. This peer-reviewed funding, which takes the form of major grants extending over a number of years, is available for projects both inside and outside Canada and has supported archaeological research in many parts of the world.

Important archaeological projects have been carried out by classical archaeologists from the University of Toronto, the University of Alberta, McMaster University, McGill University, the University of British Columbia, and the University of Laval. Egyptian archaeology has been vigorously pursued by archaeologists from the University of Toronto, while the University of Calgary has become a center for African archaeology. Possibly the most publicized Canadian work done abroad is Donald Redford's excavations in Egypt at Karnak East in connection with the Akhenaton Temple Project. The Canadian Archaeological Institute at Athens and the Canadian Academic Centre in Italy were both established in 1978, and the Canadian Institute in Egypt was founded two years later. All three institutes facilitate archaeological research in these countries under the aegis of the Canadian Mediterranean Institute. At present, the future of this institute, and of all Canadian archaeology done abroad, is seriously threatened by continuing cutbacks in federal funding.

Despite shared methodological interests, there are few professional contacts between Canadian archaeologists excavating inside Canada and those working abroad, except at the Royal Ontario Museum or in university archaeology or anthropology departments. There is also little interaction among archaeologists studying different parts of the world. The Canadian Society for Archaeology Abroad, founded in 1969 to represent the interests of these archaeologists, has ceased to exist. Archaeologists researching abroad who do maintain contacts with archaeologists working inside Canada frequently share an anthropological interest in ecological studies and in reconstructing social life while those with a more humanistic orientation tend to avoid such contacts. This situation reinforces a division between anthropological and humanistic archaeologists, who in Canada, as in the United States, remain psychologically as well as disciplinarily isolated from one another. One bridge between these two groups is the multifaceted, Toronto-centered Dakhla Oasis Project, which has brought together both sorts of archaeologists to study the culture history of that region of Egypt from prehistoric times to the Christian period.

Conclusion

In Canada, archaeology does not constitute a single discipline or even a shared approach to studying the past. Prehistoric archaeology, as it relates both to North America and to the rest of the world, is generally located in the anthropology or archaeology departments of universities. The two Canadian archaeology departments were founded by anthropological archaeologists, and the departments share an anthropological orientation. Historical archaeology is generally taught in archaeology departments; yet, despite its importance as a practice, its institutionalization in Canadian universities remains weak. The archaeology of the literate civilizations of the Mediterranean world and the Near East is more likely to be studied in departments of classics and Near Eastern studies.

In museums, the situation is quite different. Most of them employ only archaeologists who study the history and prehistory of Canada. The one important exception is the Royal Ontario Museum, which has a large staff representing in its various departments and cross-appointments with the University of Toronto all the branches of archaeology. This is the only archaeological unit in Canada in which both the anthropological and the humanistic traditions of archaeology are substantially represented. There is no society or journal in Canada that embraces the work of all archaeologists. Proposals for formal cooperation between Canadian anthropological and humanistic archaeologists have elicited no positive response.

The relations between prehistoric archaeology and anthropology are looser in Canada than in the United States. There is no overall anthropological association, as the Canadian Anthropology Society is a grouping of social anthropologists. Archaeologists working in anthropology departments have long complained that the numerical domination of these departments by social anthropologists has kept the number of prehistoric archaeologists employed in universities low. It has also hindered the hiring of archaeologists who specialize in technical analysis, which in turn has lowered the quality of archaeological training in such departments. Even so, most prehistoric archaeologists remain unwilling to abandon their ties with anthropology, and even those who work in archaeology departments see their main interests and orientation as being anthropological. Yet a growing number of archaeologists who have found employment in cultural resource archaeology, and therefore tend to be interested exclusively in Canadian archaeology, seem to be discarding this academic loyalty to anthropology.

The basic cultural chronologies were worked out in most parts of Canada in the 1960s, at a time when archaeology was considerably more developed technically than it had been when cultural chronologies were established in the United States in the 1920s and 1930s. Canadian prehistoric archaeologists also faced the formidable task of studying a large, cold, and thinly populated country that in prehistoric times was inhabited by relatively low density, hunter-gatherer populations. As a result, regardless of their disciplinary origins, these archaeologists have shared a distinctive challenge and adopted a theoretical orientation that some U.S. archaeologists have recognized as distinctive (Binford 1989, 7).

Still, as funding has become increasingly the responsibility of provincial and local authorities, Canadian archaeology has been characterized by growing regional isolation. The publications and annual meetings of the Canadian Archaeological Association have not provided the common direction and unity of purpose that was once supplied by the National Museum. No comprehensive account of Canadian prehistory existed until the publication of the first volume of the *Historical Atlas of Canada* in 1987, and its prehistoric section was largely the work of archaeologists employed by the Archaeological Survey of Canada. Books synthesizing the whole of Canadian prehistory are only now being written. Lacking a firm center or a clear image of itself, Canadian archaeology often seems to be disintegrating into a number of marginal and rather ill-favored pieces of the North American cultural mosaic. Yet, as in other aspects of Canadian life, a shared approach may in the long run more than compensate for a lack of organization and common purpose.

Bruce G. Trigger

Acknowledgments
The author thanks Jane H. Kelley and David B. Burley for their comments.

References
Binford, L. R. 1989. *Debating Archaeology.* San Diego: Academic Press.

Burley, D. V. 1994. "A Never Ending Story: Historical Developments in Canadian Archaeology and the Quest for Federal Heritage Legislation." *Canadian Journal of Archaeology* 18: 77–134.

Carlson, R. L. 1973. "The Discipline of Archaeology in Canada: An Interim Report to the Canada Council." Manuscript.

Connolly, John. 1977. "Archaeology in Nova Scotia and New Brunswick between 1863 and 1914 and Its Relationship to the Development of North American Archeology." *Man in the Northeast* 13: 3–34.

Dickson, L. 1986. *The Museum Makers: The Story of the Royal Ontario Museum.* Toronto: Royal Ontario Museum.

Forbis, R. G., and W. C. Noble. 1988. "Archaeology." In *Canadian Encyclopedia,* 2d ed., 1: 91–94. Edmonton: Hurtig.

Jenness, D. 1932. "Fifty Years of Archaeology in Canada." *Royal Society of Canada Anniversary Volume, 1882–1932.* Toronto: Royal Society of Canada.

Kelley, J. H., and R. F. Williamson. 1993. "Archaeology in the 90s: A Canadian Perspective." Manuscript.

Killan, G. 1983. *David Boyle: From Artisan to Archaeologist.* Toronto: University of Toronto Press.

McKay, A. G., ed. 1976. *New Perspectives in Canadian Archaeology.* Ottawa: Royal Society of Canada.

Martin, P. S., G. I. Quimby, and D. Collier 1947. *Indians before Columbus.* Chicago: University of Chicago Press.

Noble, W. C. 1972. "One Hundred and Twenty-five Years of Archaeology in the Canadian Provinces." *Canadian Archaeological Association Bulletin* no. 4: 1–78. (Truncated and abridged version in *The Development of North American Archaeology,* pp. 49–83. Ed. J. E. Fitting. Garden City, NY: Anchor Books, 1973.)

Trigger, B. G. 1978. "William J. Wintemberg: Iroquoian Archaeologist." In *Essays in Northeastern Anthropology in Memory of Marian E. White,* pp. 5–21. Ed. W. E. Engelbrecht and D. K. Grayson. Occasional Publications in Northeastern Anthropology, no. 5. Rindge, NH: Department of Anthropology, Franklin Pierce College.

Wright, J. V. 1985. "The Development of Prehistory in Canada, 1935–1985." *American Antiquity* 50: 421–433.

Caribbean

In 1963, French West Indian archaeologists initiated a series of biennial meetings called the International Congress for the Study of Pre-Columbian Cultures of the Lesser Antilles (Map 1). Over the next decades, so many specialists in the prehistory of the rest of the West Indies, Venezuela, and the Guianas began to attend these meetings that the name was changed to the Congress for Caribbean Archaeology.

The term *Caribbean* is not used in this context to the refer to the entire Caribbean basin but to a culture area that existed in the eastern half of the basin during pre-Columbian times (Willey 1971, 360–393). The western half of the basin formed a separate intermediate area, called that because it lay between the centers of civilization in MEXICO and PERU (Map 2). Few intermediate-area specialists come to the Caribbean congresses; they have little incentive to participate because the problems they study differ from those in the eastern half of the basin.

During prehistoric times, the two areas constituted separate interaction spheres (Caldwell 1966, 338), kept apart because the people living there were unable to travel back and forth across the Caribbean Sea. The inhabitants of the two spheres developed differently because they were unable to exchange artifacts, customs, and beliefs. Christopher Columbus's introduction of European ships, capable of traveling on the high seas, remedied this difficulty and made possible a single circum-Caribbean sphere, with its own set of problems.

This article focuses on the Caribbean sphere and its problems, but it is not entirely limited to pre-Columbian times. It also covers the disappearance of the native peoples as they came into contact with European, African, and Asian immigrants. It thus includes the indigenous side of the so-called Columbian exchange of cultural, linguistic, and biological traits that took place in the circum-Caribbean sphere (Crosby 1972).

Research within these limits has progressed through a sequence of four stages, during which the participants expanded to increasingly high levels of abstraction, each made possible by the results achieved on the previous levels. The initial stage may be called that of artifactual research because it was marked by the discovery, collection, and interpretation of structures and manufactures. In the second stage, chronological research, Caribbeanists began to organize their finds into systems of areas, periods, and ages. In the ensuing stage of culture-historical research, they used those systems to differentiate human populations or peoples, each with its own distinctive culture, and to investigate the peoples' ancestries, that is, their cultural heritages. In the final stage of sociocultural research, they focused on the societies into which the population groups organized themselves and studied the ways in which these social groups used and modified both their cultural and their natural heritages (Rouse 1986, Fig. 30).

Artifactual Research

Archaeology began in the Caribbean area, as elsewhere, with the discovery, description, and identification of buildings, tools, and other artifacts—and with their removal to private homes and public museums. At first, these items of material culture were collected individually; later, they were excavated in the form of assemblages from the sites where they had been deposited.

So far as is known, the first European settlers did not undertake archaeological research. It was not until 1740 that an explorer named Nicolas Hortsmann reported the discovery of petroglyphs (rock carvings) in the present country of Guyana (Osgood 1946, 21). In 1749, Father Juan de Talamanco, a Spanish historian and archaeologist, made a pioneer study of four carved stone figures of Taino Indian deities *(zemis)* that had been sent to him from the northern part of the Dominican Republic, and in 1775, Pedro del Prado, a Cuban, wrote about a stool *(dujo)* of the Tainos that had been found in the eastern part of his country (Ortiz 1935, 71–72).

The first known exhibition of artifacts took place in Puerto Rico in 1854. It featured the collection of Jorge Latimer, a local merchant, that was eventually acquired by the Museum of Natural History of the SMITHSONIAN INSTITUTION, Washington, D.C. (Coll y Toste 1907, 30–31). In 1867, the government of British Guiana (now Guyana) established a museum to house

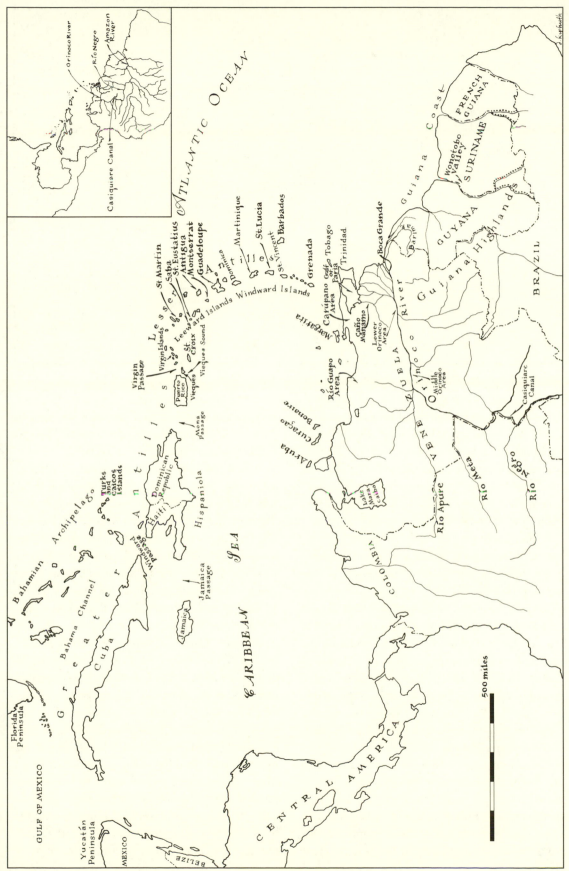

Map 1. The Caribbean Basin (after Rouse 1992, Fig. 1)

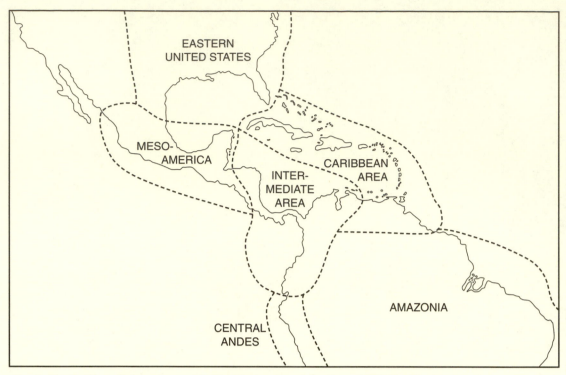

Map 2. *The Caribbean Culture Area and Its Neighboring Areas (after Rouse 1964, Fig. 2)*

items obtained from the local Indians and their sites. This museum, which bears the name of Walter Roth, a longtime director, includes natural as well as cultural objects. Its holdings in the former field are dominant, as is the collection in the Smithsonian's Museum of Natural History (Osgood 1946, 40–41).

Other museums founded at the time concentrated on culture rather than nature. Some, such as the Museo Montané at the University of Havana, were modeled after the present Musée de l'Homme in Paris, which covers the whole range of the discipline of anthropology, including artifacts obtained through ethnological study of contemporary peoples as well as archaeological research. Still other museums preferred to approach the artifacts from the standpoint of the disciplines of history and art; the Departmental Museum in Fort-de-France, Martinique, is an example.

Educational institutions have been slower to engage in the collection and exhibition of human remains. Toward the close of the nineteenth century Luis Montané, a Cuban who had studied at the Sorbonne in Paris, founded a Department of Anthropology at the University of Havana and initiated an extensive program of local research that resulted in the establishment of the museum that bears his name.

When the United States acquired Puerto Rico from Spain in 1898, its Smithsonian Institution asked J. Walter Fewkes, a staff member of the now-defunct subsidiary known as the Bureau of American Ethnology, to assess the anthropological resources of the nation's new possession. Fewkes (1907) published a large volume summarizing current knowledge of the ethnology and archaeology of Puerto Rico and the neighboring islands.

In 1911, George G. Heye of New York City invited Fewkes to write a companion volume on the West Indian artifacts in his privately owned Museum of the American Indian, Heye Foundation (Fewkes 1922). Heye subsequently hired excavators such as Theodoor de Booy (1919) and Mark R. Harrington (1921) to expand his museum's collections. The scientific value of their research was lessened by the fact that Heye insisted upon personally cataloging the finds only by site and not also recording the assemblages within the sites from which they had come. The Smithsonian Institution took over

Heye's museum in 1991 and is converting it into a National Museum of the American Indian, with the mission of preserving and displaying the cultural heritage of the indigenous inhabitants of the New World, a mission for which the museum will be eminently suited because of the high quality of its artifacts.

In 1915, the New York Academy of Sciences undertook excavations in Puerto Rico as part of its scientific survey of Puerto Rico and the Virgin Islands. J. Alden Mason (1941), a participant in this program, made the first systematic excavation of West Indian ball and dance courts at the site of Caguana (Capá). His finds went to the American Museum of Natural History in New York City, which catalogued separately the assemblages obtained from the site's various structures. This was a major improvement over the previous procedure of treating artifacts individually, and it made possible subsequent advances to higher levels of interpretation.

Ceremonial structures like those at Caguana were easily identified because their courts were lined with embankments and upright stone slabs, sometimes decorated with petroglyphs (Fig. 1). These ball courts have been intensively investigated in recent years (see Alegría 1983 for a summary), but the same cannot be said for houses. They were built of perishable materials and situated away from the refuse where the archaeologists of the time were digging in search of artifacts. Only during the 1990s have traces of multiple house posts been found in refuse-free soil (see, e.g., Versteeg and Schinkel 1992). Burials, too, have received relatively little attention because most of them contain few grave goods. Excavation in refuse heaps has recently improved by taking into consideration the processes of deposition, disturbance, and decay (Siegel 1992).

Over the years, important prehistoric sites have been preserved by converting them into public reserves. Parks on the Palo Seco midden in Trinidad (Bullbrook 1953) and at the Caguana ball and dance courts in Puerto Rico are good examples. Alegría (1983) has faithfully restored the courts at the latter site, has constructed a museum alongside them, and made Caguana a mecca for local schoolchildren and tourists.

With the shift of interest from individual artifacts to assemblages came a realization that the latter contain not only artifacts but also human skeletal material, food remains, charcoal, and other traces of human activity. These kinds of remains also began to be recovered in order to fill out the archaeological record, although they were little studied at the time.

Caribbeanists processed the artifacts by grouping them into classes, each defined by a complex of shared attributes, which is known as its *type*. Because pottery and items made of flint are abundant, complex, and variable, they were subjected to additional treatment. Vessels, potsherds, and, more recently, worked flint were broken down according to their features and then grouped into classes, each defined by its shared attributes. The defining traits are sometimes called types, like the attributes diagnostic of classes of whole artifacts, but most Caribbeanists prefer to call them *modes* in an effort to avoid confusion between the two categories. Types are the units of choice in studying artifacts from the standpoint of their use, and modes are preferred in approaching them from the viewpoint of their manufacture (Pantel 1988; Rouse 1972, 45–55).

Interest in artifacts has declined as the supply of quality specimens has dwindled and professional archaeologists have added chronological, culture-historical, and sociocultural research to their repertoire. Only avocational archaeologists continue to be preoccupied with the artifactual level. As elsewhere, it has been difficult to persuade them to catalog their finds so as to make them usable on the more abstract levels of interpretation.

The rise of conservation archaeology in the final decades of the twentieth century has led to an increase of professional activity on the artifactual level. Assemblages of remains that are in danger of being destroyed by the construction of roads, buildings, and other kinds of structures are now being removed to museums and other repositories for safekeeping. Work of this kind has been most intensively done in Puerto Rico and the American Virgin Islands, where the antiquity laws of the United States apply and federal conservation funds are

Figure 1. Ball and Dance Courts at Caguana, Puerto Rico. (Top) Row of stone slabs lining the central dance court, the petroglyphs marked with chalk to show more clearly. (Courtesy of José R. Oliver) (Bottom) The large, square central dance hall is left of center, the central ball court just beneath it. (Courtesy of A. Gus Pantel)

available, but it is also common in many other parts of the Caribbean area, notably in the French West Indies and Venezuela (Wagner 1978).

Chronological Research

By the 1920s, professional archaeologists had accumulated enough assemblages to use as the basis for setting up sequences of local periods, and by the 1930s, they had formed sufficient sequences to begin synthesizing them into regional charts or chronologies. As in other parts of the world (see, e.g., Willey and Phillips 1958), they placed the local periods whose assemblages were most alike at the same heights in the charts on the assumption that the inhabitants who were able to mutually influence each other would have produced the most similar assemblages. They checked their results by hypothesizing the existence of horizons, that is, local complexes of cultural traits presumed to have been contemporaneous, and by determining whether these "time markers" actually did have a horizontal distribution on their charts. If they did not, the charts and hypotheses were reconciled in an effort to produce the most accurate and most practicable systems of local periods within which to organize the assemblages.

Gudmund Hatt, a professor at the University of Copenhagen, pioneered the new approach. In 1924, he undertook excavations in the formerly Danish part of the Virgin Islands, which the United States had just purchased from his country. He classified his finds into three successive groups and named each group after sites from which he had obtained typical assemblages: (1) Krum Bay, (2) Coral Bay–Longford, and (3) Magens Bay–Salt River. He placed (1) at the beginning of his sequence because it lacked ceramics and put (2) before (3) because, wherever the two occurred in the same site, the assemblages belonging to (2) underlay those in (3). He also noted that (2) was characterized by white-on-red-painted pottery, which had not previously been found in the Greater Antilles, whereas the modeled-incised pottery of (3) resembled that of the Taino Indians, who occupied the Greater

Antilles in Columbus's time (Hatt 1924; Birgit F. Morse, personal communication).

In 1935, Cornelius Osgood, professor and curator of anthropology at Yale University, established a Caribbean anthropological program with the intention of tracing the spread of cultural traits from South, Middle, and North America into and out of the West Indies. He sent Froelich G. Rainey and IRVING ROUSE, his first two graduate students, to the West Indies with this aim in mind. Like Hatt, they realized that they would first have to do chronological research. Rainey, assisted by Rouse, set up a sequence of local periods in Haiti, which, like Hatt's, consisted of a preceramic period followed by two ceramic periods. The first of the two was marked by local pottery, and the second by pottery in the Taino style resembling that encountered by Hatt in the Virgin Islands. Rainey then went to Puerto Rico where he was able to distinguish two ceramic periods comparable to those Hatt had found in the Virgin Islands (Rainey 1940, 1941).

Rainey named the two ceramic periods in his Haitian sequence after typical sites, as Hatt had done in the Virgin Islands, but preferred to call the two Puerto Rican periods *Crab* and *Shell* in recognition of the fact that such food remains were dominant in their respective assemblages. He was ahead of his time in calling attention to this shift in the local diet, but Rouse found when he continued the Puerto Rican research that ecofacts such as food remains do not provide an adequate basis for chronological research because their presence in archaeological assemblages depends upon their availability and crabs and edible shellfish are limited to the coasts of large islands such as Puerto Rico. In his doctoral dissertation, therefore, Rouse (1939) substituted the names of typical sites for *Crab* and *Shell*, following the example of Hatt in the Virgin Islands and Rainey in Haiti.

Rouse also synthesized the three established sequences into a regional chronology and continues to refine and expand this chronology as new information becomes available, adding other local sequences to his charts as they have been formulated (Fig. 2).

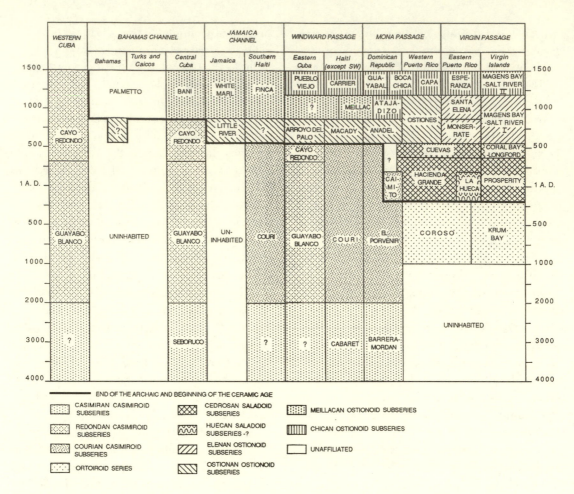

Figure 2. Chronology of the Greater Antilles (after Rouse 1992, Figure 14)

Ripley P. Bullen (1964) pioneered the development of local sequences for the Windward Islands in the southern half of the Lesser Antilles, and Louis Allaire (1973) synthesized them into another regional chronology, which he has been modifying and expanding as new data have become available. Only two peripheral groups of relatively small islands still lack adequate chronological control, the Leewards between the Windwards and the Greater Antilles and the Bahamas north of the latter. Local sequences of periods are currently being formulated for both these regions (e.g., Berman and Gnivecki 1994; Hofman 1993).

Chronological research has also spread to the mainland part of the Caribbean area but has not been so systematically done there. In 1946, Rouse worked out a sequence of periods for the island of Trinidad, just off the mouth of the

Orinoco River, in collaboration with J. A. Bullbrook, an oil geologist with previous archaeological experience in the Sudan (Bullbrook 1953; Rouse 1947). In 1950, Professor José M. Cruxent invited Rouse to join him in establishing a regional chronology for Venezuela (Cruxent and Rouse 1958–1959). The results of both projects have been refined and expanded by subsequent investigators (Barse 1989; Gassón and Wagner 1991; Sanoja and Vargas 1983). Sequences of local periods have also been constructed for Guyana by Evans and Meggers (1960) and for the former Dutch colonies by archaeologists from that country (e.g., Versteeg and Bubberman 1992). Only in French Guiana has archaeology not yet advanced beyond the stage of artifactual research.

The introduction of radiometric dating in the 1950s led to a temporary decline of interest in the use of chronological charts as many Caribbeanists assumed that the newly developed techniques of measurement rendered the charts obsolete. Experience has shown, however, that neither is sufficient by itself. The results of the two procedures need to be checked against each other in order to identify and eliminate invalid dates and to improve the accuracy of the charts.

The charts and dates have been called measures of absolute time because their temporal values remain the same throughout the regions covered. Caribbeanists also work with measures of relative time known as *ages,* which vary from place to place. Five ages are distinguished: lithic, which is marked by stone chipping; archaic, by the addition of stone grinding; ceramic, by the first appearance of pottery; formative, by the development of ball and dance courts; and historic, by the introduction of writing. These ages have an irregular distribution when inserted in the chronological charts because the innovations that define them took place at different times in different places (Fig. 2).

Culture-Historical Research

Chronological charts, dates, and ages play a number of roles in research on the final two levels of interpretation. They may be used at the start of a project to identify sites, artifacts, and other information pertinent to the problem under study and to retrieve these data from the ground or from storage. To assist in doing the latter, the Yale Peabody Museum, which is now computerizing its Caribbean collections, is adding the name of the local period when each item was produced to the information already recorded about the nature of the item and the locality from which it came (Hill and Rouse 1994).

More important, the chronological systems have added a new dimension to the study of the history of cultural traits envisaged by Osgood when he founded the Yale Caribbean program. They have made it possible to reconstruct the trajectories of traits as they spread from period to period as well as from area to area and to study the changes that took place en route. For example, prior to the construction of chronological charts and the advent of radiometric dat-

ing, it was assumed that the custom of building ball and dance courts had diffused from Mexico to the Greater Antilles because there are superficial similarities between the courts in the two regions. Thanks to chronological research, local archaeologists have been able to show that the Antillean courts originated in Puerto Rico during the latter part of the first millennium A.D. and spread east and west from there without ever reaching Jamaica or central and western Cuba, the parts of the Antilles closest to Mexico. The courts became simpler as they spread (González Colón 1984; Rouse 1992, 112–116).

West Indian scholars originally assumed that all their finds had been produced by the ethnic groups who inhabited the area in the time of Columbus, that is, by the Guanahatabeys (also known as Ciboneys), Igneris, Tainos, and Island-Caribs (Map 3). For example, Heye attributed all of the Lesser Antillean artifacts in his Museum of the American Indian to the Island-Caribs. And when the Swedish archeologist Sven Lovén wrote his scholarly summary of West Indian archaeology and ethnology in the 1930s, he began it with a statement that all four ethnic groups had come full-blown from either North or South America (Lovén 1935, 2). That assumption relieved him of the necessity of studying the evolution of the groups' cultures, since that would have taken place before they reached the islands. He only needed to concern himself with the histories of individual traits.

Lovén's assumption soon began to be contradicted by the results of chronological research. Some sequences of local periods in the Greater Antilles have now been extended back to ca. 4000 B.C. (Rouse 1992, Fig. 14), and the ethnic groups encountered by Columbus could hardly have retained their separate identities over such a long period of time. Consequently, we must distinguish the historic ethnic groups from their prehistoric ancestors and predecessors.

Ethnic groups are defined in terms of sociocultural criteria, which are difficult to infer from prehistoric remains—hence the position of sociocultural research at the end of the sequence of stages under discussion here. In the absence of adequate knowledge of sociocultural criteria, Caribbeanists have formulated prehis-

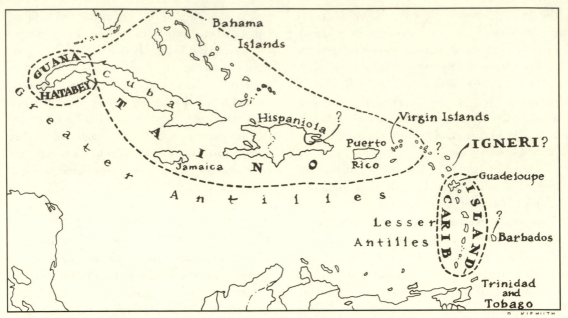

Map 3. Ethnic Groups in the West Indies at the Time of Columbus (after Rouse 1994, Fig. 1)

toric peoples and cultures, as the original title of their congresses indicates. They have defined each people by its culture and each culture by its material remains and have worked back from the cultures of the historic ethnic groups to those of the prehistoric peoples, using the so-called direct historical method.

They have approached this task by assuming that in the absence of evidence to the contrary, the inhabitants of each local period constituted a separate people, with its own distinctive culture. Since local peoples and cultures are too small to be directly equated with the ethnic groups, they have had to be grouped into larger units for the purpose of correlation. In other words, they have had to be organized into cultural taxonomies.

Cruxent and Rouse (1958–1959) formed such a taxonomy while constructing regional chronologies in Venezuela. During the course of that research they tested the alignment of the local periods in their charts by studying the distributions of single traits and complexes of traits. They applied the term *horizon* or the phrase *horizon style* to the traits or complexes that had a horizontal distribution and referred to the traits and complexes that had irregular distributions as *traditions,* following the example of Willey (1945).

They also began to pay attention to the totality of traits present within each period, that is, to the periods' cultures. They assigned the cultures that looked alike to separate classes regardless of their chronological position. They considered calling these classes of cultures *traditions,* because they are irregularly distributed on the charts, but rejected that idea because it might cause their research on the history of classes of cultures to be confused with their study of the history of classes of artifacts and features, that is, of cultural traits. They decided to call the classes into which they had grouped their cultures *series* and to limit their use of the word *tradition* to classes of artifacts and features, defined by their types and modes, respectively. Other Caribbeanists have preferred to apply *tradition* indiscriminately to both kinds of units.

Rouse (1964) introduced the concept of series or whole-culture traditions into the West Indies, and it has been almost universally adopted there. Vescelius (1986) subsequently proposed that each series be divided into subseries, which has been done throughout the West Indies but not so widely on the mainland. Each series has been named by adding the suffix -oid to the name of a period in which it occurred, and each subseries has been named by substituting the suffix -an. As elsewhere (see, e.g., Lumbreras 1974), these suffixes indicate the degree of similarity and difference among the groups of local peoples and cultures to which they refer (Rouse 1986, 10–11, 117–120).

The taxonomy of peoples and cultures thus established has been primarily used to trace the origin and development of the Tainos, whom Columbus encountered in the northern part of the West Indies (Map 3). By plotting the distributions of the ethnic groups, subseries, and series on chronological charts, the students of this problem have been able to identify Meillacan and Chican, the latest two subseries within the Ostionoid series, as Taino (Fig. 2). They have traced the ancestry of the Tainos back from these two subseries to a previous Ostionan Ostionoid subseries and thence through a Cedrosan Saladoid subseries—which occupied the Lesser Antilles, the northern half of the Guianas, and the eastern coast of Venezuela around the time of Christ—to a Ronquinan Saladoid subseries, which had previously arisen in the Orinoco Valley (Rouse 1992, 71–137).

Most attention has been paid in recent years to the central part of this trajectory, that is, to the expansion of the Cedrosan Saladoid peoples from the Guianan and east Venezuelan coasts to the Lesser Antilles and Puerto Rico at the entry into the Greater Antilles. We have found that the migrants proceeded selectively, settling first on large, mountainous islands with extensive river systems like those along which they had lived on the mainland. They quickly displaced the previous Ortoiroid inhabitants of the Lesser Antilles and Puerto Rico but came to a halt at a frontier on the eastern top of Hispaniola and remained there for some 500 years before being able to displace the Casimiroid peoples who inhabited the bulk of Hispaniola and all of Cuba. While living on that frontier they evolved into the Ostionoid peoples and cultures who eventually became the Tainos of the historic age.

From time to time, participants in the research on Taino ancestry have proposed other, mutually contradictory migration hypotheses. One archaeologist or another has concluded that each of the Saladoid and Ostionoid subseries was the result of a separate migration from South America into the West Indies. The

Figure 3. Taino three-pointed Zemi (after Rouse 1992, Figure 29a)

proponents of the various hypotheses have been unable to agree on them, nor have they been able to agree on the places of origin in South America. These conflicts have arisen because the advocates of the alternative hypotheses have limited themselves to ceramics. To be successful in reconstructing population movements one must take into consideration all aspects of culture for which there is any archaeological documentation. In other words, one must classify whole assemblages, not just the ceramic parts of the assemblages.

Because Caribbeanists have done just that in the case of the Saladoid series, they have been able to reach a consensus that its peoples migrated from the South American mainland. Most also conclude that the Saladoids evolved into the Ostionoids and thence into the Tainos after they reached the Greater Antilles. Studies of the origin and development of settlement patterns, ball and dance courts, subsistence agriculture, tools and ornaments, art, and the three-pointed type of zemi all indicate the validity of this sequence of events. For example, three-pointers are now known to have been brought into the West Indies by the Saladoids and to have been handed down by them through the Ostionoids to the Tainos. The tools became larger and began to be elaborately carved under the influence of Casimiroid art (Fig. 3).

Physical anthropological and linguistic research has shed further light on the origin of the Tainos. Tacoma (1991) has noted significant differences between the human craniums and long bones from archaic- and ceramic-age burials on the island of Aruba off the coast of Venezuela dating from before and after the time of arrival of the Saladoids in the West Indies. These differences support the hypothesis of a migration from South America. By contrast, Budinoff (1991) has found that the human skeletal material associated with Saladoid and Ostionoid pottery at the Maisabel site in Puerto Rico is essentially the same, which indicates local development within the Antilles.

Linguists have assigned the language of the Tainos in the northern part of the West Indies and that of the Igneris and Island-Caribs in the southern part to the Arawakan family and have concluded that the two diverged from Proto-Northern, a previous member of the language family. They have reason to believe that the Proto-Northern language was present in the Orinoco basin at the time when the Saladero series was there and that it spread into the West Indies and diverged into the Taino and Igneri/Island-Carib languages while the Saladoid peoples were expanding there and evolving through the Ostionoid series into the Taino ethnic group. Hence, two independent sets of conclusions, based respectively upon physical anthropological and linguistic research, mutually support the culturally based hypotheses of Saladoid migration and Ostionoid development (Rouse 1986, 120–156).

Linguists have traced the ancestry of the Taino language farther back into the central part of the Amazon basin. Donald Lathrap (1970) has been inspired by this conclusion to search for ceramic evidence that the ancestral cultures also came from there. Other archaeologists, mindful of the fact that languages and cultures often come from different places, have cited contrary evidence favoring an origin of the ancestral cultures in the Andes (Rouse 1992, Fig. 7). Neither argument is conclusive, no chronological research has yet been done along either route, and little is known about the nonceramic aspects of the local cultures.

Attempts to trace the ancestry of the Island-Caribs back from their homeland in the southern part of the Lesser Antilles to the Guianas have likewise been inconclusive. Members of that ethnic group told the European colonists that they had come from the mainland, but archaeologists have been unable to confirm that statement because they have not yet succeeded in identifying Island-Carib remains. The archaeologists' procedure may have been faulty. They have assumed that the arrival of the Caribs was a movement of peoples and their cultures, to be studied in the same way as the arrival of the Saladoid peoples, when it may instead have been a movement of immigrant social groups to be studied by the methods of sociocultural rather than culture-historical research. Carib war parties may have invaded the Windward Islands but have been too small in number to have been able to replace the previous Igneri population, and they may have become assimilated in that population, adopting its language and much of its culture.

There is some reason to believe that the ancestors of the Guanahatabeys came from Middle America (Rouse 1992, 20–22). Oliver (1989) has traced the Caquetio Indians of northwestern Venezuela back to the central part of the Orinoco Valley. Research on the fate of the Caribbean Indians during the historic age remains to be considered. This subject especially interests the inhabitants of the Spanish-speaking countries because many of them are descended from the Tainos. Most early Spanish colonists were men who obtained wives by marrying Taino women, and as a result, their offspring are racially, linguistically, and culturally mixed.

Students of the subject have been primarily concerned with the survival of biological, linguistic, and cultural traits into the historic age (e.g., García Arévalo 1988) and their spread to other parts of the world (Crosby 1972). Because the Tainos were the first Native Americans to have intensive contact with Europeans and Africans, they are the source of a large number of the New World traits that spread to the Old World, such as corn (maize), sweet potatoes, tobacco, rubber, and rubber-ball games. Many of the names for these items come from the Tainos. Conversely, the Tainos bore the brunt of the introduction of Old World diseases into the New World. This fact, combined with their intermarriage with the colonists, caused them to become extinct only decades after the arrival of Columbus, and as a result, it has been difficult to find Taino sites dating from the historic age (Rouse 1992, 138–172).

The descendants of the British, Danish, Dutch, and French colonists who settled alongside the Spaniards in the northern part of the West Indies are less interested in their Taino predecessors because the latter had disappeared before they arrived. These people prefer to study the remains of their own ancestors. In Jamaica, where the present population is almost entirely African-American, much work is being done on the slave quarters on sugar plantations and on the dwelling sites of escaped slaves.

Conditions are different in the Windward Islands, which are closer to South America. For several centuries after the extinction of the Tainos, the Island-Caribs continued to live there on islands not yet colonized by Europeans. So far, attempts to locate their remains have been unsuccessful.

While conserving the ruins of the first European settlement in South America, at Nueva Cadiz on Cubagua Island, Venezuela, Cruxent identified and excavated the quarter occupied by Indian slaves the Spaniards had brought there to dive for pearls (Rouse and Cruxent 1963, 134–138). The Indian quarters in the mission sites of Martinique, Trinidad, and Venezuela have received less attention. The subject does not greatly interest the modern inhabitants of those places because they do not trace their descent from the aborigines.

Sociocultural Research

On the final level of interpretation, Caribbeanists have shifted their attention from the peoples who produced the local cultures to the societies who used them (Watters 1976, 6). In doing so, they have focused on the societies' activities.

These scholars have been attracted to the study of societies by the presence of chiefdoms among the Tainos in the Greater Antilles and the Caquetios in western Venezuela (Spencer and Redmond 1992; Wilson 1990). Indeed, the term *chief* comes from the Taino language. The remains of the Tainos and their ancestors provide an opportunity to examine the rise of chiefdoms in isolation, uninfluenced by direct contact with previously developed chiefdoms or states.

Bernardo Vega (1980) once tried to trace the boundaries of the Taino chiefdoms by correlating them with the limits of the latest archaeologically defined peoples and cultures in Hispaniola, but he had little success. The two kinds of units appear to have had different distributions and to equate them is like treating apples as oranges.

Better results have been achieved by using the direct historical method, that is, by deriving models of the Taino chiefdoms from the ethnohistoric evidence and projecting the models back into prehistory along the Tainos' ancestral line. The historic chiefdoms consisted of relatively large groups of villages, each with its own chief, that owed allegiance to hierarchies of district and regional chiefs (Wilson 1990). The historic chiefdoms were also marked by ceremonial centers (i.e., clusters of ball and dance courts), elaborate burials, special types of ornaments, and intensive trade. Study of the spatial and temporal distribution of these criteria in the Greater Antilles during prehistoric time indicates that the local chiefdoms began to evolve during the late ceramic age and reached maturity in the formative age (Fig. 2).

Citing archaeological evidence that Bahamian villages were divided into halves, Keegan and Maclachlan (1989, 615–616) have theorized that if and when these halves split apart and became separate villages, they may have retained their affiliations and, as a result, have come to be ruled by district chiefs. The two scholars note that the Spaniards encountered such an incipient chiefdom on Aklin Island in the southern Bahamas and hypothesize that continued evolution farther south in Hispaniola would have led to the emergence there of regional chiefs and, hence, of the full chiefdoms encountered by Columbus.

The probability that their conclusions are correct is heightened by the fact that they obtained them by working within the direct line of ancestry of the Tainos as established on the previous, culture-historical level of interpretation. Without knowledge of this ancestry, the sociocultural researchers would have been prone to error. For example, in a separate study Keegan (1992, 17–18) assumed that the Dominican Republic sequence of Musiepedro (also known as

El Caimito), Atajadizo, and Guayabal cultures comprised a single, unilinear development when in fact the first of the three was separated from the other two by the frontier between the Casimiroid and the Ostionoid peoples noted above (Fig. 2). When unable to find ethnohistorical evidence that can be projected directly backward along the Tainos' ancestral line, Caribbeanists have made use of knowledge about the chiefdoms on the mainland of South America that share a common ancestry with the Tainos (e.g., Siegel 1992; Spencer and Redmond 1992). As a last resort, they have also formulated and tested models obtained through the study of chiefdoms elsewhere in the world, notably POLYNESIA, but the conclusions reached through indirect and general analogy are less reliable than those based on direct analogy because chiefdoms have developed under different conditions elsewhere in the world.

To put this point another way, sociocultural researchers in the Caribbean area have wisely chosen to take into consideration the culture-historical setting in which the behavior they are studying took place. They have also taken into consideration the natural-historical setting. For example, Haviser (1978) investigated the utilization of terrestrial resources on the island of Curaçao by plotting their distributions in the vicinity of the local settlements, and Watters (1982) and Keegan (1989) examined the balance between the use of terrestrial and maritime resources. In addition, Watters (1980) and his colleagues are examining how societies with similar cultural ancestries adapted to differences in their natural environments.

In studying the behavior that took place within the various natural- and cultural-historical settings, the sociocultural researchers have progressed beyond the norms formed by classification on the previous levels of interpretation, that is, beyond the types, modes, and cultures produced by grouping artifacts, their features, and their assemblages into classes and defining the classes in terms of their shared attributes. They focus instead on variations from the norms and, by so doing, have been able to fill significant gaps in our knowledge of conditions during prehistoric times.

Their research on variations in behavior provides those of us who continue to work on previous levels of interpretation with the information we need to avoid overclassifying our finds by assigning the products of variant behavior to classes. For example, research on the distributions of cultural traits within local areas has shown that the diagnostic or normative traits tend to be concentrated in the core parts of the areas and that the traits on boundaries tend to vary because of peripheral lag and influence from neighboring cultures. Discovery of this phenomenon has alerted Caribbeanists to the danger of classifying frontier dwellers as separate peoples and cultures. They have also avoided the trap of using single-activity sites as the basis for forming separate cultures.

Research on variation in behavior has further led to an awareness of cultural pluralities, such as the presence of intrusive wares in local pottery. For example, each of the local styles or complexes within the Cedrosan Saladoid subseries contains two wares, one characterized by white-on-red painted designs (wor) and the other by zoned, incised crosshatching (zic). Studies of the distribution of the two have indicated that the Cedrosan Saladoid potters added zic ware to their previous wor ware while living on the coast of South America and then took the two to the Antilles as plural ceramic complexes. Chanlatte Baik (1981) instead regards them as independent complexes introduced into the West Indies by a different series of local peoples—despite the fact that they occur in the same assemblages everywhere except at the northern end of the Saladoid expansion where a divergence into separate peoples and cultures appears to have taken place, reversing the convergence at the beginning of the migration (Rouse 1992, 85–90).

The activity that currently attracts the most attention among Caribbean archaeologists is subsistence. Specialists in zooarchaeology and paleobotany do most of the research on this subject. They originally studied the ecofacts obtained during artifactual research (Wing 1962) but soon began to do their own fieldwork using improved techniques for the recovery of remains.

The zooarchaeological laboratory in the Florida Museum of Natural History at the University of Florida has led the way. Beginning in the 1960s, its staff, students, and associates have found that the original Saladoid migrants placed a relatively high emphasis on terrestrial rather than maritime resources, presumably because they had originated in the interior of South America, and that seafood became more important to them during Ostionoid time, in part because of the development of deep-sea fishing.

Rainey's discovery of a change in diet from land crabs among the Saladoid peoples to marine shellfish among the Ostionoids is a case in point. The shift has been variously attributed to the overhunting of crabs, to a change in climate that may have decimated them, and to an outbreak of disease among them (Goodwin 1979, 370–375, 381–382; Jones 1985; Keegan 1989). Alternatively, the Ostionoid peoples may simply have lost the Saladoid peoples' taste for crabs.

In the 1970s, the Museo del Hombre Dominicano established a laboratory for the study of food remains. Among its achievements has been recovery of the pollen of a number of wild vegetables eaten by the Casimiroid and Ostionoid peoples (Veloz Maggiolo, Ortega, and Caba Fuentes 1973, 169–170). Members of the museum staff have also reached conclusions about changes in the natural environment, such as the extinction of ground sloths, which they attribute to overhunting by the Casimiroids (Veloz Maggiolo and Ortega 1976, 160–162).

Mainland archaeologists have paid more attention to agriculture than to food gathering. They have obtained not only culture-historical but also isotopic evidence, the latter by analyzing human bones, that the initial Saladoid farmers cultivated primarily manioc (cassava) and carried it with them into the Antilles where it was still the staple crop when Columbus arrived. By that time, however, maize had replaced it as the staple in the Orinoco Valley, presumably because maize compensated for a deficiency of protein in the local diet (van der Merwe, Roosevelt, and Vogel 1981; Roosevelt 1980). The fact that maize did not also become the primary crop in the Greater Antilles is further evidence against the conflicting hypotheses

of migration of one or more Ostionoid subseries from the mainland.

Caribbeanists have also paid considerable attention to patterns of settlement. By plotting the distribution of dwelling sites in Puerto Rico period by period, Rouse (1952) was able to follow the expansion of the ceramic-age inhabitants of that island from their initial settlements on the coastal plains through the foothills and mountain valleys into the uplands. It was this gradual adaptation to life on a large island that eventually made it possible for the Ostionoids to replace the Casimiroids on the still-larger islands of Hispaniola and Cuba.

Keegan (1992) has used a different approach in studying the settlement of the Bahamas. Choosing the route that seemed to him most likely to have been taken by the first settlers and assuming that they reached its end shortly before their encounter with Columbus, he has calculated their time of arrival in the Bahamas by applying to the length of his chosen route the average rate of expansion in other parts of the world. Simultaneously, Berman and Gnivecki (1994) have established a local sequence of periods for the central Bahamas, have dated it radiometrically, and have inferred the migration route from the close resemblance between the initial assemblages in their sequence and an Ostionan Ostionoid assemblage found in eastern Cuba. Their date of ca. A.D. 600 agrees with the one obtained by Keegan, and their conclusions about the migration route are close to his. Hence, their results, achieved through culture-historical research, confirm his, which were obtained through sociocultural research.

Sullivan (1981) and Keegan (personal communication) have found that at a somewhat later date the Meillacan Ostionoid peoples of northern Hispaniola traveled regularly to and from the Turks and Caicos Islands at the eastern end of the Bahamian archipelago in search of local resources such as salt and turtles. Eventually, Bahamians settled there and traded the commodities back to the larger island.

J. K. Kozlowski (1974) has hypothesized that the Casimiroid peoples of the previous archaic age moved up and down the great river valleys of Cuba and Hispaniola in order to obtain seasonally available foods, but Dominican archaeologists doubt that this happened. Other investigators have focused upon individual valleys or stretches of coast in order to be able to examine the distribution of settlements in greater detail. The work of Rodríguez (1990) in the Loíza Valley, the largest valley in Puerto Rico, is a good example.

There has also been considerable interest in religion and art, the former because it permeated so many aspects of the Tainos' culture and the latter because of the Tainos' propensity to portray deities in their art. Columbus commissioned Ramón Pané, a friar who accompanied him on his second voyage, to make a study of Taino religion. Pané spent four years in northern Hispaniola, learning the Tainos' language, observing their rituals, and listening to their songs and stories, and then submitted a relatively detailed report to Columbus (Arrom 1988). His work has been called the first anthropological research in the New World, and its results have been widely used to draw conclusions about religious practices and beliefs from the archaeological remains of the Tainos and their direct ancestors (e.g., Arrom 1989). Most recently, Roe (1994) has broken new ground by undertaking a componential analysis of ceramic- and formative-age art.

Much has been done, too, to identify items of long-distance trade and to determine their sources. Students of this activity have learned that the Saladoid migrants remained in contact with their ancestors in South America for some time after they entered the West Indies but broke that contact off shortly after the time of Christ (Rouse 1992, 85). The Ostionoids resumed contact ca. A.D. 1200, concomitant with the rise of chiefdoms. There was extensive commerce in ornaments of precious stones along the coasts and rivers of the South American mainland and out into the West Indies during both periods (Boomert 1987; Lathrap 1973). In addition, we now have evidence that cast gold-copper ornaments were traded into the West Indies from northern South America during Saladoid as well as late Ostionoid (i.e., Taino) times (Siegel and Severin 1993). Only sheet-gold ornaments were produced in the is-

lands, where that metal was a sign of rank among the Tainos.

In the absence of adequate evidence about other forms of contact between the local societies, such as intermarriage, play, politics, and warfare, Caribbeanists have subsumed all such activities with trade under the heading of interaction. The Caribbean culture area is a particularly good place to study this process because the Orinoco Valley and the islands of the West Indies proper form a linear sequence connected by the river's strong flow and by the fact that almost all of the islands are within sight of each other. Consequently, the local archaeology provides a wealth of information about the effect of geographical factors on the process of interaction.

Caribbeanists have sought to identify interaction spheres in the Orinoco Valley and the West Indies by studying the similarities in culture among local areas. Rouse (1992, 84–85) has concluded that the land surrounding the Gulf of Paria, including the Barrancas area just above the Orinoco delta, northwestern Guyana, and Trinidad and Tobago Islands, comprised such a sphere during the first half of the first millennium A.D. It was characterized by the Barrancoid ceramic series, whose influence extended as far upstream as the first rapids in the upper middle part of the Orinoco Valley and as far out into the West Indies as Antigua in the center of the Lesser Antilles (Barse 1989).

When I constructed my chronological charts for the Greater Antilles, I arranged their columns in order of the distribution of the ceramic- and formative-age cultures and then found, to my surprise, that the lithic- and archaic-age cultures had interrupted distributions (Fig. 2). Seeking a reason for this discrepancy, I found that I had grouped together the columns on either side of the passages between islands because they constituted separate "passage areas" during the ceramic and formative ages. If I had instead arranged the columns island by island, the local cultures of the lithic, archaic, and historic ages would all have had continuous distributions because each island comprised a culturally homogenous area during those ages. (The present division of the island of Hispaniola between the Haiti and the Dominican Republic is an exception.)

The reason for this discrepancy is to be found in a statement of the Spanish settlers that the Tainos on the eastern end of Hispaniola and the western end of Puerto Rico visited each other on a regular basis just to pass the time of day. The inhabitants of the adjacent ends of neighboring islands thus appear to have interacted more closely with each other than they did with the peoples on the opposite ends of their own islands, presumably because they had learned to travel more easily by water while living along the great river systems in South America and had carried this skill to the West Indies. On the contrary, the lithic-, archaic-, and historic-age peoples all came from areas where land travel was dominant (Rouse 1982, 48).

This discussion of sociocultural research illustrates the value of working on all four levels of interpretation. Caribbeanists would have accomplished little if they had jumped directly from artifactual to sociocultural research, bypassing the studies of chronology and of cultural and natural history; if they had done so, they would have deprived themselves of the opportunity to test assumptions made on the first and last levels by means of research on the intervening levels. All four levels are essential to the ultimate goal of archaeology, which is to learn as much as possible about humans in the past.

Irving Rouse

See also Florida and the Caribbean, Historical Archaeology

References

Alegría, R. E. 1983. *Ball Courts and Ceremonial Plazas in the West Indies*. Publications in Anthropology, 79. New Haven: Department of Anthropology, Yale University.

Allaire, L. 1973. *Vers une préhistoire des Petites Antilles*. Fond St-Jacques, St-Marie, Martinique: Centre de Recherches Caraïbes de l'Université de Montréal.

Arrom, J. J. 1988. *Ramón Pané, "Relación acerca de las antigüedades de los Indios": El primero tratado escrito en América*. 8th ed. Mexico City: Siglo Veintiuno Editores.

———. 1989. *Mitología y artes prehispánicas de las Antillas*. 2d ed. Mexico City: Siglo Veintiuno Editores.

Barse, W. P. 1989. "A Preliminary Archeological Sequence for the Upper Orinoco Valley, Territorio Federal Amazonas, Venezuela." Ph.D. dissertation, Catholic University of America, Washington, D.C.

Berman, M. J., and P. L. Gnivecki. 1994. "The Colonization of the Bahamas Archipelago: A View from the Three Dog Site, San Salvador Island." In *Proceedings of the Fourteenth Congress of the International Association for Caribbean Archaeology*, 170–186. Ed. A. Cummins and P. King. St. Michael: Barbados Museum and Historical Society.

Boomert, A. 1987. "Gifts of the Amazons: 'Green Stone' Pendants and Beads as Items of Ceremonial Exchange in Amazonia and the Caribbean." *Antropológica* (Caracas) 67: 33–54.

Booy, T., de. 1919. *Archaeology of the Virgin Islands*. Indian Notes and Monographs, 1. New York: Museum of the American Indian, Heye Foundation.

Budinoff, L. C. 1991. "An Osteological Analysis of the Human Burials Recovered from an Early Site Located on the North Coast of Puerto Rico." In *Proceedings of the Twelfth Congress of the International Association for Caribbean Archaeology, Cayenne, French Guiana, July / August, 1987*, 45–51. Ed. L. S. Robinson. Martinique.

Bullbrook, J. A. 1953. *On the Excavation of a Shell Mound at Palo Seco, Trinidad, B.W.I.* Publications in Anthropology, 50. New Haven: Department of Anthropology, Yale University.

Bullen, R. P. 1964. *The Archaeology of Grenada, West Indies*. Florida State Museum, Contributions, Social Sciences, 11. Gainesville: University of Florida.

Caldwell, J. R. 1966. "The New American Archaeology." In *The New Roads to Yesterday: Essays in Archaeology*, 333–347. Ed. J. R. Caldwell. New York: Basic Books.

Chanlatte Baik, L. A. 1981. *La Hueca y Sorcé (Vieques, Puerto Rico): Primeras migraciones agroalfareras Antillanas: Nueva esquema para los procesos culturales de la arqueología Antillana*. Santo Domingo: Privately printed.

Coll y Toste, C. 1907. *Prehistoria de Puerto Rico*. San Juan: Tipografía Boletín Mercantil.

Crosby, A. W., Jr. 1972. *The Columbian Exchange: Biological and Cultural Consequences of 1492*. Contributions in American Studies. Ed. R. H. Walker. Westport, CT: Greenwood Press.

Cruxent, J. M., and I. Rouse. 1958–1959. *An Archeological Chronology of Venezuela*. 2 vols.

Social Science Monographs, 6. Washington, DC: Pan American Union.

Cummins, A., and P. King, eds. 1994. *Proceedings of the Fourteenth Congress of the International Association for Caribbean Archaeology Barbados, 21–28 July 1991*. St. Michael: Barbados Museum and Historical Society.

Evans, C., and B. J. Meggers. 1960. *Archeological Investigations in British Guiana*. Bureau of American Ethnology, Bulletin 177. Washington, DC: Smithsonian Institution.

Fewkes, J. W. 1907. "The Aborigines of Porto Rico and the Neighboring Islands." In *Twenty-fifth Annual Report of the Bureau of American Ethnology for 1903–04*, 17–220. Washington, DC: Smithsonian Institution.

———. 1922. "A Prehistoric Island Culture Area of America." In *Thirty-fourth Annual Report of the Bureau of American Ethnology for 1912–13*, 49–273. Washington, DC: Smithsonian Institution.

García Arevalo, M. 1988. *Indigenismo, arqueología, e identidad nacional*. Santo Domingo: Museo del Hombre Dominicano and Fundación García Arevalo.

Gassón, R., and E. Wagner. 1991. "Los otros 'vestigios de la Atlántida,' o el surgimiento de la arqueología moderna en Venezuela y sus consequencias." In *Tiempos de Cambio: La Ciencia en Venezuela 1936–1948*, 215–240. Ed. Y. Fraites and Y. Texeral Arenal. Caracas: Fondo Editorial Acta Científica Venezolana.

González Colón, J. 1984. "Tibes: Un centro ceremonial indígena." M.A. thesis, Centro de Estudios Avanzados de Puerto Rico y el Caribe, San Juan.

Goodwin, R. C. 1979. "The Prehistoric Cultural Ecology of St. Kitts, West Indies: A Case Study in Island Archaeology." Ph.D. dissertation, Arizona State University, Tempe.

Harrington, M. R. 1921. *Cuba before Columbus*. 2 vols. Indian Notes and Monographs. New York: Museum of the American Indian, Heye Foundation.

Hatt, G. 1924. "Archaeology of the Virgin Islands." In *Proceedings of the Twenty-first International Congress of Americanists 1*, 29–42. The Hague.

Haviser, J. B., Jr. 1978. "Amerindian Cultural Geography on Curaçao." Ph.D. dissertation, University of Leiden.

Hill, M., and I. Rouse. 1994. "Computerization of the Caribbean Archaeological Collections." *Dis-covery 24*, no. 2: 18–21. Peabody Museum of Natural History, Yale University.

Hofman, C. L. 1993. "In Search of the Native Population of Pre-Columbian Saba (400–1450 A.D.): Part One, Pottery Styles and Their Interpretation." Ph.D. dissertation, University of Leiden.

Jones, A. R. 1985. "Dietary Change and Human Population at Indian Creek, Antigua." *American Antiquity 50*, no. 3: 518–553.

Keegan, W. F. 1989. "Transition from a Terrestrial to a Maritime Economy: A New View of the Crab/Shell Dichotemy." In *Early Ceramic Population Lifeways and Adaptive Strategies in the Caribbean*, 119–128. Ed. P. E. Siegel. International Series 506. Oxford: BAR.

———. 1992. *The People Who Discovered Columbus: The Prehistory of the Bahamas*. Gainesville: University Press of Florida.

Keegan, W. F., and M. D. Maclachlan. 1989. "The Evolution of Avunculocal Chiefdoms: A Reconstruction of Taino Kinship and Politics." *American Anthropologist 91*, no. 3: 613–630.

Kozlowski, J. K. 1974. "In Search of the Evolutionary Pattern of the Preceramic Cultures of the Caribbean." *Boletín del Museo del Hombre Dominicano 9*, no. 13: 61–79.

Lathrap, D. W. 1970. *The Upper Amazon*. Ancient Peoples and Places, 70. New York: Praeger Publishers.

———. 1973. "The Antiquity and Importance of Long-distance Trade Relationships in the Moist Tropics of Pre-Columbian South America." *World Archaeology 5*, no. 2: 170–186.

Lovén, S. 1935. *Origins of the Tainan Culture, West Indies*. Göteborg: Elanders Bokfryckeri Äkfiebolag.

Lumbreras, L. G. 1974. *The Peoples and Cultures of Ancient Peru*. Translated by B. J. Meggers. Washington, DC: Smithsonian Institution Press.

Mason, J. A. 1941. *A Large Archaeological Site at Capá, Utuado, with Notes on Other Porto Rican Sites Visited in 1914–15*. Scientific Survey of Porto Rico and the Virgin Islands, 18:1. New York: New York Academy of Sciences.

Merwe, N. van der, A. C. Roosevelt, and J. C. Vogel. 1981. "Isotopic Evidence for Prehistoric Subsistence Change at Parmana, Venezuela." *Nature 292*, no. 5823: 536–538.

Oliver, J. R. 1989. "The Archaeological, Linguistic, and Ethnohistorical Evidence for the Expansion of Arawakan into Northwestern Venezuela and

Northeastern Columbia." Ph.D. dissertation, University of Illinois at Urbana-Champaign.

Ortiz, F. 1935. "Historia de la arqueología Indocubana." In *Cuba antes de Colón*, 2: 23–457. Ed. M. R. Harrington. Havana: Colección de Libros Cubanos 33, Cultural.

Osgood, C. 1946. *British Guiana Archeology to 1945*. Publications in Anthropology, 36. New Haven: Yale University.

Pantel, A. G. 1988. "Precolumbian Flaked Stone Assemblages in the West Indies." Ph.D. dissertation, University of Tennessee, Knoxville.

Rainey, F. G. 1940. *Porto Rican Archaeology*. Scientific Survey of Porto Rico and the Virgin Islands, 18:2. New York: New York Academy of Sciences.

———. 1941. *Excavations in the Ft. Liberté Region, Haiti*. Publications in Anthropology, 24. New Haven: Department of Anthropology, Yale University.

Rodríguez, M. 1990. "Arqueología del Río Loíza." In *Proceedings of the Eleventh Congress of the International Association for Caribbean Archaeology, San Juan, July and August 1985,* 287–294. Ed. A. G. Pantel, I. Vargas, and M. Sanoja. San Juan: Fundación Arqueológica, Antropológica, e Histórica de Puerto Rico, Universidad de Puerto Rico at Río Piedras, and Forest Service of the U.S.A. Department of Agriculture.

Roe, P. G. 1994. "Cross-Media Isomorphisms in Taino Ceramics and Petroglyphs from Puerto Rico." In *Proceedings of the Fourteenth Congress of the International Association for Caribbean Archaeology Barbados, 21–28 July 1991,* 637–680. Ed. A. Cummins and P. King. St. Michael: Barbados Museum and Historical Society.

Roosevelt, A. C. 1980. *Parmana: Prehistoric Maize and Manioc Subsistence along the Amazon and Orinoco*. New York: Academic Press.

Rouse, I. 1939. *Prehistory in Haiti: A Study in Method*. Publications in Anthropology, 21. New Haven: Department of Anthropology, Yale University.

———. 1947. "Prehistory of Trinidad in Relation to Adjacent Areas." *Man* 47, no. 103: 93–98.

———. 1952. *Porto Rican Prehistory*. Scientific Survey of Porto Rico and the Virgin Islands, 18:3,4. New York: New York Academy of Sciences.

———. 1964. "Prehistory of the West Indies." *Science* 144, no. 3618: 489–513.

———. 1972. *Introduction to Prehistory: A Systematic Approach*. New York: McGraw-Hill.

———. 1982. "Ceramic and Religious Development in the Greater Antilles." *Journal of New World Archaeology* 5, no. 2: 45–55.

———. 1986. *Migrations in Prehistory: Inferring Population Movement from Cultural Remains*. New Haven: Yale University Press.

———. 1992. *The Tainos: Rise and Decline of the People Who Greeted Columbus*. New Haven: Yale University Press.

———. 1994. "Les origenes et le développement de la culture Taïno." In *L'Art des sculpteurs Taïnos: Chefs-d'oeuvre des Grandes Antilles Precolombiennes,* 12–17. Ed. J. Kerchache. Paris: Musées de la Ville de Paris.

Rouse, I., and J. M. Cruxent. 1963. *Venezuelan Archaeology*. New Haven: Yale University Press.

Sanoja, M., and I. Vargas. 1983. "New Light on the Prehistory of Eastern Venezuela." *Advances in World Archaeology* 2: 205–244.

Siegel, P. E. 1992. "Ideology, Power, and Social Complexity in Prehistoric Puerto Rico." Ph.D. dissertation, State University of New York at Binghamton.

Siegel, P. E., and K. P. Severin. 1993. "The First Documented Gold-Copper Alloy Artifact from the West Indies." *Journal of Archaeological Science* 20, no. 1: 67–79.

Spencer, C. S., and E. M. Redmond. 1992. "Prehistoric Chiefdoms of the Western Venezuelan Llanos." *World Archaeology* 24, no. 1: 135–155.

Sullivan, S. D. 1981. "Prehistoric Patterns of Exploitation and Colonization in the Turks and Caicos Islands." Ph.D. dissertation, University of Illinos at Urbana-Champaign.

Tacoma, J. 1991. "Precolumbian Human Skeletal Remains from Curaçao, Aruba, and Bonaire." In *Proceedings of the Thirteenth International Congress for Caribbean Archaeology, Held in Curaçao on July 24–29, 1989,* 802–812. Ed. S. Ayubi and J. B. Haviser. Willemstad: Archaeological-Anthropological Institute of the Netherlands Antilles.

Vega, B. 1980. *Los cacicazgos de la Hispaniola*. Santo Domingo: Ediciones Museo del Hombre Dominicano.

Veloz Maggiolo, M., and E. Ortega. 1976. "The Preceramic of the Dominican Republic: Some New Finds and Their Possible Relationships." In *Proceedings of the First Puerto Rican Symposium in Archaeology,* 147–201. Ed. L. S. Robinson. San Juan: Fundación Arqueológica, Antropológica, e Histórica de Puerto Rico.

Veloz Maggiolo, M., E. Ortega, and A. Caba Fuentes. 1973. *Los modos de vida Meillacos y sus posibles orígenes (un estudio interpretativo).* Santo Domingo: Museo del Hombre Dominicano.

Versteeg, A. H., and F. C. Bubberman. 1992. *Suriname before Columbus.* Paramaribo, Suriname: Stichting Surinaams Museum.

Versteeg, A. H., and K. Schinkel, eds. 1992. *The Archaeology of St. Eustatius: The Golden Rock Site.* Amsterdam: St. Eustatius Foundation and Foundation for Scientific Research in the Caribbean Region.

Vescelius, G. S. 1986. "A Cultural Taxonomy for West Indian Archaeology." *Journal of the Virgin Islands Archaeological Society* 10: 36–39.

Wagner, E. 1978. "Problemática de la destrucción arqueológica y la ética del arqueólogo." In *Proceedings of the Seventh International Congress for the Study of Pre-Columbian Cultures of the Lesser Antilles, Caracas, July 11–16, 1977,* 345–349. Ed. J. Benoit and F-M. Mayer. Montreal: Centre de Recherches Caraïbes, Université de Montréal.

Watters, D. R. 1976. "Caribbean Prehistory: A Century of Researchers, Models, and Trends." M.A. thesis, University of Nevada at Reno.

———. 1980. "Transect Surveying and Prehistoric Site Locations on Barbuda and Montserrat, Leeward Islands, West Indies." Ph.D. dissertation, University of Pittsburgh.

———. 1982. "Relating Oceanography to Antillean Archaeology: Implications from Oceania." *Journal of New World Archaeology* 5, no. 2: 3–12.

Willey, G. R. 1945. "Horizon Styles and Pottery Traditions in Peruvian Archaeology." *American Antiquity* 11, no. 1: 49–56.

———. 1971. *An Introduction to American Archaeology.* Vol. 2, *South America.* Englewood Cliffs, NJ: Prentice-Hall.

Willey, G. R., and P. Phillips. 1958. *Method and Theory in American Archaeology.* Chicago: University of Chicago Press.

Wilson, S. N. 1990. *Hispaniola: Caribbean Chiefdoms in the Age of Columbus.* Tuscaloosa: University of Alabama Press.

Wing, E. 1962. "Succession of Mammalian Faunas on Trinidad, West Indies." Ph.D. dissertation, University of Florida, Gainesville.

———. 1989. *Mitología y artes prehispánicas de las Antillas.* 2d ed. Mexico City: Siglo Veintiuno Editores.

Cartailhac, Emile (Edouard Phillipe) (1845–1921)

Emile (Edouard Phillipe) Cartailhac was born in Marseilles, France. He became a geologist and worked with Edouard and Henri Filhol at the Musée d'Histoire Naturelle in Toulouse, and it was those two men who encouraged his interest in prehistory. In 1866, Cartailhac moved to Paris where he was influenced by French prehistorians GABRIEL DE MORTILLET and HENRI BREUIL. Cartailhac and Mortillet were the founders of the International Congress of Anthropology and Prehistoric Archaeology, which held its first meeting in Neuchâtel, Switzerland, in 1866. In 1869, Cartailhac bought the journal founded by Mortillet, *Materiaux pour l'histoire naturelle et primitive de l'homme,* an important publication for promoting prehistory and anthropology. Cartailhac edited and published the journal until 1890 when it was amalgamated with the *Revues d'Anthropologie and d'Ethnologie* to form *L'Anthropologie.*

Cartailhac is most famous for his role in the authentication of Paleolithic cave art. In the late nineteenth century quantities of moveable Paleolithic pieces of art, engravings, and sculptures on bone, ivory, and antler wood were exhumed from prehistoric sites along with animal and human bones and stone tools. These cave sites were occasionally decorated with engravings and representations on their walls and ceilings, and the idea that early prehistoric humans could create art as well as stone tools was rejected by Cartailhac and many other archaeologists, who argued that this cave art was neither old nor authentic. By the beginning of the twentieth century, however, this view began to be debated as more discoveries of carvings and cave paintings were made at sites that were clearly from the Upper Paleolithic period. The study of ethnology had grown, and there was now evidence of this kind of art, some of it contemporary, all over the world.

In 1902, Cartailhac and Breuil rediscovered and explored the magnificent cave of ALTAMIRA in Spain. First found in 1879 by a local landowner and his daughter, the cave had been considered a forgery, rejected as an example of prehistoric art, and neglected. Visiting it certainly changed Cartailhac's mind—perhaps the

Howard Carter (left) at the entrance of Tutankhamun's tomb in Luxor, 1922 (Ann Ronan Picture Library)

cave's vastness, the fact that it was so obviously and beautifully painted, or the fact that the animals it portrayed were so identifiably extinct— had such force that he wrote "Mea Culpa of a Skeptic" that same year in which he apologized and recognized the authenticity of Paleolithic cave art. Breuil and Cartailhac went on to explore the cave of Niaux in the Ariège in 1906.

Tim Murray

See also Rock Art

Carter, Howard (1874–1939)

Born in London, the son of a talented painter and illustrator, Carter grew up in Norfolk. At the age of fifteen he first visited the country home of Baron Amherst of Hackney, whose important collection of Egyptian antiquities were to influence and inspire Carter's interest in archaeology. Baron Amherst was a supporter of the Egyptian Exploration Fund and it was via this connection that Howard Carter was hired as a draftsman and copyist by the Archaeological Survey of Egypt. He received some training in Egyptology and hieroglyphics at the BRITISH MUSEUM before leaving for Egypt in 1891.

Carter proved his worth as a competent and committed archaeological draftsman, going on to join SIR FLINDERS PETRIE at excavations at El-Amarna in 1892. Here Carter received training as an excavator from the best Egyptologist of his time. Carter's rapidly growing proficiency as an excavator and site manager, as well as an illustrator and photographer, was recognized when he was appointed to the post of chief inspector of antiquities in Upper Egypt and NUBIA in 1900. During the four years he spent in this position Carter undertook important conservation work but was left little time to excavate. However he was able to carry out detailed surveys of the Valley of the Kings, eventually locating the tombs of Thutmosis I and Queen Hatshepsut.

In 1904 Carter became chief inspector of Lower Egypt, but due to a diplomatic row he left the antiquities service and supported himself as an archaeological illustrator and draftsman, buying and selling in the antiquities trade and acting as a guide for wealthy visitors to the Valley of the Kings. In 1909 Carter was hired as expert assistant by Lord Carnarvon, who had decided he would like to try excavating in the Valley of the Kings. The two excavated other sites in Egypt for five years before they were allowed to work in the Valley of the Kings from 1914. World War I put their project on hold; then from 1918 to 1922 they searched the valley for a promising site. By this time Carnarvon had become disenchanted, and by 1922 he had decided this would be their last year. In November Carter telegraphed him in Britain to return: "At last have made wonderful discovery . . . a magnificent tomb with seals intact . . ."

Carter's long training in the practical business of excavating tombs, as well as his skill in recording their contents, made him an ideal person to undertake the task of clearing and documenting the tomb of TUTANKHAMUN. But his lack of formal education, his uneasiness about his social position, his obstinacy, and his lack of diplomacy were problematic. Tutankhamun's tomb transformed him from being an unknown journeyman excavator to a great archaeological discoverer. Clearing and cataloguing the finds changed archaeology in Egypt forever, and strife between Carter and the Antiquities Department lasted for decades. Carter's greatest gift to Egyptology and posterity was not a monumental scholarly work or new insights into the nature of ancient Egyptian life, but the eight years he spent organizing and supervising the work of a large team of photographers, conservators, and illustrators who patiently catalogued and recorded the contents of the tomb of this minor Pharaoh.

When work on the tomb finally finished in 1932 Carter spent much of his time in Luxor dreaming of discovering the tomb of Alexander the Great, or in London going about his business in the antiquities trade. He received few academic and public honors. He died in London in 1939.

Tim Murray

See also Egypt, Dynastic; Egypt Exploration Society
References
For references, see *Encyclopedia of Archaeology: The Great Archaeologists, Vol. 1,* ed. Tim Murray (Santa Barbara, CA: ABC-CLIO, 1999), p. 300.

Casa Grande

Casa Grande, located on the Gila River between Phoenix and Tuscon, Arizona, is a large Hohokam Classic–period ruin. Casa Grande is Spanish for Great House, and this structure is part of a large site with numerous compounds. Prehistoric occupation of the Southwest spans 12,000 years, and Casa Grande is the type-site (an exemplary site; the best example of a type of site) for the Hohokam Classic Period, A.D. 1100 to 1300. Named the first federal reservation for a prehistoric ruin in the United States, Casa Grande Ruins National Monument, the site includes a great house, ball court, and many compounds. No other great houses have been found, although two others may have been built between the Salt and Gila rivers.

The archaeology of Arizona has a long, complex history of exploration and excavation by amateurs and professionals. During the time of discovery in Arizona, research was aided by private funding, the creation of national monuments, and university research institutions. In

1935 several prominent publications were started across the United States: AMERICAN ANTIQUITY, the *Journal of the Society for American Archaeology*, and *The Kiva*. Casa Grande Compound A was excavated in the early 1900s by Jesse Walter Fewkes of the newly formed Bureau of American Ethnology. Organized archaeological research began in 1927 with HAROLD S. GLADWIN's expedition to Casa Grande to conduct stratigraphic excavation, which revealed evidence of two peoples and two potteries on the site. Gladwin founded the Gila Pueblo Archaeological Foundation, which is credited with consolidating the Hohokam research to a definite culture. In 1930 Emil W. Haury became Gladwin's assistant director, and his subsequent report on the Snaketown site defined Hohokam culture.

The particular housing style of Casa Grande is distinctive for the Hohokam Classic period. Casa Grande walls were built of piled-up adobe that was then dried and sometimes smoothed, polished, and plastered. The roof was made of juniper, pine, fir, and mesquite wood. The house had a lower story that was filled in, creating a mound, second and third stories with five rooms, and a top story with a single tower-like room. A compound was created by building walls surrounding the house.

Research on the Hohokam period reveals dramatic changes in architecture, pottery, and funeral customs. Changes have been attributed to causes as varied as drought, culture collapse, and migration. As in most southwestern sites, control of water is essential to survival. Casa Grande's location is a key to its function. Located at the end of an irrigation canal, it may be that the farmers controlled the water from the canal.

Danielle Greene

See also United States of America, Prehistoric
References
McGuire, Randall H., and Michael B. Schiffer. 1982. *Hohokam and Patayan: Prehistory of Southwestern Arizona*. New York: Academic Press.
Ortiz, Alfono, vol. ed. 1979. *Handbook of North American Indians: Southwest, Volume 9*. Washington, DC: Smithsonian Institution.
Reid, Jefferson, and Stephanie Whittlesey. 1997. *The Archaeology of Ancient Arizona*. Tucson: The University of Arizona Press.

Çatal Huyük
See Turkey

Catherwood, Frederick (1799–1854)

Frederick Catherwood and JOHN LLOYD STEPHENS brought the great indigenous American civilizations of Central America to the attention of the world in the 1840s. Not only were Catherwood's detailed drawings evidence of this great unknown culture, but they also remain valuable sources for details of Maya glyphs.

Catherwood was born in London, trained as an architect, and became an accomplished artist and architectural draftsman. He spent many years traveling in Greece and the Near East studying archaeological sites and drawing ruins. He and the antiquarian Robert Hay worked together on one of the first attempts to record Egyptian temples and monuments.

Catherwood returned to England, where the exhibition of his Near Eastern drawings brought him to the attention of the American adventurer John Lloyd Stephens, who had himself spent many years touring the archaeological sites of Greece, the Near East, and Egypt. The two developed a friendship based on their shared interest in archaeological exploration. It was Catherwood who alerted Stephen to two small books on the ruins of Central America, and together they began to plan an expedition to this unexplored region. Catherwood joined Stephens in New York where he had established a successful architectural practice. In the meantime Stephens wrote and published *Incidents of Travel in Arabia Petraea* in 1839 and another book about Greece, Turkey, Russia, and Poland, both of which became best-sellers and made him the fortune that was to finance an archaeological expedition to Central America.

The exotic ruined temples in the steamy jungles of Central America had, by this time, been noted by French explorers and artists such as Guillermo Dupaix and Jean Frederic Waldeck, and had provoked some interest in New York and Europe. In 1839, after Stephens managed to secure a useful presidential appointment as a diplomatic minister in Central America, the pair traveled to BELIZE. The physical difficulties

A drawing by Frederick Catherwood of El Castillo pyramid from Chichén Itzá, Yucatán, Mexico (Dover Pictorial Archive)

of traveling in Central America at this time were enormous—it was the rainy season and the jungle had overgrown known sites. Catherwood and Stephens made their way to Copan, where Indians were hired to clear vegetation off stelae. This done, Catherwood, his ankles in mud and continually bitten by mosquitoes, began to record the complex art of an unknown civilization on damp paper. He and Stephens found fifty pieces of sculpture during the first two hours of exploring Copan, and they were to spend months surveying and recording the site with a compass and tape. Stephens's vivid written descriptions were well matched by Catherwood's painstaking drawings of stelae, sculpture, and architectural details. Catherwood's plan of the site of Copan was so good that it remained the authoritative source for the next fifty years.

Catherwood and Stephens decided to visit the site of PALENQUE on their way back to the United States via MEXICO. They were undeterred by the fact that this site was a thousand miles away from Copan, that no one had ever traveled to it via Guatemala City, that the Yucatán was in state of civil war, that the local inhabitants were

hostile, and that it was, once again, the rainy season. Their effort was rewarded by the magnificence of the ruins. Once again conditions were appalling and they were both ill, but Catherwood's recordings of the palace, its bas-reliefs, and its hieroglyphics were outstanding. The two traveled on to the site of Uxmal, at which they could only spend a few days due to exhaustion and illness. Indeed Catherwood was only well enough to draw for one day and had to be carried to the coast on a litter. They returned to New York after ten months of traveling, and on June 25, 1841, *Incidents of Travel in Central America, Chiapas and Yucatán* was published to great interest and acclaim.

Fifteen months later Stephens and Catherwood returned to the Yucatán once again. Catherwood brought with him the new daguerrotype apparatus and he and Stephens spent two months at Uxmal mapping, surveying, and drawing. After this they traveled via the wells of Bolonchen to CHICHÉN ITZÁ and then on to Cozumel and Tulum, once again mapping, surveying, and drawing, and returned to New York in 1842. *Incidents of Travel in the Yucatán* was published nine months later, and was also an outstanding success. It also marked the end of their involvement with the Maya. Both Catherwood and Stephens pursued their careers in other directions, either alone or as partners, such as in the Panama railroad project in 1849.

Stephens died in 1852, his life shortened by the complications of various tropical diseases. Catherwood died in 1854, one of three hundred passengers to go down with the S.S. *Arctic* in the middle of the Atlantic Ocean.

Tim Murray

See also Guatemala; Maya Civilization

Caton-Thompson, Gertrude (1888–1985)

Born in London and educated in Eastbourne, Caton-Thompson was from an upper-middle-class family, and the early death of her father made her financially independent for the whole of her life. Until World War I she enjoyed an active social life in London and the country, and she traveled, describing her trips to Italy and Egypt during this time as the source of her later interest in archaeology.

In 1917 she was employed by the Ministry of Shipping and promoted to a senior secretarial post in which she attended the Paris Peace Conference. She declined a permanent appointment in the civil service and in 1921, aged 33, began her archaeological studies under Margaret Murray, Dorothea Bate and Sir W. M. FLINDERS PETRIE at University College London. Caton-Thompson joined Petrie's excavations at ABYDOS in Upper Egypt in 1921 and Murray's excavations in Malta in 1922. She spent the next year at Newnham College, Cambridge, attending courses in prehistory, geology, and anthropology.

In 1924 she returned to Egypt to work with Petrie and Brunton at Qau. While they investigated the cemetery, Caton-Thompson excavated the predynastic settlement site at Hemamieh and discovered the Badarian civilization. With Guy Brunton she wrote *The Badarian Civilization* (1928).

In 1925, accompanied by the Oxford geologist Elinor Gardner, Caton-Thompson began the Archaeological and Geological Survey of the

Gertrude Caton-Thompson (Hulton Getty)

northern Fayum, one of the first interdisciplinary surveys on settlement patterns and sequences in Egypt. Between 1927 and 1928 she excavated and worked with Gardner in northwestern Egypt on the desert margins of Lake Fayum, discovering two unknown Neolithic cultures that were later proven to be part of the Khartoum Neolithic. Their findings were published in *The Desert Fayum* (1934).

In 1929 Caton-Thompson was invited by the British Association for the Advancement of Science to investigate the great monumental ruins at GREAT ZIMBABWE in southern Africa. She confirmed that these ruins belonged to an indigenous African culture and dated them to the eighth or ninth centuries A.D., producing evidence of Zimbabwe's links with Indian Ocean trade. One of her assistants on this project was the young Oxford graduate KATHLEEN KENYON. Caton-Thompson's conclusions were published in *The Zimbabwe Culture* (1931). In 1930 she and Elinor Gardner collaborated again on excavations of prehistoric sites at the Kharga Oasis. These were the first Saharan oasis sites to be excavated, and the first in a large research program on the investigation of the Paleolithic of

North Africa, culminating in the book *Kharga Oasis in Pre-history* (1952).

Caton-Thompson's last excavations in 1937 were of the fourth and fifth centuries B.C. Moon temple and tombs at Hureidha in the Hadhramaut of southern Arabia (now Yemen). These were the first scientific excavations in southern Arabia, and she was accompanied on this trip by Elinor Gardner and Dame Freya Stark. Their findings were written up in *The Tombs and Moon Temple of Hureidha, Hadramaut* in 1944.

Between 1940 and 1946 Caton-Thompson was president of the Prehistoric Society, the only woman to hold this position. In 1944 she was elected a fellow of the British Academy and became a fellow of University College, London. She retired from field work after World War II, but continued to research and visit excavations in East Africa. In 1946 she was awarded the Huxley Medal of the Royal Anthropological Institute, and in 1954 the Burton Medal from the Royal Asiatic Society. In 1954 she was made an honorary fellow of Newnham College Cambridge, and received an honorary Litt.D. from Cambridge University. Between 1946 and 1960 she was a governor of the School of Oriental and African Studies in London. In 1961 she became a founding member of the British School of History and Archaeology in East Africa (later the British Institute in East Africa) and served on its council for ten years, becoming an honorary member. Although Caton-Thompson was widely regarded as being an archaeologist of formidable skill and determination, she never sought a position in a museum or a university. It has been rumored that she was once offered the prestigious Disney chair of archaeology at the University of Cambridge and that she refused it. It is true that her personal wealth allowed Caton-Thompson the freedom to work outside the constraints of an institution, and there can be no doubt that she used this advantage to make highly significant contributions to the archaeology of Africa and Arabia.

Tim Murray

See also Africa, South, Prehistory; Egypt: Predynastic

Caylus, Comte de (1692–1765)

Anne-Claude-Philippe de Tubières-Grimord, Comte de Caylus, was an antiquary and dilettante of the early-eighteenth century who traveled widely engaging in excavation (especially in Asia Minor) and observation. French art historian Alain Schnapp (1996, 238–242) has noted that Caylus, through an extensive system of contacts built up through patronage and a common interest in the ancient past, was able to conceive of the goals of the antiquary more broadly than others before him.

Committed to publication (especially his seven-volume *Recueil d'antiquités égyptiennes, étrusques, greques, et romaines* published between 1752 and 1757) and careful illustration and observation, Caylus developed a rational basis for the description and classification of the large number of objects in his collection, and in doing so, he influenced the course of French antiquarian studies in the eighteenth century.

Tim Murray

References
Schnapp, Alain. 1996. *The Discovery of the Past.* London: British Museum Press.

Celeia

The pre-Roman site of *Keleia* (Celje) is located in the southeastern part of the Savinja valley, at the foot of the Karavanke and Savinjske Alps, in Central SLOVENIA. An early Iron Age settlement was located at Miklav-ki hrib, on the southern edge of the modern town of Celje. "The Amber Road," a prehistoric trade and exchange route linking the Baltic with the northern Adriatic, ran through this area. A LA TÈNE settlement was occupied by the Celtic Taurisci tribe, who minted their own currency in the town. In the first century B.C. the settlement became part of the *Regnum Noricum* (the Kingdom of Noricum), an entity formed by Celtic tribes of the Eastern Alps. The Romans annexed the kingdom in 15 B.C. and made it the province of Noricum during the reign of Claudius (A.D. 41–54). Celeia was raised to the status of *Municipium* (*municipium Claudium Celeia*). Itineraries (such as *Tabula Peutingeriana, Itinerarium Burdigalense, Itinararium*

Antonini) bear witness to the location of the town on the *Aquileia-Emona-Poetovio* road. The Roman town name is recorded on over a hundred inscriptions and on numerous milestones.

The town covered an area of about sixty-five hectares and had about 10,000 inhabitants at its peak during the second and third centuries when, to a large extent, it retained its Celtic character. The autochthonous component was reflected in onomastic material, the worship of Celtic divinities such as Epona, Noreia, Celeia, etc., and in the archaeological remains. Celeia did not exhibit a regular insular layout, because it developed out of a pre-existing settlement. Houses were located along roads, some of which were paved in the town's center and, in some sections, lined with colonnades. Excavations have revealed houses that were adorned with mosaics and frescos, dated from the first to the fourth century. A second-century Roman temple was located on the southern edge of the town. The forum, as yet not excavated, was probably situated in the southwestern part of the town.

Cemeteries were located in the western, southern, and northern parts of the town, along roads leading to EMONA, Neviodunum, and Poetovio. Marble vaults for some of the local eminent politicians can also be found some fifteen kilometers west of Celeia, where their estates were situated. The town wall was built after the great flood of the river Savinja at the end of the third century. The town was the seat of a diocese in the Early Christian period (fifth and early sixth centuries A.D.). A church decorated with richly colored mosaics, donatorial inscriptions, and a baptisterium were recorded, dating from this period. After the fall of the Roman Empire, the town was abandoned and its former inhabitants sought refuge in isolated upland settlements.

The first reports of the collection and protection of Roman monuments in Celje date from the end of the fifteenth century. Some of the monuments were incorporated into buildings and churches during the sixteenth through the eighteenth centuries. The foundation of the Municipal Museum (*Mestni muzej*) in 1882 helped to protect extant monuments and led to the first organized archaeological excavations of the site in 1889.

Irena Lazar

References

Šašel, J. 1970. "Celeia." RE Suppl. 12, 139–148 (*Opera Selecta* [1992]: 583–587).

Celts

Ancient Sources

The name *Keltoi* (Celts), probably a corruption of another Greek word, *Galatoi,* was first used by Greek writers in possibly the early sixth century B.C. Avienus, in his *Ora maritima* written in the fourth century A.D., claimed to be using sources dating from the sixth century B.C., including a sailing manual known as the *Massiliot periplus.* Avienus referred to Great Britain as Albion and Ireland as Iernè, and he also mentioned Ligurians in southern France being pushed southward into Iberia by Celts.

Around 500 B.C., Hecataeus of Miletus, writing on the Phocaean Greek settlement at Massalia (Marseilles), placed it in the land of the Ligurians while identifying nearby Narbo (Narbonne) as Celtic. In 480 B.C., Herodotus, with a rather jumbled geographical sense, recorded that *Keltoi* were to be found at the headwaters of the Danube, near the city of Pyrene on the Turkish coast, and west of the Pillars of Hercules (Gibraltar). By this period, there is archaeological evidence of goods traded by Greeks to peoples in FRANCE and by Etruscans (as exemplified by a wealthy woman's grave of the late sixth century found at Vix on the river Saône in central France), so first-hand information from Greek travelers would have been available. Although it seems highly doubtful that any one term was applied universally to the indigenous peoples of Europe north of the Alps, it seems only sensible to use two names almost interchangeably, following Julius Caesar, who wrote in the mid-first century B.C. of the inhabitants of what is now central France that the Romans called them Gauls, but they called themselves Celts.

In the mid-sixth century B.C., Greek exchange links with "barbarian" centers north of

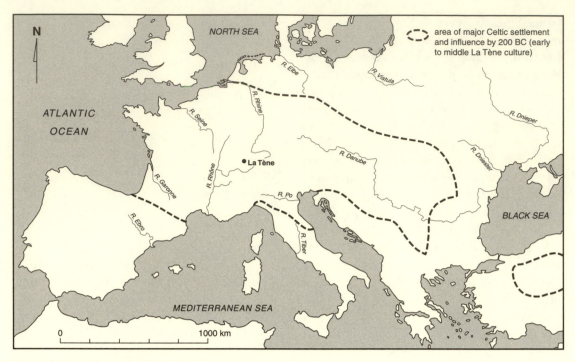

Areas of Celtic Influence by 200 B.C.

the Alps—in northern FRANCE, Rhineland Germany, SWITZERLAND, and AUSTRIA—were disrupted by the destructive power of an alliance between the Phoenician colonies of the western Mediterranean with the Etruscans and by the Persian occupation of eastern Greece and, for a brief period, of mainland Greece itself. Etruscan contacts developed in their place, because while Etruscan expansion into southern Italy was blocked by Greek settlements (or Magna Graecia), the Etruscans did consolidate their power in the region of the Po River in northern Italy.

In the first two decades of the fourth century B.C., three tribal groups named Galli, or Gauls (the Boii, Cenomani, and Insubres), and later the group known as the Senones invaded northern Italy from across the Alps. The Boii possibly originated from Bohemia while the others were most probably from northeastern France, where the district of Champagne showed signs of depopulation at this time. The sources for this movement of peoples include the Roman and Greek historians Livy (59 B.C.–A.D. 17), who was born in the Padua region of Italy, and Polybius (ca. 200–122 B.C.), who dated the arrival of the Gauls two centuries earlier.

The newcomers offered a serious threat to

Etruscan power and settled in the Po Valley, where archaeological evidence of destruction and of new settlement in harmony with the indigenous population can be seen at such places as Bologna, Spina, and Monte Bibele. As Livy recounts, in 390 B.C., Rome was almost destroyed by the Gauls, who took six of its seven hills and nearly ended Roman power, which had flourished in the wake of the Etruscans' defeat. A further six attacks were made on Rome between 367 and 320 B.C., and the Gauls later joined Hannibal's troops to attack Rome in 218 B.C.

Further east in the Mediterranean, Celts were fighting as mercenaries in the Greek world from 369 B.C., when the Greek historian Xenophon (ca. 430–ca. 360 B.C.) records that Dionysius of Syracuse lent 200 Celts to aid the Spartans against his enemies in Thebes. Celts and the Celtic culture also spread east down the Danube River as far as Hungary, and Alexander the Great met and negotiated with Celts in 335 B.C., when they boasted that they feared nothing but that the heavens might fall on them. Their petition to settle in Greece having been denied, in 281 B.C. they killed the Macedonian king, Ptolemy Keraunos, and moved into Thrace.

In 279 B.C., groups of Celts invaded Greece and attacked the sanctuary of Apollo at Delphi, and may even have sacked it, but they were driven out. Some settled in the Balkans, where the Celtic capitol of Tylis was established somewhere in what is now Bulgaria, while others crossed into Anatolia (now central Turkey), where they were known as Galatae, or Galatians. They proved to be destabilizing intruders until they were defeated in about 233 B.C. by Antigonos I, and later by his son Eumenes II, who in thanks dedicated a sanctuary to Athene Nikephoros where the famous statues of the *Dying Gaul* and the *Gaul Killing Himself and His Wife* were first displayed. Known now only from Roman copies made in the second century A.D., these statues originally formed part of a victory complex incorporating, on the temple's balustrade, a frieze of military trophies that showed weapons and armor that were comparable to those of contemporary central and western Europe.

The Renaissance and After

Many Greek and Roman sources refer to Celts, and some of them are not just geographical descriptions but also refer to physical appearance, social customs, and traits such as boastfulness. Many of these sources were lost in the upheavals of the fifth century A.D. and later following the collapse of the Roman Empire. It was not until the Renaissance and the fifteenth century A.D. that many of these sources once again became available in western and central Europe and were once again widely used by scholars.

In Britain, this "rediscovery" of past societies led to the recognition of "ancient Britons" in the writings of antiquarians such as that of the first state archaeologist, WILLIAM CAMDEN in *Britannia* 1586, and a century later, JOHN AUBREY's great but never published work, *Monumenta Britannica,* begun in 1663. It was observed that classical writers, in writing about Britain, had mentioned, not Celts, but "Pretanni." In 1723, WILLIAM STUKELEY (1687–1765), who helped found the SOCIETY OF ANTIQUARIES OF LONDON in 1717, entitled his unpublished draft of a study of the great Neolithic stone circle of AVEBURY "The History of the Temples of the Ancient Celts." Stukeley was both the great recorder of

An elaborate Battersea shield made in bronze in the first century B.C. by Celts and discovered in London (The Art Archive / British Museum)

prehistoric antiquities, such as Avebury and Stonehenge, and also the ancestor of modern Druidism and "Celtomania." EDWARD LHWYD (1660–1709), assistant keeper and later keeper of the ASHMOLEAN MUSEUM in Oxford, England, the oldest public museum in Europe, identified Welsh, Irish Gaelic, Scottish Gaelic, and Gaulish as different variants of Celtic languages deriving from invaders. This was a brave claim even for its day since the question of the origins and subsequent insular developments of Celtic remains a fraught topic.

There are no surviving pre-Roman texts since presumed Continental early Celtic speakers, although aware of writing, chose to pass wisdom orally, and writing that does exist from northern Italy, Spain, and southern Gaul is restricted to inscriptions. The earliest of these are in what is called a Lepontic script and dates to about 600 B.C. There is, in fact, much uncertainty as to whether there is, for example, any real evidence for the introduction of Celtic into the British Isles before the sixth century B.C., and there is absolutely no evidence of where or when Celtic speakers first reached Ireland.

Another problem concerns the traces of what have been claimed to be the Celtic or, following Pliny, the Celt-Iberian culture of central Spain. Arguments are divided between a settlement of the region from, and a much more complex admixture of various introduced elements with, the autochthonous population of the high Mesetas. Clearly, the Greek colonial settlements from the mid-first millennium played an important role, as can be seen in both metal types and pottery, although it is noticeable that objects typical of the late Hallstatt and LA TÈNE phases in central and western Europe are almost totally absent. By the third century, the Celt-Iberians had developed their own script.

In Continental Europe, pioneering Celtic studies were very much the product of the emerging democracies that accompanied the American and French Revolutions in the last quarter of the eighteenth century when there was a universal search for national roots. Rediscovery of the Celts, archaeologically speaking, took place at the time of the creation of romanticism, which was itself a child of new nationalisms. The Europe formerly divided by class changed to a Europe divided by ethnic solidarity and focused on the nation state while making obeisance to the rights of the masses. Among these romantic manifestations were the "translations" in 1762–1763 by James Macpherson of poems attributed to a completely fictitious third-century-B.C. poet, Ossian, which took Europe by storm. This bogus mythology was welcomed as the true "Celtic twilight" by painters such as Angelika Kaufmann and Jean-Auguste Dominique Ingres, who in 1812–1813 painted the *Dream of Ossian*. A little earlier, in 1802, Anne-Louis Girodet de Roussy Triosson, in his massive work presented to Emperor Napoleon, depicted Ossian welcoming into Valhalla the dead French heroes of the war of liberty against the Prussians.

Muddled mythologies apart, the beginning of a serious interest in folk music reflected in the number of "Scottish" compositions by composers such as Haydn, Beethoven, and Mendelssohn also point to the re-creation of the Scottish Celts as a symbol of the new Europe of "the age of the democratic revolution." Within Britain, the rediscovery of this mythical Celtic past coincided with the destruction of the Scottish highlands after the 1745 Jacobite rebellion and its brutal repression by the Duke of Cumberland—and the end at that time of Scottish aspirations to independence. "Celts" or "Scots" could be enclosed between book covers or presented in genteel concert halls just as nature, no longer a threat in a period of urbanization and industrialization, could be domesticated and hung on walls as landscape painting.

In 1816, Danish archaeologist CHRISTIAN JÜR-GENSEN THOMSEN published his THREE-AGE SYS-TEM of stone, bronze, and iron, and between 1846 and 1865, Johann Georg Ramsauer, surveyor of the imperial salt mines at Hallstatt in upper Austria, discovered a rich cemetery of about 1,000 graves associated with one phase of the prehistoric mines, dating from the seventh to fifth centuries B.C. Ramsauer claimed that the graves were Celtic, a matter still disputed although Hallstatt became the name generally applied to temperate Europe until the first half of the Iron Age. Because of the preservative effects of salt, much fabric, leather, and worked wood were also found in Hallstatt's three major areas of prehistoric mining. The mining techniques seem to have been borrowed from those used much earlier in mining the copper of the eastern Alps, with shafts extending up to 350 meters below the surface, and it was clearly a hazardous occupation. Although much of this material was discovered accidentally in the course of more recent mining activities, a major examination of the ancient mining system has been carried out by Fritz Eckart Barth, and Roy Hodson has applied modern statistical analyses to the contents of the cemetery.

Old Wealth, Modern Discoveries

The Hallstatt Iron Age is generally distinguished by its rich barrow burials, usually comprising multiple burials around one central grave, which is generally within a wooden funeral chamber. In the later Hallstatt period, the funerary goods enclosed in the chamber often included a four-wheeled wagon, personal ornaments of sheet gold, and imported Greek and Etruscan goods associated with the funerary feast, which included vessels for wine mixing and drinking and, in the case of males, antenna-hilted iron swords. The first early–Iron Age "princely" tombs located in France are in Burgundy, where the site of Magny-Lambert (seventh century B.C.) was excavated in 1872 by the Commission for the Topography of the Gauls, and Apremont was discovered in 1879. The most spectacular site is the grave of the thirty-seven-year-old "princess" of Vix (ca. 500 B.C.), which was discovered in 1953 on the banks of the River Seine below the contemporary fortified hilltop settlement of Mont Lassois. This grave contained the largest known Greek-made bronze krater, or wine-mixing vessel, 1.64 meters high and weighing 208.6 kilograms, as well as a gold neck ring, possibly from Iberia. Even more recently, a settlement has been found close to the grave, with several fragmentary statues of draped figures, but although claimed as contemporary, these may be later than the grave.

Baden-Württemberg in southwestern Germany, on the other side of the Alps from upper Austria, contains another concentration of rich Hallstatt burials. These include the huge (originally ten meters high), Magdalenenberg-bei-Vilsingen, Inzighofen-Vilsingen (seventh century B.C.), Böblingen (seventh–fifth centuries B.C.), and the barrows at Heiligenbuck and Bad Cannstatt (later sixth century B.C.). There are also sites in Alsace and Switzerland. Of the German princely graves found, that of the Hohen Asperg is in the shadow of a fortified hilltop settlement.

The easy visibility and rich grave goods of these tombs made them of major interest to nineteenth-century excavators, just as they had been to tomb robbers over the previous centuries, and most princely tombs were also near settlements. Perhaps the best excavated is at Eberdingen-Hochdorf, which was excavated in 1978–1979. This rich late Hallstatt tomb contained a unique bronze couch with caryatid cas-

tors decorated in a style that reflects the so-called situla art of the eastern Alps and the area around the head of the Adriatic. As well as the usual drinking vessels, there were nine drinking horns, a massive Greek bronze cauldron with a capacity of some 500 liters, and a quiver full of arrows. There was a considerable quantity of gold work, including shoe covers as well as a neck ring made specifically for the burial (punches for the decoration were found in the covering mound). Careful laboratory work was also able to establish that the cauldron had contained mead and that the body had been kept for several months before being interred. Excavation of the nearby settlement has revealed a princely residence, which continued in use until the early La Tène period, whereas most other Hallstatt sites in the region seem to have been abandoned earlier.

One of the most important centers in the region is the nearby settlement of Heuneburg near the headwaters of the Danube River, which was intensively excavated from 1950 to 1979. First constructed about 650 B.C., the defenses went through a number of rebuilding stages over their 200-year history, the fourth comprising a three-meter-thick enclosing mud-brick wall, which reflects eastern Mediterranean construction methods if not actual Mediterranean builders. A number of destruction periods finally resulted in the burning and final abandonment of the site in the earlier sixth century, presaging a new phase in the Iron Age of the region. In close proximity to Heuneburg was an area of open settlement and a group of large burial mounds, the largest of which, the Hohmichele, originally had a diameter of some eighty meters and a height of about fifteen meters. Although the main central burial chamber had been robbed in antiquity, one of the outer satellite graves contained the remains of a man and a woman together with a four-wheeled wagon and associated fittings.

All of these early–Iron Age sites are grouped near trade routes to the south, at or near the headwaters of the Rhone or Saône Rivers, or near the east-west trading route provided by the Danube River. Even in the 1850s, when the first of the rich chieftains' burials were being discovered and while there was continuing debate as to whether these were relics of the Romans or of local Teutonic tribes, the presence in the graves of imports from the Mediterranean was recognized as being significant.

La Tène and the Rise of a New Power North of the Alps

During the fifth century B.C., the Hallstatt centers of power gradually waned, and there are signs that there was unrest: rich barrow burials were robbed, and princely centers, such as at Heuneburg, were destroyed. The old centers were apparently replaced in status by centers of power to the north and west, in the Champagne-Ardennes region of northern France and Belgium, in the iron-rich Hunsrück-Eifel region between the Rhine and the Mosel Rivers, and in Bohemia. The burial mounds of this period are smaller, there are fewer southern imports (and those are mostly Etruscan), and the types and styles of weapons and ornaments change. Lost wax casting was replaced by bivalve molds for bronze ware and the hammering and stamping of sheet gold. The style of decoration changed, too, from simple rectangular incised designs to the creation of fantastic beasts or ambiguous human heads on fibulae, neck and arm rings, belt hooks, horse harnesses, and chariot fittings in the fifth century B.C. This period lasted until the expansion of the Roman Empire over territories from Britain to Romania and from Italy to Jutland during the period from the late second century B.C. to the later first century A.D.

The first attempt to establish a relative chronology for the Iron Age was made by the Swede HANS HILDEBRAND in 1872. He was followed by the great French archaeologist GABRIEL DE MORTILLET in 1875 and then by Otto Tischler in 1881, whose scheme was in turn refined by the Bavarian PAUL REINECKE in a number of papers beginning in 1902. As a result, La Tène is still generally divided into early, middle, and late (or I, II, and III) in France, Italy, and Switzerland and into A, B (=I), C (=II), and D (=III) in Austria, Germany, the CZECH REPUBLIC, and the rest of central and eastern Europe. Although this chronology, which is largely based on the analysis of cemetery evidence in south-

ern Germany and western Switzerland, has undoubtedly been applied too readily to very different bodies of material, with the exception of the British Isles, it has not been superseded or challenged.

The site of La Tène is on the northernmost tip of Lake Neuchâtel in western Switzerland. The collector Hansli Kopp began gathering material from the lake in 1857, and the artificial lowering of the Jura Lakes system between 1868 and 1900 led to systematic excavation by Émile Vouga, beginning in 1885, and his son, Paul Vouga, commencing in 1906. After 1872, the site's name became accepted as designating the second phase of the Iron Age. Most of what was found in the Vougas' excavations was iron, wood, and wickerwork, including the piles of a collapsed bridge, iron swords, decorated scabbards, spearheads, shield bosses, fibulae, belt hooks, axes, knives, and shears. There were few or no female objects and virtually no pottery, glass, or bronze, but there was a considerable amount of cattle and horse bones and some human skeletal remains, including skulls with clear cut marks. With the exception of coins and iron swords and their scabbards, the bulk of material from La Tène remains scientifically unstudied, and the site is now largely assigned to the period of maximum Celtic expansion, with the La Tène C (III) tree-ring dating of wooden shields giving a date of 229 B.C. There is still disagreement as to whether it was a ritual site or a trading post.

From the earlier La Tène phase (ca. 500–300 B.C.), high-status graves provide evidence of long-distance trade, particularly in coral, amber, cowrie shells from the eastern Mediterranean, and even silk, but imports were fewer and generally comprised bronze Etruscan situlae (containers), with the importance of Etruria north of the Alps first being recognized by Herman Gunthe in 1871. The drinking service was still part of the funerary rite, but it now consisted of Etruscan bronze *stamnoi* (double-handled wine-mixing jars and bronze spouted flagons) and either imported or locally made Celtic imitations. One of these, with a close affinity to one discovered in a chariot grave at the salt-mining complex at Dürrnberg-bei-

Hallein to the west of Hallstatt, was found in a grave below the defended settlement of Glauberg northeast of Frankfurt, the most northerly of the early La Tène princely complexes. Clearly, the local production of prestige goods followed the trading patterns of the southern imports.

Below the defended settlement of the Glauberg a cursus (a ritual monument made up of parallel bars and external ditches) and three warrior graves, two with bronze wine flagons, Have been found. Most remarkable are fragments of at least four deliberately broken statues—one, complete save for his feet, is a warrior with sword, shield, and Mediterranean-looking cuirass and crowned with a strange heraldic, balloonlike headdress such as is commonly found with other early La Tène depictions of the human head. Statuary of any sort from the early La Tène period is extremely rare, and the most likely source of inspiration for such figures lies in the territory of Picenum in central Italy.

Although mining activities continued at Hallstatt, the site itself seems to have declined in contrast to those at Dürrnberg, an Iron Age salt-mining center forty kilometers west of Halstatt in Austria, where salt-mining activities continued from the later seventh century until the second century B.C. At Dürrnberg the houses of the mining community and their related small-scale cemeteries have been the focus of a series of continuing excavation projects, most recently concentrated on the examination of the ancient mine shafts and associated works. Although the graves only occasionally contain Mediterranean imports, their relative wealth must have been a direct result of the bartering strength represented by the salt, which was much in demand south of the Alps. Visitors from the south not only lived but also died on the Dürrnberg as can be deducted by some of the "foreign" elements in the graves.

Another intriguing link between north and south is the hoard of neck and arm rings found high in the Swiss Alps at Erstfeld, near the St. Gotthard Pass and some distance from the new centers of power. One of the later "princely" graves is that at Waldalgesheim, near Bonn, where in 1970 Ernest A. Werth identified

"Gaulish copies" among the fine metalwork. The grave contained a bronze flagon decorated with a carefully laid out compass design as well as objects in a new style that has been named after the site. It can be demonstrated that the gold neck and arm rings in the grave were produced by at least three different craftsmen, and analysis has also suggested that the decorated neck ring and the pair of arm rings were made from melted-down gold staters (coins) of Philip II of Macedon.

Although "the early style" makes use of curvilinear decoration, it is often static, and the newer "vegetal" style, as exemplified by the gold rings from Waldalgesheim, is based on a writhing plant tendril within which, from time to time, hidden faces lurk, or as the founding father of early Celtic art studies, Paul Jacobsthal, wrote in 1941, in Cheshire Cat fashion, now visible, now hidden. This style became geographically widespread at a time in the late fourth century B.C. when classical sources report invasions and settlement in the Po Valley in northern Italy while regions of northeastern France lost population. In France, there was a major development of wheel-thrown pedestaled painted pottery with vegetal designs, showing the possible influence of Italo-Greek red-figure pottery. Certainly, in northern Italy graves have been found that contain typical La Tène B weapons and fibulae together with local pottery.

In northeastern France, what may regarded as the first scientific excavation of a La Tène cemetery was carried out by an officer of the Corps Royal des Ingénieurs Géographes (Royal Corps of Geographic Engineers). The barrow burials were mostly excavated in the nineteenth and early twentieth centuries by collectors who were not averse to robbing each others' excavations, and that fact and the sale of objects to other collectors have made the accurate attribution of nineteenth- and even earlier-twentieth-century finds in this region uncertain. It has also meant the loss to France of major pieces, such as a large collection assembled from 1863 by Léon Morel, a local tax collector in Champagne, and a unique pair of locally produced bronze-spouted flagons and an attendant pair of Etruscan stamnoi discovered in 1927 at Basse-

Yutz on the banks of the Mosel River. Both ended up in the BRITISH MUSEUM, owing to, in the former case, lack of money to purchase them for the French nation and, in the latter case, total ignorance and lack of interest on the part of the Musée des Antiquités Nationales and the LOUVRE. Still, it must be noted that it was Gabriel de Mortillet who in 1871 noted the similarity between metalwork found in the Marne region of France and that from graves at the site of the Etruscan city of Marzobotto near Bologna in Italy, thus for the first time identifying archaeological evidence for the Gaulish invasion of Italy recorded by the classical writers.

In France, as elsewhere, archaeology was used to bolster national pride, with excavations undertaken by the Emperor Napoleon Bonaparte and later by Napoleon III, who decided to write a history of Julius Caesar. In order to create a map of the Gauls in the first century B.C., Napoleon III set up a commission in 1858 to locate the places written about by Caesar in his *De bello gallico,* which were largely *oppida* (large-scale defended settlements) constructed of cross-timbers held together with iron nails and faced with stone blocks *(muri gallici).* Napoleon III's interest in locating and excavating key sites of the late La Tène period that were described by Caesar continues today. At Mont Beuvray near Autun (ancient BIBRACTE, where Caesar overcame the displaced Helvetii), where excavations started in 1865, work by an international team continues with the support of the president of France. An even more symbolic site of French aspirations to a great past is Mont Auxois (ALESIA), where Caesar recorded in detail his defeat of the Averni assembled in 52 B.C. under their chief Vercingetorix, who six years later was led to a horrid death through the streets of Rome.

The late La Tène period was one of increased centralization and tribal identity, and the latter can be particularly observed in the increased use of coinage. Coinage was introduced to Celtic warriors when, during the period of expansion of the fourth and third centuries B.C., Celts served increasingly as mercenaries in various parts of the Hellenistic world. The first native coins were struck at the beginning of the

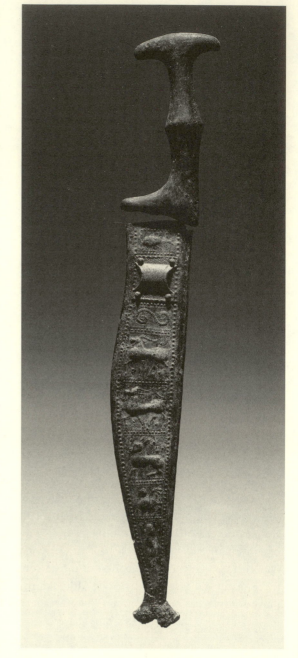

A sixth-century A. D. bronze Celtic dagger and scabbard with figures of animals (The Art Archive / Museo Civico Belluno / Dagli Orti [A])

third century B.C. in the silver-rich eastern part of Europe, and they most closely follow the Macedonian prototypes. In the west, gold was the standard, and, although by no means the only prototype, it was the coins of Philip II of Macedon that most commonly were the models. At first prized simply as a sign of conspicuous wealth and source of precious metal, as exemplified by the gold from the late-third-century Waldalgesheim chariot grave, increasingly—and of particular value to the archaeologist—coin types indicate local tribal areas, although with the expansion of trading between centers, coins of high value became distributed far beyond their point of origin.

Certain features of the *oppida,* which evolved in the course of the second century B.C. as tribal centers supported by open settlements and individual farmsteads, point to the evolution of urbanization for the first time north of the Alps. The degree to which this development may have been influenced by the nature of the town planning of contemporary Mediterranean society is a matter of debate, but it is clear from modern excavations of 200 or so sites in Hungary, the Czech and Slovak republics, Switzerland, Luxembourg, and France that there are considerably more variations than Caesar's general description might lead one to expect. Even so, the similarities in the association of the *oppida* and their attendant open sites with such activities as large-scale pottery making, smelting and the forging of iron, glass production, and the minting of coins remain as valid today as when first noted by French proto-historian JOSEPH DÉCHELETTE.

Déchelette excavated Mont Beuvray and was struck by the similarity in material from the French site and material obtained, largely unsystematically, at Stradonice in Bohemia and published in 1903 by Josef Píc, the head of the Archaeology Department of the National Museum in Prague. Déchelette translated Píc's excavation report and elaborated his own views in his massive *Manuel d'archéologie préhistorique, celtique et gallo-romain,* which was first published between 1908 and 1914 but in many ways has never been superseded.

Modern Research and the
Case of the Vanishing Celts
A long series of excavation campaigns at Manching near the Bavarian town of Ingolstadt that commenced in 1938 marks the most thorough examination of an *oppidum,* although to date, only a fraction of the 380-hectare site with

its roughly circular 7-meter-long *murus gallicus* (Gallic wall) has been examined. The site, a center of the Vindelici, the dominant tribe of the region until subjugated by Rome in 15 B.C., evolved from a series of settlements with their attendant cemeteries in the third century B.C. to the main enclosure, which evolved over a couple of generations during which time signs of burning indicate the strength of local rivalries. Inside the enclosure, regular habitation areas and industrial zones repeat patterns discovered elsewhere. Long-range trade and perhaps intermarriage are indicated by the occasional discovery of forms of female ornaments originating in the alpine region. Even more striking is the discovery of a model tree with ivy leaves made of gold-foil-covered wood whose parallels are with Italo-Greek gold work. The existence of a tree cult was recorded by classical historians.

Other evidence of later La Tène cult practices come from the vicinity of a number of square- or rectangular-banked enclosures, several with deep well shafts and square internal structures. At least some of the latter have been interpreted as temples, and among finds that seem to support their ritual use are the striking heraldic wooden animal figures from a well at Fellbach-Schmiden outside Stuttgart, which date to the late second or early first century B.C., and the somewhat older stone head of a Celt accidentally discovered in several pieces in a pit just outside a rectangular enclosure, which may have had a ritual purpose, at Mšecké Zehrovice west of Prague.

In the nineteenth century, only in France was it possible to combine both Gauls and Romans in a construct of national identity—the Franks, who had given their name to the country, vanished below the horizon of popular interest. In other parts of Europe, however, the Celts, unlike Germans, Slavs, and Hungarians, were not associated with national governments nor, except in Ireland, with aspirations to separate nationhood. Since World War II, the Celts, with their widespread historical presence across Europe, Turkey, and North Africa, have been seen as an antidote to the type of essential or genetically based racism that caused the Holocaust. As the precursors of national states, they seem to offer a unifying past shared by the countries of the emerging European Union. In the former socialist republics of central and eastern Europe, Iron Age archaeology gave archaeologists a route to pursue that gave them the opportunity of meeting other Europeans rather than concentrating on local, possibly nationalist, archaeology.

In the 1960s and 1970s, Slavs replaced Celts as the center of state-sponsored research activities, and with the break-up of the Russian-dominated eastern bloc and with the European Union becoming larger and more integrated, the Celts were increasingly seen as symbols of a transnational identity. The Council of Europe even appointed a committee to establish a "pan-European Celtic heritage trail," and a huge exhibition, *I Celti*, held at the Palazzo Grassi in Venice in 1991, had as its subtitle, *The Origins of Europe*. The introduction to the exhibition's massive catalog states: "This exhibition is a tribute both to the new Europe which cannot come to fruition without a comprehensive awareness of its unity, and to the fact that, in addition to its Roman and Christian sources, today's Europe traces its roots from the Celtic heritage, which is there for all to see" (Moscati 1991, 11). Since a historic Celtic presence and a La Tène material culture have been recorded in modern nations from TURKEY to Great Britain and from Egypt to DENMARK, the catalog's claim was intended to be comprehensive rather than exclusive. The impulse behind the European Union was basically both idealistic and practical—to prevent national rivalries causing a third world war by creating such close social and economic ties across the Continent that such a war would become impossible.

But while Continental Europeans were seeing Celts as a symbol of unity in the early 1990s, some British writers were beginning to denounce the concept of a Celtic past as divisive, even dangerously racist, and modern Celticism as fake. In 1983, the Marxist historian Eric Hobsbawm had already written of "the invention of tradition" in post-1745 Scotland, and ten years later, the English writer Malcolm Chapman argued that Celts as such had never existed and *Celts* was merely a generic term that denoted "the other." A number of English archaeologists leaped on this idea to argue that, be-

cause archaeology as a means of constructing culture history has been used to bolster unacceptable theories of nationhood and superior identity, the construct of an ancient Celtic society is essentially racist and dangerous. They argued that ethnic nomenclatures should not be used to denote past peoples known mainly on the basis of their material remains. But the same charge might be laid against the use of such labels as "Scythians," "ancient Egyptians," and even "Romans." Ultimately, the argument rests upon ideas of how ethnicity is formed, and it seems paradoxical that the hypothesis of an ancient Celtic society—whether in the British Isles or on the Continent—should be regarded as racist.

The counterargument has been that the ancient sources should not be dismissed as though Herodotus, Polybius, Livy, and Caesar were totally ignorant of their own world. It seems preferable to adopt a model of ethnicity that is not genetically determined but composed of a number of intersecting factors in which ethnicity is multiple, depending on situation and changes over time. Finally, support for the retention of the terms *Celt* and *Celtic* may be found in another quotation, this time from an English-born professor of Celtic studies working in Wales: "We have Celtic language and Celtic ethnicity, which . . . often go together, and also Celtic archaeology and Celtic art, which must be placed further off. All those uses of 'Celtic' have some historic validity and are far too useful to abandon" (Sims-Williams 1998, 33).

Vincent Megaw and Ruth Megaw

References

Birkhan, Helmut. 1999. *Kelten / Celts: Bilder ihrer Kultur / Images of their Culture*. Vienna: Verlag der Österreichischen Akademie der Wissenschaften.

Chapman, Malcolm. 1992. *The Celts: The Construction of a Myth*. London: St. Martin's Press.

Cunliffe, Barry. 1997. *The Ancient Celts*. Oxford: Oxford University Press.

Green, Miranda, ed. 1995. *The Celtic World*. London: Routledge.

Hobsbawm, Eric, and Terence Ranger, eds. 1983. *The Invention of Tradition*. Cambridge: Cambridge University Press.

Jacobsthal, Paul. 1944. *Early Celtic Art*. Oxford: Oxford University Press.

James, Simon. 1993. *Exploring the World of the Celts.* London: Thames and Hudson.

———. 1999. *The Atlantic Celts: Ancient People or Modern Invention?* London: British Museum Press.

Jones, Siân, ed. 1997. *The Archaeology of Ethnicity: Constructing Identities in the Past and Present.* London and New York: Routledge.

Megaw, Ruth, and Vincent Megaw. 1989. *Celtic Art from Its Beginnings to the Book of Kells.* London: Thames and Hudson.

———. 1999. "Celtic Connections Past and Present: Celtic Ethnicity Ancient and Modern." In *Celtic Connections: Proceedings of the Tenth International Congress of Celtic Studies,* 19–81. Ed. Ronald Black, William Gillies, and Roilbeard Ó Maolalaigh. East Linton: Tuckwell Press.

Moscati, Sabatini, ed. 1991. *The Celts.* London: Thames and Hudson.

Piggott, Stuart. 1989. *Ancient Britons and the Antiquarian Imagination.* London: Thames and Hudson.

Powell, T. G. E. 1980. *The Celts.* Rev. ed. New York: Thames and Hudson.

Rankin, H. D. 1987. *Celts and the Classical World.* London and Sydney: Croom Helm.

Sims-Williams, Patrick. 1998. "Celtomania and Celtoscepticism." *Cambrian Medieval Celtic Studies* 36: 1–35.

Cesnola, Luigi Palma di (1832–1904)

General Luigi Palma di Cesnola typifies the rapacious style of mid-nineteenth-century "archaeological" activity in the eastern Mediterranean. He had a varied and adventurous life, which included service in the American Civil War. Later, while resident in CYPRUS between 1865 and 1875 (and accredited as both the U.S. and the Russian consul), he arranged excavations at numerous sites and opened many thousands of Bronze and Iron Age tombs in the search for antiquities. The bulk of his vast collection of was eventually acquired by the Metropolitan Museum in New York City, and in return, Cesnola was appointed director of the museum in 1879. His methods both in the field and at the museum led to much criticism, especially regarding his practice of reconstructing statues from scattered pieces.

David Frankel

References

Tomkins, C. 1989. *Merchants and Masterpieces: The Story of the Metropolitan Museum of Art.* New York: Henry Holt.

Chaco Canyon

Chaco Canyon is a natural canyon with thirteen major Native American ruins, which was named a National Historical Park in 1907. The park is located in the northwest quadrant of New Mexico. Chaco Canyon's abandonment by the Western Anasazi people remains one of the great mysteries of Southwestern prehistory. The abandoned sites contain large multistoried ruins along the Chaco River, a tributary to the San Juan River. The canyon sustained 1,500 years of prehistory and over a century of scholarly research.

Chaco Canyon was first described by Gregg in 1844. Archaeological work was begun by Adolf Bandelier, then NELS NELSON (1914), EDGAR LEE HEWETT (1906), Judd (1922), ALFRED KIDDER (1915), and Mera (1935). Work was later continued by Hayes (1975) and Judge (1976). Over the years, the major research questions considered (1) the origins of specific culture traits in modern Eastern Pueblos, (2) cause for abandonment before European contact, and (3) the role of environment in social organization for people who depend on agriculture.

Studies of change over time in Chaco Canyon are observed through changes in ceramic styles, architectural details, settlement patterns, migration, and social interaction. The semi-arid climate with unpredictable rainfall is a major component as well, and may have contributed to the abandonment of Chaco Canyon after crop failures. Climate study has been an essential part of research on Chaco Canyon. Modern patterns have been compared to ancient patterns through tree-ring dating, or dendroclimatological reconstruction. Fossil pollen (palynological) studies and temperature studies also contributed to reconstructing dwelling and growing cycles. Tree-ring data for Chaco Canyon during A.D. 650–1150 show more-than-average rainfall and then a drier-than-average time afterward. At that time the former adaptations to drought may no longer have been effective.

The early theoretical approach to Southwestern prehistory characterized sites by a chronology of culture groups. Culture groups are described by region-wide changes in house and ceramic styles across the whole area, not just one site in the region. The Chaco Canyon culture group is defined by a series of ceramic and house style combinations. As part of the San Juan drainage, Chaco Canyon has Basketmaker III type settlements, which have been radiocarbon dated to A.D. 500–700. Basketmaker III sites typically are villages with shallow pit houses, storage pits, and widespread ceramics, which indicate sedentism. Also in the San Juan drainage, there is variation in house shape and interior features, such as the "sipapu," an opening symbolic of the place where humans first came into the world. Cultivated foods, such as corn, beans, and squash, as well as wild piñon and Indian rice grass, are important in the Chaco Canyon sites. Some game animals hunted were rabbits, deer, and antelope.

Chaco Canyon sites are divided into Pueblo I, Pueblo II, and Pueblo III village types. Pueblo I style, found by survey and excavation, dates from A.D. 700 to A.D. 900. As documented by Hayes (1975), Judd (1924), and Truell (1976), architectural changes feature above-ground rectangular rooms; and ceramic changes feature neck-banded gray utility ware. Villages in Pueblo I times show increased population, migration and expansion into the mountains, and campsites for seasonal activities. Pueblo II village types, dating from A.D. 900 to A.D. 1100, show population shifts, ceramic changes to Red Mesa black-on-white, pit and surface houses, and the use of masonry. In Chaco Canyon, population increased and the rate of change increased. Eighty percent of the ceramics were not made locally and seem to be traded in from the south; also the kiva (meeting house) style is slightly different. These changes indicated possibly more social interaction and networking with neighbors. Pueblo III villages, A.D. 1100 to A.D. 1300, have Chaco Canyon black-on-white ceramics and more notable archaeological features such as kivas, field and irrigation systems, roads and trails, and small items. Of the two housing styles at this time, Hosta Butte and Bonito, it is the Bonito phase that Chaco Canyon is famous for according to Hayes: towns of large, multistory buildings with 288 rooms on average; interior courtyards; great kivas; and decorative masonry.

Chaco Canyon's spectacular architecture features great kivas, large-diameter subterranean rooms with a raised firebox and roof support. Other remarkable features include the irrigation and field systems (RG Vivian 1970, 1976) that collected runoff from the cliff tops and channeled it down to the houses. Also, well-marked roads radiate from Chaco Canyon (Lyons and Hitchcock 1977) that are straight and wide, indicating a lot of planning and labor, especially for people who did not use wheels. Lyons and Hitchcock speculate the roads were used to bring bulk agricultural produce to the canyon. Pueblo III also shows some luxury items, particularly at the Bonito sites, such as cylindrical vases, cooper bells, turquoise, inlay pieces, mosaics, and even Macaw skeletons.

Various explanations are possible for the differences of Bonito towns during the Pueblo III period from other locations and periods. R. G. Vivian (1970) suggests the difference between sites shows changing social organization concerning the control of water resources and labor organization. Ferdon (1955) suggest that Bonito towns were trading bases, and part of a long-distance trade network coming out of MESOAMERICA. Therefore, Chaco Canyon residents may have adopted aspects of technology and ceremony brought up from Mesoamerica. Chaco Canyon is exceptional because there is no analog in modern Pueblo people; the towns in the canyon experienced tremendous but short-lived growth and an enormous labor pool was involved in nonessential work such as masonry veneers. Altogether these elements may have been the result of social organization changes brought about in response to extreme environmental changes, especially in available water. Most likely, a form of ranked society or chiefdom emerged over redistribution of food and water.

Danielle Greene

See also United States of America, Prehistoric Archaeology

References

Lister, Robert H., and Florence C. Lister. 1981. *Archaeology and Archaeologists: Chaco Canyon.* Albuquerque: University of New Mexico Press.

Ortiz, Alfonso, vol. ed. 1979. *Handbook of North American Indians: Southwest, Volume 9.* Washington, DC: Smithsonian Institution.

Champollion, Jean-François (1790–1832)

Although he was to gain lasting fame as the person most responsible for the decipherment of Egyptian hieroglyphics, Champollion was famous long before Egypt. By the age of 16 he could speak and read six ancient oriental languages, in addition to Latin and Greek, and at 19 he became a professor of history at the university in Grenoble in France.

The initial breakthrough in understanding ancient Egyptian hieroglyphics was the result of a study of the Rosetta Stone by a young English physicist, Thomas Young. The stone had been seized from the defeated French army in Egypt and presented by George III to the BRITISH MUSEUM. It was Young who realized that the stone was engraved with three versions of the same text—one in Greek, one in demotic Egyptian, and the last in ancient Egyptian hieroglyphs.

Champollion built on Young's work and took it further still, establishing an entire list of hieroglyphic signs and their Greek equivalents. Champollion recognized that some of the hieroglyphs were alphabetic, some were syllabic, and some were determinative, i.e., standing for a whole idea or object previously expressed. While his theories were bitterly disputed by other scholars at the time, this fundamental classification proved to be the key to understanding and translating this ancient writing system and contributed to the recognition of the study of linguistics as a scientific discipline.

Champollion became curator of the Egyptian collection at the LOUVRE in 1826, conducting an archaeological expedition to Egypt in 1828. In 1831 the chair of Egyptian Antiquities was created especially for him at the College de France. In addition to an Egyptian grammar (1836–1841) and an Egyptian dictionary (1842–1843),

Jean-François Champollion (Ann Ronan Picture Library)

his works included *Précis du système hiéroglyphique* in 1824 and *Panthéon égyptien ou collection des personnages mythologiques de l'ancienne Egypt* in 1823–1825.

Tim Murray

See also Egypt, Dynastic; French Archaeology in Egypt and the Middle East

Chan Chan

Chan Chan, the capital of the Chimú state, is located in the Moche Valley of PERU near the modern city of Trujillo. Excavation of Chan Chan was begun in 1969 by Michael Moseley and Carol J. Mackey and continues under the Peruvian Instituto Nacional de Cultura. The site is believed to have been established around A.D. 850 and to have continued to flourish until the Inca conquest in about 1470. It grew prodigiously during its 600-year history, spreading to over twenty square kilometers. Unfortunately, Chan Chan has been badly affected by looting.

Tim Murray

References

Moseley, Michael E., and Kent C. Day, eds. 1982. *Chan Chan: Andean Desert City.* Albuquerque: University of New Mexico Press.

Chang, Kwang-chi (1931–2001)

Born in Beijing, CHINA, Kwang-chi Chang was the second child of Chang Wojun, a well-known Taiwanese historian. During his childhood years, Chang witnessed the corruption of the government, the suffering of ordinary people, and the invasion of the Japanese; he was also influenced by leftist ideology. Chang left Beijing for Taiwan with his family in 1946 when Taiwan was returned to China after its Japanese occupation. His experience in Beijing led him to develop a strong nationalist consciousness and sympathy for socialist beliefs, which later caused him to be jailed for a year as a political prisoner in Taiwan when he was eighteen. This experience apparently had a great impact on his decision to become an anthropologist in order to understand "why humans are the way they are" (Chang 1998, 75).

Chang was always a top student throughout his school years and was the favorite student of LI CHI (known as the father of Chinese archaeology for his contribution to the excavations at ANYANG) in the Department of Anthropology at Taiwan University. In 1955, Chang started his graduate studies in the Department of Anthropology at Harvard University, working with H. Movius, Jr., C. Kluckhohn, GORDON R. WILLEY, and L. Ward. After receiving a Ph.D. in 1960, he taught for many years at Yale University, where he established himself as a first-rate scholar in the discipline. In 1977 he returned to Harvard as the John E. Hudson Professor of Archaeology. He then became a member of the National Academy of Sciences in the United States and also served as vice-president of Academia Sinica in Taipei in the mid-1990s.

For decades, Chang's major contributions have bridged the gap between eastern and western archaeologists by presenting Chinese archaeology to anthropological circles in the western world. He, however, did not limit his interests to Chinese archaeology. During the 1960s and 1970s he stood at the forefront of U.S. anthropology with regard to archaeological theory and was a leader in general methodological debates in archaeology and in the study of settlement patterns. As a native of Taiwan, he was a major player in establishing the field of Taiwanese archaeology. From the 1980s, in addition to academic pursuits, he made a tremendous effort to build collaborative relationships with archaeologists in the People's Republic of China. In the 1990s, he overcame all political and administrative barriers to initiating the first Sino-American collaborative field project in China since the World War II. This project in Shangqiu, Henan, is dedicated to searching for the origins of the Shang dynasty, which has been a long-standing question haunting several generations of Chinese archaeologists (Ferrie 1995).

Over the years, Chang published numerous articles and monographs in English and Chinese, and the list of his publications is forty-one pages long (Murowchick 1999). His scholarly masterpieces include four editions of *Archaeology of Ancient China* (1963, 1968, 1977, 1986), *Shang Civilization* (1980), and *Art, Myth, and Ritual* (1983). These have been the most comprehensive and authoritative accounts of Chinese archaeology available in the English language for several decades, and they have been translated into many languages. His publications in Chinese have been equally influential. Presenting many fresh views of Chinese civilization, his *Six Lectures in Archaeology* (1986) and *The Bronze Age of China* (1983), both published in Beijing, have especially enlightened archaeologists in China.

In addition to archaeology, Chang had broad interests in many fields including art history, cultural anthropology, history, paleography, the anthropology of food, and sport. For four decades he "brought up" several generations of East and Southeast Asian archaeologists, and his former students are now spread over many parts of the world including North America, Europe, Asia, and Australia. Known to his colleagues, friends, and students as "K. C.," Chang was a kind, warm, sympathetic, hardworking, and charismatic man with great wisdom and an excellent sense of humor. His extraordinary determination to overcome any difficulties in life is evident in his struggle with a devastating illness, which eventually claimed him in January 2001.

Li Liu

References

Chang, Kwang-chih. 1998. *Fanshuren de gushi* [Memoirs of a Year of My Youth]. Taipei: Lianjing.

Ferrie, Helke. 1995. "A Conversation with K. C. Chang." *Current Anthropology* 36, no. 2: 308–325.

Murowchick, Robert. 1999. "Bibliography of Works by Kwang-chih Chang." *Journal of East Asian Archaeology* 1, nos. 1–4: 1–42.

Chavín

Chavín is thought to have been a dominant culture in ancient PERU between about 900 and 200 B.C. It was comprehensively defined by JULIO TELLO in the 1930s, but the nature and extent of the Chavín culture continues to be hotly debated. Although the core of Chavín culture can be discussed without difficulty at the type site of Chavín de Huantar, it now seems likely that Chavín art styles (particularly textiles) and larger-scale urban sites (found in the initial period and early-horizon deposits of sites in the northern highlands and the coastal areas of Peru) may have developed prior to the foundation of Chavín de Huantar. Thus, Tello's original conception of Chavín as being the progenitor culture of civilization in the Andes is now questionable.

Tim Murray

References

Burger, Richard L. 1992. *Chavín and the Origins of Andean Civilization*. London: Thames and Hudson.

Moseley, Michael E. 1992. *The Incas and Their Ancestors*. London: Thames and Hudson.

Chichén Itzá

Chichén Itzá, one of the largest and most important of the Maya ruins, is located on the low, broad plain that forms the northern part of MEXICO's Yucatán Peninsula. This peninsula is composed of limestone (it is an ancient, shallow seafloor), and there is little surface water in the region: the rain soaks through the thin soil and forms caves below the surface. If the roofs of these caves collapse, sinkholes (*cenotes* in Spanish, from the Maya word *tz'onot*) are formed. Chichén Itzá has several of these sinkholes within the confines of the site. The term *Chichén Itzá,* which means "the mouth of the well of Itza," is derived from the name of the largest of these sinkholes—the so-called Sacred Well. Chichén Itzá has been the source of considerable controversy over the years, largely involving the ethnic identity of the "Itza" and the two rather distinct architectural and art styles that exist at the site. Even the chronology of the site has long been in dispute. Traditionally, Chichén Itzá's history has been divided into two major phases. In the earlier phase (ca. A.D. 800–1000) the site was purely Maya, and its buildings were in a regional style called Puuk (Puuc). Then, around A.D. 1000, the site was taken over by a group whom some identified as the "TOLTECS," from the site of Tula some 70 kilometers north of Mexico City. The Toltec foreigners (according to this traditional view of Chichén Itzá history) gained control of the site through conquest, and they controlled much of the northern part of the Yucatán Peninsula until shortly after A.D. 1200.

There are several problems with this reconstruction, which is still common in popular literature. For example, the dedication date (carved in Maya hieroglyphs) of the Great Ballcourt at Chichén Itzá was 18 November 864—impossibly early for a building argued to be one of the sites's quintessentially "Toltec" buildings. Additionally, "Maya" architecture and art at Chichén Itzá are not as clearly separated and consistently overlain by "Toltec" architecture and art as was once thought. The current view is that there is considerable overlap between the two styles, although how much overlap is still a source of dispute, as is the absolute chronology of the site. It has been argued by some that Chichén Itzá may represent a kind of "cosmopolitan style" of art and architecture, borrowing freely from several areas for inspiration. Further, the art and architecture of Chichén Itzá seems to reflect a different order of government at this northern Yucatán site. There are none of the grandiose portraits of individual kings that are the hallmark of the kingdoms to the south. Rather, the hieroglyphs of Chichén Itzá describe a multiplicity of contemporary individuals, and the site's art shows parades of lords: it appears that the site may have been ruled by some sort of council rather than a single succession of kings.

Who were the Itza, the people who are said to have ruled Chichén Itzá? Later descriptions call the Itza foreigners and tricksters and portray them as "lewd" and unable to speak fluently. This depiction clearly indicates that they were foreigners—but whether they were Toltecs from Tula (the traditional view) or some other group has remained a subject of debate. Much evidence points to the southern Gulf of Mexico region where Mexicanized Maya groups lived and honed their skills as some of Mesoamerica's greatest long-distance traders. More recently, evidence has arisen to indicate that the Itza might have been refugees from the internecine warfare of the southern Maya lowlands in the late-classic period. The name *Itza,* in fact, shows up in classic-period texts from Motul de San José, a site not far from Tikal, so we know that some Itza lived and ruled there. Maya chronicles describe a long series of migrations from the Itza homeland until these people founded and settled in Chichén Itzá.

Dominating the site of Chichén Itzá are the buildings arranged on a huge platform that is 450 by 600 meters in area. Near the center of this platform is the so-called Castillo, or Castle, the tallest temple-pyramid at the site. On the western edge of the platform is the largest ball-court in Mesoamerica. The Great Ballcourt is richly decorated with imagery symbolizing the Mesoamerican mythology of creation and the sacred charter of government, as well as murals that document the wars of conquest that gave the victors the right to rule.

Chichén Itzá is also famous for its Sacred Well, which was used as a place of ritual offerings by the Maya even after the site was abandoned. The well has been dredged several times, and thousands of archaeological pieces have been recovered. These include huge numbers of carved jade artifacts; wooden objects such as scepters, weapons, and idols; ceramics; balls of resin incense; human bones; and bells, disks, and figurines of gold. Chichén Itzá in general and the Sacred Well in particular were used as places of pilgrimage well into the Spanish colonial period, much to the consternation of the Spanish priests and administrators.

According to legend, the city fell through sorcery and trickery, but almost certainly its demise was due to fighting among rival lineages.

Maya chronicles from the Spanish colonial period say that in A.D. 1221, the ruler of Chichén Itzá was defeated by the ruler of the nearby, emergent city of Mayapan and that the Itza were driven from their capital. Today Chichén Itzá is one of the most frequently visited archaeological sites in Mexico. It is a dramatic location, with broad vistas punctuated by some of the most grandiose pyramids and decorated temples in the entire Maya area.

Peter Mathews

See also Maya Civilization

Childe, Vere Gordon (1892–1957)

Vere Gordon Childe, the most celebrated archaeological synthesizer and theorist of his generation, was born in North Sydney, Australia, 14 April 1892. He graduated from Sydney University in 1913 with first-class honors in Latin, Greek, and philosophy. At Oxford University in England, his interest in European prehistory was aroused by a desire to locate the homeland of the Indo-Europeans. He returned to Australia in 1916 and became involved in anticonscription and Labour politics, serving from 1919 to 1921 as private secretary to John Storey, the Labour premier of New South Wales.

After the defeat of the Labour government of New South Wales in 1921, Childe returned to the study of European prehistory, paying special attention to the Balkans. In 1925, he published *The Dawn of European Civilization,* a milestone in the development of culture-historical archaeology. Childe combined the concept of "the archaeological culture," refined by the German archaeologist GUSTAF KOSSINNA to try to trace the histories of specific peoples in the archaeological record, with the diffusionism of the Swedish archaeologist OSCAR MONTELIUS. Montelius believed that in prehistoric times technological skills had spread to Europe from their place of origin in the Middle East. Like his Oxford mentors, ARTHUR EVANS and JOHN MYRES, Childe stressed the creativity with which Europeans had utilized this knowledge.

Childe was the Abercromby Professor of Prehistoric Archaeology at the University of Edinburgh from 1927 to 1946 and professor of European archaeology and director of the Institute of Archaeology at the University of London from 1946 until he retired in 1956. Throughout these years he carried out numerous archaeological excavations and surveys in Scotland and also visited many excavations in Europe and the Middle East.

Although Childe was primarily a European prehistorian, for the rest of his life he sought a better understanding of cultural change. Beginning with *The Most Ancient East* (1928), he sought to delineate the revolutionary impacts that the development of agriculture and bronze working had on various parts of the Middle East and Europe. Instead of treating technological innovation as an independent variable that brought about cultural change, he sought to trace the reciprocal relations between it and specific environments, economies, and political systems. He saw changes occurring in a multilinear, not a unilinear, fashion.

In 1935, Childe visited the Soviet Union. Although he disapproved of the dogmatism imposed on Soviet archaeologists, he was impressed by the attention being paid to how ordinary people lived in prehistoric times and by Marxist interpretations of cultural evolution. In *Man Makes Himself* (1936) and *What Happened in History* (1942), Childe examined, from an evolutionary perspective, how elites and inflexible belief systems could halt economic and social progress but only at the cost of undermining a society's ability to compete with more progressive neighbors.

After World War II, disillusionment with the declining quality of Soviet archaeology led Childe to acquire a more profound understanding of Marxism as an analytical tool and to try to apply it to the interpretation of archaeological data. He attempted to reconcile the observation that all human behavior is culturally mediated with a materialist view of causality. In *Prehistory of European Society* (1958), he stressed that social and political organization provided the framework within which all archaeological data could most productively be understood.

Troubled by failing health and fearing that incipient senility was preventing him from devising new procedures for inferring social organi-

zation from archaeological data, Childe, jumped to his death from a cliff in the Blue Mountains of Australia on 19 October 1957.

Bruce G. Trigger

References
For references, see *Encyclopedia of Archaeology: The Great Archaeologists,* Vol. 1, ed. Tim Murray (Santa Barbara, CA: ABC-CLIO, 1999), pp. 398–399.

Chile
Prescientific Period (1400–1830)

Pre-Columbian society described the past as a series of mythical epochs, and this idea was documented at the time of European contact by the first chroniclers of the sixteenth century. Even today, some ethnic minorities can retell the ancient epic stories about their origins. There are descriptions dating from the sixteenth century of "excavations" of Indian tombs in search of buried treasure or motivated by curiosity abut the rituals of Indian "paganism." Of great importance for the study of pre-Columbian society are the numerous ethnohistoric documents generated by the Spanish administration during the period of Indian resistance. In fact, from the examination of these records, architectonic, ritual, and material culture traits have been explained and are of prime importance in the reconstitution of archaeological events.

During the sixteenth century, the Spanish encountered colossal ruins in the middle of a living Inca society that were evidence of a distant past. The invaders' medieval worldview, along with their creationist dogmas and limited biblical chronology, did not stimulate the need to systematically record such ruins. However, some chroniclers proposed that ancient hunters must have carried out the first peopling of the Americas. Others, such as Father Lozano, writing in the early seventeenth century, devoted himself to the study of the origin of the Indians of the New World and West Indies *(Orígen de los indios del Nuevo Mundo e Indias Occidentales).*

Between the eighteenth and nineteenth centuries, various European travelers and scientists on neocolonial and scientific explorations visited the New World, and their accounts provide important descriptions that can be linked to archaeological data. We know of several excavations in the Atacameño territory further south; an Inca fortress in Tagua was explored, and between 1851 and 1900 a series of unscientific excavations (huaqueos) in search of "mummies" or dehydrated corpses and their associated assemblages took place at a cemetery on the Loa River. The collections recovered from these excavations were shipped to museums in Paris, Madrid, Oslo, and New York.

The written accounts of explorers and scientists proved to be of great value, as they constituted the archaeological and ethnohistoric foundation from which an archaeological discourse could be nurtured. During the 1970s, Jorge Hidalgo presented the first proposal for a scientific Chilean ethnohistory and thus became the pioneer of the discipline of archaeology in Chile.

Prescientific Pioneers (1830–1890)

In Europe in 1836, CHRISTIAN JÜRGENSEN THOMSEN published his classic THREE-AGE SYSTEM and thus inaugurated archaeology as a scientific discipline sustained by Darwinian evolutionism. Thomsen's scheme paralleled the geological concept of SIR CHARLES LYELL of a greater temporal depth for humanity and was framed within the context of the natural sciences. As a result, two explanatory proposals for human history were postulated. The first propounded the diversity of all living organisms as a consequence of the earth's antiquity in a gradual evolutionary process. The second was a stratigraphic proposition, which defined an "extended chronology" in accordance with the great French anatomist and paleontologist Georges Cuvier's postulates and surpassing the biblical limits of 6,000 years.

In this postcolonial intellectual environment, recently opened up by universal philosophical reason, European scientific currents of thought made an impact on the debates between Chilean liberals and conservatives. They determined the dispute between "progress" and "backwardness."

After the mid-nineteenth century, the endorsement of the new scientific doctrines of evolutionism and positivism constituted the mission statement of the "modern" intellectual vanguard. A pioneer in this movement was Rodolfo A. Phillipi, an Austrian exile in Chile whose academic background in the natural sciences (medicine, botany, and zoology) influenced his archaeological observations as an employee of the Chilean government. Another important participant was Letelier, who was not religious and a firm empiricist. Letelier advocated an end to the "short biblical chronology" in favor of a more "extensive" chronology. He went even further and proposed a "prehistory of America," which would become a reality six years later with the publication of the monumental work of José T. Medina.

Toward the end of the nineteenth century, the French archaeologist JACQUES BOUCHER DE PERTHES successfully combined paleontology, geology, and archaeology with stratigraphic methods to create the scientific foundations of the discipline of archaeology, which enabled it to leave behind its antiquarian antecedents. Boucher de Perthes's proposals reached the New World via evolutionism, but there was no archaeological evidence akin to the spectacular findings in the Old World. Although Indian "megalithic ruins" were common in the Americas, and these exotic and abandoned ruins motivated a series of notable expeditions during the nineteenth century, Chile remained a far away place with limited archaeological attraction.

The natural sciences were influential in the founding of the important Museum of Natural History in Santiago (1830), a similar one in Valparaiso (1876), and a southern replica at Concepción (1902). These museums, the result of modern European ideas, researched and presented the whole evolutionary-biological circuit from fossils to static displays of Indian artifacts, which were regarded as some sort of more recent fossils.

The first scholar to value the archaeological past of Chile was the historian and bibliographer José T. Medina. His analysis, although not strictly linked to the naturalism in vogue, covered all of the national territory except for the north of the state, which was the subject of an ongoing dispute with PERU and BOLIVIA. He compiled major ethnohistoric sources to make sense of the various indigenous entities of an ethnological and archaeological nature. He also described various private and state-owned collections, and on the basis of these descriptions, he went into the field to search for evidence to verify the existence of ruins. Medina's reports included graphic records and a good knowledge of foreign references, to the point that he suggested homotaxic relationships (that is, classified as being the same) with Old World prehistory.

According to Medina (1882), who followed the lead of other prehistorians, events of the past had to be known in order to glance at the future of humankind. Medina lived surrounded by friends such as Luis Montt and Rafael Garrido, all collectors of Indian antiquities, in a period when historians like Benjamín Vicuña Mackenna were locating Inca ruins throughout central Chile. Medina recognized the potential of nonmonumental archaeology, advancing some analyses on ceramics, mummified bodies, and fortifications and proposing a classificatory scheme linked to the Bronze Age. Medina, of course, was not unfamiliar with the issue of Inca ("Peruvian") influence, which he accepted despite its short duration, thus setting the stage for a debate that would take place later.

Medina's period of influence was important because of the conditions that produced new knowledge concerning ethnography, prehistory, linguistics, and the exploratory nature of the institutions and publications of the Old World. Archaeological finds were recognized as being related to ethnic survivals, including the more "primitive" relics of the southern tip of South America, which justified evolutionary views of the time. Although foreign scholars described their anthropological observations, the local intelligentsia was still at odds with a nationalist state concerned with the forced assimilation of ethnic minorities, even at the expense of their virtual extermination. So while many nationalist Latin American states were promoting "native" studies so as to consolidate their national identity as part of a process of modernization, Chile was preoccupied with formalizing national pride via a search for cultural roots, uncompromised by its contemporary Indian victims.

This period corresponds with the military occupation of the Araucanian regions of south-

central Chile even while southern antiquities were arousing the interests of both scholars and collectors. The colonial elite gave way to a progressive liberal oligarchy, and during this period, after the so-called pacification campaign aimed at the "Chileanization" of the southern regions, some scholars went into the field intent on archaeological and ethnographic rescue. The ethnological and/or archaeological perception of the Indian world that prevailed during this time was similar to that of the European attitude toward its ancient and primitive cultures but with a limited historic depth. These Indian groups were incapable of incorporating themselves to the positivist civilizing process.

Two important events mark the conclusion of the processes that were to have an impact on the future of archaeology as a scientific discipline in Chile. In 1878, a novel archaeological exhibition was inaugurated in Santiago, and two years later, the Anthropological Society published a series of books on archaeology and ethnology that led to American antiquities becoming fashionable. Their main promoters were Medina and Phillipi, the latter a naturalist and closer to the discipline of archaeology. But the notion of progress prevalent at that time did not include a humanist view. After all, Darwin himself in 1842 had described the southern American Indians as "savages" and was mainly interested in their teeth in order to verify the extent of their modern humanity. In this context, the material remains of the past pertained mostly to other "savages" who were regarded more as geological fossils than as modern humans.

During this period, archaeology based its principles on two disciplines, the bibliographic-ethnohistoric approach and naturalism, both of which would dominate it until the present day. The latter was substantiated by recognizing the evolutionary processes to which all living organisms are subject, and in this context, the development of the natural sciences would be decisive for the succeeding multidisciplinary analyses.

At the end of the nineteenth century, many "fine-looking" archaeological pieces, recovered by antiquarians without regard to their archaeological context, formed the first private and state-owned collections. Many archaeological expeditions had revealed a horizontal perspective without systematic prospecting. The construction of a respectable image for the national state of Chile had begun. This state sought an understanding of the vernacular, as an instrument of legitimization and as the new non-Indian national symbol, but with no links to the indigenous populations who lived on the fringes and margins of civilization.

The Scientific Systematic Embryo (1890–1919)

Scholars began to place themselves within a naturalistic and inductive-descriptive theoretical-methodological paradigm based on the principle that all qualities are measurable. Since there was no systematic program of archaeological study, archaeologists were self-taught, with enthusiasm and French romanticism making the still largely unknown ethnic and archaeological potential attractive. Expeditions were sponsored by museums of natural sciences, scientific societies, incipient universities, etc. A series of excavations and ethnographic and ethnolinguistic salvage projects were organized under the banner of different evolutionary perspectives (autochthonous versus diffusionist), resulting in the first cultural taxonomies and physical anthropology measurements. During this time, to satisfy the taxonomic obsession of researchers, Indians were forced to live out their lives in museums, thus guaranteeing access to their remains once they died.

Interest in ethnography and physical anthropology increased with the founding of the German Scientific Society directed by Phillipi and the Scientific Society of Chile, of French ideological inclination, directed by A. Obrecht and with the establishment of such institutions as the national museums of natural history and the incipient University of Chile. Thus, an embryo of anthropological studies that would hierarchically structure the intellectual life of Santiago, Valparaiso, and Concepción became apparent.

The evolutionary-positivist paradigm of the natural and empirical sciences initially caused the development of archaeology as a scientific discipline. However, in Europe, this paradigm confronted the metaphysical idealism of the German philosopher Wilhelm Friedrich Hegel, from which the materialist thesis would emerge, which would eventually have an impact in Chile. The so-called early-twentieth-century cultural history and the North American cultural relativist schools emerged as reactions on the part of Euro-American idealists to late-nineteenth-century positivism.

The debate centered on evolutionists versus anti-evolutionists, between the followers of Lamarck and Charles Lyell and the supporters of Georges Cuvier and Alexander von Humboldt. The former were adherents of chrono-stratigraphic reconstructions and their relationship to anthropological vestiges; the latter were followers of a creationist school that lacked sequential profundity. Argentinean evolutionists like Ambrosetti, Debenedetti, Outes, and Lehmann-Nitsche were frequently cited in Chile by the first systematic scholars such as Latcham and MAX UHLE. The same was not the case for the works of Moreno, Bormeidter, and others, which lacked the properly documented, or chronologically arranged, data that were essential for the comparative method, which was in vogue at the beginning of the twentieth century.

However, orthodox Argentinean evolutionists led by the Ameghino brothers were unaware of the precise nature of the Paleolithic artifacts embedded in Miocene strata. During the International Congress of Americanists in Buenos Aires in 1895, ALES HRDLICKA shattered the largely autochthonous and hyperevolutionist Ameghinian thesis that had dated Argentinean artifacts and human fossil remains back to the Tertiary period. As a consequence, the antiquity of human occupation in Chile would be substantially reduced during this period, to shorter chronologies that remained impervious to substantial changes.

Another trans-Andean debate characteristic of this period was related to the northern Andean regions of ARGENTINA and Chile. Monuments are conspicuous in these regions, and the Inca presence was well documented in the preceding period. The debate concerned the nature of the Inca as civilizing agents. Under the banner of pseudonationalism, "Peruvian" influence was denied, particularly in those territories that were subject to territorial disputes. The patrimony of living indigenous peoples was totally and deliberately ignored, perceived as a separate entity without any history or links to archaeological remains. This "Chileanization" of ethnic territories, which legitimized the official view of racial and cultural uniformity, transformed Chile into a country devoid of Indians or ethnic diversity. Santiago became the place where centers of exclusive exotic Indian (dead or alive) exhibits were staged for the gratification of a still essentially ethnocentric anthropological science. The materials for these exhibitions came from the vanquished ethnic territories or from far away relic areas where only missionaries, some state officials, and daring travelers would venture.

With the collapse of the evolutionists, a new way of doing archaeology was inaugurated, primarily by Max Uhle, who provided a modern diachronic reconstitution of pre-Inca populations of northwestern Argentina through the identification of ceramic styles and diagnostic indicators that enabled him to establish sequences and correlations with the Peruvian-Bolivian Andes. Uhle was a field investigator who, on the basis of his anti-evolutionary diffusionist thesis, was able to see the evidence reflected in the data, and thus he inaugurated comparative analysis between the Andean core and the marginal zones. Uhle enlightened this epoch with his sound German prehistoric methodology, completely detached from approaches such as those of Eric Boman, whose explanations of the archaeological context of the sites were based solely on the ethnohistoric documentation and who relegated archaeology to bibliographical research.

At the beginning of the twentieth century, these changes in archaeological practice were marked by events such as the Fourth Scientific Congress held in Santiago in 1908. This congress brought together renowned scholars involved in the initial stages of anthropology and archaeology in South America, including Max Uhle, Ricardo Latcham, Aureliano Oyarzún, and Martin Gusinde. In 1911, the Museum of Ethnology and Anthropology was founded in Santiago, a result of Max Uhle's appointment in Chile, after his successful and prestigious performance over seven years in the United States, Peru, Bolivia, and ARGENTINA. Also in 1911, the Museum of Ethnology's cultural-history approach was initiated by the appointment of the German ethnologist Martin Gusinde, who was the finest representative of the Vienna model of cultural cycles. Throughout twelve years of intensive ethnological and physical anthropology fieldwork, Gusinde amassed one of the most valuable museum collections, in its day considered to be one of the most ancient in the Americas.

By 1910, the Ameghinian thesis had been completely discredited in the face of Euro-American proposals that made unilineal evolutionism unsustainable. It was only then that ethnic or archaeological issues, per se, were pursued as worthy objects of study under the new Euro-American historicist approach, which was dedicated to the compilation of national cultural values in the context of the ascent of the new scientific-academic intelligentsia. Between 1909 and 1911, new publications were edited by the Chilean Society for Folklore, the Chilean Society of History and Geography, the Natural Sciences Society, the national museums, and the University of Chile. By 1910, there had been a subtle shift toward the chronological models of North American archaeology. This type of archaeology was based on explanatory models drawn from theories on diffusion and migration, based on the widely held and common belief that people do not make innovations on their own but instead rely on foreign influences.

During the first decade of the twentieth century, articles published in the journals *Ethnologica* (Colonna) and *Anthropos* (Vienna) generated critical theoretical changes in archaeology in Chile. These journals disseminated the current methods of cultural history and greatly influenced Gusinde in Chile and later O. Menghin in Argentina, who initiated a new style of scientific-totalitarianism alien to any form theoretical and ideological pluralism. The vacuum left by nineteenth-century evolutionist and positivist-rationalist views was filled by a group from the Museum of Ethnology headed by Uhle, Oyarzún, and Gusinde. This group joined together under the banner of the historic-particularist paradigm and the tenets of the cultural-history school of Vienna, which was characterized by religious anti-evolutionist and overtly racist views. The group's work was also inspired by the translations of Oyarzún (Orellana 1979), the writings of Koppera and Schmidt and other classics by Ratzel Frobenius and FRITZ GRAEBNER, culminating in the Argentinean studies of Imbelloni, Bórmida, and Menghin.

Adherence to the culturalist current by Chilean intellectuals at the beginning of the twentieth century becomes understandable because in Argentina at the same time the opposite Ameghinist thesis was in vogue. During this period in Chile, all work that legitimized the superiority of certain peoples and races over others was very popular.

During the first decade of the twentieth century, while those scholars who closely adhered to the cultural-history school produced descriptive and speculative studies, other scholars made systematic contributions to the production of a documented database. Between 1900 and 1938 there was a methodological crisis caused by the abandonment of stratigraphic-naturalistic principles in favor of the hasty excavations of Indian tombs with the sole purpose of recovering artifacts to fill state museums. It has been acknowledged that these excavations were unsystematic and that no refined methods were applied to clarify cultural history in terms of pre-Inca sequences and developments in regional diversity. At the same time, from at least 1911 on, scholars in other countries were using stratigraphic methods, but the application of these methods was not popular in Chile where, with the exception of the northern and southern confines of the country, chronological frameworks were not thought to provide reliable sequences and contexts.

In this milieu, Uhle and Latcham made major contributions to the discipline. These two archaeologists were the products of German and British academic environments, which they would later incorporate with Euro-American influences. Max Uhle based his research in Chile (from 1911 to 1919) on the cultural-history paradigm. His pan-Andean archaeological perspective and his cutting-edge methods, synthesized into the Euro-American stance, enabled him to carry out contextualized excavations that made him the forerunner of modern empiricists. He enhanced the chronological, sequential, and distributive adjustments between peripheral and core cultures, based on the extension of the Tiwanaku and Inca guiding horizons, and as a result he wrote the first pre-Columbian cultural history, with its very own methods. Uhle's results remained in use until their harmonious integration into the modern investigations of JUNIUS BOUTON BIRD (1943) and even more recent investigations (Schaedel 1957).

During the first two decades of the twentieth century, then, various distant events had an impact in Chile. The first systematic physical anthropology studies began under Ales Hrdlicka, and the peopling of the Americas was established as a post-Pleistocene event (W. H. HOLMES). However "ancient" Paleolithic stations were recorded at Taltal in northern Chile, which helped to continue the debate on the earlier origins of humans in the Americas. The first stratigraphic excavations were carried out, and Max Uhle began to work in South America, where he was regarded as the father of Andean archaeology.

The Ameghinian School had been discredited to the point of oblivion by the application of stratigraphy, the discovery of rock art, the excavation of cemeteries, and the recovery of surface collections from ancient workshops. Initial excavations were in the desert, where monumental sites were more visible and profuse, in order to supply collections for state museums and private collectors. These excavations were undertaken with ethnohistoric sources rather than archaeological field-recording methods in mind. The scholars were erudite bibliographers who witnessed the erosion of any great antiquity for humans in the Americas, and in this context, Uhle's innovative role was decisive for the success of Chilean archaeology.

Transitional Interface (1919–1961)
Uhle's theories and practice were followed by the majority of Chilean senior researchers such as Ricardo Latcham (1928, 1938), who adopted his chronological sequence in spite of the fact

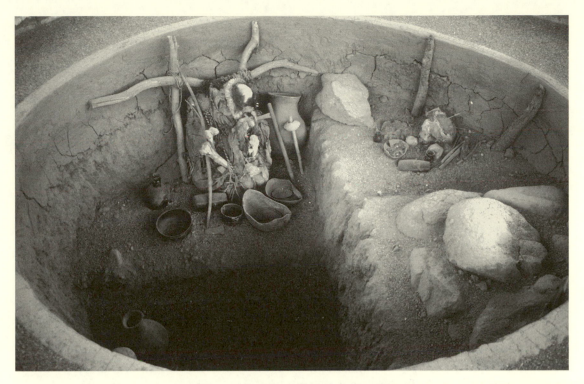

Ancient burial ground, San Pedro de Atacama, Chile (Chris Fairclough Colour Library)

that this generation was not accustomed to the transference of knowledge at the pupil level. Latcham's perspective of Chilean anthropology was influenced by classic British empiricism, which was geared toward the systematic arrangement of data rather than to theoretical reasoning, thus promoting an upsurge in the publication of valuable monographs in both material culture and regional archaeology and their trans-Andean connections (Latcham 1928, 1938). More an avid reader than a fieldworker, Latcham incorporated into the National Museum of Natural History his affinity for physical anthropology through studies in ethnography, ethnohistory, ethno-agriculture, and ethnozoology as well as his own specialty in engineering to benefit the understanding of pre-Columbian metallurgy.

Latcham did not rely on excavated data, and he was unable to use it with the same detail as Uhle. In this sense, his archaeological principles were intertwined with ethnohistoric sources. He played a leading role in anthropology until the 1940s when his colleague Grete Mostny began her scientific investigations. Mostny had

taken refuge in Chile to escape racist persecution in Vienna, and with a doctorate in Egyptology, Mostny would eventually lead the National Museum toward its higher objectives of combining science with popular communication.

Latcham's work centered on the study of the Mapuche, on physical anthropological studies, and on the compilation and interpretation of archaeological and ethnohistoric data. In addition, he also initiated courses on prehistoric Chile in 1936 at the University of Chile. He rejected proposals that stemmed from historical materialism, thus consolidating the success of the Vienna school in relation to the southern peoples of Tierra del Fuego.

The downfall of the fascist regimes in Europe in 1945 resulted in an influx of migrants to South America, including the cultural historians Marcelo Bórmida in 1946 and Osvaldo Menghin and Vladimiro Male in 1948. These scholars, along with Casanovas and Canals Frau, consolidated the hegemonic movement during times of academic repression in Argentina. The most important representative of this movement was the prehistorian Osvaldo Menghin, whose influence, especially his approach to the stone tool collections of northern Chile, was largely felt in the research and academic program at the University of Chile and research conducted in Patagonia and the south-center part of the country.

This late renewal of the cultural-history thesis was not popular in Chile, but among its final outcomes were a study on the Mapuche (Oyarzún in Orellana 1979). Julius Spiner, a lawyer from Vienna, became professor of prehistory at the University of Valparaiso and taught the next generation of archaeologists. He excavated at the Atacama oasis with Mario Orellana, but he failed to overcome the limitations of his orthodox methodology. Menghin's influence was felt in the adoption of what was considered to be the only modern method, in which cultural components recorded in Chile were compared as "global phenomena," but in contrast to the Argentinean acceptance of *"Kulturkreise"* Menghin had had limited influence in Chile.

Between 1925 and 1949, North American archeologists began to position themselves around the most important archaeological ruins and sites across the world and to disseminate their theories, methods, and resources. A. L. Kroeber, ALFRED V. KIDDER, J. H. Rowe, IRVING ROUSE, WILLIAM DUNCAN STRONG, W. Bennet, Junius Bird, C. Evans, and Betty Meggers arrived in the Andean regions. Bird (1943) and Bennet headed south, taking their cutting-edge methodologies with them. Archaeological work by M. Posnansky in Bolivia and JULIO TELLO in Peru made an impact in Chile at about the same time that Uhle ceased to be a major protagonist and Latcham was the only alternative leader.

Starting in 1940, the influence of the innovative scholars from the early part of the twentieth century began to decline or was revised by a new generation of archaeologists consisting of foreigners such as Junius Bird, resident scholars such as Grete Mostny and Francisco Cornely, and the first full-time Chilean archaeologist, Jorge Iribarrean. All were involved with the transitional interface between the Medina-Uhle-Latcham triad and the generation educated in the 1960s.

Along with the British missionary Dillman Bullock, Francisco Cornelly is considered to be the cofounder of the Museum of Angol (in 1943), and Francisco Fonck, founder of the Museum of Villa del Mar, is considered to be the pioneer of regional studies. Cornelly was a German art scholar who began his career collecting Indian antiquities. His first excavations were done in the Auracania, in south Chile, and around 1934 he settled first in Atacama and then in Coquimbo, where he founded the Archaeology Museum of La Serena (1942) and the Archaeological Society (1944). He edited some enduring publications and made known the Molle and Diaguita cultures of the semi-arid northern part of Chile. In 1959, Cornelly was replaced by his friend and collaborator, the young and talented Jorge Iribarren.

Through the work of Junius Bird (1938a, 1938b, 1943), the North American school propagated a stratigraphic method centered more on the occupational than on the funerary context, and this method contested more-traditional strategies. The work of both Bird and Iribarren abounded in new theoretical, methodological, and empirical proposals, and a passion for bibliographic resource in conjunction with fieldwork characterizes Iribarren's work. Putting aside his own ideological principles, Iribarren was able, during the height of academic repression, to protect those scholars who were subjected to humiliation by the military regime. Mostny, with an extensive academic production, concentrated her efforts on the National Museum of Natural History, where she was surrounded by notable group of collaborators such as J. Montané, E. Durán, S. Quevedo, and R. Stehberg. Along with this endeavor she continued her efforts to disseminate information through the creation of scientific youth groups.

During this period, the published works of Bird (1938a, 1938b, 1943), Mostny (1954), Latcham (1938), Iribarren (1961), Schaedel (1957), and Rydén (1944) were obligatory reading for the members of any research project in Chile. The University of Chile had been strengthened by the creation of the Center of Anthropological Studies (1950), and from this center Richard Schaedel and his local associates in the 1960s reactivated the discipline based on the work of Bird and Uhle through the use of a modern chronological, ecological, and adaptive analysis in the northern half of the country. Meanwhile, W. Mulloy's proposals about Easter Island drew Chile even closer to North American methodologies, and in this context, the Center of Anthropological Studies became the generator of scientific groundwork groups in Chile led by Carlos Munizaga, Francisco Reyes, Alberto Medina, Jorge Kaltwasser, Bernardo Berdichewsky, Ximena Bunster, Mario Orellana, Gonzalo Figueroa, and Juan Muziaga, the founder of scientific physical anthropology in Chile. Although Osvaldo Menghin's visit to this center clarified matters and methods related to issues of parietal (rock and cave) art, the Patagonian sequence, and his exploration in the south-central part of the country, his cultural-history proposals did not become popular.

A scientific movement originating in the provinces linked up with the scientific circle of the capital. This movement had its antecedents in the foundation of museums in Valparaiso, Viña del Mar, Angol, Punta Arenas, and La Serena, of which the Museum of Archaeology of La Serena constituted the most prestigious center of research and periodical publications. Like the museum in La Serena, the Museum of Viña del Mar was a front-line research center when it began using the excavation methods of "contextual cross-sections" and "determination of original floors" in 1955. In 1957, R. P. Le Paige founded the Archaeological Museum at the Casa Parroquial de San Pedro Atacama, and in 1959, Percy Dauelsberg founded the Regional Museum of Arica. During the following period, a process of regionalization took place in Chilean archaeology.

North American diffusionist explanations had ceased to be satisfactory explanations for the peopling of the Americas before 1961. The idea that all forms of progress and civilization were dispersed to marginal areas from Mesoamerican and Andean heartlands came under serious critical scrutiny. Psychological explanations of the past became inadequate, and the hierarchical ordering of differences began to compete with the search for regularities. This was a response to an inductivist approach that led more to descriptivism per se and resulted in

a growing awareness that a dialectic deductive-inductive approach was needed, which would move closer to theories that would provide the next generation of archaeologists with better research objectives for sites and collections.

Professional Scientific Development (1961–)

The American ethnologist and archaeologist JULIAN STEWARD had an enormous influence on the generation of the 1950s and 1960s through the publication of his book the *Handbook of South American Indians,* but there were also other major influences. Carlos Ponce, working with a team of national colleagues, was applying stratigraphic excavation methods at Tiwanaku; Luis Lumbreras excavated Chavín and proposed a critical reading of the North American-Andean literature; Stig Rydén finished his monograph on Chile and Bolivia; and in Argentina, Alberto Rex González published his chrono-stratigraphic work. These young scholars, who kept in permanent contact with each other, were the authors of publications that became compulsory reading for the archaeological generation of the 1950s and 1960s. Many new technical and methodological strategies would emerge from this interrelationship, such as Childean evolutionism and a reevaluation of "garbage collections" as opposed to *belles pieces,* or great art objects. Most important, the chronological archaeology that would set this generation apart began, and the first modern and reliable synthesis of regional sequences emerged.

During the first decade of the twentieth century, reactions against unilineal evolutionism were channeled through the diffusionist school, which was inclined toward the hierarchical transmission of change rather than conservative social structures. The important issue for this school was the determination of cultural "emission" and "reception," which denied local creativity or the existence of autochthonous evolutionary developments mature enough to assimilate and internally process change. There was a growing need to look for more pluralist theses, which would complement Boasian ideas that firmly opposed the idea of the biological inferiority of the American Indian and the evolutionary notion that distinguished between superior and inferior societies. The best of European evolutionism was appropriated to reconfigure cultural relativism, which represented an inductivist tendency that firmly encouraged praxis in the field and empirical data accumulation. In this context, more-objective analyses based on typological taxonomies emerged and would be the platform from which Chilean cultural ecology would surface, which occurred before the rise of systemic archaeology.

During the first part of this period, all Chile's archaeologists were Boasian positivists, rejecting rationalism because it had made a spectacle out of archaeology by burdening it with "discoveries" that lacked any professional rigor. At the time, cultures were identified in chronological and spatial order through the utilization of such an overwhelming inductive approach that it prevented any nonempirical prejudice, and thus culture was set at the center of social life. Evolutionary and transcultural changes were inserted into society independent of their social consciousness. Empiricist archaeology was debilitated by this type of idealist analysis, which was completely detached from the material nature of the archaeological data and whose causation studies were based on ethnographic analogy and other sorts of inferences of dubious value. The excessive use of chronologies and chorologies per se was debated, as were the abstract statistical typologies that had reduced societies to largely ceramic cultures. It was in this context that evolutionary functionalism arrived, arranging settlement archaeology hierarchically and opening up new avenues for research from the 1970s onward.

This period also witnessed the emergence of the first multidisciplinary endeavors in collaboration with specialists from the hard sciences. The University of Chile published specialized editions, and methodologies and techniques were optimized owing to more sustained contacts with foreign academics. At the same time, qualified scholars were now distributed across almost all of Chile, and Roberto Montandon, the pioneer of monumental restoration, began his early work in 1950; it would be continued later by Eduardo Muñoz.

It is acknowledged that North American influence started in 1960 when internal, or independent, cultural changes began to be identified as paralleling the appraisal of adaptive roles that went beyond environmental determinism. The European contribution to social evolution, along with methodological renovation by means of the unorthodox analyses of collections, and the concepts of association by superimposition proposed by the GORDON CHILDE–MORTIMER WHEELER duo were also important influences. Notions implying that typology was equal to chronology and that similarity was akin to synchronicity were gradually abandoned. Nevertheless, the diffusionist criterion was still prevalent in reference books, which continued to assert a greater antiquity for stone tool industries such as the Gatchi-Atacama without any scientific basis.

The downfall of empiricism and its subsequent return shrouded by a more scientific, neopositivist orientation merited the development of an improved explanatory and predictive capacity, which drew archaeology even closer to the social sciences. This change enabled further advances in Childean materialistic ontological proposals and with the opposed idealistic tendencies that viewed reality in a culture by itself.

In this period, pioneering investigators initiated a renovation movement through the establishment of regional archaeological museums, and the expansion of academic expertise reached its pinnacle with the publication in 1989 of a new Chilean prehistory edited by the Chilean Society of Archaeology. Other events include the beginning of systematic training in archaeology at the Universities of Chile and Concepción and the First International Archaeological Congress held in 1961 in Arica, organized by the Regional Museum of Arica and supported by the University of Chile. Two years later, in 1963, the First National Congress of Archaeology was held in San Pedro Atacama, sponsored by the museum's founder, Gustavo Le Paige, with the assistance of the Universidad del Norte. This event marked the emergence of the Chilean Archaeological Society to promote and regulate archaeological research and incorporate all scholars in archaeology. The society has published the proceedings of national congresses held so far, and the national and international congresses held in Viña del Mar a year after the congress in San Pedro Atacama indicate that the scholars from this museum, headed by Jorge Silva, Julio Montané, and Virgilio Schiappacasse, among others, have attained genuine prestige.

It was not by chance that the International Congress of Arica took place in the northern part of Chile, for it was precisely in this region that the modern inter-Andean style of "doing" archaeology had caught on, a style promoted by newsletters and informal meetings held by colleagues such as P. Dauelsberg, L. G. Lumbreras, C. Ponce, G. Vescelius, J. Montané, and L. Núñez. Since the beginning of the 1960s the most important archaeological collections have been located in the northern part of the country. The regional universities took charge of this process, building up an enormous register that in San Pedro Atacama alone would extent to half a million archaeological items. Participants of the Arica congress included Percy Dauelsberg, Guillermo Focacci, Luis Alvarez, Carlos Munizaga, Gret Mostny, Jorge Iribarren, Jean Christian Spani, Gustavo Le Paige, and Lautaro Núñez, along with scholars from neighboring countries, Luis Guillermo Lumbreras and Carlos Ponce, Julio Montané, Mario Orellana, Hans Niemeyer, Virgilio Schiappacasse, and Jorge Silva. As a whole, these groups shared common aspirations, which after the San Pedro de Atacama congress, constituted a point of reference uniting past with new generations formed at the universities.

During the 1960s, the beginning of a more systematic and professional Chilean archaeology was firmly established. The younger generation of university-educated archaeologists such as G. Ampuero, M. Rivera, P. Núñez, O. Silva, F. Bate, O. Ortíz, J. Palma, E. Durán, and S. Quevedo presented their first work at a congress held in Viña del Mar in 1964. Around this time Zulema Seguel, a French prehistorian, arrived in Concepción and began to teach prehistory and encourage research in it.

Although the schools of anthropology were in Santiago and Concepción, archaeological and museographic research spread across the country, toward the south, under the tutelage of Mateo Martinic and Dillmann Bullock, whose museum in Angol was established through the support of the latter's missionary activities. Toward the north as far as Arica, Antofagasta, and San Pedro de Atacama, the work of Dauelsberg and his associates, and by Gustavo Le Paige and his young colleagues constituted the first examples of systematic research. Since 1957, researchers such as Percy Dauelsberg, Luis Alvarez, and Guillermo Focacci, along Gustavo Le Paige and Lautaro Núñez, have lived in the northern part of the country where they conducted their first field projects. Not knowing the significance of diffusionism or relativism, this generation of scholars endeavored to obtain relevant data from collections and mentors as well as the details of archaeological methods and techniques. This was the last stage before the professionalization of the discipline.

For the youth of the 1960s, the only possible means of achieving a professional career was through the University of Chile in Santiago. It was, however, in the History Department of the Pedagogical Institute of Macul where the efforts of G. Mostny, M. Orellana, and B. Berdischewsky were first realized in 1962 in the form of an archaeology course designed for history teachers who would spread across the countryside and play an important role in archaeology. The enthusiastic participation of students from the University of Chile ensured the immediate success of this first educational program, which had graduates such as Gonzalo Ampuero, Julia Monleon, Osvaldo Silva, Mario Rivera, Victoria Castro, Carlos Thomas, Eliana Durán, Silvia Quevedo, Omar Ortíz, Luis Briones, Patricio Núñez, Carlos Orrejola, and Julie Palma. From the start, the connection to history led to the perception of archaeology as a kind of "ancient" history in which the sources that led to a hypothesis were subject to a rigorous internal critique. The universal perception of the developments of past societies was envisioned, and there was a sincere concern to confer a temporal, spatial, and contextual meaning to the prehistoric cultural diversity of the country.

The time had come to synthesize population data according to time, space, and culture. The well-preserved coastal and interior contexts of the north displayed collections that demanded considerable taxonomic efforts, which emphasized primarily subsistence data rather than symbolic or ideological considerations. Within this empiricist framework, ethnohistoric approaches were kept to a minimum and rendered undesirable. This was the situation that prevailed until the 1970s, when J. Murra and J. Hidalgo presented their innovative proposals at the Congress of Archaeology and the Multidisciplinary Congress on Andean Man, respectively, and their proposals were accepted.

It was also a period of continuous contact and collaboration with North American archaeologists and scientists, contact that helped resolve concrete issues and allowed for models to be tested outside the academic milieu. More recently, other North American agencies, such as the National Geographic Society and the Smithsonian Institution, have funded research by local investigators utilizing North American standards that have furthered archaeological advancement. In general terms, the outcome of the collaboration with North American scientific missions that began in the 1930s has been a positive one, mainly because of a shared responsibility for projects that distanced itself from any form of scientific imperialism.

This renewed environment, the theoretical-methodological proposals of the new archaeology, descriptivism, structuralism, and historic materialism began an enriching process of academic debate. However, this efflorescence was short lived. An "antiseptic" form of archaeology characterized the period between 1973 and 1990, corresponding to the military regime's political dominance. In the milieu of academic cutbacks and persecution, archaeologists, although scientifically valid, were for obvious reasons cautious in their theoretical and ideological opinions.

In 1973, Chile reinstated a socialist regime and there was a more open environment in which academic freedom was encouraged and the theoretical underpinnings of historical materialism and Marxism were intensely debated. During the period of time immediately before the subsequent military coup, a certain theoret-ical intolerance, derived from political tensions, was felt. Nevertheless, during the Congress on Andean Man, J. Murra and T. Lynch presented their groundbreaking thesis on verticality and the seasonal round, which remains the guide, even now, to the principal explanatory approaches to mobility and change in the Andes. These approaches are an example of how different theoretical stances coexisted in a plural academic environment before it was suppressed during the years of the military regime.

On the Latin American stage, the so-called social archaeology thesis succeeded in systemizing Childe's precursory ideas and historic materialism. A meeting in Teotihuacán in 1976 resulted in the Latin Americanization of this proposal at a time when the use and abuse of the modes of production were generating the first confusing signals of the materialist discourse. Nevertheless, failure to recognize the importance of these endeavors is as untenable as denying the contribution of the Soviet school to the understanding and reconstruction of daily life based on the detailed knowledge of labor processes. The latter, understood as observed practices involving specific techniques (that would leave particular wear patterns), has correctly directed us to an understanding of cultural change as an expression of internal developments during the course of the social system.

Under the military regime most schools of archaeology were closed down, and only the one located at the University of Chile remained open under the direction of Mario Orellana and Carlos Munizaga. Academia was obviously hampered by the military regime despite the fact that during the first decade after the military coup North American processual archaeology reached the country. Models of postprocessual archaeology were superimposed onto North American ecosystemic models and assisted in a theoretical upgrading during the years of academic repression in Chile.

During the military dictatorship, the principal European, North American, and Latin American currents were known at the University of Chile through the limited literature that reached the country. In this manner, different anthropological trends were disseminated, first among investigation projects situated in the north and later to those situated in the central and southern parts of the country. Considerable time had to pass, however, before academics could present more valid scientific proposals, although Orellana has argued that some museums situated in the north of the country were not only unaffected by the military regime but actually benefited from it. Closer analysis contradicts this assumption.

To the young generation of investigators who began their academic careers during the early years of the military regime, the long years of postponement and frustration represented an excruciatingly pathetic hiatus. The events were dramatic because, between 1973 and 1975, the schools of anthropology and archaeology at the Universities of Concepción and Norte were shut down. In 1980, the University of Chile was cut off from its regional campuses located in the northern part of the country. Those campuses were the seats of the Program of Archaeological and Museum Investigations, and of those programs, only an isolated museum course remained at the University of Antofagasta. The Universidad del Norte was dismantled, and its campuses were segregated along with their research units and museums; only the Museum of San Pedro Atacama was retained.

Archaeologists who were exiled and never returned include J. Montané, F. Bate, B. Berdichewsky, and O. Ortíz, and some anthropologists and archaeologists who were acquitted (but nevertheless imprisoned) were incorporated into other universities in the country. Of the network of University of Chile museums that were cofounded by B. Marinov and P. Núñez, only one remains, at the University of Antofagasta; the rest were taken over by fragile municipal governments. At the same time, the law office of the Central House of the University of Chile in Santiago proceeded in 1974 to clear management positions, an opportunity that this author, along with a dozen other affected scholars, took advantage of and in so doing, distanced ourselves from our universities of origin.

The civilian groups of the Universidad del Norte linked to the military junta neutralized student resistance in Arica by founding an archaeological museum in 1986. The groups that supported the creation of an Institute of Anthropology in 1983 provided resources for its infrastructure, and its directorship alternated among P. Dauelsberg, G. Focacci, and M. Rivera during the military regime. The Chilean Archaeological Congress of 1974 was canceled because of political allegations presented by one of the historians of Chilean archaeology.

The creation of the School of Anthropology at Antofagasta in 1971 represented one of the most important contributions to the discipline made by the Universidad Católica del Norte. The foundation of this school was in great part achieved by the joint efforts of Guacolda Boisset, the Department of Archaeology, and the associated Regional Museum. Twenty archaeologists from the north graduated in 1976, the first generation to obtain postgraduate degrees (C. Santoro, I. Muñoz, V. Standen, G. Castillo, M. Cervellino, M. A. Costa, C. Moragas, among others), and its members were tutored by academics who had achieved a regional identity, such as G. Boisset, B. Bittmann, A. Llagostera, L. Núñez, N. Vergara, V. Bustos, J. Munziaga, and H. Garcés.

During the years of the military regime, some significant contributions to the discipline were made by individuals rather than by institutions. Good examples include advances in the archaeology of central Chile based on reliable sequences and the well-documented definition of cultural complexes by F. Falabella, R. Stehberg, E. Durán, L. Cornejo, T. Planella, and others. Investigators such as F. Mena, M. Massone, C. Ocampo, and C. Prieto in the territory of Tierra del Fuego reactivated the study of hunter gatherers and created a suitable environment in which to undertake collaborative research with Argentinean colleagues. Paleo-Indian investigations started by Montané were taken up in central Chile, and in the arid and semiarid north, institutional and individual projects never halted, as is shown by the proceedings of the various archaeological congresses, the creation of the Institute of Archaeology in San Pedro Atacama, and the foundation of various state-funded museums.

After the return to democracy in 1991, the consequences of the academic impoverishment of the preceding years had to be dealt with. There was a need for more locally based theoretical paradigms and for the optimization of the formation of academic groups. Various theoretical approaches, such as the cognitive, historicist, structuralist, neopositivist, symbolist, materialist, and postprocessualist approaches, have been helpful and will continue to be useful in maximizing the interpretative options of past events. In this context, the changing perspectives of the present range from a genetic neodiffusionism to a static deductive localism, from morphological discourse to the legitimization of computerized verification per se, and from an aversion to globalizing materialistic views to sterile descriptivism.

Some analytical models have recently surfaced in Chile that offer unequivocal signs of theoretical and methodological advancements. For example, the fact that the peopling of the coast of the country took place at such an early date (10,000 years ago) has reopened the relevant issue related to the articulation of two synchronic socio-adaptive processes: the Andeanization and maritimization of Chilean society.

Aside from the reconstitution of the general and specific behavior patterns and the ideological perceptions of the human phenomenon, there were also utopian aspirations to attract the younger generations of investigators to the quest for a vision of the society of the future. The aspirations of the newest generations of archaeologists are geared toward finding jobs and toward more specialized knowledge but with less alienating theory. In this sense, their propositions are perceived as consistent and well documented. Thus, it is now necessary to employ postgraduate archaeologists and to generate a museological (museum studies) policy that will contribute to a new educational strategy.

Epilogue

We should expect the emergence of "other" archaeologies later on, related to the 500 years of recent existence: colonial, industrial, subaquatic, urban, and forensic archaeology. The last is of particular importance as can be seen by detailed expert assessments made public during the judicial processes surrounding the "disappearances" that occurred during the military regime.

Another expected outcome would be the optimization of current knowledge about the original inter-American cultural processes, through the 30,000 to 12,000 years of human occupation, making it more difficult to divide it into two areas of study: prehistory and history. In a similar vein, it would be appropriate to find an approach with the discipline of history based on theories, methods, and techniques proper to archaeology in order to elucidate a reconstitution of the greater history of the Latin American peoples both before and after the linkage to the history of the west. In this context, we should strive to advance toward an appropriate paradigmatic synthesis, which would integrate the best of the proposals on particularities and regularities, in an explicit discourse directed toward those peoples who, until now, have received only the official and elitist histories.

I am describing an archaeology incorporated into a scientific and multidisciplinary history of the peoples of the Americas, a history that would go beyond its "intellectual" orientations, not forgetting its social meaning and its objectivity, to a proper understanding of the complexity of past and present human behavior. In today's world, when many people proclaim that history is defunct, archaeologists and their "extended chronologies" are the best equipped to attempt to change this apathy to a historic utopia, one that ascends from the depth of human nature and aspires to the sustainability of human society in search of the ideal of transformations that are more just and ecumenical.

A. Lautaro Núñez;
translated by Armando Anaya Hernández

References

Bird, J. B. 1938a. "Antiquity and Migrations of the Early Inhabitants of Patagonia." *Geographical Review* 28, no. 2: 250–275.

———. 1938b. "Before Magellan." *Natural History* 41, no. 1: 16–79.

———. 1943. "Excavation in Northern Chile." *Anthropological Papers of the American Museum of Natural History* 38, part 4. New York.

———. 1946. "The Archaeology of Patagonia." In *The Marginal Tribes: Handbook of South American*

Indians, 17–29. Vol 1. Ed. Julian Steward. Bureau of American Ethnology, Bulletin 143. Washington, DC: Smithsonian Institution.

———. 1988. *Travels and Archaeology in South Chile.* Iowa City: University of Iowa Press.

Darwin, Charles. 1886. *A Naturalist's Voyage: Journal of Researches . . . during the Voyage of the H.M.S. "Beagle" round the World . . ..* London: J. Murray.

Hildalgo, Jorge. 1972. *Culturas protohistóricas del Norte de Chile: El Testimonio de los Crónistas.* Santiago: Editorial Universitaria.

Irilbarren Charlin, Jorge. 1961: "La cultura de Huentelauquén y sus correlaciones." La Serena.

———. 1962. "Correlations between Archaic Cultures of Southern California and Coquimbo, Chile." *American Antiquity* 27, no. 3: 424–425.

Gusinde, Martin. 1986. *Die Feurerland Indianen* (Los Indios de Tierra del Fuego, 1918–1924). Buenos Aires: Centro Argentino de Etnologia Americana.

Latcham, Ricardo. 1928. "Metalurgia atacameña." *Boletín del Museo Nacional de Historial Natural* 15: 107–151.

———. 1938. *Arqueología de la Región Atacameña.* Petroglifos: Prensas de la Universidad de Chile.

Medina, José. 1882. *Les aborígines de Chile.* Santiago: Guttenberg.

Meggers, Betty. 1963. *Aboriginal Cultural Development in Latin America.* Washington, DC: Smithsonian Institution.

———. 1972. *Prehistoric America.* Chicago: Aldine, Atherton.

Menghin, Oswald. 1957a. "Vorgeschichte Amerikas." In *Abriss de Voreschichte,* 162–218. Ed. R. Oldenbourg. Munich.

———. 1957b. "Das protolithikum in americka." *Acta praehistorica* 1: 5–40.

———. 1957c. "Estilos del arte rupestre de patagonia." *Idem:* 57–87.

———. 1957d. "Las piedras de tacitas como fenómeno mundial." *Bol. Museo Arqueológico de la Serena* 9: 3–12.

Montane, Julio. 1960. "Elementos precerámicos de Cahuil (Prov. Santa Cruz.)" *Museo Arqueológico de La Serena, Notas del Museo* 8.

———. 1964. "Fechamiento tentativo de las ocupaciones humanas en dos terrazas a lo largo del litoral chileno." *Arqueología de Chile Central y zonas vecinas.*

———. 1968. "Paleo-Indian Remains from Laguna de Tagua-Tagua, Central Chile." *Science* 161: 1137–1138.

Mostny Glaser, Grete. 1954. *Culturas preColombinas de Chile.* Santiago: Editorial de Pacifico.

———. 1971. *Prehistoria de Chile.* Santiago: Editorial Universitaria.

Orellana, M. 1977. *Comienzos de la ciencia prehistórica en Chile.* Santiago: Universidad de Chile.

———. 1979. *Informe preliminar sobre la tercera campaña arqueológica Argentina en Tierra del Fuego.* Buenos Aires: Colegio de graduados en Antropologia.

Orellana, Mario Rodriguez. 1979. *Aureliano Oyarzun Navarro, 1858–1947. Estudios antropologicos y arqueologicos.* Santiago: Editorial Universitaria.

———. 1982. *Investigacione y terias en las arqueológia de Chile.* Santiago: Centro de Estudios Humanisticas, Universidad de Chile.

Rydén, Stig. 1944. *Contributions to the Archaelogy of the Río Loa Region.* Göteborg.

Schaedel, R. P., and C. Munizaga. 1957. "Arqueologia chilena. Contribuciones al estudio de la region comprendida entre Arica y La Serena." Santiago: Centro de Estudios Antropológicos, Universidad de Chile.

Steward, J., ed. 1946–1950. *Handbook of South American Indians.* 6 vols. Washington, DC: Bureau of American Ethnology, Smithsonian Institution.

China

The birth of modern Chinese archaeology in the early twentieth century was a product of the introduction of western scientific methods, the rise of nationalism, and the search for the cultural origins of the nation. These three factors have had a continuing influence on the development of the discipline, with the consequence that archaeology in China has been firmly placed in the general field of history. Its research orientations and interpretations have been significantly affected by the different political agendas of the nation—especially the ever-changing concept of nationalism in particular eras.

Formative Period (1920s–1940s)

The beginnings of modern archaeology in China can be traced to 1928, when the Institute of History and Philology, Academia Sinica, launched the excavation of Yinxu, a capital city

1. Zhoukoudian	13. Qianshanyang	25. Majiabang	36. Yuchanyan
2. Yangshao	14. Qujialing	26. Songze	37. Xianrendong
3. Anyang	15. Dawenkou	27. Liangzhu	38. Diaotonghuan
4. Chengziyai	16. Cishan	28. Mancheng	39. Chengtoushan
5. Doujitai	17. Jiangzhai	29. Mawangdui	40. Sanxingdui
6. Lantian	18. Liuwan	30. Mausoleum of the	41. Dayangzhou
7. Miaodigou	19. Daxi	First Emperor Qin	42. Xinglongwa
8. Banpo	20. Honghuatao	31. Jinniushan	43. Niuheliang
9. Erligang	21. Caoxieshan	32. Longgupo	44. Taosi
10. Erlitou	22. Hemudu	33. Pengtoushan	45. Yanshi Shang city
11. Fengxi	23. Sanyuangong	34. Jiahu	46. Xiaoshuangqiao
12. Beiyinyangying	24. Shixia	35. Bashidang	47. Yuanmou

Archaeological Sites in China

of the late Shang dynasty, at Xiaotun in ANYANG, Henan Province. This was the first state-sponsored archaeological project in China, and fifteen seasons of excavation took place between 1928 and 1937 (when the Sino-Japanese War broke out). This series of excavations at Anyang was not a random occurrence but was preceded by several lines of cultural, political, and technological development, which served as the foundation for the establishment of archaeology as a new discipline.

Historical Context of Chinese Archaeology

There has been a tradition of interest in antiquarianism throughout Chinese history. Many antiquities were thought to possess a divine nature, and some bronze vessels were regarded as symbols of power and authority. This tradition encouraged the collecting and recording of ancient artifacts and, at the end of the nineteenth century, led directly to the discovery and decipherment of oracle bone inscriptions of the Shang dynasty. The discovery of the original source of the oracle bones at Xiaotun in Anyang further facilitated the identification of Yinxu at that site.

The emergence of nationalism at the beginning of the twentieth century was a significant political stimulus to the development of modern archaeology. At the same time, many revolutionary intellectuals became discontented with the sense of China under the Manchus as politically and militarily inferior to the force of foreign countries, and this discontent led to an awakening of nationalism. Liang Qichao, a Confucian reformer, was the first to heighten Chinese national consciousness, particularly in response to Japanese aggression. He pointed out in 1900 that the people of China had failed to give a name to their own country and that they referred to themselves by dynasties rather than by country. The word *China (Zhongguo),* Liang noted, "is what people of other races call us. It is not a name the people of this country have selected for themselves" (Liang 1992, 67–68).

In the early twentieth century, the concept of nationalism was ethnically centered on the Han Chinese, and minority groups were largely neglected (Dikotter 1992, 123–125; Townsend 1996). This situation was explicitly addressed by Sun Yat-sen when he said, "China, since the Qin and Han dynasties, has been developing a single state out of a single race" (Sun Yat-sen 1943, 6). According to Sun, although the Chinese people were distinct from all other "races" of the world, the boundaries of the race were drawn along the borders of the Chinese state and no comparable ethnic distinctions were made within China itself. Minority peoples were thus expected to adjust their beliefs and behavior if they wished to be counted among "the Chinese people" (Fitzgerald 1996, 69). Within this broad political climate, many Chinese intellectuals constantly endeavored to promote the self-consciousness of national identity, and the search for Chinese cultural origins became an important part of their intellectual agenda. The initial impetus for archaeological research was closely tied to this issue.

It should be noted that after the 1911 revolution, as the revolutionaries gained power and controlled the country, the concept of nationalism moved away from a racial/ethnocentric orientation to one of a state-based political entity. In time, the Nationalist government prescribed an elaborate cultural regimen to assist the peoples of Tibet, Mongolia, Manchuria, Xinjiang, and the Han regions to achieve a thorough comprehension of their common racial identity (*wuzu gonghe,* a republic of five nationalities) and to recover the sentiment of "central loyalty" toward the state (Chiang Kai-shek 1947, 10–13). However, this new concept of nationalism, which included multi-ethnic groups, seems to have been practiced more in the political arena than in the cultural domain, with the dominant ideology in China remaining centered on the cultural superiority of the Han race. The yellow emperor *(Huangdi),* a legendary sage king, was continuously elevated to the status of the founding ancestor of the Han Chinese as a symbol of national identity (Liu 1999).

It was only after the 1950s, under communism, that multi-ethnic nationalism began to affect archaeology, which is evident in the shift of emphasis from the central plains *(Zhongyuan)* to a focus on multiregional development. It is not surprising, therefore, that the choice of locations for early excavations by Chinese archaeologists was based on the primary concern of the search for the indigenous cultural origins of the Han Chinese. Moreover, influenced by the May Fourth Movement of 1919, the traditional Confucian ways of learning were criticized while western science and field methodology became influential (Li 1977, 34–35; Xia 1979). A group of young historians, referred to as "doubters of antiquity" *(yigupai)* and led by Gu Jiegang (1893–1979), developed a skeptical view of textual accounts of Chinese history. Their mission was to search for scientific evidence to reconstruct Chinese history (Schneider 1971). Archaeology, therefore, was endorsed by the *yigupai* as a scientific device to achieve this goal.

In the early twentieth century, modern archaeological fieldwork methods were introduced into China by western scholars, but they were not, however, necessarily archaeologists. The major investigations by foreigners included surveys of Paleolithic sites in Ningxia, Inner Mongolia, and northern Shaanxi Province by

E. Lecent and P. Teilhard de Chardin; excavations of *Homo erectus* remains at Zhoukoudian near Beijing by O. Zdansky, D. Black, and J. F. Weidenreich; and excavations of a Neolithic site at Yangshao in Henan by Swedish geologist JO-HAN GUNNAR ANDERSSON.

Zhoukoudian is located at a cluster of limestone hills in Fangshan county, forty-eight kilometers southwest of Beijing. It became world famous after some of the earliest human fossils were discovered there in limestone caves. The site and its abundant fossils remains—referred to as dragon bones *(longgu)* by the locals—was first discovered in 1918, and large-scale excavations followed in 1927 under the leadership of the Geological Survey of China. During the first year of excavation, an extremely well-preserved hominid lower molar was discovered and was named *Sinanthropus pekinensis,* or Peking Man (now classified as *Homo erectus pekinensis*), by the Canadian anatomist Davidson Black. In 1929, the Chinese scientist PEI WENZHONG (Pei Wen-chung) discovered a complete skullcap of Peking Man. In the following years, until the excavations were interrupted by the war in 1937, a large workforce essentially "mined" the deposits at the cave site, removing over half a million tons of material in the quest for fossils (Jia and Huang 1990; Wu and Lin 1983).

The hominid fossils found before the World War II, and subsequently lost in the confusion during the war, were studied by the German paleontologist J. F. Weidenreich. Based on twelve morphological features present in both Peking Man and modern peoples of East Asia, he concluded that some of the genes of the Peking Man had been transmitted to the modern Mongoloid populations who inhabit the same region of the world (Weidenreich 1943). This view, although controversial, was later adopted by many Chinese archaeologists to support the multiregional development theory of human evolution (Chen 1999b; Wu and Olsen 1985).

An equally important discovery around this time was the Yangshao culture found by Andersson. He was employed by the Chinese government in 1914 to conduct geological surveys, but his achievements in archaeology surpassed those

in geology. Andersson first participated in the early expeditions at Zhoukoudian, but what made him famous was Yangshao village in Henan, where he found and undertook the first excavation of a Neolithic site in China. The name of this village was then used to designate the first recognized Neolithic material assemblage in the region: the Yangshao culture. Andersson asserted that the Yangshao material remains belonged to the ancestors of the Han Chinese, but he suggested that the Yangshao pottery was probably transmitted from the West, as the stylistic patterns of Yangshao painted pottery looked similar to those from the Anau culture in Turkey and the Tripolje Culture A in southern Russia (Andersson 1923). As a result, Andersson's diffusion hypothesis initiated a decades-long debate on the origins of Chinese culture and civilization (Chen 1997, 1999c).

It should be noted that not all foreign expeditions in China were for scientific archaeological fieldwork. After the Opium War in 1840, China was forced to open its doors to the world and soon became an antiquities hunting ground for foreign imperial powers as well as for adventurers from Europe, North America, and Japan—such as AUREL STEIN, Sven Hedin, D. Klementz, and P. Pelliot—who searched for exotic antiquities from the Far East, especially in the northwestern part of China (Chen 1997, 42–51). These activities began when the government was weak and local officials were corrupt, which meant that the treasure hunters were able to carry away large quantities of artifacts from China to their own countries without significant opposition.

The behavior of these treasure hunters in China was humiliating to the Chinese, who had a strong nationalist consciousness, especially historians and archaeologists (Brysac 1997). Such activities, which were later stopped by the Chinese government, have had a long-term impact on state policies regarding the handling of cultural relics and excavations in China, policies that include the prevention of the export of antiquities from China and prohibitions on foreigners unilaterally conducting archaeological work in China (Chang 1999b, 33–37, 176–180).

Beginning of Modern Chinese Archaeology

Although the scientific field methods used by the western archaeologists enlightened Chinese scholars, the general western research orientations were not considered satisfactory. Paleolithic and Neolithic remains were thought by Chinese scholars to be too remote to be connected directly to early Chinese history (Li 1968). Andersson's proposal, which traced the origins of the Yangshao culture to the Near East, was even less appealing. As one scholar complained, "the foreign archaeologists in China do not pay any attention to the material which represents indigenous Chinese culture, but are only interested in the remains which indicate cultural connections between China and the West" (Fu 1996, 191).

Excavations in Anyang

During the 1920s, a group of Chinese scholars who had received training in modern archaeology at western universities returned to their homeland embued with a great nationalist spirit. The first was LI CHI, a Ph.D. trained in physical anthropology at Harvard University, and he, with others, launched a series of archaeological research projects in 1926. Excavations in ANYANG from 1928 to 1937, organized by Li Chi in his position at the Institute of History and Philology, Academia Sinica, were the first attempts to search for indigenous Chinese cultural origins through archaeology.

The excavations in Anyang yielded numerous material remains, including hundreds of bronze objects, nearly 25,000 pieces of inscribed oracle bones, bronze workshops, palace and temple foundations, and large royal tombs. These discoveries proved the site to be a capital city of the late Shang dynasty and for the first time provided archaeological evidence confirming the existence of an ancient indigenous Chinese culture (Li 1977).

The excavations in Anyang not only marked the beginning of modern field archaeology conducted by Chinese scholars in China but also became a field station where many leading Chinese archaeologists were trained. Most associates of Li Chi who worked in Anyang (such as Tung Tso-pin, Kao Ch'ü-hsun, Shih Chang-ju,

Liang Siyong, Guo Baojun, Yin Da, and XIA NAI) became the first generation of Chinese archaeologists and dominated the field for decades on both sides of the Taiwan Strait (Chang 1986b).

In spite of the success of the archaeological work in Anyang, there was still a gap in the evidence of material cultures between the historical Shang dynasty and the Neolithic Yangshao, as the latter was then regarded as a cultural diffusion from the Near East. Chinese scholars were still dissatisfied with the general notion that predynastic cultures in China were derived from ripples of influence extending from the West. Fu Sinian (1934) made the objection that the study of Chinese history by foreigners was mainly focused on Sino-foreign relationships, which was only a "semi-Chinese" (ban Han) endeavor. However, he continued, the more important issues to be studied were those "completely Chinese" (quan Han), that is, concerned with building the basic structure of Chinese history.

Discovery of the Longshan Culture

The cultural disconnection between Yangshao and Anyang encouraged archaeologists to search for the direct progenitor of the Shang, and the general consensus among archaeologists and historians was that the most likely area was in eastern China. After work at Anyang was halted around 1930 owing to civil war, the excavation team moved its operations to Chengziyai in Longshan township, Shandong Province, where Wu Jinding's previous preliminary surveys revealed potential archaeological discoveries (Fu 1934; Li 1990).

The excavations at Chengziyai were more fruitful than the excavators had expected. Distinctive from the Yangshao painted pottery, the black pottery from Chengziyai was similar to the Neolithic remains found at Hougang in Anyang, which lay directly beneath the Shang cultural remains. Uninscribed oracle bones found at Chengziyai provided an even more direct link between the Longshan and Shang cultures. The Longshan culture of black pottery in the east (representing indigenous Chinese culture) thus came to be viewed as a system independent of the Yangshao culture of painted pottery in the west (thought to be the result of foreign diffusion). Chinese archaeologists hoped that "if we can trace back the distribution and development of the black pottery culture at Chengziyai, most problems in the formative period of Chinese history would be resolved" (Li 1990, 193). Therefore, as Li Chi further pointed out, this discovery not only identified a homeland for a part of the Shang culture but also made a major contribution to knowledge about the origins of Chinese civilization.

Excavations at Doujitai in Shaanxi Province
While the Academia Sinica headed by Li Chi was working in Henan and Shandong, the National Beiping Academy, led by Xu Xusheng, carried out excavations at Doujitai in Shaanxi Province in 1934–1937. The intention was to search for the prehistoric origins of the Zhou dynasty. SU BINGQI, who later became the paramount senior archaeologist in China, participated in this project and established his first research achievement on ceramic typology, focusing on changing forms of the *li* vessels (Falkenhausen 1999a; Su 1948). Su regarded *li* as a vessel form that was a diagnostic for ethnic affiliations and Chinese civilization. His approach turned into a model in an archaeological methodology for several generations of Chinese students to follow.

Western Origin, Dual Origins, and Indigenous Origin of Chinese Civilization
The origins of Chinese culture have been a most sensitive issue in Chinese archaeology. Upon his discovery of the Yangshao culture, Andersson determined to find the route of eastward cultural diffusion in northwestern China. Based on his findings in the Gansu region, Andersson established a sequence of ceramic cultures that perfectly supported his hypothesis. According to this sequence, the Yangshao culture was preceded by the indigenous Qijia culture in western China, so the western origin of Yangshao pottery became logical.

The discovery of the Longshan culture in the 1930s changed the paradigm of the solely western origin for Chinese civilization inferred from Yangshao painted pottery. The Longshan culture, which was characterized by black pottery, was thought to represent the indigenous Chi-nese culture, which arose in eastern China and was contemporary with, but independent of, the Yangshao culture in western China. As a result, a new concept for the dual origins of Chinese civilization was put forward: while the Yangshao culture diffused from west to east, the Longshan culture moved from east to west. The two traditions were thought to have encountered one another and mixed, and later became the progenitor of the Shang civilization (Chang 1999a; Chen 1997, 217–227, 276–281; Liang 1959). This proposition dominated archaeological circles until the 1950s.

During the Sino-Japanese War (1937–1945) and the subsequent civil war (1945–1949), major archaeological projects were halted although some fieldwork was still occasionally carried out in peripheral regions. Xia Nai participated in the Academia Sinica's expedition in the northwestern part of the country, where his excavations yielded stratigraphic evidence indicating that the Qijia culture was in fact later than the Yangshao culture. This conclusion challenged Andersson's sequence of prehistoric cultures in western China and therefore his theory on the western origin of the Yangshao culture. Xia Nai's victory over Andersson on this issue became legendary and inspired Chinese archaeologists for decades.

During this formative period of the discipline, Chinese archaeologists struggled to achieve two primary objectives: to defend their belief in the indigenous origins of Chinese culture against foreign diffusionism and to reconstruct a reliable cultural history based on material remains in order to clear up the uncertainties in textual records that had been attacked by historical revisionists known as "the doubters of antiquity." These objectives, in turn, determined the nature of archaeology as an enterprise closely aligned to the ethnic nationalism that was centered on the Han Chinese.

Development of Archaeology in the People's Republic of China
When the Communist Party took over China in 1949, the archaeologists in the Institute of History and Philology at the Academia Sinica were split into two groups. Li Chi and several of his colleagues moved to Taiwan while Xia Nai and

Liang Siyong stayed on the mainland. Xia Nai was the one who eventually gained the most international recognition in the discipline (Falkenhausen 1999b). For the rest of the twentieth century, archaeological fieldwork, research, and training developed rapidly, but dramatic fluctuations occurred as a result of various political waves. Archaeological activities can be divided into three periods: before, during, and after the Cultural Revolution (1966–1977).

Archaeology before the Cultural Revolution (1950–1965)

Soon after the founding of the People's Republic of China in the 1950s and early 1960s, archaeologists were in great demand by the state as the country underwent tremendous construction. In 1950, the Institute of Archaeology, led primarily by Xia Nai, was established under the Academia Sinica (AS), which changed its name to the Chinese Academy of Social Sciences (CASS) in 1977. The Archaeology Program, headed by Su Bingqi, was set up in 1952 under the Department of History at Beijing University. These two institutions were the leading forces at that time in conducting archaeological research and in training young archaeologists. Many provinces also set up archaeological institutes or management of cultural relics bureaus, which were primarily involved in salvage archaeology.

In addition to Beijing University, two other universities (Northwestern and Sichuan) also started archaeology programs to train students, and the number of professional archaeologists multiplied from a mere handful before 1949 to more than 200 by 1965. The first C-14 laboratory was set up in 1965 at the Institute of Archaeology, and it was soon followed by a second one at Beijing University. The first archaeological journals, the so-called three great journals—*Kaogu* [Archaeology], *Kaogu xuebao* [Acta Archaeologica Sinica], and *Wenwu* [Cultural Relics]—were established in Beijing.

Paleolithic Archaeology

PALEOLITHIC ARCHAEOLOGY was carried out by the Institute of Vertebrate Paleontology and Paleoanthropology at the Academia Sinica. The number of excavated Paleolithic sites increased from three locations before 1949 to more than a dozen distributed in many parts of the country. Excavations at Zhoukoudian were resumed after the 1950s, and to date, that site has yielded hominid fossils of more than forty individuals dating from 550,000 to 250,000 years ago, more than 100,000 stone artifacts, and a large number of mammalian fossils. In addition, cranial remains of *Homo erectus* dating to 700,000 years ago were discovered in Lantian, Shaanxi Province, and two incisors of *Homo erectus* dating to 1.7 million years ago were found in Yuanmou, Yunnan Province. Homonid fossils and stone implements belonging to archaic *Homo sapiens* and *Homo sapiens sapiens* have been found in many locations over northern and southern China (Chen 1999b; Wu and Olsen 1985).

Neolithic Archaeology

Most fieldwork projects in the 1950s were carried out in the Yellow River valley in connection with hydraulic construction in the region. The excavations at Miaodigou in Shanxian, Henan Province, were a breakthrough and completely changed the proposition of dual origins for Chinese civilization. Archaeologists identified a ceramic assemblage, named the Miaodigou Phase II, that represented a transitional culture between Yangshao and Longshan (Institute of Archaeology, Academia Sinica 1959). This discovery clarified the relationship between the Yangshao and Longshan cultures as successive rather than contemporaneous. Chinese civilization, therefore, seems to have been derived from a single source—the Yangshao culture, which originated in the central plains region (Chang 1963; Chen 1999c).

It should be noted that the first attempt to interpret ancient Chinese history with a Marxist model of social evolution can be traced back to GUO MORUO's *A Study of Ancient Chinese Society* (1930). Under the Communist regime, and influenced by Soviet archaeology, many Chinese archaeologists wanted to employ the Morgan-Engels evolutionary theory in archaeological practice, and this Marxist interpretation of Chinese history was then seen as a new mission for the discipline in addition to the search for Chinese cultural origins. The most successful application of this evolutionary scheme in archaeology was the analysis of a Yangshao site at Banpo near Xi'an, Shaanxi Province. The excavations, led by Shi Xingbang, revealed a large portion of a Yangshao settlement. Based on burials and residential patterns, the Banpo Neolithic village was described as a matrilineal society in which women enjoyed high social status and in which "pairing marriage" was practiced (Institute of Archaeology, Academia Sinica 1963). Such statements soon became standard in many interpretations of Neolithic sites dating to the Yangshao period, and the classic evolutionary model was commonly accepted among Chinese archaeologists.

Archaeology of the Three Dynasties: Zia, Shang, and Zhou

Shang archaeology was still a focus of research. Anyang resumed its importance as a center of archaeological excavations and yielded royal tombs, sacrificial pits, craft workshops, and inscribed oracle bones. These finds enriched the understanding of the spatial organization of the site (Institute of Archaeology, Chinese Academy of Social Sciences 1994). In the early 1950s, Shang material remains that could be dated to a period earlier than Anyang were first recognized at Erligang, near Zhengzhou, Henan Province. A fortified Shang city belonging to the Erligang phase was then found at Zhengzhou. The enormous size of the rammed-earth enclosure (300 hectares in area) and abundant remains found at the site (craft workshops, palace foundations, and elite burials) indicated that it may have been a capital city before Anyang (Henan Bureau of Cultural Relics 1959). This discovery encouraged archaeologists to search for the earliest remains of the Xia and Shang dynasties.

Inspired by ancient textual records, Xu Xusheng led a survey team in western Henan Province to explore the remains of the Xia dynasty. His endeavor soon proved fruitful when the team discovered a large Bronze Age site at Erlitou in Yanshi (Xu 1959). The Erlitou site was dated earlier than the Erligang phase, and subsequent excavations yielded a large palatial foundation, indicating the high rank of the site. The site was then designated as the type site of

Bronze ritual vessel of the Shang period, twelfth century B.C. *(Image Select)*

the Erlitou culture, which preceded the Erligang phase of the Shang (Institute of Archaeology, Chinese Academy of Social Sciences 1999).

The discovery of Erligang and Erlitou generated considerable debate on many issues: whether Erlitou was a capital city of the Xia or the Shang, which phases of the Erlitou culture belong to the Xia or the Shang cultures, and which capital cities named in ancient texts corresponded to Erligang and Erlitou. Most arguments were made on the basis of textual records that were written thousand of years after the existence of the Xia and Shang and reinterpreted by many individuals afterward. As people used different textual sources, which frequently contradicted one another to support their opinions, these debates have continued for decades without reaching a consensus (Dong 1999).

Between the mid-1950s and early 1960s, excavations at Fengxi, Chang'an, Shaanxi Province, revealed a large Bronze Age site, and it was determined that the site was the location of the capital cities of the western Zhou: Feng and Hao. These finds established the cultural sequence and chronology of the Zhou archaeological record (Institute of Archaeology, Academia Sinica 1962).

Archaeological research during this period primarily focused on the central plains of the Yellow River valley, where a clear sequence of cultural development could be traced from the Yangshao to the Longshan to the three dynasties. Many Neolithic sites in southern China were also found and excavated, such as Beiyinyangying near Nanjing, Qianshanyang in Zhejiang Province, and Qujialing in Hubei Province. These sites, however, yielded neither a material assemblage as old as the Yangshao culture, which was viewed as the earliest Neolithic culture, nor a continued sequence illustrating a regional cultural development. They were regarded as the peripheries of the central plains with minor significance for Chinese civilization. Such a paradigm of ancient Chinese cultural development was accepted by archaeologists in China and abroad, not only because of the limitations of the archaeological findings, but also because the traditional view of Chinese civilization focused on the central plains.

Archaeology during the Cultural Revolution (1966–1977)

Similar to other disciplines in academic institutions, archaeology stalled during the early part of the Cultural Revolution. Research and teaching were replaced by insurrection, and most junior members of archaeological institutes and students in universities were busy criticizing senior archaeologists and professors. However, excavations never completely stopped as continued construction projects always required salvage archaeology.

It was also soon recognized by the leaders of the Cultural Revolution that archaeology could serve as an instrument of propaganda for political purposes. Sending museum exhibitions of archaeological findings to foreign countries was considered useful in improving China's international relationships and promoting China's image as a great civilization. Moreover, the highly developed material culture from ancient times could reconfirm the Chinese people's national pride, and the wealth discovered from elite burials could be used for the education of the people in terms of class consciousness. Cultural relics unearthed in the People's Republic of China were displayed for the first time in Paris and London in 1973 in order to demonstrate the glory of the Chinese civilization and the achievements of archaeology in the new China (Xia 1973). Elaborately constructed architecture, burials, and artifacts were interpreted as testimony of class repression and exploitation of the poor by the rich.

To meet the new demands, the three major archaeological journals—*Kaogu, Kaogu xuebao,* and *Wenwu,* which were discontinued in 1966—resumed publication in 1972. *Wenwu* turned into a very popular magazine, as most journals with intellectual contents in social sciences had been stopped. Between 1972 and 1977, eight new archaeology programs were established in universities (Shanxi, Jilin, Nanjing, Xiamen, Shandong, Zhengzhou, Zhongshan, and Wuhan) in order to train much needed archaeologists for the rapidly expanded discipline (Chinese Archaeology Association 1984, 227–236).

Excavations of Neolithic sites were carried out in many regions, such as Dawenkou in Shandong Province, Cishan and Honghuatao in Hebei Province, Jiangzhai in Shaanxi Province, Liuwan in Qinghai Province, Daxi in Sichuan Province, Caoxieshan in Jiangsu Province, Hemudu in Zhejiang Province, Sanyuangong in Hunan Province, and Shixia in Guangdong Province. These sites provided rich information for the understanding of prehistoric development in different regions. In addition, by 1977 the radiocarbon laboratories in the Institute of Archaeology and Beijing University had published four sets of C-14 dates, providing some very early absolute dates from Neolithic sites outside the central plains, which revolutionized archaeological research.

The discoveries of several Neolithic sites in southern China were especially important. The Hemudu site in the lower Yangzi (Yangtze) River valley yielded the earliest evidence of rice cultivation in China, as radiocarbon dates pointed to a period as early as the Yangshao culture. The Hemudu culture seems to have been succeeded by a series of Neolithic assemblages, referred to as Majiabang, Songze, and Liangzhu, which formed a continued cultural sequence in the region. These new data seriously challenged the traditional view, which regarded the central plains as the only center for the development of Chinese civilization. For the first time, the notion of a single origin of Chinese Neolithic culture needed to be reconsidered (Xia 1977) in light of the fact that southeastern China may have played an important role in the development of Chinese civilization (Su 1978).

The discoveries that made the most newspaper headlines during the Cultural Revolution were elite tombs that had been discovered accidentally (Qian, Chen, and Ru et al. 1981). In 1968, for example, western Han royal tombs belonging to the prince Liu Sheng and his wife Douwan (ca. 113 B.C.) were found in Mancheng, Hebei Province. Among some 4,000 grave goods, two jade burial suits, each made of more than 2,000 jade wafers of different shapes tied with gold thread, were the most astonishing finds (Institute of Archaeology, Chinese Academy of Social Sciences, and Hebei 1980).

In 1972, an elaborately furnished western Han burial at Mawangdui in Changsha, Hunan Province, was unearthed. After removing many layers of clay, charcoal, wooden chambers, coffins, and silk garments, a corpse, nearly 2,000 years old, of the lady Dai, was revealed. The body was in perfect condition with no sign of decomposition, and the 138.5 melon seeds preserved in her esophagus, stomach, and intestines indicated the lady's last meal shortly before her death (Hunan Provincial Museum and Institute of Archaeology 1973).

In 1976, archaeologists excavated a very well-preserved Shang royal burial, tomb number five, in Anyang. Based on bronze inscriptions found in the burial, the tomb was determined to have belonged to one Fuhao, who was referred to as a consort of King Wuding in oracle-bone inscriptions. In addition to the large number of bronze and jade artifacts unearthed from the tomb, this discovery was significant because, for the first time, a named individual in oracle-bone inscriptions was identifiable in an archaeological context (Institute of Archaeology, Chinese Academy of Social Sciences 1980).

The discovery that attracted the most international attention was the underground terracotta army found in 1974 at the mausoleum of the first emperor of the Qin dynasty (221–206 B.C.), Qinshihuangdi, at Lishan, Lintong, Shaanxi Province. Deposits located to the east of the mausoleum include four large pits, three of which contain more than 7,000 life-sized terracotta warriors and horses. In the same year as the discovery, pit number one, the largest of four, which measures 12,600 square meters in area and 4.5–6.5 meters in depth (Shaanxi Institute of Archaeology 1988) was excavated. Five years later, the first on-site museum was built over the pit so that visitors could look down over railings at the rows of clay warriors and horses as well as at the processes of excavation of the site. Excavations have continued ever since, and three pits have been covered by on-site museums, attracting millions of visitors from all over the world. The mausoleum was listed as a World Heritage Site by the United Nations Educational, Scientific, and Cultural Organization in 1987.

In spite of numerous new discoveries, archaeological theoretical interpretations during the Cultural Revolution were dry and dogmatic, an inevitable consequence of the political climate of the era. Tightly controlled foreign policies eliminated the exchange of information between China and western countries, and the only theoretical frameworks applicable at the time were Marxism and Maoism. Mortuary and settlement data obtained from many Neolithic sites were commonly used to support Morgan-Engels or Marxist-Leninist propositions such as the emergence of private property, class differentiation, the practice of matrilineal or patrilineal social organizations, and the formation of the state as the result of class conflict. In some publications, which were purely data descriptions, Marxist and Maoist slogans were routinely inserted into the contents but appeared superficial and far-fetched. The lack of fresh theoretical approaches prevented archaeologists from engaging in critical discussions, and the rapid accumulation of archaeological data also forced scholars to become preoccupied with constructing the sequence of material culture rather than with theoretical thinking about it. Chinese archaeology, therefore, largely remained artifact oriented.

Archaeology in the Post–Cultural Revolution Era (1978–)

After the Cultural Revolution, the relatively relaxed political atmosphere and the practice of economic reform promoted new developments on all fronts of Chinese archaeology. Salvage excavations conducted by regional archaeological institutes have been the most in demand, as a decentralized economic system stimulated construction projects across the country. Support from the central government has been shrinking, and most provincial institutes have become financially dependent on salvage archaeology. By 1978, a total of eleven universities had developed archaeology programs, training hundreds of archaeologists each year. These new graduates soon became the backbone of local archaeological institutes. The number of archaeological periodicals had multiplied from "the great journals" to a list of some 140 periodicals on archaeology-related subjects by 1991, most of which are published on a local level (Falkenhausen 1992). As a result, provincial archaeological institutions became increasingly independent of control by the Institute of Archaeology in Beijing with regard to administrative, academic, and financial aspects (Falkenhausen 1995).

Policies of economic reform have also opened China's doors to the world. Scholarly exchange between China and western countries has been encouraged, and western archaeological methods and theories have been brought in. Archaeologists in China found themselves facing new challenges from the outside world. During the 1980s and 1990s, as Deng Xiaoping was searching for a way for China to become a Chinese-style socialist country, archaeologists were struggling to find a way to make an archaeology with Chinese characteristics. There have been some increased nationalist feelings among many Chinese intellectuals, partially in reaction to the rapidly changing relationships between China and the rest of the world, and archaeology in this era has been strongly influenced by new concepts of nationalism.

As an enormous amount of archaeological data on all periods has been accumulated since the end of the Cultural Revolution, and three major topics have become the focal points of Chinese archaeology: the origins of early humans, the origins of agriculture, and the origins of civilization.

Paleolithic Archaeology and the Multiregional Model of Human Evolution

By the 1990s, more than sixty sites containing human fossils had been recorded as well as many more sites that have yielded Paleolithic artifacts. As world Paleolithic archaeology has been engaged in the debate between "the out-of-Africa" and "the multiregional-development" schools, evidence from China has become crucial. The majority of Chinese archaeologists and paleontologists support the multiregional development model, arguing for an independent system of evolution from *Homo erectus* to *Homo sapiens* in East Asia (e.g., Wu 1995). Some have gone even further and attempted to find evidence of the earliest hominids in China. The argument for indigenous evolution in east Asia is primarily based on two factors. First, similar to Weidenreich's observation, paleontologists continue to find morphological characteristics that are shared by hominid fossils and modern populations in the same region. Second, archaeologists have defined regional lithic traditions throughout the Paleolithic period in China that appear to be distinct from those in Africa and Europe (Chen 1999b).

The driving force for archaeologists has been to find evidence of the earliest hominid remains and the missing links in the developmental progress of modern humans in China. New evidence remains promising for the current evaluation and debate about human evolution. In 1984, for instance, a nearly complete skeleton of archaic *Homo sapiens* was found at Jinniushan (Gold Ox Hill) in Liaoning Province in 1984. The fossils were dated to 310,000–160,000 years ago, making the skeleton one of the earliest examples of this taxonomic group. Some typical morphological features of the skull are observable in earlier hominids and modern populations in the region, which seems to fit a model of local evolution (Chen, Yang, and Wu 1994).

It should be noted, however, that some recent claims about the early hominids might be problematic and lack credibility in light of the data; it has been suggested that some archaeologists have been too eager to find the first man-made stone tool in China (Lü 2000). In 1985, cranial remains of *Homo erectus* associated with stone tools were found at Longgupo in Wushan (now belonging to Chongqing), Sichuan Province. The stratum containing the hominid fossils was dated to 2 million years ago, which makes the Longgupo fossils the earliest example of *Homo erectus* in China. The reliability of the dates, however, is open to question (Huang and Ciochonetal 1995).

Even before visiting the Zhoukoudian site, Lewis Binford and Chuan Kun Ho challenged the long-established conclusions that Peking Man controlled fire and that the Zhoukoudian cave was the home of Peking Man (Binford and Ho 1985). Many Chinese archaeologists were outraged, and Jia Lanpo, one of the excavators of Zhoukoudian, defended Peking Man's reputation with great passion (Jia 1991). The strong reaction from the Chinese archaeological community is understandable when the issue is placed in the context of rising nationalism in China. Within the framework of the regional evolutionary model, Peking Man appears to have been regarded as one of the direct, but remote, ancestors of the nation.

The Origins of Food Production

When the Hemudu site (ca. 7000 B.P.) in the lower Yangzi River Valley was excavated in 1974, it was claimed that the large quantity of rice remains found there was the earliest evidence of domesticated rice in the world. However, rice production at Hemudu was in a somewhat advanced stage, and the origin of rice cultivation was still an open question. In the 1980s, rice remains dated to 8000–9000 B.P. were found at Pengtoushan and several other sites in the middle Yangzi River Valley, which was regarded as a possible center for the origins of rice domestication. The great potential of finding the earliest evidence of rice production in southern China attracted both Chinese and western archaeologists, and more excavations employing new methods and techniques—including flotation, phytolith analysis, and isotopic analysis—were carried out in the 1990s. Consequently, rice remains dated to 8000–9000 B.P. or earlier were found at Jiahu in southern Henan Province, Bashidang and Yuchanyan in Hunan Province, and Xianren-

dong and Diaotonghuan in Jiangxi Province (Chen 1999a; Lu 1999).

Excavations at the cave sites Xianrendong and Diaotonghuan, conducted by a Sino-American collaborative project led by Yan Wenming and Richard MacNeish, yielded long sequences of cultural development, suggesting that rice domestication can be traced back to a period as early as 10,000–11,000 B.P., followed by the earliest pottery making in 9000–10,000 B.P. (Mac-Neish and Libby 1995; Zhao 1998). The origin and rapid expansion of rice cultivation from the Yangze River Valley may imply the introduction of languages and genes from southern China to broader territories in adjacent regions (Higham and Lu 1998). Southern China may have also been one of the places where the earliest pottery was invented (Chen 1998). These findings have certainly promoted the significant role that China has played in world history.

The Origins of Civilization

The years since 1980 have witnessed a radically changed view of the development of Chinese civilization in archaeology, with a shift from the concept of a central-plains-centered tradition to that of a multicentered parallel development. This change was not simply a product of political propaganda, and it did not happen overnight. It has gradually emerged and crystallized as the result of a complex interplay of several factors. These include voluminous new archaeological discoveries made in areas outside the central plains, traditionally regarded as the core area of Chinese civilization; the recognition of diversified regional cultural traditions based on these new findings; a changing view of nationalism in recent years; and increased confidence in the credibility of the textual record.

New Archaeological Discoveries

Since the end of the Cultural Revolution numerous archaeological discoveries have been made—most of them in areas outside the central plains. In southern China, new evidence indicates that this region not only had its own indigenous origins of Neolithic traditions (earliest rice and pottery) but that it evolved into complex societies at same time as, if not earlier than, the central plains. Southern China also witnessed highly developed Bronze Age cultures with characteristics distinctive from those of the central plains. Several Neolithic walled settlements have been found in the middle and upper Yangzi River Valley, and one found at Chengtoushan in Hunan Province (ca. 4000 B.C.) is the earliest example of a walled settlement in China.

Distinctive elite tombs filled with large quantities of jade objects on artificially made earth mounds have been discovered in the Liangzhu culture in the lower Yangzi River Valley, and the high level of craftsmanship reflected in jade manufacture and the construction of large burial mounds have led some archaeologists to argue for the existence of early states in the Liangzhu culture (ca. 3200–2000 B.C.). Sacrificial pits containing large numbers of bronze figurines, life size or bigger, have been discovered at Sanxingdui in Sichuan Province in the upper Yangzi River Valley, revealing a previously unknown kingdom with a highly developed bronze culture contemporary with the Xia and Shang dynasties. A large tomb filled with hundreds of bronze and jade objects was found at Dayangzhou in Jiangxi Province in the middle Yangzi River Valley, which indicates the existence of an advanced bronze culture with strong indigenous characteristics along with influences from the central plains.

In northeastern China, the Neolithic tradition now can be traced back to the Xinglongwa culture (6100–5300 B.C.) in Liaoning and Inner Mongolia, which may have demonstrated a fully developed agricultural society. Complex societies seem to have evolved around 3500 B.C. in this region, as is indicated by the construction of a large public edifices in the late Hongshan culture, especially at the Niuheliang site, which yielded stone monuments with well-furnished elite burials and remains of a large architectural foundation associated with life-size female figurines (known as the Goddess Temple). This broad region later became the homeland of pastoralism and nomads whose interaction with agricultural populations dominated the political arena in the following millennia. These astonishing discoveries changed the traditional view, which regarded peoples outside the central plains as barbaric and uncivilized.

In eastern China, including Shandong and northern Jiangsu Provinces, archaeologists discovered the earliest Neolithic assemblage at Houli in Shandong Province (ca. 6200–5600 B.C.), which was followed by the Beixin, Dawenkou, and Longshan cultures, forming another regional tradition of cultural development. Many elaborately furnished elite burials and more than a dozen walled settlements dated to the Dawenkou and Longshan periods (ca. 4100–2000 B.C.) have also been found, generating more claims for the emergence of state-level societies in the Neolithic period in this region.

In the central plains, primarily including the middle Yellow River, the Fen River, and the Wei River Valleys and regarded as the center of Chinese civilization, archaeological discoveries seem to demonstrate a cultural tradition that may not have been much more advanced than those on "the peripheries" during the Neolithic period. As in other regions, the Neolithic traditions of the central plains can be traced to the Peiligang culture 7000 B.C., which was followed by a continued development of the Yangshao and Longshan cultures. Although rich elite burials dated to the Longshan period have been discovered at Taosi in Shaanxi Province and walled settlements belonging to the late Yangshao and Longshan have been found in Henan Province, these features are not unique and are certainly not earlier than those in other regions (for brief information on the major discoveries in the Neolithic period and the three dynasties, see Ren and Wu 1999; Wang 1999). Diversified regional cultural traditions are easily observable based on these new data, which have encouraged new interpretations concerning the origins of civilization.

Multiregional Development of Civilization in China
Initiated by Su Bingqi, a research model known as *quxi leixing*—the regional systems and local cultural series—was proposed in the early 1980s (Su and Yin 1981; for a review of Su's framework see Wang 1997). The model is based mainly on ceramic assemblages, with an emphasis on the independent development of and interaction among different regional cultural traditions. The *quxi leixing* concept was intended to provide a methodological framework for the re-

construction of Chinese prehistory, as it shifted away from the center-periphery model to a multiregional approach to the development of Chinese civilization.

As stated by Su Bingqi (1991), after 10,000 B.P., six relatively stable regional divisions (quxi) formed within the area embraced by historical China. The six regional cultures are further divided into a number of local phases (leixing). Each of these regions, according to Su, had its own cultural origins and developments and interacted with the others in the developmental processes of Chinese civilization. Yan Wenming suggested a similar model as "the unity and variability of Chinese prehistoric culture," seeing the central plains as the center of the flower and cultural traditions and the surrounding areas as layers of petals (Yan 1987). Instead of giving equal weight to all regional cultures implied in Su's hypothesis, Yan's model emphasizes the leading role of the central plains in the movement toward civilization while acknowledging the existence of elements of civilization in the peripheries in prehistory.

The general trend shifting from a monocentered to a multicentered development of Chinese civilization, as Lothar von Falkenhausen (1995, 198–199) observed, is also reflected in the four editions of the *Archaeology of Ancient China* by KWANG-CHIH CHANG, which have been the most comprehensive and authoritative sources of Chinese archaeology in English for decades. In the first three editions, published in 1963, 1968, and 1977, the central plains was seen as the nucleus from which complex society and dynastic civilization rose. In the fourth edition, published in 1986, this view was replaced by the concept of "a Chinese interaction sphere," covering a geographic dimension much broader than the central plains, which formed the foundation for the development of the three dynasties (Chang 1986b, 234–242). Such a change of paradigm in Chinese archaeology seems to integrate very well with a new perspective in the reconstruction of national history.

Nationalism, National History, Legends,
and Origins of Civilization in Archaeology
Since its birth, Chinese archaeology has had one clear objective: to reconstruct national history.

The concept of nation, and thus of national history, however, has changed over time, as the tasks of reconstruction have been inevitably affected by new perspectives of national history.

As the state has attempted to bring China's multi-ethnic population into a viable political entity since the1950s, the concept of the Chinese nation has become equivalent to that of the state, best described by Fei Xiaotong (1989) as a single entity with multiple components (duoyuan yiti). According to Fei, China as a nation (a substance without self-consciousness) has gradually come into existence through thousands of years. This formative process was amalgamative, with a dominant core constituted first by the Huaxia and then by the Han people. However, the cultural interaction between the Huaxia-Han and other groups was not a one-way diffusion but a mutual influence. This national entity now, according to Fei, includes all nationalities (more than fifty) and covers the entire territory of modern China. It seems that this new concept of nationalism fits relatively well with the archaeological *quxi leixing* paradigm and, in particular, with "the unity and variability" hypothesis. Evidently, the archaeological and sociological models mutually support each other in constructing national history.

With increased knowledge of regional archaeological cultures, scholars have developed a strong willingness to construct cultural history based on archaeological material remains and the historical record. There has been a tendency to identify archaeological cultures and phases, sites, and even artifacts directly with specific ancient groups of people or places named in legends or historical literature. The continuing debates on the cultural identification of several Bronze Age cities—such as Erlitou, Erligang, and, most recently discovered, Yanshi Shang city near Yanshi and Xiaoshuangqiao near Zhengzhou—best exemplify this attempt. By doing so, archaeological assemblages (mainly pottery typology) become historically meaningful, although the logical connections between the two sets of information—ceramic typology and ethnic affiliation—have not been made explicit.

The phrase "five-thousand-year history of civilization" has been commonly used in China to summarize national history, and archaeology is pledged to trace the origins and to demonstrate the processes of this history. Since recorded dynastic history did not begin until about 2000 B.C., much effort has been made to connect regional Neolithic cultural developments with the activities of predynastic legendary kings and sages in order to fill the time gap of 1,000 years. Attempts have also been made to link certain cultural achievements with the dawn of civilization, such as the manufacture of jade objects and the construction of large ceremonial monuments, which are traceable to the Neolithic period.

As a consequence, not only are legends read as reliable history and used to interpret Neolithic archaeology, but the origins of Chinese civilization are pushed back 1,000 or more years to match counterparts in MESOPOTAMIA and Egypt (Su 1988, 1997). In the early twentieth century, when the *yigupai* questioned traditional texts, they hoped that archaeologists would uncover reliable ancient history from the field. For many archaeologists today, these legendary accounts are like blueprints for reconstructing prehistory, and the *yigupai* have become the target of criticism (Li 1994).

A state-directed project in the 1990s pushed this endeavor to its peak. In a visit to Egypt, Song Jian, the state counselor *(guowu weiyuan),* was introduced to a detailed chronological record of dynastic Egypt that started from 3100 B.C. Dissatisfied with the Chinese dynastic chronology, which is not only 1,000 years later but also less precise than that of Egypt, Song Jian called for a project to reconstruct an accurate chronology of the three dynasties so that Chinese civilization would be comparable to Egypt's (Song 1996). This project, known as the Xia-Shang-Zhou Chronology Project, was officially launched in 1996. For nearly four years, some 170 experts in history, archaeology, astronomy, and radiocarbon-dating technology were involved in the project, focusing on nine primary research topics, which were further divided into thirty-six subtopics. The budget was about 17 million yuan (US$2.1 million), and archaeology certainly benefited from such a generous financial commitment from the state,

which supported some major excavations. The project achieved four objectives (Jiang 1999):

1. to provide accurate dates for a time period from the conquest of the Shang by the Zhou to the beginning of recorded chronology in 841 B.C.
2. to determine relatively accurate chronology for the late Shang period
3. to define a relatively detailed time frame for the early Shang period
4. to outline a basic time frame for the Xia dynasty

The chronology of the three dynasties has indeed become more precise and detailed than before, but the project has not made Chinese civilization temporally comparable with some older civilizations in other parts of the world.

Encouraged by the achievement of the Xia-Shang-Zhou Chronology Project, a new research organization, the Center for the Study of Civilization, was recently established in the Department of Archaeology at Beijing University. Archaeologists are now determined to find the ultimate origins of Chinese civilization, which ought to be embedded in the Neolithic cultures (Center for the Study of Ancient Civilization, Beijing University 1999).

International Collaborative Research in China
Since the 1980s, scholarly exchange between China and foreign countries has increased dramatically. It has also moved on from exchanging ideas at international conferences to conducting field research. In 1991, the Chinese National Bureau of Cultural Relics released a document on policies for Sino-foreign collaborative research in archaeology (National Bureau of Cultural Relics 1992), which, after more than forty years, reopened the door to foreign archaeologists wanting to working on Chinese archaeology.

Many collaborative projects have been carried out in recent years in regions across the country, international scholarly exchange has introduced western theories to China, and these theories have, to some extent, enriched research orientations and interpretations. New methods and technologies have been introduced in fieldwork and laboratory analyses, including, to name a few, the use of the flotation method in recovering macrofaunal and macrofloral remains; full-coverage regional survey methods, the incorporation of regional survey with geoarchaeology, GIS (geographic imaging systems) applications, and remote sensing in the study of settlement patterns; mineralogical studies of archaic jade; the development of interdisciplinary approaches such as zooarchaeology, ethnobotanical study, and environmental archaeology; and the employment of advanced laboratory technology such as AMS (accelerator mass spectrometry) dating methods, genetic studies, and the analyses of phytoliths, isotopes, and stone tool use wares. The introduction of these methods and techniques has brought Chinese archaeological research to a higher level of sophistication than before.

A new generation of Chinese archaeologists, who received Ph.D.s from foreign universities in North America, Europe, Australia, and Japan during the 1990s, has either returned to China or worked in archaeological institutions outside China. With their up-to-date knowledge of western archaeological methods and theory, they have made important contributions by introducing new ideas of study and employing new methods and techniques in collaborative research projects. The discipline has become more international than ever during this golden age of Chinese archaeology.

Interestingly, the research orientations of the joint collaborative projects seem to follow some traditional patterns. Most projects initiated by western archaeologists have primarily focused on Paleolithic and Neolithic sites, or on cultures in peripheral areas, which appeal to internationally oriented research topics, while projects designed by overseas Chinese archaeologists tend to focus on the central plains in search for the processes of Chinese civilization.

The development of Chinese archaeology, therefore, has intertwined with the ever-changing political environment of the twentieth century. Archaeologists have worked extremely hard to overcome all kinds of economic, social, and political difficulties during many different politically turbulent eras, and they have made extraordinary contributions to the field. Our understanding of ancient China has markedly improved because of their archaeological achievements.

In many cases, archaeology has been driven by changing concepts of nationalism and has been used as an instrument to support, rather than to evaluate, particular theories, political themes, and agendas. In other situations, it has provided independent data for the creation of new paradigms, which have changed traditional perspectives of China's national history. State-promoted nationalism has indeed played an important role in shaping the discipline. However, many individual archaeologists, have spontaneously exercised nationalist ideology in their research. For them, the building of national history implies dignity and pride as human beings.

China is certainly not the only nation in which archaeology is relevant and meaningful primarily in the context of the connection between modern cultural and national identities and ancient indigenous traditions (e.g., Kohl and Fawcett 1995). Therefore, in spite of the growing influence of western ideology and technology over the past decades, which in many cases has been positive, the general objective for mainstream Chinese archaeology does not seem to have changed; the discipline remains committed to the reconstruction of national history.

That mission will probably continue to dominate the discipline for many years to come. It is possible, however, that more varied research approaches will emerge in future. Although some archaeologists will continue to pursue regional historical issues, others may become engaged in theory building and cross-cultural comparative studies, which will develop the discipline from a more international perspective.

Li Liu and Xingcan Chen

References

Andersson, G. J. 1923. "An Early Chinese Culture." *Bulletin Geological Survey of China* 5: 1–68.

Binford, Lewis, and Chuan Kun Ho. 1985. "Taphonomy at a Distance: Zhoukoudian, 'the Cave Home of Beijing Man?'" *Current Anthropology* 26, no. 4: 413–442.

Brysac, Shareen B. 1997. "Last of the 'Foreign Devils.'" *Archaeology* November–December: 53–59.

Center for the Study of Ancient Civilization,

Beijing University. 1999. *Gudai wenming yanjiu tongxun*. Vol. 1. Beijing: Beijing University.

Chang, Kwang-chih. 1963. *The Archaeology of Ancient China*. New Haven: Yale University Press.

———. 1986a. *The Archaeology of Ancient China*. 4th ed. New Haven: Yale University Press.

———. 1986b. "Xia Nai (1910–1985)." *American Anthropologist* 88: 442–444.

———. 1999a. "China on the Eve of the Historical Period." In *Cambridge History of Ancient China: From the Origins of Civilization to 221 B.C.* Ed. Michael Loewe and Edward L. Shaughnessy. Cambridge: Cambridge University Press.

———. 1999b. *Kaogu renleixue suibi*. Beijing: Sanlian Press.

Chen, Teimei, Yang Quan, and Wu En. 1994. "Antiquity of *Homo sapiens* in China." *Nature* 368: 55–56.

Chen, Xingcan. 1997. *Zhongguo shiqian kaoguxueshi yanjiu*. Beijing: Sanlian Press.

———. 1998. "Searching for the Early Neolithic in China." *Documenta Praehistorca* 25: 17–26.

———. 1999a. "Earliest Evidence for Rice Cultivation in China." *Indo-Pacific Prehistory Association Bulletin* 18 (*Melaka Papers, 2*): 81–93.

———. 1999b. "Zhongguo gurenleixue yu jiushiqi shidai kaogu wushi nian" [Fifty Years of Palaeoanthropology and Paleolithic Archaeology in China]. *Kaogu* 9: 1–10.

———. 1999c. "Zhongguo shiqian kaoguxue yanjiu de xinlu licheng" [On the History of the Study of Prehistoric Archaeology in China]. In *Liangzhu wenhua yanjiu*, 141–149. Beijing: Kexue Press.

Chiang Kai-shek. 1947. *China's Destiny and Chinese Economic Theory*. London: Dennis Dobson.

Chinese Archaeology Association. 1984. *Zhongguo kaoguxue nianjian*. Beijing: Wenwu Press.

Dikotter, Frank. 1992. *The Discourse of Race in Modern China*. Stanford: Stanford University Press.

Dong, Qi. 1999. "Xi 'Yanshi Shangcheng yu Xia Shang wenhua fenjie' de yanjiu mailu" [Analysis of the Research Strategies on the Yanshi Shang City and Xia and Shang Cultures]. *Zhongguo lishi bowuguan guankan* 1: 4–11.

Falkenhausen, Lothar von. 1992. "Serials on Chinese Archaeology Published in the People's Republic of China." *Early China* 17: 247–296.

———. 1995. "The Regionalist Paradigm in Chinese Archaeology." In *Nationalism, Politics, and the Practice of Archaeology*. Ed. Philip L. Kohl and Clare Fawcett. Cambridge: Cambridge University Press.

———. 1999a. "Su Bingqi." In *Encyclopedia of Archaeology: The Great Archaeologists*, 2:591–599. Ed. Tim Murray. Santa Barbara, CA: ABC-CLIO.

———. 1999b. "Xia Nai." In *Encyclopedia of Archaeology: The Great Archaeologists*, 2:601–614. Ed. Tim Murray. Santa Barbara, CA: ABC-CLIO.

Fei, Xiaotong. 1989. "Zhonghua minzu de duoyuan yiti geju" [The Pattern of Single Entity with Multiple Components in China]. In *Zhonghua minzu duoyuan yiti geju*, 1–36. Ed. Fei Xiaotong. Beijing: Zhongyang Minzu Xueyuan Press.

Fitzgerald, John. 1996. "The Nationless State: The Search for a Nation in Modern Chinese Nationalism." In *Chinese Nationalism*, 56–85. Ed. Jonathan Unger. Armonk, NY: M. E. Sharpe.

Fu Sinian. 1996. "Kaoguxue de xinfangfa" [New Methods in Archaeology]. In *Fu Sinian xuanji*, 185–191. Ed. Yue Yuxi, Li Quan, and Ma Liangkuan. Tianjin: Tianjin Renmin Press. Reprinted from *Shixue* 1 (1930).

Henan Bureau of Cultural Relics. 1959. *Zhengzhou Erligang*. Beijing: Kexue Press.

Higham, Charles, and Tracey L.-D. Lu. 1998. "The Origins and Dispersal of Rice Cultivation." *Antiquity* 72: 867–877.

Huang, W., and Russell Ciochonetal. 1995. "Early *Homo* and Associated Artifacts from Asia." *Nature* 378: 275–278.

Hunan Provincial Museum and Institute of Archaeology, Chinese Academy of Science (CAS). 1973. *Changsha Mawangdui yihao Hanmu*. Beijing: Wenwu Press.

Institute of Archaeology, Academia Sinica. 1959. *Miaodigou yu Sanliqiao*. Beijing: Kexue Press.

———. 1962. *Fengxi Fajue Baogao* [Report of Excavations at Fengxi]. Beijing: Wenwu Press.

———. 1963. *Xi'an Banpo*. Beijing: Wenwu Press.

Institute of Archaeology, Chinese Academy of Social Sciences. 1980. *Yinxu Fuhao mu*. Beijing: Wenwu Press.

———. 1994. *Yinxu de Faxian yu Yanjiu*. Beijing: Kexue Press.

———. 1999. *Yanshi Erlitou*. Beijing: Wenwu Press.

Institute of Archaeology, Chinese Academy of Social Sciences, and Hebei Provincial Management Department of Cultural Relics. 1980. *Mancheng Hanmu fajue baogao*. Beijing: Wenwu Press.

Jia, Lanpo. 1991. "Guanyu Zhoukoudian Beijingren yizhi de ruogan wenti" [On Some Issues concerning the Zhoukoudian Beijing Man Site]. *Kaogu* 1: 62, 77–84.

Jia, Lanpo, and Huang Weiwen. 1990. *The Story of Peking Man.* Beijing: Foreign Language Press.

Jiang, Linchang. 1999. "Xia Shang Zhou duandai gongcheng de shishi yu jinzhan" [Conduct and Progress of the Xia-Shang-Zhou Chronology Project]. *Zhongguo wenwubao* 23 (June).

Kohl, Philip, and Clare Fawcett, eds. 1995. *Nationalism, Politics, and the Practice of Archaeology.* Cambridge: Cambridge University Press.

Li Chi, 1968. "Anyang fajue yu Zhongguo gushi wenti" [Excavations at Anyang and Some Issues on Ancient Chinese History]. In *Guoli zhongyang yanjiuyuan lishi yuyan yanjiusuo jikan,* vol. 40. Reprinted in *Li Chi kaoguxue lunwenji,* 796–822. Ed. Chang Kwang-Chih and Li Guangmo. Beijing: Wenwu Press, 1990.

———. 1977. *Anyang.* Seattle: University of Washington Press.

———. 1990. "Chengziyai fajue baogao xu" [Preface in the Excavation Report of Chengziyai]. In *Li Chi kaoguxue lunwenji.* Ed. Chang Kwang-chih and Li Guangmo, 189–193. Beijing: Wenwu Press. Reprinted from *Dongfang zazhi* 32, 1 (1934): 11–17.

Li, Xueqin. 1994. *Zouchu yigu shidai.* Shenyang: Liaoning Daxue Press.

Liang Qichao. 1992. "Zhongguo jiruo suyuan lun" [On the Source of China's Weakness]. In *Liang Qichao wenxuan* 1: 64–90. Ed Xia Xiaohong. Beijing: Zhongguo Guangbo Dianshi Press. Reprinted from *Qingyibao* 77–80 (1901).

Liang, Siyong. 1959. "Xiaotun, Longshan, yu Yangshao" [Xiaotun, Longshan, and Yangshao]. In *Liang Siyong kaoguxue lunwenji,* 91–98. Beijing: Kexue Press.

Liu, Li. 1999. "Who Were the Ancestors? The Origins of Chinese Ancestral Cult and Racial Myths." *Antiquity* 73: 602–613.

Lu, Tracey Lie Dan. 1999. *The Transition from Foraging to Farming and the Origin of Agriculture in China.* BAR International Series 774. Oxford.

Lü, Zun'e. 2000. "Guanyu xunzhao renlei zuxian jiqi wenhua wenti de jidian renshi" [Some Thoughts on Searching for Human Ancestors and Their Cultures]. *Zhongguo wenwubao,* 26 January.

MacNeish, R. S., and J. Libby, eds. 1995. *Origin of Rice Agriculture: Preliminary Reports of the Sino-American Jiangxi Project.* Publication in Anthropology no. 13. El Paso: El Paso Centennial Museum, University of Texas.

National Bureau of Cultural Relics. 1992. "Zhonghua renmin gongheguo kaogu shewai gongzuo guanli banfa" [Regulations for the Management of Foreign Country Involved Archaeology in the People's Republic of China]. In *Zhonghua renmin gongheguo wenwu faqui xuanbian,* 337–341. Ed. National Bureau of Cultural Relics. Beijing: Wenwu Press.

Qian, Hao, Chen Heyi, and Ru Suichu. 1981. *Out of China's Earth: Archaeological Discoveries in the People's Republic of China.* New York: Harry N. Abrams.

Ren, Shinan, and Wu Yaoli. 1999. "Zhongguo xinshiqi shidai kaoguxue wushi nian" [Fifty Years of Neolithic Archaeology in China]. *Kaogu* 9: 11–22.

Schneider, Laurence A. 1971. *Ku Chieh-kang and China's New History: Nationalism and the Quest for Alternative Traditions.* Berkeley: University of California Press.

Shaanxi Institute of Archaeology. 1988. *Qinshihuang ling bingmayong keng yihaokeng fajue baogao.* Beijing: Wenwu Press.

Song, Jian. 1996. "Chaochu yigu, zouchu mimang" [Beyond the Doubting History and out of the Mist]. *Guangming Daily,* 16 May.

Su Bingqi. 1948. *Doujitai donggouqu muzang: Shaanxi kaogu fajue baogao.* Vol. 1., pt. 1. Beijing: Guoli Beiping Yanjiuyuan Shixue Yanjiusuo.

———. 1978. "Luelun woguo dongnan yanhai diqu de xinshiqi shidai kaogu" [Neolithic Archaeology on the Southeast coast of China]. *Wenwu* 3: 40–42.

———. 1988. "Zhonghua wenming de xin shuguang" [New Dawn of Chinese Civilization]. *Dongnan wenhua* 5: 1–7.

———. 1991. "Guanyu chongjian Zhongguo shiqian shi de sikao" [Some Thoughts about the Reconstruction of Chinese Prehistory]. *Kaogu* 12: 1109–1118.

———. 1997. *Zhongguo wenmingqiyuan xintan.* Hong Kong: Shangwu Yinshu Guan.

Su Bingqi, and Yin Weizhang. 1981. "Guanyu kaoguxue wenhua de quxi leixing wenti" [On the Issue of the Distribution and Development of Regional Cultures in Chinese Archaeology]. *Wenwu* 5: 10–17.

Sun Yat-sen. 1943. *San Min Chu I: The Three Principles of the People.* Trans. Frank W. Price, ed. L. T. Chen. Chungking: Ministry of Information.

Townsend, James. 1996. "Chinese Nationalism." In *Chinese Nationalism,* 1–30. Ed. Jonathan Unger. Armonk, NY: M. E. Sharpe.

Wang, Tao. 1997. "The Chinese Archaeological

School: Su Bingqi and Contemporary Chinese Archaeology." *Antiquity* 71: 31–39.

Wang, Wei. 1999. "Xia Shang Zhou kaoguxue wushinian" [Fifty Years of Xia, Shang, and Zhou Archaeology]. *Kaogu* 9: 23–34.

Weidenreich, F. 1943. "The Skull of Sinanthropus Pekinensis." *Palaeontologia Sinica,* new ser. D, no. 10, whole ser. 127. Chungking: Geological Survey of China.

Wu, Rukang, and John W. Olsen, eds. 1985. *Palaeoanthropology and Paleolithic Archaeology in the People's Republic of China.* New York: Academic Press.

Wu, Rukang, and Lin Shenglong. 1983. "Peking Man." *Scientific American* 248, no. 6: 78–86.

Wu, Xinzhi. 1995. "The Continuity of Human Evolution in East Asia." In *The Origins and Past of Modern Humans as Viewed from DNA,* 267–282. Ed. S. Bremmer and K. Hanihara. Singapore: World Scientific Publishing Company.

Xia Nai. 1973. "Bali London zhanchu de xinzhongguo chutu wenwu zhanlan xunli" [Exhibitions of Cultural Relics Unearthed from the New China in Paris and London]. *Kaogu* 3: 150, 171–177.

———. 1977. "Tan shisi ceting niandai he Zhongguo shiqian kaoguxue" [Carbon–14 Dating and Chinese Prehistoric Archaeology]. *Kaogu* 4: 217–232.

———. 1979. "Wusi yundong he Zhongguo jindai kaoguxue de xingqi." *Kaogu* 3: 193–196.

Xu, Xunsheng. 1959. "1959 nian xia Yuxi diaocha 'Xiaxu' de chubu baogao" [Preliminary Report of the Surveys in the Ruins of Xia in 1959]. *Kaogu* 11: 592–600.

Yan, Wenming. 1987. "Zhongguo shiqian wenhua de tongyixing yu duoyangxing" [Unity and Variability of Prehistoric Chinese Culture]. *Wenwu* 3: 38–50.

Zhao, Zhijun. 1998. "The Middle Yangtze Region in China Is One Place Where Rice Was Domesticated: Phytolith Evidence from the Diaotonghuan Cave, Northern Jiangxi." *Antiquity* 72: 885–897.

Christy, Henry (1810–1865)

Born in London into a wealthy stockbroking Quaker family, Christy became such a successful banker that by 1850 he was able to spend more time pursuing his antiquarian interests and traveling. His trips to Scandinavia in 1852 and 1853 visiting museums provoked his interest in prehistory.

In 1856 his interest in ethnology took him to North America and MEXICO, where he befriended and traveled with anthropologist EDWARD TYLOR (1832–1917). Together they visited and studied the ruins of TEOTIHUACÁN, Xochichalco, and Cholula.

In 1862 Christy began funding and working with French paleontologist ÉDOUARD LARTET (1801–1871) exploring the caves of Vezere in southwestern France. They discovered the sites of Gorge d'Enfer, LAUGERIE HAUTE, LA MADELEINE, LE MOUSTIER, and les Eyzies, all of which had an enormous impact on contemporary understanding of the French Paleolithic. From evidence at Le Moustier, the Mammoth and Great Cave Bear periods were recognized as contemporaneous. From evidence at La Madeleine, the Reindeer age was better understood. Christy also funded work with Lartet in the Perigord (Dordogne) region that provided evidence for the existence of Paleolithic cave art. Much of the material found became part of the Musée des Antiquites Nationales at Saint Germain-en-Laye. Lartet (one of the giants of the history of prehistoric archaeology) was immensely fortunate in his association with Christy and their partnership made a fundamental contribution of the first rank to our understanding of human prehistory.

Christy was editing a volume of their results when he died. *Reliquiae Aquitanicae* (1875), a classic in European Paleolithic archaeology, was completed at the expense of Christy's estate by geologist Thomas Jones.

Tim Murray

See also France; Paleolithic Archaeology

Clark, Sir Grahame (1907–1995)

Grahame Clark is by general consent the only British prehistorian of the twentieth century whose importance rivaled that of VERE GORDON CHILDE. His career spanned almost the whole century as well as the emergence of modern archaeology. His first book was published in 1932, and his last appeared in 1992. Clark went up to Peterhouse College, Cambridge, in 1926 completed his Ph.D. in 1930. His dissertation was later published as *The Mesolithic Age in Britain* (1932). Miles Burkitt supervised Clark's doctorate, but it was probably DOROTHY GARROD, an active excavator, who had a greater influence on him. Clark lectured in Cambridge from 1935 to 1952 when he became Disney Professor of Archaeology. He retired from the chair in 1974 but actively wrote and researched until his death. The list of his publications is phenomenal.

While Disney Professor, he employed ERIC HIGGS and DAVID CLARKE and created an exciting environment for students from Britain and other parts of the world at Cambridge University. These contacts and a significant program of overseas excavations were the result of Clark's interest in world prehistory.

Clark's long career covered more ground that that of almost any other archaeologist of the twentieth century. He is not identified with the analysis of one kind of archaeological material, nor indeed with an interest that is restricted to one aspect of prehistory. Clark has been universally linked with the Mesolithic site of Star Carr in Yorkshire in England. However, even that work should be viewed in the larger context of Clark's overall career, for it was but one element on a broad canvas, prepared over the decade before excavation and retouched and developed many years later. Clark frequently switched his focus and interest; he would introduce ideas and study topics and then move on.

Although Clark was not regarded as a founder of "the new archaeology," at least some of its concepts were present in his writings during the 1950s. He did not carry the radiocarbon revolution to its conclusion, although he had used early radiocarbon results to demonstrate that the northern and western European Neolithic was far older than previously supposed. Clark moved on to consider hunter-gatherer landscape use and suggested the hierarchical taxonomy of human groupings in the Paleolithic northern European plain. It was left to others to identify these as biologically based mating networks, and meanwhile, Clark was engaged in the investigation of cultural diversity. His last

book, *Space, Time and Man* (1992), discussed the human ability to conceive of and organize time and space in ways that other species cannot.

Peter Rowley-Conwy

References

For references, see *Encyclopedia of Archaeology: The Great Archaeologists,* Vol. 2, ed. Tim Murray (Santa Barbara, CA: ABC-CLIO, 1999), pp. 525–529.

Clark, J. Desmond (1916–)

John Desmond Clark is preeminent among twentieth-century archaeologists working in Africa. More than any other individual he has shaped African prehistory, and his visions have established or structured almost all of the prehistoric research now under way on that continent. Desmond Clark was born in London and attended Christ's College, Cambridge, where he studied archaeology and anthropology under Miles Burkitt and GRAHAME CLARK, who taught him the importance of the paleoenvironment in archaeology and how changes in that environment might influence human behavior.

In 1937, Clark went to work in Northern Rhodesia (now Zambia) as secretary of the Rhodes-Livingstone Institute in Lusaka and as curator of the Rhodes-Livingstone Memorial Museum in Livingstone. He reorganized the museum, created thematic exhibits of both archaeological and ethnological materials, and wrote an accompanying handbook. The museum proved to be popular with local people and schoolchildren and after World War II attracted foreign tourists visiting nearby Victoria Falls. Later the museum was to be the site of Clark's annual Winter School in Archaeology. Clark also established the National Monuments Commission to protect archaeological sites in Northern Rhodesia.

During the 1930s, Clark was one of the few professional archaeologists in southern Africa. He began his fieldwork with the geologist Basil Cook from Johannesburg, and his study of the stone tools and fossils of the Old Terrace gravels of the Zambezi River in Northern Rhodesia resulted in his first publication in 1939. He obtained a research grant to do additional excavations at Mumbwa, and a 1942 report recorded a sequence of Stillbay, Rhodesian Wilton, and

J. Desmond Clark (H. J. Deacon)

Iron Age seasonal occupations. During World War II he traveled to Kenya, Ethiopia, British Somaliland, and Madagascar, where he renewed his friendship with LOUIS and MARY LEAKEY. The results of these travels, the material he collected, and the sites he surveyed were the basis of his highly respected book *Prehistoric Cultures of the Horn of Africa* (1954).

In 1947, Louis Leakey organized and hosted the First Pan-African Congress on Prehistory, and it brought together for the first time almost everyone interested in African prehistory—archaeologists, quaternary geologists, and paleontologists from twenty-six countries and from all parts of Africa and abroad. The congress gave those who attended the opportunity to meet and learn what others were doing and to discuss mutual problems. It was a landmark event for African prehistory and for Clark. Over the next decade he worked in the upper Zambezi Valley, dug the late–Stone Age cave of Nachikufu, and reexamined the Broken Hill site where the "Rhodesian man" had been found in 1921. He took leave and returned to Cambridge where he received his doctorate in 1951, writing his thesis on his work in the Zambezi Valley and the Horn of Africa.

The Second Pan-African Congress was held in 1952 in Algiers, and Clark was president of the prehistory section. Stimulated by the congress papers and collections, Clark proposed a correlation of prehistoric cultures north and south of the Sahara. Although the model he proposed is now known to be incorrect, it was Clark's first attempt to view African prehistory as a whole. In 1953, Clark found the most important site of his career at Kalambo Falls in Northern Rhodesia, and the publication of his research there established him as one of the two leading African prehistorians—the other being Louis Leakey. Clark assembled a diverse group of scholars and used a multidisciplinary approach to reconstruct the paleoenvironments of the site. A number of students and young scholars, including many who are now major figures in prehistoric studies in Africa and elsewhere, participated in the excavation and the writing of the reports.

During the 1950s, Clark published forty-six papers in addition to the proceedings of the Third Pan-African Congress held in 1955 in Livingstone and his synthesis, the *Prehistory of Southern Africa*. He continued to excavate in Angola and in the Zambezi Valley. In 1961, he became a professor in the Department of Anthropology at the University of California at Berkeley, and there he and other colleagues established a research and graduate-training program in African prehistory and related disciplines that soon became the most distinguished center for such studies in the world. By the time Clark retired from teaching in 1986, ten Africans from six different countries had received their doctorates under his direction. These African graduates are now university teachers, museum directors, and heads of antiquities organizations in their own countries. During this period Clark also expanded his research interests to Malawi, the central Sahara, central Sudan, and Ethiopia.

The breadth of Clark's personal experience in African prehistory is unique, not only because of the range of the areas he has studied but also because of the diversity of topics and their chronological range. His greatest contribution has been his ability to place the mass of data in its broader context and to write, edit, or coordinate insightful syntheses such as *Prehistory of Africa* (1970) and the *Atlas of African Prehistory* (1967).

Fred Wendorf

References

For references, see *Encyclopedia of Archaeology: The Great Archaeologists, Vol. 2,* ed. Tim Murray (Santa Barbara, CA: ABC-CLIO, 1999), pp. 754–757.

Clarke, David Leonard (1936–1976)

David Leonard Clarke, a British archaeologist, never directed a major excavation but was noted for his outstanding contributions to theoretical archaeology. He studied the ceramic vessels of the Beaker assemblage of the third millennium B.C. in Europe and gained his accreditation as an archaeologist more in the Continental museum tradition than in the British excavation mode. Clarke remained in Cambridge, England, all his professional life, and his career spanned only ten years from the completion of his Ph.D. to his sudden death in 1976.

He is famous for radicalizing British archaeology, and in *Analytical Archaeology* (1968), Clarke argued that archaeology must become a science by developing an explicitly archaeological theory based on general systems theory. Clarke argued that the variability in cultural assemblages required attention. Cultural assemblages varied—there were no discrete cultures, only overlapping suits of slightly different collections of items—and the artifacts varied as well. Concentrating on the special but calling it typical, in the sense of the unique and supposedly diagnostic, could lead to conclusions quite different from those reached when looking at the most common or typical forms. The variability in specific types of objects was a fascinating insight into the obvious. Variability of form suggested to Clarke a past of unceasing fluctuation. He believed that what was possible for biology should be feasible for culture, with variability lodged within a taxonomic frame for ordering the allocation of entities to classes, not directed to a systematic operational concern with the causes and effects of variability.

His second profound contribution to archaeological theory was the recognition of the critical importance of scale in our understanding of the past and the different scales of phenomena within it. If archaeology was to be systematic, as Clarke wished, it was not difficult to envisage that the established rigor and precision should be extended to include precise statements about magnitude and variability. Clarke's great insight was that by extension, the rigor of acquiring data should also be applied to its interpretation.

Clarke wanted to find the taxonomic system that meshed all archaeological phenomena together, coinciding, by accident or intent, with "natural" categories of culture, and doing for archaeology what the sixteenth-century Swedish biologist Carolus Linnaeus had done for biology. Even without a high-level theory, a system of classification that coincided with a natural taxon would allow coherent research propositions, just as it did for biology before the modern synthesis. The addition of variation to the description of archaeological entities should lead toward a proper theory of culture. In this respect, Clarke had something in common with "the new archaeologists" in the United States. The correct procedure, whether based on Hempellian logic in the U.S. scheme or taxonomy in Clarke's scheme, was intended to produce good and appropriate theories.

The quandary at the core of Clarke's agenda is the absence of a systematic high-level theory about what matters—an explanation of the nature of human behavior. This weakness was common to the entire program of the new archaeology, and it still is a fundamental limitation of archaeological theory. No current paradigmatic position in archaeology has overcome this quandary.

Roland Fletcher

References

For references, see *Encyclopedia of Archaeology: The Great Archaeologists,* Vol. 2, ed. Tim Murray (Santa Barbara, CA: ABC-CLIO, 1999), pp. 866–868.

Classification

Classification is the most fundamental of all interpretive activities, not only in archaeology but also in all of science. There comes a time, sooner or later, when the sheer accumulation of data requires its subdivision into groups before any other analytical or interpretive procedures can be undertaken. In archaeology, this has been true in the case both of artifacts and of cultures. As a result, archaeological classification has a long history, and in the broadest sense it probably dates back to the beginnings of archaeology itself. Beginning in the early nineteenth century, scientific classification developed hand in hand with scientific archaeology.

Preliminary Considerations and Definitions

If classification is the most fundamental of interpretive activities in archaeology, it is also one of the most complex and one of the most controversial. There are, to begin with, two quite different kinds of archaeological classifications, respectively, of artifactual finds and of "cultures" (variously also designated as horizons, patterns, aspects, etc.). The procedures involved are so different for both cases, and the characteristics of the classifications themselves so different, that their histories must be considered separately. There are, in addition, classifications of such things as house types, burial types, and decorative styles that fall somewhere between artifact classifications and culture classifications. They are classifications of abstractions rather than of concrete things, but they are confined in each case to one particular kind of abstraction while culture classifications are based on a whole range of abstractions involving different kinds of evidence.

Culture classifications are akin to, and in some sense derived from, the historian's traditional practice of periodizing the past—as, for example, into successive phases that are called Tudor, Jacobean, and Restoration. In archaeology, however, culture classifications attempt to encompass and to summarize both the spatial and the temporal variability of archaeological remains, creating units of analysis that are believed to represent the normative culture of a certain specific region during a specific interval of time. The Fort Ancient Culture of the Ohio River Valley and the Tripolye Culture of Neolithic Eastern Europe are examples of culture classification. Very frequently these schemes have a genetic character akin to that in language

classification; that is, they recognize "parent" and "daughter" cultures in a chronological sequence.

Artifact classifications are usually nongenetic. They are however enormously variable, depending partly on the nature of the material being classified. The two most common kinds of artifact classifications are those of pottery and lithics (especially projectile points), but the salient features that are considered in the two cases are quite different. Pottery classifications are usually designed for use with small fragments; as a result, they place emphasis on stylistic and componential features rather than on overall form, which often cannot be determined. Projectile point classifications, on the other hand, are designed for use on whole specimens or large fragments and are based largely on criteria of form. The variables to be considered in classification also depend on what characteristics have been found to be temporally or chronologically significant; for example, color in the case of most pottery classifications but not in most lithic classifications.

However, the most important differences among artifact classifications depend on the purposes for which they were developed. A major distinction can be made between basic or essentialist classifications, which are designed to yield information about the material being classified, and instrumentalist classifications, in which the classified material is used for some purpose external to the material itself, such as the dating of archaeological sites. Essentialist classifications are often developed for the instruction of a wider public, for example, through museum displays and popular books, while instrumentalist classifications are developed only for "in-house" use among archaeologists and find expression chiefly in technical monographs. There are also purely ad hoc classifications whose only purpose is convenience: very often, to permit the description of a large and diverse mass of material in a limited number of monograph pages (see Adams and Adams 1991, 157–168). Most archaeological bead classifications seem to fall into this last category.

Many, but not all, artifact classifications are typologies—here defined as classifications that have been made for the specific purpose of sort-

Reconstructing vases at the British Museum (Gamma)

ing entities into discrete categories for purposes of statistical treatment. In such a system, the categories must be mutually exclusive and not overlap, so that each individual artifact or shard is assigned to one and only one category. Moreover, the set of categories must be comprehensive so that there is "a pigeonhole for every pigeon." These features are not necessary in a classification that is made only for communication purposes; such a system may consist of a set of norms that overlap at the boundaries (see Adams and Adams 1991, 76–90). Typological classification is a relatively recent feature of scientific archaeology and is important chiefly when typological data are to be used quantitatively, or statistically. Consequently, it is a feature of artifact classifications rather than of culture classifications.

Many but not all classifications, both of artifacts and of cultures, have a hierarchical feature; that is, the smallest classificatory units are grouped into larger and more inclusive units in the same way that biological species are grouped into genera. This feature is especially prevalent in pottery classifications like the "type-variety system" that has been widely used in North and Central America (Smith, Willey, and Gifford 1960; Wheat, Gifford, and Wasley 1958). Such hierarchical classifications will be here designated as taxonomies.

Renaissance and Enlightenment Foundations

The archaeology of today is an outgrowth of what was earlier called antiquarianism. It is usually said to have had its beginnings in the Renaissance period, fifteenth to sixteenth centuries, when royal and noble patrons paid for field excavations in Italy and Greece that would yield objets d'art for their private collections. Before long, the antiquarian fever spread to England, where its focus shifted from classical antiquity to the megalithic remains of late prehistory. The objects recovered from these early diggings were displayed in "cabinets of curiosities"—often a whole room or several rooms in a nobleman's palace might be devoted to such displays. Later, a great many of the collections found their way into museums; indeed, they formed the original nuclei of some of Europe's earliest museums.

Every collector developed his or her own system for displaying the collected antiquities, as, a little later, did the museums that inherited them. Although none of these systems have survived, we may assume that at least some of them involved primitive, ad hoc classifications, perhaps according to the materials employed, artistic similarities, or places of finding. This type of ad hoc classification, while it has been partially superseded by other and purportedly more scientific systems, has by no means disappeared from archaeology. For example, it is still a common practice to divide up the total assemblage of material to be described in an archaeological monograph according to the material employed, so that there are separate chapters on pottery, objects of stone, objects of bone, and the like.

If the Renaissance was preeminently an era of discovery and collecting, the Enlightenment—essentially coeval with the eighteenth century—was above all an era of systematization. The dominant concern during the Enlightenment was to bring order and system to the mass of materials and facts that had been collected, not only in the natural world but in the social and political spheres as well. This effort resulted in a proliferation of botanical, zoological, and geological classifications, best exemplified by the "system of nature" developed by the Swedish botanist Carolus Linnaeus in the eighteenth century (Linnaeus 1735). At the same time, the moral philosophers, especially in France and in Scotland, developed logically coherent social and political schemata, including what came to be known as the three-stage schema of prehistory. This framework envisioned successive hunter-gatherer, pastoral, and agricultural stages in human development and was proposed almost simultaneously by Turgot in France and by Ferguson and Millar in Scotland (Meek 1976).

In the broadest sense, the classificatory methods of Linnaeus and other naturalists provided a methodological foundation for the later development of artifact classification while the three-stage schema of the moral philosophers was equally basic, at least conceptually, to the subsequent development of culture classification. However, the real development of classification as an essential, rather than merely an incidental, feature of archaeology had to wait for the beginnings of scientific archaeology, which came about only when the true antiquity of the human race began to be recognized. That recognition was one of the signal achievements of the nineteenth century.

The Beginnings of Scientific Archaeology

Scientific archaeology arose from the recognition that material remains from the past can be sources of information as well as of aesthetic enjoyment. Once that happened, scientific classification followed more or less inevitably. Artifacts began to be classified first and foremost with an eye to the information they could yield, information about themselves and about their makers and their times.

Scientific advances in archaeology have often begun in areas where the archaeological record was scantiest; where, in other words, careful and precise investigation was required to extract any information from the little that has survived from the past. This was undoubtedly the reason why European scientific archaeology, including classification, had its beginnings in Scandinavia, a region that was outside the realm both of classical antiquity and of the prehistoric megalith builders. Scandinavians at the outset of the nineteenth century were gripped by the same spirit of nationalism that affected nearly all European peoples, and like many of the others, they began to regard prehistory as an essential part of their national heritage. Without major architectural monuments or conspicuous objets d'art, however, they had a much more difficult job recovering that heritage than their neighbors in the more southern countries. It was in that context that scientific archaeology had its beginnings, mostly in DENMARK.

The Danes pioneered in the development of both culture classification and artifact classification. In the beginning, the two went hand in hand, but with the dominant concern always on the classification of cultures, since that was an essential step in the reconstruction of national prehistory. Artifact classification was ancillary, or instrumental; that is, it was undertaken, not to learn about the artifacts themselves, but to define the artifact types that were diagnostic attributes of each particular culture. There was a special interest in those types that could be recognized as "index markers" for particular cultural periods, akin to the "index fossils" of the geologist and the paleontologist. This instrumentalist function remains an important consideration in artifact classification to the present day, particularly in the Old World.

The Development of Culture Classification in the Old World

As far back as 1776, Scandinavian scholars had recognized that in their countries there were some archaeological sites that yielded only stone-cutting tools, others had both stone and copper, and still others had stone, copper, and iron (Daniel 1967, 90). In the early nineteenth century, Vedel Simonsen wrote specifically of a Stone Age, a Copper Age, and an Iron Age as stages in the prehistory of Scandinavia (Simonsen 1816–1819). It was CHRISTIAN THOMSEN, however, who first gave wide publicity to what has come to be called the THREE-AGE SYSTEM when he arranged all of the prehistoric collections in the newly opened Danish National Museum into separate Stone Age, Bronze Age, and Iron Age assemblages in 1819. In order to achieve this comprehensive separation, he studied not only the cutting tools but also all of the different prehistoric remains at his disposal, including such things as pottery and ornaments, classifying them as Stone, Bronze, or Iron Age according to the contexts in which they occurred. The three-age system was thus from the beginning both a culture classification and a kind of artifact classification.

Thomsen's contribution to the three-age system was basically museum oriented, and it was left to several colleagues, most notably JENS JACOB WORSAAE, to give it wider recognition through published works (especially Worsaae 1843). For some time, however, there was resistance to the scheme in other countries, where scholars tended to regard it as a strictly Scandinavian phenomenon. In the competitive nationalist spirit of the times, they were perhaps hoping to discover uniquely different cultural sequences for their own countries. Still, by the 1850s, discoveries in England, Ireland, and Switzerland had convinced at least some scholars that the scheme had a wider validity. A little later it was found to accord perfectly with the worldwide schemata of cultural evolution proposed by sociologist Herbert Spencer (1855), ethnologist John Lubbock (LORD AVEBURY)(1865), anthropologist Lewis Henry Morgan (1877), and other pioneer evolutionists, and its acceptance became universal. Indeed, it has remained at the foundation of nearly all cultural classification systems in Europe and the Near East to the present day.

The three-age system could be regarded as a mere periodization, exemplifying a procedure that had long been common among historians. However, it was also the first archaeological culture classification insofar as it created a set of mutually exclusive categories to which both sites and artifacts were to be assigned.

French prehistorians, working in the middle of the nineteenth century, made an important addition to the three-age system when they recognized the existence of two stone ages: an earlier period characterized by the exclusive use of chipped stone tools and a later period having also ground and polished tools. In *Pre-historic Times*, first published in 1865, the English prehistorian John Lubbock gave these phases the formal names by which they are still known: Paleolithic, or Old Stone Age, and Neolithic, or New Stone Age.

It was also the French prehistorians of the later nineteenth century who first revealed the great variety of Stone Age cultures and the very long time span that they had occupied. ÉDOUARD LARTET, excavator of many Paleolithic sites in the Dordogne and Vezere regions of France, offered a four-stage periodization based on the kinds of mammal bones that were found in the sites: first aurochs and bison, then reindeer, then mammoth and woolly rhinoceros, and finally, cave bear. However, this periodization was soon superseded by the more comprehensive Stone Age classification of GABRIEL DE MORTILLET, which, like the earlier classificatory systems of Thomsen and Lubbock, was based on the internal evidence of distinctive artifact types rather than on the external evidence of paleontology.

The de Mortillet system as originally proposed (Mortillet 1869) comprised four stages, Mousterian, Solutrean, Aurignacian, and Magdalenian, each named after a "type site" in central France where the remains had first been identified. In a modification three years later, the author temporarily dropped the Solutrean but added a Chellean at the beginning. An important distinction was now also made between the first three stages, which were called Lower Paleolithic, and the last stage, called Upper Paleolithic. The latter was distinguished from its three predecessors by the use of bone and horn as well as stone tools. In a further modification in 1883, the author restored the Solutrean, as an Upper Paleolithic stage, and also added a Thenaisian period at the beginning of the sequence and a Robenhausian at the end (Mortillet 1883). The former was an eolithic period, represented by crudely chipped stones that had not yet attained any standardized forms, and the Robenhausian was actually a Neolithic period based on recent finds in Switzerland.

The de Mortillet scheme continued to undergo modifications, first at the hands of its original author and then by a host of successors. By the end of the nineteenth century, the Aurignacian had been restored to its original position in the Upper Paleolithic and an additional very important stage, the Acheulian, had been added to the Lower Paleolithic. The Thenaisian and Robenhausian were never generally accepted as part of the Paleolithic chronology, although de Mortillet himself always believed in them.

As GLYN DANIEL (1950, 106) observed, the de Mortillet system "became an accepted canon of prehistory," and in many respects it remains so today. Part of its appeal lay in the fact that the entire system was strictly chronological and unilineal, each stage succeeding the preceding with no allowance for concurrent, spatial variation in culture in different parts of Europe. As such, it was wholly consistent with the unilinear theories of social evolution that gained general acceptance in the latter part of the nineteenth century. In the broadest sense, it may be said that evolutionism, biological and social, provided the ideological framework within which archaeological classification developed for more

than half a century. The most imaginative prehistorians, like Lubbock, attempted to combine the artifactual evidence of prehistory with the ethnographic evidence on which social evolutionists chiefly relied to produce comprehensive cultural descriptions of prehistoric life at its various stages of development. It was thus the prehistorian and the ethnographer together who provided the nineteenth century with its particular progressivist vision of prehistory.

Modified innumerable times, the de Mortillet system, with its basic division into Lower and Upper Paleolithic, still remains at the core of Old World Paleolithic classifications. There is now some allowance for concurrent spatial variations within the system, particularly in the Upper Paleolithic where phases like Tardenoisian and Tayacian are considered to be localized adaptations to particular circumstances. The scheme nevertheless remains at heart a chronological one.

It was recognized from the beginning that the European Neolithic stage had been far shorter in duration than the Paleolithic, enduring perhaps not more than a few thousand years. Yet European scholars at the end of the nineteenth century were so wedded to a unilinear vision of cultural evolution that they at first tried to fit all of the known varieties of Neolithic culture into a single developmental succession, as they had done in the case of the Paleolithic. However, the Neolithic archaeological record was far richer and more diverse than that of the Paleolithic, encompassing not only tool types but also pottery, houses, and burials. As the full diversity of these remains came to be recognized, the effort to fit them all into a strictly evolutionary and unilinear sequence became insupportable. As a result, the classification of Neolithic cultures in Europe and the Near East came to be based as much on the recognition of spatial differences as it was on temporal differences.

The great systematizer for the European Neolithic, as well as for the Bronze and Iron Ages, was yet another Scandinavian, OSCAR MONTELIUS. Through detailed study of artifact collections from all over Europe he worked out a series of regional chronologies and then went on to suggest an overall periodization into which they would all fit. His periodization encompassed four stages for the Neolithic and five stages for the Bronze Age (Montelius 1903). Other scholars working at about the same time subdivided the prehistoric Iron Age into two phases. The Montelius scheme combined and elaborated upon the features of the Thomsen and de Mortillet classifications in that culture periods were defined both by the materials employed in tool manufacture and by diagnostic characteristics of the tools themselves. In effect, the new method substituted diagnostic assemblages for individual diagnostic tool types as the basis for the definition of cultures and culture periods. This approach, which Montelius called "the typological method," has since been widely employed by European prehistorians although it has come in for substantial criticism in the recent past.

Although the cultural chronologies of Montelius and his colleagues, like those of Thomsen and de Mortillet, were based on the recognition of supposed continent-wide similarities, those similarities were attributed for the first time to cultural diffusion rather than to evolutionary processes. This new perspective went hand in hand with the general adoption of the concept of culture among both ethnologists and prehistorians at the end of the nineteenth century. Different prehistoric assemblages were now seen as representing the work of ethnically distinct peoples who had continually borrowed ideas from one another. At least in the Neolithic and Bronze Ages, widespread cultural similarities were now seen mostly as the result of those borrowings.

The Montelius chronology of roman-numbered Neolithic (I-IV) and Bronze Age (I-V) stages is still occasionally employed by European prehistorians insofar as it provides a handy set of typological-chronological pigeonholes into which particular cultures can be placed. However, modified versions of the scheme have a much more basic role in the classification of Aegean and Near Eastern cultures, where scholars still routinely assign sites and cultures to the Early, Middle, or Late Bronze Age and to numbered subdivisions of these periods.

Although the general typological method of Montelius has remained in use among European prehistorians to the present day, no one since Montelius himself has proposed an overall, formal schema for the classification or periodization of European and Near Eastern prehistory. The nearest thing to overall synthesis is found in the works of English archeologists GORDON CHILDE (1925) and GRAHAME CLARK (1952), but both of those scholars made use of the culture classifications already in use rather than proposing new ones.

A new and highly formal methodology for the development of culture classifications was proposed in 1968 by DAVID CLARKE (1968, 187–398). In the broadest sense, it represented a refinement of the typological method in which artifacts were to be clustered into types, types into assemblages, and assemblages into cultures using highly rigorous criteria of inclusion at each level. However, this discussion was purely programmatic. Clarke did not go on to propose an actual classification based on his system, nor did the Soviet prehistorians who discussed and debated the methods of culture classification in rather similar terms during the same period (Klejn 1982). The time/space grid of European prehistory that remains in actual everyday use among prehistorians is still very largely an extension of the ones created initially by Christian Thomsen, de Mortillet, and Montelius, and it is based on their typological methodology.

The underlying conceptual model for Old World Paleolithic classification has always been chronological and evolutionary while the underlying model for Neolithic and Bronze Age classification has been mostly geographical and diffusionist. It may be noted that the same is generally true in the classifications of African Paleolithic and Neolithic cultures, which have been undertaken almost entirely by European-trained scholars (Trigger 1989, 135–138).

Culture Classification in the New World
Although the classification of prehistoric cultures in Europe and the Near East was always overshadowed by a concern for chronology and a belief in evolutionary progress, these factors

were almost wholly lacking in early North American archaeology. There was a nearly universal belief that the native inhabitants had arrived in the Western Hemisphere only within the last two or three millennia and that their cultures had undergone little or no significant advance during the subsequent interval. At the same time, however, ethnographers could recognize the enormous diversity of culture exhibited by present-day Indians in different parts of the continent, and it was expected, correctly, that the same diversity would be encountered in the archaeological record. As a result, culture classification in North America from the beginning came to emphasize geographical rather than chronological variation.

If the informing framework for Old World cultural classification was the theory of social evolution, the informing framework for New World classification was the culture-area concept. In simplest terms, this concept involves the recognition that cultures in different regions show a high degree of similarity to one another but differ from those in neighboring regions as a result partly of historical diffusion but mostly of adaptation to differing environmental resources. Culture-area theory, unlike early evolutionary theory, places a heavy emphasis on specialized adaptation.

American prehistorians had the enormous advantage, which the Europeans lacked, of observing the living, immediate descendants of the peoples whom they were studying archaeologically. Inevitably, American archaeology developed and has retained a close alliance with ethnology, and the basic framework followed in classifying prehistoric cultures reflects, at least in a general way, the model employed in classifying the living Indian cultures. This culture-area model was developed initially by ethnologists at the Smithsonian Institution at the end of the nineteenth century. The earliest formulation, published in 1896, envisioned sixteen culture areas in North and Central America: Northwest Coast, Southwest, Great Plains, and so on (Mason 1896). The culture areas were differentiated most importantly by modes of subsistence (maize agriculture, forest hunting, fishing, collecting, etc.) but also by commonalities of technology, housing, social organization, and religion.

Archaeologists, assuming that the remains they dug were immediately ancestral to living Indian cultures, tended for a time to take the culture-area theory as a given. Moreover, their excavations for a long time failed to uncover any conspicuously stratified sites or any evidence of genuinely primitive Paleolithic-type cultures, thus seemingly confirming the general belief in a recent migration of the Indians from the Old World. As investigations progressed, however, two things became apparent: first, there was considerable diversity among the prehistoric cultures even within certain culture areas, and second, there had indeed been substantial developmental change in many of the prehistoric cultures. This realization led, in the 1920s, to a widespread recognition of the need for a classification of the prehistoric American cultures that would be independent of existing ethnographic classifications.

The first Pecos Conference, held in New Mexico in 1927, marks the beginning of formal classification in American prehistory. The conferees agreed to divide the prehistoric Pueblo culture (now called Anasazi) into seven developmental stages, each marked by distinctive pottery types, house types, and settlement patterns as well as certain other cultural criteria (Kidder 1927). Although this division was, strictly speaking, a periodization rather than a classification, it set a pattern of systematization that was soon widely copied in other parts of North America. Within a very few years, several other cultures had been defined and periodized not only in the Southwest but in the Midwest, Northeast, and other areas. Within two decades, systematic cultural classifications had been developed for nearly the whole of North America, as well as for parts of Central and South America (Martin, Quimby, and Collier 1947). Cultures and their subdivisions were defined on the basis of a wide variety of culture traits, artifactual and architectural, but projectile points were always treated as primary in the definition of preceramic cultures while pottery types played the same role in the later cultures.

The proliferation of named cultures led, at

least in some quarters, to a perceived need for more formal systematics. In 1934, Winifred and Harold Gladwin published a short monograph entitled *A Method for the Designation of Cultures and their Variations* (Gladwin and Gladwin 1934). Their approach was strictly chronological and culture-historical, and it was based on an analogy with biological classification. The metaphor they used, however, was that of describing a tree. In the beginning, according to the Gladwin scheme, there were a few widespread and generalized regional roots. These in the course of time had given rise to stems, stems had subdivided into branches, and branches had subdivided into phases. In the U.S. Southwest (where the scheme was developed) there was an original southwestern root, which gave rise to stems that we now call Anasazi, Hohokam, and Mogollon (the Gladwins used different terms); the Anasazi stem in its turn had in time split into the Chaco, Mesa Verde, and Kayenta branches, and the Kayenta branch (to take one example) had split into Tsegi, Jeddito, and various other phases.

At nearly the same time, archaeologists in the Middle West were developing a fundamentally different classificatory system that ignored history altogether and was based purely on typological resemblances between artifacts and artifact groups. Formally designated the Midwestern Taxonomic Method, it came to be known popularly as the McKern System because it was first described in print by W. C. McKern (McKern 1939), although it had actually been formulated at a series of archaeological conferences several years previously.

The Gladwins' system was essentially a splitting system, but the Midwestern System was conceived by its authors as a lumping system. The latter began at the lowest level by recognizing foci, which were made up of groups of sites in a localized area, that shared a very large number of traits in common. Foci were grouped into aspects, which shared some but not as many traits in common; aspects were in turn lumped into phases, and finally phases were grouped into patterns, representing the highest and most generalized level in the system. The original scheme comprehended only two patterns for the whole eastern United States, the

Woodland and the Mississippian. The Midwestern System was devised to a considerable extent for the study and classification of museum and private collections, most of which were poorly dated, and for that reason it did not have a specifically chronological dimension. Phases, aspects, and foci might be either temporal or geographical variants of the parent pattern.

The Gladwin classificatory system involved too much speculation about historical connections to be congenial to most archaeologists, and it was never adopted, except by the Gladwins and their close associates. The McKern System, on the other hand, has been widely, though not very systematically, employed in many parts of North America besides the Midwest, but it has never been accepted as providing a fully satisfactory overall schema for the classification of North American prehistory. Like nearly all classificatory devices, it has been found to work better in some places and at some periods than at others.

Meanwhile, the discovery of so-called early man (now usually called Paleo-Indian) remains in the 1930s added a new and unexpected chronological dimension to American prehistory. Paleolithic-type remains were found that must date back at least several thousand years, and they could not be definitely related to the later Indian cultures. In classifying these early remains, American prehistorians followed much more closely the model of de Mortillet than their own methodology in dealing with the later culture. That is, the various Paleo-Indian cultures, like Clovis and Folsom, were treated strictly as chronological subdivisions in a single linear progression. This approach seems to be supported both by distributional evidence and by subsequent radiocarbon dating, but it probably owes something to the influence of the Old World Paleolithic canon as well.

In 1958, GORDON WILLEY and Philip Phillips proposed a comprehensive chronological schema for all of the native cultures of the New World (Willey and Phillips 1958) in which the prehistoric cultures were assigned to five developmental stages: lithic, archaic, formative, classic, and postclassic. This involved no formal systematics; it was a simple evolutionary chronology somewhat akin to the European three-age system, though paying more attention to ecological factors. This schema has proved useful for the evolutionary pigeonholing of specific prehistoric cultures, but it makes no effort to express historical relationships among them, as the Gladwin and McKern systems are intended to do.

The Gladwin and McKern systems remain almost the only efforts to introduce anything like formal or rigorous systematics into the classification of New World cultures, and neither has come into general use. Insofar as formal methods have been employed, they have largely been devoted to the differentiation of sequential phases within the same culture (e.g., Pueblo I-V) rather than to the differentiation of spatially distinct cultures. Overall, archaeological culture classification in the Americas remains mostly an ad hoc process, guided by no rigorous rules, and the same is true for Europe and Africa. There is a continuing, largely unexamined premise that preceramic cultures are defined most importantly by projectile point types and ceramic cultures, by pottery types. The establishment and acceptance of a particular culture, and of its successive phases, is still very much a matter of dialogue among the relevant specialists, resulting eventually in a general agreement on norms and boundaries.

Although there has been a great deal of highly sophisticated debate about the epistemology as well as the methodology and the utility of artifact classification, there has been relatively little debate concerning culture classification. There is, rather, a general recognition that archaeological cultures are for the convenience of the archaeologist so that the question of their "reality" does not arise.

The Development of Artifact Classification

Scientific artifact classification developed initially as an adjunct to culture classification. The early prehistorians, like Thomsen and de Mortillet, were not really interested in tools and pots as evidence of activities, technologies, or thought patterns but only as identifiers of chronological horizons. The objective in artifact classification was to identify those types that could be associated specifically with the Stone, Bronze, or Iron Age and could help in the allocation of sites to one or another of those periods. Individual types were of course defined on the basis of formal characteristics, but they were then grouped together on the basis of chronological contexts rather than the internal evidence of form or function.

So long as they were undertaken for purposes of culture definition and of site attribution, artifact classifications were dominated by the concept of "the index fossil." That is, primary attention was given to those artifact types that were found to be diagnostic of specific periods. On the other hand, artifact types that were considered nondiagnostic were often ignored. Thus, for example, Mediterranean archaeologists gave names and definition to a few pottery types, like Minyan Ware, that had a high degree of historical significance, but a great many other and more ubiquitous pottery wares went unnamed. In the same way, North American prehistorians developed comprehensive and highly detailed classifications of projectile points, but nothing comparable was done for the more generalized stone tools like scrapers and choppers.

A long step forward was taken when Montelius introduced the typological method in the latter part of the nineteenth century. Using this procedure, cultures and chronological horizons were defined on the basis of total assemblages rather than of a few diagnostic types, and as a result, artifact classifications became more comprehensive. There was not, however, any attempt to introduce formal systematics into the classifications.

Not all nineteenth-century artifact classifications were instrumentalist. The problem confronting the museum curator was fundamentally different from that of the field archaeologist, since a museum's mission is to inform or entertain the public rather than to answer culture-historical questions. Moreover, a great many museum collections had been donated by amateurs, with little or no accompanying provenience information. This was especially true in the case of arrowhead collections, which have always had a special fascination for Americans. As a result, museums often developed purely formalistic artifact classifications based on criteria of size, shape, and color alone (e.g., Rau 1876). When using this procedure, groups of similar-appearing artifacts were displayed together without any consideration for their times or places of origin. This tradition persisted in the display of many kinds of museum materials until well into the twentieth century.

General A. H. PITT RIVERS, often regarded as the father of scientific archaeology in Great Britain, went beyond other museum curators in combining classificatory formalism with evolutionism. So committed was he to a unilinear evolutionary perspective that he arranged all of the objects in his vast collection—both ethnographic and archaeological—into what he believed to be developmental sequences without any reference to their place of origin (Pitt Rivers 1874). Pitt Rivers may thus have been the first prehistorian to employ purely logical seriation, although the technique had certainly been used earlier by art historians. Combined with more formal typology, it would later by used by scholars like SIR WILLIAM MATTHEW FLINDERS PETRIE and Alfred L. Kroeber to develop culture sequences in areas where direct chronological evidence was lacking. That is, types were initially defined on formal grounds and then arranged into what appeared to be logical developmental sequences.

The single most important revolution in artifact classification came about as a result of the introduction of frequency seriation in the early decades of the twentieth century. This procedure grew out of a recognition that cultures generally change gradually rather than cladistically. At any given time, some types of artifacts are always coming into use while others are going out. After the passage of a generation or two all of the same artifact types may still be in use as at the beginning, but some will have increased in frequency while others will have decreased. Accordingly, cultures and their various developmental phases need not always be recognized by diagnostic artifact types or assemblages; they can also be recognized by diagnostic frequencies of artifacts, even when there are no individually diagnostic types.

The frequency seriation method appears to have been pioneered by two scholars working at nearly the same time in different parts of New Mexico. Excavating in the Tano ruins near the Rio Grande, NELS C. NELSON was able to assign the various ruined pueblos to five successive chronological periods on the basis of pottery wares and ware percentages present or absent (Nelson 1916). Before he could make numerical calculations, however, Nelson first had to identify and name all of the different wares present in his collections. At about the same time, Alfred L. Kroeber was collecting potsherds from the surfaces of ruined pueblos in western New Mexico (Kroeber 1917), and without any excavation at all, he was able to suggest a sequence of the ruins based on the frequency or infrequency of particular wares. Once again, this method necessarily involved an initial classification of the wares. Later, Kroeber was to apply the same principles in the classification of pottery collections and of culture horizons in Peru (Kroeber 1944).

Frequency seriation introduced for the first time the procedure of quantification in artifact classification, and this procedure involved two important methodological correlates. First of all, if types were to be treated quantitatively, classifications had to be fully comprehensive; there had to be a type category for every shard or point. Moreover, the categories had to be mutually exclusive. In other words, the classification had to be a true typology. Second, the frequency seriation approach had the effect of partially decoupling artifact classification from culture classification. That is, types might not necessarily be diagnostic of any one period or even of any one culture yet their relative frequency could help in the definition of periods and cultures.

The activities and the success of Nelson and Kroeber inaugurated an era of almost feverish identification and naming of prehistoric pottery types, first in the southwestern United States and before long in neighboring areas as well. Once again, as in the case of culture classification, the proliferation of newly proposed types led to a perceived need for more formal systematics. Here again, the Gladwins took the lead when they published *A Method for the Designation of Southwestern Pottery Types* (Gladwin and Gladwin 1930). The authors recognized that many southwestern pottery types had been widely traded so they were important components in the ceramic assemblages not only of their makers but of neighboring cultures as well. Indeed, in the case of some types, the specific region of origin was far from certain. The Gladwins therefore suggested that pottery classification should be decoupled from culture classification, in effect breaking with a tradition that had been prevalent for 100 years. Pottery types, they said, should not be named after the presumed cultures of their makers (as, for example, the Maya orange) but should instead be given names that were free of cultural or chronological implication. They proposed a system of binomial designation, such as "Tularosa black-on-white"; the first element is a geographical name (usually from the site or area of first discovery), and the second describes the surface color or configuration. This suggestion has since been widely followed in the naming of pottery types in many parts of North America.

Although the Gladwins proposed the rules for pottery classification, it was another southwesterner, Harold S. Colton, who undertook the arduous and painstaking task of putting them into operation. Colton and several associates systematically examined several million potsherds from northern Arizona and eventually produced the monumental *Handbook of Northern Arizona Pottery Wares* (Colton and Hargrave 1937), which included minutely particularized descriptions and illustrations of no fewer than 150 types. The Colton scheme had also a hierarchical or taxonomic feature: it began with a basic division between oxidized and reduced types, subdivided each into groupings called wares, then subdivided many of the wares into series, and finally subdivided each ware or series into types. The hierarchical approach has not found general acceptance in other areas, but the individual Colton wares have nearly all stood the test of time, owing largely to the painstaking effort that went into their original definition. At the same time that Colton was working in Arizona, Florence Hawley produced

a *Field Manual of Prehistoric Southwestern Pottery Types* (Hawley 1936), based mainly on New Mexico materials, and J. A. FORD was introducing similar analyses and descriptions of pottery types in the Mississippi Valley and eastern North America (Ford 1938). Subsequently, comprehensive pottery classifications have been developed for just about every part of North, Middle, and South America.

The frequency seriation method was originally developed in the study of pottery distributions, and it is still much more often applied to pottery than to other materials. In the 1940s and 1950s, however, FRANÇOIS BORDES introduced a similar approach in the study of lithic materials from French Paleolithic sites (Bordes 1950, 1961), and his method required a far more precise and comprehensive typology of stone tool types than had previously been attempted. The Bordes method has proved generally effective on its home ground, and attempts have been made to employ it in many other parts of Europe, the Near East, and Africa. Field-workers tried originally to employ the same actual tool types that had been designated by Bordes in France, assuming them to be universal in distribution, but they were unsuccessful. The general conclusion now is that the frequency seriation method itself works well with Paleolithic stone tools but the actual types must be separately classified for each area (Kolpakov and Vishnyatsky 1989).

The partial decoupling of artifact classification from culture classification had a kind of liberating effect on the study of artifacts. No longer treated simply as culture markers, they could be studied more nearly as autonomous data, giving evidence of technologies, activity patterns, and even thought patterns that were not necessarily culture specific. Moreover, by 1940 many North American prehistorians had come to feel that the older, instrumental artifact classifications had done their job insofar as a series of cultures and culture sequences had been devised for nearly the whole continent. It was time therefore to develop new classifications for new purposes.

In effect, North American prehistorians after 1940 ceased to be concerned exclusively with culture-historical issues. There was a common feeling that once all the different cultures had been defined and had been placed in their proper temporal order, it was time to move on to new questions. The result was a series of self-proclaimed "revolutions" in American archaeology, each of which had an impact, at least theoretically, on the processes of artifact classification. With each new change of paradigm, archaeologists often found that their previously established type concepts were not adequate to the questions that were now being asked.

The first "revolution," beginning around 1940, was strongly influenced by concurrent developments in ethnology. It was argued at the time that the appropriate task of the anthropologist, both in ethnology and in archaeology, should not be simply to look at culture and history from the outside but, rather, to "get inside the minds of the people," to see the world as much as possible as they saw it. This would later be called the "emic" approach to the study of culture as opposed to the "etic" approach that analyzed culture only from the viewer's perspective.

In the field of artifact classification, it was argued that archaeologists had been splitting hairs over minute differences in pottery temper or the length-width ratio in arrowheads because these differences proved useful for the chronological ordering of sites even though they might have been accidental or meaningless to the actual makers of the artifacts. There was, as a result, a certain turning away from the strict formalism that had characterized the previous generation of classifiers. The basic idea now was that artifact types should be essentialist rather than instrumentalist, they should represent "mental templates" in the minds of the makers, and they should ignore variations and variables that seemed to be unintentional. However, there was never complete agreement as to how this essentialism was to be determined. One school, championed by Alex Krieger (1944) and IRVING ROUSE (1960), argued that the most sharply demarcated types could be safely assumed to represent the intent of the makers. These types would have a maximum of internal cohesion and external isolation, to use a phrase that later became popular. Another school, best represented by WALTER TAYLOR (1948, 114–123), apparently believed that prehistoric peoples thought more in functional than in formal terms and therefore recommended an approach to classification based more on the function than on the form of objects. Critics were able to suggest, however, that neither approach necessarily captured the original thinking of the artifact makers. Sharply demarcated types represented habitual behavior on the part of the artifact makers that might, or might not, have been a reflection of conscious intent while functional types necessarily reflected the archaeologist's own system of logic (Ford 1954).

In the end, the would-be revolution of the 1940s had much more effect on the formation of typologies and taxonomies that it had on individual types. Types themselves continued to be designated on formal grounds of shape, size, decoration, and so on. There was a continuing and largely unexamined assumption that whatever criteria appeared salient to the archaeologist must have been salient to the makers as well. Once designated, however, individual types were now often clustered into larger categories on the basis of presumed use rather than of appearance; in other words, into functional rather than formal taxonomies. Pottery vessels were grouped together on the basis of their presumed use for cooking, food serving, storage, etc., rather than on the basis of shared patterns of decoration.

The supposed emic, or functional, revolution had not proceeded very far when it was overtaken in the 1960s by the self-proclaimed "scientific revolution" ushered in by "the new archaeologists." These archaeologists shared with their predecessors the belief that artifact types should in some sense be "real" rather than mere heuristic constructs of the archaeologist; therefore, there was, at least for a time, a continued assumption that "reality" must reflect the intent of the makers. However, "reality" was now to be determined by strictly scientific and empirical procedures without recourse to interpretation or context. The touchstone of reality was replicability. Any type proposed by one archaeologist should be capable of confirmation by others, using properly scientific measures. Types, like other scientific propositions, should be regarded as propositions to be tested (Hill and Evans 1972). As a result, there was a renewed emphasis on formal systematics, exemplified especially in the work of David Clarke (1968, 187–229), Robert Dunnell (1971), and Dwight Read (1974).

The renewed emphasis on formality and rigor led to an important methodological innovation: the use of statistics and the definition of types by attribute clustering rather than by object clustering (Spaulding 1953). The archaeologists' traditional procedure of partitioning a body of collected material into types through visual inspection and the observation of similarities was now thought to be too intuitive. Instead, a list was to be made of all the attributes of size, shape, color, and so on that were exhibited by all the objects in a collection individually. Types were then to be defined by clusters of attributes that occurred together with a frequency greater than chance, as revealed through the use of accepted statistical measures. Such a procedure would, in theory, result in "finding the joints in nature" and would eliminate all subjective judgment and all historical interpretation from the process of classification. The attribute-clustering approach came to be known as "agglomerative" in contrast to the older method of partitioning, which was called "divisive."

In the beginning, the major difficulty in statistically based classification lay in the enormous number of separate calculations that had to be made in order to determine the randomness or nonrandomness of a nearly infinite number of attribute combinations. That difficulty was overcome in the 1970s, however, through the use of computers. There followed a decade of experimentation with computerized systems of classification, which, it was hoped, would finally achieve the elusive goal of automatic classification (see especially Whallon and Brown 1982). Before long, the search for automatic and absolutely "natural" classification became an end in itself, rather than a means to an end, and as such it considerably outlived the new archaeology paradigm that had given it birth.

It was eventually realized, however, that the goal of automatic classification was not practically attainable. The coding of more and more variables simply resulted in the generation of more and more types; far more than were useful for any practical purpose. Indeed, the ultimate logical outcome of computerized classification was a series of classifications in which every object constituted a separate type. In the end, there was a general, though not universal, acknowledgment that types that were not produced for any specific purpose were also not useful for any specific purpose.

As a result there has been, since the early 1980s, a considerable loss of faith in the possibilities of computerized classification and, with it, a loss of interest in the subject of classification in general. The postmodern fashion of the 1990s represented in many ways a reversion to the perspective of the 1940s, once again condemning formal typological constructs precisely because they had been made to serve the archaeologists' own purposes.

The successive changes of direction and of interest that have taken place since 1940 have resulted in far more theoretical and programmatic literature than actual, in-use classifications. The concern of most authors has been to propose new methods of classification rather than to develop actual classifications based on those methods. Insofar as the new methods have been put to practical use, it has been almost entirely at the level of individual assemblages. There has been, as a result, a proliferation of ad hoc classifications, each archaeologist developing his or her own system as a way of dealing with, and publishing, his or her own finds. For the most part, these individual systems have not proved capable of generative use and have not passed into what might be called the public domain. The archaeological type concepts and typological systems that remain in general, region-wide use are still very largely those that were developed, chiefly for the instrumentalist purpose of culture classification, more than half a century ago.

Other Archaeological Classifications
Although the vast majority of archaeological classifications are concerned either with cultures or with artifacts, there are also classifica-

tions of house and building types, of burial types, of petroglyph and pictograph types, and of artistic styles. Some of these classifications, like some of the artifact classifications, predate the beginnings of scientific archaeology. As far back as the 1750s, WILLIAM STUKELEY devised a classification of British earth mounds and megalithic monuments. A generation later, RICHARD COLT HOARE and WILLIAM CUNNINGTON proposed a fivefold classification of English barrow types. In North America, antiquaries CALEB ATWATER in 1820 and Squier and Davis in 1848 proposed classifications of earth mound types.

The classification of houses and of burials has always gone hand in hand with culture classification, much as did the classification of artifacts before the 1930s. Indeed, the various monument types designated by Stukeley, Colt and Cunnington, and Atwater were initially regarded as the primary diagnostics for the recognition of different cultural periods. Later, house types took their place along with pottery and projectile points as defining characteristics of the various Neolithic cultures of the Old World, as well as of prehistoric American cultures. The importance of house types in culture classification is particularly evident in the U.S. Southwest, where each of the major cultures (Anasazi, Hohokam, Mogollon, and Hakatayan) is characterized by its own distinctive form of dwelling, as are the different developmental phases in some of the cultures. Burial types on the other hand have played an especially important role in defining the early cultures of the Nile Valley, where evidence of housing is largely lacking. In NUBIA, at the beginning of the twentieth century, GEORGE A. REISNER recognized and differentiated a whole succession of previously unfamiliar ancient cultures on the basis of burial types alone (Reisner 1909).

Unlike artifact classifications, the classifications of house types and burial types have never really been decoupled from the larger objective of culture classification. Although prehistoric dwellings have been extensively studied from the standpoint of function and of ecology, their formal partitioning into types still serves mainly for the identification of cultures and of horizons. The case is somewhat different, however,

in the classification of petroglyphs and pictographs, since many of these cannot be associated with specific peoples or time horizons. Classifications of rock art therefore tend to be more strictly formal and essentialist, based strictly on the exhibited characteristics of the drawings. There is not, however, any one generally accepted classification, or system of classification, of rock art. Every region has its own scheme based on its own distinctive body of material.

Theory versus Practice: The Typological Debate

As long as the basic aim in artifact classification was to define cultures and sequences, the actual procedures involved in the classification were generally regarded as nonproblematical. Artifact types were accepted or rejected on the grounds of their recognizability and their utility or nonutility for the reconstruction of culture history, and the question of their objective reality or meaningfulness to their makers did not arise. Debate often occurred over the legitimacy or the utility of individual types, but it did not touch upon the general methods or the purposes of classification itself.

However, the major shifts of interest that occurred after 1940 gave rise not only to new approaches to classification but also to an extensive and often heated dialogue about the nature and the meaning of classification itself. In one form or another, this discussion persists down to the present day, particularly in North America, where it has been given the name, "the typological debate." The accumulated body of theoretical and programmatic literature is enormous, yet it bears surprisingly little relationship to what goes on in the practical domain, and it must therefore be discussed independent of actual field practice.

The most fundamental issue that has been debated concerns the "naturalness" or "artificiality" of types, which was raised initially in the context of the "functional revolution" in the 1940s but in one guise or another continues to be debated down to the present day. There is general agreement that "artificial" (i.e., instrumentalist) types can be created that are useful for some archaeological purposes; the question is whether or not there can also be "natural" (i.e., essentialist) types that have objective existence independent of any purpose of the typologist. The question in simplest terms is, Can types exist independent of purposes?

Both the erstwhile functionalists of the mid-century era and the new archaeologists of the next generation attempted to answer this question in the affirmative. It is evident, however, that the conception of what constitutes "naturalness" was quite different in the two cases. For the functionalists, it was a wholly emic concept, identifying that which was meaningful to the artifact makers and users. For the new archaeologists, despite their occasional assertions to the contrary, it was basically etic, identifying that which was discoverable through statistical procedures. There were contemporary critics of both approaches who continued to insist that types cannot be wholly separated from the archaeologists' cognition, which in turn is shaped by his or her purposes. It remains true in any case that nearly all of the artifact types that are in general everyday use were developed for avowed culture-historical purposes while it has so far been possible to develop purely formal and purpose-free classifications only in the case of specific, limited assemblages.

Another issue raised in the typological debate was that of emic versus etic classification, although those two terms were not generally employed during the earlier phases of the debate. The mid-century functionalists insisted that the artifact types previously in use were somehow "wrong" because they were purely heuristic constructs while the proper aim of archaeology should be to understand (and classify) from the perspective of those who were studied. As applied to artifact classification, however, this approach proved to be less revolutionary than some of its proponents believed. It did not really affect the way that individual types were defined, only the way in which they were grouped into larger taxa.

Eventually, it was recognized that the categories created by the functionalists were ultimately those that responded to the archaeologists' own logic and that the actual perspective of the prehistoric artifact user was beyond recovery. As a result, the functional approach, as an alternative to formal classification, died out after a generation or so, although it continues to be widely employed as a way of grouping artifacts for publication in monographs. It is noteworthy, however, that postmodernists are now raising the same questions about formal typologies that the functionalists raised, that is, casting doubt on the typologies because they reflect the categorical logic of the archaeologists' own culture. But while the functionalists had believed that the prehistoric native's outlook should be privileged, if only it could be recovered, the postmodernists now insist that nothing should be privileged.

Yet another issue raised in the debate was that of lumping versus splitting. Although it had long been recognized that some classifiers were naturally "lumpers" while others were "splitters," the difference became a methodological issue with the introduction of statistical procedures in the late 1950s and even more with the advent of widespread computer use a generation later. Types had traditionally been devised by a partitioning or splitting procedure, dividing up a collection of material into recurring and visibly distinct types. In this approach, types were recognized first, and their specific defining attributes were then discovered through rigorous analysis. On the other hand, the method of attribute clustering is necessarily a lumping procedure in which attributes are defined first and are then clustered together to define types. There continue to be advocates of both approaches, as well as people who believe that these are alternate routes that will ultimately arrive at the same end. It remains true, however, that most of the artifact types that are in general use today were devised by the older splitting procedure.

The typological debate has been conducted mainly by North American prehistorians, particularly as regards the use of computers in classification. Since the 1960s, there has also been a somewhat different typological debate among European prehistorians, a debate that emphasizes methods rather than objectives. In the Old World, the influence of de Mortillet and Montelius remains strong, and it is still generally taken for granted that the proper purpose of artifact classification is to aid in the development of culture classifications, particularly with chronologies. Debate, therefore, has been largely concerned with the best way of achieving that purpose (cf. especially Graslund et al. 1976; Klejn 1982).

Adams and Adams (1991, 278–304) have undertaken a review and critique of the typological debate, and they argue that much of the debate has been misplaced, partly because it has ignored the question of purpose and partly because it has failed to grasp the full complexity of type concepts. Types necessarily have material, cognitive, and representational dimensions—the actual objects, the archaeologists' mental perception of the objects, and the words and pictures that are used to convey those understandings. The three dimensions are not wholly interdependent in that any one of them can be changed without necessarily affecting the other two.

Adams and Adams go on to assert that just about everything that has been written about archaeological types is partly true and partly not true because the types that are actually in regular use are partly natural and partly artificial, partly essentialist and partly instrumentalist, partly formal and partly functional. An infinity of types may be actually present in the material, but the archaeologist inevitably selects from among them those that are useful for some purpose by choosing to emphasize some attributes and ignore others. The authors conclude that the ultimate touchstone of artifact types is that they must be consistently recognizable and they must be demonstrably useful for some purpose.

It remains to add that the vast majority of artifact classifications have always been and are ad hoc schemes, devised to permit the archaeologist to describe a large and diverse body of material in a limited number of pages. From this perspective, just about every archaeologist is also a typologist, and just about every monograph involves its own typology.

William Y. Adams

References

Adams, W. Y., and E. W. Adams. 1991. *Archaeological Typology and Practical Reality: A Dialectical Approach to Artifact Classification and Sorting.* Cambridge: Cambridge University Press.

Bordes, F. 1950. "Principes d'une methode d'etude des techniques et de la typologie du paleolithique ancien et moyen." *L'Anthropologie* 54.

———. 1961. *Typologie du Paleolithique ancien et moyen.* Bordeaux: Impremeries Delmas.

Childe, V. G. 1925. *The Dawn of European Civilization.* London: Kegan Paul.

Clark, J. G. D. 1952. *Prehistoric Europe: The Economic Basis.* London: Methuen.

Clarke, D. L. 1968. *Analytical Archaeology.* London: Methuen.

Colton, H. S., and L. L. Hargrave. 1937. *Handbook of Northern Arizona Pottery Wares.* Bulletin 11. Flagstaff: Museum of Northern Arizona.

Daniel, G. 1950. *A Hundred Years of Archaeology.* London: Gerald Duckworth.

———. 1967. *The Origins and Growth of Archaeology.* Harmondsworth, Eng.: Penguin Books.

Dunnell, R. 1971. *Systematics in Prehistory.* New York: Free Press.

Ford, J. A. 1938. "A Chronological Method Applicable to the Southeast." *American Antiquity* 3, no. 3: 260–264.

———. 1954. "The Type Concept Revisited." *American Anthropologist* 56, no. 1: 42–54.

Gladwin, W., and H. S. Gladwin. 1930. *A Method for the Designation of Southwestern Pottery Types.* Medallion Papers 7. Globe, AZ: Gila Pueblo.

———. 1934. *A Method for the Designation of Cultures and Their Variations.* Medallion Papers 15. Globe, AZ: Gila Pueblo.

Graslund, B., et al. 1976. "Relative Chronology: Dating Methods in Scandinavian Archaeology." *Norwegian Archaeological Review* 9, no. 2: 69–126.

Hawley, F. M. 1936. *Field Manual of Prehistoric Southwestern Pottery Types.* Bulletin 291. Albuquerque: University of New Mexico.

Hill, J. N., and R. K. Evans. 1972. "A Model for Classification and Typology." In *Models in Archaeology,* 231–273. Ed. David L. Clarke. London: Methuen.

Kidder, A. V. 1927. "Southwestern Archaeological Conference." *Science* 66, no. 1716: 489–491.

Klejn, L. S. 1982. *Archaeological Typology.* International Series 152. Oxford: British Archaeological Reports.

Kolpakov, E. M., and L. B. Vishnyatsky. 1989. "The Bordes Method?" *Norwegian Archaeological Review* 22, no. 2: 107–118.

Krieger, A. D. 1944. "The Typological Concept." *American Antiquity* 9, no. 3: 271–288.

Kroeber, A. L. 1917. *Zuni Potsherds.* New York: American Museum of Natural History, Anthropological Papers 18, no. 1: 7–36.

———. 1944. *Peruvian Archaeology in 1942.* Publications in Anthropology 4. New York: Viking Fund.

Linnaeus, C. 1735. *Systema naturae.* Leiden: Theodorus Haak.

Lubbock, J. 1865. *Pre-historic Times. as Illustrated by Ancient Remains. and the Manners and Customs of Modern Savages.* London: Williams and Norgate.

McKern, W. C. 1939. "The Midwestern Taxonomic Method as an Aid to Archaeological Culture Study."*American Antiquity* 4, no. 4: 301–313.

Martin, P. S., G. I. Quimby, and D. Collier. 1947. *Indians before Columbus.* Chicago: University of Chicago Press.

Mason, O. T. 1896. "Influence of Environment upon Human Industries or Arts." *Annual Report of the Smithsonian Institution for 1895,* 639–665. Washington, DC.

Meek, R. L. 1976. *Social Science and the Ignoble Savage.* Cambridge: Cambridge University Press.

Montelius, O. 1903. *Die typologische Methode: Die alterend Kulturperioden im Orient und in Europa.* Stockholm: Slebstverlag.

Morgan, L. H. 1877. *Ancient Society.* New York: Henry Holt.

Mortillet, G. de. 1869. "Essai de classification des cavernes et des stations sous abri, fondee sur les produits de l'industrie humaine." *Comptes Rendu de l'Academie des Sciences.*

———. 1883. *Le prehistorique.* Paris: Alcan.

Nelson, N. C. 1916. "Chronology of the Tano Ruins, New Mexico." *American Anthropologist* 18, no. 2: 159–180.

Pitt Rivers, A. H. 1874. "On the Principles of Classification Adopted in the Arrangement of His Anthropological Collection Now Exhibited in the Bethnal Green Museum." *Journal of the Anthropological Institute of Great Britain and Ireland* 6: 293–308.

Rau, C. 1876. "The Archaeological Collections of the United States National Museum in Charge of the Smithsonian." *Smithsonian Contributions to Knowledge* 22, Article 4.

Read, D. W. 1974. "Some Comments on Typologies in Archaeology and an Outline of a Methodology." *American Antiquity* 39, no. 2: 216–242.

Reisner, G. A. 1909. *Archaeological Survey of Nubia.* Bulletin 3.

Rouse, I. D. 1960. "The Classification of Artifacts in Archaeology." *American Antiquity* 25, no. 3: 313–323.

Simonsen, V. 1816–1819. *Udsiqt over Nationalhistoriens aeldste og maerkeligste Perioder.* Copenhagen.

Smith, R. E., G. R. Willey, and J. C. Gifford. 1960. "The Type Variety Concept as a Basis for the Analysis of Maya Pottery." *American Antiquity* 25, no. 3: 330–340.

Spaulding, A. C. 1953. "Statistical Techniques for the Discovery of Artifact Types." *American Antiquity* 18, no. 4: 305–313.

Spencer, H. 1855. *Social Statics.* London.

Taylor, W. W. 1948. *A Study of Archeology.* Memoir 69. Menasha, WI: American Anthropological Association.

Trigger, B. G. 1989. *A History of Archaeological Thought.* Cambridge: Cambridge University Press.

Whallon, R., and J. A. Brown, eds. 1982. *Essays on Archaeological Typology.* Evanston, IL: Center for American Archaeology Press.

Wheat, J. B., J. C. Gifford, and W. Wasley 1958. "Ceramic Variety, Type Cluster, and Ceramic System in Southwestern Pottery Analysis." *American Antiquity* 24, no. 1: 34–47.

Willey, G. R., and P. Phillips. 1958. *Method and Theory in American Archaeology.* Chicago: University of Chicago Press.

Worsaae, Jens J. A. 1843. *Danmarks oldtid Oplyst ved Oldsager og Gravhoie.* Copenhagen: Selskabet for Trykkefrihedens rette Brug.

Claustra Alpium Iuliarum

Claustra Alpium Iuliarum is a late Roman defensive system in western SLOVENIA, northwestern Croatia, and northeastern ITALY. The term *Claustra Alpium Iuliarum* was first found in the texts of the Roman officer and historian Ammianus Marcelinus, who wrote in the fourth century A.D., and it was frequently used by many other ancient writers. The name Julian Alps was used in ancient times for the mountainous ridge extending from the Gail River valley (Carynthia in southern Austria) in the north to the mountain of Ucka (Istria in northwestern Croatia) in the south. Today, the name Claustra Alpium Iuliarum is normally applied to the remains of partially explored walls and fortifications in this region.

When constructing the defensive system, the Romans took advantage of the difficult terrain between the Roman towns of Tarsatica (Rijeka in northwestern Croatia), Tergeste (Trieste in northeastern Italy), Emona (Ljubljana in central Slovenia), and Forum Iulii (Cividale in northeastern Italy). The defensive system aimed at controlling all land routes and passages from the Balkans to Italy, and it consisted of a series of barrier walls in valleys and signal towers, small fortifications, and *castella,* or forts, which were built using prehistoric and early Roman constructions. As an organized military system, it belongs to the third and fourth century A.D., but some parts were used later as well.

Bojan Djuric

References
Šašel, J., and P. Petru, eds. 1971. *Claustra Alpium Iuliarum.* Ljubljana: Fontes.

Colombia

Among the most important sources for modern Colombian archaeologists are the writings of the Spanish conquistadores. The documents left by these soldiers, priests, administrators, and specially appointed chroniclers of the Indies of the sixteenth and seventeenth centuries are used in various ways: to complement the later periods of local or regional archaeological sequences, as a tool for interpreting the function or significance of archaeological sites or aspects of culture, and, finally, in conjunction with twentieth-century ethnographic studies used to build evolutionary type classifications of cultures. Perhaps that is why the sixteenth century is taken as a starting point by some of the authors who have dealt at length with the history of the discipline (Duque 1965, 1967, 1970; Burcher 1985; Londoño 1989; Uribe 1979; Jaramillo 1994). The works of these authors are the main sources for this entry.

A number of the sixteenth- and seventeenth-century writers—the priest Juan de Castellanos in his *Elegies of Illustrious Men of the Indies,* Friar Pedro Simón in his *Historical Notices of the Conquests of Terra Firme in the West Indies,* and Lucas Fernández de Piedrahita, author of the *General History of the New Kingdom of Granada*—had antiquarian interests. Their writings included discussions of the peopling of the new continent and of related factors such as changes in sea level. The importance of their work, however, is somewhat diluted by the unavoidable biblical frame of reference, for some of them were convinced that American Indians were the descendants of the Lost Tribes of Israel. (Unless otherwise stated, Spanish is the original language of the publications and journals mentioned in this entry; full bibliographical details can be found in Bernal [1970], Enciso and Therrien [1996], and Bermeo [1990]).

The systematic looting of Indian tombs was one way in which the Spaniards obtained the gold that they coveted and that was the driving force behind the conquest. Means of recognizing tombs by marks on the surface and ways of distinguishing rich graves from poorer ones were frequently described; in his *Historical Compilation,* for example, Friar Pedro de Aguado described the rich tombs of the lower Sinú River basin as well as those of the Muisca area, in the upland plateau of the Eastern Cordillera (a mountain range).

Early on, the Spanish crown issued laws to ensure its share of the profits from the looting of shrines and tombs, and lawsuits and quarrels between crown and church over the possession of gold idols obtained in these places were not infrequent. Regrettably tomb looters remained a step ahead of antiquaries and later archaeologists during the centuries that followed. This was the case with San Agustín in the upper reaches of the Magdalena River, the country's most famous archaeological region, through which the Spaniards passed in the sixteenth century. At that point monolithic sculpture was already a feature of the past, and the statues, within artificial mounds, were not visible. By the eighteenth century, when Friar Juan de Santa Gertrudis visited the region, looting had started. His *Marvels of Nature* was the first written account of the region, although he described monuments as images of Catholic religious dignitaries "sculpted by the devil." He traveled extensively in the southwestern part of New Granada (as the country was known by that time) and wrote about the ancient burials of various parts of it.

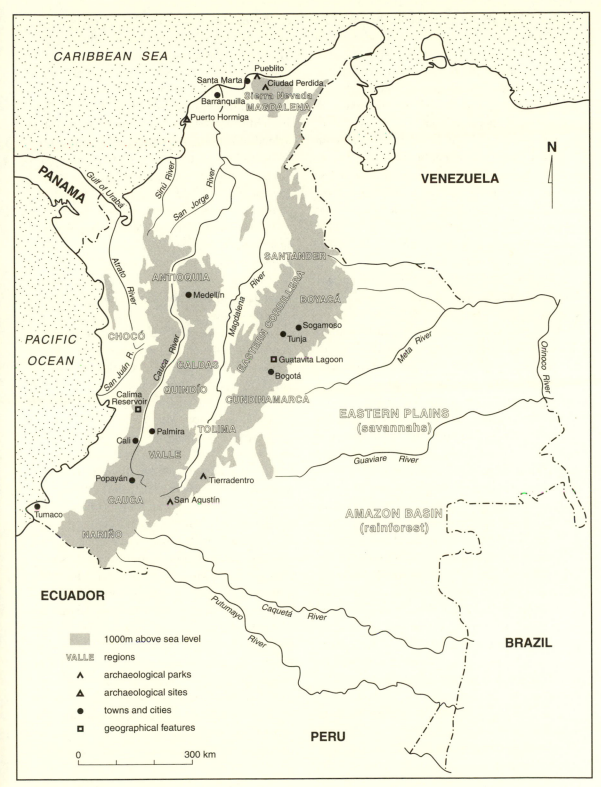

Archaeological Sites in Colombia

Aside from the friar's recounting of his travels, little antiquarian material has been found thus far in the documents of the eighteenth century. This may be due to a lack of interest on the part of archaeologists, many of whom consider that their period of study ends with the sixteenth century; for them, although the seventeenth century might be of faint interest, the eighteenth is more or less outside their boundaries. This situation is beginning to change, partly because historians are demanding that archaeologists resolve certain questions that documents cannot address. In 1983 an earthquake destroyed much of Popayán, one of the few towns that had maintained a well-preserved colonial urban center, and exposed the foundations of many ancient buildings, thereby opening up a rich field for archaeological investigations.

The final years of the eighteenth century marked the beginning of institutionalized scientific activity. A rising demand in Old World markets for certain products of the American colonies may account for the particular orientation of this interest. King Charles III of Spain ordered botanical expeditions to be organized in MEXICO, PERU, and New Granada, the last being undertaken by José Celestino Mutis. This Spanish savant managed to attract a group of young and enthusiastic local intellectuals to join his ambitious endeavor, and for decades they carried out extensive fieldwork, collecting botanical speciments and various kinds of samples and information as their interests extended into the fauna and other natural resources and the customs of the land. Within this framework Francisco José de Caldas, an astronomer and geographer, visited San Agustín in 1779 and recognized its stone statues as the product of a former Indian population and work that ought to be studied properly.

The enthusiasm of the expedition members was enlivened by the 1801 arrival of Baron Alexander von Humboldt, a German naturalist and explorer whose antiquarian interests and descriptions ranged from petroglyphs in the Orinoco River basin to the Muisca and their legend of a chieftain covered in gold dust (*el dorado*) who used to throw golden offerings into a sacred lake. Humboldt had accepted the calendar hypothesis of Fr. José Domingo Duquesne, who had described one elaborately engraved Muisca stone as a calendar and taken it as proof that this group had achieved a degree of civilization comparable to that of Mesoamerican societies. Although the calendar hypothesis was subsequently proved wrong, Humboldt's prestige helped to legitimize the Indian past in the intellectual milieu of the time. As part of the New Granada upper class, the expedition's scientists were affected by current philosophical trends from the aftermath of the French Revolution, and they were active in organizing a revolt against Spanish rule. With the wars of independence the expedition came to an end, not least because some of its members, such as the great Caldas, paid for their political activism with their lives.

Soon after the achievement of political independence in the 1820s, attempts were made to rebuild what had been destroyed, including the effort to replace dead scientists with foreign ones. The Mining School was created along with the National History Museum (which brought in Jean Baptiste Boussingault, an expert in mines) and, in 1824, the National Museum, among whose exhibits was a Muisca mummy. However, political independence did little to change the country's social and geographic profile: the upper-class, landed Granadian aristocracy replaced the Spaniards in the higher echelons of civil, military, and religious administration; slavery continued in a modified way; and a hierarchy with castelike nuances placed tribal Indians and peasants of mainly indigenous and African ancestry in the bottom social ranks. The country was made up of culturally differentiated provinces, poorly integrated and isolated by rugged geography. During the nineteenth century the republican government was involved in an ongoing quest for an appropriate political organization, resulting in eight constitutional changes that were invariably preceded or followed by civil wars.

Most notable during the second and third decades of the nineteenth century were the visits and memoirs of various European travelers whose interest in Colombia had been sparked by Baron von Humboldt. Boussingault visited San

Agustín; a captain named Cochrane dug a number of Muisca tombs in the area around Guatavita, with what was apparently an antiquarian interest; and John P. Hamilton referred to various unsuccesful attempts, dating from colonial times, to drain the lake that contained the El Dorado treasure. Auguste Le Moyne, a French diplomat, recorded how many Granadians dug up ancient tombs in search of treasure, and he described the the colorful lore that developed around this activity. A decree issued in 1833 gave the discoverers of Indian tombs and temples rights over them, thus stimulating tomb looting.

Antiquarian interests managed to survive through the efforts of individuals such as Manuel Vélez, a collector and keen observer of finds in the provinces of Cundinamarca (on the upland plateau surrounding Bogotá) and Antioquia. In a letter to Boussingault, first published in 1847 in the *Bulletin of the French Geographical Society,* Vélez proposed a new interpretation of these finds. He believed that they were not, as was commonly thought, the products of barbarians who deserved to be conquered and catechized in the sixteenth century. Instead, he argued, they were the products of rich, powerful, and perhaps even civilized groups. He hypothesized that these superior nations had vanished before the conquest. In 1848 Gen. Joaquín Acosta published the *Historical Compendium of the Discovery and Colonization of New Granada,* in which the Muisca and other sixteenth-century populations were given as much importance as the entries on the Spanish conquerors.

A renewal of scientific interest was triggered by plans for further integration of the republic into world markets. It was again felt that the information available on human and natural resources was far from adequate for the task, so a new expedition, geographic this time—the Comisión Corográfica—was launched in 1850. At the same time, various academic institutions were created, and others, such as the National Museum, were improved. Although the expedition lasted less than a decade, its achievements were many in a number of scientific fields, and pre-Columbian remains were recorded and drawn. Agustín Codazzi, an Italian geographer, was the expedition's director and carried out what can be described as the first systematic study of San Agustín, comprising an illustrated catalog of the statues, a properly surveyed plan of their location (and of the area), and an interpretation of their meaning. Codazzi believed that the San Agustín monuments were religious in nature and that the statues were not isolated pieces but part of a building or structure. Another member of the expedition, Manuel Ancízar, had the task of describing the customs of the different races making up the population of the Eastern Cordillera, together with the ancient monuments and natural curiosities of this region.

The most notable contribution at this time was that of Ezequiel Uricoechea, an accomplished naturalist and philologist whose interests extended to ethnology and the study of Muisca goldwork. In his *Memoirs of Neogranadian Antiques,* published in Berlin in 1854 and perhaps the first book that could be called an archaeological text, he described the archaeology of the middle Cauca Valley, but his main emphasis was on the technology of Muisca votive figures. This same emphasis on the Muisca characterizes the work of Liborio Zerda; his interest was prompted by Adolf Bastian, who had visited the country in search of Indian antiquities on behalf of the Berlin Ethnographical Museum. Zerda's contri butions to journals in 1883 were published as *El Dorado: A Historical, Ethnological and Archaeological Study of the Chibcha [Muisca],* and for the first time the historical base of the legend was outlined. The 1860s and 1870s were remarkable for the attention that was paid, between civil wars, to cultural heritage. In 1865 the first legal guidelines for the protection of monuments were issued, and the National Museum was attached to the newly organized but short-lived Institute of National Arts and Sciences before being transferred, in 1867, to the recently founded National University.

By the 1870s interest in another region was increasing. In 1871 Andres Posada Arango presented his *Essay on the Aboriginal Cultures of the State of Antioquia in Colombia* to the French Anthropological Society. In 1885 Manuel Uribe Angel published the *General Geography and Historical Compendium of the State of Antioquia* in Paris. At this time Antioquia comprised the modern departments of Caldas, Quindío, and Risaralda. These regions, which were densely populated until the sixteenth century, were depopulated by the conquest. Between 1840 and 1895 settlers from northern Antioquia moved back into the area in increasing numbers, attracted by the richness of its prehispanic tombs—particularly those that yielded items of the Quimbaya gold style in Quindío. Some of these new finds of pottery and other materials were sold to collectors. The best known of these individuals was Leocadio María Arango, who founded a private museum in Medellín, considered by the French traveler Pierre D'Espagnat in 1897 to be much superior to the display of aboriginal antiques at the National Museum in Bogotá. Another well-known collector in Antioquia was Vicente Restrepo, a historian and author of *The Chibcha [Muisca] before the Spanish Conquest*. He was also a metallurgist and a partner in a photographic studio that produced visiting cards that featured illustrations of pre-Columbian gold pieces together with other more conventionally fashionable motifs.

By the beginning of the 1880s the Ministry of Public Education issued a circular letter requesting the donation of objects (which were now referred to as archaeological works rather than antiquities) to the National Museum. A revival of scientific interest resulted in a new state-sponsored venture, the Comisión Permanente. For the first time pre-Columbian antiquities as objects of study had the same status as plants, rocks, minerals, and animals; and ethnological questions were considered relevant to the history of the republic. Jorge Isaacs (better known as a poet and novelist) was part of the commission, and after its dissolution he continued to travel to and study the Atlantic coastal region and parts of the adjacent Sierra Nevada; he became increasingly interested in indigenous groups and prehispanic objects, explaining the latter in terms of the former in his *Study of the Tribes of [the State of] Magdalena*.

These early collections attracted the attention of European scholars. Some artifacts had made their way overseas to museums and into private collections and were available for study. (The acquisition process was begun by the mu-

seums in 1849 and was pursued more actively after 1870.) Goldwork was particularly appealing, and it was studied by a number of scholars (see Londoño 1989). The first Congress of Americanists was held in 1875, and papers on the archaeology of Colombia were read at this and subsequent congresses. For the eleventh congress, held in 1892 (the year of the four-hundredth anniversary of the first European contact with America), various scholars read papers on the archaeology of Colombia. Among them was Soledad Acosta de Samper, the daughter of the Joaquín mentioned earlier and the only woman antiquarian of the nineteenth century. At the congress she read a paper on "The Aboriginal Populations of the Territories Which Today Form the Republic of Colombia at the Time of the Discovery of América." Ernesto Restrepo Tirado (son of the Vicente mentioned earlier) published *Studies on the Aborigines of Colombia* and *An Ethnographical and Archaeological Essay on the Province of the Quimbayas* and years later wrote his *History of the Province of Santa Marta,* the outcome of research conducted at the National Archive in Bogotá and the General Archive of the Indies in Seville, Spain.

Spain celebrated the four-hundredth anniversary with an exhibition on the history of the Americas. One participant, Colombia, exhibited a set of remarkably beautiful pre-Columbian gold items from the Quindío region, known as the Quimbaya Treasure, and several private collections. The latter were subsequently on display in the Universal Exhibition of Chicago in 1893, but the Quimbaya Treasure was presented to the Queen Regent of Spain in gratitude for diplomatic services rendered, and she passed it on to the Archaeological Museum of Madrid. Many twentieth-century Colombians were greatly chagrined by this donation because the Quimbaya Treasure was placed in a Spanish rather than a Colombian museum; the treasure has since become a symbol of the loss of many other aspects of national heritage to foreign collectors and museums due to a lack of interest on the part of government officials.

Paradoxically, although antiquarian studies during the second part of the nineteenth century increased in importance and acquired indepen-

Gold seated figure from Quimbaya, Colombia, fourteenth–fifteenth century (Image Select)

dent status, there was a movement away from fieldwork and toward armchair studies, a trend that extended into the first decades of the twentieth century. Carlos Cuervo Márquez was an exception in this regard. A historian and Colombia's first field archaeologist, he excavated in San Agustín, in the eastern plains of the Orinoco basin, and in a new region that came to be known through him as the Tierradentro; this area would become famous for the polychrome paintings and sculptures on the chamber walls of the pre-Columbian tombs found there. Márquez was the first to make a detailed description of the Tairona stone architecture in the Sierra Nevada of Santa Marta. His most important publication was *Prehistory and Travels* (1893), which was republished in 1920 as *Archaeological and Ethnographical Studies.* Another work that was not written by a scholar but that contained useful archaeological information was *Remembrances of Tomb Looting in Quindío* by Luis Arango Cano.

During the last years of the nineteenth century some efforts were made by the state to inspire antiquarian activity, but for the most part the field remained the province of independent scholars, who were in contact with Europe and with current scientific trends. Most of them were professionals, but archaeology was not taken seriously and was considered a hobby; moreover, their interests were focused on pre-hispanic antiquities and the Spanish chronicles. A number of these chronicles were not available in Colombia, either because they were out of print or because they were still archival material. As a result of the enthusiasm of these researchers, however, several of these works were reprinted and important documents were published. Mi-grations, especially movements of Caribs, and the distribution of traits and prehispanic objects were the subjects that most interested scholars. The emphasis on migrations lent a certain time depth to their views, but there was also a ten-dency to relate prehispanic objects of any age to sixteenth-century chiefdoms and groups. A re-grettable result of inertia, this tendency still sur-vives in many general or popular presentations of Colombian archaeology (see Botiva et al. 1989 for an effort to counteract that tendency).

In 1902 the Academy of History and Antiqui-ties was created under the protection of the state, and the Academy of the History of Antio-quia was founded two years later in Medellín. Between 1910 and 1920 the National Museum acquired various large private collections. De-spite these changes, however, relatively little ar-chaeological research was conducted in Colom-bia during this period. To some degree this was the result of the hegemony of the conservative party, strongly backed by the Catholic Church and the landowners, for whom the history of the country started with the introduction of Spanish civilization. These parties attributed the backwardness of the contemporary, mainly ru-ral mestizo population to the degradation of an originally blemished Indian ancestry.

With some exceptions, it was mainly foreign scholars who explored Colombia and discovered the rich variety of regional cultures and styles, in addition to the historically better documented Muisca and Quimbaya. The ever popular San Agustín was chosen by the German archaeolo-gist Konrad Theodor Preuss, who carried out the first systematic archaeological excavations in the area in 1914. He transported a number of the most remarkable statues, carved on huge stone slabs, to the Berlin Ethnographical Museum. As a reaction to this notable feat, pre-Columbian monuments were declared part of the history of the nation in 1918 and placed under the protec-tion of the Ministry of Public Instruction. Two years later there was a ban on taking monuments and objects into public or private ownership outside of Colombia without permission from the Academy of History.

This new legislation did not prevent J. Alden Mason of the Field Museum of National History in the United States from taking, in 1922, a siz-able collection of pottery, bone, and stone arti-facts from the first archaeological excavations in Pueblito and other Tairona sites in the Sierra Nevada de Santa Marta. However, it did enable the Santa Marta custom authorities to refuse to ship the collection without due permission. A request for permission was rejected by the Na-tional Academy of History but later granted by the Ministry of Public Instruction.

Other expeditions included those of Henry Wassén in what is today known as the Calima region and that of Sigvald Linné, who explored the northern Pacific Coast near the Gulf of Urabá. This was part of the king of Belgium's romantic quest for the site of Santa Maria La Antigua del Darién, the first Spanish settlement in mainland South America. This region was as exotically tropical and remote to Colombian scholars, who were mainly based on the cool highland plateau of Bogotá, as it was to the northern Europeans. Geographic barriers to travel remained largely unconquered well into the twentieth century, and for some regions commercial air transport (organized very early in Colombia) arrived before roads or railways.

In the 1930s the defeat of the conservative party that had governed Colombia for the previ-ous three decades allowed the winning liberal party to carry out its ambitious plan to modern-ize the country. This effort began at the founda-tions—with profound changes to agrarian and educational policies. Within the intellectual mi-lieu there was reform in the arts, politics, and social sciences, and the Mexican Revolution and the Indian uprisings in the Cauca region re-ceived much attention. Bachué, goddess of the sixteenth-century Muisca pantheon, was chosen as the emblem of a group of intellectuals who wanted to change the prevailing inferiority complex of the nation (the result of its mixed cultural legacy) and sought inspiration and values in Colombia's autochtonous, Indo-American ancestry. Among these intellectuals was Gregorio Hernández de Alba, who was commissioned by the Ministry of Education (formerly the Ministry of Public Instruction), along with the Spanish archaeologist José Pérez de Barradas, to carry out excavations in San Agustín in 1937. The following year, under the same ministry, he created the National Archaeological Service to study and protect the pre-Columbian past and to exert control and provide technical assistance in that regard. Although its aims were ambitious and its economic resources and personnel modest, the service managed to cover a lot of ground and carry out multiple and diverse activities. Under its aegis the archaeological parks in San Agustín and Tierradentro were created. They had been set up by legislation in 1931 and 1935 that gave the state the power to acquire land for the purpose; and each park now boasted a park warden! Legislation passed in 1931 that ordered the foundation of a specialized museum in ethnology and archaeology was actualized in 1938, as the result of an exhibition to commemorate the four-hundredth anniversary of the city of Bogotá. This provided an excuse to incorporate the old National Museum collection, to attract donations, and to obtain extra funds to buy private collections.

The Archaeological Service offered lectures for the general public and for schoolchildren, and it established contacts and exchanges with universities and scientific centers outside the country, especially in France and the United States. The last and most important of all these new initiatives was the publication of the journal *Bulletin of the Archaeological Museum,* established in 1943 and replaced two years later by the *Bulletin of Archaeology.*

Into this very fertile ground in Colombia European intellectuals and exiles from the Spanish civil war and Nazism were welcomed. Many married Colombians and settled in and worked for the country for the rest of their lives. Austrian-born Gerardo Reichel-Dolmatoff, the archaeologist best known internationally, was part of this group.

By 1939 specialized courses in anthropology and archaeology were taught in the recently established Social Sciences Section of the Teacher's Training College (Escuela Normal Superior) under the supervision of the German professor Justus W. Schottelius. Shortly afterward the National Ethnological Institute was founded under Paul Rivet (the director of the Museum of Man in Paris who had fled occupied France). This organization provided training for professionals prepared to carry out basic research in archaeology, physical anthropology, linguistics, and ethnology rather than specializing in any one field. Rivet believed that in a rapidly developing country where many indigenous cultures and archaeological sites were about to disappear without trace, it was vital to get researchers into the field as quickly as possible and for them to have a broad range of skills. Rivet's best-known work, *The Origins of American Man,* combined diffusionism with the ideas from the cultural-history school, and, for better or worse, this became the orientation of his and following generations of Colombians (see Gnecco 1995 for a withering critique).

The new institution had financial backing from the French government for many years, and it not only encouraged young researchers but also provided modest financing and even a new venue for publishing results: the *Review of the National Ethnological Institute.* Luis Duque Gómez, Julio César Cubillos, and Eliécer Silva Célis began systematic surveys of different regions and published detailed excavation reports. Alicia Dussán, the most remarkable of the first generation of Colombian women archaeologists (working side by side with her husband, Gerardo Reichel-Dolmatoff), started to explore the northern Atlantic lowlands. Together they spent the next decades on research projects that ranged from the discovery of one of the earliest examples of pottery in the Americas (Puerto Hormiga, dated to approximately 3500 B.C.) to excavations at early formative sites and at precontact villages and small towns with stone architecture in the Sierra Nevada of Santa Marta. As part of the Yale Archaeological Expedition Wendell C. Bennet surveyed museum and private collections and published, in English, the first modern archaeological appraisal of the country as a whole—*Archaeological Regions of Colombia: A Ceramic Survey.*

In 1945 the Archaeological Service merged with the Ethnological Institute, a move considered necessary to end the "divorce" between archaeology and ethnology. At the time members of the institute included the German geographer Ernesto Guhl and the Russian-born German historian Juan Friede, anticipating interdisciplinarity change thirty years before it was advertised as the great innovation of archaeological studies in the 1980s. Between 1946 and 1947, in a move to spread the benefit of its activities to at least the western and most populated portion of the country, the institute created a number of local branches and encouraged the formation of regional museums. As a result of this policy the Ethnological Institute of the Department of Magdalena was founded in the town of Santa Marta, under the direction of Gerardo Reichel-Dolmatoff. The Atlántico branch in Barranquilla was directed by Carlos Angulo Valdés, whose lifelong interest has been the archaeology of the Caribbean lowlands. Another branch in Popayán was set up as a joint venture with the University of Cauca, where Henry Lehmann was establishing a museum. The Antioquia branch, with its headquarters in Medellín, had links with the university department, and a museum was started through the acquisition of the highly important private collection formed by Leocadio María Arango. This branch was directed by Graciliano Arcila Vélez, whose main interests lay in the Urabá region. On the outskirts of the town of Sogamoso, a branch with a museum was set up inside an archaeological park on the proposed location of the Sun Temple of the Muisca. This branch was directed by Eliécer Silva Célis, who made this enterprise his lifelong interest.

By 1947 the institute administered a number of archaeological parks—San Agustín, Tierradentro, Facatativá (near Bogotá), Sogamoso—and was starting another one in Pueblito. The Cauca branch had begun to train researchers, and there were ambitious plans for further branches in the Chocó and Nariño regions. In 1948, however, the liberal reforms, although by now much attenuated, paradoxically induced a violent backlash by the extreme political right. The populist liberal presidential candidate was assassinated, and his working-class supporters reacted by rioting. Colombia was plunged into another civil war, which climaxed in a harsh, conservative regime. Although there was respite after "pacification" during the military dictatorship, the causes and embers of the backlash survived and very slowly evolved into internal guerrilla warfare. There were no casualties among archaeologists, and none of the institutes or museums or libraries suffered from extensive fire or pillage, but something barely definable was irretrievably lost—the sense of being part of a group with an adventurous mission. Occasional harassment of intellectuals became part of the political climate of the times, and keeping a low profile was the safest position. Some managed to escape by enrolling in postgraduate courses in the United States or in Europe; others found themselves a niche away from the turmoil. Through isolation, archaeologists managed to survive unscathed, but the isolation persisted when it was no longer a political necessity. Perhaps this fact explains both the petty bickering that tainted academic exchanges and the provincialism that has warped the outlook of some scholars.

By 1953 the Ethnological Institute had shed some of its parks and branches and was reorganized (still within the Ministry of Education) as the Colombian Institute of Anthropology (ICAN). Its two periodical publications were merged into the *Revista Colombiana de Antropología* [Colombian Revew of Anthropology]. The institute lapsed into relative obscurity. It managed to continue to train anthropologists, many of whom were medical doctors, architects, lawyers, and other professionals for whom anthropology was a second career; very few of these individuals would work in the field on a full-time basis. Nevertheless, the 1950s were not without some success—and the foundations for the prosperity of the next decades were laid down. Many titles in history and related subjects, essential reading for archaeologists today, were printed or reprinted at this time (and alas, never again), some by the Collection of the Presidency of the Republic.

The most important event of the 1950s was the establishment of the Gold Museum as a permanent public exhibition. Its origins go back much further. Many years before, the Bank of the Republic, which bought gold from mines as well as pre-Columbian metal items to melt down for the country's reserves, had begun to preserve some of the most outstanding archaeological items sold to it. In the 1930s the bank actively pursued a policy of acquiring individual objects as well as outstanding private collections to prevent them from being taken out of the country. By 1944 these objects were displayed in a room to which only very distinguished individuals were invited. The bank began to publish books on archaeology and goldwork and to acquire pottery objects as well. By 1959 it housed its museum in a specially designed vault in its main offices at a newly built bank, and entrance was no longer restricted. Two years later ambitious plans for an independent site were under way.

In the 1960s two influential summaries of Colombian archaeology were published internationally and in English. One of these was by Angulo and appeared in *Aboriginal Cultural Development in Latin America: An Interpretative Review,* edited by Betty Meggers and Clifford Evans (1963). The other was a volume in the series *Ancient Peoples and Places,* in which Reichel-Dolmatoff (1965) outlined the clearest and most comprehensive interpretation of the country's pre-Columbian past that has been written to date.

Colombia was enjoying a period of relative peace after its two political parties opted to take turns in power instead of fighting over the next two decades. With severe restrictions on imports, national industry was flourishing, and the international demand for coffee (then Colombia's main export) was growing. The recently founded, private University of the Andes was training the upper echelons of technicians needed to manage the imported technology that was fundamental for modernization. Since the Ministry of Education had decreed in 1962 that anthropology should be taught at universities rather than by the Institute of Anthropology, the institute's last batch of anthropologists graduated in 1963. The University of the Andes started a Department of Anthropology under the direction of Gerardo Reichel-Dolmatoff, seconded by his wife, Alicia. The National University also began to train anthropologists in the 1960s, albeit sporadically at first. During the following decade the University of Antioquia in Medellín and the Universidad del Cauca in Popayán followed suit. Nevertheless, between 1963 and 1978, about 70 percent of those receiving B.A.s in anthropology graduated from the University of the Andes. The Reichel-Dolmatoffs' time at the University of the Andes ended when, against all expectations, the shock waves of the 1968 student upheaval in Europe hit that stronghold of the middle and upper classes. Although relatively short, their tenure there was a remarkable boost to archaeology, since they managed to inspire a "1940s-style" need for urgent fieldwork. They attracted a number of foreign scholars who came to teach and carry out research, among them Sylvia Broadbent, who, through systematic excavations in Muisca territory, set up a first chronological framework for the Muisca and preceding occupations in the region.

By the 1970s Gonzalo Correal, working for the ICAN, began his research on the largely unknown Paleo-Indian period; his program was known as "Man and Environment in the Pleistocene," and it lasted nearly three decades. Most of the fieldwork was on the Sabana, the upland plateau around Bogotá, and it was often conducted in partnership with the Dutch palynologist Thomas van der Hammen, whose ongoing research projects, starting in the 1960s, laid the foundation for the environmental archaeology of the 1980s and 1990s. At about the same time, Carlos Angulo Valdés, working from his headquarters at the Universidad del Norte in Barranquilla, pursued his own long-term program of research in the Atlantic lowlands; he was one of the group of archaeologists who used the methods of ceramic seriation developed by Evans and Meggers. He focused primarily on the formative period, with his work on the site of Malambo as a starting point In southwestern Colombia Julio César Cubillos, at the University of the Valle in Cali, carried out extensive fieldwork in the valley of the Cauca River. The university acquired an important collection that formed the basis of the archaeological museum named after this scholar.

The 1970s were remarkable for the "new winds" blowing through the archaeological world with the foundation, renewal, or reinforcement of various, mainly state-connected institutions involved in research, publication, and/or pre-Columbian heritage management. In Cali what was originally a branch of the SMITHSONIAN INSTITUTION of Washington was reorganized as the Institute for Scientific Research of the Cauca Valley (INCIVA). *Cespedesia,* its journal, though primarily focused on botanical matters, has published many articles on archaeology and history. In 1968 the Gold Museum opened in a new building designed to meet the most up-to-date specifications, high security among them. Here the remarkable and extensive collection of gold artifacts was exhibited in the best didactic manner and made accessible to a wider public. It became the best-loved museum in the country and gained international renown as a result of its policy of sending temporary exhibitions all over the world, accompanied by attractive catalogs with original contributions by experts (see, for example, Bray 1987). The museum also provided the research platform from which its two archaeologists, Ana María Falchetti and Clemencia Plazas, seconded by Juanita Sáenz, launched their long-term project of mapping and exploring the thousands of hectares of raised fields, housing platforms, and causeways in the seasonally flooded plains of the lower San Jorge River. Over the following decades the museum opened branches in the capital cities of several departments.

The Bank of the Republic also set up the Foundation for National Archaeological Research (FIAN). Initiated by Luis Duque (at that time director of the Gold Museum), it was originally oriented toward the preservation of monuments in San Agustín, and it funded research in this area. Over time this foundation has financed research all over the country on a one-person, one-project basis for up to a year. Between 1972 and 1984 it financed 106 projects, of which 30 percent were for fieldwork and theses of undergraduates. In 1978 it started publishing the best

fieldwork reports and by 1984 boasted twenty-eight titles (FIAN 1985a). This foundation has perhaps been the single most important factor in promoting research into all aspects of Colombian archaeology, and it has managed to continue its activities, relatively unscathed by financial cuts, into the twenty-first century.

Another state bank, the Popular Bank, has taken a similar path, although on a more modest scale, through its Fund for the Promotion of Culture. Purchases made over a number of years enabled it to amass a large collection of pre-Columbian pottery and found two archaeological useums: the Casa del Marqués de San Jorge in Bogotá and La Merced in Cali. Its publication series included a number of titles in archaeology as well as new editions of the writings of several Spanish chroniclers whose work was of great interest to archaeologists. The fund established an annual prize for the best archaeological research, an unfortunately short-lived program. Among the projects recognized by this program was the work Alvaro Chavez and Mauricio Puerta had carried out in Tierradentro.

The Colombian Institute of Anthropology began to share its location in a nineteenth-century stone prison with the National Museum and appears to have lost much of its former drive. The few young graduates from the University of the Andes who found a job there made little difference in this regard. The ICAN was soon to be incorporated into the newly created Colombian Institute of Culture (COLCULTURA) under director Alvaro Soto, one of Reichel-Dolmatoff's pupils. Combining personal dynamism and professional connections, he managed to increase the budget, augment the institute's staff of researchers, and establish strategic research stations in areas of the country in need of fieldwork. Working from the Nariño station Maria Victoria Uribe explored that little-studied region and established links with the results obtained by Ecuadorean scholars on the southern extensions of the area. The most outstanding archaeological project was the extensive exploration of Tairona sites on the northwestern slopes of the Sierra Nevada de Santa Marta. For several hundred years this area had been abandoned to the forest and practically uninhabited, but it was recolonized by farmers from the central Andean region who had been displaced by the civil war of the 1950s. Gilberto Cadavid and Luisa Fernanda Herrera de Turbay documented 200 sites. The last of these, located in the Buritaca River basin, was the site of a Tairona town with an elaborate stone infrastructure that had been plundered by tomb looters. However, due to its inaccessibility (hence the nickname Ciudad Perdida, or Lost City), the site was still relatively well preserved. The ICAN plunged into the adventure of restoring it (under the direction of Gilberto Cadavid and Ana María Groot) at enormous cost, since the work necessitated a large staff dependent on supplies delivered by helicopter. Undoubtedly a site of remarkable beauty and charm, with incalculable historical and didactic importance, its preservation since 1976 as another archaeological park, with a permanent staff supported under the same costly conditions, has drained most of the funds the ICAN received for its Archaeological Division.

There was a considerable influx of foreign scholars into Colombia due to events related to World War II and its aftermath. Many were doctoral aspirants carrying out fieldwork for their theses and were generally backed by grants. Most returned to their countries of origin, and only a few remained in Colombia. Among these were Marianne Cardale Schrimpff, who arrived to study textile techniques of contemporary Indian groups as a means to understand the production of archaeological ones, and Ann Osborn, whose ethno-archaeological studies among the Uwa (Tunebo) Indians are remarkable. Other scholars observed the minimum etiquette and remained in contact with local colleagues, among them Karen Bruhns after her research in the middle Cauca Valley. Some, such as Henning Bischoff, who carried out research in the Caribbean lowlands, returned for further periods of fieldwork. Unfortunately, a number of opportunists who had been welcomed and given support then went away and forgot the obligations incurred—such as sending copies of their reports. Opinion is divided about the passing of Law 626, another of Soto's feats. It established the rule that those in charge of foreign research projects should share a percentage of their funds with local scholars. This law frightened off a number of bona fide scholars, and when it was applied too literally, it filled the ICAN's storage space with junk, yet it also enabled a number of students to be part of an international research project in which they could acquire field and laboratory experience.

Foreign scholars were not the only ones who provided this invaluable service. Gonzalo Correal (by now a member of the teaching staff of the Department of Anthropology at the National University), in spite of very modest funding, carried out many of his excavations at early hunter-gatherer sites with his students and made a point of training them in lithic analysis and bone identification. Among those students whose names were well known by the 1990s, Gerardo Ardila stands out for his attempts at interpreting very early societies through fieldwork among the Makú (a group of hunter-gatherers of the Guaviare River forest, who remained isolated until very recently).

Over the following decades the ICAN suffered various ups and downs, and it gradually shed archaeologists, losing prominence in research. At the same time the FIAN and several regional universities and institutions gained strength. However, legislation from as far back as 1963 ensured that the ICAN would retain an important role in Colombian archaeology. By law this institute had the power to grant or deny permission for archaeological excavations, and although this rule did not deter commercial grave diggers, it could hardly be ignored by bona fide excavators. ICAN staffers were was also obliged to visit the site of any accidental finds of pre-Columbian objects made in the course of public works and to instruct local authorities to halt work if necessary and to salvage heritage sites or objects. This role was maintained against the inclinations of some of the directors, who were faced with diminishing budgets and rapid increases in emergency archaeology of all kinds, as well as the burden of policymaking and innumerable other administrative duties. Miriam Jimeno's two terms as director (from the mid-1980s to the mid-1990s) were exceptional in that the institution enacted a policy of fortifying the ICAN and accepting new challenges.

Diverse trends mark the archaeology of the 1980s. On the one hand the FIAN sponsored one-person, short-term projects in traditional site-oriented archaeology all over the country, and for publication it favored thorough site reports rather than fanciful flights into newfangled theories; it also welcomed research in subjects such as ethnology, geology, history, and biology where this provided answers to archaeological questions. Noteworthy are the various studies by Anne Legast on the identification of animals represented in archaeological objects. On the other hand long-term regional projects became quite frequent. Among the first was the Swiss-sponsored Calima project carried out in collaboration with the ICAN; a number of scholars participated in this project—notably, Warwick Bray, Leonor Herrera, and Marianne Schrimpff. The project had a strong interdisciplinary component and focused on landscape and changes in agricultural adaptations. It reinforced a trend that Correal and van der Hammen had initiated and Angela Andrade had followed: the study of *terra preta* (anthropic) soils in the Amazon region, carried out jointly with the soil scientist Pedro Botero (who would become the much sought after soil consultant on many excavations). Luisa Fernanda de Turbay, a palynologist, is also a popular consultant, as well as the director of another interdisciplinary group that carried out a long-term project on anthropic soils and cultivars in the Amazon basin. She is the founder of Erigaie, a private consultancy enterprise that offers pollen analysis as well as the identification of animal bone and plant material.

Jean François Bouchard of the National Center for Scientific Research in Paris introduced French-style excavations with his long-term work in the Tumaco region, carried out with anthropology students. Two further projects, both influential in the sense of training students and orienting the next generation in methodology and theory, concentrated on the San Agustín area. The more modest version, directed by Héctor Llanos of the Department of Anthropology of the National University, was supported by successive grants from the FIAN. It aimed to establish the geographic limits of the San Agustín culture and to study the dynamic relationship between human settlement patterns and the environment. The second project, directed by Robert Drennan of the University of Pittsburgh in collaboration with the University of the Andes, carried out an ambitious regional survey in the La Plata area, a region adjoining San Agustín and sharing many of its cultural traits but little studied at that time. Drennan's main interests have been demographic trends, the distribution of population, and the rise of sociopolitical complexity. Shovel tests were carried out in the field by small battalions of students, the most promising of whom were given financial support to obtain postgraduate degrees at the University of Pittsburgh. Out of this group came several of the brilliant young people who made their names in the 1990s, such as Augusto Oyuela, known for both his research on the Tairona occupation in the foothills of the Sierra Nevada de Santa Marta and the surrounding lowlands and his work on the preceramic period in the Atlantic lowlands, and Carl Langebaek, well known for his research in the Muisca region and, recently, in Tierradentro. Others obtained postgraduate degrees through different channels: Felipe Cárdenas and José Vicente Rodriguez in physical anthropology, a subject that had been almost abandoned since the 1940s, are both influential for their teaching and training at University of the Andes and National University, respectively.

In southwestern Colombia Cristóbal Gnecco has concentrated on preceramic lithic assemblages, Diógenes Patiño has studied the southern Pacific lowlands, and Carlos Armando Rodríguez has worked on the Cauca Valley. Roberto Lleras, working from the Gold Museum, has achieved new insights into Muisca metalwork, and Eduardo Londoño, who concentrates on ethnohistorical research, is editor of the *Bulletin of the Gold Museum* (started in 1978), which celebrated the arrival of the new millennium by going wholly virtual—the first casualty of the Internet craze. This generation also includes those who chose to stay and make the most of opportunities in Colombia, such as Héctor Salgado, for many years director of the archaeological division of INCIVA in the Department of Valle and now at the University of Tolima, Camilo Rodríguez, who also works in Tolima, and Monika Therrien, who works on colonial archaeology.

In the first half of the 1990s the growth of rescue (paid or contract) archaeology, which had started in the 1970s, reached its peak. Paradoxically, although funds available per project were much above what could be expected in sponsored academic archaeology, the quality of analysis was often mediocre or worse, even when taking into account the special constraints inherent in this activity. However, there were notable exceptions, and under expert guidance some researchers have made important contributions. Outstanding examples are the work on lithic assemblages carried out by Carlos Eduardo Lopez in the Magdalena River plain and in Antioquia, as well as the River Porce Project directed by Neyla Castillo, whose work filled the preceramic void for the region and enlarged the area of the distribution of the mysterious "incised brownware" first defined by Bennet and further contextualized by Karen Bruhns. In Manizales María Cristina Moreno channeled profits from paid archaeology into the renovation of the Archaeological Museum of the University of Caldas, which possesses an outstanding collection for the middle Cauca region.

Even if the results of certain projects are not always up to academic standards, the importance of enforcing the inclusion of preventive archaeology in the preliminaries of any project cannot be underestimated. ICAN has spent a lot of time and energy coordinating regional institutions to present a single front to contractors and to try to enforce minimal rules for practitioners, as contracts were frequently won by undergraduates or unemployed anthropologists or other social scientists not qualified in archaeology. In the late 1990s these efforts suffered a serious setback, paradoxically through circumstances that promised more protection for archaeological heritage. In 1991 a new Colombian constitution was drawn up as a part of efforts to democratically counteract the political ills besetting the country—the production of outlawed drugs, corruption, and guerrilla and paramilitary warfare. Alvaro Botiva, an ICAN archaeologist lobbying with the Constituent Assembly, was influential in getting two articles included in the new constitution to clearly place all items of cultural heritage under the protection of the state. In principle this was a legal tool of great utility, but its drawback was tied to the fact that a new constitution must be translated into laws and decrees; years later when archaeological heritage legislation was considered, it was included in a package with "culture" in general and inefficiently lobbied in congress by COLCULTURA. At the same time, the big state companies of the mining sector were more efficient and managed to make the articles relevant to archaeology ambiguous, with the legal obligation for contract archaeology dependent on *knowledge* of the existence of sites in the area to be affected rather than on the *presumption* of their presence (as had been the case before). This change has greatly increased the risks to sites and reduced the time available for their study before they are destroyed. The economic recession that hit the country in 1997 has slowed building and mining activities and hence the risk of destruction of little-studied areas, but at the same time, it has reduced the amount of funds available for sponsored research, left institutions facing reductions in personnel, and even run the risk of total disappearance due to cutbacks in government spending recommended by the World Bank. ICAN has suffered two restructurings over the last few years, one in 1997 when COLCULTURA (of which it was part) was upgraded to the Ministry of Culture and another in 2000 when it was combined with the Institute of Hispanic (i.e., colonial) History and renamed ICANH. The new institution has a lively and laudable publication policy, but it appears to be turning its back on urgent and difficult issues such as leadership in policy setting and heritage management.

At the turn of the twenty-first century the number of potential archaeologists, among them those with postgraduate qualifications, has increased, even as funds for research in the social sciences have steadily diminished; those moneys available are allocated to subjects related to strife, aggression, war, and peace. However, this is not the most difficult aspect of the situation at the beginning of the twenty-first century. Today even fewer areas are considered to pose "only" moderate risk for fieldwork. The huge demand for illegal drugs in the United States and other parts of the world and the determination of the United States to ignore the lessons of its own history (i.e., that prohibition does not work) have devastated Colombia in two ways: through the spraying of forbidden crops and extensive adjacent areas with toxic chemicals and through the war between guerillas and paramilitaries for control of large tracts of the country. As a result of these and other circumstances, the better-trained and more promising professionals in every field tend to leave the country or are being absorbed by bureaucracy, and quite often they direct their stunted energies into rather sterile criticism of what has been achieved since the mid-1900s. (These achievements are considered by some to fall short of "science" due to their supposed lack of explanatory value.) But the pendulum is swinging. Postmodernism has reached archaeology somewhat belatedly but in a deadly form, to judge by a very recent proposal (see Gnecco 1999) that archaeology should comply with the demands of Indian communities who are reshaping their past according to their present ambitions. It is not quite clear if this implies going against the available archaeological evidence.

Leonor Herrera

References

Arocha, Jaime, and Nina de Friedemann. 1984. *Un siglo de investigación social: La antropología en Colombia.* Bogotá: Editorial Etno.

Bermeo Rojas, Jorge. 1990. "Bibliografía de la cultura agustiniana." *Informes Antropológicos* 4: 140.

Bernal, Segundo. 1970. *Guía bibliógrafica de Colombia de interés para el antropólogo.* Bogotá: Universidad de los Andes.

Botiva, Alvaro, Gilberto Cadavid, Leonor Herrera, Ana María Groot de Mahecha, and Santiago Mora. 1989. *Colombia prehispánica: Regiones arqueológicas.* Bogotá: Instituto Colombiano de Antropología.

Bray, Warwick. 1987. *The Gold of El Dorado.* London: Royal Academy.

Burcher De Uribe, Priscilla. 1985. *Raíces de la arqueología en Colombia.* Medellín: Universidad de Antioquia.

Chavez, Milcíades. 1986. *Trayectoria de la antropología Colombiana.* Bogotá: Colciencias.

Duque Gomez, Luis. 1965. "Prehistoria, etnohistoria y arqueología." In *Historia extensa de Colombia,* vol. 1, tomo 1. Bogotá: Academia Colombiana de Historia.

———. 1967. "Prehistoria: Tribus indígenas y sitios arqueológicos." In *Historia extensa de Colombia,* vol. 1, tomo 2. Bogotá: Ediciones Lerner.

———. 1970. "Notas sobre la historia de las investigaciones antropológicas en Colombia." In *Apuntes para la historia de la Ciencia en Colombia* 1: 213–235. Bogotá: Colciencias.

Enciso, Braida, and Monika Therrien, comps. 1996. *Compilación bibliográfica e informativa de datos arqueológicos de la sabana de Bogotá, siglos VIII al XVI.* Bogotá: Instituto Colombiano de Antropología.

FIAN (Fundación de Investigaciones Arqueológicas Nacionales). 1985a. *Informe de labores 1972–1984 y manual para la presentación de proyectos.* Bogotá: Fundación de Investigaciones Arqueológicas Nacionales del Banco de la República.

———. 1985b. *Proyectos de investigación realizados entre 1972 y 1984.* Bogotá: Fundación de Investigaciones Arqueológicas Nacionales del Banco de la República.

Friedemann, Nina S. De, and J. Arocha. 1979. *Bibliografía anotada y directorio de antropólogos colombianos.* Bogotá: Sociedad Antropológica de Colombia.

Gnecco, Cristóbal. 1995. "Praxis científica en la periferia: Notas para una historia social de la arqueología colombiana." *Revista Española de Antropología Americana* 25: 9–22.

———. 1999. *Multivocalidad histórica: Hacia una cartografía postcolonial de la arqueología.* Bogotá: Universidad de los Andes.

Jaramillo, Luis Gonzalo. 1994. "Colombia: A Quantitative Analysis." In *History of Latin American Archaeology,* 49–68. Worldwide Archaeology Series 15, Aldershot, UK.

Jimeno Santoyo, Miriam. 1990–1991. "La antropología en Colombia: Ponencia al Seminario Balance y Perspectivas de la Antropología en América Latina y el Caribe." *Revista Colombiana de Antropología* 18: 53–65.

Langebaek, Carl Henrik. 1994. "La elite no siempre piensa lo mismo: Indígenas, estado, arqueología y etnohistoria en Colombia (siglos XVI a inicios del XX)." *Revista Colombiana de Antropología* 31: 121–143.

Llanos Vargas, Héctor. 1999. "Proyección histórica de la arqueología en Colombia." *Boletín de Arqueología*.

Londoño Velez, Santiago. 1989. *Museo del Oro: 50 años*. Bogotá: Banco de la República.

Meggers, Betty J., and Clifford Evans, eds. 1963. *Aboriginal Cultural Development in Latin America: An Interpretative Review*. Washington, DC: Smithsonian Institution.

Reichel-Dolmatoff, G. 1965. *Colombia*. London: Thames and Hudson.

Rodriguez, Carlos Armando. 1986. "50 años de investigación arqueológica en el Valle del Cauca." *Boletín Museo del Oro* 16: 17–30.

Uribe T., Carlos. 1979. "La antropología en Colombia." *América Indígena* 40, 2: 281–380.

Colonial Williamsburg

See Williamsburg

Colt Hoare, Sir Richard (1758–1838)

Born into an aristocratic banking family, Colt Hoare was financially independent and thus able to pursue a career of leisure. After the premature death of his wife he assuaged his grief by traveling around Europe for two years, a journey that stimulated his interest in monuments and antiquities. He returned to Britain to become Baron Hoare in 1787, then continued his European travels, visiting archaeological sites and drawing them for the next three years, until the French Revolution made it impossible to remain on the continent.

It was this impasse that caused him to visit Wales, England, and Ireland, drawing the monuments of his own country. Between 1812 and 1821 he illustrated and published the two-volume *Ancient History of North and South Wiltshire* and the *History of Ancient Wiltshire*. These contained accounts of Stonehenge and AVEBURY, of Roman roads and sites, and of hundreds of barrows that he had explored with his protégé WILLIAM CUNNINGTON. These books can be seen as the first attempts at recording the archaeology of a particular region.

Colt Hoare was a fellow of the Royal Society and the SOCIETY OF ANTIQUARIES OF LONDON, and he wrote numerous books, printed for private circulation, on history, architecture, and the archaeological sites, artifacts, and monuments of Europe, England, Wales, and Ireland. He financed his own archaeology team—composed of Cunnington, draftsman Philip Crocker, and special workmen—and he believed that excavations should be able to answer questions about the past. Unfortunately the answers to the big questions, such as who it was who actually built the monuments he caused to be excavated or recorded, remained elusive.

Colt Hoare saw himself as a historian, with his arguments based on facts and not on speculation, as were those of WILLIAM STUKELEY. He was one of the first of the new generation of Romantic aristocratic gentlemen who were travelers, adventurers, artists, and journalist-writer-historians who were also keen barrow diggers. Such antiquaries featured strongly in the pursuit of the understanding of the past during last years of the eighteenth and the early nineteenth centuries, their position both chronologically and ideologically somewhere in between the antiquarians of the Enlightenment, and the professional archaeologists of the mid-nineteenth century.

Tim Murray

See also Britain, Prehistoric Archaeology

Computer Applications in Archaeology

The application of computers to deal with archaeological problems has evolved from the statistical applications of the late 1950s and early 1960s to the current information technology (IT) approach. The development of ever-more user-friendly computer technology has encouraged the adoption of computers among a wider range of archaeologists than just those interested in quantitative analysis. It has been argued that the growing popularity of computer use is mainly owing to the fact that it can facilitate enormously the dissemination of archaeological information to a more generalized public at a relatively low cost. Some archaeologists have even seen the adoption of IT in archaeology as a subdiscipline in its own right. A series of specialized journals and regular meetings attest to this trend, for example, the annual Computer Applications and Quantitative Methods in Archaeology Conference, which, after more than twenty-five years, attracts a growing number of archaeologists from around the world.

This trend has been characterized as a step forward to the ultimate full-fledged embracing of IT by archaeologists. In an evolutionary scheme akin to the Danish archaeologist C. J. THOMSEN's THREE-AGE SYSTEM, the evolution of computer applications in archaeology can be considered as follows: the 1960s were the age of exploration; the 1970s, the age of implementation; the 1980s, the age of exploitation; and the 1990s, the age of information.

Quantitative Applications
In the 1960s, the age of exploration, statistics represented the main practical application of computers to archaeology. The facts that the statistical packages used were developed for mainframe computers and that archaeologists interested in this type of analysis had to have certain knowledge of the programming languages limited the generalized adoption of computers to a certain extent. Nevertheless, toward the second half of the 1970s, there was a noticeable shift in how archaeologists approached their data.

Archaeologists became aware of the need to present and analyze their data in a numerical form, and this shift was fostered by the development of radiocarbon dating, on the one hand, and the development of easier programming languages—e.g., Fortran—on the other. Although statistical applications experienced a decline in the mid-1980s, perhaps as a reaction against the alleged scientism of processual archaeology on the part of postprocessual archaeologists, the development of commercial statistical packages for the personal computer (PC), along with the impact of multivariate statistics, provoked a resurgence of this approach in the 1990s. Overall, it can be said that statistics has remained a favored computer-based application in archaeology throughout time.

Equally favored since the 1970s has been the use of computers in database management. Originally designed to keep museum and site inventories on mainframe computers, the de-

velopment of PC-based programs (e.g., Dbase, Access) has sparked interest in this application. Currently, the development of metadata (i.e., data that documents information about datasets while allowing the expedient transfer and sharing of data between users) has opened the possibility of having access to the enormous resources contained in museum collections and site reports from other research institutions.

Artificial Intelligence and Expert Systems
The 1980s witnessed the emergence of what was presaged as being a revolutionary approach to archaeological problem solving: artificial intelligence (AI) and expert systems. Simply described, AI is a system by which computers are programmed to process data following a rationale similar to that of the human brain. In other words, the goal was to teach computers how to "think" like people. An outcome of AI was the development of expert systems, or programs that can replicate the combined knowledge of human experts addressing a specific problem in order to solve it. By mimicking the advice-giving capabilities of human experts, expert systems can offer intelligent advice or make an intelligent decision about how to solve a problem.

The proponents of this new methodology believed the multidisciplinary nature of the archaeological issues provided the ideal environment in which expert systems could thrive. However, despite the initial clamor and success stories in other disciplines, expert systems have not been fully embraced by archaeologists. Its critics argued that despite the expedient access to expert knowledge that expert systems offered, their main drawback lay in their limited or nonexistent ability to reproduce the uniquely human capabilities of common sense, creativity, and learning. Furthermore, some archaeologists expressed concern that an overreliance on expert systems could be detrimental to the development of archaeological theory.

Attempts to overcome some of the limitations were undertaken, but apparently the momentum was lost. Expert systems gained a moderate level of popularity in archaeology toward the latter part of the 1980s but eventually lost favor and have been practically abandoned, although this by no means implies that they are completely defunct, and it would not be surprising to see them reemerge.

Computer Graphics

It is apparent that the increasingly accessible prices of hardware and the development of more user-friendly software have greatly promoted the use of computers by archaeologists to address all sorts of issues. It is owing to this availability that we have witnessed a dramatic adoption in the application of computer graphics and virtual reality (VR) techniques for the display and analysis of archaeological data. Computers have long offered obvious advantages to archaeological documentation in the recording of excavation plans, artifact illustration, and the processing and presentation of results from scientific analysis, and these advantages are augmented by the ability to apply computer-generated graphics in reconstructive models of archaeological sites and structures. In this field, VR has had a considerable impact on how archaeological data is displayed.

The basic components of VR have been developed since the early 1960s, but the limitations of the available hardware at that time made its use prohibitive, except for those institutions that could afford it, like the military. Nonetheless, the ongoing developments of computer technology and decreasing prices have allowed a more widespread access to this technique. However, the embracement of VR has not been an easy process. The complexity of the graphics needed to reproduce the real world hindered its full acceptance for some time. The first attempts at VR renderings ended up being a disappointing imitation of reality, and the initial hype it created soon simmered down. As a response to this early rejection, current VR systems are more likely to attempt to "simulate" rather than imitate reality, which means that VR graphics will represent models of reality, not reality itself. There is a qualitative difference in this conception since simulated objects are ideal mathematical constructs that are displayed outside reality; consequently, the need for fully immersive systems is removed.

Another initial problem of VR graphics was that performance was dependent on the type of

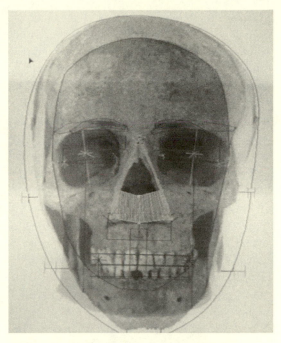

Reconstruction of a man's face from the skull using digital technology (Gamma)

computer platform being used and the level of technical expertise of the user. To cope with these limitations, more-accessible programming languages have been developed since the mid 1990s—such as Virtual Reality Modeling Language (VRML) and Quick Time Virtual Reality (QTVR)—which are intended to become the standard languages for interactive simulations on the worldwide web.

Despite the simplification of the programming language, the production of computer-generated graphics is still a complex process comprising two stages: the modeling and the rendering. In the former, the geometric characteristics of the objects to be created are specified. In the latter, the model created is converted into pictures of the objects, which are then displayed from different perspectives. Simple objects can be created using "primitives," simple predefined geometric shapes, e.g., cubes, spheres, cones, and cylinders. More-complex objects like landscapes or complex buildings cannot be properly modeled with primitives, and in these cases, the simplest building block used is a face of a polygon, and thousands of individual faces may be required.

The results thus obtained can indeed be impressive, but the ongoing issue is whether archaeologists using this technology are merely obtaining pretty pictures or whether these graphic renderings will be of any assistance in the process of deriving better interpretations of the data. That computer-generated graphics can offer much more to archaeology than just pretty pictures is a position that has been adopted by various enthusiasts of these techniques. The insight that can be gained in terms of the social and political relationships reflected in the use of space, and even the construction of detailed models of the actual excavation process of archaeological sites for educational and analytical purposes, have been highlighted as obvious advantages.

What is immediately apparent is that computer graphics can increase public attention with regard to archaeology. The models represent a powerful and persuasive means of conveying to a much wider public the ideas and interpretations that the archaeologist distills from the data. For museums, computer graphics offer the possibility to enhance the way in which collections are presented to the public, for computer-generated graphics can allow the visitor to view the site from various perspectives—a bird's-eye view, walk around it, walk inside it—and thus obtain a more comprehensive impression of how the site may have been seen by its original users. Equally important, three-dimensional documentation of heritage structures can offer great advantages for the referencing and archiving undertaken by government agencies in charge of managing cultural resources.

Computers and Archaeological Knowledge

Although the creation of impressive images and the expeditious and effective manipulation of huge databases are without doubt of great appeal, archaeologists who embrace this technology should proceed with caution. They have to be aware that the sophisticated presentation of data may blind the uncritical eye to the fact that only a minuscule part of the whole may have been captured—and that it may represent our own subjective perception of that reality.

The very nature of the interpretative illustrations of archaeological sites and monuments generated by computer graphics has sparked an increasing amount of discussion. These discussions have centered mainly on the implicit assumption that the images are an all-inclusive, accurate interpretation of the past while, in fact, they may lack a rigorous scientific basis and perhaps represent more of the artist's impression.

It is undeniable that information technology is making groundbreaking contributions to archaeology, but it is not known how exactly this "new" technology impacts archaeological theory and what the consequences will be in terms of production and the dissemination of knowledge. Since the first incorporation of the computer as an analytical tool, in the midst of the paradigmatic shift that the processual archaeology was generating, there was an awareness on the part of some people of the growing need to have dual and simultaneous advances in method and theory.

The relationship between technological development and theory development is akin to what has been identified by some scholars as the interaction between tools and problems. Archaeologists now have access to a revolutionary tool that can handle enormous quantities of data, the computer, but tools can acquire a life of their own, computers in the information age may even come to dominate an entire period of thought. Throughout the history of science we see instances in which the solution to specific problems was delayed by the lack of appropriate tools to address the relevant issues. On the other hand, the availability of certain tools has allowed us to perceive problems, and formulate questions, that otherwise might have remained unidentified. This improved perception can lead to the formulation of new questions that may have a considerable impact on the development of our theoretical underpinnings.

The challenge of this age of information according to its proponents is the "democratization" of knowledge. In other words, not only will the information age facilitate communication among scholars, but it is hoped that it will actually promote international cooperation in archaeological issues.

The democratization of knowledge is an issue that looms large in the minds of those archaeologists who are fully engaged in bringing archaeology up to speed in the information age. It has been noted that since its insertion in the social sciences in the nineteenth century, archaeology has been part of a paternalistic civilizing process. In this sense, the Internet offers the great possibility of radical changes in the hierarchical structure of archaeological knowledge. In the view of these specialists, the growing accessibility to the Internet poses new possibilities in the dissemination and creation of new knowledge, thus making it more difficult for the academy (those professionals inside of universities) to have exclusive control of it.

Armando Anaya Hernández

References

Dingwall, Lucie, Sally Exon, Vince Gaffney, Sue Laflin, and Martjin van Leusen, eds. 1999. *Archaeology in the Age of the Internet.* Proceedings of the Twenty-fifth Anniversary Conference, University of Birmingham, April 1997. BAR International Series 750. Oxford: British Archaeological Reports.

Reilly Paul, and Sebastian Rahtz, eds. 1992. *Archaeology and the Information Age, A Global Perspective.* London and New York: Routledge.

Costa Rica and Nicaragua

In her history of Central American archaeology, DORIS STONE observed that "early archaeology in lower Central America was primarily a part of exploration; sites and surface finds were discovered and described by observant travellers, engineers (and) art historians" (1984, 13). It is true that in the earlier days of exploration and initial investigation—the early and mid-twentieth century—Central American archaeologists were widely traveled and conversant with the prehistoric sites and artifacts of more than one, and frequently all, of the Central American countries. For example, Harvard archaeologist Samuel Lothrop worked in GUATEMALA, EL SALVADOR, Nicaragua, Costa Rica, and PANAMA, and one of his final publications was a synthesis of lower Central America. Harvard ethnologist Herbert Spinden worked in El Salvador and MEXICO, but also wrote extensively about Costa Rica and Nicaragua. Harvard student Doris Stone worked in Costa Rica and Honduras, but has also published widely about the prehistory of other countries in the isthmus.

Of present-day researchers, perhaps only Payson Sheets, who excavated in Panama, Costa Rica, and El Salvador and conducted survey activities in Nicaragua, or Ronald L. Bishop, who conducted extensive analytical programs with jade and ceramic data from Panama, Costa Rica, Nicaragua, Honduras, El Salvador, and Guatemala, approach this breadth of coverage.

Beginning in the early twentieth century, regional syntheses included Costa Rica and Nicaragua (*see* Joyce 1916; Spinden 1917; Lothrop 1966; Baudez 1970; Willey 1971; Stone 1972, 1977; Ferrero 1977). Joyce's synthesis was based on museum collections, while Lothrop, Baudez, GORDON WILLEY, Stone, and Ferrero reflected the gradual growth of the archaeological database; their regional syntheses became increasingly data-based through time.

A number of summary volumes on research in the area have appeared since 1980 (*see* Lange and Stone 1984; Lange 1984; Lange, Sheets, Martinez, and Abel-Vidor 1992; Lange 1992; Graham 1993). In addition to regional overviews, the publications have more complete bibliographic resources for Costa Rican and Nicaraguan archaeology. An annotated bibliography of Central American archaeology and pre-Columbian art is in preparation.

Improved transportation and logistical conditions, as well as changes in archaeological paradigms, methodologies, and analytical possibilities, have affected Nicaraguan and Costa Rican archaeology, just as they have elsewhere. Where entire regions were once available only by horse, mule, on foot, or by dug-out canoe, there are now paved roads. Expanding populations and new communities provide communications and other support in what were once vast empty spaces. Where the dating of ceramic types, or entire sites, was once dependent on cross-association with the better-studied adjacent areas on the southern and eastern frontier of the Maya lowlands, radiocarbon dating has provided a firm chronological basis.

This entry places the history of Costa Rican and Nicaraguan archaeology within the broad outlines established for American archaeology (Willey and Sabloff 1993). However, archaeologists who are nationals of Central American countries often see the development of Latin American archaeology as having its roots in the intellectual history of that region. As Fonseca (1992, 13–15) noted (translation mine):

> The archaeological tradition that has most influenced Latin America, and therefore Costa Rica, is that of North America. . . . [A]s inheritors of European ethnocentrism, the colonizers of North America reserved the concept of history to the study of their own origins, and the related origins of those peoples who influenced the development of their culture (in this case Native Americans). . . . The history of archaeology has acquired different characteristics from country to country, and from region to region. In Costa Rica, archaeologists recently began to explain our ancient history.

This tendency to identify with "our" native ancestors, and to see their remains as the roots of the national heritage, persists even though the Spanish eliminated as much as 95 percent of the indigenous population.

Furthermore, the contrasting histories of the national political systems in Nicaragua and Costa Rica have greatly impacted the development of archaeology. With longer-term stability in the university and museum systems (reflecting stability in the broader political, social, economic, and cultural dimensions of society) Costa Rica has a larger and more mature corps of archaeologists (and auxiliary museum and collaborative specialists such as botanists, chemists, etc.) than does Nicaragua.

Nicaragua

Archaeologically, this is by far the least known of the Central American republics. While there was a great deal of nineteenth century interest, and detailed summaries (Lange et al. 1992; Arellano 1993) have been written, Nicaragua is still little known, particularly in the north and east (see map).

The Non-Scientific/Speculative Period, 1492–1840

Numerous early accounts by Spanish chroniclers contain limited descriptions of goldworking, settlement patterns, subsistence practices, and religious activities. These reports

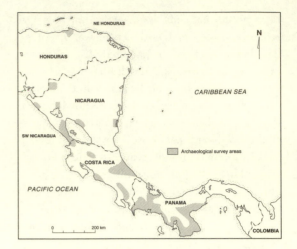

Central American Archaeological Survey Areas

were utilized by late-nineteenth and early-twentieth-century researchers to speculate about external cultural contacts and influences, which were presumed to have been primarily Mesoamerican. These same data, and more recent historical overviews and secondary sources (*see* Radell 1969; MacCloed 1973; Newson 1987; Incer 1990) are being utilized by contemporary researchers to test models of social organization, to supplement archaeological data in the development of cultural-historical sequences, and to define patterns of localized development and regional interaction.

Scientific Research, 1840–Present

Classificatory and Descriptive Period, 1840–1914. Ephraim G. Squier, who had been educated as an engineer, was the United States charge d'affaires to the republics of Central America during the mid-nineteenth century. He published (1852) still-important baseline data on the stone statuary and petroglyphs of Isla Zapatera and other islands in Lake Nicaragua.

Another traveler, Frederick Boyle, described the area of Chontales, and reported seeing pothunters destroying sites and tombs. Boyle not only wrote down his travel observations, but was also, according to Stone (1984, 25), "the first to notice the difference between the monoliths of Chontales, Niquiran, and others in Nicaragua . . . Boyle also illustrated Luna Ware, shoe vessels, and stone faces from Ometepe and Zapatera islands, Mombacho, and Chontales."

Earl Flint and J. F. Bransford conducted some of the first documented excavations in Nicaragua, and their collections are now in the SMITHSONIAN INSTITUTION and in the PEABODY MUSEUM at Harvard University. Flint presented the first scientific report on the famous footprints of Acahualinca, but unfortunately assigned them an excessively speculative age of more than fifty thousand years! Bransford was with a U.S. Navy medical group and took advantage of being in Nicaragua to explore certain aspects of its prehistory. His report described work on Ometepe Island and in the isthmus of Rivas, and illustrated both one of the earliest (Bocana Zoned Incised) and latest (Luna Polychrome) ceramics types known from the area.

Carl Bovallius was a Swedish naturalist who recorded drawings of statues, petroglpyhs, and artifacts, primarily from Zapatera Island. Already in the nineteenth century this island had become a standard stop on the archaeological tour. Karl Sapper also traveled through the area and filed cursory reports on the sites and artifacts he encountered. As a geographer, his environmental and physical descriptions are perhaps of even greater interest.

Classificatory and Historical Period, 1914–1940. While Herbert Spinden never actually conducted archaeological research in either Nicaragua or Costa Rica, his interest in Central American and Mayan archaeology inspired him to suggest models that influenced other scholars who did work in the two countries.

As Doris Stone (1984, 17) noted: "Spinden . . . broadened Lehmann's concept of the archaeological culture center to include three provinces of lower Central America (a) northern Honduras east of La Ceiba and eastern Nicaragua north of Rivas and west of the forest zone; (b) southern Nicaragua; and (c) northern Costa Rica, subdivided into six sections." While based on linguistic data that were not universally accepted at the time, Spinden's model was the first careful attempt to divide prehistoric Nicaragua and Costa Rica into cultural/geographical areas.

Chronological Concerns, 1914–1949. While the historical period ends in 1940 with Willey and

Jeremy Sabloff's scheme, it lasted until into the early 1960s in Nicaragua, where there was a distinct time lag in the development of scientific archaeological research and the establishment of national and regional cultural chronologies. In other parts of Latin America (Mexico, PERU, etc.) chronological sequences had been developed since the 1920s.

Samuel K. Lothrop did not excavate during his sojourn in Costa Rica and Nicaragua in the 1920s. Like Bransford, he originally went to the area as an employee of the United States government, and took advantage of the slow pace of official business to pursue his interests in archaeology. He attempted to relate his descriptive corpus of ceramics to known chronologies from southern MESOAMERICA and Mexico, and, perhaps more importantly, created a two-volume visual museum (Lothrop 1926) of the pre-Columbian ceramic art of Nicaraguan and Costa Rica.

In Nicaragua, a locally defined cultural historical sequence began to emerge only at the very end of the 1950s, when the Institute for Andean Research's "Program on the Inter-relationship of New World Cultures" permitted Gordon Willey and Albert H. Norweb to survey and test a number of sites on the isthmus of Rivas. Wolfgang Haberland also contributed to the development of the Nicaraguan chronological framework with his work on Ometepe with Peter Schmidt in the early 1960s. This also created the first example of methodological contrast, with Hno. Hildeberto Maria carrying on thematic studies on rock art and petroglyphs at the same time that Haberland and Schmidt were conducting their cultural-historical research.

Willey, Norweb, and Haberland's work also marked the beginning of the qualitative imbalance between Costa Rican and Nicaraguan research, with the Nicaraguan sequences being primarily dependent on cross-dating with the better chronometrically controlled sequences (*see* Appendix III; Lange and Stone 1984) from Costa Rica. After thirty years, additional chronometric data from Pacific Nicaragua were obtained by Salgado at the Ayala site in 1992–93 (see below).

Context and Function, 1940–1960. There was little archaeological activity in Nicaragua during this period, although various authors continued to publish on the trinity of stone statuary, footprints, and petroglyphs.

The Beginning of the Explanatory Period, 1960s. In the development of Nicaraguan archaeology, the concerns with context and function of the preceding period were combined with the first efforts at explanation. In addition to their chronology building efforts, Haberland and Schmidt also contributed to the explanation of certain aspects of the archaeological record including shamanism and specialized site use, such as the Concepcion volcano site, El Respiradero.

The Explanatory Period: New Data and Interpretations, 1960s and 1970s. Lydia Wyckoff continued chronology building on the Pacific Coast, while Richard Magnus initiated the first survey and stratigraphic testing on the Atlantic watershed and produced the first chronological sequence for that region. He also searched for data to explain coastal adaptation and to interpret possible connections with other cultural areas. Magnus was instrumental in bringing Nicaraguan nationals such as Silvia Montealegre Osorio, Anibal Martinez, and Franzella Wilson into active participation in archaeological research. In 1973 and 1974, Neil Hughes salvaged mortuary remains and related ceramic and ecological data from a sewer installation in downtown Managua.

Karen Olsen Bruhns initiated a project to study the interrelationships of various styles of Chontales statuary, but lacked a firm chronological linkage between the statues and the established ceramic sequence. She also conducted some work on Zapatera Island in conjunction with the statuary research.

The Explanatory Period: Continuing Methodological and Theoretical Innovations, 1970s–1980s. Healy (1980) analyzed part of the collections from Willey and Norweb's efforts and significantly refined the typology and sequence from the Rivas area of Nicaragua. Nonetheless, the gap between the time of excavation and the time of analysis and publication clearly transcends the era of emphasis on chronological sequence and

local/regional cultural histories and the era of more expansive, if somewhat less precise, model building and systematic explanation.

The first intensive effort to train Nicaraguan nationals in archaeology occurred during the first years of the revolutionary Sandinista government (1979–1985). Most of the archaeologists currently working for the National Museum of Nicaragua received their first opportunities during this era. Various rescue projects were conducted at different sites, primarily on the Pacific Coast by Rigoberto Navarro, Anibal Martinez, Edgar Espinoza, Ronaldo Salgado, Rafael Gonzalez, and Jorge Zambrana. The initial development of a national park system also provided brief protection for important sites such as Isla el Muerto, Isla Zapatera, and Isla Ometepe in Lake Nicaragua. A group from the Milwaukee Public Museum recorded the important petroglpyhs from Isla el Muerto. Much of this research was motivated by the interest and dedication of Amelia Barahona, then director of cultural patrimony.

In 1983, Frederick W. Lange, Payson D. Sheets, and Anibal Martinez carried out a rapid reconnaissance of sites on the Pacific coast of Nicaragua, as well as some sites to the east of lakes Managua and Nicaragua. These studies produced a better map of local Nicaraguan prehistoric development, as well as gathering the obsidian and ceramic specimens that integrated Nicaraguan data with similar databases from southern Mesoamerica and northwestern Costa Rica.

Other important projects carried out by the National Museum of Nicaragua in the 1980s included excavations at the colonial site of Leon Viejo, and at other sites in the Managua urban and Pacific coastal regions. In 1987, Mario Molina and Jorge Levano developed a master plan for the management of the Leon Viejo site. The economic situation that developed during the 1980s made archaeological research increasingly opportunistic and salvage oriented.

These projects were dependent almost exclusively on foreign funding and initiatives, although they were required to involve Nicaraguan counterparts in the fieldwork. Primary among these was the French Archaeological

Mission under the auspices of CEMCA (Centre d'Études Mexicaines et Centramericaines), headquartered in Mexico City. Beginning in 1984, Dominique Rigat and Franck Gorin worked first in the Chontales area east of Lake Nicaragua, and later in the Lake Managua basin in the north central part of the country. These projects contributed to the goal of a national inventory of archaeological sites that is being supported by the Organization of American States, and in Chontales they recovered stone statuary from a dateable context. The research also contributed significantly to our understanding of differences in regional settlement patterns, and in the distribution of imported obsidian, locally available lithic materials, southern Mesoamerican ceramics, and Greater Nicoya ceramics.

Navarro (1993) and Espinosa (1993) have provided brief reviews of some of the projects from the 1980s and the early 1990s.

Recent Developments, 1990s. The first years of the 1990s make it clear that the greatest era of research in Nicaraguan archaeology lies in the future. A Swedish archaeological project, under the direction of Lars Radin, embarked on a first-ever detailed mapping project of Zapatera Island. Laraine Fletcher from Adelphi University (New York) is meeting both national site inventory and settlement pattern and chronological sequence development in unknown areas with a project in the Esteli-Somoto area in north central Nicaragua. Nicaraguan archaeologists (Ronaldo Salgado, Jorge Zambrana, Edgard Espinosa, and Rafael Gonzalez) are participating actively in both of the projects, and gradually assuming increased analytical and reporting responsibilities.

Silvia Salgado, a Costa Rican graduate student at SUNY-Albany, obtained dissertation funding from the National Science Foundation to initiate a project at the Ayala site, near Granada. While she was also able to refine the early part of the regional sequence, her main emphasis was on site hierarchies and internal site organization. She also recovered southern Honduran ceramics that further blurred the poorly defined boundaries between the north-ern edge of "Greater Nicoya" and the southern "frontier" of Mesoamerica.

Nicaraguan archaeologists, as well as some of the foreign archaeologists working in Nicaragua, participated in a National Science Foundation–sponsored conference on the future of research in Greater Nicoya in Costa Rica in May of 1993. The Organization of American States funded the first training course for archaeologists in Nicaragua, from February to June of 1993. The course was extremely successful and benefited from participation by university professors and students and employees of other government institutions in addition to the national museum. Arellano (1993) has edited a volume recapitulating the last thirty years of archaeological research in Nicaragua.

None of the universities in Nicaragua currently offers a degree in archaeology and there are no university-employed archaeologists. The National Museum of Nicaragua employs four archaeologists, all of whom have been trained "on the job" working with foreign archaeological projects; none of the four has a degree in anthropology/archaeology. Of similar concern is the lack of a national archaeological journal (such as *Vinculos,* published by the National Museum of Costa Rica) to provide a local outlet in Spanish of Nicaraguan research, and to educate the government and the public about the importance of protecting and studying the nation's cultural heritage. Despite this somewhat gloomy reality some progress is being made by dedicated archaeologists, working under difficult circumstances.

Costa Rica

Costa Rican archaeology has experienced greater development than has archaeology in Nicaragua. The shift from reliance on foreign archaeologists to a primary dependence on country nationals has largely been completed in Costa Rica. Various authors (*see* Arias 1982; Corrales 1987; Fonseca 1992) have examined the development of archaeology in Costa Rica, and in this section their approaches are merged with the Willey and Sabloff framework. For example, Arias (1982, 4; translation mine) observed that:

An analysis of the theoretical and methodological changes that have occurred in Costa Rican archaeology is not a easy task . . . the models that have been used up to now are the Cultural Historical model and the Cultural Process model, with an additional period that we might call the pre-paradigm period in which there was no theoretical model to guide archaeological investigation.

The Non-Scientific/Speculative Period, 1492–1840

Arias (1982, 4) referred to this as the Pre-Paradigm Period, characterized by the speculations of early chroniclers and conquistadors and later travelers who wrote about the "lifestyles" of the unknown peoples they encountered. They reported customs that were strange, exotic, and foreign to the rapidly dominant European culture.

Scientific Research, 1840–Present

The Classificatory-Descriptive Period, 1840–1914.

This period includes Fonseca's (1992, 15) "period of the pioneers of Costa Rican archaeology" (1850–1925) in which he mentions both Anastasio Alfaro and Carl V. Hartman as being inseparable from the pioneer archaeological effort. Alfaro was trained in museum work at the Smithsonian Institution, "excavated" at the site of Guayabo de Turrialba, and in 1887 founded the National Museum of Costa Rica. Hartman, a Swedish botanist like Bovallius, provided some of the first knowledge of mortuary patterns in Costa Rica, conducting research at both Las Mercedes on the Atlantic watershed and at Las Guacas on the Nicoya peninsula. His practice of carefully recording excavation contexts produced volumes of information that are still of great use.

Taking a broader approach, Arias classified the entire period from 1840 to 1960 as the "synchronic descriptive period," which focused on describing cultures as composed of particular norms and customs, but without an emphasis on temporal change or interrelationships between groups.

Echoing Fonseca's statement, Stone (1984, 27) suggested that Anastasio Alfaro could be considered "the father of Costa Rican archaeology." I would narrow that accolade slightly to a more specific recognition as the father of "museum archaeology" in Costa Rica.

Both Bransford and Flint, previously mentioned in the section on Nicaragua, crossed briefly into northwestern Costa Rica and recorded data from the areas of the Bay of Culebra and the Bay of Salinas, respectively. This was an early reflection of the historical and political unity of the Rivas and Nicoya areas, and an early indication of the relative unity of "Greater Nicoya," a concept later further developed by Lothrop (1926), Norweb (1964), and Lange (1971).

The Classificatory-Historical Period, 1914–1940.

In the local Costa Rican sequence, this correlates roughly with Fonseca's (1992, 15) "Period of Synchronic Description" (1925–1960). Certain aspects of the previous period continued, as reflected in the studies of Jorge Lines and the early publications of Doris Stone and Samuel Lothrop, but overall there was little archaeological activity.

Chronological Concerns, 1914–1940.

As in Nicaragua, in Costa Rica we see a time lag in the development of local chronological sequences when compared with such developments in other parts of the Western Hemisphere. Until the early 1960s, Costa Rican archaeology was dependent on cross-dating with external sequences.

Context and Function, 1940–1960.

During this period Carlos Aguilar Piedra began to train as an archaeologist with studies in Mexico and at the University of Kansas, and in 1953 became professor of archaeology and the main force behind the development of the archaeology program at the University of Costa Rica. He conducted research at the highland site of Retes in the 1950s and sparked public interest in Costa Rican archaeology with the discovery of wooden artifacts preserved beneath a volcanic ash fall. He is the father of modern archaeology in Costa Rica.

This also was the period during which mod-

Table 1. Periodization of Costa Rican and Nicaraguan Archaeology

Wiley and Sabloff (1980)	Fonseca (1992)	Arias (1982)	Corrales (1987)
			Research Design Archaeology (1985–present)
Explanatory-Cont Method Theoretical Innovation (1970s)	Explanatory/ Diachronic 1975–present		
Explanatory-New Data (1960s–1970s)		Explanation of Sociocultural Processes (1970–present)	Priority of Salvage Archaeology (1974–1985)
Explanatory-Begin (1960s)	Descriptive Diachronic (1960–1975)	Diachronic (1960–1970)	
Classificatory-Historical-Context and Function (1940–1960)	Descriptive Synchronic (1925–1960)		
Classificatory-Historical Chronological (1914–1940)	Pioneros (1850–1925)		Official Collecting (1887–1974)
Classificatory-Descriptive (1840–1914) Speculative (1492–1840)		Descriptive Synchronic (1840–1960)	

ern Costa Rica was first conceptually divided into three archaeological areas: northern Pacific, Central Valley and Atlantic watershed, and southern Pacific, with these subdivisions facilitating more detailed control of the slowly developing archaeological data base. As Fonseca (1992, 15) noted, these three cultural and geographical areas coincided with the names of the three indigenous groups first encountered by the Spanish: Chorotega, Huetar, and Boruca. Fonseca points out that a mistake was made at this stage of Costa Rican archaeology in assuming that artifacts found in these areas were automatically made by these peoples. We now know that the contact period cultural appellations have relatively unreliable direct and historical utility beyond the first century or so before the Spanish invasion.

Fieldwork undertaken between 1959 and 1967 resulted in the first chronological sequences for Costa Rica. Under the auspices of the Institute for Andean Research, the Interrelationship of New World Cultures Project under Claude Baudez and Michael Coe developed the basis for the central developmental sequence for northwestern Costa Rica, and Samuel Lothrop developed an initial sequence for the southern Pacific region. Wolfgang Haberland, Laura Laurencich Minelli, and Maria Bozzoli de Wille also contributed to our chronological knowledge of southern Costa Rica, and the close and across-the-border relationship of this area to western Panama.

Beginning of the Explanatory Period, 1960s. Arias (1982, 4) described Kennedy's developed sequence for the Reventazon Valley and Aguilar's sequence for the Guayabo de Turrialba region as the beginnings of the concern with chronology. Matthew W. Stirling also contributed important chronological information to our knowledge of the Atlantic watershed.

In 1969, Lange conducted research in northwestern Costa Rica and broadened the application of the Coe and Baudez chronological sequence. Assuming more of a cultural and ecological approach, he focused on relationships of riverine and coastal adaptation and challenged the long-held assumption that there had been strong Mesoamerican influence in this region.

Explanatory Period: New Data and Interpretations, 1960s and 1970s. Fonseca (1992, 15) designated the period between 1960 and 1975 a "Period of Descriptive Chronology," an accurate representation of local developments in Costa Rica. He also observed (1992, 16) that this was the period in which the diachronic concept of cultures and societies was finally accepted. At the same time Aguilar and Snarskis developed chronological sequences for the Central Valley and Atlantic watershed, and Sweeney completed analysis of some of Coe's earlier work in northwestern Costa Rica. All of these efforts resulted in there being at least a broad chronological framework for the entire country.

Explanatory Period: Continuing Methodological and Theoretical Innovations, 1970s–1980s. Arias (1992, 5) classified this explanatory period as still part of the process of consolidation and as principally characterized by the concern for the explanation of sociocultural processes, with an emphasis on human ecology. Citing Binford, Arias commented that regional studies were the most appropriate means of studying social processes and cultural change, while also noting that it was necessary to continue to develop chronological sequences as an aspect of, but not

the principal objective of, research. She also noted the important transition from speculating about to explaining Costa Rica's past. This transition still largely remains uninitiated, and local newspapers still give credence to wildly speculative explanations about particular sites and cultural historical relationships.

For Fonseca (1992, 15) this was the "Period of Diachronic Explanatory Models." Inspired by the administration of Costa Rican President Daniel Oduber (1974–1978) and National Museum of Costa Rica director Luis Diego Gomez, the first two major site surveys and hypothesis testing projects were initiated. The Bay of Culebra project focused on the development of coastal adaptation in northwestern Costa Rica, and the Guanacaste-San Carlos Project was designed to study the relationships between the Pacific and Atlantic watersheds. Michael J. Snarskis continued with testing and mapping numerous large architectural sites on the Atlantic.

Hector Gamboa was head of the department of anthropology and history at the National Museum of Costa Rica during this period. His understanding of Costa Rican prehistory and his great diplomatic skills, which helped to blend the interests of foreign and national researchers, were essential to the growth in research in Costa Rica during this time.

Oscar Fonseca obtained his M.A. in anthropology from the University of Pittsburgh in 1977 and returned to Costa Rica to assume a pivotal role in the further development of the anthropology and archaeology teaching program at the University of Costa Rica. The University of Costa Rica also began an intensive reevaluation of the site of Guayabo de Turrialba, and used this to support the field training of a whole generation of young Costa Rican students. During this time, Oscar Fonseca, Luis Hurtado de Mendoza, Michael Snarskis, and to a lesser extent Lange supported a significant increase in archaeological training at the university. Unfortunately, the number of available jobs quickly was outpaced by the number of students graduating from the university. Costa Rica has been slow to see the advantages of adding archaeologists to the staffs of the Ministry of Tourism, the National Park Service, the Ministry of Housing, and the like.

In 1977, Costa Rican author Luis Ferrero published the first detailed summary of Costa Rican prehistory. In conjunction with the beginning of the publication of the journal *Vinculos* by the National Museum of Costa Rica in 1975, Ferrero's volume complemented the important function of placing essential data, in Spanish, about Costa Rican prehistory in the hands of Costa Rican students and public.

In the early 1980s Robert Drolet initiated the Boruca Dam–Rio Terraba project in southern Costa Rica, and research on the Bay of Culebra continued under a cooperative arrangement between the National Museum of Costa Rica and the University of California, Los Angeles. Payson Sheets initiated the Lake Arena project in the cordillera of Guanacaste and demonstrated the utility of applying remote sensing technology to Costa Rican archaeology. Winifred Creamer conducted an extensive survey and testing program on the Gulf of Nicoya.

The late 1970s and 1980s saw the definitive transition to vesting principal research responsibilities with Costa Rican archaeologists at the University of Costa Rica and at the National Museum of Costa Rica. Aida Blanco conducted research at the site of Ochomogo in the central highlands, and collaborated with Maritza Gutierrez and Silvia Salgado in the rescue archaeology of the Cenada market site in the metropolitan San Jose area. Magdalena Leon focused on the archaeology of the metropolitan area. Ricardo Vazquez conducted research at the central highland site of Agua Caliente. Sergio Chavez, Ana Cecilia Arias, Maureen Sanchez, Myrna Rojas, Carlos Valdesperras, and Floria Arrea conducted research at central valley sites. Francisco Corrales and Ifigenia Quintanilla developed long-term research in the Central Pacific region, and Olman Solis conducted microsettlement research at one of the sites in the area. Blanco and Juan Vicente Guerrero conducted extensive rescue operations at the La Ceiba in Guanacaste. Marlin Calvo, Leidy Bonilla, and Silvia Salgado mapped and tested a salt production site on the south shore of the Bay of Culebra.

Some of these projects were rescue oriented, while some were pure research in orientation (*see* Lange and Norr 1986). Corrales (1987) has discussed this transition in more detail. Of particular importance were the expansion of research efforts into the Central Pacific coastal region and greatly increased efforts in the Central Valley.

Recent Developments, 1990s. The construction on the Bay of Culebra tourist project began, and research directed by Ellen Hardy was conducted under a contract between the Ministry of Tourism and the National Museum of Costa Rica. There were also signs that the long waiting Boruca Dam impoundment was under reconsideration. Jeffrey Quilter has continued Drolet's research in the Rio Grande de Terraba region, and Aida Blanco is both conducting research and directing a regional museum in the San Isidro region.

In addition, Ifigenia Quintanilla is developing a greatly expanded contextual database for one of Costa Rica's best known prehistoric enigmas, the stone balls of the Diquis region. The French team of Claude Baudez, Sophie Laligant, Natcha Borgnino, and Valerie Lauthel conducted stratigraphic research in the Diquis area that helped to refine the sequences developed by Lothrop and Haberland. John Hoopes has initiated long-term research in the Golfito area.

In an ongoing collaboration between rescue and academic archaeology, the National Museum is also involved in a massive salvage project in the area of the Cañas-Liberia irrigation project in the northwestern region. Research by University of Costa Rica archaeologists is largely restricted to the Central Valley, and the teaching program at the university has been weakened by the departure of some key professors and by a shift in emphasis by the social science division of the university. While not an archaeologist, Adolfo Constenla is making important linguistic contributions (1991) to our understanding of the period immediately preceding the Spanish invasion.

The 1990s saw the first steps toward collaboration between the archaeologists of Costa Rica and Nicaragua. In 1993 they participated in a National Science Foundation–sponsored workshop to discuss the future of research in

Greater Nicoya and in the first training course for young archaeologists to be sponsored in Central America by the Organization of American States.

Conclusion

In this entry, Costa Rica and Nicaragua have been dealt with as two separate entities. In terms of the history of archaeology as it has been practiced in the two countries, this is perhaps the best method. However, in terms of reflecting the prehistory of the two countries, it creates artificial barriers. Nicaragua and Costa Rica share prehistoric cultural communalities along both the Pacific and Atlantic coasts, and Costa Rica has communalities with Panama in the south; Nicaragua with Honduras and El Salvador in the north.

These communalities were recognized by some of the more observant early explorers and archaeologists. These have more recently been concretely demonstrated by instrumental analyses of jade and ceramics conducted by Ronald L. Bishop of the Conservation Analytical Laboratory of the Smithsonian Institution, and obsidian analyses conducted by Fred Stross and Frank Asaro of the Lawrence Berkeley Laboratory at the University of California.

Not only in reviewing the history of Costa Rican and Nicaraguan archaeology but also in foreseeing its future we see the long-term need for balance between cultural and historical studies and the testing of systems and models. There are still vastly unknown areas of Central America (the Nicaraguan and Costa Rican segment of the map is reproduced on page 374) for which we still need the most basic cultural and historical data with which to formulate problems of broader and more general interest.

The history of Nicaraguan and Costa Rican archaeology began with the explorations of early travelers, developed with the assistance of foreign archaeologists, and is gradually becoming the primary responsibility of country nationals. The late 1970s and the early 1980s were a golden age for the development of national archaeology in both countries. In Costa Rica this momentum has been maintained, while in Nicaragua it has stalled temporarily.

Nicaragua and Costa Rica are on the verge of developing the basis for collaboration that is essential for regional studies and for approaching many of the cultural and historical problems that need to be researched. It is hoped that when the next history of the archaeology of these two countries is written, a heightened level of cooperation between the universities, museums, and professional communities will be one of the highlighted themes.

Frederick W. Lange

See also Rouse, Irving

References

Arellano, Jorge Eduardo, ed. 1993. *30 Años de Arqueologia en Nicaragua.* Managua: Instituto Nicaraguense de Cultura.

Arias, Ana Cecilia. 1982. "La Arqueologia en Costa Rica: Vision general de su desarrollo historico." In *Boletin,* Asociacion Costarricense de Arqueologos, pp. 4–6. San Jose: Jimenez and Tanzi Printing.

Baudez, Claude F. 1970. *Central America.* Geneva: Nagel Publishers.

Constenla, Adolfo. 1991. *Las Lenguas del Area Intermedia: Introduccion a Su Estudio Areal.* San Jose: Editorial de La Universidad de Costa Rica.

Corrales, Francisco. 1987. *La Arqueologia de Rescate y el Museo Nacional de Costa Rica.* Tercera Conferencia del Nuevo Mundo Sobre Arqueologia de Rescate. Carupano.

Espinosa, Edgar. 1993. Diez Años en la Arqueologia de Nicaragua. In *30 Años de Arqueologia en Nicaragua.* Edited by J. E. Arellano. Managua: Instituto Nicaraguense de Cultura.

Ferrero, Luis. 1977. *Costa Rica Precolombina.* San Jose: Editorial Costa Rica.

Fonseca, Oscar M. 1992. *Historia Antigua de Costa Rica.* Coleccion Historia de Costa Rica. Editorial Universidad de Costa Rica, San Jose.

Graham, Mark Miller, ed. 1993. *Reinterpreting Prehistory of Central America.* Niwot: University Press of Colorado.

Healy, Paul F. 1980. *The Archaeology of the Rivas Region, Nicaragua.* Waterloo, Ontario: Wilfred Laurier University Press.

Incer, Jaime. 1990. *Viajes, Rutas, y Encuentros, 1502–1838.* San Jose: Libro Libre.

Joyce, Thomas A. 1916. *Central American and West Indian Archaeology, Being an Introduction to the Archaeology of the States of Nicaragua, Costa Rica, Panama, and the West Indies.* New York: Putnam.

Lange, Frederick W. 1971. *Culture History of the Sapoa River Valley, Costa Rica.* Beloit, WI: Beloit College, Logan Museum of Anthropology, Occasional Papers No. 4.

——. 1984. "The Greater Nicoya Archaeological Subarea." In *The Archaeology of Lower Central America.* Edited by F. W. Lange and D. Stone. Albuquerque: University of New Mexico Press.

Lange, Frederick W., ed. 1992. *Wealth and Hierarchy in the Intermediate Area.* Washington, DC: Dumbarton Oaks.

——. 1993. *Precolumbian Jade: New Geological and Cultural Interpretations.* Salt Lake City: University of Utah Press.

Lange, Frederick W., and Lynette Norr, eds. 1986. "Prehistoric Settlement Patterns in Costa Rica." *Journal of the Steward Anthropological Society* 14 (1982–1983). Steward Anthropological Society, Urbana.

Lange, Frederick W., Payson D. Sheets, Anibal Martinez, and Suzanne Abel-Vidor. 1992. *The Archaeology of Pacific Nicaragua.* Albuquerque: University of New Mexico Press.

Lange, Frederick W., and Doris Z. Stone, eds. 1984. *The Archaeology of Lower Central America.* Albuquerque: University of New Mexico Press.

Lothrop, Samuel K. 1926. *Pottery of Costa Rica and Nicaragua.* Contribution, no. 8, 2 vols. New York: Heye Foundation, Museum of the American Indian.

——. 1966. Archaeology of Lower Central America. In *Handbook of Middle American Indians,* vol. 4. Edited by R. W. Wauchope. Austin: University of Texas Press.

MacCloed, Murdo J. 1973. *Spanish Central America: A Socioeconomic History, 1520–1720.* Berkeley: University of California Press.

Navarro, Rigoberto. 1993. Labor del Departamento de Arqueologia (1980–1985). In *30 Años de Arqueologia en Nicaragua.* Edited by J. E. Arellano. Managua: Instituto Nicaraguense de Cultura.

Newson, Linda. 1987. *Indian Survival in Colonial Nicaragua.* Norman: University of Oklahoma Press.

Norweb, Albert H. 1964. Ceramic Stratigraphy in Southwestern Nicaragua. In *Actas y Memorias* del XXXV Congreso Internacional de Americanistas (Mexico, 1962). Vol. 1, pp. 551–561. Mexico.

Radell, David. 1969. "Historical Geography of Western Nicaragua: The Spheres of Influence of Leon, Granada and Managua, 1519–1965." Ph.D. dissertation, University of California.

Spinden, Herbert J. 1917. *Ancient Civilizations of Mexico and Central America,* Handbook Series no. 3. New York: American Museum of Natural History.

Squier, Ephraim G. 1852. *Nicaragua: Its People, Scenery, Monuments, and the Proposed Interoceanic Canal.* 2 vols. New York.

Stone, Doris Z. 1972. *Pre-Columbian Man Finds Central America.* Cambridge, MA: Peabody Museum Press.

——. 1977. *Pre-Columbian Man in Costa Rica.* Cambridge, MA: Peabody Museum Press.

——. 1984. "A History of Lower Central American Archaeology." In *The Archaeology of Lower Central America.* Edited by F. W. Lange and D. Stone. Albuquerque: University of New Mexico Press.

Willey, G. R. 1971. *An Introduction to American Archaeology: South America.* Englewood Cliffs, NJ: Prentice Hall.

Willey, G. R., and J. A. Sabloff. 1993. *A History of American Archaeology.* 3d ed. San Francisco: W. H. Freeman.

Cotter, John L. (1911–1999)

One of the pioneers in establishing historical archaeology in North America, John L. Cotter had an earlier career in prehistoric studies. As a graduate student, he helped excavate the famous Paleo-Indian site of Lindenmeier in Colorado (1934–1936) and the Clovis typesite at Blackwater Draw, New Mexico (1936–1937). After receiving his master's degree in anthropology from the University of Denver in 1935, he worked extensively in the southeastern United States, especially in Kentucky and along the Natchez Trace Parkway in Mississippi. Administratively, he also had experience in southwestern prehistory, serving during the 1940s as the National Park Service supervisor for the Tuzigoot National Monument in Arizona.

Cotter's primary contribution was helping to establish historical archaeology in North America. In 1953, he was assigned by the National Park Service to JAMESTOWN, VIRGINIA (the first permanent English settlement in America in 1607), and there he directed—with the help of Edward B. Jelks, Louis Caywood, Joel

Shiner, and Paul Hudson—three seasons (from 1954 to 1956) of extensive fieldwork. In 1958, this project and the earlier pioneering excavations on the site by J. C. HARRINGTON (1936–1941) were described and published in Cotter's classic work, *Archaeological Excavations at Jamestown, Virginia*.

After working at Jamestown, Cotter returned to Philadelphia, where he had previously done graduate work at the University of Pennsylvania (1936–1937), and completed his doctorate in anthropology there in 1959. Although almost fifty years old, he set out to use the city and its institutions to build his newly adopted specialization. His primary employment was as the northeast regional archaeologist (1957–1970) for the National Park Service office in the city, but it was his secondary affiliations with the University of Pennsylvania and its University Museum that gave him a broader base for building American historical archaeology. Cotter worked in three different but equally constructive settings: as an educator, as an active field archaeologist, and as a professional organizer for the discipline.

In 1960, at the invitation of the new Department of American Civilization at the University of Pennsylvania, Cotter taught a class entitled "Problems and Methods of Historical American Archaeology," the first academic class anywhere in the United States and elsewhere to carry the designation, "historical archaeology." For almost twenty years he taught a series of courses that introduced students to this new subject, and because the city itself was the site explored, he helped to create urban historical archaeology in America. In 1992, he coauthored with Daniel G. Roberts and Michael Parrington *The Buried Past: An Archaeological History of Philadelphia,* the first such synthesis for a major U.S. city.

Much earlier, in January 1967, he was one of a small group of established scholars who assembled in Dallas, Texas, and founded the Society for Historical Archaeology. Cotter served as the society's first president (1967) and coedited the initial volume of its journal, *Historical Archaeology*. Twice he invited the new society to meet in Philadelphia, first to celebrate the county's bicentennial (1976) and six years later

to mark the city's three-hundredth anniversary (1682–1982).

Shortly before his death, the Society for Historical Archaeology created the John L. Cotter Award in Historical Archaeology to honor his memory and to recognize the achievements of researchers (including students) at the start of their professional careers.

Robert L. Schuyler

See also Historical Archaeology
References
Cotter, John L. 1958. *Archaeological Excavations at Jamestown, Virginia*. Archaeological Research Series, no. 4. Washington, DC: National Park Service.
Cotter, John L., Daniel G. Roberts, and Michael Parrington. 1992. *The Buried Past: An Archaeological History of Philadelphia*. Philadelphia: University of Pennsylvania Press.

Crawford, O. G. S. (1886–1957)

O. G. S. Crawford was born in India and grew up with aunts in England. He took an Oxford degree in geography, and the subject of his short thesis was a field survey of archaeology in the Andover district of England. He went to the Sudan to excavate with the Wellcome expedition until World War I began; then he served in the Royal Flying Corps as an observer, was shot down, and became a prisoner of war.

After supplying archaeological details to correct revised editions of Ordnance Survey maps, Crawford was appointed in 1920 as the survey's first archaeological officer, a post he held until his retirement in 1946. Visible monuments and earthworks had been recorded since the survey's first mapping of Britain early in the nineteenth century, but Crawford extended and developed this work into a much fuller record of the nation's visible archaeology, drawing on both scattered or systematic records in other institutions and new field surveys. As well as providing better archaeological notice in the ordinary maps, he surveyed for and drew up a remarkable series of period maps, beginning with *Roman Britain* (1924), the best being, in Crawford's own view, the two sheets of *Britain in the Dark Ages* (1935).

O. G. S. Crawford (Ann Ronan Picture Library)

Wartime experience with flying and photography made Crawford a pioneer archaeological air-photographer (though he was not the very first as air photographs of Stonehenge had been taken from a balloon in 1905). He worked at first by searching out the archaeological features on military photographs, which had, of course, been taken with other purposes in mind. In 1922, he lectured with aerial photographs of Hampshire that showed the archaic "Celtic" field systems of late prehistory. That success led to the publications *Air Survey and Archaeology* (1924); *Wessex from the Air* by Crawford and Alexander Keiller (1928), which reported the results of special flying over Wessex to take new photographs from a hired airplane; and the textbook *Air Photography for Archaeologists* (1929). In these publications, the distinctive earthwork traces from English prehistory were better defined, and the characteristics of later distractions, e.g., pillow mounds built as artificial rabbit warrens, were identified.

Those founding texts of air photography report observations made just in time to record the earthworks of the southern England chalk land before plowing ripped them up. There is an astonishingly crisp detail on a great many of the early classic photographs. Building on the access the survey had as a state agency to military and other government aerial photographs, Crawford made it the focus for the new discipline. After retiring from the survey, he took up fieldwork again in northeastern Africa. In 1927, Crawford founded the journal *Antiquity,* which he edited until his death.

Much of the archaeological record of the Ordnance Survey was lost in the bombing of its Southampton office in 1940. Reorganizations many years later transferred the survey's archaeological interests into those of the royal commissions for ancient monuments in England, Scotland, Wales, and Northern Ireland, where they are combined also with the aerial-photographic archive as part of the present consolidated field and survey records of each nation's archaeology.

In *Man and His Past,* begun during World War I and published in 1921, Crawford set out the enduring fundamentals of his view of archaeology, which I think might best be described, in its developed form, in terms of its being a "topographical landscape history." He valued the enormous mass of information in, for example, the many large-scale manuscript maps that had been made of country estates over the decades, and he photographed these maps at the survey to bring the scattered reports into a centralized archive record. The weakness of the previous topographic work lay in its woolly and unhistorical approach. The idea of classifying human settlements by their function and position in a structured landscape was sound, but one needed a clear framework of chronology and some decent knowledge of function to put it into some reasoned order. There is now a distinctive style of British landscape archaeology that combines detailed study and mapping of surface earthworks with aerial photography and limited excavation at those points where key relationships may be shown stratigraphically; this robust and practical approach owes much to Crawford's influence and example, which was perfectly straightforward and very well thought through. (Crawford once said to English archaeologist SIR MORTIMER WHEELER about *Antiquity,*

"What I want is simple, clear-minded stuff that any intelligent fool can understand.") This approach is not usually theoretical in a self-consciously explicit way, but still it is not unsystematic.

Contemporaries saw Crawford as a distinctive individualist with a strong and independent spirit. Wheeler told with relish the scandal that echoed around archaeological Wales when Crawford received Welsh archaeologists visiting his excavation wearing *shorts*—"Thereafter for thirty seven years he was one of my closest friends, and his boyish glee in calling the bluff of convention never left him." Crawford's autobiography is full of tales of conflict between his free spirit and the bureaucratic systems of the Ordnance Survey.

Crawford's later work *Archaeology in the Field* (1953) shows him drifting away from his early principles, and his last work, *The Eye Goddess* (1957), is alarmingly lacking in that robust good sense and clear attention to good chronology that before had been the Crawford style. In 1955, however, Crawford wrote a good autobiography, *Said and Done*.

Christopher Chippindale

References

Crawford, O. G. S. 1921. *Man and His Past.* London: Milford.

———. 1924a. *Air Survey and Archaeology.* Ordnance Survey Professional Papers, new series, 7. Southampton: Ordnance Survey.

———. 1924b. *Map of Roman Britain.* Southampton: Ordnance Survey.

———. 1929. *Air Photography for Archaeologists.* Ordnance Survey Professional Papers, new series, 12. London: Ordnance Survey.

———. 1935. *Map of Britain in the Dark Ages.* 2 sheets. Southampton: Ordnance Survey.

———. 1953. *Archaeology in the Field.* London: Phoenix House.

———. 1955. *Said and Done: The Autobiography of an Archaeologist.* London: Phoenix House.

———. 1957. *The Eye Goddess.* London: Phoenix House.

Crawford, O. G. S., and A. Keiller. 1928. *Wessex from the Air.* Oxford: Oxford University Press.

Cunningham, Alexander (1814–1893)

Alexander Cunningham went to India from England as an army engineer in 1833 and fell, as a young man, under the influence of JAMES PRINSEP, who had undertaken the task of reorienting the research interests of the members of the Asiatic Society of Bengal founded in 1784. The society was the focal point of European research activities in India, and under Prinsep's secretaryship these interests veered from mere literary speculations to field investigations.

By the mid-1830s, Cunningham was assisting Prinsep with his research, in particular with the study of Kharosthi, the principal ancient script of the Indian northwest. Until 1842, as his publications show, Cunningham was interested principally in the study of coins and seals—some of them Roman—that were then being found in profusion in the northwestern part of India. He never lost this early interest in scripts and coins, and his publications, such as *Inscriptions of Asoka* (1877), *Coins of Ancient India from the Earliest Times down to the Seventh Century* A.D. (1891), and *Coins of Mediaeval India from the Seventh Century down to the Muhammadan Conquests* (1894), are eloquent testimony to its persistence in his life.

Another major line of investigation pursued by Cunningham was in the area of ancient Indian architecture. He published a detailed study of ancient temples in Kashmir in the *Journal of the Asiatic Society of Bengal* in 1848 and followed that work with *The Bhilsa Topes,* a study of the Buddhist stupas at Sanchi and in its neighborhood (1854); *The Stupa of Bharhut* (1879); and *Mahabodhi, or the Great Buddhist Temple under the Bodhi Tree at Bodh-Gava* (1892).

Cunningham also contributed a great deal to the elucidation of various historical problems related to ancient India, and his analyses of dynastic issues in his Archaeological Survey of India Reports constitute the primary evidence of this contribution. Another of his abiding interests was the study of ancient Indian historical geography based on both archaeological surveys and textual material. This study culminated in the publication of *The Ancient Geography of India* (1871).

However, it is for his Archaeological Survey of India Reports that Cunningham maintains a permanent place in the history of Indian archaeology. Of the twenty-three volumes published in this series between 1862 and 1887, twelve were written by Cunningham himself, two were written by him in collaboration with an assistant, and the rest were written by his three assistants in the Archaeological Survey of India—J. D. Beglar, A. C. L. Carlleyle, and H. W. Garrick. As far as the archaeology of the area between the northwestern hills and Bengal is concerned, these reports constitute a major source of information even today.

The Archaeological Survey of India was established by the government of India in 1861 mainly owing to Cunningham's persuasion. He became its first director-general/director on his retirement from military service. After four years the survey was disbanded to be reestablished in 1870–1871, with Cunningham again in charge. He retired from this duty in 1885. His main interest in archaeology was topographical, and he followed the routes traveled by Alexander the Great and two famous Chinese pilgrims, Hiuen Tsang (seventh century A.D.) and Fa-Hian (fifth century A.D.), and identified and described ancient sites along the way. Some of the most important ancient city sites of India owe their identifications to him. He was not much of an excavator, but he mapped out sites on a scale that has not yet been equaled in India.

Dilip Chakrabati

See also South Asia

Cunnington, William (1754–1810)

A middle-class cloth merchant who, like his wealthy patron, SIR RICHARD COLT HOARE, developed a passion for excavating English barrows and graves. He lead Colt Hoare's archaeology team, and with draftsman Philip Crocker surveyed a huge part of Wiltshire, locating ancient sites and earthworks. It was Cunnington who supervised the excavation of some 379 barrows and who ensured that observations were recorded accurately and carefully. He also divided barrows into five types and used stratigraphy to identify primary and secondary burials. While coins were used to date some barrows,

Cunnington argued that it was possible that graves with only stone artifacts in them might be earlier than those that contained metal ones. Notwithstanding these advances in fieldwork methods and in the analysis of artifacts neither Cunnington nor his patron Colt Hoare was able to convincingly demonstrate a relative chronology for these English monuments.

Tim Murray

See also Britain, Prehistoric Archaeology

Curtius, Ernst (1814–1896)

Curtius was born in Lubeck and studied philology and philosophy in Bonn, Gottingen, and Berlin. In 1837 he traveled to newly independent GREECE and visited the site of Olympia, the excavation of which was to become his lifelong work. He returned to Germany and obtained his doctorate in Halle in 1841. In 1844 he was appointed tutor to the German Crown Prince, the future Emperor Friedrich III, and professor of classical philology in Berlin. In the same year he published his most important work, a two-volume description of the Peloponnese, which was the result of his travels in the 1830s.

In 1856 Curtius returned to Gottingen as professor of classical philology and archaeology. He published *Griechische Geschichte,* which became the most widely read Greek history written in German, republished five more times. In 1868 he moved to Berlin as professor of classical archaeology. HEINRICH SCHLIEMANN's successes at Troy led to German government support of Curtius's long-planned excavation of Olympia. In 1874 he signed an agreement with the Greek government that not only allowed German scholars exclusive rights to excavate Olympia, but also provided for the exhibition of finds at the site. This was the first government-supported excavation in Greece, and it became a model for other countries who wished to work there and respect Greek antiquities and the right of the Greek government to keep them. Curtius also helped to found the German Archaeological Institute (DEUTSCHES ARCHÄOLOGISCHES INSTITUT) in Athens.

Olympia was excavated between 1875 and 1881 (and again from 1936 to 1941 and since

1952). Excavations revealed the layout of Greece's most important and largest religious shrine, locating the temple of Hera, the great altar of Zeus, and the Olympic stadium. The only major surviving sculpture by Praxiteles, "Hermes carrying the infant Dionysus," was also unearthed at the site. Model techniques of excavation and stratigraphy were employed at the site, and the amount of valuable sculptural, numismatic, and epigraphic material found was very great. The results were edited by Curtius in five volumes. While Curtius's primary achievement was his organization and editing of the excavations at Olympia, he also inspired many scholars with his love of Greece and its past.

Tim Murray

See also German Classical Archaeology

Cushing, Frank Hamilton (1857–1900)

Cushing was born in Pennsylvania and grew up near Albion in New York State. His poor health as a child resulted in a circumscribed but intense education in the fields and woods of his immediate environment. It was during his explorations that Cushing was to find the Indian arrowhead that stimulated his lifelong interest in ethnology. At eighteen he studied natural science at Cornell University and wrote an article about the natural history of his neighborhood in New York. This was published by the SMITHSONIAN INSTITUTION, whose staff were so impressed that they offered him a job.

In 1879 Cushing was appointed to the new Bureau of American Ethnology, which was closely connected to the Smithsonian Institution. Under the directorship of geologist and explorer JOHN WESLEY POWELL (1834–1902) the Bureau became the center for anthropological research in North America. While its mandate was to study the ethnography and linguistics of Native American people so as to better administer Indian affairs, the bureau also had a considerable impact on the development of North American archaeology.

The bureau maintained the view that there was no real difference between indigenous American peoples in the nineteenth century and their prehistoric ancestors. In an environment that denied indigenous American peoples their histories, archaeologists gained insights into the past by working closely with ethnologists and modern native people. In this way prehistoric archaeology was defined as a branch of anthropology.

Cushing and his Bureau colleague J. W. Fewkes (1850–1930) pioneered this approach, known as the direct historical method. They used ethnographic parallels to interpret, by analogy, the activities of prehistoric people. Cushing was so interested in the processes by which the artifacts he found were made that he became a master of indigenous technologies, arts, and crafts.

His outstanding achievements include his studies of the Zuni Pueblo Indians, made over the five years that he lived with them, his explorations of ancient pueblos in the Salt River Valley in Arizona, and his investigations of the ancient inhabitants of Key Marco, Florida. His *Zuni Creation Myths* (1896) and *Zuni Breadstuff* (1920 republished) remain ethnological classics.

Tim Murray

See also United States of America, Prehistoric Archaeology

Cyprus

The history of archaeology on the Mediterranean island of Cyprus exemplifies issues common to many areas. Several intertwined themes are discussed in this entry—largely within a general chronicle of discovery and research with a concentration on the prehistoric periods—including issues of nationalism, colonialism, and gender alongside academic traditions in constructing local archaeological practice and styles. The impact of specific political events and other factors provides a significant background, structuring both attitudes and developments. The influence of individual researchers is also especially marked in the archaeology of so small an area.

In the middle of the nineteenth century, many foreign officials resident in Cyprus began

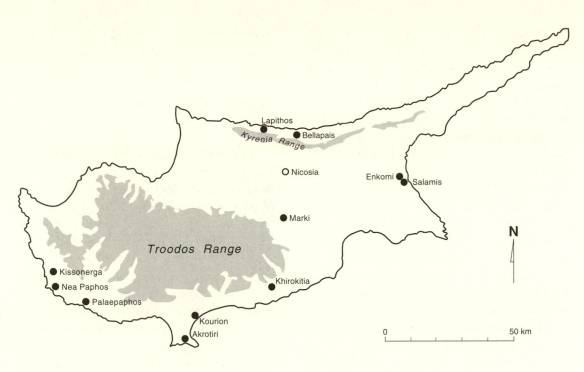

Archaeological Sites in Cyprus

to collect and excavate for antiquities, motivated less by academic concerns than by a spirit of acquisitiveness and competition, sometimes enhanced by financial motives. A more circumspect attitude toward the Ottoman rulers of Cyprus might have been appropriate for consular officials like Sir Robert Hamilton Lang, but when official permits were not forthcoming, excavation and the subsequent exportation of antiquities continued nonetheless.

The most flamboyant and active of these early predators was the Russian and American consul, General LUIGI PALMA DI CESNOLA. His vast collections, obtained by large-scale plundering of tombs and other sites, were exported from the island after 1870. Most of this material—over 10,000 items—was finally purchased by the Metropolitan Museum in New York City, and part of the deal resulted in Cesnola's appointment as the first director of that museum. Lavish publications did little to allay scholarly disapproval of Cesnola's methods and abilities. His brother, Major Alexander Palma di Cesnola, continued the family tradition by excavating in Cyprus in the 1870s for a British collector who subsequently sold the material in Great Britain.

Other consular collectors began to move be-

yond simple acquisition. Thomas Backhouse Sandwith is generally credited with being the first to attempt to establish a pottery sequence, initially presented in a paper to the SOCIETY OF ANTIQUARIES OF LONDON in 1871. Most antiquarian activity on the island was more concerned simply with acquisition until a major political development in 1878 led to the establishment of British rule.

Although Cyprus was administered by Britain, it remained a part of the Ottoman Empire until 1914 when it was formally annexed to the British Empire. Initial administration of the Ottoman antiquities laws was inadequate, despite the establishment of a museum in 1883, and the situation did not change significantly for some decades. One immediate reaction to the British takeover was an upsurge of interest on the part of professional archaeologists, especially those based at the BRITISH MUSEUM. From 1879 onward, Max Ohnefalsch-Richter worked at numerous sites on behalf of the British Museum, which thereby obtained a significant share of the finds. Other British museums also obtained small collections by contributing to the costs of fieldwork.

A major development was the foundation of the Cyprus Exploration Fund in 1887 to provide a more professional approach to research by the British archaeological establishment. The impetus for this development was clearly from classical, rather than western Asiatic, archaeologists, as the former found Cyprus to be a freely accessible field as it was the only area for classical archaeology under British rule. This move can be seen as part of a generally negative attitude toward TURKEY and the Ottoman Empire by western Europeans and the extension of a long-standing philhellenic attitude. These biases—cultural, political, and academic—resulted in several factors that were to have lasting effects on archaeological research on the island. One is the tendency to view the island from the Hellenic west, rather than the east, and a related tendency to see Cyprus as an intermediary between the two cultural hemispheres of Asia and Europe. Another—no less important—factor was the establishment of English as the first language of Cypriot archaeology instead of either Greek or Turkish.

The Cyprus Exploration Fund sponsored the excavation of several sites on the island during most of the1890s, principally under the aegis of the British Museum. The various participants brought an increased professionalism to the archaeology of the island, although work was not always up to contemporary standards. The research of one member, JOHN L. MYRES, was of a far higher quality than that of his colleagues, and the *Catalogue of the Cyprus Museum,* published by Myres and Ohnefalsch-Richter in 1899, and Myres's subsequent *Handbook of the Cesnola Collection of Antiquities* (1914), established many of the basic structures that still condition archaeological thought. For example, his classification of pottery provided the basis for all future work. Another crucial development was the introduction of the formal divisions of the Bronze Age, following the system developed on Crete by SIR ARTHUR EVANS and applied more widely in the Aegean.

An equally, if not more, significant development occurred in the 1920s. As the result of an accidental meeting with Luki Pierides, a scion of an important Cypriot family whose members had a long-standing and sophisticated interest in the history and antiquities of the island, the

Swedish classical archaeologist Axel Persson sent a doctoral student to work on the island. EINAR GJERSTAD's thesis, *Studies on Prehistoric Cyprus* (Gjerstad 1926), reviewed all available data on the Bronze Age and supplemented that data with new stratigraphic excavations at several sites.

Gjerstad revised and elaborated earlier pottery classifications, he used technological and formal characteristics to segment wares into typological series with clear chronological associations, and the proportional seriation of wares in his stratified sequences replaced the earlier presence/absence seriations used for tomb material by Myres. This change allowed Gjerstad to subdivide the Bronze Age into finer chronological units, which he did by developing a formal tripartite division for each of the three major periods—an approach that Myres criticized. Myres would have preferred to see the introduction of a more fluid system, along the lines of the sequence-dating system developed by WILLIAM MATTHEW FLINDERS PETRIE in Egypt, but Myres's suggestion was never followed and Cypriot archaeology has remained structured by Gjerstad's rigid set of chronological referents.

The dominance of Gjerstad's approach was ensured by the work of the Swedish Cyprus Expedition, which changed the archaeological landscape of the island. Following his doctoral research, Gjerstad devoted himself to raising funds for a major research project on Cyprus, and from 1927 to 1931, he and three Swedish colleagues excavated their way around the island. They formed an exceptionally efficient and professional team, and as they dug, they processed the finds, and within a few years the basic volumes of site reports were published. It took another forty years for the final summary volumes to appear, but these included more comprehensive studies of material and were not confined to the immediate results of the expedition.

The Swedish Cyprus Expedition was not the only expedition working on the island, but its work was by far the most substantial in scale. From the 1930s onward, the pace of research increased. Minor work—such as rescue excavations of tombs discovered during building works or being plundered by looters—was carried out by staff of the Department of Antiquities, and PORPHYRIOS DIKAIOS was the most important of these workers. In 1931–1932, he carried out major excavations at the early Bronze Age cemetery at Bellapais-Vounous, but his most significant work for the next thirty years was on earlier sites.

His highly professional and extensive excavations at a series of Neolithic and Chalcolithic settlement sites, such as KHIROKITIA-VOUNI, were matched by model site reports. In establishing the basic structures for research Dikaios attempted to place his sites in an evolutionary scheme, tracing developments from one cultural system to another. Many of the difficulties of dating and cultural associations that he grappled with have now become redundant as a result of radiometric dating techniques, but his work is a classic example of the influence of technique and approach on explanation. Many aspects of terminology and the definition of cultures and periods introduced by Dikaios have affected later research.

In contrast to the earlier periods, the archaeology of the early and middle Bronze Ages has until recently been based almost exclusively on tomb material. Dikaios's work at Bellapais-Vounous was followed by equally extensive excavations by James Stewart, and both projects were initiated largely to salvage material before tombs could be robbed. The value of goods from Bronze Age tombs also encouraged museum-funded research, for foreign excavators could, until Cypriot independence in 1960, expect a generous share of the material excavated. A change in the policy regarding the export of antiquities has had a significant effect on the style, or even the possibility, of fieldwork. It is unlikely, for example, that many teams, including the Swedish Cyprus Expedition, could have obtained the funds to carry out their work without the promise of material rewards to sponsoring countries or institutions.

Apart from the massive losses of material through the looting of sites and the dispersal of thousands of items by nineteenth-century collectors, Cypriot material from scientific excavations is also distributed all around the world, and the attempt to catalog holdings in public museums through the gradual production of a corpus of Cypriot antiquities has done a little to overcome this problem. The series, initiated by Paul Åström, is a specifically Cypriot version of the *Corpus Vasorum antiquorum,* and it fits well with the object-oriented approach that is common to most Cypriot archaeology.

James Stewart followed his excavations at Bellapais by embarking on a massive early Bronze Age project, but by time of his death in 1962 only an abstract had been completed as one of the final volumes of the Swedish Cyprus Expedition. Stewart's exhaustive undertaking involved a comprehensive corpus and a complex, idiosyncratic classification of pottery, refining and developing on the ware series set up by Gjerstad, coupled with an intricate—many would say unusable—typology of shape. Stewart could develop a chronology of individual artifacts and tomb groups, but other aspects of analysis or explanation could only be addressed by generalized, ad hoc interpretations of behavior: the primary interest was in developing an artifact-based historical narrative.

Until recently, much of Cypriot archaeology has been characterized by a primarily historical approach, although different issues affect the questions addressed in different periods. The late Bronze Age, in contrast to the preceding periods, is well represented by excavations of settlements, especially the large cities that developed on the coast at that time. These, and the rich tombs associated with them, provide an array of more complex and exotic items, for at the time Cyprus was part of the international trading systems of the eastern Mediterranean. Goods were exported to and imported from Egypt, the Levant, Anatolia, and the Aegean. The rich tombs of the period, with their gold jewelry and exotic pottery, encouraged excavation early on, and the presence of Mycenaean types was of particular interest, for they were tangible evidence of an association with Greece.

Modern Greek Cypriots are naturally interested in when Greeks first came to the island and when the Greek language was introduced, but both earlier and more recent archaeologists have been similarly influenced, especially as the initial researchers came to the island from the

Bust of thirty-year-old bearded man from the classic period, 500 B.C., now in the Louvre (Gamma)

Aegean world. Philhellenic strands within scholarship and nationalism have to some extent encouraged a perception of more significant relationships westward, while equally strong, if not stronger, eastern associations have often been played down. These underlying factors also fit most comfortably with a general culture-historical approach to archaeological explanation, identifying specific events and peoples. Similarly, the archaeology of later periods in Cyprus, especially those of historical periods, tends to follow the established, more art-historical frameworks of research, like elsewhere in the Mediterranean.

While Cyprus was a British colony the director of the Department of Antiquities, like the directors of other government departments, was British even though highly qualified Cypriot archaeologists, such as Dikaios, carried out world-class research. After independence in 1960, control passed entirely into Cypriot hands, but that change did not lead to a reduc-

tion in the scale or intensity of foreign research work on the island. Instead, the first Cypriot director of the Department of Antiquities, VASSOS KARAGEORGHIS, encouraged international expeditions. This tradition of hospitality continues, and each year up to twenty foreign teams from a wide array of countries excavate on the island. Karageorghis imposed one inflexible rule: he insisted on adequate publication, and that policy has recently been reinforced by the current director, Sophocles Hadjisavvas. Karageorghis himself led by example, producing comprehensive site reports on his own major excavations at sites such as SALAMIS, Kition, and Maa. A major research component is an integral part of the duties of all staff members in the Department of Antiquities, along with curatorial and administrative responsibilities and the constant demands of salvage excavations.

In 1974, Turkish forces invaded and occupied the northern part of the island. An exchange of populations followed, with Greek-speaking, Christian Cypriots moving south and Turkish-speaking, Muslim Cypriots concentrating in the north. The island remains divided, but except for Turkey, no countries recognize the legitimacy of the Turkish administration in the north. The only internationally accepted legal authority is the government of the Republic of Cyprus, which is, in practice, the government of Greek Cyprus with effective control in the south.

The political situation has had a dramatic impact on archaeological research. Quite apart from the destruction and looting of sites and collections in inadequately policed areas, there has been no formal archaeological work in the Turkish-controlled north since 1974. The Department of Antiquities was always dominated by Greek-speaking Cypriots, who now can operate only in the south, and all foreign archaeologists, too, work only in the south. In a purely legalistic sense, excavators in the north would be digging illegally as it is not likely that they would have a permit from the accepted authorities, but most excavators also have closer personal associations with Greek Cypriots and Greek Cyprus. It is possible to argue that the original philhellenism of the earlier generations of archaeologists has carried through to modern researchers and has been reinforced by dealings with the better-educated Greek Cypriot officials and scholars. The situation may have biased some aspects of earlier research, but since 1974, it has had a dramatic practical effect as all recent excavations are concentrated in one part of the island so that a significant bias in primary data is gradually being created.

This bias is best illustrated by a long-term regional project directed by Edgar Peltenburg. Relocating his research from the north coast after 1974, Peltenburg has carried out extensive excavations at a series of Chalcolithic sites on the south coast, principally at Lemba and Kissonerga. When combined with Dikaios's earlier work, there is now a solid basis for a discussion of the earlier prehistoric periods along the southern coast but little immediate prospect of comparative data from the northern half of the island.

Archaeologists from eighteen different nations have attended conferences in Cyprus, and apart from Cypriot scholars, the most active participation came from France, Great Britain, and the United States, the last clearly increasing in quantity. This increase has been partly promoted by the establishment of the Cyprus-American Archaeological Research Institute in Nicosia, which until recently was the only foreign institution of its kind on the island. There is now also a Cypriot section of the Athens Archaeological Society based in Nicosia.

Although excavations dominate Cypriot research, there has been a long tradition of archaeological survey. During the 1950s, Hector Catling established the Cyprus Survey within the Department of Antiquities, and he led a team of Cypriot archaeologists on a series of extensive surveys with the long-term view of covering the whole island. This ambitious plan could not be carried out, but Catling's initial studies of settlement pattern provided the basis for later more sophisticated work by Nicholas Stanley Price and Steven Held, both looking at the earlier prehistoric periods. David Rupp's Canadian Palaepaphos Survey Project has been the most substantial regional survey project; it used conventional survey strategies to document sites within a large river valley. Surveys by

Bernard Knapp in the northwestern foothills of the Troodos have introduced more complex methods of off-site recording and analysis.

The relocation of refugees after 1974, coupled with a boom in tourism, led to large-scale developments in southern Cyprus, which has placed excessive pressure on many important sites. Although some rescue work can be carried out, Cypriot heritage managers are severely hampered by inadequate resources and ineffective penalties imposed on offenders. The impact of tourism on both site management and developing archaeological practice and theory is almost entirely negative. Specific, more impressive sites—mainly those of later antiquity, such as PAPHOS—provide the main focus for tourists. Those sites and associated information in museums reinforce a formal, object-oriented, and simple culture-historical view of the past.

Since the early 1970s there have been sporadic attempts at processual or "new" archaeology. Nicholas Stanley Price, working on the early prehistoric periods, and David Frankel, working on the middle Bronze Age, were among the first to introduce a more self-conscious concern with method and theory and an analytical approach to data to derive behavioral rather than historical explanations of the past. This trend is especially marked in prehistoric archaeology, rather than that of later antiquity, as can be seen in papers given at a conference on early society in Cyprus held in 1988 (Peltenburg 1989).

Among current modern approaches are Steven Held's ecologically based analysis of colonization and settlement pattern, Alain Le Brun's symbolic analysis of features at Khirokitia, Bernard Knapp's processual and postprocessual discussions of the late Bronze Age, Jenny Webb and David Frankel's consideration of discard and site formation, and Priscilla Keswani's analyses of the development of hierarchies. Ceramics still provide the basis for much of Cypriot archaeology, but there are significant moves away from the older typological approaches, as is illustrated by many of the papers given at a conference on Cypriot ceramics (Barlow, Bolger, and Kling 1991).

Despite these developments, Cypriot archaeology as a whole, especially that of late antiquity, remains firmly within a tradition that emphasizes excavation, description, and culture-historical explanation. Its greatest strength lies in this primary concern for data and a well-established tradition of substantial site reports providing the basis for explanations of all kinds.

David Frankel

See also Enkomi-Ayios Iakovos; Kourion; Pieridou, Angeliki; Taylor, Joan du Plat

References

Åström, P. 1971. *Who's Who in Cypriote Archaeology: Biographical and Bibliographical Notes.* Studies in Mediterranean Archaeology 992. Göteborg, Sweden: Paul Åströms Forlag.

Åström, P., E. Gjerstad, R. S. Merrillees, and A. Westholm. 1994. *The Fantastic Years on Cyprus: The Swedish Cyprus Expedition and Its Members.* Studies in Mediterranean Archaeology Pocketbook 79. Jonsered, Sweden: Paul Åströms Forlag.

Barlow, J. A., D. L. Bolger, and B. Kling, eds. 1991. *Cypriot Ceramics: Reading the Prehistoric Record.* Philadelphia: University of Pennsylvania Press.

Gjerstad, E. 1926. *Studies on Prehistoric Cyprus* Uppsala.

Goring, E. 1988. *A Mischievous Pastime: Digging in Cyprus in the Nineteenth Century.* Edinburgh: National Museums of Scotland.

Held, S. O. 1990. "Back to What Future? New Directions for Cypriot Early Prehistoric Research in the 1990s." *Report of the Department of Antiquities, Cyprus* 1–43.

Karageorghis, V. 1999. *Excavating at Salamis in Cyprus 1952–1974.* Athens: A. G. Leventis Foundation.

Karageorghis, V., ed. 1985. *Archaeology in Cyprus 1960–1985.* Nicosia: A. G. Leventis.

Merrillees, R. S. 1975. "Problems in Cypriote History." In *The Archaeology of Cyprus: Recent Developments,* 15–38. Ed. N. Robertson. Park Ridge, NJ: Noyes Press.

Peltenburg, E. 1989. *Early Society in Cyprus.* Edinburgh: Edinburgh University Press.

Webb, J. M., and D. Frankel. 1995a. "Gender Inequity and Archaeological Construction: A Cypriot Case Study." *Journal of Mediterranean Archaeology* 8, no. 2: 93–112.

———.1995b. "'This Fair Paper, This Most Goodly Book': Gender in the Archaeology of Cyprus, 1920–1990." In *Gendered Archaeology: Proceedings of the Second Australian Women in Archaeology Conference,* 34–42. Research Papers in Archaeology and Natural History. Ed. J. Balme and W. Beck. Canberra: Australian National University.

Cyriac of Ancona (1391–1454)

Regarded by many scholars as the earliest archaeologist, Cyriac of Ancona (whose real name was Ciriaco de' Pizzicolli) was, beginning in 1423, an inveterate traveler throughout Greece and along the Mediterranean coast of Turkey with a passion for collecting inscriptions. The latter he derived from monuments, which he also drew. Although much of his work was destroyed, some fragments of his drawings survive (Schnapp 1996, 110–114).

Tim Murray

References

Schnapp, Alain. 1996. *The Discovery of the Past.* London: British Museum Press.

Czech Republic
Background

The Czech Republic lies in central Europe and since the sixth century A.D. has been inhabited by Czechs who speak a Slavic language but whose culture has been more Western European in style since the Middle Ages. At that time the territory, almost identical with its present frontiers, formed the Kingdom of Bohemia, part of the Holy Roman Empire of the Middle Ages. Later it was integrated into the Austrian Empire, and in 1918 it gained new independence under the name of Czechoslovakia. It became an island of western-type democracy in the 1930s, when all the surrounding countries were ruled by authoritarian or fascist regimes. In an act of appeasement Czechoslovakia was given to Adolf Hitler by the west European powers in 1938. It was occupied by Germany in 1939, and at the end of World War II the Great Powers decided at Yalta that Czechoslovakia should belong to the Russians after the war. It remained formally independent, becoming a Soviet satellite state. After a short period of liberalization in the 1960s it was occupied by the Soviet army in 1968 to stop what seemed to be a development toward democracy. It regained full independence in

1989 during the process of the disintegration of the Soviet empire, and it is now striving to revitalize contacts with western democracies that were severed in 1938. The eastern part of Czechoslovakia, Slovakia, chose independence in 1992, so what remained is the Czech Republic. From the geographic point of view and also historically, the Czech Republic has been divided into two parts: the west is called Bohemia, the east, Moravia.

The archaeological record of both Bohemia and Moravia began in the early Paleolithic period. It was richly structured into settlement sites, cemeteries (both "flat" and those with surviving barrows), hoards, fortifications, ritual monuments, and so forth. The number of sites runs to the thousands, and most of them are polycultural. Settlement sites, whose mutual distance is from 1 to 3 kilometers in many instances, mostly consist of underground features filled with cultural deposits full of shards (since the Neolithic period), animal bones, and other finds, but there are few superimposed layers. "Pagan" graves preceding the ninth century A.D. usually contain grave goods (pottery, stone, bronze, and/or iron artifacts). In consequence of the rich artifactual record, most of the post-Mesolithic sites can be classified with the accuracy of plus or minus 100 years. All these circumstances create very good conditions for detailed archaeological research.

The Beginnings of Archaeological Interest

The Czech chronicler Kosmas, who died in A.D. 1125, mentioned a barrow near Prague where a legendary Czech military leader of the ninth century should have been buried. This is an early example of the interpretation of an archaeological monument. Similarly, Václav Hájek of Libočany, writing in 1541, believed that the Marcomanian king Marobuduus (first century A.D.) had his seat at Závist near Prague, a place that is now known as a late–LA TÈNE period oppidum (fortified town). His interpretation was nearly correct from the chronological point of view, which may have been a matter of chance, but it should be kept in mind that Hájek was unusually good at inventing details when historical evidence failed him; apparently he had a good model of the past.

The first exact field observation was that of Karel Škréta, a painter who in 1668 made a drawing of the siege of Libice, an early medieval stronghold in Bohemia. Although he placed the historically attested battle of the tenth century into the eastern part of the site (with a gothic church, etc.), he also faithfully recorded the empty western part, consisting of bare fields surrounded by a simple rampart. One flat place in the fields has been described by Škréta as "ruins"; this is exactly where excavations of the 1950s unearthed the ground plan of a tenth-century church lying in the center of the original stronghold. All this is not very surprising to those who know that peasants of the late-medieval period (and much earlier times) correctly identified long-deserted earthworks as ancient forts and barrows as ancient graves. Many Iron Age hill-forts carry the name *Hradiště*, which means hill-fort in Czech; this also applies to cases where the ramparts are barely visible.

The first recorded collection containing archaeological objects was that of the Bohemian King Rudolph II, who was also a Roman emperor. It was kept in the royal palace in Prague and enriched by the king himself by means of excavations of a Bronze Age cemetery in Silesia, which in Rudolf's time belonged to the Kingdom of Bohemia. The excavation took place in 1577, and Rudolph unearthed one of the vessels with his own royal hands.

The Romantic Period

As in most European countries, archaeological activities in Bohemia and Moravia greatly increased in the romantic period from the end of the eighteenth century onward. The main idea was the belief that prehistory as recovered by archaeology was a backward projection of history, with the same "nations" and the same habits as recorded in the earliest written documents. There was no knowledge of the great antiquity of the human race; in fact, very few people ever considered the question of what preceded the Celtic, Germanic, and Slavic "nations" in central Europe. Therefore, the romantic query did not demand any systematic handling of the archaeological finds, which were simply believed to be illustrations of ancient his-

Artifacts from the tomb of the Bohemian king Premysl Otakar II in St. Vitus Cathedral (ca. 1370s) (Hulton Getty)

tory. Archaeology could supply details unmentioned in written documents, but it did not produce historical sources that could compete with written evidence. Archaeology did not have any specific problems of its own; the relevant questions were supplied by history. In this way the romantic paradigm was fully subordinated to history.

However, this was also the period of important discoveries. For example, K. J. Biener von Bienerberg, a military engineer, excavated several urnfields in the vicinity of Hradec Králové from 1768 to 1776 and later published his results in three volumes. He unsuccessfully tried to distinguish Slav and Germanic pottery. A hoard of Celtic coins (some forty kilograms of gold) was found near Podmokly in 1771, but most of the metal was melted down to mint the coins of the owner of the estate. This find has aroused much interest in archaeology.

There were many excavations in the first half of the nineteenth century, some of them published. M. Kalina von Jäthenstein, to give just one example, published a book titled *Pagan Sacrificial Places, Graves and Antiquities in Bohemia* (in Czech) in 1836. It was a complete survey of Czech archaeological material, full of "unscientific," romantic stuff, and assembled in cooperation with another "field archaeologist" named Václav Krolmus. The other excavations and publications of this period may be less impressive in their individuality, but they were many.

In a way, Josef Dobrovský, an extremely clever and able philologist and historian, was an exception in the romantic atmosphere of his time, for he tried to solve, on the basis of the archaeological record, the problem of whether the ancient Slavs incinerated their dead (Dobrovský 1786). In his case, finds were not used as mere illustrations, but the framework remained romantic.

Nationalism was not a great problem in the

eighteenth century, but it rose to importance in the nineteenth. A nice example in this regard involved the forgeries of allegedly early-medieval manuscripts written in Czech that were "discovered" in 1817 and 1819. Being well written, they influenced one part of Czech archaeology until the beginning of the twentieth century, as many influential historians and archaeologists accepted them as facts (e.g., P. J. Šafařík in 1836 and later F. Palacký, J. L. Píč, and others).

The romantic paradigm of archaeology faced a crisis when it became clear that it was unable to answer its own questions, in spite of the fact that the number of finds substantially increased. This development, however, did not take place in a vacuum: it was stimulated by changing ideologies reflecting changing social structure. It is often believed that the rise of the middle class and the beginning of the industrialization of the country can be held responsible for the development. Details of the complicated processes that took place within the society of the nineteenth century have not yet been sufficiently studied.

The Beginning of Formalism
The beginning of archaeology has often been identified with the creation of the first formal system of archaeological finds (the THREE-AGE SYSTEM). It may not be chance that this attitude toward the "beginning" of archaeology came from modern archaeologists who themselves were proponents of formal (typological) archaeology. The romantic period seemed to them to be unscientific, apparently because it relied so heavily on models derived from outside (from history). There is no obvious reason, however, why the beginning of archaeology should be set as late as the introduction of the three ages.

The three-age system was well known and adopted in Czech lands soon after it was proposed in DENMARK. J. E. Vocel, the first Prague professor of archaeology, was its partisan, and J. V. Hellich, a custodian of the archaeological collection at the National Museum in Prague, used it in a handbook on Czech archaeology, written in 1943. The opposition of German specialists to the three-age system, however, could not be entirely dismissed and resulted in a conditional adoption of the ideas of the three ages by some Czech archaeologists.

It is worth noting that Vocel tried to subdivide the Bronze Age on the basis of the chemical composition of bronze artifacts. This is an example of how early formal archaeologists were still looking for chronologically sensitive attributes of artifacts before finding them in terms of shape and decoration. The romantic paradigm did not end abruptly with the three-age system, as it was permanently regenerated by the nationalism of the nineteenth century, which was especially active in central Europe. It was only at the end of the century that the national ambitions of at least some nations of the central European states (including those of the Czechs) were satisfied and they became more or less politically stable. This created the necessary conditions for an almost complete (but temporary) abandonment of romantic and nationalist concepts.

Developed Formal Archaeology
The three-age system was not entirely satisfactory, not only because of persisting nationalism but also because some countries had many archaeological finds that showed a good deal of formal variability that could not be explained by means of the three basic periods. By the end of the nineteenth century Bohemian and Moravian archaeology had its basic classificatory framework, going far beyond the three-age system, and this framework did not change substantially afterward.

This achievement was the logical consequence of the greatly enlarged effort of many Czech archaeologists in the second half of the nineteenth century who excavated new sites and tried to classify their finds into more detailed subdivisions. The final form of the achievement is connected with the names of Lubor Niederle, Karel Buchtela, Inocenc L. Červinka, and Jaroslav Palliardi (mainly for the Neolithic period). The first two archaeologists based their classification on the monumental collections of the National Museum in Prague, which were greatly enriched by Josef L. Píč and his friends. Píč, an unusually active curator of the National Museum, promptly published his finds, which enabled his opponents to use them to discredit his arguments. Although he tried to work independently in creating a nonformal and more or less romantic paradigm of his own, Niederle (then already a professor of prehistoric archaeology at Charles University in Prague) was well aware of the parallel work being done elsewhere in Europe, which, however, he and Buchtela did not accept unconditionally. With the exception of some supposedly romantic points primarily concerning several assumed migrations, their paradigm was formal, that is, based on shape, decoration, and similar characteristics, as observed on individual artifacts. Červinka, working in Moravia and closely following Niederle and Buchtela, based his views on the collections of a number of local archaeologists, and Palliardi built on excavations of his own.

In spite of the fact that there were romantic elements in the works published around the turn of the twentieth century, such works were basically not nationalist, for their main problems were connected not with the "nations" known in central Europe at the beginning of written history but with the formal aspects of the archaeological record.

These achievements, however, were not isolated in Europe, and they were not the first of their kind. By the 1870s many archaeologists in other parts of Europe (OSCAR MONTELIUS in Sweden was the most prominent representative of the current) began to look for finer divisions of the archaeological record, inspired, directly or indirectly, by Charles Darwin's evolutionary theories (which, however, explained the variability of nature). Their work was unusually successful, leading to detailed chronological schemes, one part of which (for the Bronze Age and the beginning of the Iron Age) is still used. The studies were undertaken mainly in Scandinavia and later in Germany in the period from 1890 through 1910. They are generally known under the name *typology,* as the chronological schemes were constructed on the basis of the "evolution" of archaeological types (usually a parallel evolution of several types for each period).

The contribution of Czech lands to these schemes has already been mentioned. Czech archaeologists not only created typological sequences for their own regions but also supplied important parts of the evidence on which other specialists could build. An important Czech contribution to the typological endeavor, which deserves to be mentioned in more detail, was achieved by the Moravian archaeologist Jaroslav Palliardi, who proposed a detailed chronology (with twelve phases) of the Moravian Neolithic and Eneolithic periods. The conclusions he arrived at by the end of the nineteenth century are still valid; they were, in fact, so much ahead of their time that they were not developed further until the late 1950s. This was partly caused by the fact that their final form only appeared when the views of GUSTAF KOSSINNA, a prominent German professor of philology, started to occupy the minds of official archaeologists. Although Palliardi demonstrated that the individual Neolithic and Eneolithic cultures represented consecutive chronological phases, Kossinna's adherents considered them to be more or less contemporaneous groups covering different ethnic wholes. However, it clearly followed from Palliardi's chronology that "Nordic elements," such as the funnel beakers, appeared very late in the Moravian sequence and therefore could not be considered responsible for the appearance of civilization throughout Europe, as maintained by Kossinna. Palliardi's findings contradicted Kossinna (and even his nonradical followers) to such a degree that almost no archaeologist had the courage to mention them.

The First Half of the Twentieth Century

The three-age system and the recognition of the "diluvial" age of humans that followed had one great nonformal consequence: it became clear that humankind was of great antiquity, and it was to be expected that the "nations" known at the beginning of written history could not account for everything in the past; after all, much history was not mentioned in any written documents. This idea was taken up by a number of archaeologists, first of all by Kossinna, who began to look for ancient Indo-Europeans and their origins in the archaeological record. Formal archaeology was so successful in drawing formal differences among chronologically and spatially distinct finds that it seemed logical to use these differences to answer some of the old romantic questions. This current was openly nationalistic and often even racist, which also accounted for its aggressiveness. As happened many other times during the development of archaeology, these ideas combined with ideology, this time mainly with the German nationalism that was gradually developing into Nazi ideology based on racism. This deviation of the human mind ended with the close of World War II, leaving a theoretical vacuum not only in Germany but also in many countries of central and southeastern Europe. It became impossible to hold old nationalist views (whether in the authentic German form or reversed to meet the criteria of other kinds of nationalism [possibly anti-German]), but there was no alternative at hand. In some countries this tendency is still perceptible.

Another influential current in central European archaeology of this period was the diffusion theory of the Vienna ethnological school, a form of which became a constituent part of VERE GORDON CHILDE's writings. The theory originally assumed that culture had spread throughout the world from a limited number of *Kulturkreislehre,* but this idea was later dropped in favor of "pure" diffusion. The diffusion concept has by and large spread into archaeology in the form of a hunt for influences, whether from the north or from the southeast.

The reason why this entry addresses the central European intellectual environment at such length in connection with Czech archaeology is because Czech archaeology was largely professionalized in the twentieth century, and professional people are always much more aware of theory than are their amateur colleagues. In central Europe, however, theory was traditionally supplied by literature written in German, the best-known second language of most educated people in the Czech countries during the times of the Austrian monarchy. Thus, the influence of literature written in German was strong in Czech archaeology, as it was in Hungary and Poland. It is therefore rather surprising that Czech archaeology as a whole was conspicuously resistant to the Kossinna form of nationalism, which appeared in only a very few papers after the war. The resistance of mainstream Czech archaeology to such views may have been related to the fact that there was no local fascist tradition that would make it ideologically acceptable to reverse Kossinna, transforming his teaching into another sort of nationalism.

Taking the preceding paragraphs into account, it is easier to understand the achievements of Czech archaeology between the two world wars. The results of the preceding generations were largely fortified, and a solid basis for further development was created. The formal typological approach found expression in the earlier part of the period in the works of Albín Stocký and Josef Schránil. Theoretically and methodologically they represent more or less a prolongation of the first decade of the century, bringing the views of Niederle, Buchtela, and others to perfection. "Influences" became a standard concept, and many migrations were described.

The same background can be observed with regard to Stocký's and Schránil's pupils. Jaroslav Böhm, however, produced, in addition to a few typological studies, at least two books for the general public containing unconventional ideas. Jan Filip created mostly arid typology, and Jiří Neustupný was more orientated toward cultural history. But in the interwar period there were still many nonprofessional archaeologists working in various fields of the discipline, some of whom achieved better results than their professional colleagues, mainly by not being so strongly determined by the ruling, official paradigms of their time. This observation applies especially to Jan Axamit, Bedřich Dubský, Karel Žebera, Ladislav Hájek, František Vildomec, and Vilém Hrubý. Some of the amateur archaeologists of this period later became professionals, employed by new archaeological institutions.

In addition to the theoretical achievements within the framework of formal archaeology, the period between the two world wars brought an important consolidation of archaeological institutions. The university now regularly produced professional archaeologists, the National Museum got a modern system of collections that could be used by everybody, and the newly founded State Archaeological Institute promised to become a center for heritage management. As will be explained shortly, these undeniable achievements were lost in the postwar socialist period.

The Socialist Period

Ideologically, the socialist period began just after World War II as nationalist propaganda stressed the allegedly close relationship between Czechs and Russians. This propaganda found immediate reflection in archaeology: archaeology was expected to demonstrate the eastern connections of the Czech nation, proving that the "Slavs" arrived very early from the east. This point was directed against the Germans, with whom the Czechs have, in fact, more in common than with the Russians. Most archaeologists did not recognize the ideological background of these views and actively participated in the officially supported boom of "Slavic archaeology" especially if no explicit ideological statements were required, and there were no direct nationalist implications. This period ended in 1968; thereafter anything "Slavic" became ideologically untenable because it was a reminder of the Russian military invasion. There was a subperiod just after the mid-1960s, preceding the liberalization of 1968, when achievements of Czech scientists in general were evaluated on the basis of references in the West: the regime recognized that it could not rely on reports put out by the party bureaucracy that ruled the institutes.

Contrary to the expectations of many western archaeologists, Marxism never became a widespread topic in Czech archaeology. However, statements on theory running against Marxist ideology would have been punished, something that automatically put an end to all discussions of major theoretical issues. Any theoretical debate had to have the usual dogmatic form, full of quotations from Karl Marx (see Neustupný 1967), but there were not many publications of this sort. Marxism was completely dropped after 1968, as some of its ideas apparently seemed dangerous to the communist ruling class; all that remained was the usual Marxist political rhetoric. But the situation in West Germany—where, despite the absence of Marxist ideological pressure, there was no discussion of theory in the 1950s through to the 1980s—makes it uncertain whether theoretical issues would have been raised by Czech archaeologists of that period if there had not been any communist regime. Marxist philosophy, however, had one positive effect in that every university student had to study the works by Marx and Friedrich Engels. Consequently, many students became acquainted with some kind of philosophy and a sort of anthropology, although a part of the related reading was purely political (see Neustupný 1991).

As real archaeological theory, being ideologically controlled, was dangerous to touch, most archaeologists refused to go near it. It was also dangerous to write positively about anything coming from the West. To proclaim oneself to be a "New Archaeologist," for example, was a risk that nobody took. In this situation many archaeologists preferred nontheoretical topics within the tradition of formal, typological archaeology; the main problems discussed in archaeological writings were chronology and cultural influences, assumed to come predominantly from the southeast. At the same time, the large-scale contemporaneity of prehistoric cultures was taken for granted, and this, of course, opened the door to the equation of archaeological cultures with ethnic units; the assumption of many migrations was a logical result. This kind of archaeology may have been a protest against the communist regime because it was utterly nonideological (see Kuna 1993), or at least not favorable to socialism, whereas an active engagement in communist ideology was otherwise required in any other sphere of life. New Archaeology and the beginnings of postprocessual archaeology were largely missed in this deformed intellectual environment.

In this way it happened that Czech archaeologists became very good at typological chronology (cf. Krumphanzlová 1972), and their detailed schemes created in the 1950s and 1960s are still valid; they became the basis for local sequences all over central Europe. Either they were applied directly or they stimulated similar schemes to originate elsewhere as parallels. Czech archaeologists have also achieved positive results in the study of the natural environment and the spatial structure of sites. Problems involving the latter concern ensued not only from theoretical considerations but also from the unusually large rescue excavations that took place, by and large in northwestern Bohemia. This region was the only one to have an effective rescue team (a branch of the Prague Academy Institute) as early as the end of the 1950s; tens of hectares were continuously stripped and covered by rescue excavations in front of open coal mines, leading to the creation of an unusually rich archaeological record (see Neustupný 1994).

In the 1950s and 1960s archaeology was lavishly supported by the state for ideological reasons, and major amounts of money went to large-scale excavations. This, however, was done at the expense of rescue work, museums, and universities, which were allotted very limited funds. Moreover, the large excavations, mostly led by the institutes of the Academy of Sciences, often remained unpublished for decades, so their great informative potential was partly wasted. But in spite of this, these excavations have brought much new knowledge, which has not yet been fully used. The support for excavations substantially diminished in the 1970s when they began to necessite a growth in rescue work paid by the developers.

The Postsocialist Period

The power structures introduced by the communists had a devastating effect on Czech archaeology. In the postsocialist period almost nothing was normal: how could it have been without the imposition of the all-pervasive party control? The party disappeared by 1989, but the institutions created for its maintenance partly remained. At the beginning of the period it seemed that the transition to a normal state would be fast and easy, but such hopes have not been realized, mainly because many individuals succeeded in keeping their microenvironments unchanged. The previous system has been replaced by liberal mechanisms of self-rule in the field of research. As Czech society as a whole is successfully and rapidly moving toward a market economy based on private property and toward western-type democracy, the state of Czech archaeology is likely to change in the future.

The "Prehistories" of the Czech Republic

There are many summary works on Bohemian, Moravian, and Czechoslovak prehistory, far more than in other countries. The likely reason for this is that Bohemia and Moravia are geographically well defined by mountains, having no or sparse archaeological finds in border areas; thus, it is not necessary to draw artificial limiting lines along modern frontiers while compiling archaeological evidence.

Leaving aside the purely antiquarian lists of monuments, the first summary books are those by J. E. Vocel (1845, 1853, 1866). They were followed by a series of books, beginning with the works of Buchtela and Niederle (Buchtela 1899; Niederle and Buchtela 1910) and leading to those of Schránil (1928), Böhm (1941), Neustupný (1946), Filip (1948), and Neustupný (1968). All these writings are based on similar methodological and theoretical grounds (formal typological approach, interest in influences and limited migrations, little interest in economy and social relations). The last-named book, however, was concerned with ecological evidence and issues.

New principles were introduced by Evžen and Jiří Neustupný in 1961. The influences and migrations were kept to a minimum, and economic and social questions were discussed on an unprecedented scale. In this sense their work went far beyond the typological paradigm. Bohemian archaeology was influenced by the two preceding books (especially by their systematic discussions of prehistoric economy and society and their summaries of the environmental evidence), but otherwise it remained within the traditional typological current. The most recent attempt (Neustupný 1994), a textbook for schools, suppresses the typological detail and tries to explain the past in terms of the practical function, social meaning, and symbolic significance of the archaeological record.

The Organization of Archaeological Research

The first type of organization in which archaeology was performed on a professional or semi-professional level was the museum. The National Museum in Prague (originally the Museum of the Kingdom of Bohemia) and the Moravian Museum in Brno, both founded in 1818, were followed by Olomouc (in northern Moravia) and other smaller museums that became centers of archaeological research, and they continued to be so during the second half of the nineteenth century. In addition to the large museums many local museums were opened in which amateur archaeologists were especially active at the end of the nineteenth and in the first half of the twentieth centuries.

The second centers of archaeological research were the universities. The Charles University in Prague, founded in 1348, has had a chair of Bohemian antiquities since 1850. Jan Erazim Vocel, a partisan of the three-age system who compiled a book on Bohemian antiquities (Starožitnosti země české, 1866), was its first professor of archaeology. In 1898 Lubor Niederle was appointed the first professor of prehistoric archaeology, and since that time the chair has been occupied permanently (except during World War II, when Czech universities were closed by the Germans). Yet though Charles University educated several professional archaeologists, most of them in the second half of the twentieth century, it never became the center of Czech archaeology. It did not perform any major excavations, and its staff was always limited to a very few persons. Nonetheless, it produced a number of outstanding professional archaeologists on a high level. The Brno University in Moravia has had a chair of prehistoric archaeology since 1933, and in many respects it has been more active archaeologically than Charles University in Prague. At present archaeology is also taught at a number of smaller universities, but none of them has a chair of archaeology.

The network of museums and universities was supplemented by the State Archaeological Institute in 1919 (with a Brno branch in 1941). Originally, the institute was a small body occupied mainly with fieldwork. It became the core of the Archaeological Institute of the Czechoslovak Academy of Sciences, founded in accordance with the Russian template in 1953. As a result of that move any hopes of Czechoslovakia getting an institution to take over the care of archaeological monuments and rescue excavations vanished.

The foundation of the Czechoslovak Academy of Sciences was a part of the program to unify the Soviet empire by building comparable structures everywhere; the goal in creating this institute was to easily control the sphere of science and humanities from one communist party center. This meant an incredible degree of centralization, with more than half of all Czech archaeologists directly attached to this institute (others were attached indirectly). The Prague Archaeological Institute had some 200 employees in 1989, and there was another but smaller institute in Brno. Museums and universities were not allowed to grow in this phase, and in the first twenty years there was no body responsible for rescue excavations (later, this responsibility was partly assumed by the Academy Institutes). All theoretical activities were supposed to be done by the academy, whose leading position in the field of science was embodied in law. Directors of the institute became the rulers of Czech archaeology.

The socialist regime fostered people of mediocre intellect in general, and most of those in archaeology were not exceptions to this rule. To achieve anything after the Russian invasion of Czechoslovakia, one had to be a member of the Communist Party or a secret police agent. Individuals in both these categories were active in archaeology. For the most part only children of reliable party members were allowed to study "ideological" subjects, and archaeology was considered to be one of them. In view of these facts it is surprising that a fair number of talented people escaped the attention of the party and became good archaeologists. This often happened at the cost of them joining the party. After the "capitalist revolution" in 1989, several groups of archaeologists, doing mostly rescue work, separated from the Institutes of the Academy in 1993. But otherwise the situation had not changed in principle by the middle of 1994 and the Academy of Sciences, with its large, Russian-type institutes, survives as the last socialist institution in the Czech Republic.

The main archaeological journal, *Památky Archeologické,* was founded in 1854. Originally, it contained articles on both archaeology and the history of art; it has since turned into a purely archaeological journal with two issues per year. Recently, it has been published in English, German, and French to inform archaeologists abroad.

Another journal that covers the whole territory of the Czech Republic is *Archeologické Rozhledy,* founded in 1949 to replace *Obzor Prehistorický* (published from 1922 to 1950) in an effort to get archaeology under reliable control after the communist takeover. *Archeologické Rozhledy* is published in four or six issues per year and primarily contains articles in Czech, with foreign language summaries; some of the articles are fully in English, French, or German.

Moravia had its own journal, called *Pravěk,* from 1903 to 1927 (it did not appear regularly). There has been an effort recently to start publishing a new series of this journal (so far one issue came out in 1992). In addition, Brno University and a number of museums (mainly the National Museum in Prague and the Moravian Museum in Brno) regularly publish archaeological articles in their own periodicals.

Archaeologist had their societies rather early. The first of them was the Archeologický sbor Národního Muzea (the Archaeological Committee of the National Museum, founded in 1843), and subsequently there were several other. The most important among them was Společnost československých prehistoriků (after World War I) and Moravský archeologický klub. After the communist takeover they were all replaced by a single organization called Společnost československých Archeologů; being put under the control of the Academy of Sciences, its importance was negligible.

Evžen Neustupný

References

Biener von Bienenberg, K. J. 1778–1785. *Versuch über einige merkwürdige Alterthümer im Königreich Böhmen.* Hradec Králové.

Böhm, J. 1936. "Sto let systému tří period." *Obzor Prehistorický* 10: 301.

———. 1941. *Kronika objeveného věku.* Prague: Družstevní Práce.

Buchtela, K. 1899. Die Vorgeschichte Böhmens (*Věstník slovanských starožitností*).

Červinka, I. L. 1902. *Morava za pravěku.* Brno.

Dobrovský, J. 1786. Ueber die Begräbnissart der alten Slawen (*Abhandlungen der königlichen Gesellschaft der Wissenschaften*). Prague.

Dubský, B. 1949. *Pravěk jižních Čech.* Blatná: Bratři Římsové.

Filip, J. 1948. *Pravěké Československo* (La Tchécoslovaquie préhistorique.) Prague.

Fridrich, J., ed. 1994. *25 Years of Archaeological Research in Bohemia* (Památky archeologické-Supplementum 1). Prague: Archaeological Institute.

Kalina von Jäthenstein, M. 1836. *Böhmens heidnische Opferplätze, Gräber und Alterthümer* (Pagan sacrificial places, graves and antiquities in Bohemia). Prague.

Krumphanzlová, Z., ed. 1972. *Vývoj archeologie v Čechách a na Moravě 1919–1968* (The Development of Archaeology in Bohemia and Moravia 1918–1968). Archeologické studijní materiály 10. 2 vols.

Kuna, M. 1993. Post-processual Archaeology from a Post-Marxist Perspective. *Archeologické Rozhledy* 45: 390–395.

Neustupný, E. 1967. *K počátkům patriarchátu ve střední Evropě* (The beginnings of patriarchy in Central Europe). Rozpravy ČSAV 77/2. Prague.

———. 1991. "Recent Theoretical Achievements in Prehistoric Archaeology in Czechoslovakia." In *Archaeological Theory in Europe: The Last Three Decades,* 248–271. Ed. I. Hodder. London: Routledge.

———. 1994. "Settlement Area Theory in Bohemian Archaeology—Teorie sídelních areálů." In *25 Years of Archaeological Research in Bohemia* (Památky archeologické—Supplementum 1), 248–258. Prague: Archaeological Institute.

Neustupný, J. 1946. *Pravěk lidstva.* Prague: Orbis.

———. 1968. "150th Aniversary of the National Museum in Prague." *Current Anthropology* 9: 221–224.

Niederle, L. 1893. *Lidstvo v době předhistorické.* Prague.

———. 1902. *Slovanské starožitnosti.* Prague.

Niederle, L., and K. Buchtela. 1910. *Rukověť české archeologie.* Prague.

Píč, J. L. 1899. *Starožitnosti země České*. Vols. 1.1–3.1. Prague.

Šafařík, P. J. 1836. *Archeologické starožitnosti*. Prague.

Schránil, J. 1928. *Vorgeschichte Böhmens und Mährens*. Berlin und Leipzig: Walter de Gruyter.

Sklenář, K. 1969. "Nástin vývoje prehistorického bádání v Čechách do rokul 1919." *Zprávy Československé společnosti archeologické* 11: 1–91.

———. 1981. "The History of Archaeology in Czechoslovakia." In *Towards a History of Archaeology*, 150–158. Ed. G. Daniel. London: Thames and Hudson.

———. 1983. *Archaeology in Central Europe: The First 500 Years*. New York: St. Martin's Press.

Vocel, J. E. 1845. *Grundzüge der böhmischen Altherthumskunde*. Prague.

———. 1853. *Archäologische Parallelen*. Vienna.

———. 1866. *Pravěk země české*. Prague.

D

Daniel, Glyn (1914–1986)

Glyn Daniel grew up in the Vale of Glamorgan in southern Wales, was educated at Barry Grammar School, then went to St. John's College, Cambridge, on a scholarship in 1932. He switched from geography to archaeology and was at St. John's all the rest of his life.

Daniel's first research on the megalithic monuments of the British Isles was later enlarged by studying their cousins in France and across Europe as a whole. His work was published as *The Prehistoric Chamber Tombs of England and Wales* (1950) and *The Prehistoric Chamber Tombs of France* (1960). It was a large task, in the late 1930s, simply to collate knowledge of the chamber tombs and then to relate them to their sister monuments scattered across western Europe.

Working within the "moderate-diffusionist" framework for European prehistory associated particularly with the work and name of VERE GORDON CHILDE, Daniel devised a scheme (1941) for a dual colonization of western Europe by megalith builders: a passage-grave tradition originating in the eastern Mediterranean and a gallery-grave tradition originating in the western Mediterranean, which between them explained the pattern in northwest Europe, the region where the diffusionist impulse had spread the habit of megalithic building. Like other schemes diligently built to explain European prehistory with slight and ambiguous chronological evidence, this one collapsed in the 1950s when calibrated radiocarbon chronology showed that the northwest European megaliths, especially those in Brittany, were earlier than, or as early as, their supposed ancestors in Mediterranean lands. Instead, Daniel was

able to enjoy the role that his native Wales played in originating a style and craft of stone-building through Atlantic Europe that was older than the pyramids of Egypt.

It seems in retrospect that it was not helpful to concentrate research on megaliths as a defined class on their own. The techniques of building with great blocks are much the same everywhere, because the engineering options are few, so similarities of form can only be weak proof of cultural affinity or any direct historic connection. Recent study has instead preferred to integrate examination of the megaliths with evidence from nonmegalithic contexts of the same periods. Even that is still not an easy task because the artifactual evidence that can be used in dating is even now often slight or uncertain; it was certainly impossible to find it a good basis for systematic megalithic study in the prewar and preradiocarbon era.

In 1943, Daniel published *The Three Ages,* a study of the Scandinavian development in the early nineteenth century of a Stone Age/Bronze Age/Iron Age division of early European archaeology, the key insight in ordering the artifacts that made studying prehistory possible in that century. This was the first of many studies by Daniel in the history of archaeology, including *A Hundred Years of Archaeology* (1950), *The Idea of Prehistory* (1962), *The Origins and Growth of Archaeology* (edited, 1967), and *A Short History of Archaeology* (1981), that set out the essentials of the nineteenth-century story especially as they have now come to be generally understood. Implicit in this important part of Daniel's writing, though not unnecessarily emphasized, is the insight that we do not excavate the simple *facts* of ancient matters. Archaeological knowledge depends also on the attitudes and values of the inquirer; the advances in the developing history of archaeology came from new opportunities that resulted from changing frames of ideas as well as from new field discoveries.

In 1952, Daniel participated in an archaeological quiz show on British (BBC) television, *Animal, Vegetable, Mineral?* and soon became its chairman. For each show, three experts (of whom SIR MORTIMER WHEELER was the regular performer with the best style and panache) would examine mystery objects from a museum collection and try to identify just what they were and where they came from. The program was an unprecedented success in the "strange and heady days" of early British television, and Daniel was voted "Television Personality of the Year" in 1955. Looking now at the few minutes of black-and-white film that survive, it is not easy to see why the program caught the public imagination so. Rather than allowing himself to be pulled further into the television world, Daniel stayed with archaeology and later was much involved in the guidance of the long-running BBC archaeology series *Chronicle*.

In 1955, Daniel began to edit a new series of books for Thames and Hudson, *Ancient People and Places,* which ran to over 100 volumes, and in 1957, he succeeded O. G. S. CRAWFORD as editor of the journal ANTIQUITY. As a journal and book editor, knowledgeable in the ways of television and with a lively sense of what was new and exciting, Daniel had great importance (not always visible) from the 1950s onward; in the modern phrase, he was a great "networker." Knowing everyone, always interested in the gossip as to who had found what and said what, he had an influential hand in many useful innovations, and much was done, written, and published that might not have occurred without his cheery and steel-centered encouragement. A long series of his students went on from St. John's to successful careers in archaeology; Glyn was especially proud of 1962 when Barry Cunliffe, Colin Renfrew, and two other members of St. John's all got first-class degrees. Cambridge recognized Daniel's diverse service, in his college as well as in the university, and that his work was much broader than the conventional research of a narrow academic career by electing him Disney Professor of Archaeology in 1974, in succession to SIR GRAHAME CLARK. When Daniel retired in 1981, he was succeeded by his student Lord Renfrew.

Daniel published an excellent fat autobiography, *Some Small Harvest,* which is full of lively and telling stories, in 1986, the year of his retirement after thirty years of editing *Antiquity* and the year of his death. He was survived by his wife, Ruth, production editor for *Antiquity* and the less public partner in a celebrated Cambridge double act for the forty years since their marriage in 1946.

Christopher Chippindale

References

Daniel, Glyn E. 1986. *Some Small Harvest: The Memoirs of Glyn Daniel.* London: Thames and Hudson.

Dart, Raymond Arthur (1893–1988)

Born near Brisbane, Queensland, Australia, Dart graduated from the University of Queensland in 1913 with a science degree. He studied medicine at the University of Sydney and after completing his master's degree in anatomy, and his medical degree in 1917, joined the Australian Medical Corps in France and England from 1918 to 1919. After the war he worked with SIR GRAFTON ELLIOT SMITH, demonstrating anatomy at University College London, and then in 1920 won a Rockefeller Foundation fellowship to the United States. He first studied at the University of Cincinnati but then spent most of his time in the anatomy department at Washington University in St. Louis, Missouri. In 1922 Dart became professor of anatomy and dean of the medical school at the University of Witwatersrand in SOUTH AFRICA, and he built up these institutions until 1943, creating the Raymond Dart Collection of Human Skeletons while teaching there. He retired in 1958 but continued to work as an honorary professorial research fellow at the Bernard Price Institute for Palaeontological Research in Witwatersrand for six months of the year and as professor at the Avery Postgraduate Institute in Philadelphia, U.S.A., for the other six months, until the age of ninety-three. The In-

"Peter" van Riet Lowe (right) with (from left to right) Raymond Dart, Robert Broom, and Abbé Breuil examining an "ape-man" skull (H. J. Deacon)

stitute of the Study of Man in Africa was founded at the University of Witwatersrand in his honor.

Dart is best known for the discovery and interpretation of the fossilized child's skull found in a limestone deposit at the Buxton Limeworks near Taung in northern Cape Province, South Africa, in November 1924. In an article in *Nature* in February 1925, Dart argued that the Taung skull was evidence for the presence of an anthropoid ape in Africa that, based on elements of its morphology, had become more human. He called it *Australopithecus africanus,* and while it did not fit into the ape family, Dart could not (at first) classify it as a member of the family *Hominidae* either, because of its small brain size.

For the next twenty-five years the place of *Australopithecus* and its significance was disputed and Dart's expertise attacked. Dart argued that the size of the Taung brain was not as important as its form, and that other early humans had shown that the principle of mosaic evolution was possible. This meant that some parts of the body hominized before others, and not just the brain (as argued by Elliot Smith and Sir Arthur Keith with the PILTDOWN evidence). In the case of the Taung skull, dental and postural hominization were evident even if an increase or hominization of the brain was not. By the 1950s Dart had been vindicated by more *Australopithecus* discoveries in South Africa, by Robert Broom at Sterkfontein, and in Kenya, by LOUIS LEAKEY. During the same period Piltdown was proven to be a fraud, and *Australopithecus* was finally classified as an ancestral hominid.

Dart also proposed that before the Stone Age there had been a Bone Age or "osteodontokeratic culture"—when *Australopithecus* had used the bones, teeth, and horns of their animal prey as tools and implements. Dart based this argument on his extensive study of thousands of fossilized and broken bones from the *Australopithecus*-bearing cave of Makapansgat in the northern Transvaal. The new discipline of *taphonomy* was effectively born out of attempts to disprove this last of Dart's hypotheses.

Tim Murray

Dasgupta, Paresh Chandra (1923–1982)

P. C. Dasgupta was primarily an art historian interested in the early historic terracottas and later sculptures of West Bengal before he was made the director of the West Bengal State Directorate of Archaeology and Museums in Calcutta in the early 1960s. His subsequent career is an excellent example of how important a role even amateurs can perform in modern archaeology, especially in the Third World, by their sheer enthusiasm.

Stone Age sites had been known in West Bengal before, but the number of discoveries Dasgupta made in this field far outstripped any significant work done earlier. One of his sites, Susunia, is undoubtedly the only major primary Acheulian site in eastern India, rich in both faunal and lithic remains. Interestingly, his amateurism meant that he was instrumental in preventing the full potential of the site from being realized because he employed a large number of workmen to only pick up artifacts. Neolithic-Chalcolithic sites were well understood in many other parts of India by 1960, but nothing was known of them in West Bengal. Dasgupta soothed regional pride by finding a large number of them over a wide area, and although he did not do justice to the major site he excavated in this context, that of Pandu Rajar Dhibi, his report (Dasgupta 1964) was for many years the only definitive publication on the stratigraphy of such a site in West Bengal.

Dasgupta's department soon built up what was to become the largest archaeological collection from Bengal. The museum that was established after he had retired in the late 1970s reflects his enormous enthusiasm and support for Bengal archaeology, and those who work in the region will always feel indebted to him.

Dilip Chakrabarti

References
Dasgupta, P. C. 1964. *Excavations at Pandu Rajar Dhabi.* Calcutta.

Dating

Establishing the age of objects, landscapes, or contexts is one of the primary tasks of the archaeologist. It has also proved to be among the most difficult. Archaeology's twin roots in the humanities and in sciences such as geology and paleontology provided two types of answers to the question, how old? Although antiquarians, historians, and philosophers long pondered the history of people before writing, it was only in the nineteenth and twentieth centuries that the discipline of archaeology was able to make great strides in developing reliable means of assigning age and chronological relationship.

From the humanities, particularly through the study of material culture, archaeologists have developed schemes of relative dating based on the close analysis of the forms and functions of artifacts. In this endeavor strong links with CLASSIFICATION (taxonomy) and typology were forged that depended on the development of consistent rules for describing artifacts and the contexts in which they were found. The earliest relative chronologies, such as the THREE-AGE SYSTEM, were founded upon description, taxonomy, and the development of typology. But in the absence of a means to establish relative age, such classifications and typologies were, in essence, ahistorical and potentially circular in their logical forms.

Geology and paleontology provided the basis of a solution. The principle of relative dating (that is, establishing that one thing is relatively older or younger than another thing) was based on the notion of stratigraphy. In this sense it was understood that following the law of superposition (by which what is on the top is assumed to be younger than what is on the bottom), the relative ages of artifacts could be established on the basis of their relative positions within a stratigraphic profile. Advances in the degree to which antiquarians and archaeologists in the nineteenth century understood the principles of stratigraphy (and site formation) were matched by an increasing sophistication in the ways in which they were able to apply them.

The work of Scandinavian archaeologists such as JENS JACOB WORSAAE, SOPHUS MÜLLER, and OSCAR MONTELIUS and Egyptologists such as W. M. FLINDERS PETRIE was particularly significant in the development of the relative-dating technique of seriation. These advancements were supported by painstaking research into the nature and distribution of artifact assemblages across space and time (as defined by the chronological relationships established through stratigraphy and typology). Such research allowed archaeologists to document a phenomenon in the human use of material culture that had temporal implications. Put simply, seriation acknowledges that artifacts change in their forms and in their styles of decoration over time. Archaeologists such as Petrie were able to use empirical evidence from excavations to establish that change in such forms and styles had a history that was generally repeated—an artifact in its earliest appearance was rare, it then became more popular (and hence more numerous), and, as fashion moved on, it eventually became rare once again before finally vanishing. Petrie's great contribution to the method of seriation was to harness his empirical information to construct frequency diagrams for artifacts of various types at various stratigraphic levels, thus creating "battleship curves" that plotted the "life histories" of artifact form and style.

Notwithstanding the great advances made in relative chronologies based on the analysis of artifacts and their stratigraphic contexts, archaeologists were significantly hampered by their inability to quantify time. Without quantifiable time they could establish the direction of history, but they could not explore significant elements of process that require a means of establishing rate and duration. The establishment of high human antiquity, which was first achieved in the mid–nineteenth century by scholars such as HUGH FALCONER, JOSEPH PRESTWICH, ÉDOUARD LARTET, and JACQUES BOUCHER DE PERTHES, was limited in its impact precisely because it was essentially based on relative chronology. Archaeologists had to wait until well into the twentieth century before reliable means of establishing the absolute ages of objects or their stratigraphic contexts could be established, but when this was achieved the practice of archaeology was transformed to its core.

Of course, archaeologists had long been aware that ancient societies had their own sense of time and succession, creating calendars that, when deciphered (as in the case of MESOAMERICAN calendrical systems), provided absolute dates with great precision. Indeed, it was the linking of these calendars and lists of kings and dynasties (especially in Egypt and the Middle East) that allowed Petrie and Montelius (and, of course, VERE GORDON CHILDE) to construct a notional "history" for late-European prehistory. However, although it was widely accepted that constructing such histories was a valuable undertaking, it was also understood that the reliability of such histories rested on assumptions about duration and processes that were difficult to independently test. Dates derived from the study of ancient coins and inscriptions certainly assisted (and continue to assist) the archaeologist in refining chronology, but of themselves they did not overcome the limitations of the approach. This accomplishment had to wait for the application of science-based dating methods to archaeology.

During the twentieth century archaeologists were presented with a constant flow of techniques for dating either archaeological objects or archaeological contexts or both. The first of these, dendrochronology, or tree-ring dating, was pioneered by A. E. DOUGLASS in the first two decades of the century. Although it was originally developed in the Southwest of the UNITED STATES, the technique has been used in other parts of the world with varying degrees of success (Baillie 1982). The story of dendrochronology mirrors that of other science-based dating technologies in the twentieth and twenty-first centuries in that the techniques themselves become the subject of continuing research and development. Although the great proliferation in absolute dating technologies that occurred in the twentieth century has often been explained as stemming from a desire to encompass more time with greater precision, it is also true that the archaeological scientists who create and employ such techniques also need to devote considerable research time to understanding their nature, prospects, and limitations.

This is perhaps most apparent in the development and application of radiocarbon dating. Given that this was the first dating technology that depended on the establishment of regular, time-dependent processes (in this case radioactive decay), archaeologists and archaeological scientists have been researching C-14 dating since its development by WILLARD LIBBY in 1952. Radiocarbon dating has become the most widely used absolute dating technology all over the world. Indeed, one of its very great strengths has been its capacity to create a "world prehistory"—a framework within which archaeologists could compare what was happening in parts of the world that had, at that time, little or no shared history (Bowman 1990). However, virtually from the time the technique was first applied to archaeological contexts, practitioners have recognized and worked to correct limitations in the technology—an effort that has led to the development of a thriving industry in dating research and the education of archaeologists in the business of collecting samples and interpreting dates. After some fifty years of research we now have enhancements of Libby's original technique that can deliver more accurate absolute dates over longer time periods.

Some limitations in radiocarbon dating have been overcome by the development of new technologies such as luminescence dating (Aitken 1985), which themselves have become the subjects of ongoing research. Given that dating is so central to the business of doing archaeology in the early twenty-first century, any reputable undergraduate archaeology textbook contains exhaustive descriptions of techniques for dating materials as diverse as the enamel on teeth or the products of volcanic eruptions in the very remote human past. The identification of regular decay processes occurring in nature is an ongoing task designed to assist the archaeologist in obtaining absolute dates from seemingly intractable materials and to improve our confidence in the reliability and precision of such dates. Notwithstanding the great success achieved by dating specialists in the twentieth century, we should never forget that although the development and application of the technologies is important, the task of making sense of them remains firmly in the province of the archaeologist.

Tim Murray

References
Aitken, M. J. 1985. *Thermoluminescence Dating.* London: Academic Press.
———. 1990. *Science-based Dating in Archaeology.* London: Longman.
Baillie, M. G. 1982. *Tree-ring Dating and Archaeology.* London: Croom Helm.
Bowman, S. 1990. *Radiocarbon Dating.* London: British Museum Publications.

Davis, Edwin Hamilton (1811–1888)

Davis was born at Hillsboro in southern Ohio, a town surrounded by a number of circular, square, and octagonal earthworks that were the cause of much speculation. From his earliest years Davis was interested in the origins of the mounds and their builders. He graduated from the Cincinnati Medical College in 1837 and settled down to practice medicine in Chillicothe, Ohio, but his interest in the earthworks continued. Davis financed the surveying of 100 of these, and the stratigraphic excavation of others, by newspaper editor-turned-archaeologist Ephraim G. Squier. Consolidating their data with the findings of other researchers on prehistoric earthworks from all over the eastern UNITED STATES, Davis and Squier co-wrote *Ancient Monuments of the Mississippi Valley* (1847), the SMITHSONIAN INSTITUTION's first publication. It remains an important source of information for archaeologists to this day. Squier and Davis supported CALEB ATWATER's Moundbuilder theory, and while this precluded speculation on the origins of mounds and earthworks, they did speculate on their possible uses.

Davis collected artifacts from the mounds that were regarded as surprisingly advanced artistically. Most of his collection was acquired by the Blackmore Museum in Salisbury, England, while a smaller part is in the American Museum of Natural History in New York City. Davis was professor of medicine at the New York Medical College from 1850 to 1860, and maintained his interest in archaeology, appearing as a regular lecturer on archaeology to various learned societies.

Tim Murray

Dawkins, Sir William Boyd (1837–1929)

Born in Shropshire, England, Dawkins studied geology at Oxford and after graduating in 1860 worked for the Geological Survey of England.

In 1869 he was appointed curator at the Manchester Museum and lecturer in geology at Owens College in Manchester. In 1874 the college became the Victoria University of Manchester (now Manchester University) and Dawkins became its first professor of geology, a position he held until his retirement in 1909.

Dawkins became interested in Paleoanthropology in 1859 when he helped the Rev. J. Williamson explore the Wookey Hole, a cave in the Mendip Hills in southern England, in search of evidence of early humans in England. At the same time WILLIAM PENGELLY and HUGH FALCONER were interpreting prehistoric material found at BRIXHAM CAVE in Devonshire to the same end. While in his first book, *Cave Hunting* (1874), Dawkins cautiously supported the idea of early human antiquity, by his second, *Early Man in Britain* (1880), he argued that human antiquity was only as old as the Pleistocene period (10,000 years ago). Dawkins believed that the mammalian extinctions at the close of the Tertiary period would have also included humans—if they had existed at all. Based on the fossil remains in river-drift terraces or cave sites, Dawkins argued that humans first appeared in Europe during the middle Pleistocene period. He criticized French archaeologist GABRIEL DE MORTILLET for excluding regional variations in early human evidence, and went on to suggest that differences in assemblages might also be the result of tribal or ethnic variations, or of access to raw materials.

Dawkins maintained his position on human antiquity despite subsequent developments in Paleoanthropology, but remained active in scientific debates, including that of the great antiquity of Piltdown man. Despite regarding the arguments for Piltdown as "heresy," he was to become close friends with Sir Arthur Keith, who at that time was vigorously supporting the finds from Piltdown.

Dawkins became a Fellow of the Geological Society in 1861 and received the Lyell Medal in 1889 and the Prestwich Medal in 1918. He was knighted in 1919.

Tim Murray

See also Britain, Prehistoric Archaeology; Piltdown Forgery

A page from the Dead Sea Scrolls (Gamma)

Dead Sea Scrolls

Widely acknowledged as a highly significant collection of Hebrew and Aramaic manuscripts, the Dead Sea Scrolls were originally discovered in 1946 in a cave near the Dead Sea at Khirbet Qumran in what is now Israel. Further discoveries were made in caves along the northwestern margin of the Dead Sea. The manuscripts have been dated to a period between the last two centuries B.C. and the first century A.D. and represent primarily religious texts. They are still being studied by scholars from all over the world.

Tim Murray

See also Syro-Palestinian and Biblical Archaeology
References
Silberman, Neil Asher. 1994. *The Hidden Scrolls: Christianity, Judaism, and the War for the Dead Sea Scrolls.* New York: G. P. Putnam's Sons.

Déchelette, Joseph (1862–1914)

Déchelette is considered one of the first professional archaeologists in FRANCE, not only because he was paid by an institution to conduct his work, but also because his social and financial situation allowed him to devote himself full-time to research on a European scale. His career was relatively brief—roughly fifteen years between 1899 when he retired from his manufacturing business and 1914 when he died as a result of action during World War I. Déchelette was a self-taught scholar, never belonging to the academic elite or sharing in its exclusive focus on classical archaeology. He was, both socially and intellectually, above the level of local scholars and amateurs, who were limited to their arrondissement or canton. He was a correspondent of the Institut de France and the Société des Antiquaires, a member of the Comité des Travaux Historiques, a divisional inspector of the Société Française d'Archéologie, and a conservator of the Antiquites et Objets d'Art du Departement de la Loire.

Déchelette's success in the field of protohistoric archaeology was no accident, and in the no-man's-land between history and prehistory he pioneered what innovations were possible at the frontier where different disciplines meet.

Faced with a fragmented discipline in which archaeological remains were interpreted in isolation, Déchelette gathered together scattered records, connected disparate data and defined a relevant method that would work for all the periods covered by archaeology. He acquired an encyclopedic knowledge that enabled him to tackle problems from a synthetic perspective. When the publisher Picard proposed a manual of national archaeology, Déchelette was the obvious person to do it, writing the four volumes of the *Manuel d'archeologie prehistorique, celtique et galloromaine* between 1908 and 1914.

Déchelette was also one of the first archaeologists to examine the structure of empirical archaeological information. His 1904 publication *Les vases ceramiques ornes de la Gaule romaine* probably gives the best account of his method. The analysis of decorative techniques coupled with the identification of categories of vases clarified the apparent chaos of the sherds and indicated the existence of a series of workshops ranked in time and space. It was thus possible to discern the general development of the ceramic industry in the Gallo-Roman era, which coincided with a gradual shift in the centers of production from northern Italy to the banks of the Rhine.

On a more detailed level the study of the decorative motifs and the stamped forms allowed archaeologists to identify each workshop by the individual output of its potters. In turn researchers could then trace how techniques and decorative themes were transmitted from workshop to workshop or even from potter to potter. The next step could be an analysis of the changes in the iconographic repertory, thereby moving from a technochronological study of the archaeological materials to questions of economic history or historical anthropology.

Déchelette, the father of French protohistory, was not a creative genius. He was a conscientious worker who applied himself enthusiastically to his archaeological pursuits in his retirement as he had done to his career in manufacturing.

He was awarded the Legion d'Honneur and given an honorary doctorate by the University of Freiburg. He was a foreign member of the Academies of Madrid and Stockholm and a contributing member of the Deutsches Institut and of the Archaeological Societies of London, Edinburgh, Dublin, Copenhagen, Brussels, Prague, and Hamburg.

Laurent Olivier; translated by Judith Braid

References

For references, see *Encyclopedia of Archaeology: The Great Archaeologists, Vol. 1,* ed. Tim Murray (Santa Barbara, CA: ABC-CLIO, 1999), 287–288.

Deetz, James J. F. (1930–2001)

After receiving his B.A. (1957), M.A. (1959), and Ph.D. (1960) from Harvard University, James J. F. Deetz taught at the University of California at Santa Barbara (1960–1978), Harvard University (1965–1966), Brown University (1967–1978), the College of William and Mary (1977–1978), and the University of California, Berkeley (1978–1993). He then became the David A. Harrison Professor of New World Studies at the University of Virginia. Deetz is acclaimed as a masterful teacher who entertains and inspires the students who flock to his ever-popular courses.

The author of over sixty articles and books that are influential in both historical and prehistoric archaeology, Deetz was admired for his clear and accessible writing. His Ph.D. dissertation, *The Dynamics of Stylistic Change in Arikara Ceramics* (1965), was heralded for its innovative statistical analyses of artifact variation as a means of delineating shifts in social organization and patterns of kinship among the Arikara Indians of the Missouri River Valley before and after European contact. His next book, *Invitation to Archaeology* (1967), was used extensively as a textbook for introductory classes in archaeology, and his popular introduction to historical archaeology, *In Small Things Forgotten* (1977), remains in wide distribution and has had multiple printings. Deetz's *Flowerdew Hundred* (1993) received the 1994 James Mooney Award from the Southern Anthropological Society and the 1995 Distinguished Book Award of the Society of Colonial Wars, New York.

From 1967 to 1978, Deetz served as assistant director of Plimoth Plantation, conducting excavations at a number of historical sites in and around PLYMOUTH, MASSACHUSETTS, including seventeenth-century Pilgrim settlements. From 1982 until the time of his death he was director of research and a member of the board of directors of the Flowerdew Hundred Foundation, Hopewell, Virginia, where he directed field schools and summer institutes in American historical archaeology, sponsored by the National Endowment for the Humanities, at seventeenth-, eighteenth-, and nineteenth-century sites at FLOWERDEW HUNDRED PLANTATION. From 1984 Deetz held the post of honorary visiting professor of historical archaeology at the University of Cape Town, SOUTH AFRICA, and from 1983 he conducted research on the British colonial frontier of the eastern Cape as part of his broader investigation of the comparative archaeology of English colonialism.

Grounded in structuralism, Deetz's approach was synthetic, working from data outward, emphasizing qualitative as well as quantitative evaluations, incorporating multiple and complementary lines of evidence, and allying historical documents closely with excavated evidence. His interest lay in the details of the everyday lives of, for example, early settlers, indigenous peoples, colonists, and African Americans, and his method comprised probing diverse categories of material culture such as houses, gravestones, ceramics, musical instruments, and clay pipes. By examining the products of individuals, Deetz brought to light the underlying cultural rules that generate the patterns of thought which are manifest in social behavior and material culture.

Mary C. Beaudry

References

Deetz, J. 1963. "Archaeological Investigations at La Purisma Mission." In *UCLA Archaeological Survey Annual Report 1962–1963,* 165–241. Los Angeles: Department of Anthropology-Sociology, University of California at Los Angeles.

———. 1965. "The Dynamics of Stylistic Change in Arikara Ceramics." *Illinois Studies in Anthropology* 4. Urbana: University of Illinois Press.

———. 1967. *Invitation to Archaeology.* Garden City, NY: Natural History Press. Translated into Japanese, Tokyo: Tuttle-Mori Agency, 1988.

———. 1971. *Man's Imprint from the Past: Readings in the Methods of Archaeology.* Boston: Little Brown and Company.

———. 1977. *In Small Things Forgotten: An Archaeology of Early American Life.* Garden City, NY: Anchor Books.

———. 1988a. "American Historical Archaeology: Methods and Results." *Science* 239 (22 January): 362–367.

———. 1988b. "History and Archaeological Theory: Walter Taylor Revisited." *American Antiquity* 53, no. 1: 13–22.

———. 1988c. "Material Culture and Worldview in Colonial Anglo-America." In *The Recovery of Meaning: Historical Archaeology in the Eastern United States,* 219–235. Ed. M. P. Leone and P. B. Potter, Jr. Washington, DC: Smithsonian Institution Press.

———. 1989. "Archaeography, Archaeology, or Archeology?" *American Journal of Archaeology* 93: 429–435.

———. 1993. *Flowerdew Hundred: The Archaeology of a Virginia Plantation, 1619–1864.* Charlottesville and London: University Press of Virginia.

Deetz, J. F., and E. S. Dethlefsen. 1964. "Death's Heads, Cherubs, and Willow Trees: Experimental Archaeology in Colonial Cemeteries." *American Antiquity* 31, no. 4: 502–510.

Dendrochronology

See Archaeometry; Dating; Douglass, Andrew Ellicot

Denmark
Discoveries and Scholars

Although archaeology is a young science, it is rooted in a centuries-old tradition as part of the aristocratic passion for collecting. The princely collections of curios fashionable during the Renaissance also contained prehistoric artifacts. They were few in number, since excavations had not yet begun and treasure hunting was only practiced on a small scale in northern Europe. Objects recognized as archaeological were primarily monuments: grave mounds, dolmens and runic stones, and prehistoric remains were rare in this period. Until the end of the reign of King Christian IV, treasure trove material was regarded as a source of state income and melted down. Not until King Frederik III established his Kunstkammer (Chamber of Arts) in 1663 were treasure troves awarded antiquarian status and placed on exhibition.

This situation changed abruptly after the agrarian reforms of the 1780s, which increased the destruction of burial mounds. Although treasure and hoard finds turned up in newly cultivated areas and were more common, thousands of prehistoric remains were being destroyed. This alarming situation led to the establishment in 1807 of the Royal Commission for Antiquities and a national museum, housed in the loft of the Trinitatis Church in Copenhagen. Questionnaires were sent to all clergy and other interested private citizens to obtain a comprehensive survey of the nation's antiquities, and the results were published, but museum accessions were still few.

CHRISTIAN JÜRGENSEN THOMSEN, a merchant with no academic qualifications, was appointed secretary of the Royal Commission for Antiquities. He systematically rearranged the museum's collections, registered accessions, and in 1819 opened the museum to the public via free, weekly, guided tours that he conducted himself. In a short time the museum became an object of great interest throughout Scandinavia. During the fifty years (up to 1865) that Thomsen was in charge—ending as the director of five museums—the foundations of the collections were laid, and the number of accessions rose steadily (in Thomsen's time there were 540 each year). This led to the acquisition in 1832 of four to five rooms in the Christiansborg Palace and still more in 1838, occasioned by the visit of the Russian czar-prince. Finally, in 1854, the museum was housed in Prinsens Palace, where it is still to be found, having undergone extensive alterations and additions in the 1930s. A major factor in the progress of archaeology was Thomsen's principle that the collections should be open to everyone and that guided tours could instruct people about the past and create an interest in antiquities among all classes of society. Thomsen thus established a practice fundamental to all museums today.

In this period only a few random excavations were carried out. Finds were acquired primarily from the many destroyed burial mounds, and they were cataloged and exhibited. A lack of transportation prevented frequent field trips, and museum work was carried out on a part-time and unpaid basis until JENS JACOB WORSAAE received the first royal appointment to the position of inspector for ancient monuments. Great importance was attached to developing contacts with interested collectors and dealers, through the increasing popularity of archaeology at a time of a national economic depression, and the payment of rewards to the finders.

From 1855 onward a growing number of provincial collections were established. With the collecting activity of King Frederik VII as a model, many aristocratic private collections were established in the decades after 1850, and a corresponding number of private citizens' collections were begun in towns. An expanding market for artifacts developed. In these decades the destruction of burial mounds reached a climax as a result of the new prosperity and the many subsequent advances in agriculture.

Worsaae became a museum curator in 1866 in the midst of this sudden expansion. He rearranged the collections, and the National Museum, having created new positions and received special grants, began a more systematic excava-

Gundestrup bowl discovered in Denmark (Image Select)

tion program. Thomsen's students were often out on fieldwork. The great Iron Age bog finds at Thorsbjerg, Nydam, Kragehul, and Vimose were excavated and published by Conrad Engelhardt. The first rich grave finds from the Roman Iron Age from Varpelev and Valløby were published by C. F. Herbst and Engelhardt; Worsaae excavated at the Jelling burial mounds and at Danevirke, and as early as the 1850s he collaborated with the zoologist JAPHETUS STEENSTRUP and the geologist Johann Forchammer in excavating oyster-shell middens that he interpreted as the remains of Stone Age hunting people. From 1873 forward a program of conducting regular local parish visits, made possible by the many new railway lines, was carried out, resulting in new finds and excavations. (Unfortunately, the railways also destroyed a fair number of burial mounds, as did the new roads.) Museum accessions rose in this period to an average of 810 a year.

After Worsaae's sudden death in 1885, the dominant figure in Danish archaeology was SO-PHUS MÜLLER, who became curator of the National Museum in 1892. Projects begun by Worsaae were carried on (including the interdisciplinary study of kitchen middens, the results of which were published in 1900), many new finds were published (such as the sun-chariot from Trundholm and the silver cauldron from Gundestrup), and most large-find groups were reassessed. Among the new activities carried out was the major single-grave project in Jutland, designed to save some of the thousands of grave mounds being destroyed in those years. A regional study of settlements was initiated, and the first Maglemosian habitation site was excavated by Georg Sarauw. The large Iron Age graveyards in Jutland were also systematically studied by C. Neergaard. In fact, a large part of the National Museum's work now focused on Jutland. Systematic excavation techniques were developed, and Müller gradually created his own staff of assistants. During this period, until Müller's retirement in 1921, find accessions reached their peak and stabilized, coinciding with the consolidation of agriculture.

Whereas Worsaae had embraced decentralization and recommended that each county should have its own curator, Müller sought to concentrate all scientific and administrative control in the National Museum. The "old" provincial museums were placed under the administration of the National Museum in 1887, which also directed all excavations and was entitled to all the important finds. This led to the systematic looting of thousands of burial mounds in Jutland by dealers, and Müller began a ruthless, systematic fight against looting by means of proclamations, pamphlets, and popular meetings. With the spread of education and the gradual improvement of social conditions among the rural proletariat, itinerant dealers of looted goods slowly vanished from the scene.

The development of provincial museums in these years took a new direction in many places. Interest in peasant culture rose significantly over the whole of Scandinavia, coinciding with the growth of industrialization, and a large number of folk museums were established. Between 1855 and 1929 seventy-five local history museums were also founded.

New nature-conservation legislation was passed in 1937, which protected all prehistoric remains in situ. Between 1937 and 1957 all parishes in Denmark were inspected by staff from the National Museum. Undisturbed and particularly significant burial mounds and monuments (24,000 in total) were placed under complete protection, and all the 78,000 burial mounds that had been plowed were protected against excavation and destruction. All previous conservation had been voluntary, and thus 7,500 prehistoric sites were already protected when the new legislation was passed. Preservation initiatives had been started by the Commission for Antiquities in 1807, and between 1927 and 1934 nearly 100 sites a year were placed under protection. The new legislation, however, ensured a uniform legislative and administrative framework within which antiquities could be safeguarded as part of the natural and cultural landscape.

Equally important was the 1929 establish-

ment of a lectureship in prehistoric archaeology at the University of Copenhagen. With Johannes Brøndsted as lecturer and, from 1941, as professor, a new generation of young archaeologists were trained there—individuals who would influence the development of Danish archaeology until the present day; the chair of archaeology established in Århus in 1949 guaranteeed scientific continuity. In 1932 and 1933 Brøndsted became curator of the first department of archaeology at the National Museum. A few years earlier, in 1928, the journal *Fra Nationalmuseets Arbejdsmark* was established to provide popular information on archaeology, and was published by the National Museum. Several new staff members were appointed, the first and most important of whom was Therkel Mathiassen, who laid the basis for a new tradition in the regional surveying of settlements and their environments.

There was a gradual but significant decline in the number of new grave and hoard finds brought to the museums during these years, partly because certain find groups were nearly exhausted and partly because of the conservation legislation; the growing interest in settlement finds may also have been relevant. A new type of active archaeologist arose as a result of the attention Mathiassen paid to this group of sites. The popularity of archaeology drew people into the field. During the same period Gudmund Hatt carried out his classic, pioneering work—the registration of Iron Age field systems and the excavation of their house sites. For the third time a research program was begun on an interdisciplinary basis, this one involving the Ertebølle culture and the development of early agriculture, but now, for the first time, interpretations were aided significantly by pollen analyses. The Mose (i.e., bog) Laboratory was set up during the war, and in 1956 the eighth department of the National Museum was established to deal with pollen analysis, C-14 DATING, and similar matters. Among new sites investigated in this era were the large-scale excavations of Trelleborg and Fyrkat.

All these trends were followed and further developed during the 1960s and 1970s by a growing staff of archaeologists. This period was characterized by steadily improving methods of recording and excavation, resulting in the accumulation of essential new knowledge on both detailed and comprehensive levels. The composition of settlement layers was recorded in terms of its archaeology, geology, and botany. Crumbling skeletal remains were exposed in graves with a brush or recorded by means of phosphate analysis. The use of machinery to uncover large surface areas also added to the knowledge of the nature of settlements, since it thereby became possible to expose whole villages. In this way the work of the Settlement Committee (established by the Research Council) was extremely important. Excavation activity also increased with the setting up of the Fortidsmindeforvaltning (Administration of Ancient Monuments), which began the excavation of endangered sites, or rescue archaeology, as laid down in a revision of the Act of Conservation in 1969.

The last two decades of the twentieth century saw the interlinked expansion and development of rescue archaeology and museums. Museums in Denmark took over the practical responsibility of carrying out all rescue archaeology. This initially caused expansion, but since the mid-1980s there has been stagnation. Because so many museums were involved and because a good number of them were small, the demands of modern, large-scale rescue excavations could not be met, and the museums were not helped by legislation, basically unchanged since 1969, that left postexcavation work unfinanced and unpaid for by private developers. (This legislation is about to be revised in accordance with the Malta Convention of the European Parliament.) As a result a large number of young Danish archaeologists migrated to find work in other countries, especially Norway and Sweden. Because rescue archaeology is the motor of the archaeological environment in all industrialized countries, Danish archaeology is now at a watershed. Will it reform legislation and the framework of rescue archaeology and enforce a new dynamic? Or will it remain within the traditional framework of museum archaeology?

Research Objectives and Milieus

Thomsen began a scientific tradition that was as important as his museum work in the development of archaeology in that he created a milieu for archaeological research—a precondition for the development and continuity of every field of study. This goal was reflected in his comprehensive correspondence, in which he shared all his knowledge and experience and thereby decisively influenced the development of museums and archaeology in Scandinavia.

An important figure in the field of scholarship at that time was Thomsen's contemporary C. C. Rafn, who in 1825 was a founding member of the Society of Northern Antiquaries (it became a royal society three years later). Rafn was the prime mover in the society, which was to become the foremost scientific medium for Danish archaeology. Its growing membership, at home and abroad, helped to give Danish archaeology a prominent place during the middle and latter part of the nineteenth century. This was also the time when a special French edition of the society's annual publication was issued (at that time French was the main language of Danish archaeology). The society published Icelandic manuscripts, partly for scholars and partly for the general reader. This effort soon gave the society a sound economic footing, which was further enhanced by the 1837 publication of the international best-seller *Antiquitates Americanae*. The society's scholarly reputation, as well as its capital, increased steadily during the nineteenth century, partly because a growing proportion of its core membership consisted of scientists, heads of state, princes, and other prominent figures from all over the world. From 1832 on archaeology was represented in the periodical *Nordisk Tidsskrift for Oldbyndighed*, retitled *Antiquerisk Tidsskrift* after 1936. These journals were succeeded in 1866 by *Aarbøger for nordisk Oldkyndighed*. During their first few decades, however, they primarily served the study of history and philology. To change this situation required an improvement in the status of archaeology, reflected both in greater activity and in an archaeological objective defined in terms of social and cultural history. This change was brought about by Thomsen's followers in the years after 1850, with Worsaae as the guiding spirit.

The ground had already been prepared in the 1840s when the young Worsaae elegantly re-

A well-preserved Stone Age tumulus at Roddinge, Denmark, containing two chambers (Ann Ronan Picture Library)

futed some of the period's more imaginative manifestations of archaeological enterprise. These included a body found in a bog at Harald-skjaer that was alleged to be that of Queen Gun-hild, known as the wife of Erik Bloodaxe; and the dramatic Runamo runic inscriptions that— subjected to Worsaae's critical scrutiny— proved to be not the work of humans but natural cracks and crevices. This caused a sensation because on this occasion a young student academically demolished some of the most eminent scholars of the time, as was confirmed later during a debate in the Academy of Sciences and Letters. By his effective and tactically well chosen criticism of a few examples of the erroneous and uncritical use of archaeological sources, Worsaae had achieved an important victory for the independence of the new science. This success was followed by a demonstration of how archaeological sources might contribute to the knowledge of prehistoric cultures, in Worsaae's popular book, designed for the general reader entitled *Danmarks Oldtid oplyst ved Oldsager og*

Grachøie [Denmark's Prehistory as Revealed in Antiquities and Burial Mounds]. First published in 1843, the work was translated into German in 1844 and English in 1849. Built around Thomsen's THREE-AGE SYSTEM, it emphasized the inadequacy of written sources, argued against legendary traditions, proposed a process of culture-historical evolution, and gave the three ages an approximate dating.

The period between 1850 and 1875 was a turning point for the development of the natural and historical sciences throughout Europe. In archaeology Thomsen's three-age system was seen to be valid by the larger part of the scholarly and archaeological world. In Denmark itself archaeology was established as an independent discipline. Thomsen's system was also developed chronologically, and dates were provided. The archaeological community in these decades was dynamic and open to new ideas, with no sharp divisions between professional and amateur archaeologists or between the various disciplines of social and cultural history. There was as yet no formal archaeological training. The subsequent fifty years were a time of consolidation and stabilization during which the many problems formulated by Worsaae were tackled and few new problems arose. Under Sophus Müller archaeology followed a narrower path. A well-defined scientific methodology was worked out, both in resolving chronologies and in excavation, and at the same time there were stricter demands placed on archaeological work.

Another equally essential archaeological prerequisite was the working out of a well-defined scientific method to build a chronology. It was soon realized that it was possible to establish a "developmental series" of artifacts, which could be divided according to type. When these type series were compared with one another, in the context of closed finds, the main periods could now be subdivided with great accuracy. Formerly, divisions had primarily been based on differences; now they were based on graduated similarities. This method had been developed in Sweden in the 1870s by HANS HILDEBRAND and OSCAR MONTELIUS, who gave it its methodologically most precise version under the name of typology. In fact, typology reflected a general methodological tendency in contemporary archaeological research, which was probably one reason why Müller argued so vehemently against it. In his opinion it was nothing new.

The decades around the turn of the nineteenth century thus saw two major achievements: a representative collection was acquired as a result of substantial accessions, and with this collection as well as improved typological methods, chronological systems were finally worked out. Broadly speaking, later research has only added minor chronological adjustments. Bronze Age chronology was the first to find its final version in 1885, followed by Iron Age chronology and, after the turn of the century, Stone Age chronology. Only the Old Stone Age was still inadequately studied, and settlements from the other periods also began to attract scholarly attention. It was now possible to show the distribution over large geographic areas of specific artifact types, and typological studies not of chronological changes but of geographic ones could demonstrate the spread of

cultural influences, often from south to north. The distribution areas of specific artifact types were termed *culture groups,* and these groups were identified with different peoples. One such culture group, the single-grave culture, had been discovered in systematic excavations in Jutland, and it was thought to represent a new immigration from the southeast. Worsaae's desiderata had now been fulfilled. In this period similar theories of culture were also being worked out in philology, anthropology (the study of races), and ethnography (the culture-group theory in Europe, the Boas school in the United States). There was widespread interest in cultural diffusion, which was linked with theories on migration and so forth. Race, language, and culture were the basic elements. Archaeologists managed to date the Bronze and Iron Age periods by linking finds from the north with those from the south, found in Greece and Egypt. This fundamental progress enabled Sophus Müller to give the first truly comprehensive account, in 1897, of cultural developments in Danish prehistory.

Under Müller and his successor, C. Neergaard (who served from 1921 to 1933), the research milieu was restrictive, and rigid lines of demarcation were drawn in many directions. Müller laid down the objectives that all had to pursue, and he controlled publication rights. Consequently, able assistants with an independent outlook, such as Georg Sarauw and later on Blinkenberg, Johansen, and Hatt, eventually left the museum. Yet considerable results were obtained, and archaeological material was not allowed to remain unpublished. At the end of the nineteenth century several major works by A. P. Madsen, V. Boye, and others were published, and the monograph series "Nordiske Fortidsminder" was begun in 1889 to present important new finds.

When Johannes Brøndsted began lecturing at the University of Copenhagen in 1929 and then—almost by a palace revolution—replaced Neergaard as head of the first department of the National Museum from 1932 to 1933, an open and dynamic research environment was restored, and there was an impressive increase in activity in all areas. Contacts were reestablished with the natural science, with the university, and with amateur archaeologists. Efforts were directed toward two goals: elucidating Old Stone Age cultures and the problem of settlements in general and establishing renewed chronological studies in order to improve the older systems. The following two decades were among the most productive in the history of Danish archaeology. One major publication came after another, and to present many of the new results to an international public, *Acta Archaeologica* was founded in 1930. From 1938 to 1940 Brøndsted summarized the results in his impressive outline entitled *Danmarks Oldtid* (*Denmark in Olden Times*). The book covered no new theoretical ground, but it did present the picture of Danish prehistory with more detail and subtlety than ever before. This book was followed by a steadily increasing flow of popular books and pamphlets.

Brøndsted's students have left their mark on developments up to the present day—in positions at the National Museum, in institutes of archaeology, and in a few provincial museums. Yet a kind of dividing line appeared toward the year 1950. In 1949 P. V. Glob became a professor in Århus, as did C. J. Becker in Copenhagen in 1952. Glob devoted himself to great practical tasks—at first in the newly founded Jydsk Arkaeologisk Selskab (Archaeological Society of Jutland), as founder of the Prehistoric Museum of Moesgård, and on expeditions to the Persian Gulf and then later as keeper of national antiquities, in which capacity he no doubt was more successful than anybody else in giving archaeology a popular image. By contrast, Becker carried on the scientific traditions of the discipline in Copenhagen with special emphasis on chronological research and later settlement excavations. In subsequent decades he trained most of the younger generation of archaeologists. In this way and as editor of the chief publications, Becker helped to influence scientific developments during this period more effectively than anyone else.

There is, however, a kind of interaction between Århus and Copenhagen. In Århus an enterprising, outgoing archaeological environment was created around the Jydsk Arkaeologisk Selskab and the new journal *Kuml,* first appearing in 1961, and the atmosphere was intensified by the professor Ole Klindt-Jensen. In Copenhagen, however, a more restrictive research community developed, based on research conducted within the framework laid down by Becker. This was furthered by the publication of the new monograph series "Arkaeologiske Studier," which first came out in 1973. As a result of these opposing tendencies in Århus and Copenhagen, the period has not been characterized by fundamental methodological progress, although there has been more precise methodological formulation (by, e.g., Mogens Orsnes and Olfert Voss) and an increasing use of statistical methods. In terms of social and cultural history it has been a period of stagnation: Brøndsted and Glob have had their work reprinted, but new publications in the field have failed to produce fresh insights or information.

Since 1975 a special Danish version of the "New Archaeology" has developed—something that is less theoretical and more anchored in the archaeological material, trying to combine the English and the German traditions. This becomes apparent when looking through the major journals: *Aarbøger for nordisk Oldkyndighed* (Copenhagen), *Kuml* (Århus), *Journal of Danish Archaeology,* and *Acta Archaeologica.* One reason for the direction of Danish archaeology is that the major proponents of the New Archaeology have chosen to publish internationally. After an expansive period of new theoretical developments during the 1970s and early 1980s, some stagnation (or perhaps consolidation) has taken over. Danish archaeology has tended to become more regional than international, a development that might be linked to the lack of university departments (only two small departments exist) and the dominance of museums. During the 1980s a national research project titled "From Tribe to State" inspired a series of conferences and books on the formation of Iron Age chiefdoms and states, another example of regional perspectives dominating.

Among the new research trends since the mid-1980s the most profilic has been underwater or maritime archaeology. National surveys and large-scale rescue operations, in combination with the establishment of a new research center, have encouraged an expansion in this field. In addition, the computerization of the large national register of monument, sites, and finds during the 1980s led to developments in the application of modern methodological tools such as GEOGRAPHIC INFORMATION SYSTEMS (GIS) in settlement archaeology. The other area of expansion has resulted from the establishment of two national research centers for settlement studies during the 1990s, which have helped to analyze and publish the results of settlement excavations and projects, such as the Thy project, the Als project, or the Saltbæk Vig project, all based upon international cooperation.

Archaeology in Society

A general and well-known feature of the archaeology of many countries is that, throughout its development, it has been part of national moral rearmament, and Denmark is no exception. The "fateful years" of 1807, 1848, 1864, 1920, and 1940 to 1945 are all reflected in the archaeological activity of the time, and prehistory in these years of crisis was frequently used as a symbol of national identity. After all, it was not only through museums and archaeological books that knowledge of archaeology spread. Most of the population learned about it second- or thirdhand—primarily through the literary tradition but also in an attenuated form through school textbooks, children's books, folk high schools, and so forth. In this way knowledge of prehistory and of the past in general reached a large section of society in a complex process of dissemination, during which it underwent several changes and was used in many disguises. The question is whether it is possible to discern behind these general tendencies any important changes in the social position of archaeology and its ideological affiliations. Was archaeology used? What was it used for and by whom? We can attempt to answer these questions in several ways. The records of the National Museum, for instance, show us the route from finder to museum and the fact that that route changed. The other route, from archaeologists out to different segments of society via literature, popular outlines, and the like, is also informative. Fi-

nally, the founding of museums and the active interest shown by people outside the circle of professional archaeologists provide us with more tangible information.

There seems to be no doubt that the Commission for Antiquities was set up as the indirect result of the Romantic movement and the national defeats of the time. There is also no doubt that during its first fifty years, archaeology in Denmark was a leisure pursuit of the educated upper class. So-called popular backing was found only on a small scale. The clergy and local government officials (magistrates and county prefects) played a crucial role by maintaining contact with the Museum of Antiquities during this early period. But it was the payment of rewards that counted among those people who actually made the finds, since their standard of living was miserably low throughout most of the nineteenth century. The educational ideas that were part of the archaeological effort were expressed by archaeologists and the educated upper class of government officials and landowners.

Those who were to become enlightened by the past were not themselves actively involved in this process. The initiatives came from the people at the top. Several attempts were made at the time to set up public archaeological collections in the provinces, often attached to a county library (i.e., as part of the educational effort). But they were only attempts. Both administratively and ideologically, archaeology remained an integral part of the period's autocracy.

In the interwar years between 1850 and 1864, five provincial museums were established in rapid succession: Ribe, Odense, Århus, Viborg, and Ålborg. They were founded by the educated upper middle class of the towns and not by the social group with which they were most concerned—the local peasants—at a time when the towns were experiencing rapid population increases and economic expansion. By this point archaeology had won general recognition as an important branch of national history, which was further emphasized by King Frederik VII's active interest in the field. Moreover, investigations were begun during these years at a number of national monuments, such as Jelling and Danevirke, and in Denmark's relationship with Germany archaeology was used as a political weapon. Worsaae denied German claims of ethnic and cultural affinities between South Jutland and Germany in his 1865 publication of Schleswig's prehistoric monuments. So, too, did Sophus Müller when he wrote about South Jutland's prehistory in 1913 and 1914. On the whole, the discussion of such nationalist themes has always thrived in times of national crisis or consolidation.

The great period of museum foundation occurred at the end of the nineteenth century and in the first decades of the twentieth (up to and including the 1930s). This was also a time of expansion for the folk high schools. The farmers and peasantry were the new dominant class. While they organized themselves politically and economically—forming the Venstre (Left) party, cooperative societies, banks, and so on—the folk high schools provided their cultural education. Farmers and peasants were taught a sense of cultural and historical identity by these schools, which spread and renewed fundamental national values, as reflected, for instance, in the high school songbooks. And as a result of this farmers and schoolteachers began to establish their own museums, the folk and regional museums. These institutions expressed the cultural self-assurance of farming people as keepers and intermediaries of the old vanishing peasant culture. They also reflected the desire for a more tangible historical identity based on the districts they lived in and knew well. As a further sign of this phenomenon, a large number of county historical journals were published beginning at the turn of the century. New social groups had become exponents of archaeological activity and of historical activity as a whole. For these people both history and prehistory had a definite function, giving perspective and meaning to their own roles in transmitting historical traditions. At the same time, it should be remembered that below the new class of independent farmers there still existed a large and uneducated rural proletariat, many members of which emigrated to the United States in the 1880s and 1890s. They did not receive their share of the progress until the smallholders' legislation and social reforms of the twentieth century.

As the records of the National Museum demonstrate, teachers replaced the clergy as museum middlemen. In fact, schoolteachers played a major role in the archaeological and historical work of this period. In keeping with these developments, Müller saw archaeology as a product of the new era: as he observed, "Rather than tracing its ancestry to the Middle Ages, in the manner of aristocrats, the study of prehistory prefers to regard itself as a child of the new era, born as an ordinary citizen in the dawn of the Century of Liberty."

The period between 1930 and 1950 was a time of consolidation, during which the cultural activities in the countryside were continued—for example, in youth and gymnastic clubs and in regional historical societies. A growing number of interested individuals, with affiliations to the tradition of regional history, became actively involved as amateur archaeologists and made their own collections, many of which became the nuclei of small, regional museums. These private collectors—many of them gardeners or working men and women—had a different background from their predecessors. Amateur archaeologists, the active collectors, became a new concept. This tendency toward a proliferation of archaeological interest has been accentuated since 1980. In the towns a new and large circle of educated, middle-class readers are reached primarily through the periodical *Skalk* but also through an increasing number of popular archaeological books, for which there is now a ready market. The readers are not actively involved in archaeology; rather, they see it as something exciting and interesting—as entertainment. This attitude is underlined by the way prehistory is presented: as "newspaper items" in *Skalk,* as prehistoric news in the form of sensational and exciting new finds, in the slightly piquant and macabre appeal of Glob's book *The Bog People,* and so forth. Archaeology long ago abandoned its nationalistic commitment and has become entertainment for the rising middle classes. New types of exhibitions and museums also seek to attract this public. The national commitment to use archaeology has continued mainly among nonarchaeologists, most explicitly in the writings of Martin A. Hansen.

During the period 1975 to 2000 archaeology in Denmark was professionally consolidated. This effort was mainly linked to the expansion of local and regional museums. After a period of stagnation during the 1950s and 1960s, these institutions became the driving force in local cultural revivals. The modernization of Danish society increased the demand for and interest in local histories and identities, and museums successfully took on the job of meeting those needs. New grassroots movements formed local archives to supplement this development. History since industrialization became a major interest, as it presented a parallel story to the present-day transformations of society and landscape. And since 1985 public interest has increasingly focused on monuments and landscapes as part of a revitilization of local tourism and recreation.

Kristian Kristiansen

Acknowledgments

Gratitude is expressed to Jens Henrik Bech, Lotte Hedeager, Jorgen Street-Jensen, Birgitte Kjae, Viggo Nielsen, and Olfert Voss for their critical comments and supplementary information during the final preparation of this article.

References

Christensen, Aksel E. 1969. Vikingetidens Danmark.: Pa oldhistorisk baggrund. Kobenhavn: Det kgl. Nordiske Oldskrifts-Selskab 1831: Om nordiske Oldsager og deres Opbevaring.

Earle et al. 1998. "The Political Economy of Late Neolithic and Early Bronze Age Society: The Thy Archaeological Project." *Norwegian Archaeological Review* 31, 1: 1–28.

Klindt-Jensen, O. 1975: *A History of Scandinavian Archaeology*. London: Thames and Hudson.

Kristiansen, K. 1996. "The Destruction of the Archaeological Heritage and the Formation of Museum Collections: The Case of Denmark." In *Learning from Things*. Ed. David W. Kingery. Method and Theory in Material Culture Studies. Washington, DC: Smithsonian Institution Press.

Thomsen, C. J. 1849. *A Guide to Northern Antiquities*. London.

Worsaae, J. J. A. 1849. *The Primeval Antiquities of Denmark*. London.

Desor, Edouard (1811–1882)

Born near Frankfurt, Germany, but of French origin, Edouard Desor played an important role in the development of archaeological research in SWITZERLAND after the middle of the nineteenth century. Desor's intellectual path was eventful. While studying law in Germany, his political activities in the liberal movement forced him into exile, first in Paris, then in Bern, Switzerland, where he met and developed a friendship with the naturalist Louis Agassiz, whom he then followed to Neuchâtel, Switzerland.

As the young master's right-hand man, Desor found himself among Agassiz's disciples and became immersed in the intense dynamic of research in what was a "scientific factory," in the words of his friend Carl Vogt. He studied the natural sciences—geology, paleontology, and above all, glaciology—during some of the group's risky explorations in the Alps. In 1848, he followed Agassiz to the United States, where they fell out. While Agassiz was teaching at Harvard University, Desor undertook different geographical, geological, and zoological tasks and surveys for the U.S. government. Four years later he returned to Switzerland to teach geology in Neuchâtel.

Desor's curiosity was universal, both in the natural sciences and in prehistoric research, which he only discovered in 1854 following the work of FERDINAND KELLER on the lake dwellers. His easy social nature and his facility of expression, as much as his liking for travel, enabled him to be in constant contact with most Swiss and foreign prehistorians and naturalists. Thus, Desor chaired the first international congress of prehistory ("paleoethnology") in his adoptive town of Neuchâtel in 1866.

He inherited a considerable fortune after his brother died, which gave him financial security while he studied and published. It also allowed him to keep an open house for guests who wished to participate in scientific debates, and this venue became famous in Neuchâtel. He continued to be involved in politics, initially on behalf of the Radical (progressive) Party, which elected him president of the Swiss Federal Assembly.

Desor studied the palafittes, or pole dwellings, of Lake Neuchâtel, but he also studied those of other lakes, both Swiss and foreign. He even started lake-dwelling research in northern Italy. His studies sought to clarify the differences between Neolithic and Bronze Age sites by defining reference corpora. He was one of the few people to question whether the so-called dwellings on water were warehouses rather than houses. He became interested in the problems of trade, and the relationships between land and lakeside dwellings, but, unlike most of his contemporaries, he always remained cautious about ethnic assimilations and peoples' migrations. Desor worked to familiarize Swiss scientists with Nordic Mesolithic and French Paleolithic research. He closely followed French archeologist GABRIEL DE MORTILLET's work on the origins of man.

Desor is most famous for his work at the site of LA TÈNE in Switzerland, and he excavated several mounds in the Neuchâtel area. He was the first to propose a chronological division of the Iron Age (Desor 1865, 1866, 1868). He argued that the mounds (or tumuli), even without any iron objects, such as those at Favargettes, belonged to the earliest part of the Iron Age, like the Hallstatt sites, whereas the sites of La Tène, Tiefenau (Bern), and ALESIA (France) represented a second development, or a later Iron Age. Alesia provided a certain chronology, thus joining prehistory to history.

Desor made few detailed studies on precise subjects, but his insatiable curiosity encouraged him to try to find out all the facts he could about archaeology. With his open mind and his great scientific rigor, he considerably widened the field of prehistoric research.

Marc-Antoine Kaeser

References

Aspes, A. 1994. "A History of Research on the Lake-Dwellings in Northern Italy." *Bulletin of the XIII Congress of the International Union of Prehistoric and Protohlstoric Sciences—Forli, Italy, 1996* 2: 75–78.

Desor, E. 1865. *Les palafittes ou constructions lacustres du Lac de Neuchatel.* Paris: Reinwald.

———. 1866. "Discours d'ouverture du Congres International Paleoethnologique de Neuchatel, 1866." *Materiaux pour l'histoire primitive et naturelle de l'homme* (September–October): 471–482.

———. 1867. "Discussion sur la premiere epoque du fer." In *Congres internanon d'anthropologieet d'archéologie préhistoriques. Compte rendu de la 2me session, Paris, 1867,* 291–296. Paris: Reinwald.

———. 1868. "Le tumulus des Favargettes." *Musée Neuchatelois* 5: 229–242.

Desor, E., and L. Favre. 1874. *Le bel âge du bronze lacustre en Suisse.* Paris and Neuchâtel: Sandoz.

Favre, L., and F. Berthoud. 1883. "Edouard Desor: Discours prononcés à l'ouverture des cours de l'Academie de Neuchâtel le 12 avril 1882." *Musée Neuchatelois* 20: 29–74.

Kaenel, G. 1990. *Recherches sur la période de La Tène en Suisse occidentale: Analyse des sépultures.* Cahiers d'archeologie romande 90. Lausanne: Bibliotheque Historique Vaudoise.

———. 1991. "Troyon, Desor et les "Helvetiens" vers le milieu du XIXe siecle." *Archaologie der Schweiz* 14: 19–28.

Rivier, H. 1931. "La Société neuchâteloise des Sciences Naturelles 1832–1932. Notice historique publiée à l'occasion de son centenaire (Chapters II–III, 1833–1882)." *Bulletin de la Societé Neuchâteloise des Sciences Naturelles* 56: 18–47.

Schaer, J.-P. 1994. "Pierre Jean Edouard Desor (1811–1882)." *Histoire de l'Université de Neuchatel,* Vol. 2, *La seconde Academie.* 403–408. Hauterive: Université de Neuchâtel/Attinger.

Deutsches Archäologisches Institut (DAI)

The antecedents of the Deutsches Archäologisches Institut (DAI, German Archaeological Institute) lie in the Instituto di Corrispondenza Archeologica, which was founded in Rome in 1829 by a group of antiquarians, artists, and diplomats. The purpose of the institute was the promotion of the study of classical art, epigraphy, and topography. The Prussian crown prince (later King Friedrich Wilhelm IV) was its first patron, and in 1832, when Eduard Gerhard, the person most responsible for the creation of the institute left Rome for Berlin, the organization moved with him.

Beginning in 1859, the links between the institute and first the Prussian and later the German governments became closer until it became a government operation and the name was changed to the Deutsches Archäologisches Institut. Since the turn of the twentieth century, the

DAI has grown from a focus on Italy to encompass a German interest in the archaeology of Greece and the Middle East. As such, it has become a major source of finance and administration for German archaeological activity and is a highly respected publisher of field and laboratory research pursued under its auspices.

Tim Murray

See also German Contributions to the Archaeology of the Classical World

Dezman, Dragotin (1821–1889)

The Slovenian archaeologist, natural scientist, and politician Dragotin Dezman (also known as Carl Deschmann) introduced and developed scientific and professional archaeology in SLOVENIA. He first studied medicine, law, and natural sciences at Vienna University; was curator of the Provincial Museum of Carniola (Landes Museum fur Krain) in Ljubljana from 1852 to 1889; and in 1864 was made president of the Museum Society of Carniola and also a member of the Anthropological Society of Vienna.

As a natural scientist, Dezman devoted the first decades of his research and museum work almost entirely to his specialities: zoology, botany, and geology. However, in 1875 he discovered pile dwellings at the site of LJUBLJANSKO BARJE in Slovenia, and from then on he focused most of his work on prehistoric archaeology. From 1875 to 1877 he conducted several excavations of pile dwellings and uncovered some interesting artifacts such as wooden architectural remains, clay figurines, richly ornamented pottery, and the earliest metal finds in Slovenia. He published only short reports and notices of this work.

In the 1880s, he extended his prehistoric research to include the entire province of Carniola, the core province among Slovenian lands in the Austro-Hungarian Empire. He published the first syntheses on the prehistory of this province, "Prahistorische ansiedlungen und Begrabnisstatten" and "Zur Vorgeschichte Krains" in 1880 and 1891, respectively.

Dezman considered prehistoric archaeology to be a natural science founded on empiricist and evolutionist anthropological bases. He tried to follow the development of archaeology in Europe and to apply the best standards of those positivist disciplines to his work. For example, he was able to distinguish the LA TÈNE finds in Carniola only a year after the Iron Age was divided into the Hallstatt and La Tène periods. He maintained contacts with many of the most important institutions and scholars in central Europe and even beyond. He integrated the Provincial Museum into the international museum network, and after his important discoveries at Ljubljansko Barje, he organized the First Austrian Congress of Anthropology and Prehistory in Ljubljana in 1879. As an important personality in political and cultural life (mayor of Ljubljana 1871–1873, member of Parliament in Vienna 1873–1879), he succeeded in developing the new Museum Palace, which was officially opened in 1888. On that occasion he published a modern guidebook to the museum's collections, of which the prehistory collection was the most prominent.

Predrag Novakovic

References

Dezman, D. 1880. "Prahistorische ansiedlungen und Begrabnisstatten." In Krain I. Bericht, *Denkschriften der k.k. Akademie der Wissenschaften, Matematisch-naturwissenschaftliche Classe* 42, 1–54. Vienna.

———. 1888. *Fuhrer durch das Krainische Landes-Museum Rudolfinum in Laibach.* Ljubljana.

———. 1891. "Zur Vorgeschichte Krains." In *Die osterreichisch-ungarisch Monarchie in Wort und Bild, Karnten und Krain,* 305–324. Vienna.

Gabrovec, S. 1971. "Stopetdeset let arheologije v Narodnem muzeju." *Argo* 10, no. 1.

Lozar, R. 1941. "Razvoj in problemi slovenske arheoloske vede." *Zbornik za umetnostno zgodovino* 17.

Dikaios, Porphyrios (1904–1971)

Porphyrios Dikaios studied archaeology in GREECE, Britain, and FRANCE. He was the curator of the Cyprus Museum from 1931 to 1960, acting director of the Department of Antiquities during World War II, and director from 1960 to 1963. He made major contributions to Cypriot archaeology through his excavations at numerous sites of many periods, the more important of which include Neolithic Khirokitia-Vouni

(1936–1946) and Sotira-Teppes (1947–1956), early–Bronze Age Bellapais-Vounous (1931–1932), and late–Bronze Age ENKOMI (1947–1957). His work on the earlier periods in CYPRUS, summarized in his contribution to the fourth volume of *The Swedish Cyprus Expedition*, is of particular significance, both in providing primary data and in the analytical and conceptual frameworks he developed, which still structure much current research. His substantial publication on the excavations at Enkomi remains the starting point for research on the later prehistory of the island.

David Frankel

References

Price, Stanley. n.d. 1979. "On Terminology and Models in Cypriot Prehistory." In *Studies Presented in Memory of Porphyrios Dikaios*, 1–11. Ed. V. Karageorghis. Nicosia: Lions Club.

Stylianou, N., ed. 1998. *Photomosaic: Pictures through the Years by Porphyrios Dikaios.* Nicosia: Cultural Services, Ministry of Education and Culture.

Dolní Vestonice

Excavated by the Czech archaeologist Karel Absolon (1887–1960), Dolní Vestonice is a complex of six open-air sites in Moravia, CZECH REPUBLIC, dating from the Upper Palaeolithic period (about 25,000 years ago). The site features an accumulation of bones from over 100 woolly mammoths, hearths, pits, evidence of round dwellings, and a number of burials. Subsequent work in the mid-1980s revealed more burials. The LITHIC technology (featuring burins, scrapers, and backed blades) is classified as Eastern Gravettian. Perhaps most remarkable of all is the abundance of fired clay, including one complete "Venus" figurine and the remains of two simple kilns, which together are the earliest evidence for pottery anywhere in the world.

Tim Murray

Domestication of Plants and Animals

The domestication of wild plants and animals (which is a characteristic of the Neolithic period in any given region) has been a worldwide phenomenon occurring independently in southwest

Clay "Venus" from Dolní Vestonice, Gravettian, 24,800 B.C. (Ancient Art and Architecture Collection Ltd.)

Asia, parts of North, Central, and South America, CHINA, and Africa. This change in human behavior arose following the trend toward exploration of a more broad-spectrum economy in the Mesolithic period (approximately 12,000 years ago), when people expanded their hunting and fishing repertoire to include previously unexploited species. Between 10,000 and 5,000 years ago, farming, pastoralism, and sedentism were being adopted on a large scale, although by no means universally.

Domestication of wild species results when humans take control of an animal's or a plant's reproductive cycle, causing genetic and phenotypic change. The degree of control people have over their environment can be measured on a continuum, ranging, for example, from herding wild animals to breeding them for specific preselected traits, and it can exist for hundreds of

Painting of herdsmen with cattle, from the tomb of Nebarnun, 1400 B.C. (Image Select)

years as minimal intervention. The process of increasing control is also known as "the emergence of food production," representing a shift in focus from the end product (the dead animal or harvested plant) to the living organism and its secondary products (such as milk or wool or seeds for replanting) (Meadow 1984).

Food production and domestication are visible in the archaeological record through such sources as (1) metric evidence (size), (2) morphology (shape), (3) age/sex profile in an archaeological assemblage, and (4) geography (presence of a species outside its natural range) (Bogucki 1999). In general, domesticated plants increase in size as people select for higher yield per plant, and domesticated animals decrease in size as people select for docility. Morphological changes in plants include the shift from a brittle to a flexible rachis (the stem connecting the seed to the stalk), as people harvest and cultivate seeds that remain on the plant after others have scattered. In animals, morphological changes include the twisting and spiraling shapes of horn cores in goats and sheep and an increase in meat and wool bearing. Animal domestication also results in the retention of juvenile physical characteristics into adult-

hood, such as short muzzles in dogs and small tusks in pigs.

Quantities and proportions of plants as well as the age and sex profile of animals at a site can be used to distinguish economic strategies ranging from hunting and gathering to cultivation and pastoralism. A concentration of a few plant species may indicate intensive gathering or cultivation rather than opportunistic collection. A large quantity of immature animals in a faunal profile rather than a generalized assemblage could reflect domesticated herds in which only a few older individuals were kept for breeding. Finally, the spread of plant and animal species outside their ancestral range can usually be linked to human intervention and encouragement.

Although animal and plant domestication arose independently in several parts of the world, the search for the earliest origins of agriculture has focused on three archaeological regions in the Near East: the Levant (ISRAEL, Syria, and JORDAN), Anatolia (modern TURKEY), and the Zagros Mountains (IRAN and Iraq). The Natufian culture of the Levant (12,500 years ago) has been identified with the earliest sedentary communities, dependent on the harvesting of wild cereals and the hunting of gazelles at sites such as Jericho and Abu Hureyra (Bogucki 1999). By 10,000 years ago the descendants of the Natufians, whose culture is known as Pre-Pottery Neolithic A, had adopted a strategy involving the domestication of emmer wheat, einkorn wheat, and barley, followed by the domestication of sheep and goats. These founder crops and animals of the Near East—emmer and einkorn wheat, sheep, and goats—were transported with the spread of agriculture through southeastern Europe to western Europe, reaching the British Isles by 4,000 to 3,000 years ago (Haviland 2000).

Agriculture developed independently in East Asia from two centers, the Huanghe or Yellow River valley in northern China, where foxtail millet was domesticated, and the middle Yangzi River in southern China, which was the source of domesticated rice. Archaeological evidence places the origins of rice crops at about 8,500 years ago (Bogucki 1999). In West Africa crops such as sorghum, pearl millet, watermelon, black-eyed peas, and kola nuts were domesticated, and they spread through central Africa with the migration of Bantu speakers (Haviland 2000).

MESOAMERICA is the site of the earliest domestication in the New World. There, archaeologists have long sought the origin of maize, believed to have originated in wild teosinte (found in the Valley of MEXICO) and been domesticated as early as 7,000 years ago, after which it spread throughout the New World (Pringle 1997). Some of the earliest examples of the domesticated dog have been found in North America, dating back almost 15,000 years, although this animal was domesticated independently in many areas of the world. In addition, North Americans were the first to domesticate the sunflower, squash, marsh elder, and chenopod by about 4,000 years ago (Smith 1995), and they also adopted maize and beans introduced from Mesoamerica. South American domesticates include the bottle gourd, cotton, and, later, the potato and manioc, as well as animals such as guinea pigs, llamas, alpacas, and ducks.

The mechanisms and motivations behind the beginnings of food production continue to be explored. We know that the switch from hunting and gathering to cultivation and herding did not arise from new knowledge about the reproduction of plants and animals, for people had a deep understanding about their environment long before they chose to adopt agriculture. Additionally, the transition to an agricultural economy entailed many disadvantageous conditions and an overall decline in health and longevity. For instance, sedentism and population increases coincided with an increase in communicative diseases, some of them created by new waste-disposal problems. And agriculture provided a less stable subsistence base: farmers became vulnerable to crop failure, and since they were invested in permanent settlements, they could no longer move on when local food resources were depleted. Consequently, archaeologists are concerned with discovering the possible pressures that caused people to adopt a stressful and potentially dangerous subsistence strategy involving sedentism, cultivation, and animal raising.

The first cultigens, such as maize, wheat, and barley, grow easily in a disturbed habitat, and they may have propagated themselves around peoples' living areas. But these plants selected for domestication were not first-choice foods for foragers. Instead, early farmers sacrificed flexibility, diversity of diet, and access to first-choice foods in exchange for permanent, year-round settlement with a nearby food supply.

Possible reasons for this shift include environmental factors such as food shortages, population pressure, and climatic drying and cultural developments such as adaptation to sedentism and changes in band organization beginning in the preceding Pleistocene society (Bogucki 1999). Previous theories explaining the emergence of food production, proposed by archaeologists such as VERE GORDON CHILDE, ROBERT BRAIDWOOD, Kent Flannery, and Andrew Moore, primarily dealt with environmental and population pressures on foraging societies. More recently, social factors have been examined for their contributing role in the dramatic shift in subsistence strategy that occurred in the Neolithic (Bogucki 1999).

Thalia Gray

References

Bogucki, P. 1999. *The Origins of Human Society.* Malden, UK: Blackwell Publishers.

Haviland, W. A. 2000. *Human Evolution and Prehistory.* Fort Worth, TX: Harcourt College Publishers.

Meadow, R. 1984. "Animal Domestication in the Middle East." In *Animals and Archaeology,* vol. 3, *Early Herders and Their Flocks.* BAR International Series 202. Ed. J. Clutton-Brock and C. Grigson. Oxford: British Archaeological Reports.

Pringle, H. 1997. "The Slow Birth of Agriculture." *Science* 282: 1446–1450.

Rindos, D. 1984. *The Origins of Agriculture: An Evolutionary Perspective.* Orlando, FL: Academic Press.

Smith, B. 1995. *The Emergence of Agriculture.* New York: W. H. Freeman. (Scientific American Library).

Dorpfeld, Wilhelm (1853–1940)

Dorpfeld was employed as an architectural draftsman at the excavation of Olympia, under the supervision of the great German classical archaeologist ERNST CURTIUS. It was Dorpfeld who had shown HEINRICH SCHLIEMANN around the site of Olympia in 1876, which Schliemann visited after he had been accused of amateur and unscientific excavation methods. Dorpfeld was familiar with the technical side of the excavations and so impressed Schliemann that he was eventually hired to work at the site of Troy, in Hisarlik in Turkey.

From 1882 to 1890, Dorpfeld was Schliemann's assistant. He began at Troy during Schleimann's third season of excavations, after Schliemann had once again been criticized by journalists and some archaeologists for being a treasure hunter and a fraud—and this despite the friendship of the great German archaeologist RUDOLF VIRCHOW. So Dorpfeld was employed for scholarly credibility, and wisely so as it turned out. He clarified the stratigraphy of the walls and allowed a better understanding of the evolution of the structures on the site. He corrected Schliemann's mistake of attributing the burnt layer to the second rather than the third layer from the bottom. Dorpfeld also discovered that the city continued outside the walls and was present in Hissarlik in March 1890 when the international panel of archaeologists assembled by Schliemann decided that the site was indeed the remains of ancient Troy.

Dorpfeld went on to assist Schliemann at the excavation of the city of Tiryns in the Peloponese from 1884 to 1885. The floor plan of the palace was uncovered and Dorpfeld discerned the floor plans of two buildings similar in structure to that of Temple A at Troy. He identified this architectural form as the Homeric megaron. The other major find at Tiryns were Mycenean wall-paintings. While the site was a disappointment to Schliemann, for Dorpfeld it was a great success, as it was he who located the architectural remains and the wall paintings.

In 1886 Schliemann and Dorpfeld excavated at Levadia, where they searched unsuccessfully for the site of the Oracle of Trophonius. They also returned to Orchomenos, where Dorpfeld cleaned out and drew up a more accurate plan of the tomb. Together they visited Crete to look at the site at Knossos—but Schliemann considered the rights to excavate the site to be too expensive.

Dorpfeld traveled with Schliemann to London to help mount a response to critics of the interpretation of their finds from Tiryns and escorted Schliemann's body from Naples, where he had died, back to Athens, where he was buried.

Succeeding Schliemann, Dorpfeld used more refined excavation methods, identifying nine levels and revising Schliemann's chronology and stratigraphy at Hissarlik, proposing that Troy VI, not Troy II, was the Homeric city. In 1893 and 1894 Dorpfeld confirmed the late Bronze Age date of Troy VI. He subsequently excavated on Levkas, which he identified as Homeric Ithaca, the home of Odysseus.

Tim Murray

Douglass, Andrew Ellicot (1867–1962)

Born in Windsor, Vermont, and a graduate of Trinity College, Connecticut, in 1889, Douglass joined the Harvard College Observatory, which marked the beginning of a long and eminent career concerned primarily with astronomy. Douglass helped to establish and operate three major astronomical observatories—the Harvard College Observatory at Arequipa, Peru; the Lowell Observatory in Flagstaff, Arizona; and the Steward Observatory at the University of Arizona in Tucson—before he became involved in archaeology.

Douglass's interest in the effects of sunspots on terrestrial weather led him to investigate the annual growth layers of Arizona pines for variations in tree-ring width. He discovered a relationship between rainfall and tree growth, and between cyclical variations in tree growth and sunspot cycles. Looking for extensive tree-ring records to substantiate his theories, Douglass asked archaeologists in Tucson for pieces of wood from the ruins of a southwestern pueblo. Within a decade he was able to date some of these wooden remains back to A.D. 100, and others to A.D. 700, providing archaeology with a valuable tool for establishing an independent chronology. Douglass went on to develop the study of tree-rings into the science of dendrochronology. Tree-ring DATING has made substantial contributions to archaeology in the Arctic, Britain, Central Europe, and the Mediterranean Basin. Douglass also provided dendro-climatic and dendro-environmental reconstructions for archaeology.

He retired from astronomy to found and direct the Laboratory of Tree-ring Research at the University of Arizona, which he helped to establish as the preeminent center for dendrochronological research.

Tim Murray

Dubois, Eugene (1858–1940)

Born in the NETHERLANDS, Dubois studied medicine at the University of Amsterdam until 1884. He worked as an assistant to the Anatomist Max Furbringer from 1881 until 1887, and lectured in anatomy from 1886 to 1887. Inspired by the work of Ernst Haeckel, Dubois resigned from the university and left for the Dutch East Indies (now INDONESIA) to search for evidence of early human beings. Haeckel had claimed that humankind had descended from a group of apes in Asia, and not in Africa as Dar-

win had suggested. This argument was based on a few anatomical resemblances between modern humans and the gibbons of ISLAND SOUTHEAST ASIA.

Supported by the Dutch colonial government, Dubois searched for human ancestral remains in Java and Sumatra from 1888 to 1895. The skullcap, thighbone, and a few teeth of a *Pithecanthropus erectus*, along with other fossils, were found near the village of Trinil on Java between 1891 and 1893. Dubois believed these remains, known as "Java man," to be the missing link between apes and humans, and he returned to Europe to convince the scientific community of their importance.

Dubois's fossil finds were the first hominid remains to be accepted as material proof of human evolution, and a significant number of scientists regarded them as proof of a chain of connection between humans and their primitive ancestors. The debate about their significance led to the development of an evolutionary interpretation of extant European Neanderthal remains, leading to further development of the new science of paleoanthropology.

Dubois became professor of crystallography, mineralogy, paleontology, and geology at the University of Amsterdam in 1899 and withdrew from the debate on *Pithecanthropus*. He continued with paleontological and anatomical research, pioneering allometric relations between brain and body size in vertebrates and hominids. This work convinced him that vertebrate evolution had not proceeded in a linear nor a gradual way, but through quantum changes. He maintained that *Pithecanthropus* was the missing link between primates and hominids, and he would not accept that other pithecanthropine finds, made in Java in the 1930s by von Koenigswald, were much closer to *Homo sapiens* that he had originally argued. He retired in 1929.

Tim Murray

References

Theunissen, Bert. 1989. *Eugene Dubois and the Ape-Man from Java: The History of the First Missing Link and Its Discoverer*. Dordrecht; Boston: Kluwer Academic Publishers.

Duff, Roger Shepherd (1912–1978)

Roger Duff was born in Invercargill on the south island of New Zealand and attended Otago University and Canterbury University College. Duff was introduced to Pacific ethnology and archaeology by Dr. H. D. Skinner, director of the Otago Museum and a well-known archaeologist. Duff became director of the Dominion Museum (now the National Museum) in Wellington, a position he held from 1948 to 1978.

Duff received a Doctor of Science Degree from the University of New Zealand in 1951 for his most famous work on the Moa-hunter period of Maori culture, which has since been reprinted numerous times. This monograph became the foundation for the integration of modern Maori and Polynesian history based on Duff's archaeological and ethnological understanding of the Pacific. In his analysis of material excavated from burial sites at Wairu Bar, Duff confirmed that the Maori Moa-hunters were truly Polynesian peoples, rather than Melanesian as had formerly been thought. Based on the highly developed stone-adzes Duff was later to describe eastern Polynesian culture as "Neolithic."

Duff received a number of awards including the Smith Medal from Otago University for anthropological research and the Hector Medal from the Royal Society of New Zealand.

Tim Murray

See also New Zealand: Prehistoric Archaeology; Papua New Guinea and Melanesia; Polynesia

Dugdale, Sir William (1605–1686)

The son of a Warwickshire gentleman, Dugdale became a lawyer. His interests in antiquities and local history were encouraged by local antiquarians William Burton, author of the *Description of Leicestershire,* and Sir Simon Archer, the owner of a historic collection relating to Warwickshire. During the 1630s and 1640s Dugdale researched the histories of Warwick county's families, and this brought him to the attention of the well-connected and aristocratic antiquarians of London, Sir Henry Spelman, Sir Christopher Hatton and Thomas, the Earl of Arundel. They invited him to London and eased his way into the world of national antiquarianism. They also

Sir William Dugdale (Hulton Getty)

encouraged him to research the monastic foundations of England with another antiquarian, Roger Dodsworth of Yorkshire.

To this end Dugdale was provided with access to records in the Exchequer and the Tower of London, major depositories of ancient documents dating back to the Middle Ages. The library of Sir Robert Cotton, another antiquarian, was also opened to Dugdale. His patrons recommended that he become a Herald, a position that included lodgings at the Office of Heralds in London and a small income. With the political crisis between Parliament and King James II, Dugdale was dispatched by Sir Christopher Hatton to record as many as possible of the coats of arms, inscriptions with details of kinship lines, and church records on stone, glass, brass, and paper, which the antiquarians knew would be targets for destruction by the Puritans during the impending civil war.

In 1648, with the collapse of the Royalist cause, Dugdale went to France where he continued his research, but on French records about English monasteries. He returned to England to work with Dodsworth to complete their *Monasticon* and to publish his *History of War-*

wickshire. After the Restoration Dugdale published the second volume of *Monasticon,* and wrote a history of the Cathedral of St. Paul's in London. Supported by the new chancellor, Clarendon, and the new archbishop of Canterbury, Sheldon, Dugdale went on to complete the unfinished works of his first patron, Spelman, who had died in 1641. These included Spelman's glossary of words and terms in Anglo-Saxon and Norman law.

Dugdale wrote a history of the law, lawyers, and the Inns of Court entitled *Origines Juridiciales* (1666) and the *Baronage of England* (1676) a genealogical history of the English aristocracy since Saxon times. Most of Dugdale's work involved the recovery of historic material about the great institutions of the Middle Ages, and it was a significant achievement given the number of old records and their state of neglect and disorder. He did benefit from the work of other scholars, such as Dodsworth and Archer, and he often published composite antiquarian studies. However in the seventeenth century antiquarian research was cooperative, and Dugdale became the center of such work as an advisor on archival searches. He was unusual among his contemporaries in that he did write up and publish most of his work, even if it took over twenty years to do it. He wanted above all else to ensure that the record of the past was preserved and that it was "straight." Dugdale was a typical late-Renaissance historiographer who reconstructed a manuscript-based past. He was seen as old fashioned by Restoration scientific antiquarianism.

In 1662 he wrote the *History of Imbanking and Drayning of Diverse Fennes,* a departure from his usual patient and methodical documentary research. This Dutch-inspired engineering project, which changed parts of Norfolk and Cambridgeshire from swamps to fertile agricultural land, exposed Dugdale to geology and natural history and the history of technology—to the kind of ideas and areas of study that were to be the foundation of restored King Charles II's Royal Society, the new antiquarianism.

Some of Dugdale's works were contentious, especially the *Monasticon.* The Reformation tended to make anything about Britain's Roman Catholic past unpopular, and the book was much criticized when it was first published. His book on the drainage of the fens was seen as a political apology, an attempt to disguise and justify the great wealth the project engendered for some. He greatly encouraged other antiquarians such as Anthony Wood of Oxford and his son-in-law, Elias Ashmole, and Dugdale did encourage and help JOHN AUBREY, who disliked archival research. However, he remained unimpressed by Aubrey's multidisciplinary antiquarianism, his new ideas about fieldwork, and his speculation on the origins of AVEBURY and Stonehenge. Dugdale was knighted in 1677.

Tim Murray

SOUTH ORANGE PUBLIC LIBRARY

3 9507 00112286 9

WITHDRAWN